Portugal

If Spain is the head of Europe,
Portugal, set at its western extremity,
where land ends and sea begins,
is as it were the crown on the head.

Luís de Camões
The Lusiads, Canto III

G. Guittard/HOA QUI

Portugal evokes the days of the great explorers, ships sailing out towards uncharted seas and a New World, yet it is also a land steeped in the nostalgia or *saudade* expressed in the popular *fado* tradition of song. The landscapes, too, reflect a range of diverse impressions: the grandiose Douro valley is striated by vineyards where the harvest is bottled as Port wine; brightly painted boats bob in the ports of coastal fishing villages; the Alentejo plain rolls away south-ward to a far distant horizon; below the red cliffs of the Algarve lie sandy beaches and emerald inlets; the old villages are enlivened by colourful traditions.

The Portuguese are fond of dichotomy: witness the peaceful cohabitation of religious fervour and extra-vagant night-life, or the strength of their attachment to rural identity coupled with the development of leading industries. The capital city of Lisbon is the symbol of the harmony between the future and the past. As the city celebrates the 500th anniversary of Vasco da Gama's journey of discovery to India, it opens the door to the 21st century in Expo'98; the international exposition is devoted to the world's oceans.

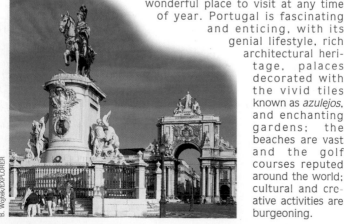

This dynamic and optimistic nation, which has seen spectacular economic development since joining the European Union in 1986, is a wonderful place to visit at any time of year. Portugal is fascinating and enticing, with its genial lifestyle, rich architectural heri-tage, palaces decorated with the vivid tiles known as *azulejos*, and enchanting gardens; the beaches are vast and the golf courses reputed around the world; cultural and cre-ative activities are burgeoning.

B. Wojtek/EXPLORER

Contents

Key — 4

How to use this guide — 5

Map of principal sights — 6

Map of touring programmes — 8

Map of places to stay — 9

Introduction — 11

The land of Portugal — 12

Government — 17

Historical table and notes — 18

The Great Discoveries — 23

Art and architecture — 27

Azulejos — 35

Literature — 37

Cinema — 39

Traditional and festive Portugal — 40

Food and wine — 48

Sights — 55

The Madeira Archipelago — 260

The Azores Archipelago — 285

Practical information — 321

Planning your trip — 322

Getting there — 323

Getting around — 323

Accommodation — 325

Eating out — 326

General information — 326

Shopping — 328

Recreation — 329

Calendar of events — 331

Further reading — 333

Glossary — 334

Admission times and charges — 326

Index — 357

Key

★★★ Worth a journey
★★ Worth a detour
★ Interesting

Tourism

⊙	Admission Times and Charges listed at the end of the guide	►►	Visit if time permits
	Sightseeing route with departure point indicated	AZ B	Map co-ordinates locating sights
🏛🛆🛆🛆	Ecclesiastical building	🇿	Tourist information
	Synagogue – Mosque		Castle, historic house – Ruins
	Building (with main entrance)	∪ ✿	Dam – Factory or power station
■	Statue, small building	☆ ∩	Fort – Cave
⊥	Wayside cross	⛏	Prehistoric site
◎	Fountain	▼ �	Viewing table – View
	Fortified walls – Tower – Town gate	▲	Miscellaneous sight

Recreation

	Racecourse		Beginning of waymarked footpath
	Skating rink		
	Outdoor or indoor swimming pool	♦	Outdoor leisure park/centre
⌂	Marina, moorings		Theme/Amusement park
⌂	Mountain refuge hut		Wildlife/Safari park, zoo
	Overhead cable-car	⊛	Gardens, park, arboretum
	Tourist or steam railway	◉	Aviary, bird sanctuary

Additional symbols

══ ══	Motorway (unclassified)	✉ ◎	Post office – Telephone centre
❶ ❶	Junction: complete, limited	✉	Covered market
⊨ ══	Pedestrian zone		Police station (Gendarmerie) – Barracks
⊥═══⊥	Unsuitable for traffic, street subject to restrictions	⚠	Swing bridge
⊞⊞ ----	Steps – Footpath	∪ ✕	Quarry – Mine
🚆 🚌	Railway – Coach station	🅑 🅕	Ferry (river and lake crossings)
⊡++++⊡	Funicular – Rack-railway		Ferry services: Passengers and cars
—•— ◉	Tram – Metro station	⇌	Foot passengers only
Bert (R.)...	Main shopping street	③	Access route number common to MICHELIN maps and town plans

Abbreviations

G	District government office (Governo civil)	M	Museum (Museu)
H	Town hall (Câmara municipal)	POL.	Police (Polícia)
J	Law courts (Palácio de justiça)	T	Theatre (Teatro)
		U	University (Universidade)

Symbols specific to this guide

℗	Pousada (hotel run by the State)	❸	Hotel described in this guide

How to use this guide

The summary maps on pages 6-9 are designed to assist you in planning your trip: the **Map of Principal Sights** identifies major attractions, the **Touring Programmes** proposes regional driving itineraries and the **Places to Stay** map points out plesant holiday spots as well as various recreational facilities. We recommend reading the **Introduction** before your trip as the background information on history, the arts and traditional culture can make your visit more meaningful.

Portugal's principal natural and cultural attractions are presented in alphabetical order in the Sights section, which concludes with an island by island description of Madeira and the Azores. Portuguese place names are used throughout this guide to ensure easy on-sight orientation. Commonly used Portuguese words appear in the glossary at the end of the guide. The clock symbol (⊘) placed after sight names refers to the admission times and charges section in the **practical information** chapter, where you will also find a wealth of travel tips, addresses and a calendar of events.

This guide is designed to be used in conjunction with the detailed Michelin road **maps 940 and 441** (1:400 000) and the Michelin **map 39** to Lisbon (1:10 000). Cross-references to these maps appear in blue print under chapter headings. In this guide you will find selected hotel and restaurant recommendations in the **Travellers' addresses** for Lisbon, Porto, Coimbra, Évora, Faro and Óbidos. For a wider selection, consult the annually updated **Michelin Red Guide Portugal** or **España-Portugal**, which also include numerous town plans.

Consult the comprehensive index when looking for specific place names, historic figures or practical information.

We greatly appreciate your comments and suggestions. Write to us at the address shown on the inside cover or at our Web site: www.michelin-travel.com.

Boa viagem!

X. Testelin/RAPHO

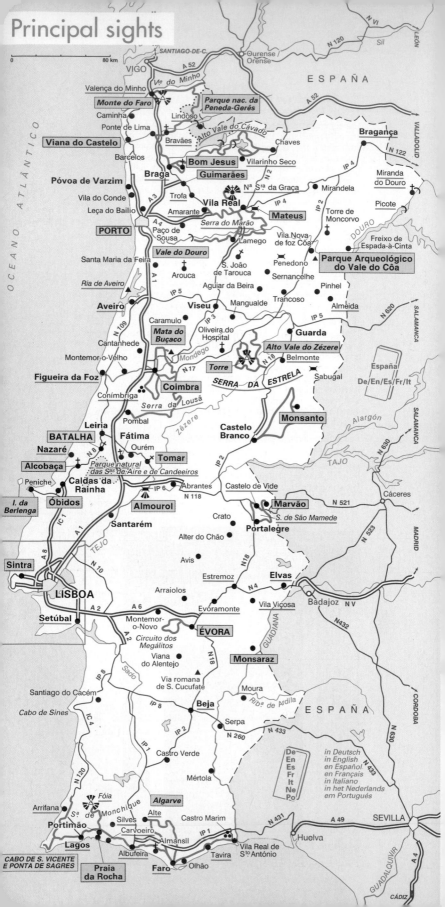

Principal sights

Worth a journey ★★★

Worth a detour ★★

Interesting ★

The names of sights described in the guide

appear in black on the map:

see the index for the page number

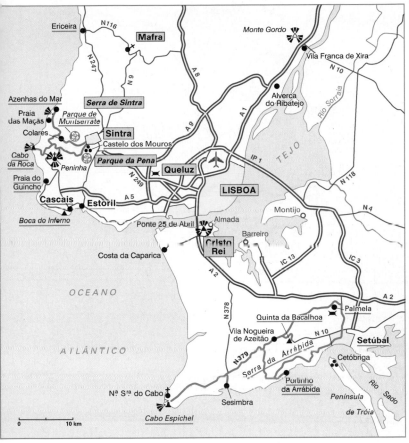

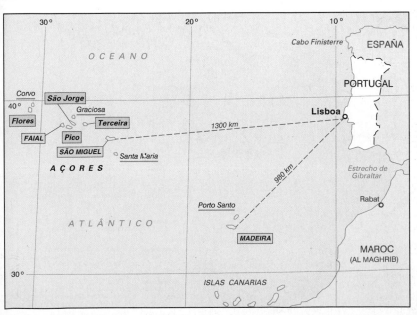

7

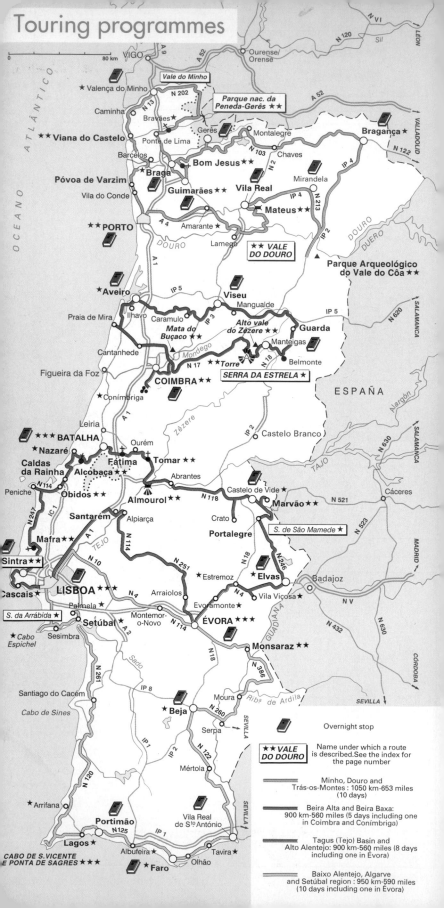

Touring programmes

Places to stay

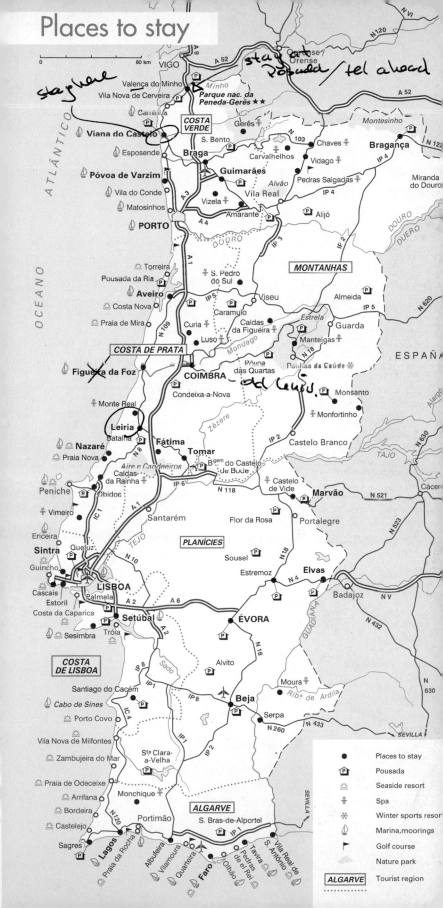

Ponta da Piedade – Algarve

G. Simeone-DIAF

Introduction

The land of Portugal

Portugal has few of the monotonous vistas as can be found in the Spanish Meseta. The continental part of the country in the southwest of the Iberian Peninsula occupies a relatively small area of 88 944sq km/34 341sq mi (560km/350mi from north to south and 220km/137mi from west to east) which has a tremendous variety of landscape. Generally speaking, the altitude decreases from the Spanish border towards the Atlantic and from north to south; the Tagus (Tejo) divides a mountainous region in the north from an area of plateaux and plains in the south. The archipelagos of Madeira and the Azores have a surface area of 782sq km/302sq mi and 2 335sq km/902sq mi respectively. *(See MADEIRA and the AZORES at the end of the guide.)*
In 1992, Portugal's population was ten and a half million.

GEOLOGICAL FORMATION

In the Primary Era the north of Portugal was affected by Hercynian folding which resulted in the emergence of hard granite and shale mountain ranges. These were worn down in the Secondary Era to form a vast plateau out of which rose erosion resistant heights such as the Serra de São Mamede. In the Tertiary Era, the raising of the Alps and Pyrenean folding led to a brutal upheaval of the plateau, dislocating it into a series of small massifs such as the Serra do Marão and Serra da Estrela. The massifs were separated by fissures near which emerged thermal and mineral springs and, especially in the north, metal deposits. The upheavals were accompanied in some cases by eruptions of a volcanic nature which formed ranges such as the Serra de Sintra and Serra de Monchique. It was at this point that the Tagus and Sado Basins were formed and the coastal plains folded into the low ranges of the Serra de Aire, Serra do Caldeirão and Serra da Arrábida. This zone of faults in the earth's crust is still subject to geological disturbance as shown in the earthquake which destroyed Lisbon in 1755 and even more recent tremors.

The coastline became less indented in the Quaternary Era through erosion of the Estremadura and Alentejo cliffs and alluvial accumulation in the Aveiro and Sines areas.

RELIEF

The Cantabrian Cordillera extends westwards into Portugal, north of the Douro, where it takes the form of massive mountain ranges separated by heavily eroded valleys.

Between the Douro and the Tagus, the Castilian Sierras extend into Portugal as particularly high relief. Monte da Torre in the Serra da Estrela is Portugal's highest mainland peak (1 993m/6 539ft). The Mondego and Zêzere valleys surround the ridge. South of the Tagus lies a plateau which drops towards the sea. Its vast horizons are barely interrupted by the minor rises of the Serra de Monchique and Serra do Caldeirão.

The 837km/520mi of coast offer incredible variety. There are interminable strands, beaches of fine sand sheltered by rock cliffs, creeks, and promontories such as those of Cabo Carvoeiro, Cabo Espichel and Cabo

de São Vicente. Vast estuaries are now occupied by the country's main ports: Oporto on the Douro, Lisbon on the Tagus and Setúbal on the Sado. Fishing harbours like Portimão have developed in bays, or, as with Peniche and Lagos, In the protection of headlands. However, most of the coast consists of flat sandy areas sometimes lined by offshore bars as in the eastern offshore Algarve and along Ria de Aveiro. The waters are cooled by a current from the Canary Islands which counterbalances the warmth of the Gulf Stream.

REGIONS AND LANDSCAPE

The areas described below correspond to the old historical provinces which closely reflected the country's natural regions. Portugal's present administrative divisions, known as districts, are also given.

The North

The old provinces of the Minho and Douro are green and heavily cultivated while the inland regions of Trás-os-Montes, Beira Alta and Beira Baixa are bleaker and drier.

Douro vineyards

G. Sioen/RAPHO

The Minho (Districts: Braga and Viana do Castelo) and the Douro (District: Porto) – The region is also known as the **Costa Verde** or Green Coast. The greater part of the Minho and Douro provinces consist of granite hills covered with dense vegetation. The exceptions to these are the bare summits of the Serra do Gerês, Serra do Soajo and Serra do Marão, which make up Peneda-Gerês National Park, and are strewn with rocky scree. The fields, enclosed by hedges and climbing vines, sometimes produce two crops a year, while here and there small clumps of eucalyptus, pines (on the coast) and oaks stud the landscape. Vineyards, orchards and meadows contribute to the rural economy. Olive, apple and sometimes orange trees grow on the sunniest slopes. The very dense population live in numerous small villages connected by winding roads which are often paved. Main roads tend to follow lush river valleys like those of the Lima and the Vez. The region, with **Porto** (in Portuguese, Oporto) as capital, is an active one which attracts more than a quarter of Portugal's population. Many industries are centred around Porto and Braga.

Trás-os-Montes (Districts: Bragança and Vila Real) – Trás-os-Montes means "beyond the mountains". True to its name, this province of high plateaux relieved by rocky crests and deeply cut valleys, stretches out beyond the Serra de Marão and Serra do Gerês. The moorland plateaux, dominated by bare summits and covered with stunted vegetation, are used for sheep grazing. Remote villages, with houses built of granite or shale, merge into the landscape. The more populous river basins around Chaves, Mirandela and Bragança, with their flourishing fruit trees, vines, maize and vegetables, seem like veritable oases in the bleak countryside. The whole area has always been affected by emigration. Today, many of the people who left are returning to build homes in the small towns.
The Alto Douro region in the south contrasts with the rest of the province by its relative fertility. The edges of the plateaux and the slopes down to the Douro and the Tua have been terraced so that olive, fig and almond trees can be grown, and particularly the famous vine which produces the grapes for port wine and *vinho verde*.

The Beira Alta (Districts: Guarda and Viseu) and Beira Baixa (District: Castelo Branco) – This region, the most mountainous in Portugal, is geographically a westward extension of the Spanish Central Cordillera. The landscape consists of a succession of raised rock masses and down-faulted basins. The mountains, of which the principal ranges are the **Serra da Estrela** and **Serra da Lousã**, have thickly wooded slopes crowned with summits, in some cases bristling with rock outcrops, but more often covered with grass on which sheep graze. Occasional reservoirs formed artificially behind dams fill the sites of ancient glaciary corries or gorges hollowed out of the quartz. Old villages look down on valley floors terraced into a chequerboard of maize and rye fields as well as olive groves.

The greater part of the population lives in the Mondego and Zêzere valleys. The Mondego Valley, a vast eroded corridor and a main communications route, is rich arable land; where the hillsides face the sun, vines may often be seen extending the vineyards of the Dão region. The Upper Zêzere Valley, known as the Cova da Beira, specialises more in rearing livestock, wheras the main town, Covilha, has an important wool industry. Around Guarda, most of the granite built villages are still protected by a castle or ramparts, reminders of former wars between Portugal and Spain.

The Centre

The Beira Littoral (Districts: Coimbra and Aveiro) — This low lying region cut by many water courses corresponds approximately to the lower valleys of the Vouga, the Mondego and the Lis. There are rice fields in the irrigated areas around Soure and Aveiro. The coast, which forms the northern part of the **Costa de Prata**, consists of long straight beaches and sand dunes anchored by vast pinewoods such as Pinhal de Leiria and Pinhal do Urso, while at Aveiro, the *ria* or lagoon provides an original touch to the scenery. Inland, the cottage gardens of wheat and maize are bordered by orchards and vines. There are also some beautiful forests, including Mata do Buçaco. The region's two main centres are Coimbra with its famous university and Aveiro with its *ria* and salt-pans.

Estremadura (Districts: Leiria, Lisbon and Setúbal) — In the past, this was the southern limit of the lands reconquered from the Moors, hence the name Estremadura which means extremity. Today, the region, which includes the Lisbon area, contains a third of the country's population.

Between Nazaré and Setúbal the countryside is gently undulating. Villages of single storey houses are surrounded by cultivated properties, which being small in the north and large in the south, are tended with minute care; fields of wheat and maize, olives, vines and fruit trees grow between clumps of pines and eucalyptus.

Along the coast, where tall cliffs alternate with attractive sand beaches, there are many fishing villages. The Serra de Sintra is a pleasant wooded range near Lisbon, while the Serra da Arrábida, south of the Tagus, provides shelter for small seaside resorts.

The region's activities are centred around Lisbon, the political, administrative, financial and commercial capital.

The Ribatejo (District: Santarém) — The Riba do Tejo, or banks of the Tagus, is an alluvial plain formed in the Tertiary and Quaternary Eras. On the hills along the north bank, the farmers cultivate a mixture of crops based on olives, vines and vegetables. The terraces along the south bank belong to large scale landowners who grow wheat and olives.

The plain, which may be flooded for irrigation, is covered with rice fields, market gardens and above all acres of grassland on which horses and fighting bulls are reared. The region, with its main centre in Santarém, is renowned for its Portuguese style bullfights known as *touradas*.

The South

The Alentejo (Districts: Beja, Evora and Portalegre) — The Alentejo, meaning beyond the Tagus *(Além Tejo)*, covers nearly a third of the total land area of Portugal. It is a vast flat plain practically without relief, except for the Serra de São Mamede. There is almost no natural vegetation; as a proverb says, "there's no shade in the Alentejo". However, in spite of the difficulties of irrigation, the land is seldom left fallow. The Alentejo, Portugal's granary, is also the region of the cork oak, the ilex (holm oak) and the olive tree; in addition plums are grown around Vendas Novas and Elvas. Flocks of sheep and herds of black pigs eke out an existence on the poorer land. The vast stretches of open countryside dotted with old villages make the region one of Portugal's most attractive.

Traditionally, the region has been one of huge estates centred around a *monte* or large remote whitewashed farmhouse, built on a rise. The other local inhabitants live in villages of low houses with big chimneys. The situation changed after the Carnation Revolution when the land reform of July 1975 split up the estates into smaller co-operatives. As this has not been very successful, there has been a return to medium and large scale properties.

The coast is generally uninviting although several seaside resorts are beginning to develop. There are few harbours apart from Sines which is well-equipped.

There are no large towns; Evora with its 35 000 inhabitants acts as the regional capital but lives mainly from tourism.

Alentejo countryside

The Algarve (District: Faro) – Portugal's southernmost province takes its name from the Arabic *El Gharb* meaning "west" for this was in fact the most westerly region conquered by the Moors. The Algarve, separated from the Alentejo by shale hills, is like a garden: flowers grow alongside crops and beneath fruit trees allowing one to see geraniums, camellias and oleanders, cotton, rice and sugar cane as well as carobs, figs and almonds. Many cottage gardens are surrounded by hedges of aloes *(agaves)*. The villages have brightly whitewashed houses with decorative chimneys. To the west rises a mountain range of volcanic rock, the **Serra de Monchique,** covered in lush vegetation. The coast is very sandy. The *Sotavento* stretch east of Faro is protected by offshore sandbanks, while the *Barlavento* section to the west consists of beaches backed by high cliffs which form an impressive promontory at Cabo de São Vicente.

Over the last few years the Algarve has undergone extensive tourist development, sometimes to the detriment of traditional activities such as fishing, canning, horticulture and the cork industry. Most of the small fishing villages have become vast seaside resorts.

The main towns are Faro, Lagos and Portimão.

PARKS AND RESERVES

A variety of conservation areas have been set up in Portugal to protect the natural beauty of the landscape as well as the local flora and fauna.

National Park – Portugal's only national park is that of **Peneda-Gerês** (72 000ha/177 919 acres) in the north.

Nature Reserves – Among Portugal's specially protected areas are the nature reserves of **Montesinho** (75 000ha/185 333 acres) near Bragança, *ALVÃO* (7 220ha/17 841 acres) near Vila Real Amarante, **Serra da Estrela** (100 000ha/247 110 acres), **Serra de Aire** and **Serra dos Candeeiros** (34 000ha/84 017 acres) near Fátima, which form a beautiful limestone landscape with many caves, **Sintra-Cascais** (23 280ha/57 527 acres), **Serra da Arrábida** (10 820ha/26 737 acres), **Serra de São Mamede** (31 750ha/78 457 acres) and **Ria Formosa** (18 400ha/45 468 acres). All these nature reserves are in mountainous regions with the exception of the Ria Formosa lagoon which is in a highly developed tourist area of the Algarve.

Conservation areas – Many areas have been singled out for the protection of their flora and fauna. Among them are mountainous regions like **Serra de Malcata** (21 760ha/53 771 acres), swamps such as **Paúl de Arzila** (535ha/1 322 acres) and **Paúl do Boquilobo** (530ha/1 310 acres), river estuaries which have a particularly rich birdlife, including the **Tagus estuary** (14 560ha/35 979 acres), the **Sado estuary** (22 700ha/56 094 acres) and **Castro Marim** (2 089ha/5 162 acres) in the Guadiana estuary, and lastly dune areas including the **São Jacinto dunes** (666ha/1 646 acres) in Ria de Aveiro and those on **Berlenga island** (1 063ha/2 627 acres).

Most of the beauty spots in Madeira and the Azores are now classified as conservation areas. *See MADEIRA and the AZORES.*

Protected landscapes – Some of Portugal's coastal areas have been declared protected landscapes to prevent them from being marred by uncontrolled building development. They include **Esposende** (440ha/1 087 acres), the **southeast Alentejo** and the **coast near Cabo de São Vicente** (70 000ha/172 977 acres).

VEGETATION

TREES AND FOREST
MAIN SPECIES

☐ Deciduous oaks	◆ Nature reserves
☐ Evergreen oaks	● Eucalyptus
☐ Pine trees	♀ Carob trees

The number and diversity of plants in Portugal is a visual reminder of the contrasts in climate and different types of soil to be found within its borders. The **robur** and **tauzin oak**, together with **chestnuts**, birches and maples, grow on the very wet peaks of over 500m/1 500ft in northern Portugal and on the Serra de São Mamede in the centre and Serra de Monchique in the south.

South of the Tagus and in the Upper Douro Valley where the summers are very dry, there are dense woods of **ilex** (holm oak) and **cork oak** which grow beside heaths and moorlands sparsely covered with cistus, lavender, rosemary and thyme. While they may be found throughout the country, cork oaks are particularly abundant in the Alentejo. Portugal is the world's leading cork producer. The **eucalyptus** mainly grows along the coast together with **maritime pines** and umbrella pines which form vast forests beside the Costa da Prata beaches near Leiria, Coimbra and Aveiro. Aleppo pines dominate in the Serra da Estrela. Eucalyptus and pines, often chosen for afforestation, are being planted on ever increasing areas of land.

Mediterranean plant species acclimatise well in the Algarve where one may see **aloes** (agaves) as well as **carob, almond, fig, orange** and **olive** trees.

Join us in our constant task of keeping up-to-date. Please send us your comments and suggestions.

Michelin Tyre PLC
Tourism Department
The Edward Hyde Building
38 Clarenson Road
WATFORD Herts WD1 1SX - U.K.
Tel: 01923 415000
Fax: 01923 415250
Internet: WWW.michelin-travel.com

Government

The Portuguese flag

The green vertical stripe at the hoist and red stripe in the fly are divided by an armillary sphere bearing the Portuguese coat of arms. The sphere supports a white shield with five blue shields, each with five white disks symbolising Christ's wounds. The seven yellow castles represent the strongholds retaken from the Moors.

POLITICAL ORGANISATION

The **Constitution** promulgated on 2 April 1976 brought in a semi-presidential form of government. **Executive power** is held by the **President of the Republic** who is elected by universal suffrage for a five-year term (renewable once). The president appoints the **Prime Minister**, who represents Parliamentary majority, and, on his suggestion, the rest of the government. The revised Constitution of 1982 has limited the president's powers although he retains the right to veto laws approved by straight majority vote in the Assembly. **Legislative power** is held by a single Chamber of between 240 and 250 members who are elected for four years. The archipelagos of Madeira and the Azores are Autonomous Regions with their own Regional Government and Regional Assembly. The Assembly is elected by universal suffrage. The President of the Republic appoints a **Minister of the Republic** for each of the Autonomous Regions, who then appoints a **Regional Government President.**

ADMINISTRATIVE ORGANISATION

The old historical provinces of the Minho, Trás-os-Montes, Douro, Beiras (Alta, Baixa and Litoral), Ribatejo, Estremadura, Alentejo and Algarve no longer fulfil an administrative role but still denote the main regions of the country.

For the purposes of tourism, Portugal is the Costa Verde and Montanhas in the north, Costa da Prata and Costa de Lisboa in the centre, Planícies and Algarve in the south, and the archipelagos of Madeira and the Azores.

Portugal's present administrative organisation is as follows:

• **Districts**: There are 18 in mainland Portugal, three in the Azores and one in Madeira. Health, education and finance are managed at district level.

• **Concelhos**: These councils represent municipal authority. There are 305 in all. A *concelho* is similar to a district borough or a canton. Each one has a town hall or *Paço do Concelho* and an executive committee or *Câmara Municipal* led by a president who acts as mayor. Both the president and the municipal assembly are elected by universal suffrage every four years.

• Lastly, each *concelho* consists of several **freguesias**, the smallest administrative unit. There are 4 200 or so *freguesias* in Portugal, responsible for keeping public records, civil status, the upkeep of natural heritage, and organising festivals and other local events.

PROVINCES AND DISTRICTS

○ Braga   District boundaries and capitals

MINHO   The old provinces

Historical table and notes

Up until the 11C, before its emergence as an independent kingdom, Portugal's history was common with the rest of the Iberian Peninsula.

9-7C BC	The Greeks and the Phoenicians establish trading posts on the coasts of the Iberian Peninsula, inhabited in the west by Lusitanian tribes, originally a Celtiberian population.
3-2C	The Carthaginians master the country; the Romans intervene (Second Punic War) and take over the administration of Lusitania, so named by Augustus. Viriate, chief of the Lusitanians, organises resistance and is assassinated in 139.
5C AD	The Suevi (Swabians) and Visigoths occupy most of the Iberian Peninsula.

Moorish occupation

711	The Moorish invasion from North Africa.
8-9C	The Christian war of reconquest of the Iberian Peninsula begins at Covadonga in the Asturias, led by Pelayo in 718. By the 9C, the region of Portucale, north of the Mondego, has been liberated.

The founding of the kingdom

In 1087, Alfonso VI, King of Castile and Léon, undertakes the reconquest of present-day Castile-La Mancha. He calls upon several French knights, including Henry of Burgundy, descendant of the French king Hugues Capet, and his cousin Raymond of Burgundy.

When the Moors are vanquished, Alfonso offers his daughters in marriage to the princes. Urraca, heir to the throne, marries Raymond; Tareja (Teresa) brings the county of Portucale, which stretches between the Minho and Douro rivers, as her dowry to **Henry of Burgundy** in 1095. Henry thus becomes Count of Portugal.

Henry dies in 1114; Queen Tareja becomes regent pending the coming of age of her son **Afonso Henriques**. But in 1128 the latter forces his mother to relinquish her power *(see GUIMARÃES)*; in 1139 he breaks the bonds of vassalage imposed upon him by Alfonso VII of Castile and proclaims himself King of Portugal under the name Afonso I; Castile finally agrees in 1143.

Afonso Henriques continues the reconquest and after the victory at Ourique (1139) takes Santarém and then Lisbon (1147) with the aid of the Second Crusade's fleet. The capture of Faro in 1249 marks the end of Moorish occupation.

Burgundian dynasty (1128-1383) – Wars with Castile

1279-1325	King Dinis I founds the University of Coimbra and establishes Portuguese, a dialect of the Oporto region, as the official language.
1369-83	Taking advantage of the trouble in Castile, Fernando I attempts to enlarge his kingdom; in failing he proposes the marriage of his only daughter, Beatriz, to the King of Castile, Juan I.
13 June 1373	First Treaty of Alliance with England (signed in London).

Battle of Aljubarrota, 15C miniature

British Library, London/BRIDGEMAN-GIRAUDON

Dom Sebastião came to the throne in 1557 at the age of three. He was educated by a Jesuit priest who instilled in him the old-fashioned values of chivalry which his romantic, proud nature was prone to exacerbate. He believed that a mission had been conferred upon him: namely, to conquer Africa from the Moorish infidels. In 1578, having made the decision to fulfil his destiny, he set sail for Morocco along with 17 000 men and the finest flower of Portuguese nobility. However, with his soldiers poorly prepared and encumbered by their stately armour under a ruthless sun, his dream was to end in brutal fashion in the muddy reaches of the Malhazin river at Alcácer Quibir, where half of his armada was to die and the other half to be taken prisoner. His body was never found. The Spanish domination which followed encouraged the development of Sebastianism, which transformed the young king into a long-awaited Messiah to save Portugal, thus enriching the Portuguese soul with yet another type of nostalgic longing (saudade).

Museu National de Arte Antiga

Dom Sebastião by Cristóvão Morais, 16C

Avis dynasty (1385-1578) – The Great Discoveries

(See The Great Discoveries later in this chapter)

1385	Upon Fernando I's death in 1383, his son-in-law Juan of Castile claims the succession; but João, bastard brother of the late king and Grand Master of the Order of Avis is acclaimed to rule; the **Cortes** in Coimbra proclaims him King of Portugal under the name **João I.** Seven days later, on 14 August, Juan of Castile confronts João of Avis at the **Battle of Aljubarrota** but fails. To celebrate his victory, João builds the monastery at Batalha. He marries Philippa of Lancaster, thus sealing the alliance with England which is to last throughout Portugal's history.
1386	Treaty of Windsor with England.
1415	The **capture of Ceuta** in Morocco by João I and his sons, including **Prince Henry**, puts an end to attacks on the Portuguese coast by pirates from Barbary and marks the beginning of Portuguese expansion.
1420-44	Settlement of the Madeira archipelago begins in 1420 and that of the Azores in 1444.
1481-95	**João II**, known as the Perfect Prince, promotes maritime exploration; however, he mistakenly rejects Christopher Columbus' project. During his reign Bartolomeu Dias rounds the Cape of Good Hope (1488) and the **Treaty of Tordesillas** is signed (1494), dividing the New World into two spheres of influence, the Portuguese and the Castilian.
1492	Christopher Columbus discovers America.
1495-1521	Reign of **Manuel I**. In order to marry Isabel, daughter of the Catholic Monarchs of Spain, he has to fulfil the condition of expelling the Jews from Portugal. This he orders in 1497 and Portugal loses a great many traders, bankers and learned men. **Vasco da Gama** discovers the sea route to India in 1498 and **Pedro Álvares Cabral** lands in Brazil in 1500. **Magellan's** expedition is the first to circumnavigate the world, in 1519-22.
August 1578	The young king **Sebastião I** is killed and succeeded by his great uncle, Henrique I, whose death marked the beginning of the end of Portugal's supremacy. To ensure Portuguese succession, three of his cousins lay claim to the crown: Dom António, Prior of Crato, the Duchess of Bragança and the King of Spain, Philip II, son of the Infante, Isabel. Philip II, who has won over the rich, gets the upper hand and arrives in Lisbon in 1580. The Prior of Crato seeks support in the Azores *(see AZORES)*.

Spanish domination (1580-1640)

1580	**Philip II** of Spain invades Portugal and has himself proclaimed king under the name Felipe I. Spanish domination lasts 60 years.
1 Dec 1640	Uprising against the Spanish; the war of restoration of Portuguese supremacy ensues. Duke João of Bragança takes the title João IV of Portugal; the **Bragança family** remain as the ruling dynasty until 1910.
1668	Spain recognises Portugal's independence.

The 18C

1683-1706	**Pedro II** on the throne.
1703	Britain and Portugal sign the Methuen Treaty and a trade treaty facilitating the shipping of port to England.
1706-50	The reign of **João V**, the Magnanimous, is one of untold magnificence — sustained by riches from Brazil — in keeping with the luxurious tastes of a king of the Baroque period. The finest testimony to the period is the monastery at Mafra *(see MAFRA)*.
1 Nov 1755	An earthquake destroys Lisbon.
1750-77	**José I** reigns assisted by his minister, the **Marquis of Pombal**. Through the latter's policies, Portugal becomes a model of enlightened despotism. Pombal expels the Jesuits in 1759.

The Napoleonic Wars

Portugal joins the first continental coalition against Revolutionary France in 1793. In 1796 Spain leaves the Convention and allies itself to France. When Portugal refuses to renounce its alliance with England, Spain invades in 1801 and the resulting war is known as the **War of the Oranges**. To ensure a strict application of the blockade on Britain, Napoleon invades Portugal but his commanders have little success in a country supported by English troops under the command of Wellesley.

The future Duke of Wellington prefers guerrilla tactics and finally forces the French from the Peninsula.

Portugal suffers violence and depredations by both armies; and the political and moral effects are tragic along with material poverty. King João VI and his family spend a long exile in Brazil (1807-1821).

The downfall of the monarchy

1828-34	**Civil War between liberals and absolutists.** In 1822 Brazil is proclaimed independent and Pedro IV, older son of **João VI**, becomes Emperor Pedro I of Brazil. In 1826, on the death of João VI, Pedro I retains the Brazilian throne and leaves the throne of Portugal to his daughter **Maria II**. A charter for a liberal constitution is adopted. Dom Pedro's brother Miguel, who has been appointed regent, champions the cause for an absolute monarchy and lays claim to the crown which he eventually obtains in 1828. A bitter struggle ensues between the absolutists and the liberal supporters of Dom Pedro. Aided by the English, Dom Pedro returns to Portugal to reinstate his daughter on the throne in 1834; the Evoramonte Convention puts an end to the Civil War. In 1836 Maria II marries Prince Ferdinand of Saxe-Coburg-Gotha who becomes king-consort the following year.
1855-90	In spite of political restlessness during the reigns of **Pedro V** (1855-61), **Luís I** (1861-89) and Carlos I (1889-1908), a third Portuguese empire is reconstituted in Angola and Mozambique. The British Ultimatum ends endeavours by the Governor, **Serpa Pinto**, to set up a territorial belt linking Angola and Mozambique.
1899	Treaty of Windsor with England.
1 Feb 1908	Assassination in Lisbon of King Carlos I and the Crown Prince. Queen Amélia manages to save her youngest son who succeeds to the throne as **Manuel II**.
5 Oct 1910	Abdication of Manuel II and Proclamation of the Republic.

The Republic

1910-33	The Republic cannot restore order. Entering into the war against Germany in 1916, and sending troops to France only aggravates the domestic situation, already critical in 1928. General Carmona then calls upon Oliveira Salazar, professor of economics at Coimbra University. **Dr. Salazar** is appointed Minister of Finance, then in 1932, Prime Minister; he restores economic and political stability but in 1933 promulgates the Constitution of the New State (Estado Novo) instituting a corporative and dictatorial regime (with newspaper censorship and the PIDE, a secret police force).

The Carnation Revolution (1974)

1939-45	Portugal remains neutral during the Second World War.
1949	Portugal is one of the founding members of NATO.
1961	India annexes Goa, a Portuguese territory since 1515.
1968-70	Salazar, whose accident near the end of 1968 prevents him from taking part in affairs of state, dies in July 1970. His successor, Caetano, continues a ruinous and unpopular anti-guerrilla war in Africa.
25 April 1974	**Carnation Revolution** (Revolução dos Cravos): the Armed Forces Movement, led by General Spínola, seizes power.
1974	Independence of Guinea-Bissau.
1975	Independence of Cape Verde Islands, Mozambique, Angola and São Tomé.
1976	New Socialist Constitution. General António Ramalho Eanes is elected President of the Republic. Independence of East Timor. Autonomy is granted to Macau (a Portuguese province in southeast China) and the archipelagos of Madeira and the Azores.
1980	The conservative party wins the general election. Sá Carneiro forms a government, but dies in a plane crash on 4 December. General Eanes's presidential mandate is renewed.
1986	Portugal becomes a member of the EEC on 1 January. Mário Soares is elected President of the Republic on 16 February.
March 1986	600 years of friendship between Britain and Portugal celebrated with Queen Elizabeth and Prince Philip's state visit.
1991	Mário Soares is re-elected president.
1994	Lisbon chosen as European Capital of Culture.
1996	Jorge Sampaio elected President of the Republic.
1998	Lisbon hosts Expo'98.

THE ANGLO-PORTUGUESE ALLIANCE

"Our Oldest Ally" – This alliance dates back more than 600 years to a treaty signed in London in 1373. This was ratified in 1386 by the **Treaty of Windsor** which followed the Battle of Aljubarrota (1385) in which English archers helped João I, the new King, and Nuno Alvares, to beat the Castilians. This treaty of perpetual peace and friendship has been reratified and invoked several times since, for military, commercial and dynastic reasons.

Military assistance began at the time of the Crusades when in 1147 the reconquest of Lisbon was achieved by Afonso Henriques with the help of an army of Crusaders on their way to the Holy Land.

Troops were sent by Richard II in 1398 to aid the expulsion of Dom Dinis, a pretender to the Portuguese throne, and again in 1415 to help the expedition to Ceuta in North Africa. In an unsuccessful attempt to break the Spanish domination of Portugal (started in 1580) Elizabeth I provided one of the pretenders to the throne, António, Prior of Crato, with an army in 1589. Military assistance continued throughout the centuries *(see the Napoleonic Wars above and box on William Carr under SINTRA).*

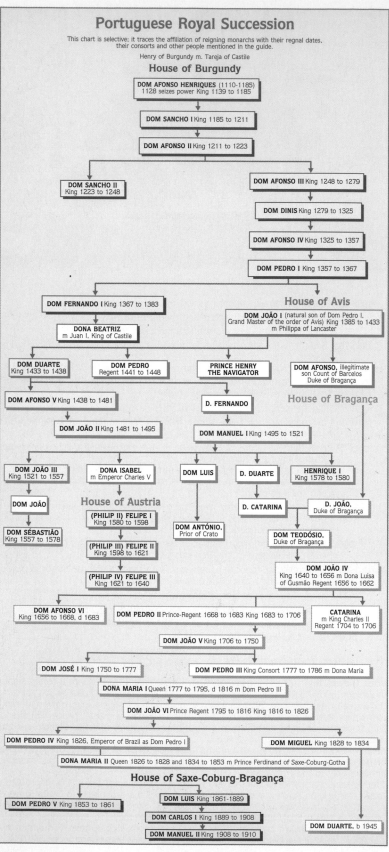

Portuguese Royal Succession

This chart is selective: it traces the affiliation of reigning monarchs with their regnal dates, their consorts and other people mentioned in the guide.

Henry of Burgundy m. Tareja of Castile

House of Burgundy

DOM AFONSO HENRIQUES (1110-1185) 1128 seizes power King 1139 to 1185

DOM SANCHO I King 1185 to 1211

DOM AFONSO II King 1211 to 1223

DOM SANCHO II King 1223 to 1248

DOM AFONSO III King 1248 to 1279

DOM DINIS King 1279 to 1325

DOM AFONSO IV King 1325 to 1357

DOM PEDRO I King 1357 to 1367

DOM FERNANDO I King 1367 to 1383

DONA BEATRIZ m Juan I, King of Castile

House of Avis

DOM JOÃO I (natural son of Dom Pedro I, Grand Master of the order of Avis) King 1385 to 1433 m Philippa of Lancaster

DOM DUARTE King 1433 to 1438

DOM PEDRO Regent 1441 to 1448

PRINCE HENRY THE NAVIGATOR

DOM AFONSO, illegitimate son Count of Barcelos Duke of Bragança

DOM AFONSO V King 1438 to 1481

D. FERNANDO

House of Bragança

DOM JOÃO II King 1481 to 1495

DOM MANUEL I King 1495 to 1521

DOM JOÃO III King 1521 to 1557

DONA ISABEL m Emperor Charles V

DOM LUIS

D. DUARTE

HENRIQUE I King 1578 to 1580

DOM JOÃO

House of Austria

(PHILIP II) FELIPE I King 1580 to 1598

DOM ANTÓNIO, Prior of Crato

D. CATARINA

D. JOÃO, Duke of Bragança

DOM SÉBASTIÃO King 1557 to 1578

(PHILIP III) FELIPE II King 1598 to 1621

DOM TEODÓSIO, Duke of Bragança

(PHILIP IV) FELIPE III King 1621 to 1640

DOM JOÃO IV King 1640 to 1656 m Dona Luisa of Gusmão Regent 1656 to 1662

DOM AFONSO VI King 1656 to 1668, d 1683

DOM PEDRO II Prince-Regent 1668 to 1683 King 1683 to 1706

CATARINA m King Charles II Regent 1704 to 1706

DOM JOÃO V King 1706 to 1750

DOM JOSÉ I King 1750 to 1777

DOM PEDRO III King Consort 1777 to 1786 m Dona Maria

DONA MARIA I Queen 1777 to 1795, d 1816 m Dom Pedro III

DOM JOÃO VI Prince Regent 1795 to 1816 King 1816 to 1826

DOM PEDRO IV King 1826, Emperor of Brazil as Dom Pedro I

DOM MIGUEL King 1828 to 1834

DONA MARIA II Queen 1826 to 1828 and 1834 to 1853 m Prince Ferdinand of Saxe-Coburg-Gotha

House of Saxe-Coburg-Bragança

DOM PEDRO V King 1853 to 1861

DOM LUIS King 1861-1889

DOM CARLOS I King 1889 to 1908

DOM DUARTE, b 1945

DOM MANUEL II King 1908 to 1910

"Our Oldest Ally", it was in these terms that Winston Churchill described Anglo-Portuguese relations in the House of Commons in 1943 when announcing the latest agreement which provided facilities for British shipping in the Azores during the Battle of the Atlantic (Portugal remained neutral in the Second World War). The alliance also included trade agreements.

As early as the 13C trade flourished in English wool and textiles and Portuguese wax, leather and skins, fruit and olive oil. The Methuen Treaty of 1703 *(see PORTO)* provided conditions for the shipping of port wine to Britain.

Many marriages further strengthened relations, among the most notable being that of Philippa, daughter of John of Gaunt, Duke of Lancaster in 1386

> ### A European dynasty with prominent connections
>
> In the 19C the Ernestine Wettins of the Saxe Coburg-Gotha branch provided sovereigns of Belgium, Bulgaria, Great Britain and Portugal. The cousins, Albert (1819-61) and Ferdinand (1816-85) were to become Prince and King-Consorts to Queen Victoria of Great Britain (1840) and to Queen Maria II of Portugal (1836), respectively. Both consorts took a keen interest in architecture and the royal residence at Pena, the hunting lodge at Bussaco, the castle at Balmoral and Osborne House on the Isle of Wight all bear their special imprint. The term Balmoral-Manueline was coined to describe the style.

to João I, King of Portugal and founder of the House of Avis which was to reign until 1580, and that of Catherine (Catarina) of Bragança with King Charles II in 1662.

THE GREAT DISCOVERIES

When asked about their history, the Portuguese willingly evoke the period of the great discoveries with pride and nostalgia. They relate how a handful of adventurous Lusitanians plied the oceans in search of new lands, intent simply on exploration rather than conquest, unlike their Spanish neighbours so proud of their *conquistadores*.

Grand designs – On 25 July 1415, a fleet of more than 200 ships under the command of Dom João I and his three sons, Prince Henry being one, set sail from Lisbon. The **capture of Ceuta** put an end to coastal attacks by pirates from Barbary resulting in Portuguese control of the Straits of Gibraltar. They also hoped the expedition would furnish them at low cost, with gold and slaves from the Sudan. The spirit of the Crusades was not altogether lacking either, given that Christians opposed Muslims throughout the venture. By landing on the African continent the Portuguese aimed to join their kingdom to that of the Christian Prester John who was said to rule a country beyond the Moorish territories. Furthermore, the idea of discovering a new world, of unveiling the unknown, was ever in the minds of men of ambition at that time.

Lastly, economic reasons were a strong incentive. Towards the end of the Middle Ages, wealth lay in the hands of those who held the monopoly to the spice and perfume trade from the Orient. In this case it was the Moors and the Venetians; the former controlled the land transport, the caravans between the present-day Persian Gulf and the Mediter-ranean, and the latter the sea transport, the shipping across the Mediterranean. In order to bypass these intermediaries, a sea route had to be found, and Henry the Navigator was to devote his life to this dream.

The Sagres School – Prince Henry the Navigator (1394-1460) retired to the Sagres Promontory together with cos-mographers, cartographers and naviga-tors to try and work out a sea route from Europe to India. The idea of rounding Africa by the south had al-ready begun to germinate in his mind and to ensure that his hypotheses should ultimately be proved correct, he called on experienced navigators to journey ever further south. **Madeira** was discovered in 1419 by João Gonçalves Zarco and Tristão Vaz Teixeira, the **Azores** in 1427 (supposedly by Diogo de Silves), and in 1434 **Gil Eanes** rounded **Cape Bojador**, then the furthest point known to western man. To guarantee the success of these expeditions the Sagres School improved the caravel itself as well as navigational instruments *(see SAGRES)*. Each time they discovered

A. Wolf/EXPLORER

Prince Henry the Navigator, 15C polyptych of the Adoration of St Vincent new land the mariners erected a **padrão**, a cairn surmounted by a cross and the arms of Portugal, to mark their presence. Above all, they established trade relations. Prince Henry inspired new methods of colonisation by setting up **trading posts** *(feitora)*, exchanges and banks. These offices, set up and run by private individuals, sometimes fostered the development of towns independent of the local powers, such as Goa. **Companies** were created to control trade in a particular commodity, of which the monopoly rights were often acquired. There were also **deeds of gift**, usually of land, to ships' captains with the charge that the area be developed.

Henry died in 1460 but the stage had been set.

Vasco da Gama, 15C painting

The great discoveries – The major discoveries were made during the reigns of João II and Manuel I who were both grand nephews of Henry the Navigator. **Diogo Cão** reached the mouth of the Congo in 1482 and the whole coast of Angola then came under Portuguese control. In 1488 **Bartolomeu Dias** rounded the Cape of Storms, which was immediately rechristened the Cape of Good Hope by Dom João II. A few years earlier **Christopher Columbus**, the Genoese navigator married to a Portuguese, had had the idea of sailing to India by a westerly route. His proposals, rebuffed in Lisbon, found favour with the Catholic Monarchs and in 1492 he discovered the New World. In 1494, under the **Treaty of Tordesillas** and with the Pope's approval, the Kings of Portugal and Castile divided the newly discovered and as yet undiscovered territories of the world between them: all lands west of a meridian 370 sea leagues west of the Cape Verde Islands were to belong to Castile, all east to Portugal. The position of the dividing meridian has led some historians to speculate as to whether Portugal knew of the existence of Brazil even before its official discovery by **Pedro Álvares Cabral** in 1500.

The exploration of the African coast by the Portuguese continued. On 8 July 1497 a fleet of four ships commanded by Admiral **Vasco da Gama** sailed from Lisbon with the commission to reach India by way of the sea route round the Cape. By March 1498 Vasco da Gama had reached Mozambique and on 20 May he landed in Calicut (Kozhicode, southern India): the sea route to India had been discovered. This epic

PRINCIPAL PORTUGUESE EXPEDITIONS (1419-1522)

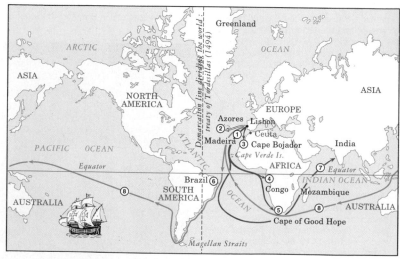

① Madeira (João Gonçalves Zarco and Tristão Vaz Teixeira, 1419)
② The Azores (1427)
③ Cabo Bojador (Gil Eanes, 1434)
④ Mouth of the Congo River (Diogo, Cão, 1482)
⑤ Cape of Good Hope (Bartolomeu Dias, 1488)
⑥ Brazil (Pedro Álvares Cabral, 1500)
⑦ Mozambique and India (Vasco da Gama, 1498)
⑧ Circumnavigation of the world (Magellan's expedition, 1522)

voyage was later sung in *The Lusiads (Os Lusíadas)* by the poet Camões. In 1501 **Gaspar Corte Real** discovered Newfoundland, but King Manuel was interested primarily in Asia. Within a few years the Portuguese had explored the coastlines of Asia. By 1515 they were in control of the Indian Ocean, thanks to fortified outposts like Goa which had been established by **Afonso de Albuquerque** in 1510.

It was, however, on behalf of the King of Spain that the Portuguese **Fernão de Magalhães** (Magellan) set out in 1519 and landed in India in 1521. Though he was assassinated by the natives of the Philippines, one of his vessels continued the journey to become the first to circumnavigate the world (1522).

In 1517 King Manuel I sent an ambassador to **China** but this expedition proved a failure and it was not until 1554 that the Portuguese were able to trade with Canton and make contact with Macau. In 1542 the Portuguese arrived in Japan where they caused political upheaval by introducing firearms. The Jesuits, whose Society of Jesus had been founded in 1540, became very active there and by 1581 there were almost 150 000 Christians.

The bonus – The Discoveries, coming in a troubled period at the end of the Middle Ages, were of very great consequence on the development of western civilisation at the dawn of the Renaissance. From the beginning of the 16C, the monopoly of the trade with India, which had always been in the hands of the Turks and the Arabs, passed to the Portuguese; Mediterranean and Baltic trading posts such as Venice, Genoa and Lübeck declined in favour of ports on the western seaboard, particularly Lisbon; merchants from northern Europe came to trade their arms, cereals, silver and

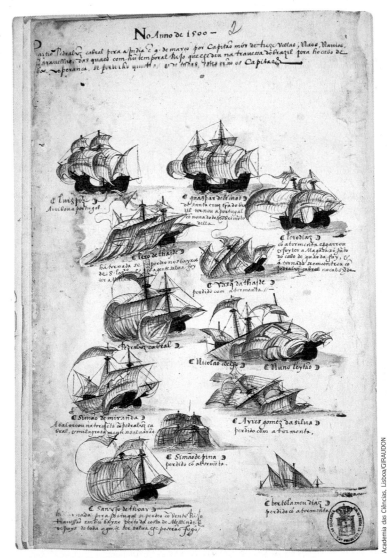

Pedro Álvares Cabral's armada – Book of the Armadas, 16C

copper for African gold and ivory, famous Indian spices – pepper, cinnamon, ginger and cloves – Chinese silks, Persian carpets and precious metals from Sumatra. New products – the sweet potato, maize, tobacco, cocoa and indigo – were introduced to Europe; gold from Africa and America flooded in through the Tagus. Portugal and Spain became great powers, establishing vast colonial empires, while the Islamic countries lost their importance.

The discovery of new lands and civilisations disrupted every sphere of universal history, not only political and economical but also cultural and religious. For instance, the discovery of the existence of formerly unknown peoples posed religious problems: did the men of the New World have a soul and were they marked by original sin? These doubts presaged the Reformation; the development of the critical approach led to the advancement of modern science; the fields of anthropology and geography expanded. The need for cheap manual labour brought about slavery; the traffic in "black ebony" introduced African Negroes to America.

Evanescent riches – Portugal, however, had overspent its strength; the population had dropped from 2 to 1 million, many having gone overseas; riches encouraged idlers and adventurers; land was not tilled and wheat and rye had to be imported; crafts and skills were lost; the cost of living rose steeply. Gold was exchanged for goods from the Low Countries and France until Portugal's riches were dissipated and virtually nothing remained. The final blow came on 4 August 1578, when the young King Sebastião I was killed at El-Ksar El-Kebir in Morocco *(See Historical table and notes)*. Two years after his death Portugal came under Spanish control.

Art and architecture

Prehistoric sites like the megaliths around Évora, the rock engravings in the Vale do Côa, as well as Iron Age ruins like those of Citânia de Briteiros, or the Roman remains at Conímbriga, Tróia and Évora will interest the lover of Antiquity. There are also small pre-Romanesque churches which recall the different architectural influences that swept across the Iberian Peninsula from the north and the east. Among them are the Visigothic (Igreja de São Pedro de Balsemão near Lamego and Igreja de Santo Amaro in Beja), the Mozarabic (Capela de São Pedro de Lourosa in Oliveira do Hospital), and lastly the Byzantine (Capela de São Frutuoso near Braga). But it is from the 11C onwards, as the country gained its independence, that Portuguese art took on a specifically national character.

THE MIDDLE AGES (11-15C)

Romanesque Art

The Romanesque influence arrived late in Portugal, in the 11C, brought from France by Burgundian knights and monks from Cluny and Moissac, it retained many French traits. Nevertheless, the influence of Santiago de Compostela, particularly in northern Portugal, produced a style more Galician than French which was further enhanced through the use of granite. Monuments have a massive and rough appearance with capitals that show the granite's solid resistance to the mason's chisel.

Cathedrals, often built by French architects, preferably on an elevation in the centre of a town, were reconstructed at the same time as local fortified castles and, therefore, often outwardly resemble them. The cathedrals in Coimbra, Lisbon, Évora, Oporto and Braga are good examples. They served as supports to the Portuguese military, at that time occupied in attacking the Moorish forces. Country churches, built at a later date, sometimes have richly carved main doorways. The interior design, frequently including pointed arches and even groined vaulting, has often been transformed by Manueline or baroque additions.

Mosteiro de Batalha

Gothic Art

While the Romanesque style blossomed in chapels and cathedrals in the north, Gothic architecture developed most vigorously at the end of the 13C in the limestone regions of Coimbra and Lisbon in the form of large monasteries. The churches, which are designed with a nave and two corresponding aisles, together with polygonal apses and apsidal chapels, retain the proportions and simplicity of the Romanesque style. The **Mosteiro de Alcobaça** served as a model for the 14C Cistercian cloisters of the cathedrals in Coimbra, Lisbon and Évora. Flamboyant Gothic found its most perfect expression in the **Mosteiro da Batalha** even though this was only completed in the Manueline period.

Sculpture – Gothic sculpture developed in the 14C for the adornment of tombs, but barely featured as decoration on tympana and doorways. Capitals and cornices were ornamented only with geometric or plant motifs with the exception of a few stylised animals or occasional human forms (capitals in the Mosteiro de Celas in Coimbra). Funerary art flowered in three centres, Lisbon, Évora and Coimbra from where, under the influence of **Master Pero**, it spread into northern Portugal, principally to Oporto, Lamego, Oliveira do Hospital and São João de Tarouca, in spite of the difficulties posed by the use of granite. The most beautiful tombs, those of Inês de Castro and Dom Pedro in the Mosteiro de Alcobaça, were carved out of limestone. Coimbra's influence continued into the 15C under **João Afonso** and **Diogo Pires the Elder**. A second centre developed at Batalha inspired by **Master Huguet** (tombs of Dom João I and Philippa of Lancaster). Statuary, influenced by the French, particularly at Braga, is typified by minuteness of detail, realism in the carving of the head and gentleness of expression.

Military Architecture

The Portuguese, in the wars first against the Moors and then the Spanish, built castles which remain today as prominent features of the landscape. The first series mark the successive stages of the Reconquest, the second, dating from the 13 to 17C, guard the major routes of communication. Most of these castles, built in the Middle Ages, have a strong family likeness. Double perimeter walls circle a keep or Torre de Menagem which was usually square, and crowned with pyramid capped merlons, a trace of the Moorish influence.

THE MANUELINE PERIOD (1490-1520)

The Manueline style marks the transition from Gothic to Renaissance in Portugal. Its name, which was only given to it in the 19C, recalls that it flowered during the reign of Manuel I. Despite the brevity of the period in which it developed, the Manueline style's undeniable originality has given it major importance in all aspects of Portuguese art.

It reflects the passion, which inspired all of Portugal at the time, for the sea and of faraway territories which had just been discovered, and manifests the strength and riches accumulating on the banks of the Tagus.

Architecture – Churches remained Gothic in their general plan, in the height of their columns and network vaulting – but novelty and movement appeared in the way columns were twisted to form spirals; triumphal arches were adorned with mouldings in the form of nautical cables; ribs of plain pointed arched vaulting were given heavy liernes in round or square relief; these, in their turn, were transformed by further ornamentation into four-pointed stars or were supplemented by decorative cables occasionally intertwined into mariners' knots. The contour of the vaulting itself evolved, flattening out and resting on arches supported on consoles. The height of the aisles was increased, so giving rise to true hall churches.

Window in the Convento de Cristo, Tomar

Y. Travert/DIAF

Sculpture – The Manueline style shows its character most fully in the form of decoration. Windows, doorways, rose windows and balustrades are covered with sprigs of laurel leaves, poppy heads, roses, corn cobs, acorns, oak leaves, artichokes, cardoons, pearls, scales, ropes, anchors, terrestrial globes, armillary spheres and lastly the Cross of the Order of Christ which forms a part of every decorative scheme.

Artists – **Boytac** was responsible for the first Manueline buildings, the Igreja do Convento de Jesus at Setúbal, and the Sé (Cathedral) at Guarda. He also contributed to the construction of the Mosteiro dos Jerónimos in Belém, Lisbon, the Igreja do Mosteiro da Santa Cruz in Coimbra and the Mosteiro da Batalha. His artistry lay in magnificent complication: twisted columns, of which he was the master, were covered with overlapping laurel leaves, scales and rings; doorways, which were a major element in Manueline art, stood in a rectangular setting bordered by turned columns crowned with spiralled pinnacles; in the centre of the whole or above it stood the Manueline emblems of the shield, the Cross of the Order of Christ and the armillary sphere.

Mateus Fernandes, whose art was distinctly influenced by the elegance of Flamboyant Gothic, brought a Manueline touch to Batalha. Decoration, which he usually designed as an infinitely repeating plant, geometric or calligraphic motif, takes precedence over volume – the doorway to the Capelas Imperfeitas (Unfinished Chapels) at Batalha is outstanding for the exuberance of its decoration.

Diogo de Arruda was the most original Manueline artist. He designed the famous and marvellously inventive Tomar window *(see TOMAR)*. Marine and nautical themes became a positive obsession with this artist.

Francisco de Arruda was the architect of Lisbon's Torre de Belém (Belém Tower). He rejected the decorative excesses of his brother, preferring the simplicity of Gothic design which he embellished with Moorish motifs.

The Arruda brothers were recognised equally as the "master architects of the Alentejo", where they displayed their skill in combining the Manueline style with Moorish themes which gave rise to an entirely new style, the **Luso-Moorish.** This is characterised by the horseshoe arch adorned with delicate mouldings. Most of the seigneurial mansions and castles in the Alentejo, as well as the royal palaces in Sintra and Lisbon, bear the stamp of this style.

Simultaneously, as Manueline architecture was reaching its peak at the end of the 15C, Portuguese sculpture came under Flemish influence due to **Olivier de Gand** and **Jean d'Ypres** – their masterpiece is the carved wooden altarpiece in Coimbra's Sé Velha. **Diogo Pires the Younger** followed, adopting Manueline themes in his work of which the best example is the font in the Mosteiro de Leça do Balio (1515).

In the early 16C artists came from Galicia and Biscay to work in northern Portugal. There they helped build the churches at Caminha, Braga, Vila do Conde and Viana do Castelo. The obvious influences in their work are Flamboyant and Spanish Plateresque. From 1517 onwards, two Biscayan artists, **João** and **Diogo de Castilho** worked successively in Lisbon, Tomar and Coimbra. Their art, which had much of the Plateresque style in it, became integrated in the Manueline style (Mosteiro dos Jerónimos).

Minor arts Manueline taste in the minor arts exhibits an exuberance in decorative motifs often inspired by the Orient. Church plate, which was particularly sumptuous in the 15 and 16C, owed much to Oriental exoticism. Pottery and china were influenced by Chinese porcelain. Furniture adopted Oriental decorative techniques with the use of lacquers (China) and inlays of marquetry, mother of pearl and ivory.

PAINTING FROM 1450 TO 1550

The Portuguese painters had to free themselves from foreign influence (in this they lagged behind the architects and sculptors, nevertheless illustrated in their own way the country's prodigious political ascent.

The Primitives (1450-1505) – The early painters were influenced by Flemish art which was introduced into Portugal partly through the close commercial ties between Lisbon and the Low Countries.

Only **Nuno Gonçalves, author of the famous São Vicente polyptych** *(see Museu de Arte Antiga in Lisbon)* remained truly original, not least in the way the pic-

The Annunciation by Freis Carlos

ture's composition evoked a tapestry more than a painting. Unfortunately none of his other works are known except for the cartouches for the Arzila and Tangier tapestries which hang in the Collegiate Church of Pastrana in Spain.

A group of anonymous "masters", including the **Master of Sardoal**, left a good many works which may be seen throughout the country's museums in the sections on Portuguese Primitives.

Among the Flemish painters who came to Portugal, **Francisco Henriques** and **Carlos Frei** stand out for their wide-ranging compositions and rich use of colour.

The Manueline Painters (1505-1550) – The Manueline painters created a true Portuguese School of painting which was characterised by delicacy of design, beauty and accuracy of colour, realism in the composition of the backgrounds, life-size human figures and an expressive naturalism in the portrayal of people's faces tempered, however, with a certain idealism. The major artists in the school worked in either Viseu or Lisbon.

The **Viseu School** was headed by **Vasco Fernandes**, known as Grão Vasco (Great Vasco) whose early works, including the altarpiece at Lamego, reveal Flemish influence. His later work showed more originality, a richness of colour as well as a sense of the dramatic and of composition (as in his paintings from Viseu cathedral which may now be seen in the town's Museu Grão Vasco). **Gaspar Vaz**, whose works may be seen in the Igreja São João de Tarouca, began painting at the Lisbon school, but in fact painted his best pictures while at Viseu.

The **Lisbon School** established around **Jorge Afonso**, painter for King Manuel I, saw the development of several talented artists:

– **Cristóvão de Figueiredo** evolved a technique which recalls the later impressionists (the use of spots of colour in place of the longer brushstrokes) and the use of black and grey in portraiture. His style was imitated by several artists including the Master of Santa Auta in his altarpiece for the original Igreja da Madre de Deus in Lisbon.

– **Garcia Fernandes**, sometimes archaic in style, showed a certain preciosity in portraits.

– **Gregório Lopes**, whose line and modelling were harsher, painted Court life. He excelled in backgrounds which present contemporary Portuguese life in exact detail (altarpiece in the Igreja de São João Baptista in Tomar). His influence may be seen in the work of the Master of Abrantes even though the latter already had a baroque style.

THE RENAISSANCE

The Renaissance style, which retained its essential Italian and French characteristics in Portugal, spread out – particularly in the field of sculpture – from Coimbra, where several French artists had settled.

Nicolas Chanterene, whose style remained entirely faithful to the principles of the Italian Renaissance, undertook the decoration of the north door of the Mosteiro dos Jerónimos in Belém before becoming the master sculptor of the Coimbra School. The pulpit in the Igreja da Santa Cruz in Coimbra is his masterpiece. **Jean de Rouen** excelled in altarpieces and low reliefs, as may be seen in the Mosteiro de Celas in Coimbra. **Houdart** succeeded Nicolas Chanterene in 1530 at Coimbra as grand master of statuary. His sculptures are easily recognisable for their realism.

The advance in architecture, which came later than in the other arts, was brought about by native Portuguese: **Miguel de Arruda** introduced a classical note to Batalha after 1533; **Diogo de Torralva** completed the Convento de Cristo in Tomar; **Afonso Álvares** began the transition to classical design by giving buildings a monumental simplicity.

CLASSICAL ART

The classical period saw the triumph of the Jesuit style with **Filippo Terzi**, an Italian architect who arrived in Portugal in 1576, and **Baltazar Álvares** (1550-1624); churches became rectangular in plan and were built without transept, ambulatories or apses.

Painting came under Spanish influence and produced only two major artists: **Domingos Vieira** (1600-78), whose portraits are vividly alive, and Josefa de Ayala, known as **Josefa de Óbidos** (1634-84). A feeling for classical composition is apparent in the work of the gold and silversmiths of the period. The 17C was marked by the Indo-Portuguese style of furniture, typified by marquetry secretaries, rare woods and ivory.

BAROQUE ART (LATE 17-18C)

The baroque style, which owes its name to the Portuguese word *barroco* – a rough pearl – corresponds, in the artistic sense, to the spirit of the Counter-Reformation.

Architecture – Baroque architecture abandoned the symmetry of the classical style and sought movement, volume, a sense of depth through the use of curved lines and an impression of grandeur. In Portugal, the beginning of baroque architecture coincided with the end of Spanish domination. In the 17C, architecture, therefore, took on an austere and simple appearance under **João Nunes Tinoco** and **João Turiano**, but from the end of the century onwards façades became alive with angels, garlands and the interplay of curving lines, particularly at Braga. The architect **João Antunes** advocated an octagonal plan for religious buildings (Igreja da Santa Engrácia in Lisbon). In the 18C

King João V invited foreign artists to Portugal. The German **Friedrich Ludwig** and the Hungarian **Mardel**, both trained in the Italian School, brought a monumental style, as can best be seen in the Mosteiro de Mafra.

True baroque architecture developed in the north and can be seen in both religious and civic buildings (Igreja de Bom Jesus near Braga and Solar de Mateus near Vila Real), where the whitewashed walls of the façades contrast with the pilasters and cornices which frame them. In Porto, **Nicolau Nasoni**, who was of Italian origin, adorned façades with floral motifs, palm leaves and swags. In Braga, architecture approached the rococo in style (Palácio do Raio in Braga, Igreja de Santa Maria Madalena in Falperra).

Decoration – *Azulejos* and *Talha dourada* were popular forms of decoration, the latter being the Portuguese name for the heavily gilded wood used in the adornment of church interiors, including, from 1650 onwards, high altarpieces which were first carved before being gilded. In the 17C altarpieces resembled doorways; on either side of the altar, surrounded by a stepped throne, twisted columns rose up while the screen itself was covered in decorative motifs in high relief including vines, bunches of grapes, birds, cherubim, etc. Altarpieces in the 18C were often all out of proportion, invading the ceiling and the chancel walls. Entablatures with broken pediments crowned columns against which stood atlantes or other statues. Altarpieces were also surmounted by baldachins.

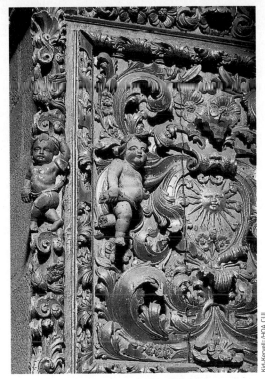

Baroque detail inside Évora cathedral

Statuary – Many statues generally in wood were to be found on the altarpieces which decorated the churches. In the 18C statuary largely followed foreign schools: at Mafra, the Italian **Giusti** and his colleagues instructed many Portuguese sculptors, among them **Machado de Castro**; in Braga, Coimbra and Oporto, **Laprade** represented the French School; however, at Arouca, the Portuguese **Jacinto Vieira** gave his carvings a very personal, lively style. The idea of the baroque cribs *(presépios)*, that can be seen in many churches, originate from southern Italy. In Portugal they are more naïve but not without artistic merit. The figures in terracotta are often by **Machado de Castro, Manuel Teixeira** or **António Ferreira**. The talent of the baroque sculptors is also evident in the many fountains found throughout Portugal especially in the Minho region. The monumental staircase of Bom Jesus near Braga is made up of a series of fountains in the rococo style.

Painting – Painting is represented by **Vieira Lusitano (1699-1783)** and **Domingos António de Sequeira** (1768-1837), the latter a remarkable portrait painter and draughtsman.

FROM THE LATE 18C TO THE 19C

Architecture – The second half of the 18C saw a return to the classical style which may be seen in the work of **Mateus Vicente** (1747-86 – Palácio Real in Queluz), **Carlos da Cruz Amarante** (Igreja de Bom Jesus), and the Lisbon architects, particularly **Eugénio dos Santos** who created the so-called Pombal style. In the late 19C when the Romantic movement favoured a revival of former styles, Portugal developed the neo-Manueline, an evocation of the prestigious period of the Great Discoveries exemplified by the Castelo da Pena in Sintra, the Palace-Hotel in Buçaco and the Estação do Rossio in Lisbon. At the same time *azulejos* were being used to decorate entire house façades.

Sculpture – **Soares dos Reis** (1847-89) tried to portray the Portuguese *saudade* or nostalgia in sculpture; his pupil, **Teixeira Lopes** (1866-1918) revealed an elegant technique, particularly when portraying children's heads.

Painting – Portuguese painters discovered the naturalistic approach from the Barbizon school in France. Two painters, **Silva Porto** (1850-93) and **Marquês de Oliveira** (1853-1927) followed the Naturalist movement, while **Malhoa (1855-1933)**, the painter of popular festivals, and **Henrique Pousão** (1859-84) were closer to Impressionism; **Sousa Pinto** (1856-1939) excelled as a pastel artist and **Columbano Bordalo Pinheiro** (1857-1929) achieved distinction with his portraits and still lifes.

THE 20C

Architecture – The influence of Art Nouveau may be seen in buildings in Lisbon, Coimbra and Leira, while one of the finest examples of Art Deco in Portugal is the Casa de Serralves in Oporto. In the thirties, the architect **Raúl Lino** built the Casa dos Patudos in Alpiarça, near Santarém. However, it was only in the fifties that a noticeable development in housing came about which may be seen in council houses, garden cities and buildings like the Museu Gulbenkian in Lisbon.

The Oporto School of architecture stands out for the modernism it advocates with internationally known architects such as **Fernando Távora** (b. 1923) and **Álvaro Siza** (b 1933) who was commissioned to restore the Chiado quarter in Lisbon which was partly destroyed by fire in 1988. The main architectural event in Lisbon in the eighties was the construction of the post-modern Torres das Amoreiras designed by **Tomás Taveira**.

Sculpture – **Francisco Franco** (1885-1955) held great sway over the official sculpture of the period, including the commemorative monuments so popular under Salazar. More recently, João Cutileiro has come to prominence with his original collection of statues (Dom Sebastião in Lagos, and Camões in Cascais), while José Pedro Croft (stonework), Rui Sanches (woodwork) and Julião Sarmento are all contemporary artists who adhere to a more conceptual style of sculpture (installations).

Painting – In the early 20C Portuguese painting mainly stuck to Naturalism; only a few artists diverged to follow the general trend; **Amadeo de Souza Cardoso** (1887-1918), a friend of Modigliani, worked in Paris assimilating the lessons of Cézanne and found his true expression first in Cubism then in a highly coloured variant of Expressionism; his friend **Santa Rita** (1889-1918) who died unexpectedly, made a great contribution to the Portuguese Futurist movement but destroyed much of his work. **Almada Negreiros** (1889-1970) was influenced by Cubism all the while remaining a classical draughtsman. He was also a poet and playwright. He painted the large frescoes in Lisbon's harbour stations in 1945 and 1948. **Maria Helena Vieira da Silva** (1908-92), who moved to Paris in 1928, derived her art from the Paris School, although in her space paintings the *azulejo* influence of pattern and colour may be seen.

Among the best known contemporary painters are Paula Rego (b. 1935), who draws upon Op-Art, Júlio Pomar, Lourdes Castro, José Guimarães and, more recently, Pedro Cabrita Reis (installations), Pedro Calapez (abstraction and volumetric forms), Pedro Portugal, Pedro Casquiero (abstraction), Graça Morais and Pedro Proença (allegorical images).

The Game of Chess by Vieira da Silva

ARCHITECTURAL TERMS

(Cadeiral: *words in blue are in Portuguese*)

Adufa: A protective lattice screen made of small strips of wood arranged on the outside of windows.

Ajimez: a paired window or opening.

Apse: the generally rounded end of a church behind the altar. The exterior is called the east end.

Altar Mor: the high altar.

Archivolt: the lower curve of an arch, from column impost to column impost, in a doorway or archway.

Armillary sphere: a globe made up of hoops to show the motions of the heavenly bodies. As the emblem of King Manuel I, it is often portrayed in Manueline art.

Artesonado: a marquetry ceiling in which raised fillets outline honeycomb-like cells in the shape of stars. This particular decoration, which first appeared under the Almohads, was popular throughout the Iberian Peninsula in the 15 and 16C.

Atlantes: supports in the form of carved male figures

Atrium: a forecourt or open central courtyard in a Roman house.

Azulejos: glazed, patterned, ceramic tiles.

M. Chaput/MICHELIN

Barbican: an outer defence of a castle, especially a watch-tower projecting over a gate or drawbridge.

Bastion: a projecting part of a fortification built at an angle of, or against the line of, a wall.

Cadeiral: the choir-stalls in a church.

Campanile: a bell-tower, often detached from the church.

Capelo Mor: the chancel or sanctuary.

Chicane: a zig-zag passageway.

Citânia: A term used to describe the ruins of former Roman or pre-Roman settlements on the Iberian Peninsula.

Coro: the part of a chancel containing the stalls and used by canons and other members of the clergy.

Coro alto: a church gallery.

Curtain wall: a stretch of wall between two towers or bastions.

Empedrado: A typical surface covering for Portuguese pavements and streets made from stones of various types and colours to create attractive designs.

Gable: the decorative, triangular upper portion of a wall which supports a pitched roof.

Glacis: an embankment sloping gently down from a fort.

Grotesque: (from *grotta* or grotto in Italian): the name given to a fantastic or incongruous ornament used in the Renaissance.

Hypocaust: a space under a floor in a Roman house where hot air or furnace gases were used for heating.

Impluvium: a square basin in the atrium of a Roman house used for collecting rain water.

Jacente: a recumbent funerary statue.

Judiaria: an old Jewish quarter.

Lantern: The part of a dome which opens laterally.

Lavabo: a fountain basin in cloisters used by monks for their ablutions.

Levada: Water which is directed through irrigation channels.

Lombard arches: a decorative device in Romanesque architecture consisting of small slightly projecting blind arcades linking vertical bands.

Machicolation: a corbelled crenellation.

Merlon: the solid part of an embattled parapet between two crenels.

Modillion: a small console supporting a cornice.

Moucharaby: a wooden lattice-work screen placed in front of a window.

Mouraria: A former Moorish district.

Mozarabic: the work of Christians living under Arab rule after the Moorish invasion of 711. On being persecuted in the 9C, they sought refuge in Christian areas bringing with them Moorish artistic traditions.

Mudejar: the work of Muslims who remained under Christian rule following the Reconquest. It is used to describe work reminiscent of Moorish characteristics which was undertaken between the 13 and 16C.

Paço: a palace or country house.

Padrão: A stone monument erected by the Portuguese to denote possession of lands they discovered.

Pelourinho: a stone pillory *(see Traditional and Festive Portugal)*.

Peristyle: a row of columns surrounding a court, garden or façade.

Pier: vertical shaft supporting an arch.

Plateresque: a style that originated in Spain in the 16C and derived from *plata:* silver, used to describe finely carved decoration as in the work of silversmiths.

Púlpito: a pulpit.

Quinta: a country estate or the main house thereon.

Retable: an altarpiece; marble, stone or wood decoration for an altar.

Rococo: a late baroque style of decoration with asymmetrical patterns involving scrollwork, shell motifs, etc.

Sé: a cathedral. From the Latin *sedes* meaning seat; here the episcopal seat or cathedral.

Solar: a manor house, town mansion or family seat.

Stucco: a type of moulding mix consisting mainly of plaster, used for coating surfaces.

Tree of Jesse: a genealogical tree showing Christ's descent from Jesse through his son David.

Talha dourada: carved, gilded woodwork typical of Portuguese baroque.

Tracery: intersecting stone ribwork in the upper part of a window, a bay or rose window.

Zimbório: The highest outer part of the cupola on a building.

AZULEJOS

Ever since the 15C the *azulejo* has been a component of the different styles of Portuguese architecture that have followed one another through the centuries.

There is some controversy as to the etymological origin of the word *azulejo*; some say it comes from *azul* meaning blue, others that it in fact derives from the Arabic *az-zulay* or *al zuleich* which means a smooth piece of terracotta.

15C Armillary Sphere

Origin – The first *azulejos* came from Andalusia in Spain where they were used as decoration in *alcázars* and other palaces. They were introduced into Portugal by King Manuel I who, having been dazzled by the Alhambra in Granada, decided to have his Sintra palace decorated with the rich ceramic tiles. *Azulejos* at that time took the form of **alicatados**, pieces of monochrome glazed earthenware cut and assembled into geometric patterns. The process was superseded by that of the **corda seca** in which a fine oil and manganese strip was used to separate the different enamels, and when fired, blackened to form an outline for the various motifs. Another method for separating the motifs was known as **aresta** and consisted of drawing ridges in the clay itself. In the 16C the Italian Francesco Nicoloso introduced the Italian **majolica** technique, in which the terracotta was covered with a layer of white enamel which could then be coloured. *Azulejos* thus developed into another type of artistic medium with a wide range of decorative possibilities. The Portuguese created a standard square with 14cm/5.5 inch sides and opened their own workshops in Lisbon.

Renaissance and Mannerist styles – Towards the middle of the 16C Flemish influence took precedence over Spanish, and more complex *azulejo* panels were used to decorate churches; the transept in the Igreja São Roque in Lisbon is a good example. *Azulejos* were in great demand for decorating summer houses and gardens. The finest examples may be seen at Quinta de Bacalhoa and date from 1565. They consist of wonderful multicoloured panels with an Italian majolica-ware quality, which illustrate allegories of great rivers and of Susannah and the Elders. The panel of Nossa Senhora da Vida, which may be seen in the Museu do Azulejo in Lisbon, dates from the same period.

Nossa Senhora da Vida (detail) 16C

The 17C – Portugal entered a period of austerity under Spanish domination. In order to decorate church walls without incurring great expense, simple monochrome tiles were used and placed in geometric patterns. The Igreja da Marvila in Santarém is a fine example. A style known as *tapete*, a sort of tile-carpet or tapestry, was developed for *azulejo* compositions, repeated in blocks of 4, 16 or 36 tiles, which resembled oriental hangings on account of their geometric or floral patterns. These large multicoloured panels, which adorned churches along with other decorative devices including gilded wood and sculpture, were manufactured on a large scale.

The restoration of Portuguese monarchy was followed by a period of great creative development. There was a return to figurative motifs on panels with illustrations of mythological scenes or caricatures of contemporary society life. As for colour, traditional blues and yellows were enhanced by greens and purples through the addition of copper and manganese; there are fine examples at the Palácio dos Marqueses da Fronteira in Lisbon. Little by little, multicoloured tiles gave way to cobalt blue motifs on a white enamel background as may be seen in the Victory Room of the Palácio dos Marqueses da Fronteira. At the same time, a great many tiles were made according to Dutch models with just a single motif, perhaps an animal, a flower or an allegory. These tiles were used to decorate kitchens and corridors.

The 18C – Tiles in the 18C were almost exclusively blue and white; a fashion that came from Chinese porcelain which was popular at the time of the Great Discoveries. *Azulejos* were decorated by true artists, masters including **António Pereira, Manuel dos Santos** and especially **António de Oliveira Bernardes** and his son **Policarpo**. Among their works are the Capela dos Remédios in Peniche, the Igreja de São Lourenço in Almansil and the Forte de São Filipe in Setúbal.

The reign of João V (1706-50) was characterised by magnificence, with the gold from Brazil funding all manner of architectural extravagance. The taste of the day was for dramatic effect

17C tapete style

which expressed itself particularly well in *azulejos*. Panels became veritable pictures, with surrounds of intermingling festoons, tassels, fluttering angels and pilasters – the **baroque style** in full bloom. The main artists at the time were **Bartolomeu Antunes** and **Nicolau de Freitas**. *Azulejos* became popular throughout Portugal, Madeira, the Azores and Brazil. The second half of the 18C was marked by the **rocaille style** (rock and shell motifs). There was a return to polychromy with yellow, brown and purple being the dominant colours; painting became more delicate; smaller motifs were popular and frames were decorated

18C panel

with scrolls, plant motifs and shells as may be seen at the Palácio de Queluz, particularly along the Grand Canal. The *azulejo* played an essential role in the reconstruction of Lisbon after the earthquake in 1755. It was used to enliven a style of architecture that was rather sober, sometimes austere. The opening of the Fábrica Real de Cerâmica in Rato in 1767 meant that *azulejos* could be manufactured in great quantity. There was a return to the *tapete* style. The **neoclassical style** during the reign of Maria I is notable for the refreshing subject matter of its tiles which were framed by garlands, pilasters, urns and foliage.

The 19C – In about 1830 the Portuguese who had gone to Brazil in search of their fortune returned home to decorate their house façades entirely with *azulejos*. This was a popular method in Brazil for protecting walls from tropical rain and humidity. As the fashion caught on, entire streets and church façades were covered in small, stamp manufactured ceramic tiles. The *azulejo* became one of the main decorative devices for shops, markets (Santarém) and stations (Évora and Aveiro), depicting trades, regional traditions and historical events.

Romanticism was given full expression by **Rafael Bordalo Pinheiro** who, once the Caldas da Rainha factory had opened in 1884, produced tiles with motifs in relief covered by a new iridescent enamel. He was the great instigator of **Art Nouveau** in Portugal. Another major artist, **José António Jorge Pinto**, specialised in allegorical panels. When **Art Deco** came in, geometric shapes dominated, producing a style that was easier to manufacture industrially. Other works appeared at the same time illustrating themes from history and folklore. **Jorge Colaço** (1868-1942) decorated the Estaçao de São Bento in Oporto and the Palácio do Buçaco with immense blue and white frescoes of historical scenes.

Present day – In the 1940s and 50s the *azulejo* regained a certain prestige and, in keeping with the architecture of the time, was used in large geometrical fescoes and friezes mainly for covering façades.

Between 1987 and 1990, famous painters including Helena Vieira da Silva, Júlio Pomar and Sá Nogueira decorated Lisbon's new underground stations with *azulejos*.

Literature

While remaining open to outside influences which are quickly and successfully assimilated, Portuguese literature is none the less original and capable of imagination. It reflects the lyrical and nostalgic spirit, the famous *saudade* of the people, as in the *fado* – and also a critical sense, rapidly inclined towards the satire of the injustice or absurdity in each era. This is why poetry has always held a privileged position with, as a figurehead defying the centuries, the monumental work of Camões.

The Middle Ages – The earliest known Portuguese literature dates from the late 12C with the poetry of the troubadours, influenced by Provençal lyricism. There were **Cantigas de Amor** for male voices, the more popular **Cantigas de Amigo** and the satirical **Cantigas de Escárnio e Maldizer** which were collected in anthologies or *cancioneiros*. The most famous of these, the *Cancioneiro Geral*, compiled by the Spaniard Garcia de Resende in the 16C, covered all the poetry written in Portuguese and Castilian over more than a century. King Dinis I, a poet himself, imposed the official use of Portuguese in the 13C. Dom Pedro was the major literary figure of the 14C. However, Fernão Lopes (born circa 1380/1390), the chronicler of Portuguese kings and queens *(Chronicles of Dom Pedro, Dom Fernando, Dom João I and Dom Dinis)*, is considered the great name in medieval literature.

The Renaissance – The 16C introduced humanism and a revival of poetry and dramatic art which can be seen at its best in works by **Francisco Sá de Miranda** (1485-1558), **Bernardim Ribeiro** (1500-52), author of the famous novel *Child and Damsel (Menina et Moça)*, **António Ferreira** (1528-69) in his *Lusitanian Poems (Poemas Lusitanos)* and *Castro* and especially **Gil Vicente** (1470-1536), a great dramatist whose 44 plays painted a satirical picture of Portuguese society in the early 16C. He began with acts *(autos)*, which were often inspired by religious themes and then moved on to tragicomedies and farces *(farses)*.

The greatest figure of the period, however, remains **Luís de Camões** or Camoens (1524-80) who, having demonstrated his virtuosity of verse in *The Lyric (A Lírica)*, shows himself to be the poet of the Great Discoveries in his vast portrait of *The Lusiads (Os Lusíadas, 1572)*, which relates to the epic voyage of Vasco da Gama in a similar way to the *Odyssey*. He led an adventurous life, which took him, among other places, to Morocco (where he lost an eye) and to Goa, and exposed him to the injustices of the world, by disappointments in love and other misfortunes.

BOYER-VIOLLET

So we ploughed our way through waters
where none save Portuguese had ever sailed before.
To our left were the hills and towns of Morocco,
the abode once of the giant Antaeus;
land to our right there was none for certain,
though report spoke of it.
And now our course took us into regions and past
islands already discovered by the great Prince Henrique.

Luís de Camões
The Lusiads, Canto V

Classicism – In the 17C during the 60 years of Spanish domination, Portuguese literature was confined to the Academies in Lisbon and the provinces; baroque affectation prevailed, but at the same time there was "Sebastianism", a belief in the return of King Sebastião, that is to say in the restoration of the country's independence. Much of the literary output consisted of chronicles and travel narratives including work by **Fernão Mendes Pinto** (1509-83) who wrote *Peregrination (Peregrinação)*. The Jesuit **António Vieira** (1608-97) revealed the growing personality of the immense colony of Brazil in his sermons and letters as a missionary.

The 18C – The Age of Enlightenment was represented in Portugal by scholars, historians and philosophers. Theatre and poetry came under French influence. **Manuel M.B. do Bocage** (1765-1805) of French descent, was the great lyric and satirical poet of the 18C.

The 19C – Romanticism took a firm hold thanks to **Almeida Garrett** (1799-1854), who was not only a poet *(Fallen Leaves – Fôlhas Caídas* and *Flores Sem Fructo)* and master of a whole generation of poets, but also a theatre reformer, playwright *(Frei Luis de Sousa)* and novelist *(Travels in My Homeland – Viagens na Minha Terra)*. Among the century's other outstanding poets were **António F. de Castilho** *(Amor e Melancolia)* and **João de Deus**.

Alexandre Herculano (1810-77) introduced the historical novel and his *História de Portugal* was a great success. Among fellow historians, mention should be made of **Oliveira Martins**. The transition to realism came about with work by **Camilo Castelo Branco** (1825-90) whose best-known novel *Fatal Love – Amor de Perdição* gives an account of society at the time. The end of romanticism was signalled by the work of the Azorian **Antero do Quental** (1842-91) whose *Odes Modernas* were an instrument of social unrest. **Eça de Queirós** (1845-1900), a diplomat and a novelist, made a critique of the morals of his day *(Cousin Bazilis, The Maias, Barbaric Prose* and *The Sin of Father Amaro – O Primo Basílio, Os Maias, Prosas Bárbaras, O Crime do Padre Amaro)*. **Guerra Junqueiro** (1850-1923) wrote satirical and controversial poems.

Contemporary authors – **Fernando Pessoa** (1888-1935), a complex and precursory genius, revived Portuguese poetry by using different names and personae, among them Ricardo Reis, Álvaro de Campos, Alberto Caeiro and Bernardo Soares, which enabled him to express himself in different styles. His *Book of Disquietude (Livro do Desassossego)* was published forty years after his death *(see also p 137)*. Among his contemporaries and successors mention should be made of his friend **Mario de Sá Carneiro** who committed suicide at the age of 26 leaving some very fine poems. **José Régio** *(Poems of God and the Devil – Poesias de Deus e do Diabo)*, **Natália Correia**, **António Ramos Rosa** and **Herberto Helder**. Among the main novelists are **Fernando Namora** *(The Wheat and the Chaff – O Trigo e O Joio)*, **Ferreira de Castro** (1898-1974) who drew upon his experiences during a long stay in Brazil *(The Jungle* and *The Mission – A Selva, A Missão)*. **Carlos de Oliveira** (1921-1981) who wrote about life in small villages *(Uma Abelha na Chuva)*. **Manuel Texeira Gomes** *(Letters with No Moral – Cartas sem nenhuma moral)*, **Urbano T. Rodrigues** *(Bastards of the Sun – Bastardos do Sol)*, **Agustina Bessa Luís** *(The Sibyl – A Sibila* and *Fanny Owen)*, as well as regionalist authors like **Aquilino Ribeiro** and **Miguel Torga**. **Vergílio Ferreira** first wrote neo-realistic novels before adopting a very personal style in which he tackles existential problems *(Aparição)*.

Over the last few decades Portuguese literature has undergone a veritable revival with writers such as **José Cardoso Pires** *(Ballad of Dog's Beach – Balada da Praia dos Cães)*, **Lídia Jorge** *(A Costa dos murmúrios, Notícia da Cidade Silvestre)*, **Vitorino Nemésio** and his beautiful novel *Mau Tempo no Canal* which takes place in the Azores, **António Lobo Antunes** *(South of Nowhere* and *An Explanation of the Birds – O Cús de Judas, Explicação dos Pássaros)*, **Sofia de Mello Breyner** whose work is mainly poetical, and **José Saramago** who mixes all the great legends and figures of Portuguese history, including João V and Fernando Pessoa in his

Fernando Pessoa (1964) by Almada Negreiros

novels *(Baltasar and Blimunda, The Year of the Death of Ricardo,* and *The Gospel According to Jesus Christ – Memorial do Convento, O Ano da Morte de Ricardo Reis, O Evangelho segundo Jesus Cristo).*

Mention should also be made of the philosopher **Eduardo Lourenço** *(O Labirinto da Saudade),* **Eugénio de Andrade,** a major, prolific, post-war poet, Almeida Faria who writes about memory, exile and nostalgia, and **Maria Judite de Carvalho** who is continuing her demanding work *(Os Armários Vazios).*

The former Portuguese colonies, particularly Brazil, contribute greatly to Lusitanian literature with authors such as **Jorge Amado,** José Lins do Rego, etc.

Angola also has a tradition of great storytellers such as Luandino Vieira *(Velhas Estórias, Nós os de Makuiusu),* Pepetela *(As Aventuras de Ngunga),* while in Cape Verde, the philologist Baltazar Lopes *(Chiquinho)* and the storyteller Manuel Lopes *(Os Flagelados do Vento Leste)* bear witness to the literary wealth of these West African islands.

Cinema

During the 1930s and '40s the development of Portuguese cinema was marked by popular-based themes, rural films and moralistic comedies with leading actors such as Beatriz Costa and António Silva. The ideology of the Salazar regime then began to dominate with the almost-official producer António Lopes Ribeiro. From the '50s onwards, directors became a fundamental part of Portuguese cinema, which became known for its creativity and independence, while the '60s were marked by the exodus of young Portuguese to France and Great Britain to study cinema. The best known directors of the time were **Paulo Rocha,** who was Jean Renoir's assistant, **Fernando Lopes** *(Belarmino)* and **António de Macedo** *(Domingo à tarde).* Paulo Rocha distinguished himself in 1963 with *The Green Years* (Verdes Anos) which made a break with films under the dictatorship and was the precursor for the "Cinema Novo" (New Cinema) movement, the equivalent of "New Wave" in France. He then went on to film in Japan *(The Island of Loves – A Ilha dos Amores* and *The Mountains of the Moon – As Montanhas da Lua).* Many directors returned to Portugal after the Carnation Revolution to make films with a militant, political bent, such as *O Recado,* which was produced during the dictatorship by **José Fonseca e Costa.** Other important directors of the period include **António Reis** *(Jaime),* **António Pedro de Vasconcelos** *(O lugar do Morto)* and **Lauro António** *(A manhã Submersa).*

Among the new generation of directors in the '80s and '90s can be included **Joaquim Pinto, João Mário Grilo** *(O Processo do Rei),* **João Botelho** *(A Portuguese Farewell – Um Adeus Portugûes* and *Three Palm Trees – Três Palmeiras),* **João César Monteiro** *(Recollections of the Yellow House – Recordações da Casa Amarela* and *God's Comedy – A Comédia de Deus)* and **Pedro Costa** *(O Sangue* and *A Casa da Lava).*

However, **Manoel de Oliveira,** who was born in 1908, has always held a very special place in Portuguese cinema. His early films were dedicated to his home town, Oporto, where he filmed from 1931 onwards. Later he turned to more imaginary themes and mainly drew upon Portuguese literature with works by Camilo Castelo Branco *(Fatal Love – Amor de Perdição* and *The Day of Despair – O Dia do Desespero),* or by Agustina Bessa Luís *(Francisca,* adapted from *Fanny Owen, Party,* written in collaboration with Oliveira). French literature also inspired him *(Le Soulier de Satin* by Paul Claudel); his *Valley of Abraham (Vale Abraão)* drew upon Flaubert's *Madame Bovary.* Luís Miguel Cintra and Leonor Silva are actors who frequently figure in his most recent films.

Valley of Abraham film by Manoel de Oliveira

Cinemateca Portuguesa

Traditional and festive Portugal

At the beginning of the 1970s it was still common to see women dressed entirely in black carrying pitchers on their heads, fishermen in traditional costume, and horse-drawn carts, but today these scenes are rare. Portugal has become a member of the European Union, the roads have been improved thus opening up hitherto isolated regions to modern life, and emigrants have returned to their homeland with new customs. However, not all aspects of traditional life have disappeared and those that remain add to the charm of a trip to Portugal. They may be seen in pottery markets, on the coast where boats are hauled up the beach on logs, and in small remote villages where carts are still in use. They are particularly deep-rooted in the northeast, the Alentejo and the Azores.

Minho

DOMESTIC ARCHITECTURE

Portugal has preserved different styles of traditional housing according to the region, most apparent in the north and in the south, that is the Alentejo and the Algarve.

The North – The most popular building material is granite. Houses are massive, with tiled roofs. As chimneys are very small or even non-existent, the smoke has to escape through gaps in the roof, the doorway or the windows. The outside stairway leads to a stone balcony or verandah large enough to be used as a living room.
In Trás-os-Montes shale is the dominant material and the houses have slate roofs.
On country estates in the Douro valley, beside simple cottages, one may see elegant manor-houses *(solares)*, which are often whitewashed.

The Centre: Estremadura and Beira Litoral – The limestone with which the houses are built adds a pleasant touch to their appearance. The façades are often ornamented with cornices and stucco; the outside staircases have disappeared.

Alentejo – The houses, built to shelter the inhabitants from the summer glare and heat, are low-lying single storey structures with whitewashed walls and minimal sized doors and windows. Nevertheless, the winters are so harsh that huge square or cylindrical chimneys (at Mourão) are also a local feature. Building materials vary according to the region: usually *taipa* or dried clay, or adobe, mud mixed with cut straw and dried in the sun, being used as they were in Moorish times. Bricks are used for decorative features, for chimneys, crenellations and verandahs, while around Estremoz marble is common.
Door and window frames are often painted blue, red or yellowy-orange.

Algarve – The white houses squat low, several juxtaposed cubes making up each dwelling. Sometimes the roof of rounded

Alentejo

tiles is replaced, in the east, by a terrace to catch rainwater or to dry fish or fruit on. The white flat-roofed houses in Olhão and Fuseta resemble the villages of North Africa. Very occasionally the terrace is replaced by a four-sided peaked roof, *telhado de tesoura*, which some attribute to a Chinese influence. Peaked roofs are mostly to be seen in Faro, Tavira and Santa Luzia. Doorways are surmounted by arches and covings. Chimneys are slender and elegant, gracefully pierced, painted white or

Algarve

built of brick laid in decorative patterns and crowned with a ball, a finial, a vase, or an ornament of some kind such as a lance or scythe.

Madeira and the Azores – In Madeira, traditional mountain dwellings have a thatched roof with two eaves which descend right down to the ground, thus covering the whole house. The main door on the front of the house is flanked by two small windows, with an occasional third one above it. All these openings are set into the wall with colourful surrounds.

Madeira

Houses in the Azores are similar to those found in the Algarve, offering a reminder of the islands' first inhabitants. However, the Empires of the Holy Ghost are brightly-coloured original buildings, similar in style to chapels, which have large windows and are used to house objects for the worship of the Holy Ghost *(See AZORES ARCHIPELAGO Traditions)*. Buildings are generally painted white with a black basalt trim.

Traditional urban features

Pavements – Throughout the country and even in the archipelagos of Madeira and the Azores, pavements and squares are paved with beautifully patterned compositions of alternating blocks of black basalt, golden sandstone, white limestone and grey granite. These are known as **calçadas**.

Granaries (Espigueiros) – The granaries, found particularly throughout the Minho, especially in Lindoso and Soajo (in the Serra do Soajo which is in the Parque Nacional da Peneda-Gerês), are small granite constructions built on piles. They serve as drying floors for maize. The sacredness of maize is symbolised by the cross on the roof.

Windmills (Moinhos) – There were about 2 000 windmills in Portugal several years ago but most have now been abandoned and are in ruins. They may still be seen on hilltops around Nazaré, Óbidos and Viana do Castelo. Those most common today are the Mediterranean type in which a cylindrical tower built of stone or hard-packed clay supports a turning conical roof bearing a mast. The mast carries four triangular sails.

Pillories (Pelourinhos) – Standing in the centre of small towns and villages is the traditional pillory where in the past brigands were exposed. In the Middle Ages, pillories were also the symbol of triumphant municipal power; only those who had power to dispense justice could erect a pillory. Many stand beside town halls, cathedrals and monasteries which were then generally seats of jurisdiction.
In the 12C, pillories were plain columns supporting a cage in which wrongdoers were locked. With time the cage lost its importance, being replaced by iron hooks to which miscreants were chained.
The **columns**, which are often cylindrical but also prismatic, pyramidal, conical or twisted (17C), may be decorated with straight or spiralling ribs, roses, carved discs, scales, knots or geometric motifs. The **superstructure** is ornamental, often deriving in design from the original cage and taking the form of a miniature cage with small columns, or

a sort of fir cone, a prism, or quite simply a flat block surmounted by small columns. The top can also be a smooth or armillary sphere (from the Manueline period), and may be crowned by a weather vane or an arm brandishing the sword of justice. In the Bragança region most of the pillories end in four arms of stone in the shape of a cross from which hang iron hooks.

Padrões – These public monuments, memorials bearing the cross and the arms of Portugal, were erected by Portuguese explorers when they reached new lands. They may be seen in former colonies and in Madeira and the Azores.

Y. Cavaille/EXPLORER

Windmills

HANDICRAFTS

Portugal's arts and crafts are remarkably varied and unpretentious. The weekly markets held in most towns and particularly the fairs, known for their crowds and colour, give a good idea of the skill of Portuguese craftsmanship.

Ceramics and pottery – There are many village potters *(olarios)* producing domestic and decorative earthenware which varies in shape and colour according to the region of origin. In Barcelos, pots are glazed, colours bright (yellows and reds) and with ornamentation consisting of leaves, stems and flowers; handsome multicoloured cocks are also made locally. Around Coimbra, the colour used is green with brown and yellow overtones and the decoration is more geometric. The potters of Caldas da Rainha use bright green and produce items with surprising shapes. Continuing the tradition set up by Rafael Bordalo Pinheiro *(see LISBON – Museu Rafael Bordalo Pinheiro)*, water jugs, salad bowls and plates are all heavily adorned with leaves, flowers, animals, etc. In Alcobaça and Cruz da Légua the potters work with more classical designs, distinguishing their ware by the variety of blues they use in its decoration.

In the Upper Alentejo (in Redondo, Estremoz and Nisa) the clay is encrusted with shining quartz particles or marble chips; in the Algarve amphorae are still made after Greek and Roman models; lastly, in the Tras-os-Montes the potters damp down their ovens at the end of the firing to give the ware a black colour.

Lace – A popular saying goes "Where there are nets, there is lace" and, in truth, lace is made virtually only along the coast (Caminha, Póvoa de Varzim, Vila do Conde, Azurara, Peniche, Setúbal, Lagos and Olhão) or near the ports (Valença do Minho, Guimarães and Sives). The only exception is Nisa. The decorative motifs used are fir cones and flowers, trefoils at Viano do Costelo where the lace looks more like tulle, and seaweed, shells and fish at Vila do Conde.

Embroidery – Madeira's embroidery is particularly well-known, although mainland Portugal also produces wonderful shawls, tablecloths and bedspreads. The best-known bedspreads *(colchas)* are from Castelo Branco and are embroidered with silk on linen. The tradition is a long-standing one and the work itself is painstaking. Bedspreads form an important part of a bride's trousseau.

Filigree work – The working by hand of gold or silver wire which reached its height in the reign of King João V (1706-50), is still held in high regard in Portugal. The chief centre is the small town of Gondomar not far from Oporto. Delicate, intricate

Museu de Cerâmica – F. Matias/ANF-IPM

Caldas da Rainha pottery

jewellery in the shape of hearts, crosses, guitars and above all caravels is fashioned from the extremely pliable wire. In the Minho, filigree earrings and brooches are worn to set off the regional costume.

Basketwork – Rushes, willows and rye straw are all used to make decorative and utilitarian wickerwork baskets. Pack saddles may be seen in the Trás-os-Montes with twin pairs of deep cylindrical baskets on either side.

Carved yoke from Minho

Weaving and carpet making – Hand weaving still flourishes in some mountain villages. Lengths of heavy frieze are woven on old looms to make capes and tippets. Guimarães specialises in bedspreads and curtains in rough cloth bordered with classical motifs in bright colours. The hemp or linen based carpets embroidered in wool at Arraiolos are the best known of their type and have simpler designs.

Woodwork – In the Alentejo a lot of items made of wood, including trays, chairs and cupboards are painted with brightly-coloured, naive motifs.

Painted whitewood is an important feature of traditional Portuguese handicraft and may be seen all over the country. Examples include ox yokes (the most famous being in the Barcelos region), painted carts (in the Alentejo and the Algarve) and carved and painted fishing boats (in the Ria de Aveiro and many of the country's beaches).

Cork – Wherever the cork-oak grows (particularly in the Alentejo and the Algarve), a local craft has developed, making cork boxes, key rings, belts, bags, etc.

> **Best known handicraft markets and fairs**
>
> **Barcelos:** pottery fair on Thursday mornings
> **São Pedro de Sintra:** antiques fair on the second and last Sunday of the month.
> **Estremoz:** pottery market on Saturdays.
> **Estoril:** handicraft fair (Feira de Artesonato) in July and August.
> **Santarém:** agricultural fair in October.
> **Golegã:** horse fair in November.

FESTIVE PORTUGAL

The Portuguese, so often contrasted with the more volatile Castilian, in spite of his reputation as a reserved character with a bent for **saudade** or nostalgia, will always greet you politely and cordially. He likes to be surrounded by friends and remains attached to tradition, periodically called to mind by innumerable local festivals organised all over the country.

Fado

A little history – There are many theories about the origin of the *fado:* a monotonous chant that derived from the troubadour songs of the Middle Ages, or, a song with Moorish or Afro-Brazilian roots.

The *fado* first appeared in Portugal in the late 18C in the form of sentimental sailors' songs. It then developed in the early 19C during the troubled times of the Napoleonic Wars, English domination and the independence of Brazil. These circumstances explain

43

the popular response to the song, with its serious subject matter, usually the forces of destiny (the name *fado* is said to come from the Latin *fatum:* destiny) or human passions. It became popular in Lisbon in 1820 with the singer **Maria Severa**. In 1833 the first *fado* houses *(casas de fado)* opened and the song took on its present form. In 1870 aristocrats adopted it as a means of expressing their romantic emotions. By the end of the century it had become a literary genre and the great poets and writers of the day tried their hand at it. A *fastida* figure began to appear in novels, wandering from *fado* house to *fado* house, sitting in a cloud of smoke, drinking and, eyes half-closed, listening to nostalgic tunes. At the beginning of the 20C the fado served as a means for critics to voice their ideological quarrels.

The singer **Amália Rodriguez** has brought the *fado* international fame, so much so that it has become the symbol of Portugal and its *saudade*.

Singing and playing the fado – The singer *(fadista)*, often a woman, is accompanied by one or two instrumentalists. The Portuguese guitar *(guitarra)* differs from the Spanish *(viola)* in having twelve strings as opposed to six, and is thus a more subtle instrument. The *fadista*, who is often dressed in black, stands straight, head thrown back, eyes half closed, and sings out in a strong, often deep, voice. The effect is very beautiful, moving and captivating. Attempts to modernise the style and develop a light-hearted *fado* with greater variety in the rhythm have been frowned upon on by some devotees.

The Lisbon *fado*, which can be heard in restaurants in the city's old quarters, more closely resembles the original *fado* form than does the Coimbra version. This latter, which is gradually dying out, is sung only by men, dressed in large black student capes. The subject matter is generally about students' love affairs with working-class women.

Places to listen to the fado – There are performances every evening in Lisbon's *fado* houses in the Alfama and Bairro Alta quarters. Unfortunately many of these places have become extremely touristic and the *fado* has lost some of its soul. However, one may sometimes be lucky enough to find a small restaurant where amateur *fadistas* sing for their own delight ... and ours *(see Travellers' addresses for Lisbon)*.

Regional life and folk dancing

The local dances reflect many provincial idiosyncrasies and even the difference in character of the people living in different regions.

Minho and the Douro Coast – The inhabitants, retiring yet very friendly, come together for harvests and grape-picking, singing to encourage themselves as they work. This same gaiety is found in their dances which are famous throughout Portugal. **Viras,** a type of round to the accompaniment of traditional songs, have a strong rhythm. The **gota** or *vira galego* is even more energetic. The **malhão** and **perim** show off the beauty of the local girls who wear attractive costumes, sometimes enhanced by a gold bracelet or other piece of jewellery.

Trás-os-Montes and the Beiras – Community life has not totally disappeared in these provinces where life is hard. Communal ovens, mills and wine presses still exist. The dances, **chulas** and **dança dos Pauliteiros,** illustrate the woman's unassuming attitude to her social position.

Beira Litoral, Estremadura, Ribatejo – Merrymaking plays a less important part in life, except between Ovar and Nazaré where the **vira** reappears. As danced by the fisherfolk of the area, the *vira* with its deft figures becomes a joy to watch while in Nazaré a further pleasure is added with the interplay of colourful petticoats worn by all the girl dancers. The wide plains of the Ribatejo are the homeland of the brilliantly costumed *campinos* or cattlemen who raise and guard the fighting bulls.

The Estremenho, or man from the Estremadura, is a fine talker and is said to be the braggart of Portugal; the Ribatejan is more reserved, and dances alone in the **fandango** and the **escovinho**. Women dress simply in short skirts, light-coloured blouses, low broad-heeled shoes and woollen scarves to cover their heads.

Alentejo – The women dress in clothes well suited to their hard work in the fields. The men, people of few words, dance while singing slow and mournful measures of **saias** and **balhas.**

Algarve – The people of the Algarve, normally rather serious, are joyful and dynamic during festivals. Their dance, the **corridinho,** has a lively rhythm.

Romarias

Romarias are religious festivals held in honour of a patron saint. The most important take place in northern Portugal, particularly in the Minho. Small *romarias* in mountain chapels last only one day, but the big ones in towns can last several days. Some social and professional groups for instance, the fishermen of Póvoa de Varzim, hold their own *romarias*.

Collection – A few days prior to the festival the organisers make a collection to meet expenses. Gifts in kind are collected in baskets decked with flowers and garlands and are then auctioned. The collections, which thus mark the start of the festivities, are

Traditional costumes

Nazaré

Nazaré

Algarve

Ribatejo

Minho

45

Festa dos Tabuleiros, Tomar

enlivened by players such as the *gaitero* or bagpiper, the *fogueteiro* or man who lights the fireworks and, in the Alentejo, the *tamborileiro* or tambourine player. Streets are carpeted with flowers.

The Candle (Círio) – The most important part of the religious ceremony is the solemn bearing of a candle, from which comes the name *círio* given to the focal point of the *romaria*, or the parading of a banner, from a sometimes distant place to the sanctuary. The candle is borne on an ox-drawn wagon or in a flower-decked farm cart; behind, led by the *gaitero*, follows a procession from which emerges the statue of a saint or the Virgin covered in garlands, lace and artificial flowers.

The procession circles the sanctuary two or three times accompanied by clamorous shouts from the crowd, musical instruments and fire-crackers. The candle or banner is then set down near the altar and the faithful advance to kiss the feet of the saint.

The "Saints of Intercession" – To win special favour from certain saints, believers perform acts of penance such as going round the sanctuary on their knees. The wax ex-votos on these occasions are often models of the organ or limb for which recovery is being sought. Matchmaking saints (St John, St Antony, St Gonsalo) were very popular in olden times; while the festivals of saints are said to protect animals (St Mamede, St Mark, St Sylvester), they were attended not only by pilgrims but also by their animals.

The traditional worship of the **Holy Ghost** is particularly deep-rooted in the Azores and Brazil. The famous *Tabuleiros* festival in Tomar, organised in the olden days by Holy Ghost brotherhoods which were founded in the 14C, continues to this day.

Popular rejoicings – Once the religious ceremonies are over, the festivities, usually a meal, dancing and fireworks, begin. Local crafts are always on sale at a *romaria*.

TOURADAS: BULLFIGHTING

The Portuguese refuse to see in a fight between a man and a bull a contest of intelligence versus instinct; for them it is a display of skill, elegance and courage; the bull is only the instrument. Unlike the Spanish *corrida*, part of the Portuguese *tourada* is performed on horseback, and the bull is not killed. The fight to the death was banned in the 18C by the Marquis of Pombal after the Count of Arcos met with an accident. Once a gentleman's pastime, the *tourada* still plays a role in social life.

Order of events – The entry into the ring by the horsemen, toreros and *forcados*, who salute the public and the authorities, is a real ceremony with special bullfighting music. The *tourada* then opens with the first horseman *(cavaleiro)* on a magnificent caparisoned stallion and dressed in an 18C style costume consisting of a gold-embroidered coat of silk or velvet, a plumed tricorn hat and shining kneeboots with silver spurs. He is accompanied by the *toureiros* in costumes of lights, brandishing pink and yellow capes. The *cavaleiro* provokes the bull and gets close enough to place the beribboned darts or *farpas*. It is a spectacular sight, with the horse wheeling deftly away when the bull charges. Bulls can often weigh about 500 kilos/1 100 lbs and when in the ring, have their horns covered with a leather thong *(emboladas)*. The rider changes horses. Then, while the *toureiros* on foot rouse the bull by flourishing their capes, the rider thrusts 4, 5, 6 *farpas* into the beast's neck, thus enraging it. With his work over and the bull showing signs of exhaustion the *cavaleiro* makes way for a team of *forcados*, men who would formerly have been armed with a kind of fork or *forcado*. The team usually consists of eight men dressed in beige, brown and red, who file into the ring. Their role is to master the bull, a stage in the contest known as the *pega*. The leader, wearing a green cap with a long point, lollops towards the bull, inciting it with a shout. He tries to seize the beast by the horns while his fellows immobilise it; if this proves too difficult, the leader has to seize the bull's withers from the side while one of the men, the *rabejador*, pulls its tail and gets whirled along behind. At this stage in some fights, a few cows, with their copper bells ringing, are sent into the ring to entice the bull to leave. The bull is then either slaughtered the next day or retired for breeding.

In traditional *touradas* there are three *cavaleiros* and several *toureiras*. Part of the fight is conducted on foot and progresses in a similar way to fights in Spain, the difference being the absence of *picadors* and rather than a sword, an artificial flower is thrust into the withers.

The bullfighting season in Portugal lasts from Easter to October; contests are usually held twice a week, on Thursdays and Sundays. The best known fights take place in the Praça de Touros in Lisbon, Santarém and Vila Franca de Xira, near the areas in the Ribatejo where the bulls are bred.

Tourada

Food and wine

COOKERY

Portuguese meals are copious and wholesome. The menu consists of several dishes, usually prepared with olive oil and flavoured with aromatic herbs such as rosemary, bay leaves, etc.

Eggs play an important part in Portuguese food: they are used in soups and often accompany fish and meat dishes, they also form part of most desserts. Rice, for which the Portuguese developed a liking following their voyages to the Far East, is the most favoured vegetable. Fried potatoes are also commonly served.

Soups – Soup is served at most meals. Among the many varieties are *canja de galinha,* chicken soup with rice, *sopa de peixe,* fish soup, *sopa de marisco,* seafood soup, *sopa de coelho,* rabbit soup, and *sopa de grão,* chickpea soup.

The most famous is the Minho **caldo verde** which is served north of the Mondego. This consists of a mashed potato base to which finely shredded green Galician cabbage is added; lastly olive oil and slices of black pudding, *tora,* are mixed in.

Bread soups or **açordas** are to be found in all regions, those of the Alentejo having many variations such as the *sopa de coentros* made with coriander leaves, olive oil, garlic and bread, with a poached egg on top.

In the south, **gaspacho,** a soup of tomatoes, onions, cucumbers and chillies seasoned with garlic and vinegar, is served cold with croutons.

Caldeirada

Fish and crustaceans – Fish is a basic element of Portuguese cuisine. Cod, **bacalhau,** is the most common fish, particularly in the north. There are, it is said, 365 ways of preparing it *(see Bacalhau à Brás recipe on page following).* Many other fish, however, are to be found in some part or other of the country: the aroma of grilled sardines wafts through the streets of every coastal town; many types of fish are put into the **caldeirada** or stew made by fishermen on the beach. You will get tunny fillets in the Algarve, river lampreys and salmon beside the Minho and shad beside the Tagus. Seafood *(mariscos)* including octopus is plentiful. Shellfish are delicious and very varied especially in the Algarve where a special copper vessel, a *cataplana,* is used to cook clams and sausages spiced with herbs.

Crayfish *(lagosta)* prepared in the Peniche way, or steamed, are rightly famous.

Meat and game – Apart from pork and game, Portuguese meat is often very ordinary. Pork is cooked and served in a variety of ways. The **leitão assado,** or roast sucking-pig, of Mealhada (north of Coimbra) is delicious. Meat from various parts of the pig can also be found in stews, in **linguiça** or smoked pigs' tongue sausages, in smoked pork fillets, *paio,* and in smoked ham, *presunto,* at Chaves and Lamego. Ham and sausages are added to the **cozido à Portuguesa,** a hotpot of beef, vegetables, potatoes and rice, also to the local tripe prepared in the Oporto way, *dobrada,* a dish of pig or beef tripe cooked with haricot beans.

Pork in the Alentejo way, or **carne de porco à Alentejana,** is pork marinated in wine, garnished with clams. Other meat is mostly minced and consumed as meat balls, although lamb and kid are sometimes roasted or served on skewers.

Cheeses – Ewes' milk cheese should be tried between October and May, notably the *Queijo da Serra da Estrela,* the *Queijo de Castelo Branco* and the creamy *Queijo de Azeitão* as well as goats' milk cheeses such as the *cabreiro,* the *rabaçal* from the Pombal region and the small soft white cheeses or *quejinhos* from Tomar, often served as an hors d'œuvre as is the fresh goat's cheese, *Queijo fresco.*

Desserts — Portugal has an infinite variety of cakes and pastries. Nearly all recipes include eggs and come in most instances from old specialities prepared in convents such as the **Toucinho-do-Céu, Barriga-de-Freira** and **Queijadas de Sintra**, with almonds and fresh sheep's milk. The dessert most frequently seen on menus, however, is the **pudim flan**, a sort of cream caramel, while the **leite-creme** is a creamier pudding made with the same ingredients. Rice pudding, **arroz doce**, sprinkled with cinnamon is often served at festive meals.

In the Algarve, the local figs *(figos)* and almonds *(amêndoas)* are made into the most appetising sweetmeats and titbits.

A particularly delicious pastry is the **pasteis de nata**, a small custard tart sprinkled with cinnamon.

Queijadas de Sintra

A "faithful friend"

Cod *(bacalhau)* has played an important role in Portugal's maritime history, and is such a standby in family dining that it is commonly known as the "faithful friend". Fished in the cold, far-off waters of Newfoundland, it had to be salted to preserve it until the fishing fleet returned home. Emblematic of Portuguese cooking, a traditional dish for Christmas, a delicacy enjoyed by fishermen and peasants alike, cod is enjoyed throughout the country, particularly served as fish balls. **Bacalhau à Brás**, a cod recipe which is originally from Lisbon, is now served the length and breadth of Portugal.

Ingredients for 4 people:
500g (about 1 pound) of cod
500g of potatoes, fried
3 medium-sized onions
5 eggs, beaten
2 cloves of garlic
4 tablespoons of oil
Chopped parsley, black olives, salt and pepper

Soak the cod overnight, changing the water several times.

Shred the cod, taking care to remove the skin and any bones, and rinse through a cloth.

Peel the potatoes and cut into strips.

Slice the onions into thin rings.

Heat the oil in a frying pan

with the garlic and remove when golden. Fry the onions until golden and add the cod. Leave on the heat for 5 minutes, add the potatoes and garlic. Season with salt and pepper and add the beaten eggs and mix well. Sprinkle with parsley and decorate with the black olives.

Drinks – Portugal produces excellent mineral waters, such as the Água de Luso and the sparkling waters of Castelo, Carvalhelhos, Vidago and Pedras Salgadas. The beer is mostly light lager type. The fruit juices, both still *(sem gás)* and sparkling *(com gás)*, are excellent and refreshing.

WINE

Portugal is the eighth largest wine-producer in the world and has a rich variety of wines, including the world famous **Port** and **Madeira**. The wines one buys locally or drinks in a restaurant at reasonable prices are of good quality, suitable for all occasions and deserve to be better known.

Port

The vines of the Upper Douro and its affluents produce a generous wine which is shipped from the city that gave it its name, Oporto, only after it has matured.

The English and Port – In the 14C some of the wines produced in the Lamego region were already being exported to England. In the 17C the Portuguese granted the English trading rights in exchange for their help against the Spanish. By the end of the 17C, once the port process had been developed, some Englishmen acquired country estates *(quintas)* in the Douro valley and began making wine. Through the **Methuen Treaty** (1703) the English crown obtained the monopoly of the Portuguese wine trade. However in 1756, to combat this English invasion, King Dom José I and the Marquis of Pombal founded the **Company of the Wines of the Upper Douro** *(Companhia Geral da Agricultura dos Vinhos do Alto Douro)* which fixed the price for all exported port. The following year the company defined the area in which port vines could be grown. Various English companies were set up, among them Cockburn, Campbell, Offley, Harris, Sandeman, Dow, Graham, etc. The Portuguese followed suit in 1830 with their own companies with names like Ferreira and Ramos Pinto. In 1868 phylloxera raged throughout the region but the vineyards were rapidly rehabilitated – many of the vineyards were grafted from phylloxera-resistant American stocks – and "vintage" port was being produced by the end of the 19C.

The vineyards – The area defined by law in 1757 for the cultivation of vines covers 240 000ha/593 000 acres of which a tenth consists of vineyards that stretch for about sixty miles along the Douro to the Spanish border. The approximate centre is situated at Pinhão. There are 25 000 vineyard owners. Port's inestimable quality is due, no less to the exceptional conditions – hot summers, cold winters, and schist soil – under which the grapes are grown and ripened, than to the processing of the fruit when harvested. The vines grow on steep terraces overlooking the Douro, a striking picture not only from an aesthetic point of view but also in terms of the extraordinary amount of work involved.

The making of port – The grape harvest takes place in late September. Men carry the bunches of grapes in wickerwork baskets on their backs. The cut grapes go into the press where mechanical crushing has taken the place of human treading which, with its songs and rhythmic tunes, was so highly picturesque. The must is sealed

WINES AND REGIONAL SPECIALITIES

Wine-producing region   ***Bucelas*** Major vineyards

off during fermentation which reduces the sugar content to the right amount, then brandy – from Douro grapes – is added to stop the fermentation and to stabilise the sugar. In the spring the wine is taken by lorry and train to Vila Nova de Gaia. Up until a few years ago it was transported 150km/90mi along the Douro to Oporto in picturesque sailing craft known as *barcelos rebelos*. Some of these boats may be seen at Pinhão and Vila da Gaia. The wine is stored with the 58 port wine companies that have set up in Vila Nova da Gaia and matures in huge casks or, more commonly, in vats containing up to 1 000ml/220 400 Imperial gallons. It is then decanted into 535 litre/118 gallon barrels *(pipes)* in which the porous nature of the wood augments the ageing process. The Wine Institute (Instituto do Vinho do Porto) sets the rules and controls the quality.

Types of port – Port, which is red or white according to the colour of the grapes from which it is made, has many subtleties – it can be dry, medium or sweet. The variety of port also depends upon the way it is made. Port aged in casks matures through oxidation and turns a beautiful amber colour; port aged in the bottle matures by reduction and is a dark red colour. The alcohol content is about 20%.

Vintage ports are selected from the best wines of a particularly fine year and are bottled after two years in casks. They then mature in the bottle for at least ten years or more before being served. Since 1974 all Vintage Port must be bottled in Portugal.

White port or **Branco** is less well known than the reds. It is a fortified wine made from white grapes. Dry or extra dry, it makes a good apéritif.

Blended ports are red ports made from different vintages from different years. The blending and ageing differ according to the quality required. They include:
– **Tinto**, the most common, which is young, vigorous, distinctly coloured and fruity.
– **Tinto-Alourado** or **Ruby**, which is older, yet rich in colour, fruity and sweet and is the result of the blending of different vintages from different years.
– **Alourado** or **Tawny** is blended with different vintages from different years and ages in wooden casks. Its colour turns to a brownish gold as it ages. It should be drunk soon after it is bottled.
– **Alourado-Claro** or **Light Tawny** is the culmination of the former.

Choosing a port – **White port** is the least expensive followed by *Tinto*, **Ruby port** and then the **Tawny ports.** Very good quality tawny ports give an indication of their age (10, 20, 30 or more years). Next come the ports which bear their vintage date *(colheita)*; they have been made with wines from the same year. The best and most expensive are **Vintage ports** and **Late Bottled Vintage Ports (L.B.V.).** The former are made with wine from an exceptionally good year and are bottled after two to three years; likewise, the latter are made with wine from the same vineyard and are bottled after four to six years. Since 1963 the French have replaced the English as the largest importers of port.

Madeira

Madeira wine, which deserves to be better known, has always been particularly popular with the English. *See the introduction to the island of Madeira.*

Other wines

Several regions in Portugal produce perfectly respectable wines which can be enjoyed in restaurants. One can ask for the *vinho da casa*, usually the local wine.

Vinho Verde – *Vinho Verde* from the Minho and the Lower Douro Valley can be white (tendency to gold) or deep red. Its name, "green wine" comes from its early grape harvest and short fermentation period which gives the wine a low alcohol content (8° to 11°) and makes it light and sparkling with a distinct bouquet and what might be described as a very slightly bitter flavour.

Dão – Vines growing on the granite slopes of the Dão Valley produce a fresh white wine as well as a sweet red wine with a velvety texture and a heady bouquet which most closely resembles a Burgundy.

Bairrada – A very old vine-growing region which produces a robust, fragrant wine.

Colares – The vines grow in a sandy topsoil over a bed of clay in the Serra de Sintra. The robust, velvety, dark red wine has been famous since the 13C.

Bucelas – Bucelas is a dry, somewhat acid straw-coloured white wine produced from vineyards on the banks of the Trancão, a tributary of the Tagus.

Other table wines – The Ribatejo vineyards produce good everyday wines; full bodied reds from the Cartaxo region and whites from Chamusca, Almeirim and Alpiarça on the far bank of the Tagus.
Also worth trying are the wines of Torres Vedras, Alcobaça, Lafões and Agueda, the Pinhel and Mateus rosés as well as the sparkling wine from the Bairrada region which goes wonderfully well with roast sucking-pig.
In the Alentejo, full-bodied reds such as Reguengos, Borba and Redondo predominate. The one exception to this is the white Vidigueira wine.
In the Algarve, a small amount of wine is still produced in Lagoa, home to the country's oldest co-operative.

Dessert wines – Setúbal moscatel from the chalky clay slopes of the Serra da Arrábida is a generous fruity wine which acquires a particularly pleasant taste with age. Fruity amber-coloured Carcavelos is drunk as an apéritif as well as a dessert wine.

Spirits – The wide variety of Portuguese brandies includes *ginginha*, cherry brandy from Alcobaça, *medronho*, arbutus berry brandy and *brandimel*, honey brandy from the Algarve. *Bagaço* or *bagaceira*, a grape marc, served chilled, is the most widely drunk.

G. Sioën/RAPHO

World Heritage List

In 1972, The United Nations Educational, Scientific and Cultural Organization (UNESCO) adopted a Convention for the preservation of cultural and natural sites. To date, more than 150 States Parties have signed this international agreement, which has listed over 500 sites "of outstanding universal value" on the World Heritage List. Each year, a committee of representatives from 21 countries, assisted by technical organizations (ICOMOS – International Council on Monuments and Sites; IUCN-International Union for Conservation of Nature and Natural Resources; ICCROM – International Centre for the Study of the Preservation and Restoration of Cultural Property, the Rome Centre), evaluates the proposals for new sites to be included on the list, which grows longer as new nominations are accepted and more countries sign the Convention. To be considered, a site must be nominated by the country in which it is located.

The protected cultural heritage may be monuments (buildings, sculptures, archaeological structures, etc.) with unique historical, artistic or scientific features, groups of buildings (such as religious communities, ancient cities); or sites (human settlements, examples of exceptional landscapes, cultural landscapes) which are the combined works of man and nature of exceptional beauty. Natural sites may be a testimony to the stages of the earth's geological history or to the development of human cultures and creative genius or represent significant ongoing ecological processes, contain superlative natural phenomena or provide a habitat for threatened species.

Signatories of the Convention pledge to co-operate to preserve and protect these sites around the world as a common heritage to be shared by all humanity.

Some of the most well-known places which the World Heritage Committee has inscribed include: Australia's Great Barrier Reef (1981), the Canadian Rocky Mountain Parks (1984), The Great Wall of China (1987), the Statue of Liberty (1984), the Kremlin (1990), Mont-Saint-Michel and its Bay (France – 1979), Durham Castle and Cathedral (1986).

In Portugal, UNESCO World Heritage sites are:

Central Zone of the Town of Angra do Heroismo in the Azores
Monastery of the Hieronymites and Tower of Belem in Lisbon
Monastery of Batalha
Convent of Christ in Tomar
Historic Centre of Evora
Monastery of Alcobaça
Cultural Landscape of Sintra
Historic Centre of Oporto

Palácio Nacional da Pena, Sintra

Sights

ABRANTES

Santarém — Population 7 349
Michelin map 940 N5

Abrantes, a town in central Portugal, occupies an open **site★** on a hillside overlooking the right bank of the Tagus. The Tramagal road, on the south side of the river, affords excellent views of this fine town of white stone.

The commanding fortress had fallen into decay more than two hundred years before the Peninsular War, when the town was entered first by French troops in 1807 and later by Wellesley who briefly made it his headquarters in 1809.

The town is also known for its delicious confections, "Abrantes straw" or *palha de Abrantes*, so-called because the eggs from which it is made leave yellow strawlike streaks.

Castelo – The way up to the fortifications (now restored) is through a maze of alleyways dazzling with flowers. The keep has been converted into a **belvedere** from which there are views, of the middle valley of the Tagus to the point downstream, where it is joined by the Zêzere, southwards to a countryside carpeted with olive trees on which, here and there, appear groups of white village houses. To the north can be seen the upstanding ranges of the Serra do Moradal and the foothills of the Serra da Estrela.

The **Igreja de Santa Maria** ⊘, rebuilt in the 15C, includes a small **museum** which contains a 16C carving of the Trinity in polychrome stone and, on the high altar, a beautiful statue of the Virgin and Child dating from the 15C. The tombs of the Counts of Abrantes date from the 15C and 16C.

AGUIAR DA BEIRA

Guarda — Population 1 264
Michelin map 940 or 441 J7

The granite houses of the town of Aguiar da Beira, which stands in the austere landscape of the Serra da Lapa, are grouped around a main square, which has kept all of its medieval character. In the centre is a 12C pillory, and framing the perimeter, a tower crowned with pyramidal merlons, a Romanesque fountain similarly crenellated and a house, typical of the Beira Region, with an outside staircase.

ALBUFEIRA★

Faro — Population 14 237
Michelin map 940 U5 — Local map see ALGARVE

Albufeira is a former Moorish stronghold that has kept its Arab name meaning "castle on the sea". Over the past few decades it has become the most famous seaside resort in the Algarve with its international visitors and fashionable nightlife. The site has been spoiled somewhat by the host of modern buildings one has to go through to reach the old fishing village in the centre. The white houses of the village form an attractive group, atop a golden coloured cliff overlooking the beach. This curves out below and is protected from the swell by the rocky headland of Baleeira, a strange crook-shaped point, to the west.

Albufeira

TOUR

Views – There are fine views of the **site★** from the signal station above the fishing harbour to the east, or from the west, heading towards Galé Beach.

The Town – Albufeira is best explored on foot. It has cobbled alleys and Moorish arches with lanterns. The streets converge on the main square, Largo E. Duarto Pacheco, where tourists gather on the large number of café terraces in the summer.

Beaches – A tunnel from the end of the main street, 5 de Outubro, leads to the bathing beach which is separated from that of the fishermen (Praia dos Barcos) by a cliff. Pleasant *corniche* streets overlook this beach with its distinctive rocks. Albufeira's town beach is very crowded in the summer. There is, however, a wide choice of quieter alternatives on either side of the town, like Galé to the west, which may be reached by car.

ALCOBAÇA★★

Leiria – Population 5 383
Michelin map 940 N3

One of the most beautiful Cistercian abbeys dating from the Middle Ages stands in the heart of the small town.

Alcobaça is set in an agricultural region at the confluence of the Alcoa and Baça rivers which gave the town its name. Its main activities are fruit growing, wine making and the production of a cherry liqueur called *ginginha*. Alcobaça is also an active commercial centre for the local pottery which is predominantly blue.

A Cistercian foundation – In 1147, in the middle of the Reconquest, Afonso Henriques, the first King of Portugal, is believed to have vowed that he would found a monastery and dedicate it to St Bernard if he managed to capture Santarém from the Moors. The legend is based on fact: Afonso Henriques did indeed found an abbey at Alcobaça which he donated to the Cistercians in 1153. At that time, land to be cleared was often entrusted to monastic orders who took it upon themselves to improve it. Alcobaça became a daughter house of Clairvaux in France and was modelled on the French abbey. Construction began in 1178 but the earliest buildings were destroyed by the Moors. Work resumed in the early 13C and the church was completed in 1253. Alcobaça developed rapidly and its abbot became one of the most influential figures in the kingdom.

A posthumous coronation – Inês de Castro, who had accompanied the Infanta Constanza of Castile to Portugal in 1340, found herself exiled from the Court by King Alfonso IV. The monarch sought in this way to separate his son, Dom Pedro, the husband of the Infanta Constanza, from the lady-in-waiting, whose beauty he had been unable to resist. In 1345, on the death of Constanza, Inês returned to her lover at Coimbra, installing herself in the Mosteiro de Santa Clara-a-Velha. The presence of Inês and her children angered Alfonso IV who, in his anxiety to keep his kingdom free from all Castilian pretensions, raised no objection to Inês' murder on 7 January 1355. Dom Pedro took up arms and laid siege but failed to capture the city of Oporto. Two years later he succeeded his father, wreaked justice on the assassins and revealed that he had been married to Inês, in secret. In 1361 he had Inês' body exhumed and, legend has it, dressed the cadaver in a purple robe, put a crown upon its head and compelled the nobility of the realm to come and kiss the decomposed hand of the "dead queen". A solemn nocturnal procession then accompanied the remains to the church of the monastery of Alcobaça.

After António Ferreira in his tragedy *Castro*, the poet Camões made this dramatic event the basis of several episodes in *The Lusiads* and in 1942, the French writer Montherlant once again took up the theme in his play *La Reine Morte*.

★★MOSTEIRO DE SANTA MARIA ⊘ *45min.*

The external appearance of the 18C Santa Maria Monastery belies the splendid Cistercian architecture within. Of the original façade, altered by successive 17C and 18C reconstructions in the baroque style, only the main doorway and the rose window remain. The statues adorning the façade represent from bottom to top St Benedict and St Bernard, the four Cardinal Virtues (justice, prudence, temperance and fortitude) and at the top, in a niche, Our Lady of Alcobaça.

★★Church

The church has been restored and in doing so, rediscovered all the nobility and clean lines of its original Cistercian architecture. It is one of the largest churches of its kind, with an impressive elevation.

Nave – The nave is very spacious; the quadripartite vaulting is supported on transverse arches which, in turn, rest on mighty pillars and engaged columns. By terminating the latter 3m/10ft above the ground the architect considerably increased the space available for the congregation and gave the church a unique perspective. The aisles have striking vertical lines; they are almost as tall as the nave is long.

Transept – The 14C tombs of Inês and Dom Pedro are in the transept. Carved in a soft limestone in the Flamboyant Gothic style, they were considerably damaged by French soldiery in 1811.

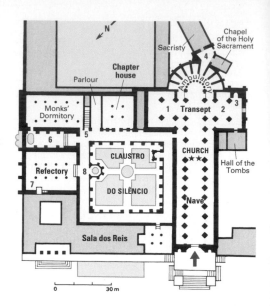

** **Inês de Castro's Tomb** (Túmulo de Inês de Castro) – *In the north transept* (**1**). The beautiful reclining figure of Inês de Castro, supported by six angels, lies upon a tomb on which the four panels are surmounted by a frieze bearing the Portuguese and Castro coats of arms. Depicted on the sides are scenes from the Life of Christ: at the head is a Crucifixion in which the Virgin may be seen mourning at the foot of the Cross. The Last Judgment which adorns the panel at the statue's feet is interesting for its particularly realistic detail; at the bottom on the left, the dead, as the tombstones rise, are standing before God in Judgment, and at the bottom on the right, the damned are being hurled into the jaws of a monster symbolising hell.

** **Dom Pedro's Tomb** (Túmulo de Dom Pedro) – *In the south transept* (**2**). Beneath a severe reclining figure, Dom Pedro's tomb depicts, on its sides, the life of St Bartholomew, the King's patron saint. The panel at the head of the tomb is occupied by a beautiful rose representing the wheel of fortune, or, according to some archaeologists, scenes from the life of Inês and Pedro, a theme taken up in the tomb's upper frieze. The panel at the foot depicts Dom Pedro's last moments. The **Transit of St Bernard** (**3**), a damaged terracotta depicting the death of the saint, stands in a chapel off the south transept. It was modelled by monks in the 17C.

Chancel – The chancel, which is based on the design of Clairvaux, is surrounded by a vast ambulatory off which open two beautiful **Manueline doors** (**4**) dating from the 16C.

Dom Pedro's Tomb

★★Abbey buildings

Claustro do Silêncio – The cloisters, which were built in the early 14C, have an attractive simplicity of line; between buttresses slender twin columns support with great elegance three rounded arches which are surmounted by a rose. The upper storey was added by Diogo and João Castilho in the 16C.

Chapter House – *Off the east gallery.* The archivolts rest on graceful small columns and vaulting in which the ribs fan out from central pillars and wall brackets.

Monks' Dormitory – A staircase (**5**) leads to the monks' dormitory, a vast Gothic hall over 60m/195ft long. Two rows of columns with capitals divide the room into three sections.

Kitchens (**6**) – The kitchens, which were enlarged in the 18C, are flanked to the east by the storeroom. The white tiled chamber is of monumental proportions, being 18m/58ft high and with enormous open fireplaces; water is laid on, flowing in as a tributary of the River Alcoa.

Refectory – The refectory is a large hall with ribbed vaulting. A stairway, built into the thickness of the wall and surmounted by a fine colonnade, leads to the reader's pulpit (**7**). Opposite the door, a **lavabo** and 17C fountain (**8**) jut out into the close.

Sala dos Reis – In the 18C Kings' Hall a frieze of *azulejos* illustrates the foundation of the monastery; the statues carved by monks represent the Portuguese kings up to Dom José I. Note also a beautiful Gothic Virgin and Child.

ADDITIONAL SIGHT

Museu da Junta Nacional de Vinho ⓥ – *1km/0.5mi along the N 8 in the direction of Leiria, on the right.*
A wine cooperative's warehouses are the setting for this wine museum with its collections of bottles (old Port and Madeira), wine vats, wine presses and stills.

ALGARVE★★

Michelin map 940 U3, 4, 5, 6 and 7

The Algarve stretches across the whole of southern Portugal. Its name derives from the Arabic *El-Gharb* meaning "west". The landscape and climate, which is mild all year round, resemble those of North Africa. The garden-like vegetation consists of figs, carobs, bougainvillaeas, geraniums and oleanders in the midst of which stand white houses with ornamental chimneys.
The fine beaches, which have been extremely popular since the 70s, have attracted extensive tourist development which has unfortunately disfigured parts of the coast. The coastline varies distinctly from east to west.

THE EAST COAST AND OFFSHORE SAND BARS

① From Vila Real de Santa António to Faro
65km/40mi – allow a day

East of Faro the coast is known as the leeward shore or *Sotavento*. The area stretching westwards from Manta Rota near Cacela Velha forms an unusual lagoon landscape closed in by sandy islets. There are boat links between the mainland and the beaches on the offshore bars as well as footbridges over the lagoon. In order to preserve this exceptional natural site, the entire coast from Manta Rota to Ançao near Quinta do Lago has been declared a protected area, namely **Parque Natural da Ria Formosa**. This is 60km/37mi long, covering 18 400ha/45 468 acres of dunes, channels and areas of great ornithological interest. The reserve is also rich in molluscs and crustaceans and is an important spawning area for fish.

Vila Real de Santo António and **Monte Gordo** – *See VILA REAL DE SANTO ANTÓNIO AND EXCURSIONS.*

Cacela Velha – This pleasant hamlet is built around the ruins of a medieval fortress and a small church with an attractive doorway. From its rocky bluff it affords a fine **view** over the lagoon and fishing boats below. During the summer, the main lake, with its two small restaurants, is a popular place to savour local Algarve delicacies.

★**Tavira** – *See TAVIRA.*

Pedras de El Rei – The holiday village of villas and attractive gardens has a rail link *(10min)* to the offshore sandbank and its beautiful beach, **Praia do Barril**.

Luz de Tavira – The Renaissance church on the village outskirts has an attractive Manueline doorway and flame ornaments around the roof.

Olhão – *See OLHÃO.*

★**Faro** – *See FARO.*

THE INTERIOR

② Circuit around Faro via the Serra do Caldeirão
107km/67mi – allow a day

This tour provides an insight into a relatively unknown area of the Algarve, between the limestone hills of the "barrocal" and the schist mountains of the Serra do Caldeirão just a few kilometres from the coast yet far from its madding crowds. The flower-decked, whitewashed villages have managed to preserve their traditional appearance, where handicrafts are still an important industry for the small local population. There is no such thing as monotony in these mountains, where the scenery changes with the seasons. In January and February the flowering almond trees carpet the mountains in a mass of white ; spring heralds the appearance of the rock-rose with its white bloom, while in summer and winter oranges stand out against the green backdrop of the cottage gardens. The year-round scents alone are worth the visit, with eucalyptus, pine, lavender and rock-rose all growing here in abundance.

Estói – *Leave Faro on the N2 heading northeast. After 10km/6mi, turn right along the Estói road (towards Tavira).*

Ruínas Romanas de Milreu ⊙ – A square-shaped apse and two marble columns are all that remain of the 1C Roman settlement Ossónoba. In the town, which was built around a temple, the brick foundations of the houses and baths surround the living quarters and pools, some of which still retain their polychrome mosaic designs. Particularly worthy of note is the **mosaico dos peixes grandes**, a mosaic of large fish on the wall of one of the pools.

J.P. Lescourret/EXPLORER

Palácio de Estói

Jardins do Palácio de Estói – *From Estói head 1km/0.5mi beyond Milreu.* A lane of palm-trees leads to the gardens. The gardens are bordered with orange trees which rise in terraces to the Baroque façade of this small 18C palace. The balustered verandas, decorated with pools, statues, busts, marble and earthenware vases, blue and multi-coloured azulejos with mythological and fantastic figures, and even some Roman mosaics from nearby Milreu, create a very picturesque sight. The overall atmosphere of these neglected gardens is one of romantic charm, rather like Italian palaces.

Return to the N 2 and head north.

São Brás de Alportel – This peaceful small town, originally named Xanabus by its Moorish founders, is built on elevated ground dotted with white houses and typical chimneys. The town used to be the country's main centre for cork extraction and still retains a few, light, cork-related industries. Algarroba pods, almonds and figs are important local crops.

Casa da Cultura António Bentes – Museu Etnográfico do Trajo Algarvio ⊙ – This ethnographic museum, housed in an attractive 19C bourgeois mansion, contains an interesting collection of old carts and carriages, dolls and typical local dress. It also houses temporary exhibitions. The beautiful garden of the Bishops of the Algarve's former residence can be seen in front of the museum.

Continue along the N2 for 14km/9mi. The road winds its way through groves of eucalyptus and pine before reaching Barranco Velho. Here, head towards Querença along the N 396.

Querença – The village nestles on the slope of a hill at an altitude of 276m/905ft. The foundation of the **Igreja de Nossa Senhora da Assunção** on the summit is attributed to the Knights Templar. Although the church was completely remodelled in 1745, it has retained its Manueline door. The interior contains some fine gilded carvings. Many of the dazzling white tumble-down houses still have their traditional wood ovens. Arbutuses abound in the surrounding fields, producing strawberry-like berries used to make the well-known **aguardente de medronho**, a local brandy.

Retrace your route, then take the road to Aldeia da Tôr, close to where you will see a Roman bridge. Head towards Salir.

Salir – There is a fine view of the mountains from the ruined Moorish castle. To the northeast of the village, the Rocha da Pena sits atop a steep, rugged hill at an altitude of 479m/1 571ft with its two walls dating from the Neolithic period. The abundant local flora and fauna, such as the fox, genet, hedgehog, royal eagle owl, Bonelli's eagle and round-winged eagle, are now protected.

Take the N 124 towards Alte.

★**Alte** – The white houses of this extremely attractive village of narrow, winding streets cling to the sides of a hill in the *serra*. In the lower part of the town, two rustic fountains, the Fonte Pequena and the Fonte Grande, and some picnic tables, provide a welcome stopping spot often used for festivals and *romarias*.

Igreja Matriz – The origins of this church are pre-16C. The exterior boasts a fine Manueline door, while the inside of one of the chapels is entirely covered with 18C azulejos. The Capela de Nossa Senhora de Lourdes also contains valuable Seville-style coloured azulejos in relief dating from the 16C.

Rejoin the N 124. At Benafim Grande, turn right on to a small road leading to the N 270, which you join at the village of Gilvrazino. Then head towards Loulé.

Loulé – The town, which was inhabited by the Romans, has preserved a few remnants from the walls of its Moorish castle. It is a large horticulture and handicraft centre and an important distribution point for produce and products from the mountain towns and villages, particularly in its lively and unusual neo-Moorish style (19C) market building, where some fine pieces of pottery can also be found. A large number of artisans carry on their traditional crafts around the historical centre, including fan palm work (hats, rafts), esparto grass (mats), leather, copper and brass, saddles and harnesses.

The surrounding countryside is covered with algarroba, almond, fig and olive trees Loulé is also famous for its Carnival, reputed predecessor of the carnival in Rio de Janeiro. The Senhora da Piedade *romaria* held on the second Sunday after Easter originates from pre-Christian times.

Museu Municipal ⊙ – The museum, located next to the castle, contains items of regional ethnography and a reconstruction of a traditional kitchen.

Igreja Matriz – *Entrance through the side door* – The church, which was founded in the 13C and is dedicated to St Clement, has been remodelled over the centuries. Its most impressive external feature is an ogival portico; the foliated capitals, a Manueline and a Renaissance chapel, are well worth seeing in its three-nave interior. The main chapel is split by a double window.

Igreja de Nossa Senhora da Conceição – The interior of the church, which is covered with beautiful 17C azulejos, contains an 18C gilded wood altarpiece.

Return to Faro on the N 125-4.

The coast near Praia da Rocha

Y. Travert/DIAF

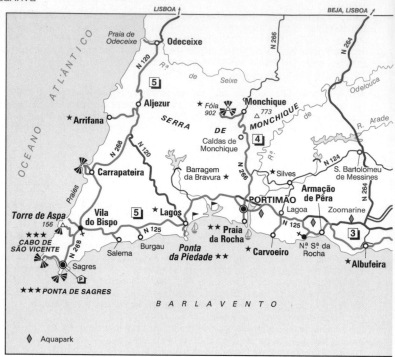

THE ROCKY COAST

③ From Faro to Portimão – *100km/62mi – allow a day*

The windward shore or *Barlaventa* is the Algarve's most famous stretch of coast. Ochre – coloured cliffs plunge down to the beach as far as Vilamoura and the turquoise sea surges into coves and grottoes. Some of these may be explored by boat. Unfortunately, the natural beauty has been marred in many places by intensive tourist development. Small harbours look lost in amongst tall white apartment blocks and in summer fishing boats are crowded out by beach umbrellas.

★Capela de São Lourenço – *See ALMANSIL.*

Quinta do Lago and **Vale do Lobo** – The two holiday villages are good examples of luxury tourist development with golf courses, country clubs and smart hotels around which are dotted splendid villas nestling among umbrella pines. There are footbridges across the lagoon to the beaches.

Quarteira and Vilamoura – *See VILAMOURA.*

★Albufeira – *See ALBUFEIRA.*

Armação de Pêra – *See ARMAÇÃO DE PERA.*

★Carvoeiro – *See CARVOEIRO.*

Portimão – *See PORTIMÃO.*

★★Praia da Rocha – *See PRAIA DA ROCHA.*

SERRA DE MONCHIQUE

④ From Portimão to Pico da Fóia *30km/19mi – about 2 hours – See Serra de MONCHIQUE*

LAGOS AND THE WEST COAST

⑤ From Portimão to Odeceixe – *140km/87mi – about 1 day*

The south coast around Lagos attracts fewer tourists and its small fishing villages have managed to keep their character. The west coast beyond Cabo de São Vicente is still very wild. Windswept and wave-battered, it consists of tall, grey cliffs at the foot of which nestle beautiful beaches approached by steep narrow roads. The landscape viewed from these beaches is often grandiose. The water is colder and

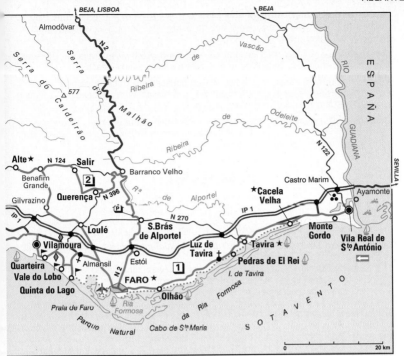

rougher than on the south coast of the Algarve and the waves are large enough for body-surfing. The hinterland is undulating, with eucalyptus, pine trees and aloes, while the bright white villages have remained unspoiled. The region is ideal for anyone seeking a quiet spot and is particularly popular with campers.

★Lagos – *See LAGOS*

★★Ponta da Piedade – *See PONTA DA PIEDADE*

Several roads lead southwards between Lagos and Vila do Bispo to beaches and fishing villages such as **Burgau** and **Salema**.

Vila do Bispo – The bright white village is a junction for roads to the north, the Algarve and Sagres. The baroque **church** ⊙ has a chancel in gilded wood and its walls are decorated with *azulejos* (1715). A door to the left of the chancel opens into a small museum of art which contains a beautiful crucifix.

★★Ponta de Sagres and Cabo de São Vicente – *See CABO DE SÃO VICENTE and PONTA DE SAGRES.*
Return to Vila do Bispa.

Torre de Aspa – *6km/4mi west. Take the Sagres road, then bear right and follow the signs.* The belvedere, which stands at an altitude of 156m/512ft, affords a beautiful **view★** of Cabo de São Vicente and Ponta de Sagres.

Waterparks

There are many recreational parks along the N 125. They have become part of the Algarve landscape and are hard to resist on extremely hot days, offering a refreshing alternative to the beaches. In general they consist of water slides of various shapes and sizes, adjoining lawns with sunshades, a snack-bar and a shop selling beachwear. They are open during the summer months and half or full day tickets can be bought.

The **Zoomarine** is more geared towards children. It has swimming pools, dolphin and parrot shows, an aquarium and other attractions. It is located on the N 125, 1km/0.6mi from Guia, towards Albufeira.

The **Big One** is near Porches, just 5km/3mi away on the road to Armação de Pêra.

Slide and Splash is on the Estômbar road, near Zoomarine.

The **Atlantic Park** is also on the N 125, 1.5km/1mi after the 4 Estradas crossroads for those visitors coming from Almansil.

The **Aqua Show** is towards Quarteira on the N 396.

Castelejo, Cordoama, Barriga and Mouranitos beaches – The beaches may be reached by car *(track access)* from Vila do Bispo. The scenery is wild and impressive with tall, grey cliffs.

Carrapateira – A road runs around the headland west of the village. There are fine views of the steep rock-face and Bordeira's long sandy beach.

Aljezur – The town consists of white-walled houses with brightly painted borders. A road from here leads west *(9km/5.5mi)* to **Arrifana**★ with its beach and fishing harbour nestling into the foot of a tall cliff.

Odeceixe – The southern approach to this attractive white village is through eucalyptus trees. A road runs for 4km/2.5mi alongside the Seixe, a small coastal river and estuary whith a **beach** at its mouth.

ALMANSIL

Faro – Population 5 945
Michelin map 940 U5 – Local map see ALGARVE

The village stretches alongside the N 125 that links Portimão to Faro.

★**Capela de São Lourenço** ⊙ – *2km/1mi east of Almansil, to the north of the road, in the hamlet of São Lourenço.*
The Romanesque chapel of St Lawrence, which was remodelled in the baroque period, is decorated inside with **azulejos**★★ dating from 1730, the work of Bernardo, an artist known as Policarpo de Oliviera Bernardes *(See Introduction – Azulejos)*. The walls and vaulting are covered with tiles depicting the life and martyrdom of St Lawrence: on either side of the chancel there are scenes depicting the blind and the distribution of moneys gained from the sale of sacred vessels; in the nave, on the south side there is a meeting between the saint and the pope, the saint in prison, and on the north side, preparation for the martyr's torture and St Lawrence on the grid being comforted by an angel. Outside, on the church's flat east end, a vast panel of *azulejos* shows St Lawrence and his gridiron beneath a baroque scallop shell.

Centro Cultural de São Lourenço ⊙ – The centre, which is located directly below the church in a typical Algarve house, organises a varied year-round music and arts programme which includes contemporary Portuguese as well as foreign performers.

B. Barbier/DIAF

Igreja de S. Lourenço

*Admission times and charges for the sights described
are listed at the end of the guide
Every sight for which there are times and charges
is identified by the symbol ⊙ in the Sights section of the guide.*

Castelo de ALMOUROL★★

Santarém

Michelin map 940 N4

The fortress of Almourol, which stands with towers and crenellations on a small rocky island covered in greenery in the centre of the Tagus, was constructed by Gualdim Pais, Master of the Order of the Templars in 1171 on the site of an earlier Roman fort.

The outstandingly romantic setting has given rise to many legends being woven around the castle. In Francisco de Morais's long prose romance of chivalry, *Palmeirim de Inglaterra (Palmeirim of England)*, duels and fights follow in quick succession at the foot of the ramparts.

Tour ⊙ – *Access from the N 3, north of the Tagus (2km/1mi east of Tancos). Leave the car along the river bank opposite the castle.* From the landing stage, there is a good view of the castle in its **setting★★**. The double perimeter wall, flanked by ten round towers, is dominated by a square keep *(access to the top by 85 steps and a low door)* commanding a panoramic **view★** of the river and its banks.

ALTER DO CHÃO

Portalegre – Population 2 794

Michelin map 940 O7

Alter do Chão stands grouped round its 14C **castle**. The upright crenellated towers overlook the main square, which is paved in a black and white mosaic pattern.

The **view** from the top of the keep looks down from a height of 44m/71ft onto the city and the surrounding olive groves.

On the square, north of the castle, a 16C marble **fountain** is surrounded by elegant slender columns, the classical capitals of which support a beautiful entablature.

AMARANTE★

Porto – Population 4 757

Michelin map 940 or 441 I5 – Local map see Vale do DOURO

Amarante is a picturesque small town, with its 16, 17 and 18C houses, complete with wooden balconies and wrought iron grilles; it is built in tiers up a hillside overlooking the Tâmega. The town, well known for its pastries *(lérias, foguetes, papos de anjo)* and its *vinho verde* wine *(See Introduction – Wines)*, comes alive each year on the first Saturday in June when it celebrates the feast day of its patron saint, Gonçalo. Gonçalo lived as a hermit in the 13C. He was also the patron saint of marriage and fertility.

SIGHTS

Ponte de São Gonçalo – This granite bridge (late 18C) spans the Tâmega. A marble plaque, on one of the obelisks at the entrance to the bridge on the left bank, recalls the successful resistance at this spot on 2 May 1809 of General Silveira, the future Count of Amarante, against a detachment of Napoleon's troops.

Igreja e Convento de São Gonçalo – The church, which was erected in 1540, possesses a side doorway adorned with three tiers of small columns in the Italian Renaissance style, crowned by a baroque pediment. A central niche at the level of the first tier contains the statue of St Gonçalo. The four statues on the piers of a loggia to the left of the doorway are of the four kings who reigned while the monastery was being constructed. A cupola, with an *azulejos* decorated lantern tower, rises above the transept crossing.

The interior, modified in the 18C, has some lovely gilded wooden baroque furnishings: an altarpiece in the chancel, two pulpits facing each other, and above all the **organ case★** (early 17C) which is supported by three Tritons. St Gonçalo's tomb (d 1259) lies in the chapel on the left of the chancel; the chapel on the right, called that of the Miracles, contains votive offerings.

At the end of the north arm of the transept, a door opens on to the plain Renaissance cloisters, which surround a fountain with grotesques.

Câmara Municipal – The town hall occupies what were formerly the conventual buildings *(in the market square, to the right of the church)*.

A small **museum** ⊙ on the first floor contains archaeological remains, sculptures and modern paintings including works by the Cubist painter, **Amadeo de Souza Cardoso** *(See Introduction – Art – 20C)*, who was born near Amarante.

Igreja de São Pedro – This 18C church has a baroque façade decorated with statues of St Peter and St Paul.

The unique nave, beneath a stucco-work barrel vault, is decorated with 17C bands of blue and yellow *azulejos*; the chancel beneath a stone vault with sunken sculpted panels, has a gilded wooden altar. There is a coffered chestnut wood **ceiling★**, with elegant carving in the sacristy.

EXCURSION

Travanca – *18km/11mi along the N 15 going towards Oporto about 45min.*
The 12C **church** forms part of an ancient Benedictine monastery (now an asylum) built in the hollow of a small wooded valley. The structure is of granite and presents a wide and robust façade in surprising contrast to the interior which, with its three aisles, is completely harmonious in its proportions.
The historiated **capitals★** adorning the doorways, the triumphal arch and the chancel are outstanding.
To the left of the church stands a machicolated tower with battlements, its doorway roughly decorated.

ARMAÇÃO DE PÊRA

Faro – Population 2 894
Michelin map 940 U4 – Local map see ALGARVE

This fishing village has become a highly developed seaside resort with tall white tower blocks fronting its immense beach.

★★Boat trip ⊙ – *As far as Cabo Carvoeiro, to the west, leaving from Armação (eastern beach).* The trip, on a calm sea, takes you past the sandstone cliffs and the rocks strangely sculpted by erosion, where you can discover 18 **sea caves★★** considered the most beautiful on the Algarve coast (Pontal, Mesquita, Ruazes, etc).

Capela de Nossa Senhora da Rocha ⊙ – *3km/2mi to the west.*
This lovely white chapel with its pointed steeple, well situated on a headland in the cliffs, has a doorway framed by two columns with sculpted capitals; the interior is covered with *azulejos* and has charming votive offerings (ships).

AROUCA

Aveiro – Population 2 340
Michelin map 940 or 441 J5

The Arouca Monastery and a few houses on its perimeter lie deep in the hollow of a small green valley surrounded by wooded heights. Founded in 716 but rebuilt in the 18C after a fire, the monastery forms a baroque but unadorned group.

Igreja do Mosteiro ⊙ – The single nave of the abbey church contains numerous gilded baroque altars and several statues in Ança stone carved by Jacinto Vieira. The 18C tomb worked in silver, ebony and quartz in the second chapel on the south side of the church, contains the mummy of Queen Mafalda (1203-52), daughter of King Sancho I; she retired here in 1217.

Coro Baixo – The lower chancel is ornamented with an 18C gilded organ loft, stalls with richly carved backs and graceful statues of religious figures by Jacinto Vieira.

Museu de Arte Sacra de Arouca ⊙ – This museum on the first floor of the cloisters contains Portuguese Primitive **paintings★** dating from the late 15 to the early 16C from the Viseu School, and works, including an *Ascension*, by the 17C artist Diogo Teixeira. There is also a statue of St Peter dating from the 15C.

Serra da ARRÁBIDA★

Setúbal
Michelin map 940 Q2 and Q3

The Serra da Arrábida rises and falls over the southern part of the Setúbal peninsula, covering 35km/22mi between Cabo Espichel and Palmela. The line of hills is made up of the ends of Secondary Era limestone deposits, pushed back, broken and buried beneath more recent deposits, and which reappear on the north side of the Tagus abutting the Sintra Massif.
The **Parque Natural da Arrábida**, which covers 10 800ha/26 688 acres between Sesimbra and Setúbal, has been created to protect the local scenery and architecture.

ROUND TOUR FROM SESIMBRA *77km/48mi – about 4 hours*

The itinerary described below takes in the two very different sides of this small range of mountains, which is a mere 6km/4mi wide. The **southern side** slopes down to the ocean, ending in cliffs 500m/1 600ft high. The indented coastline, the white and ochre colours of the limestone strata, the blue of the Atlantic, the heathlike vegetation where pines and cypresses rise out of a thick undergrowth of arbutus, myrtles and lentisks, is more reminiscent of a Mediterranean than an Atlantic landscape. Some of the creeks with their beautiful clear water and fine beaches have

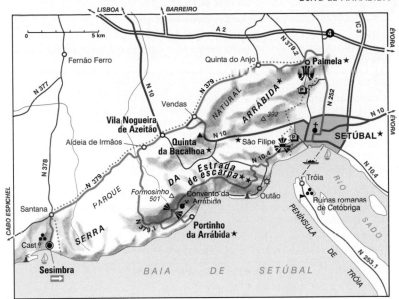

been developed for tourism. The **northern side**, which has a more rounded relief, has, where cultivated, a landscape of vineyards, orchards and olive groves and, on poorer ground, of its original brush and pine woods. The villages are prosperous and there are many *quintas*.

Sesimbra – *See SESIMBRA.*
After Santana, the N 379 taken on the right, winds between hills enlivened by orange trees and windmills.
2.5km/1.5mi before Vila Nogueira de Azeitão, turn right on N 379-1 towards Arrábida.
After a brief run through olive groves and vineyards, the road begins a winding climb through dense vegetation. The sea appears far below.
Follow the signs to Portinho.

★**Portinho da Arrábida** – The Bay of Portinho da Arrábida, at the foot of the *serra*, forms an even curve, edged by a beautiful semicircular beach of fine white sand that is very popular at weekends. A majestic rock rises out of the transparent waters. At the entrance to the village, the **Forte de Nossa Senhora da Arrábida**, a fort built in the 17C as a protection against Moorish pirates, now houses a small **Museu Oceanográfico** ⊘ with fine displays of sponges and various marine species. Steps lead from the left of the fort entrance down to a cave.
Continue along the N 379-1, leaving the lower corniche road on the right.

★★**Estrada de escarpa** – The corniche road follows a section of the mountain crestline affording views of both the northern and southern slopes. On the left there is an immediate view of Monte Formosinho (alt 499m/1 637ft) the *serra's* highest peak, and on the right of Portinho and the Sado estuary. Below, in the foreground, abutting on a cliff overlooking the sea stands the **Convento da Arrábida** that was founded by Franciscans in 1542. Several round chapels dot the mountainside. A drop in the height of the mountain crestline affords several glimpses of the interior, while the Tróia Peninsula juts out into the sea. In the final descent and in the vicinity of a cement works and its accompanying housing, Setúbal can be seen set into the back of its bay.

★**Setúbal** – *See SETÚBAL.*
Leave Setúbal heading north on the N 252 and, before the motorway, take the N 379 to the left.

★**Palmela** – *See PALMELA.*
The N 379 runs near Bacalhoa (on the N 10 opposite the Rodoviária Nacional bus station) which can be reached from Vendas on the left.

★**Quinta da Bacalhoa** – *See Quinta da BACALHOA.*
The N 10 passes through vineyards and orchards to Vila Nogueira de Azeitão.

Vila Nogueira de Azeitão – The prosperous agricultural town set amidst beautiful *quintas* is famous for its moscatel. The main street is bordered with lovely baroque fountains and the graceful buildings and gardens of the **Casa Vitícola José Maria de Fonseca**, a firm which has been making moscatel wine since 1834.
Return to Sesimbra on the N 379 via Santana.

ARRAIOLOS

Évora — Population 3 567
Michelin map 940 P6

This charming village, which stands perched on a hill in the great Alentejo Plain, is famous for its wool carpets.
The 14C castle dominates streets of white-walled houses with door and window frames painted blue.

Arraiolos carpets — In the second half of the 17C a small industry was established and grew up in the Arraiolos region, manufacturing hemp and linen carpets which were then embroidered with wool in cross-stitch and used as chest and wall coverings. The carpets first followed Indian and Persian designs with animal figures and plant motifs but soon the Oriental patterns and colourings were abandoned in favour of more popular themes in which blue and yellow predominated.
Nowadays Arraiolos carpets are on sale in the village shops and at the cooperative.

Castelo — The castle *(partially restored)* commands a fine view of the village and olive groves beyond, Divor Reservoir, and the **Convento de Quinta dos Lóios** which has been converted into a *pousada*.

AVEIRO★

Aveiro — Population 29 646
Michelin map 940 or 441 K4

Aveiro stands at the end of the Ria da Aveiro in a setting of salt marshes, lagoons and canals.

Historical notes — Like the neighbouring villages of Ovar, Ilhavo and Vagos, which now lie landlocked a couple of miles inland, Aveiro was once a seaport. It developed apace in the 15C and 16C due to Princess Joana's presence *(see below)* and as a result of the deep-sea cod fishing off Newfoundland. However, in 1575 disaster struck. A violent storm closed the lagoon; the harbour silted up and the city, deprived of its industries, fell into decline.
An effort by the Marquis of Pombal to rehabilitate it in the 18C came to nothing as did several plans to breach the strand to the sea. Finally in 1808 with the aid of breakwaters built from stones taken from the old town walls, a passage was opened once more from the lagoon to the sea; to the north of the town the Rio Novo took over the former winding course of the Vouga in a direct line.
Ceramic and chinaware industries developed locally (Ílhavo and Vista Alegre), bringing prosperity and with prosperity came expansion and artistic renown: Aveiro became a centre of baroque art with a famous school of sculpture. The town was soon adorned with monuments.

Aveiro today — The town still lives off its saltpans, grazing, rice paddies and land made fertile with seaweed gathered from the sea floor. But it remains primarily a fishing town, earning its living from the sea: lamprey and sea perch are caught in the lagoon, sardines and skate on the coast. Industry is, however, the mainstay of the region: traditional pottery making (Ílhavo, Vista Alegre), a cellulose factory, fish processing and canning, shipyards, engineering industries (bicycles, tractors, car assemblying) and iron and steel works (Ovar). Aveiro is Portugal's third largest industrial centre after Lisbon and Oporto.
Gourmets visiting the town should try the *ovos moles*, a type of egg dessert, usually served in miniature painted wooden barrels.
A great exhibition fair is held each year during March and April. In July or August, for the Ria Festival, a competition takes place on the central canal to find the best painted prow from the fleet of wide-bottomed *moliceiros (See below — Ria de Aveiro)*, used for harvesting the seaweed in the estuary.

A distinctive feature — Canals crisscross the town spanned by several small bridges; the graceful *moliceiros* as well as their mooring posts inevitably bring to mind Venetian gondolas and their *palli*. The immediate proximity of the river and its labyrinth of waterways gives Aveiro its originality.
In addition, the town centre has several lovely buildings, a fine museum, a pleasant park, and a main avenue with plenty of shade *(Avenida Dr Lourenço Peixinho)*.

★CANAL QUARTER 2hr

Some canals of the Ria de Aveiro continue right into the town; they are shored up by embankments on which the water laps over at high tide.

Canal Central (Y) — Part of it is bordered by noble dwellings, their classical façades reflected in the water, and there is a continuous spectacle of small boats, *moliceiros* or launches moving about on it, or tying up.

AVEIRO

Coimbra (R.) .... **Y** 12
Comb. da Grande Guerra (R.)... **Z** 13
Dr. Lourenço Peixinho (Av.).... **Y**
José Estêvão (R.) .... **Y** 24
Luís de Magalhães (R. do C.).. **Y** 28
Viana do Castelo (R.) .... **Y** 40
14 de Julho (Praça) .... **Y**

Antónia Rodrigues (R.) .... **Y** 3
Apresentação (Largo da) .... **Y** 4
Belém do Pará .... **Y** 6
Capitão Sousa Pizarro (H.) ...... **Z** 9
Clube dos Galitos (R.) .... **Y** 10
Eça de Queirós (R.) .... **Z** 14
Eng. Pereira da Silva (R.) .... **Y** 16
Gustavo F.P.-Basto (R.) .... **Z** 18
Humberto Delgado (Praça) ..... **Y** 21

Jorge de Lencastre (R.) .... **Y** 22
José Rabumba (R.) .... **Y** 27
Marquês de Pombal
   (Praça)................................ **Z** 31
Milenário (Praça do) .... **Z** 33
República (Praça da) .... **Y** 34
Santa Joana (Rua) .... **Z** 37
Santo António (Largo de)........ **Z** 39
5 de Outubro (Av.) .... **Y** 42

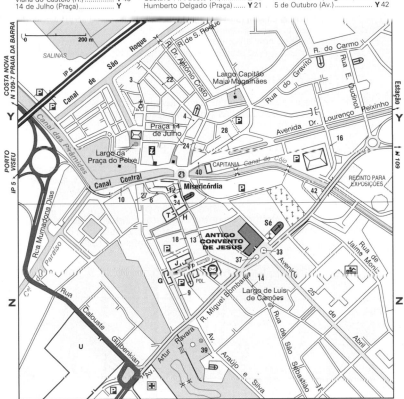

The best viewpoint is from the wide bridge-tunnel with balusters which divides it at the half-way point, and is the main crossroads in the town *(Praça Humberto Delgado)*.

Canal de São Roque (Y) – It borders the built-up area to the north, and is spanned (in front of Rua Dr. António Cristo) by an elegant stone humpback footbridge. It divides the salt marshes from the salt warehouses which line the embankment amongst the low roofed houses of the fishing quarter.

★**Antigo Convento de Jesus: Museu** ⊙ **(Z)** – *Rua Santa Joana*.
The Convent of Jesus was erected from the 15 to the 17C. Princess Joana, daughter of King Afonso V, retired here in 1472 and remained here the last eighteen years of her life. In the 18C a baroque façade was superimposed on the older front.

★**Igreja** – The church dates from the 15C, but the interior decoration was completed in the early 18C.
The interior has some exceptionally sumptuous carved and gilded wood, particularly in the **chancel**★★, a masterpiece of baroque exuberance with its columns, altars, coffered and rose ceiling beautifully intermingled and prodigiously wrought; scenes from the life of Saint Joana can be seen on *azulejos* panels. The lower chancel *(coro baixo)*, holds **St Joana's tomb**★ (early 18C). This masterpiece by the architect João Antunes, a mosaic in polychrome marble, is supported by sitting angels, also in marble.

Cloisters – The Renaissance style cloisters are surrounded by chapels, one of which contains the beautiful 15C **tomb of João de Albuquerque**. The refectory is decorated with floral *azulejos*.

★**Museu** – A tour of the museum includes a visit to the church gallery or **coro alto** which is decorated with paintings and a 14C Crucifixion in which Christ's expression changes according to the angle.
The museum itself exhibits various collections including sculptures of the Coimbra School (16C) and Portuguese Primitive paintings on wood. One of these is a lovely **portrait of Princess Joana**★ late 15C, attributed to Nuno Gonçalves – who painted the

famous polyptych of the Adoration of St Vincent – remarkable for the severe sculptural features of the young girl dressed in court finery. There are also Italian paintings (a Virgin with honeysuckle, 15C anonymous); 18C paintings on copperplate; pottery, vestments, religious objects and 17C lecterns.

In the rooms devoted to baroque art, there are statues in polychrome wood of the Aveiro Angels, a strange Holy Family in earthenware from the workshop of Machado de Castro, and a lacquered wooden writing desk. The room where Saint Joana died in 1490 is now an oratory decorated with altarpieces and gilded wood. A section on ancient carved stones completes the exhibit.

ADDITIONAL SIGHTS

Sé (Z) – Originally a simple church, the cathedral has been greatly modified since it was first built in the 16C. It has a baroque façade and inside, a strange mixture of styles; ancient and beautiful *azulejos* have been added to the renovated walls of the nave and a 17C organ has been installed in the north arm of the transept. To the left of the entrance, there is an early Renaissance Entombment.

Igreja da Misericórdia (Y) – The Church of the Misericord has an imposing 17C doorway, finely worked. Inside, the height of the nave and the 17C *azulejos* should be noted, as well as, opposite the pulpit, the churchwardens' pew.

Estação – *Take Avenida Dr. Lourenço Peixinho* (**Y**).
The *azulejos* panels which decorate the outside and inside façades of the railway station (by the platforms) are a pleasant and interesting illustration of Aveiro's monuments as well as its region, and the traditional crafts and costumes of the Ria.

B. Barbier/DIAF

Moliceiro on the Ria de Aveiro

★RIA DE AVEIRO

The Ria de Aveiro appears as a vast lagoon marked by tides, with scattered islands and crisscrossed with channels, bordered with salt marshes and pine forests, behind an offshore bar some 45km/28mi long and not more than 2.5km/1.5mi wide, with a narrow bottleneck (Barra Channel) linking it to the ocean. The lagoon takes the shape of a triangle and at high tide covers about 6 000ha/23sq mi, for an average depth of 2m/6.5ft. Very rich in fish, fertile in the parts above sea level, the *ria* is particularly famous for its seaweed which is used as a fertiliser. The seaweed is traditionally collected in **moliceiros**, flat-bottomed boats with prows curved like swans' necks and painted with naive motifs in vivid colours. They have a sail or are propelled with a pole. The rakes' prongs *(ancinhos)* for scraping or gathering up seaweed are hung around the tip of the prow. Unfortunately, the number of these boats is decreasing although there is still an annual competition for the best decorated.

Boat trips ⊘ in summer give a taste of life in the *ria*, as the craft mingle with the boats of saltworkers, fishermen, peasants and *moliceiros* collecting seaweed.

Northern arm of the ria

Bico – The interest of this small port, which is reached after crossing Murtosa, lies in the moliceiros which gather here on certain days.

Torreira – This is a small port on the *ria* where beautiful *moliceiros* may still be seen. It also fronts the sea and has developed into a resort on account of its fine sandy beach.
Between Torreira and São Jacinto there are good views of the *ria* and seaweed collectors may be seen going about their work. The Pousada da Ria, located between the two ports, has been built right down on the water's edge. The Reserva Natural das Dunas de São Jacinto is 2km/1mi before São Jacinto.

Reserva Natural das Dunas de São Jacinto – This nature reserve, which covers 666ha/1 645 acres of some of the best preserved dunes in Europe, is particularly interesting for its scenery, flora and fauna. A **visitor centre** ⊘ contains exhibitions on the reserve and there are signposted trails through pine woods and dune vegetation.

São Jacinto – The small resort in the pine woods is also a military camp and port, at the end of the north offshore bar, on the Barra Channel. Oxen can be seen hauling up the fishing boats on the beach.

Southern arm of the ria

Ílhavo – This small fishing port has an interesting **museum** ⊘ on the history of the fishing industry and the sea with models of fishing boats and *moliceiros*. There is also a display of Vista Alegre ceramics.

Vista Alegre – This town has been a manufacturing centre of fine chinaware and glass since 1824. A **museum** ⊘ in the factory premises recounts the developments of production since its earliest days.

Costa Nova – A growing family resort, shaded by umbrella pines and conveniently situated on the edge of both the Atlantic beaches and those of the lagoon. The small houses with façades decorated with vertical strips of painted wood give it a very cheerful aspect *(see photograph in Practical Information)*.

Praia da Barra – A seaside resort in full development, sheltered by an offshore bar of sand dunes, behind which there is an immense beach stretching southwards beyond Costa Nova.

AVIS

Portalegre – Population 1 893
Michelin map 940 O6

The first glimpse of Avis comes as a welcome sight as one crosses the monotonous Alentejo plateau, which is covered mostly with cork oaks and olive trees. The town, which has kept traces of its early fortifications, overlooks the confluence of the Seda and Avis rivers, now submerged below the waters of the reservoir serving the Maranhão power station, 15km/9mi downstream.
The N 243 to the south affords the best **view★** of the town. Ramparts, a few medieval towers and the church of the Convento de São Bento, rebuilt in the 17C, stand witness today of the city's brilliant past.

Two famous Battle Abbeys

On 14 August 1385 the two pretenders to the throne of Portugal, Juan I of Castile and João I, Grand Master of the Order of Avis, and their respective allies faced each other, prepared to do battle at Aljubarrota. Knowing that defeat meant Spanish domination, João I vowed to raise a superb church in honour of the Virgin if she would grant him victory. The Portuguese bowmen on foot resisted the Spanish cavalry. Portugal had secured its independence and three years later building on the **Mosteiro do Batalha** began and it remains today as a great national shrine.
319 years earlier, on 14 October 1066, William the Conqueror's first battle on English soil was fought at **Hastings** and he too built a **Battle Abbey** to commemorate the Norman victory over King Harold. However this abbey was largely dismantled at the Dissolution.

It was in this town, at the beginning of the 13C, that the military order founded in 1147 by Afonso Henriques to fight the Moors, became geographically established. The oldest order of chivalry in Europe bore several names and followed the rules of several other orders before finally becoming the Order of St Benedict of Avis. It prospered in the Tagus area until 1789.

Avis was also the cradle of the dynasty which was to reign over Portugal from 1385 to 1580. On 7 August 1385 João (bastard son of Pedro I), Grand Master of the Order of Avis, was proclaimed king under the name **João I**. In February 1387 he married Philippa of Lancaster.

Quinta da BACALHOA★
Setúbal
Michelin map 940 Q3 – Local map see Serra da ARRÁBIDA

The Quinta da Bacalhoa is on the N 10 as you leave Vila Fresca de Azitão heading towards Setúbal, opposite the Rodoviária Nacional bus station.

This seigneurial residence, built at the end of the 15C and remodelled in the early 16C by the son of Afonso de Albuquerque, Viceroy of India, has both Renaissance and Moorish styles and rich **azulejos★** decoration.

TOUR

In the manor house a graceful loggia giving onto the gardens is adorned with polychrome *azulejos* panels depicting allegories of great rivers including the Douro, Nile, Danube and Euphrates.

Gardens ⊘ – The gardens have a harmonious presentation and a pleasing freshness. In the formal garden, inspired by the style current in 16C France, clipped box trees alternate with fountains with mythological figures. An ornamental kitchen garden, where mandarin orange and walnut trees, bamboo and cinerarias grow, ends at an attractive pavilion and ornamental pool. The walls inside the pavilion are decorated with Spanish *azulejos* with geometrical patterns, but the most impressive panel is the Florentine-style depiction of **Susannah and the Elders★** which is the oldest figurative panel in Portugal (1565).

The tour ends in a walk beside a 15C gallery decorated with busts.

BARCELOS
Braga – Population 4 031
Michelin map 940 or 441 H4

Barcelos is a small attractive town on the north bank of the Cávado. It was the capital of the first county of Portugal and residence of the first duke of Bragança. It is now a busy agricultural market and a well-known centre for the production of pottery, ornamental crib figures, carved wood yokes and decorated cocks.

The **market** held on Thursday mornings, is one of Portugal's most famous.

The Barcelos Cock – A pilgrim on his way to Santiago de Compostela was accused of theft as he was about to leave Barcelos.

In spite of his honesty he found himself unable to offer a satisfactory defence and was condemned to die by hanging. He made one last plea. But the judge refused to be swayed in his condemnation of the stranger. The pilgrim, therefore, sought the protection of St James and noticing the judge's repast of roast cock, declared that in proof of his innocence, the cock would stand up and crow. The miracle occurred. The judge, in recognition of the pilgrim's innocence, set him free, and he erected a monument in memory of the miracle; it may now be seen in the municipal archaeological museum in the Former Palace of the Ducal Counts of Barcelos.

Barcelos Cocks

B. Goussé/RAPHO

OLD QUARTER

The main sights are centred around the **medieval bridge** over the Cávado in the southern part of the town.

Igreja Matriz – This 13C church, which was modified in the 16C and 18C, has a plain façade, flanked on the right by a square belfry, and a Romanesque doorway. The **interior★** is glittering with gold and bordered with Baroque chapels. The walls are decorated with 18C *azulejos*. Some of the capitals are historiated.

Pelourinho – This pillory, which was erected in the Gothic period, has a hexagonal column upon which stands a graceful granite lantern.

Solar dos Pinheiros – This beautiful 15C Gothic manor house built of granite is adorned with three-storeyed corner towers.

Ruinas Paço dos Condes de Barcelos – This 15C palace ruins are the setting for a small open air archaeological museum, **Museu Arqueológico** ⊘. Of particular interest is the 14C monument set up in honour of the Barcelos Cock *(see above)*. A vaulted chamber in the basement houses a **Ceramics Museum**.

ADDITIONAL SIGHTS

Campo da República – This vast esplanade in the centre of the town is the scene of the famous terracotta ware **market** held on Thursday mornings.

★Igreja de Nossa Senhora do Terço – *On the northern side of Campo da República.* The Church of Our Lady of Terço was formerly part of a Benedictine monastery which was founded in 1707. The walls of the nave are covered with beautiful 18C **azulejos★** depicting events in the life of St Benedict. The coffered ceiling is painted with forty scenes of monastic life. The pulpit of gilded wood is richly ornamented.

Torre de Menagem – This tower, part of the remains of the 15C ramparts, now houses the Tourist Information Centre.

Igreja do Bom Jesus da Cruz – The Church of Jesus, which is built in the northern baroque style, has an interesting plan in the shape of a Greek cross.

Mosteiro da BATALHA★★★
Leiria
Michelin map 940 N3

The Monastery of Batalha (Battle) stands in a green valley (unfortunately right beside the National 1), a mass of gables, pinnacles, buttresses, turrets and small columns – the rose gold effusion of its architecture is one of the masterpieces of Portuguese Gothic and Manueline art.

The Battle of Aljubarrota – On 14 August 1385 on the Plateau of Aljubarrota, 15km/9mi south of Batalha, two pretenders to the throne of Portugal and their respective allies faced each other, prepared to do battle: Juan I of Castile, nephew of the dead king, and João I, Grand Master of the Order of Avis, who had been crowned king only seven days previously.

The opposing forces were of very different strengths: against the organised forces and sixteen cannon of the Castilians, the Constable Nuno Alvares Pereira could only muster a squad of knights and foot soldiers. João I of Avis, knowing that defeat would mean Portugal passing under Spanish domination, made a vow to build a superb church in honour of the Virgin if she were to grant him victory. The Portuguese troops resisted and were victorious. A few days later Nuno Alvares pursued the enemy back into Spain as far as Castile.

Portugal had secured independence for two centuries.

Three years later the Mosteiro de Santa Maria da Vitória, subsequently known as the Mosteiro da Batalha, began taking shape.

The building of the monastery – Work was started by the Portuguese architect Afonso Domingues and was continued from 1402-1438 by Huguet, an Irishman, who designed in the Flamboyant Gothic style the founder's chapel where João I, his English queen, Philippa of Lancaster, daughter of John of Gaunt, and his sons lie buried. Death prevented the completion of the octagonal mausoleum (the Unfinished Chapels) of King Duarte I.

During the reign of Afonso V (1438-1481), the Portuguese architect Fernão de Evora built the so-called Afonso V cloisters in a sober style. Mateus Fernandes the Elder, one of the masters of the Manueline style, succeeded as architect, cooperating with the famous Boytac in the tracery of the arcades of the Royal Cloisters and continued the building of the chapels around the octagon. The chapels, however, were never completed, for King João III (1521-1557) abandoned Batalha in favour of a new monastery, the Mosteiro dos Jerónimos in Lisbon.

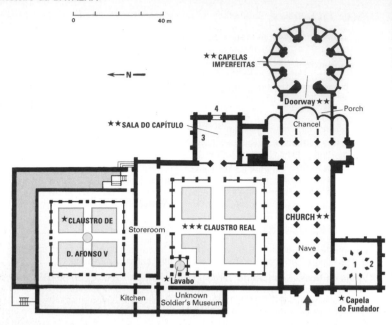

TOUR ⊘ 1hr

Exterior

The monastery, which in accordance with the Dominican rule, has no belfry, possesses innumerable pinnacles, buttresses and openwork balustrades above Gothic and Flamboyant windows. The building is in fine textured limestone, which has taken on a lovely ochre colour with time.

The complicated structure at the east end of the church demonstrates the architectural problems arising from joining on to an earlier apse an octagonal rotunda, which, by means of pillars, was to bear a vaulted ceiling.

The Founder's Chapel, off the south aisle, is surmounted by an octagonal lantern supported by flying buttresses.

The main façade is divided into three by pilasters and buttresses: the central part, decorated with a network of lancet shaped blind arcades, is pierced high up by a beautiful Flamboyant window; the main doorway is richly carved, bearing statues (new copies) of Christ in Majesty, surrounded by the Evangelists on the tympanum, the twelve Apostles on the sides, and angels, prophets, kings and saints on the covings. The doorway's proportions appeared to better advantage when the church stood, as it did originally, below the level of the terrace outside.

Interior

★★Church (Igreja) – The church's vast interior is very plain, the outstanding element being the upward sweep of the vaulting. The chancel is lit by **stained-glass windows★** which date from the 16C Manueline period and depict scenes from the Life of the Virgin and Jesus Christ.

★Capela do Fundador – This square chamber, known as the "Founder's Chapel", lit by Flamboyant windows, is covered with an octagonal lantern topped by a star shaped cupola. The massive pillars supporting the lantern are linked by festooned depressed arches.

In the centre are the tombs (**1**) of King João I and his queen Philippa of Lancaster, the two figures reclining beneath delicately carved canopies. The Avis and Lancaster coats of arms appear on the tomb. Bays on the south and west sides contain the tombs of the founder's four younger sons (Duarte, the eldest was buried in the sanctuary), Fernando, John, Pedro and Prince Henry the Navigator whose tomb (**2**) is covered with a canopy.

★★★Claustro Real– The Gothic and Manueline styles mix most successfully in the Royal Cloisters, the simplicity of the original Gothic design not being obscured by Manueline detail. The fleur-de-lys balustrade and the flowered pinnacles provide a motif which harmonises well with the Manueline tracery backing the carved marble arcades. The slender columns supporting the tracery are adorned with coils, pearls and shells.

Sala do Capítulo – The chapter house contains the tomb (3**) of the Unknown Soldier where, in fact, the bodies of two Portuguese soldiers lie. Both died in the First World War, one in France, the other in Africa.

The **vaulting***** is an outstandingly bold feat; after two unsuccessful attempts the master architect Huguet managed to launch a square vault of some 20m/60ft without intermediary supports. It was so dangerous that it is said to have been accomplished by convicts condemned to death. Huguet spent a whole night alone beneath his daring work once the last of the scaffolding had been removed.

The chamber is lit by a window containing beautiful early 16C **stained glass*** (**4**) representing scenes of the Passion.

*Monks' Lavabo (Lavabo dos Monges) – The lavabo in the northwest corner of the cloisters consists of a basin with a festooned curbstone surmounted by two smaller basins. The light, filtering through the stone tracery between the arches, gives a golden glow to the stone and the water.

This corner of the cloisters offers a beautiful view of the church dominated by the north transept bell turret.

The old refectory, which has a fine Gothic ceiling, houses the Unknown Soldier's Museum.

*Claustro de D. Afonso V – The coats of arms on the keystones to the vaulting in these fine Gothic cloisters are those of King Duarte I and King Afonso V.

Royal Cloisters, Mosteiro de Batalha

J.P. Lescourret/EXPLORER

Go round the outside of the chapter house and through the porch to the Unfinished Chapels.

★★**Capelas Imperfeitas** – Dom Duarte commissioned a vast mausoleum for himself and his descendents but he and his queen alone, lie buried in the unfinished building open to the sky. A vast transitional Gothic Renaissance porch connecting the east end of the church with the doorway of the octagonal chamber was added later by Dom Manuel. This **doorway**★★, which was initially Gothic in style, was ornamented in the 16C with Manueline decoration of a rare exuberance; it opens towards the church with a curved arch beneath a powerful multilobed arch. The cut-away ornament of the festoons as well as the detailed decoration on the covings and the columns are well worth looking at.

Seven chapels radiate from the octagonal rotunda, divided from each other by the famous incomplete pillars. These pillars are deeply carved all over, their ornament contrasting sharply with the plain lines of a Renaissance balcony added above by King João III in 1533.

BEJA★

Beja – Population 19 968
Michelin map 940 R6

Beja covers a rise on the wide Alentejo Plateau, at the watershed between the Sado Basin to the west and the Guadiana Basin to the east.

After being a brilliant Roman colony *(Pax Julia)*, the town became the seat of a Visigothic bishopric and then fell under Muslim control for four centuries. Today capital of the Baixo Alentejo, it is a town of white houses and straight streets that lives principally on the trade of local wheat and olive oil, and has the appearance of a flourishing agricultural market town.

The Portuguese Letters – In the world of literary correspondents Beja has been known for three centuries as the town of the Portuguese Nun. In 1669 a translation of the *Letters of a Portuguese Nun* written to Count Chamilly by Mariana Alcoforada, a nun in the Convento das Clarissas da Conceicão in Beja, was published in France. The five love letters, in which passion, memory, despair, entreaty and reproaches of indifference all mingle, caught the public imagination and became famous overnight. The letters' authenticity, however, was soon questioned; critics, struck by the quality of the "translation", suggested that the work had been composed in French by the writer Guilleragues, secretary to Louis XIV. Others, however, given the nobility of the sentiments, believed the letters proved the existence of a former romance of Count Chamilly, who had left in 1661 to fight in Alentejo against the Spaniards and only returned in 1668 at the end of the War of Devolution.

The Three Marias

Three Portuguese writers, Maria Isabel Barreno (b 1939), Maria Teresa Horta (b 1937), and Maria Fatima Velho de Costa (b 1938) collaborated on a controversial work, *New Portuguese Letters* (1972; English translation 1975), an anthology of poems, fictitious letters, and some of the authors' own correspondence. The book is based on an earlier collection, *Letters of a Portuguese Nun*, published in 1669 and translated into English about ten years later. The modern anthology was banned in Portugal because of its sexual frankness and open criticism of the country's opressive regime. The authors were tried and held by the authorities until the 1974 Carnation Revolution brought reform and greater freedom for artistic expression.

SIGHTS

★**Antigo Convento da Conceição** – The Poor Clares Convent, where the famous Portuguese nun lived, was founded by Dom Fernando, father of King Manuel, in 1459. The graceful Gothic balustrade crowning the church and the cloisters recalls that of the Mosteiro da Batalha. Today the convent houses the regional museum.

Museu da Rainha Dona Leonor ☉ – The baroque **church** was profusely decorated with gilded and carved woodwork in the 17C and 18C.

The walls of the cloisters on the right are covered with *azulejos*. The **chapter house** is richly decorated with beautiful 16C Hispano-Moorish *azulejos* from Seville and the vaulting is adorned with 18C floral motifs. A collection of Crucifixes is on display. The rooms beyond contain paintings including a *St Jerome* by Ribera (17C) and a 15C *Ecce Homo*.

The first floor contains the Fernando Nunes Ribeiro archaeological collection of engraved flagstones from the Bronze Age and Iron Age epigraphic stelae.

There is also a reconstruction of the cell window through which Sister Mariana Alcoforada is said to have talked to Count Chamilly.

The street opposite the convent, Rua dos Infantes, leads to **Praça da República**, the heart of the town with its pillory and town hall. A street to the right of the square leads downhill towards the castle.

Castelo ⊙ – The 13C castle's crenellated perimeter wall (housing a military museum), flanked by square towers, is overlooked at one corner by a high **keep**★ topped by pyramid shaped merlons. The first floor, which is reached by a spiral staircase, has fine star vaulting resting on Moorish style veined corner squinches. A machicolated gallery runs the full length of the wall just below the top of the keep, providing a remarkable lookout over the Alentejo Plain now covered with wheat.

★**Igreja de Santo Amaro** ⊙ – This small Visigothic church, parts of which date back to the 6C, now houses the **Visigothic art section** of the Museu da Rainha Dona Leonor. There is a collection of capitals and columns with plant and geometrical motifs. The column showing birds catching a snake is particularly interesting.

EXCURSION

São Cucufate ⊙ – *29km/18mi. Leave Beja northwards on the N 18 and at Vidigueira turn left onto the N 258; 2km/1mile after Vila de Frades, bear right (signposted).*

Excavations have uncovered the ruins of a large 4C **Roman villa** belonging to an important landowner. The building's interest lies in its two storey brick and stone construction. The upper floor is supported by a vaulted gallery, which is rare in the Iberian Peninsula. To the south are remains of a temple. In the Middle Ages, the northern part of the villa was converted into a monastery; its church contains frescoes.

BELMONTE★

Castelo Branco – Population 2 475
Michelin map 940 or 441 K7

Perched at an altitude of 600m/2 000ft on the spine of a hillock near the Serra da Estrela, Belmonte can be identified from afar by the square keep of its ancient castle. The great navigator **Pedro Álvares Cabral** who discovered Brazil in 1500 was born here. His statue stands on the main street which is named after him. The pantheon of the Cabral family has been erected in a chapel on the hill of the castle. Belmonte's history is also linked to that of Judaism in Portugal *(see box)*. Even today the town is home to the largest Jewish community in the country, and a new synagogue is currently under construction. Its isolated geographical situation undoubtedly encouraged the influx of Jews who took refuge here and continued to practise their religion in secret following the decree expelling them from the country in 1497. It is these so-called Cryptojews or *marranos* who have preserved Jewish traditions in Portugal.

Castelo ⊙ – Built in the 13-14C by King Dom Dinis I, only the keep, ringed with battlements, remains and the partly demolished enclosure, restored in 1940. The corner tower, on the right of the keep, has 17C balconies with console brackets, and the section of the wall adjoining it on the left has a double Manueline window with the Cabral family's coat of arms above it. The castle has been remodelled to include an amphitheatre for shows and concerts. The keep on the other side will soon be home to a small museum.

A walk round the perimeter wall offers a fine **view**★ of the countryside below, the Beira heights and the roof tops of Belmonte.

Igreja de São Tiago ⊙ – Next to the castle and of an earlier period but modified in the 16C, the church still has some interesting elements inside dating from the Romanesque period; a baptismal font, 16C frescos in the chancel and 12C examples on the wall to the right. The Nossa Senhora da Piedade chapel, built in the 14C, contains a strange pulpit with a sounding-board and a polychrome Pietà carved from a single block of stone, as well as capitals which refer to the exploits of Fernão Cabral I, the father of Pedro Álvares Cabral.

Panteão dos Cabrais ⊙ – The pantheon containing the tombs of Pedro Álvares Cabral and his parents is in the late 15C chapel adjoining the Igreja de São Tiago.

Capela de Santo António ⊙ – The construction of the 15C chapel in front of the church was ordered by the mother of Pedro Álvares Cabral.

Igreja Matriz ⊙ – The church, which was built in 1940, contains the picture of Our Lady of Hope, which, according to tradition, was said to have accompanied Pedro Álvares Cabral on his official voyage to discover Brazil, as well as a replica of the cross used in the first mass celebrated there. The original can be seen in Braga Cathedral.

*Torre Romana de Centum Cellas – *4km/2.5mi to the north. Take the N 18 towards Guarda then, on the right, the road to Comeal (sign marked Monumento) where there is a road leading to the foot of the tower.*
According to the excavations carried out in 1995, this impressive ruin is part of a 1C Roman villa which was connected to the tin trade along the road linking Mérida and Braga. Its square mass, made of pink granite blocks laid with dry joints, still stands with rectangular openings on three levels.

Ilha da BERLENGA★★

Leiria
Michelin map 940 N1

The Ilha de Berlenga, a reddish-coloured mass, which protrudes 12km/7mi out to sea from Cabo Carvoeiro is the main island in an archipelago consisting of a number of rocky islets, the Estelas, the Forcadas and the Farilhões.
Berlenga, 1 500m/4 921ft long and 800m/2 625ft at its widest point, reaches a height of 85m/279ft above the sea. The major attractions of this block of bare granite lie in its numerous indentations and headlands and in its marine caves.
Berlenga is famous for its underwater, line and harpoon fishing.

Access ⊙ – The boat sails parallel to the south shore of the Peniche peninsula, then passes close to Cabo Carvoeiro and the curious Crows' Ship (Nau dos Corvos), a rock resembling a ship's prow circled by screaming gulls.
It moors at the foot of an ancient fortress (1676), now an inn.

***Boat trip ⊙ – The trip is especially interesting because of the variety of small islands, reefs, arches and marine caves hollowed out of the red brown cliffs.
Among the most striking sights of the trip are, south of the inn, the Furado Grande, a marine tunnel 70m/230ft long which ends in a small creek (Cova do Sonho) walled by towering cliffs of red granite; beneath the fortress itself is a cave known locally as the "blue grotto", where light refracts on the sea within, producing an unusual and most attractive emerald green pool.

Walk – *1hr 30min.* Take the stairway from the inn to the lighthouse. Halfway up turn to look at the fortress in its **setting★; on reaching the plateau take a path on the left which goes to the west coast or Wild Coast. There is a good **view★** from the top, of the rocks, of the sea breaking below and, in the distance, the other islets of the archipelago.
Return to the lighthouse and descend by a cobbled walk, leading to a small bay bordered by a beach and a few fishermen's cottages. Halfway down, and to the left, one sees a creek where the sea roars and smashes in bad weather.

BRAGA★

Braga – Population 64 113
Michelin map 940 or 441 H4

Marked by its long clerical history, Braga is bristling with churches and monasteries and has a reputation for being rooted in the past.
Nonetheless, as the capital of the Minho, it is an active industrial centre (leather, textiles, brick manufacture, soap making, engineering and smelting). A yoke fair is still held on Tuesdays on the fairground *(largo da feira)*.

A very religious city – Bracara Augusta, an important Roman town, was made into their capital by the Suebi when they advanced upon the area in the 5C. The town was subsequently captured first by the Visigoths (who built the Igreja de São Frutuoso) and then the Moors and only regained prosperity after the Reconquest when it became the seat of an archbishopric.
From this time onwards the influence of the Church became paramount, a feature now particularly apparent in the richness of the architecture; in the 16C the archbishop and patron Dom Diogo de Sousa presented the town with a palace, churches and calvaries in the Renaissance style; in the 18C the two prelates, Dom Rodrigo of Moura Teles and Dom Gaspar of Bragança made Braga the centre of Portuguese baroque art. Braga, once the seat of the Primate of All Spain, is still strongly ecclesiastical in character. Holy Week is observed with devotion and is the occasion for holding unusual processions. The Feast of St John the Baptist on 23 and 24 June attracts crowds of local people and even many from as far as Galicia; they attend the processions, folk dancing and firework displays in the brilliantly decorated town.

★SÉ ⊙ *1hr 30min*

Only the south door and the arching over the main doorway, ornamented with scenes from the medieval *Romance of Renart the Fox*, remain from the original Romanesque cathedral. The portico with festooned Gothic arches is by Biscayan artists brought to Braga in the 16C by Diogo de Sousa. The moulded window frames date from the 17C. This same archbishop is responsible for the cathedral's east end bristling with pinnacles and balusters. The graceful **statue**★ of the Nursing Madonna (Nossa Senhora do Leite) beneath a Flamboyant canopy which adorns the east end exterior is said to be by Nicolas Chanterene.

★**Interior** – It was transformed in the baroque period. The contrast between the richness of the woodwork and the simplicity of the nave is striking. The font (**1**) is Manueline: to the right, in a chapel closed by a 16C grille, lies the bronze tomb (túmulo, 15C) of the Infante Dom Afonso.

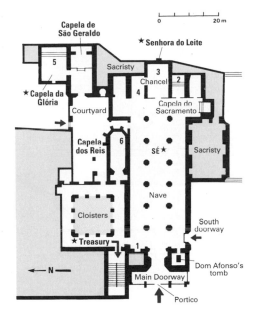

The Chapel of the Holy Sacrament (Capela do Sacramento) contains a fine 17C polychrome wooden altar (**2**) representing the Church Triumphant after a picture by Rubens.

The chancel *(no access),* which is covered with intricate ribbed **vaulting**★ in the Flamboyant style, contains a Flamboyant **altar**★ (**3**) of Ança stone carved on the front with scenes of the Ascension and of the Apostles. Above the altar is a 14C statue of St Mary of Braga. To the left of the chancel is a chapel (**4**) decorated with 18C *azulejos* by António de Oliveira Bernardes depicting the life of St Pedro de Rates, first bishop of Braga. A harmoniously baroque group is formed by the two 18C **cases**★ on either side of the balustraded organ loft.

★**Tesouro** – The cathedral treasury has a fine collection of 16-18C vestments as well as some outstanding church plate. This includes a Manueline chalice, a 14C cross in rock crystal, a 17C silver-gilt reliquary cross, a 10C Mozarabic chest made of ivory, a 16C chalice, a 17C monstrance, Dom Gaspar of Bragança's 18C silver-gilt monstrance adorned with diamonds, and several statues including a 13C Christ and St Crispin and St Crispinian, patron saints of shoemakers. There are also some 16C *azulejos* on display. The gallery or **coro alto** contains 18C gilded wooden stalls and provides a good view of the church interior.

A tour of the treasury includes the Capela de São Geraldo and the Capela da Glória.

Capela de São Geraldo – The walls of the Gothic St Gerald's Chapel are decorated with 18C azulejos illustrating the life of St Gerald who was the first archbishop of Braga.

★**Capela da Glória** – The Gothic Chapel of Glory is decorated with 14C mural paintings in the Mudejar style. The sides of the Gothic **tomb**★ (**5**) of the founder, Dom Gonçalo Pereira, in the centre of the chapel, bear reliefs of the Crucifixion and the figures of the Apostles, the Virgin and Child and clerics at prayer.

Capela dos Reis – The Kings' Chapel with Gothic vaulting resting on beautiful brackets sculpted with human heads, contains the 16C tombs (**6**) of Henry of Burgundy and his wife Teresa, parents of Afonso Henriques, the first king of Portugal, and the mummy of Dom Lourenço Vicente (14C), archbishop of Braga, who fought at Aljubarrota.

ADDITIONAL SIGHTS

Antigo Paço Episcopal (A) – The Former Episcopal Palace is made up of three edifices dating from the 14, 17 and 18C. The library, whose reading room has a beautiful gilt coffered ceiling, shelves 9C documents. The medieval north wing looks out over the pleasant Santa Bárbara Gardens (the 17C fountain of St Barbara).

Capela dos Coimbras (B) – The 16C Coimbras Chapel, next to an 18C church, has a crenellated and statue ornamented tower built in the Manueline style.

Museu dos Biscainhos ⊘ (**M¹**) – This 17C and 18C palace with its painted ceilings adorned with stuccowork and its walls decorated with panels of *azulejos* has been arranged with Portuguese and foreign furniture dating from the same period. There are carpets from Arraiolos, Portuguese silverware, porcelain and glassware.

BRAGA

Capelistas (Rua dos)............... **A** 7
Dom Diogo de Sousa
(Rua)................................ **AB** 16
Franc. Sanches (Rua)............. **B** 22
São Marcos (Rua)................. **AB** 28
Souto (Rua do) .... **AB** 33

Abade Loureira (Rua)............... **A** 3
Biscainhos (Rua dos).............. **A** 4
Caetano Brandão (Rua)........... **B** 6
Carmo (Rua do)...................... **A** 9
Central (Avenida).................... **A** 10
Chãos (Rua dos) .... **A** 12
Conde de Agrolongo (Praça) ... **A** 13
Dom Afonso Henriques (Rua) . **B** 15

Dom Gonç. Pereira (Rua)........ **B** 18
Dom Paio Mendes (Rua) .... **B** 19
Dr Gonçalo Sampaio (Rua) ..... **B** 21
General Norton de Matos (Av.) **A** 24
Nespereira (Avenida) .... **A** 25
São João do Souto (Praça) ..... **A** 30
São Martinho (Rua de)............ **A** 30
São Tiago (Largo de) .... **B** 31

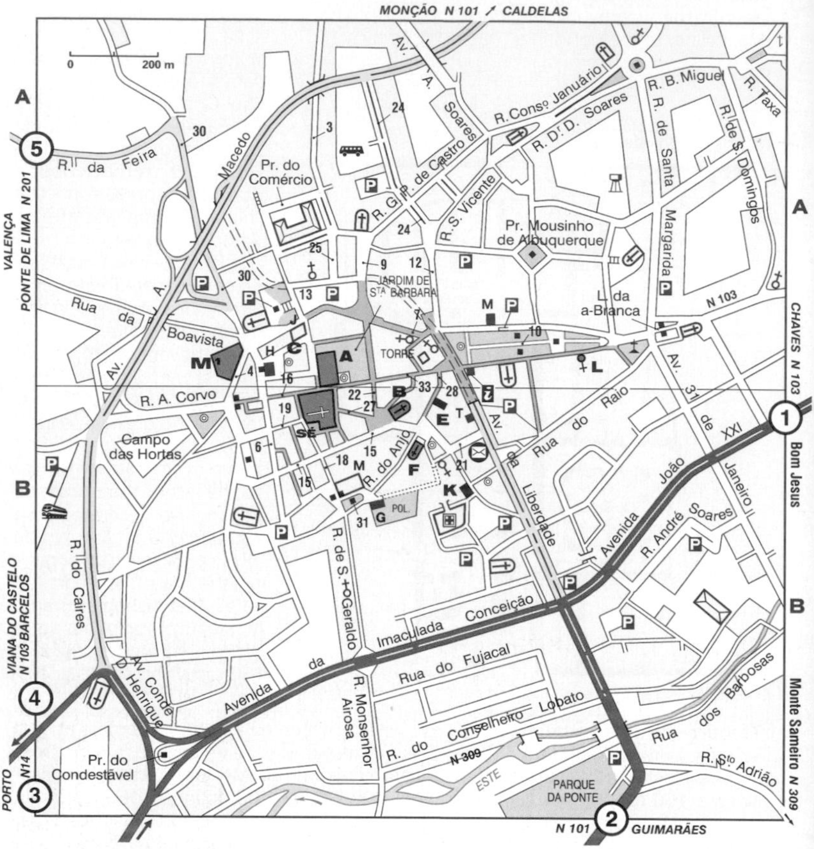

MONÇÃO N 101 / CALDELAS

A Antigo Paço Episcopal
B Capela dos Coimbras
C Fonte do Pelicano
E Casa das Gelosias
F Igreja de Santa Cruz
K Casa do Raio ou do Mexicano
L Capela de N.S. da Penha de França
M¹ Museu dos Biscainhos

The graceful suite of rooms leads onto beautiful gardens with an ornamental pool and 18C style statues.

Fonte do Pelicano (**C**) – In front of the town hall there is a lovely baroque fountain where the water spouts from a pelican and bronze cupids.

Casa das Gelosias (**E**) – The unusual House of Screens takes its name from the grilles and screens of Arabic design.

Igreja de Santa Cruz (**F**) – The Church of the Holy Cross is a 17C building in baroque style.

Casa do Raio or Casa do Mexicano (**K**) – The front of this 18C rococo residence is decorated with *azulejos*.

Capela da Nossa Senhora da Penha de França ⊙ (**L**) – The chapel is embellished with fine *azulejos* by Policarpo de Oliveira Bernardes and a 17C baroque pulpit.

EXCURSIONS

★★**Santuário do Bom Jesus do Monte** – *6km/4mi east. Leave Braga by* ① *on the town plan.* The baroque flight of steps to the Bom Jesus sanctuary is one of Portugal's most famous monuments. It is carved out of austere grey granite set off by whitewashed walls, an example of the Northern Baroque style. The different stages of construction, which spread over several decades, are apparent. The Stairway of the Three Virtues is rococo, while the church, which was built by Carlos Amarante between 1784 and 1811, is neo-classical.

The symbolism of the Via Sacra – The Holy Way, which pilgrims ascended on their knees, consists of a path bordered with chapels illustrating the Stations of the Cross, and the Stairway of the Five Senses followed by that of the Three Virtues. It represents the spiritual journey of believers who must learn to overcome their senses and attain the three virtues of Faith, Hope and Charity in order to gain salvation.

Access ⊘ – *by the funicular which climbs the 116m/381ft to the sanctuary in a few minutes;*

– by the road winding in hairpin bends through the greenery;

– by the stairway itself (about 15min), the Holy Way taken by pilgrims. This affords the best views from which to appreciate the magnificence of the baroque architecture and the natural beauty of the setting.

If you choose the stairway, leave the car in the car park near the entrance to the funicular.

A graceful portico opens onto the winding path which is bordered with chapels. At each chapel a scene from the Passion is evoked by astonishingly lifelike terracotta figures. Near each chapel stands a fountain, ornamented with mythological motifs.

The Stairway of the Five Senses – This is a double staircase with crossed balustrades; the base consists of two columns entwined by a serpent; water pours from the serpent's jaws, flowing back over the length of its body. Above the Fountain of the Five Wounds (where water falls from the five bezants of the Portuguese coat of arms), each level is embellished by a fountain designed allegorically as one of the five senses. Water springs from the eyes representing sight, from the ears for hearing, from the nose for the sense of smell and from the mouth for taste. The sense of touch is shown by a person holding a pitcher in both hands and pouring water.

The Stairway of the Three Virtues – This is adorned with fountains evoking Faith, Hope and Charity. Each balustrade is decorated with obelisks and figures from the Old Testament.

From the church parvis there is a fine **vista**★ of the baroque stairway and the town of Braga.

The **church** contains reliquaries and ex-votos. The chancel is adorned with a calvary in the same style as that of the chapels along the Way of the Cross.

Santuário do Bom Jesus do Monte

Y. Travert/DIAF

★Capela de São Frutuoso de Montélios ⊙ – *3.5km/2mi west. Leave Braga by* ⑤, *going towards Ponte de Lima; bear right at Real for São Frutuoso.*
This Visigothic chapel was incorporated into the church of St Francis (São Francisco) in the 18C. It was originally built in the 7C and is said to have been partly destroyed by the Moors and rebuilt in the 11C. Its Greek cross plan shows a Byzantine influence. The four arms were once surmounted by cupolas supported by 22 columns. The remaining capitals and friezes are decorated with acanthus leaves. A small exhibition traces the history of the chapel and includes a model showing its original appearance.
The gallery or *coro alto* in the Church of St Francis contains Renaissance stalls from Braga Cathedral.

★Round tour to the east of Braga via Bom Jesus do Monte – *44km/27mi about 3hr. Leave Braga by* ① *on the town plan.*

★★Bom Jesus do Monte – *See above.*

★Monte Sameiro – Monte Sameiro is crowned by a late 19 - early 20C sanctuary to the Virgin and is a very popular pilgrimage. A staircase (265 steps) climbs to the cupola's lantern tower (alt 613m/2 011ft) from where there is a vast **panorama★★** over the Minho; in clear weather Monte de Santa Luzia overlooking the Viana do Castelo can be seen in the northwest, the Serra do Gerês in the northeast and the Serra do Marão in the southeast. Below, in the foreground, are traces of the prehistoric city of Briteiros and, facing it, the sprawling mass of Braga.

Citânia de Briteiros – The ruins of Citânia de Briteiros stand on a hillock 337m/1 102ft high. The city existed during the Iron Age – 8 to 4C BC – and measured 250 x 150m/820 x 492ft. Three perimeter walls protected its 150 huts. Two huts have been reconstructed by the archaeologist Martins Sarmento. The objects unearthed in the course of excavations can be seen in the Museu Martins Sarmento at Guimarães.

Serra da Falperra – On a wooded slope of this small *serra* stands the **Igreja de Santa Maria Madalena**. Supposedly built by the architect of the Casa do Raio in Braga, the church has an unusual 18C rococo style façade on which there is not a single straight line.
Return to Braga by the N 309.

BRAGANÇA★

Bragança – Population 14 662
Michelin map 940 or 441 G9

Bragança, lying within the boundaries of the austere province of Trás-os-Montes, stands in a high combe at an altitude of 660m/2 165ft in the Serra da Nogueira.
The medieval city within its ramparts stands on high overlooking the modern town. The best **view★** is from the São Bartolomeu Pousada or from the chapel lookout point beside it *(2km/1mi southeast).*

The fiefdom of the House of Bragança – The medieval city was raised to the status of a duchy in 1442 and became fief to the Bragança family. This family, which had laid claim to the throne since the occupation of the country by Philip II of Spain, reigned over Portugal from 1853 to 1910. Throughout this period the title of Duke of Bragança was given to the heir to the throne.

★MEDIEVAL CITY

The city crowns a hilltop, enclosed within its long fortified walls and towers. The medieval city has an old-world atmosphere with its quiet, flower-decked narrow streets and gentle birdsong.

Castelo ⊙ – The castle, which was built in 1187, comprises a tall square keep 33m/108ft high, flanked by battlemented turrets, and several towers, which house a small military museum; two halls are lit by paired Gothic windows. The panorama from the keep platform extends over the old town, the lower town and the surrounding hills.

Pelourinho – The Gothic style pillory rests on a sow hewn out of the granite which is said to date from the Iron Age.

Igreja de Santa Maria – The origins of the church date from the Romanesque period, although it was totally remodelled in the 18C. It has an elegant façade with a door which is framed by two twisted columns decorated with vine plants; inside a fine ceiling painted in *trompe-l'œil* depicts the Assumption.

Domus Municipalis ⊙ – This pentagonal-shaped building, erected in the 12C, is the oldest town hall in Portugal. It is pierced on every side by small rounded arches. A frieze of carved modillions runs beneath the roof. The interior consists of a vast chamber and, below, a basement with a former cistern.

Bragança city walls

ADDITIONAL SIGHTS

These may be seen in the lower town that was built in the 17C and 18C.

Largo da Sé – The square is adorned with a large baroque cross which was originally a pillory.

The cross is in front of the city's cathedral, which is adorned with azulejos and baroque carved and gilded altars inside.

Igreja de São Bento – This single-nave 16C church has a Renaissance-style painted wooden ceiling. The chancel, with its attractive **Mudejar ceiling**, contains a valuable 18C gilded wooden altar screen.

Igreja de São Vicente – St Vincent's church is Romanesque in origin, but was totally reconstructed in the 18C. The interior contains a profusion of *talha dourada* work from the 17C, and the chancel is topped by a gilded vault. According to tradition, it was in this church that the secret wedding between Dom Pedro and Dona Inês de Castro took place *(see ALCOBAÇA)*.

Museu do Abade de Baçal ⊘ – The museum is housed in the former Episcopal palace. The collections include archaeological displays, paintings, items of local ethnological interest, coins and religious art. At the entrance, a video provides an insight into Trás-os-Montes costumes, and an interactive computer provides information on the museum, the region and its monuments. The ground floor contains a fine collection of funerary steles and milestones. On the second floor, the chapel of the former palace, with its painted ceiling, displays a set of 16C and 17C ecclesiastical vestments and polychrome pictures of saints. In Room 7, a 15C Virgin with Child in gilded and polychrome wood is worthy of particular note. The museum also contains an interesting collection of goldsmiths' art.

EXCURSIONS

Parque Natural de Montesinho – The reserve covers an area of 75 000ha/ 185 333 acres between Bragança and the Spanish border and includes the *serras* of Montesinho and Corôa. The area is rich in wildlife (wild boars, foxes, wolves and birds of prey); all these are now protected within the park.

The vegetation is predominantly black oak and chestnut, with heather and rockrose at higher altitudes. This isolated region has preserved its specific rural traditions, particularly in the characteristics of its architecture, costumes and inhabitants. In **Rio de Onor**, a town which is both Spanish and Portuguese, separated by a small bridge marking the border, women can still be seen washing clothes in the river. Local customs are still much in evidence, for example in **Guadramil**, another border town.

***Igreja do Mosteiro de Castro de Avelãs** – *Take the Chaves road. Head to the right of the viaduct and turn left immediately after the bridge. Follow the signs to the Mosteiro.*
The church was part of a former Romanesque Cistercian monastery (12C). All that remains of it are the apse and the apse chapels with blind arcading. It is unique in Portugal, both in its shape and its brick construction, and is linked to other Spanish churches under the Order of Cluny on the pilgrims' route to Santiago de Compostela.

BRAVÃES★

Viana do Castelo – Population 653
Michelin map 940 or 441 G4

The church at Bravães is one of the finest Romanesque buildings in Portugal.

***Igreja de São Salvador** ⊙ – The façade of this small Romanesque church (12C) is opened by a remarkable **doorway★** whose arching is covered in an intricate decoration representing doves, monkeys, human figures and geometrical motifs; richly historiated capitals crown naïvely carved statue columns. The tympanum, resting on the stylised heads of a pair of bulls, is ornamented with two angels in adoration of Christ in Majesty.
A low relief of the Holy Lamb is carved into the tympanum (of the south doorway) which is supported by two griffins.
Inside, the triumphal arch is embellished by a frieze influenced by Arabic design.

Mata do BUÇACO★★

Buçaco Forest – Aveiro
Michelin map 940 or 441 K4

Buçaco National Park lies to the north of Coimbra near the Luso spa, crowning the northernmost peak of the Serra do Buçaco. It is enclosed by a stone wall pierced by several gates. In a vast clearing in the centre of the forest, where a wide variety of trees grow, stands a castle-like palace-hotel built in 1900 to an extraordinarily unusual design.

A well guarded forest – As early as the 6C Benedictine monks from Lorvão built a hermitage at Buçaco among the oaks and pines of the original forest. From the 11C to the early 17C the forest was jealously maintained by the priests of Coimbra Cathedral who had inherited it. In 1622 Pope Gregory XV forbade women to enter the forest on pain of excommunication.

B. Barbier/DIAF

Palace Hotel

In 1628 the Barefoot Carmelites built a community and surrounded the domain by a wall. They continued to preserve and develop the forest by planting many new varieties including maples, laurels, English oaks, Mexican cedars and cypress trees. They obtained a papal bull from Urban VIII threatening anyone damaging the trees in their domain with excommunication.

However, a decree dated 28 May 1834 abolished all religious orders in Portugal and the Carmelite friars had to leave Buçaco. The forest was taken into royal care and then came under the Water and Forest Department which continued to plant apace. Today, the 105ha/250 acres of forest in Buçaco include over 400 native varieties of tree (eucalyptus, lentisks, etc) and about 300 exotic species (ginkgos, monkey-puzzles, cedars, Himalayan pines, thuyas, Oriental spruces, palms, arbutus, sequoias, Japanese camphor trees, etc). Besides the trees there are also tree ferns, hydrangeas, mimosas, camellias, magnolias, philarias and even lilies of the valley.

The Battle of Buçaco — September 1810 found Wellington once more facing the French, this time from the "damned long hill" at Buçaco. (By this time the French had already made two unsuccessful attempts to invade and conquer Portugal; and Wellington, although he had won victories as far east as Talavera in Spain, had been forced to retreat twice to Portugal to safeguard his lines of communication and reorganise his and the Portuguese armies).

TOUR ⊙

Palace Hotel — The hunting lodge, which looks more like a stage set than a hotel, was commissioned by King Carlos and built by the Italian architect Luigi Manini between 1888 and 1907. It is a pastiche of the Manueline style and recalls the Torre de Belém and the cloisters of the Mosteiro dos Jerónimos in Lisbon. It is flanked by a small tower surmounted by an armillary sphere. The decoration inside is as exuberant as it is outside and the staircase is vast. Its walls are covered with huge *azulejos* panels by Jorge Colaço depicting episodes from Camões' **The Lusiads**, and battle scenes from the history of Portugal.

Convento dos Carmelitas Descalços ⊙ — *Below the hotel.*
The remains of the Barefoot Carmelite Convent built between 1628 and 1630 comprise a chapel, the cloisters and several monks' cells lined with cork to keep out the cold.

THE FOREST

There are several walks through the forest with its sprinkling of hermitages built by the monks in the 17C. The second walk includes an interesting Via Sacra (Way of the Cross). All the itineraries described below start from the car park beside the hotel.

★★① Fonte Fria and Vale dos Fetos
1hr 15min round trip on foot.

Ermida da Nossa Senhora de Assunção — The Hermitage of Our Lady of the Assumption is one of the ten hermitages in the forest to which the monks used to retire.

Fonte Fria — The water of the Cold Fountain rises in a cave and spills out to form a cascade down a flight of 144 stone steps; at the bottom, hydrangeas and magnolias surround the pool into which the water flows and which also mirrors some majestic conifers nearby.
The path, lined with magnificent tree ferns, rhododendrons and hydrangeas, then follows a small stream to a lake beside which stand some thuya trees.

Vale dos Fetos — This beautiful fern alley embellished with pine and very tall sequoias leads to the gate, Porta das Lapas.

Porta de Coimbra — Coimbra Gate was built at the same time as the 17C wall and has rococo decoration. Two marble plaques on the exterior façade display the text of the two papal bulls mentioned above. The gate opens onto an attractive terrace lookout where the view is particularly beautiful at sunset.

Return by way of Avenida do Mosteiro, an avenue of superb cedars.

★★② Via Sacra and Cruz Alta
1hr round trip on foot

Take Avenida do Mosteiro below the convent, then turn left for the Via Sacra.

★**Via Sacra** — The Way of the Cross was built in the baroque style in the late 17C. The chapels along the way contain life-size terracotta figures enacting the different stages of the climb to Calvary.

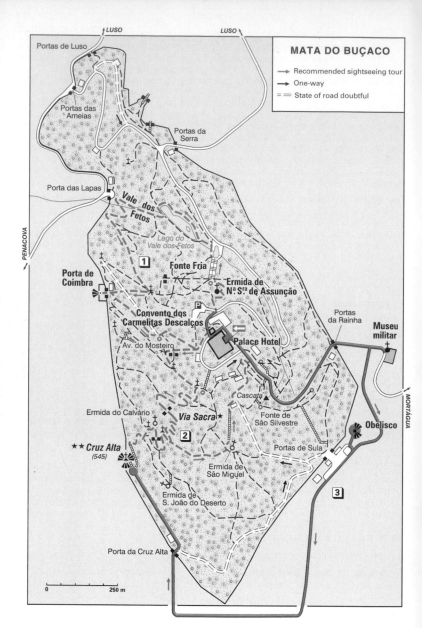

MATA DO BUÇACO

→ Recommended sightseeing tour
→ One-way
= = State of road doubtful

★★**Cruz Alta** (panorama) – Alt 545m/1 788ft. The panorama from the Cross is immense: to the right is the Serra do Caramulo; ahead a large number of white villages scattered over the coastal plain; below, the hotel emerging through forest greenery; in the distance to the left, the built-up mass of Coimbra and on the horizon on the far left, beyond the Mondego valley, the heights of the Serra da Lousã and the Serra da Estrela.

Return by the woodland paths which lead past various hermitages.

③ **The Cruz Alta by car**
6km/4mi

A few hundred yards from the hotel glance at the waterfall (cascata), fed by the **Fonte de São Silvestro** nestling amongst ferns and hydrangeas.

Museo Militar ⊘ – The military museum, which is outside the wall, features the Battle of Buçaco and the campaigns of 1810.

Obelisco – The obelisk, which is topped by a glass star, commemorates the battle of 27 September 1810. There is a wonderful **view**★ of the Serra da Estrela and the Serra do Caramulo from the monument.
The road then climbs through pine trees to the gate which leads to the Cruz Alta.

CALDAS DA RAINHA

Leiria — Population 19 128
Michelin map 940 N2

Caldas da Rainha, a spa with a long established reputation, is a large agricultural centre with a crowded market. It is famous for its **ceramics** of varied design *(See photograph in Introduction-Handicrafts)*.

The Queen's Baths (Caldas da Rainha) — In 1484 **Queen Leonor**, wife of King João II, when travelling to Batalha to take part in memorial rites on the anniversary of the death of her father-in-law Afonso V, caught sight of some peasants bathing in evil smelling steaming pools at the roadside. Intrigued, she asked for an explanation and was told that the water cured rheumatism. Thereupon, she decided to bathe before continuing on her way to Batalha. The queen then resumed her journey but had proceeded less than 6km/4mi when she began to feel the good effects of the sulphuric waters. This convinced her to immediately postpone her religious observances in order to continue the cure. The village where the queen turned round has been known ever since as Tornada (which means "return from a trip").

In 1485 Leonor's generosity impelled her to sell jewels and lace to raise sufficient funds to found a hospital in the town.

Later the queen commanded that a large park be laid out and a church built nearby.

SIGHTS

★**Grande Parque das Termas** — The delight and green freshness of the park lies in its weeping willows, palms, flowers, lawns, statues and stretches of water.

Museu José Malhoa ⊘ — The museum, which is in the park, contains 19 and 20C paintings, sculpture and pottery. Worth noting are the works of José Malhoa (1855-1933) painter of popular scenes whose best known canvases include *Promises (as Promessas)* and the *Last Interrogation of the Marquis of Pombal*. Malhoa's style is characterised by his use of intense light and colours and realistic themes.

Another painter, Columbarno (1857-1929) also known as the Master of Half Light, has left some fine portraits, notably *Boy's Head (Cabeça de Rapaz)*.

Igreja de Nossa Senhora do Pópulo — The church, which was built at the end of the 15C at the command of Queen Leonor, is crowned by an elegant belfry.

Inside, the walls are entirely covered with 17C *azulejos* and the altar frontals with fine 16C Moorish *azulejos* in relief. Above the Manueline style triumphal arch is a beautiful **triptych**★ of the Crucifixion attributed to Cristóvão de Figueiredo (early 16C).

Use the Map of Principal Sights to plan an itinerary.

CAMINHA

Viana do Castelo — Population 1 878
Michelin map 940 or 441 G3

The fortified town of Caminha was formerly part of Portugal's northern frontier defence against Galician aspirations. It occupied a key position at the confluence of the Coura and the Minho and also controlled the Minho estuary, overlooked on the Spanish side by Monte Santa Tecla. Caminha is now a fishing village and craft centre for coppersmiths.

Praça do Conselheiro Silva Torres — The square is still largely medieval in character with ancient buildings grouped round a 16C granite fountain. The 15C **Casa dos Pitas** is Gothic and its emblazoned façade is elegant with curved windows. The town hall, **Paços do Concelho** has a lovely coffered ceiling in the council chamber. The clock tower, **Torre do Relógio**, was once part of the 14C fortifications.

Go through this gate to Rua Ricardo Joaquim de Sousa which leads to the church.

Igreja Matriz ⊘ — The parish church was built in the 15-16C as a granite church fortress. Apart from a few Gothic elements such as the pinnacles, the style is basically Renaissance as is particularly evident in the façade doorways. The south door is framed by carved pilasters supporting a gallery where statues of Saints Peter, Paul, Mark and Luke stand. The pediment contains a Virgin flanked by two angels. The east end of the church is Platersque in style rather than Manueline.

Inside is a magnificent *artesonado* **ceiling**★ of maplewood carved by a Spaniard in the Mudejar style. Each octagonal panel, framed in stylised cabling, bears a rose at its centre. On the right, stands a statue of St Christopher, patron saint of boatmen. The Chapel of the Holy Sacrament, to the right of the chancel, contains a 17C gilded wood tabernacle illustrated with scenes from the Passion by Francisco Fernandes.

CANTANHEDE

Coimbra – Population 7 498
Michelin map 940 or 441 K4

Cantanhede is a large agricultural town and a commercial centre for wine, cereals and wood. The famous white marble known as Ançã stone is quarried from the countryside between Cantanhede and **Ançã** *(10km/6mi to the southeast)*. It is as easy to carve as wood and has always been popular with local sculptors and architects, particularly those of the Coimbra School *(See COIMBRA)*. The white stone turns a lovely golden colour with time, but it has a tendency to crumble and wear away.

Igreja Matriz – The parish church contains several 16C works attributed to Jean de Rouen, in particular, in the second chapel on the right, the altarpiece with a Virgin of Intercession and in the Chapel of the Holy Sacrament to the right of the chancel, two tombs surmounted by statues.

EXCURSIONS

Varziela – *4km/2mi northwest. Take the Mira road and bear left after 2km/1.2mi (signpost).*
The chapel contains an **altarpiece★** of Ançã stone attributed to Jean de Rouen. There is considerable detail in the carving which shows a Virgin of Intercession flanked by two angels and the kneeling figures of dignitaries of the Church and Court.

Praia da Mira – *17km/11mi northwest by the N 234 and N 334.*
The coast here is a vast, endless sandy beach fringed by pinewoods in the stretches where there is no housing development.
Traditional fishing methods like those once used in Nazaré may still be seen on the beach. For want of a real harbour, the large, vividly coloured fishing boats are moored on the beach. Equipped with their nets for a trip out to sea, the fishermen position their boats on small logs and roll them forward by pushing against the hull. Once the boats are in the water, they jump inside and row furiously through the surf. When they return, the boats are brought up the beach on logs with the help of a cable wound in by a tractor. The nets are traditionally trawled in by teams of oxen.

Hauling in a fishing boat

Michelin Route Planning on Internet www.michelin-travel.com.
Michelin, your companion on the road, invites you to visit our Web site and discover
European route planning on the Internet.
Whether you just want to know the distance between two points, or need a detailed itinerary, for a holiday or on business, we provide all the information necessary for accurate travel planning.

CARAMULO

Viseu – Population 1 546
Michelin map 940 or 441 K5

Caramulo is a spa at an altitude of 800m/2 625ft on a wooded hillside in the Serra do Caramulo. Parks and gardens enhance this town on the schist and granite massif which is wooded with pines, oaks and chestnuts and also has crops such as maize, vines and olives. The western slope, which descends gently towards the Aveiro coastal plain, is completely different from the eastern slope where the sharper relief is cut away by tributaries of the Mondego.

★**Museu do Caramulo** ⊘ – The museum, which is also called the Fundacão Abel Lacerda after its founder, comprises two sections.

Ancient and Modern Art Exhibition – The collections contain statues from the 15C Portuguese School including a Virgin and Child, a series of tapestries from Tournai representing the arrival of the Portugueuse in India and a large number of paintings by contemporary artists: Picasso (still life), Fernand Léger, Dufy, Dali, Braque etc.

★**Automobile Exhibition** – Some fifty vehicles, all beautifully maintained in working order, are on display in a modern building. Amongst the oldest are an 1899 Peugeot and a 1902 Darraco; the most prestigious include Hispano-Suizas, Lamborghinis and Ferraris. There are also some bicycles and motorbikes.

EXCURSIONS

★**Pinoucas** – *3km/2mi. Leave Caramulo heading north on the N 230; after 2km/1.5mi bear left on a dirt track which ends at the watchtower 1km/0.5mi further on.*
From the top (alt 1 062m/3 481ft) there is an impressive panorama over the Serra do Caramulo.

Serra do Caramulo – *7.5km/4.5mi. Leave Caramulo heading west on Avenue Abel Lacerda which becomes the N 230-3; 3km/2mi further on you pass on your left the road leading to Cabeço da Neve.*

★★**Caramulinho** – *30min round trip on foot, by a rocky path which has 130 steps cut into its face.* The tip of the Serra do Caramulo (alt 1 075m/3 527ft) makes an excellent **viewpoint** over the Serra do Lapa in the northeast, the Serra da Estrela in the southeast, the Serra da Lousã and Serra do Buçaco to the south, over the coastal plain to the west, and over the Serras da Gralheira and do Montemura to the north.

Return to the intersection with the Cabeço da Neve road, which you then take to the viewpoint.

Cabeço da Neve – Alt 995m/3 264ft. This balcony summit has a plunging **view** to the south and towards the east, over the lower wooded mountain dotted with villages, the Mondego basin and the Serra da Estrela.

*Consult the **index** to find an individual town or sight.*

CARVOEIRO★

Faro
Michelin map 940 U4 – Local map see ALGARVE

Built in a narrow indentation in the cliff, this fishing village has become a pleasant seaside resort that has not yet been spoilt by modern buildings.

Miradouro de Nossa Senhora da Encarnação – At the top of a steep slope, to the east of the beach *(in front of a chapel and a police station)*, this belvedere offers an extensive view over the cliffs of Cabo Carvoeiro.

★★**Algar Seco** – *500m/1/3mi beyond the Miradouro de Nossa Senhora da Encarnação, plus 30min round trip on foot. Leave the car in the car park.*
Below Cabo Carvoeiro, the **marine site** of Algar Seco is reached through a maze (including 134 steps) of reddish rocks sculpted by the sea in the shape of peaks, arches, rounds of Swiss cheese etc. The site gives the impression of a giant heart beating as the gaping entrances to several semi-submerged caves throb under the impact of violent whirlpools from confronting currents. On the right *(sign "A Boneca")*, a short tunnel leads under a conically formed ceiling, into a cavern (converted into a refreshment room in summer) which has two natural "windows" from which there is a view encompassing the western cliffs. On the left, a path leads to a headland from where one can see the entrance to a deep underwater cave.
The **sea caves** ⊘ of Cabo Carvoeiro can be visited by boat during the season.

CASCAIS★

Lisboa – Population 29 882
Michelin map 940 P1

Cascais is both a fishing port of age old tradition and a bustling holiday resort. The town has everything in its favour: a mild climate in which sea air combines with cool air from the Serra de Sintra and a fine sand beach lining a beautiful bay. It is progressively expanding into a smart suburb of Lisbon with its developed centre and pleasant pedestrian streets lined with shops and restaurants.

Men have appreciated this particular site since the earliest times. Prehistoric man from the Palaeolithic Era was followed in turn by Romans, Visigoths and Moors. Cascais gained its independence at the same time as Lisbon and by the middle of the 14C had acquired the status of *Vila*, but at the end of the 16C, in 1580 and again in 1597, it was sacked first by soldiers of the Duke of Alba and later by those of Mary Tudor. The earthquake of 1755 destroyed the town again, just as it was really beginning to recover. The *azulejos* which decorate the **Igreja da Nossa Senhora da Assunção** date from this period. The bent to tourism came in 1870 when the court moved to Cascais for the summer for the first time. With the court came a tradition of elegance and a group of architects. The royal palace or former citadel on the promontory which protects the bay on the southwest is now a residence of the Head of State.

> **Museu-Biblioteca dos Condes de Castro Guimarães** ⊘ – On the coast road, this 19C noble residence, with a central patio, has a collection of 17C Portuguese and Indo-Portuguese furniture and *azulejos*, 18 and 19C Portuguese gold and silver-smith work and pottery, 18C bronzes, carpets and Chinese vases, valuable books (one of which is a 16C *Chronicles of D. Afonso Henriques*) and a strange organ chest dating from 1753. In the park there is a large fountain with *azulejos*.

A selection of hotels in Cascais is listed under Travellers' addresses for Lisbon.

EXCURSIONS

★**From Cascais to Praia do Guincho** – *8km/5mi heading west on the coast road – about 30min.*
On leaving Cascais, pass the former royal palace on the left and then the municipal park on the right.

★**Boca do Inferno** – When the road turns to the right, a house and a café with a few pines standing on the left, mark the site of this **abyss**★ formed by marine erosion. The sea, entering under a rock arch, booms and crashes particularly in bad weather. The road continues as a *corniche* above the sea, offering some fine views of the wild coast. Beyond Cabo Raso (small fort), where the road turns off towards the Serra de Sintra, stretches of sand being pounded by rough seas can be glimpsed between the rocky points.

★**Praia do Guincho** – This immense beach is backed by windswept dunes and a small fort; the imposing headland, Cabo da Roca can be seen on the horizon. This is a popular spot for windsurfing.

> **Monumento a Ibne-Mucane** – *5km/3mi on the N 9 going towards Alcabideche.*
A stele, erected in honour of the Arabian poet Ibne-Mucane, who was born in Alcabideche in the 10C and is believed to be the first poet to sing of windmills praises in Europe, bears the following inscription on the stone: "If you are really a man you need a mill which turns with the clouds and is not dependent on water courses".

CASTELO BRANCO

Castelo Branco – Population 24 287
Michelin map 940 M7

The town was well fortified as it lay strategically close to the Spanish border, but it nevertheless suffered a number of invasions and occupations – events which have left few historic monuments. The maraudings of the Napoleonic troops in 1807 were among the most devastating. The scant ruins of a Templars' stronghold dominate the town. The capital of Beira Baixa is, today, a peaceful flower bedecked city living on its trade in cork, cheese, honey and olive oil; it is particularly known for the fine bed-spreads (*colchas*) embroidered in different colours by young girls, who perpetuate a tradition going back to the 17C, as each prepares her trousseau.

SIGHTS

> **Museu Francisco Tavares Proença Júnior** ⊘ (**M¹**) – Established in the old epis-copal palace, it has an interesting collection: on the ground floor, archaeological and stone relics, coins, earthenware and ancient weapons, pieces of broken flasks and Roman pottery; in the staircase, 16C Flemish tapestries *(Story of Lot)*; upstairs, other 16C Flemish tapestries, paintings of the 16C Portuguese School (a *Santo*

CASTELO BRANCO

João C. Abrunho	16
Liberdade (Alameda da)	18
Rei D. Dinis	28
Sidónio Pais	43
1º de Maio (Avenida)	46

Arco (Rua do)	3
Arressário (Rua do)	4
Bairreiro (Largo do)	6
Bairreiro (Rua do)	7
Cadetes de Toledo (Rua)	8
Camilo Castelo Branco (Rua)	9
Espírito Santo (Largo do)	10
Espírito Santo (Rua do)	12
Ferreiros (Rua dos)	13
Frei Bartolomeu da Costa (R.)	15
Luís de Camões (Praça)	19
Mercado (Rua do)	21
Olarias (Rua das)	22
Pátria (Campo da)	24
Prazeres (Rua dos)	25
Quinta Nova (Rua da)	27
Relógio (Rua do)	30
Santa Maria (Rua de)	31
São João (Largo de)	33
São João de Deus (Rua)	34
São Marcos (Largo de)	36
São Sebastião (Rua)	37
Sé (Largo de)	39
Sé (Rua da)	40
Sonhora da Piedade (Rua)	42
Vaz Preto (Rua de)	45

A Cruzeiro de São João
B Convento da Graça
M¹ Museu Francisco Tavares
Proença Júnior

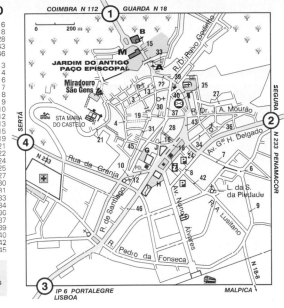

António attributed to Francisco Henriques), documents and antique Portuguese furniture (a beautiful 17C carved cupboard), and embroidered bedcovers from Castelo Branco. On the same floor there is a room devoted to modern art.

★★**Jardim do Antigo Paço Episcopal** ⊘ – The 17C gardens belonged to the Episcopal Palace and now form an unusual ensemble of topiary (clipped box trees and hedges), banks of flowers, ornamental pools, fountains and baroque statues (signs of the Zodiac, Doctors of the Church, the Seasons, the Virtues, etc).
An alley, which runs beside the Crown Lake and ends in two flights of steps, is lined by balustrades peopled with statues: the Apostles and the Evangelists on the right face, the Kings of Portugal on the left – note the irony with which the sculptor has depicted the kings who suffered Spanish domination by considerably reducing their size. The atmosphere is quite extraordinary in these magical gardens, where the overall sensation is one of timelessness.
Pass beneath the staircase which spans Rua Frei Bartolomeu da Costa.

Cruzeiro de São João (**A**) – The Manueline style (16C) twisted column is surmounted by a carved cross placed over a crown of seaweed.
Leave the car in front of the Igreja de Santa Maria do Castelo and take, on the left of the ruins of the Templars' Castle, the stairway to the Miradouro de São Gens.

Miradouro de São Gens – This shady esplanade bright with flowers affords an extensive view of the town and the surrounding landscape speckled with olive trees.

Gardens, Antigo Paço Episcopal

Convento da Graça e Museu de Arte Sacra da Misericórdia ⊘ (**B**) – Opposite the palace is the Convento da Graça, which has retained a Manueline door from its primitive early-16C construction. Inside, the home of the Santa Casa da Misericórdia, a small sacred art museum contains the statues of Queen Saint Isabel and St John of God with a pauper, a Virgin and Child, a 16C St Matthew and two marble statues of Christ on the cross.

Continue down and enter the medieval town.

Cidade Medieval – The medieval town, with its traditional stone-paved narrow streets and clothes and cages hanging from the windows, has preserved a few interesting buildings such as the former Paços do Conselho (Town Hall) on the Praça Velha, dating from the 1600s but significantly remodelled since, the 17C Arco do Bispo on the attractive Praça Camões, as well as several other delightful palaces.

EXCURSIONS

Penamacor – *50km/31mi northeast on the N 233.* Situated at an altitude of 600m/1 968ft, the village, which dates from Roman times, is crowned by a castle, the construction of which was ordered by Dom Sancho 1 in 1209; parts of the wall and the keep can still be seen today. The panoramic view over the plain and surrounding hills is impressive, and the walk through the old part of Penamacor particularly pleasant.

The **Igreja da Misericórdia** ⊘ has a fine Manueline door and a high gilded wood altar. The **Convento de Santo António** ⊘, founded in the 16C, contains a chapel with a roof and pulpit in lavish *talha dourada* style.

★★**Monsanto** – *22.5km/14mi from Penamacor. Take the N 332 as far as Medelim, and then the N 239. See MONSANTO.*

Idanha-a-Velha – *Return to Medelim and rejoin the N 332. 12km/8mi.*
This village of 90 inhabitants was a prosperous Roman settlement with its proximity to the road linking Mérida and Astorga. At first sight it seems more like an open-air museum with excavations everywhere, giving the visitor the sensation of having returned to the past. By following the signposted archaeological path you will pass by the 13C Torre dos Templários, a Templars' tower built on top of a Roman temple, the cathedral (Sé), rebuilt five times on a site with paleo-Christian origins, still comprising vestiges from all of its periods of construction, a Roman bridge, rebuilt during the Middle Ages, and many other historical remains.

CASTELO DE VIDE★

Portalegre – Population 2 558
Michelin map 940 N7 – Local map see Serra de SÃO MAMEDE

Castelo de Vide lies bunched at the foot of its castle, which stands perched on an elongated foothill of the Serra de São Mamede. It owes its attraction to old whitewashed houses stepped high up the hillside along winding alleys brilliant with flowers. The town is also a spa; its waters are beneficial for diabetes, hypertension and hepatitis.

SIGHTS

Praça de Dom Pedro V – On this square the Igreja de Santa Maria stands opposite two 17C buildings, namely the Baroque Palácio da Torre and the Santo Amaro Hospital. Also overlooking the square are a fine 18C mansion and the late 17C town hall.
Behind the Igreja de Santa Maria, take a street leading to the Fonte da Vila and the Judiaria.

★**Judiaria (Jewish Quarter)** – Arriving in a delightful little square, note the **Fonte da Vila**, a fine Renaissance fountain made of granite. Continue through the steep alleyways below the castle; the houses are whitewashed and have Gothic doorways.
At the crossroads between a street that climbs to the castle and another that runs at right angles to it, is the **medieval synagogue** which evokes the past history of the quarter.

Castelo ⊘ – *Go through the outer walls.* A stairway at the foot of a round 12C tower leads to the **keep**. From the room with a Gothic cupola and a cistern, there is a picturesque **view★** of the town.

EXCURSION

Monte da Penha – *5km/3mi south. 2km/1.2mi south of Castelo de Vide a narrow surfaced road branches off the N 246-1.*
The road climbs round rocks and pines to the Capela de Nossa Senhora da Penha (700m/2 296ft). From the front of the chapel there is a lovely **view★** of Castelo de Vide.

CASTRO MARIM

Faro – Population 4 549
Michelin map 940 U7

Castro Marim abuts on a height overlooking the ochre coloured and marshy Lower Guadiana Plain near its outflow into the Gulf of Cádiz. Facing the Portuguese town across the estuary – and the border – is the Spanish town of Ayamonte.

Castro Marim, which was already in existence in Roman times, became, in 1321, on the dissolution of the Order of Templars in Portugal, the seat of the Knights of Christ until this was transferred to Tomar in 1334.

The ruins of Castro Marim's fortified castle, which was built of red sandstone and demolished by the earthquake of 1755, stand to the north of the village, while the remains crowning a hill to the south are of the 17C Forte de São Sebastião.

> **Castelo** ⊘ – *Leave the car at the foot of the pathway marked "castelo" and walk up to the castle. The entrance is on the left.*
> Within the partly restored walls is a castle dating back to the 12C. The parapet walk affords a view over the small city with the 17C Forte de São Sebastião in the foreground, the salt marshes, the Guadiana, the bridge between Portugal and Spain, and the Spanish town of Ayamonte to the east and Vila Real de Santo António and the coast to the south.

CASTRO VERDE

Beja – Population 2 794
Michelin map 940 S5

This agricultural town owes its name to a prehistoric stronghold. On the third Sunday in October it holds a well-known agricultural and crafts fair which dates back to the 17C.

> **Igreja de Nossa Senhora da Conceição** ⊘ – The walls of this basilica are covered entirely with magnificent *azulejos*. In the nave, the tiles of the upper part represent scenes from the Battle of Ourique (a town 14km/8.5mi away) where in 1139, Afonso Henriques vanquished the Moors and was proclaimed King of Portugal *(see GUIMARÃES)*.

Alto Vale do Rio CÁVADO★

Upper Cávado Valley – Braga and Vila Real
Michelin map 940 or 441 I 4,5 G 5,6,7

The course of the Cávado river above Braga is steeply enclosed between the Serra do Gerês and the Serras de Cabreira and do Barroso. In this rocky upper valley, as in its tributary, the Rabagão, a series of dams control reservoir lakes of a deep blue colour which are surrounded by wooded mountain slopes crested by bare peaks – altogether a highly picturesque landscape.

Development – The Cávado, which is 118km/73mi long, rises to an altitude of 1 500m/4 859ft in the Serra do Larouco not far from the Spanish frontier; after crossing the 15km/11mi of the Montalegre Plateau, the river course drops sharply, losing 400m in 5km/1 300ft in 3miles as it follows a series of rock faults running northeast-southwest. The hydro-electric development of this upper valley, facilitated by the impermeable quality of the granite rocks through which the river had cut its course, began in 1946. Dams exist at Alto Cávado, Paradela, Salamonde and Caniçada on the Cávado, at Alto Rabagão and Venda Nova on the Rabagão and at Vilarinho des Funas on the Homen. These installations generate about 18% of the total hydro-electric power produced in Portugal.

FROM BRAGA TO CHAVES

235km/141mi – about half a day (not including visit to Braga) – local map see Parque Nacional da PENEDA-GERÊS.

★**Braga** – *See BRAGA.*

Leave Braga by ① *in the direction of Chaves.*

> Immediately upon leaving Braga, the Cávado valley on the left becomes deep and wild; the road climbs along the south slopes which are covered with pine trees and eucalyptus. 8km/5mi further along on the left-hand side of the road, a belevedere affords a view of the last green stretch of the valley. Beyond and to the right, a hillock crowned with rocks looks like a medieval fortress, and 3km/2mi further on, the castle of Póvoa de Lanhoso with its keeps rising up behind Pinheiro, can be seen. After this village, the Cávado Valley is hidden, while on the right the parallel valley of the Rio Ave appears, sparkling and scattered with

Alto Vale do Cávado

hamlets. Then the road climbs up through a landscape of bare and rocky crests often topped with rocks resembling ruins; on the slopes there are beautiful spherical rocks, also *espigueiros* and a few cattle.

A little before Cerdeirinhas, the N 103 turns and descends overlooking the Cávado River which it follows, running along the edge of the Parque Nacional da Peneda-Gerês.

The road then begins to wind and turn, affording precipitous **views★** of two reservoirs: the 15km/9mi long **represa de Caniçada★** and the Salamonde. Both lie below pine scattered slopes, dominated by the bare summits of the Serra do Gerês.

Bear left off the N 103 on the Paradela road over the crest of the Vanda Nova dam, at the next crossroads bear right.

As the corniche-style road rises rapidly, the **views★★** of the Serra do Gerês become even more beautiful. A little before Paradela, on the left, there is a village built on a rocky projection at the foot of a shale hillock, which has been strangely slashed and hollowed out at the back by a gigantic quarry.

The road crosses Paradela and arrives at the dam of the same name.

At Paradela you enter the eastern part of the **Parque Nacional da Peneda-Gerês National Park** known as the Barroso region where local traditions have been kept very much alive. Villagers still share a communal oven as well as an ox that they use for work in the fields.

★**Represa da Paradela** – This reservoir lake at an altitude of 112m/367ft above Cávado River has a lovely mountain **setting★**.

Pitões das Júnias, a village 15km/9mi north of Paradela, has some Romanesque ruins belonging to a Benedictine monastery which dates back to the Visigothic period in the 9C. The lichen-covered granite stone around the doorway is decorated with a frieze of stylised plant motifs. Several arches indicate where the cloisters once stood.

Return to the N 103.

The road runs alongside the **Venda Nova reservoir**.

Vila da Ponte – A village perched upon a rock spur.

After Pisões, a path to the right leads to the Alto Rabagão dam.

★**Barragem do Alto Rabagão** – The dam stands as a massive concrete wall. Go to the crest of the dam at the end of the road, where there is a good **view** over the reservoir-lake.

Return to the N 103. The road skirts the north edge of the lake before turning left to Montalegre.

Montalegre – Montalegre was built in a beautiful **setting**★ at an altitude of 966m/3 170ft. Old red roofed houses encircle the walls of the 14C castle (in ruins), the keep of which commands the wild and mountainous plateau. Looking out one can see to the northeast the Serra do Larouco where the Cávado rises.

★**Serra do Barroso** – Continuing along the N 311, pass through **Carvalhelhos**, famous for its waters *(see below)*. On the next summit, with access via a dirt road, observe the **Castro de Carvalhelhos**, a settlement dating from the Iron Age, with its foundations, doors and walls still clearly visible. A road leads from Carvalhelhos to **Alturas do Barroso**, a traditional village in these harsh, isolated mountains. From there, head to **Vilarinho Seco**, the most traditional mountain village in this area. It has no modern buildings, and the rural two-storey dwellings (with the animals and straw below) of loose, dark stone, with wooden veranda and staircase and thatch roof, appear not to have changed in centuries. Hens and goats run loose below the granite granaries, with the most frequent traffic on the street, the pairs of the impressive breed of Barroso oxen. To combat the harshness of the region, men would work together, combining their flocks and pastures, and using collective ovens, mills etc. The descent towards the N 311 passes through a landscape of haphazard round rocks which have been smoothed by erosion.

The N 308, on the plateau and lined with pine and heather, returns to the N 103. Then the road crosses arid rock-strewn moors covered with heather and cut by streams. The plateau suddenly disappears as the **view**★★ extends dramatically to take in a vast green and cultivated basin at the far end of which can be seen the low lying old villages of **Sapiãos** and **Boticas**. The road climbs through magnificent pine forests before joining the lovely agricultural Tâmega Valley to reach Chaves.

Chaves – *See below.*

CHAVES

Vila Real – Population 13 027
Michelin map 940 or 441 G7

Trás-os-Montes is an arid province, but Chaves is well favoured as it was built on the banks of the Tâmega, in the centre of a sunken basin, which is particularly fertile.

The small town of Aquae Flaviae, known to the Romans for its thermal springs, was transformed into an important stopping point on the Astorga-Braga road when Trajan built a bridge over the Tâmega, within its bounds. In 1160, after being recaptured from the Moors, Chaves was fortified to ensure its command of the valley facing the Spanish fortress of Verín. In the 17C ramparts were added, after the style of the French military architect Vauban. Even now the old castle huddled close by picturesque white houses with corbelled wooden verandas give the town considerable style.

It is now a quiet spa town *(see box)*, equally known for its excellent smoked ham *(presunto)*.

SIGHTS

Ponte Romana – One can get a general view of the bridge from the attractive gardens which run down to the river. With the passing of the years it has lost its stone parapets and even some arches, but it, nevertheless, adds considerably to the charm of the setting. The milestones at the southern end still bear legible Roman inscriptions.

Praça de Camões – Overlooking this graceful square right in the heart of old Chaves are several interesting monuments. The statue of Dom Afonso, first Duke of Bragança, stands in the middle.

★**Igreja da Misericórdia** – The façade of this small 17C baroque church is pleasantly embellished with verandas and twisted columns. The inside walls are covered with *azulejos* showing scenes from the Life of Christ and the Bible, attributed to Oliveira Bernardes. There is a large gilded wooden altarpiece; the ceiling is decorated with 18C paintings, one of which, in the centre, is a Visitation.

Museu da Região Flaviense ⊘ – This museum, which is housed in a fine 17C building, contains archaeological and ethnological collections. In a room on the ground floor are prehistoric stone relics – the main piece in the display is a megalithic **figure in human form** (about 2000 BC) – and Roman remains including sculptures and milliary columns. Upstairs there are ancient coins and a banknote plate, a magic lantern, and radio receivers dating from the early wireless days.

Paços do Concelho – The noble classical façade of the town hall looks onto the square.

Igreja Matriz – While parts of the parish church are Romanesque, it was rebuilt during the Renaissance as the doorway with carved pilasters testifies. A niche in the wall of the polygonal apse contains a granite statue of Saint Mary Major, said to be one of the oldest statues in Portugal. The chancel is topped by a ribbed vault.

Standing on the other side of the church, in another square, is a Manueline style **pillory**.

Torre de Menagem – The keep is all that remains of the castle; a massive square tower with battlements at the corners, still surrounded by its quadrangular outer wall. Built by King Dinis in the 14C, it was the residence of the first Duke of Bragança, illegitimate son of Dom João I.

Museu Militar ⊙ – This military museum covers four floors of the keep; the first two have ancient weapons and armour, the third evokes the First World War (machine guns, uniforms) and the fourth, colonial wars (Portuguese and native weapons). From the platform summit (121 steps) there is a panoramic view over the town, the ramparts and the cultivated valley of Chaves.

The waters and spas

Chaves is situated in an area rich in thermal springs which originate from the North/South fault line in the Alto Tâmega region. All these springs have their own curative virtues and are part of a general network known as the "Alto Tâmega thermal system".

Caldas de Chaves ⊙ – These hot water springs (73°C – 163°F) were already popular with the Romans, who gave the town the name of Aquae Flaviae. The waters are alkaline, warm and rich in sodium bicarbonate, and are recommended for digestive disorders, rheumatism and hyper-tension. The modern spa buildings are situated in a thermal park by the river.

Termas de Vidago ⊙ – *11km/7mi from Chaves.* This estate, in an attractive leafy park, has been totally restored and is now one of the best-equipped spas in the area. At its entrance, the majestic rose-coloured façade of the Art Deco-style Palace-Hotel transports the visitor back to the beginning of the century. This elegant ambience continues inside, with the exquisite decoration of the same period in keeping with the peacefulness of the setting. The bicarbonated water from Vidago is sold all over the country. The Vidago spa receives visitors with disorders of the digestive, respiratory and nervous systems.

Termas de Pedras Salgadas ⊙ – *31km/19mi from Chaves.* This magnificent 40-hectare/100-acre park, which is home to the spa buildings, is well worth a visit in its own right. The pervading atmosphere in the estate, which was created in 1904, and where the marks of time have been progressively repaired, is nonetheless one of abandon and nostalgia. The buildings and decoration include beautiful fountains, bathhouses and a casino, all dating from the beginning of the century. The sodium bicarbonated waters at Pedras Salgadas are recommended in the treatment of bone and digestive system disorders.

Caldas Santas de Carvalhelhos ⊙ – *30km/19mi from Chaves.* This spa resort is in a pleasant park criss-crossed by small streams and surrounded by the Barroso mountains. It is situated next to the bottling plant for this famous sparkling water, known for the treatment of digestive system and circulatory problems.

COIMBRA★★

Coimbra — Population 79 799
Michelin map 940 or 441 L4

Overlooked by the tall tower of its old university, Coimbra stands on a hillside at the foot of which flows the Mondego. Many poets, inspired by the romantic **setting★**, have immortalised the charm of the city, the first capital of Portugal, and have helped to make it a centre of fine arts and letters.

The best views of Coimbra are from Santa Clara bridge or from the Vale do Inferno viewpoint *(see below).* Although the town has spread substantially over recent decades, and has been surrounded by modern districts, the centre is still distinctly divided into the upper town (A Cidade Alta), which is traditionally the university and episcopal quarter, and the lower town (A Cidade Baixa) or shopping area.

Today Coimbra is an active industrial and commercial centre with the production of textiles (hosiery and woollen goods), foodstuffs, tanneries, potteries, photographic equipment and a truck assembly line.

There are a great many fine leather goods and clothes shops selling local products in the picturesque pedestrian streets in the centre, around **Praça do Comércio (Z)**.

From Mount Helicon to the banks of the Mondego: the University – "The first king (King Dinis) honoured the noble art of Minerva at Coimbra, calling on the Muses to leave Mont Helicon to come and play in the smiling meadows of the Mondego" – thus Camões describes the founding of Coimbra University in *The Lusiads.* In fact, it was in Lisbon that King Dinis founded the university in 1290. It was transferred to Coimbra in 1308, but was only permanently established there in 1537 when King João III installed it in his own palace. Teachers from the universities of Oxford, Paris, Salamanca and Italy were drawn to the new university, making the town one of the most important humanist centres of the period. Competition soon followed from Jesuit colleges and the university had to wait until the Company of Jesus was expelled by Pombal in 1759 before recovering its full brilliance.

The Coimbra School of Sculpture – In the early 16C several French sculptors formed a group of artists under the protection of the patron, Cardinal Georges d'Amboise, the promoter in Normandy of what was known as the "methods and style of Italy", came to work in Coimbra. Nicolas Chanterene, Jean de Rouen, Jacques Buxe and Philippe Houdart joined with the Portuguese João and Diogo de Castilho, in about 1530, to create a school of sculpture in the town. Their art was learned and sophisticated, inspired by Italian decorative forms: doorways, pulpits, altarpieces and the low reliefs surrounding altars were delicately carved out of the fine Ança stone. This new style of decoration gradually spread throughout Portugal.

Student life – The city, peaceful throughout the summer, reawakens with a start at the beginning of the academic year and the return of the 20 000 students.

Some of them, though the custom is dying out, retain traditions that go back 400 years. They drape themselves in voluminous black capes, which they fringe with cuts on the hem according to the number of times they have been disappointed in love, and adorn their briefcases with different coloured ribbons to denote their faculty. Romantics by choice, they play guitars and sing *fados* distinguishable from those of their rivals in Lisbon by the intellectual or sentimental nature of the themes. The students band themselves into groups of "republics" numbering between twelve and twenty, usually from the same region, and live communally, renting vast apartments and managing the group budget in turn.

General view of Coimbra

★OLD TOWN AND UNIVERSITY *3hr*

Park the car beside the Mondego and follow on foot the itinerary shown on the plan of the town centre.

The old town lies on the Alcáçova hill, reached by a tangle of narrow and picturesque alleys cut here and there by steps with expressive names like Escadas de Quebra-Costas: Broken Ribs Steps.

Porta de Almedina (Z A) – The gateway with an Arab name (*medina* means city in Arabic) is one of the last remaining sections of the medieval wall. It is surmounted by a tower and adorned with a statue of the Virgin and Child which stands between two coats of arms.

Paço de Sub-Ripas (ZY B) – This town house was built in the Manueline style early in the 16C. The street runs beneath a wing of the **Casa do Arco (Y C)**.

Torre de Anto (Y) – This tower, which is part of the medieval city wall, is a centre for the regional handicrafts of Coimbra.

★★Sé Velha ⊙ **(Z)** – The old cathedral was commissioned by King Afonso Henriques when Coimbra was the capital of Portugal. At that time it stood on the border between the Christian and the Muslim worlds, which explains its fortress-like appearance complete with pyramidal merlons. The cathedral, Portugal's earliest, was built between 1140 and 1175 by two French master craftsmen, Bernard and Robert, hence the similarities with French Romanesque churches modelled on that of Cluny and others in the Auvergne.

TRAVELLERS' ADDRESSES

Where to stay

Astória – Av. Emídio Navarro 21, 3000 Coimbra – ☎ (039) 220 55 – fax 220 57 – 64 rooms – 12 000/15 000$ (CC) – restaurant – air conditioning.
Frequented in former times by artists, this centrally-located hotel is housed in an elegant, turn-of-the-century Parisian-style building and has retained much of its charm.

Quinta das Lágrimas – Santa Clara, 3000 Coimbra – ☎ (039) 44 16 15 – fax (039) 44 16 95 – 35 rooms, 4 suites – 18 000/21 000$ (CC) – parking – restaurant – air conditioning.
This famous quinta (see description below) has been converted into a charming luxury hotel. It is situated in lush, green surroundings on the other bank of the Mondego, close to the city's historic centre.

Eating out

D. Luís – In the D. Luís hotel – Santa Clara – ☎ (039) 44 25 10 – 2 750$ (CC). Portuguese and international cuisine in modern surroundings. Beautiful views of Coimbra.

Real das Canas – Vila Mendes 7 – ☎ (039) 81 48 77 – 2 900$ (CC), closed Wednesdays.
Reasonably-priced restaurant serving typical Portuguese dishes. Particularly enjoyable in the evening with its beautiful view of the town and river.

Dom Pedro – Av. Emídio Navarro – ☎ (039) 291 08 – fax (039) 39 246 11 – 4 250$ (CC).
This pleasant restaurant, decorated with azulejos, is centrally located close to the river, and serves traditional cuisine.

Coimbra nightlife

The town, very quiet in the summer, comes to life during the academic year. The students start the evening by meeting at the outdoor cafés in the Praça da República. They then move on to one of the bars around the cathedral **(Aqui há Rato, Piano Negro, Bigorna Bar)**, some of which have live music, or to the nightclubs, **Via Latina** (with its outdoor terrace), **Scotch Club** (which stays open the latest) or **Urbanidades**. Bars and clubs on the other side of the river are currently in fashion, such as the nightclub/bar **1000 olhos**, just across the bridge, the **Galeria de Santa Clara** (in front of one of the side gates of Portugal dos Pequeninos), a bar and art-gallery with a pleasant garden, and, further along, the **Bar de São Francisco**.

COIMBRA

Comércio (Praça do) .... **Z**	Ameias (Largo das) .... **Z** 3	Fernandes Tomás (Rua de)...... **Z** 25
Fornao de Magalhães (Avenida) **Y**	Antero de Quental (Rua).......... **Y** 4	Guilherme Moreira (Rua).......... **Z** 31
Ferreira Borges (Rua).............. **Z** 27	Borges Carmeiro (Rua de) .... **Z** 10	Portagem (Largo do) .... **Z** 36
Sofia (Rua da)........................ **Y**	Dr João Jacinto (Rua de)............................. **Y** 18	Quebra-Costas (Escadas de)........................ **Z** 37
Visconde da Luz (Rua)........... **Y** 43	Dr José Falcão (Rua)............... **Z** 19	Sobre-Ripas (Rua de) .... **Z** 42
		8 de Maio (Praça).................... **Y** 45

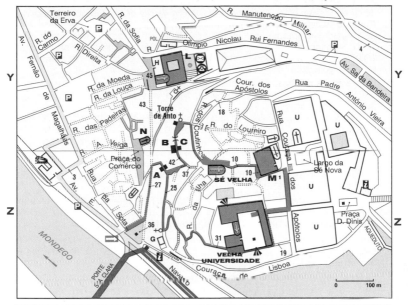

A Porta de Almedina
B Paço de Sub-Ripas
C Casa do Arco

L Mosteiro de Santa Cruz
M¹ Museu Nacional Machado de Castro
N Igreja de São Tiago

Exterior – The main façade is plain in contrast to the doorway added to the north face in about 1530. This door, which is attributed to Jean de Rouen and is, unfortunately, badly damaged, was one of the earliest examples of Renaissance influence in Portugal. On the **east side**, the tower, disfigured by the addition of a baroque lantern turret, has a beautiful, well integrated arcaded gallery where the design of the capitals shows Oriental influence.

Interior – A wide gallery above the aisles opens onto the nave by means of a graceful triforium with Byzantine capitals, which, like the lantern over the transept crossing, show Oriental influence.

The Flamboyant Gothic **altarpiece★** in gilded wood at the high altar, is by the Flemish masters Olivier de Gand (Ghent) and Jean d'Ypres. At the base, the four Evangelists support the Nativity and the Resurrection; above, surrounded by four saints, an attractive group celebrates the Assumption of the Virgin, who has been carved with a most graceful face. The top of the altarpiece is crowned with a calvary resting on a fine canopy.

In the **Capela do Sacramento★**, the chapel to the right of the chancel, there is a good Renaissance composition by Tomé Velho, one of Jean de Rouen's disciples. Below a figure of Christ in Benediction surrounded by ten Apostles, the four Evangelists face the Virgin and Child and St Joseph across the tabernacle. In front of the chapel a baptismal font in the Manueline and Renaissance styles was carved by Jean de Rouen in 1520.

To the left of the chancel, in the Chapel to St Peter adorned with *azulejos* in the Mudejar style, is a Renaissance altarpiece (in poor condition) by Jean de Rouen, representing the life of the saint.

Cloisters – *Access through the first door in the south aisle.*

The late-13C cloisters are an example of transitional Gothic architecture; they were restored in the 18C. Blind arcades are surmounted by round bays filled with a variety of tracery. In the chapter house, on the south side, lies the tomb of Dom Sesnando, first Christian governor of Coimbra, who died in 1091.

★★ **Museu Nacional Machado de Castro** ⊘ (**Z M¹**) – *As the museum is currently being renovated, the description that follows is general and only the major works are mentioned.*

The museum is in the old episcopal palace which was modified in the 16C, and is named after the sculptor Machado de Castro who was born in Coimbra in 1731. The Renaissance porch opens onto a patio-courtyard. On the west side there is a loggia built by Filippo Terzi which has a charming view over the top of the old cathedral and the lower town, as far as Mondego.

Sculpture – The museum has a particularly rich sculpture section. Near the entrance hall are several arches and columns that belonged to some 12C Romanesque cloisters. Galleries in the left wing contain medieval sculptures including a little equestrian statue of a **medieval knight★**, and a Virgin Great with Child (Nossa Senhora de Ó) by Master Pero. These are followed by works of the Coimbra School dating from the Renaissance. Among them are a Virgin Reading by Chanterene, a work by Houdart, an Entombment of eight personages by Jean de Rouen, and a Virgin of the Annunciation by the Master of Túmulos Reais. A number of 17C statues (*Pietà* in polychrome wood by the monk Cipriano de Cruz) and 18C statues, complete the collection.

Objets d'art and paintings – The first floor, with its handsome wood ceilings, including the Mudejar ceiling in the Arab Salon, has a very fine collection of Portuguese porcelain and pottery.

The section on religious, Flemish and Portuguese painting of the 15 to 17C includes altarpiece panels of Santa Clara by Isembrand, a 16C *Assumption* by the Master Vicente Gil, and *Ascension* and a *Nativity* by the 16C Masters Vicente Gil and Manuel Vicente, as well as three paintings by Josefa de Obidos.

The gold and silverware section contains some outstanding works such as the **Mendes Gueda chalice** (1152) and the **reliquary-statue of the Virgin and Child**, part of Queen Saint Isabel's treasure.

Cryptoporticus – This is in the basement, and, at first view, consists of an impressive row of wide doors. It formed the base of the ancient forum of the Roman town of Aeminium which stood on the site Coimbra occupies today.

★★**Universidade Velha** ⊙ (**Z**) – The old university is housed in buildings that once belonged to the royal palace and were restored and modified to become the Paço dos Estudos in 1540.

Porta Férrea (**Z**) – The main door opening on to the university courtyard is 17C.

Pátio – The courtyard is dominated by an 18C tower. To the left, the courtyard extends to a terrace which provides a fine panorama of the Mondego and the plain beyond. Opposite are the library and chapel and, on the right, the graceful Paços da Universidade.

COIMBRA

Antero de Quental (Rua)......... **V** 4
António Augusto Gonçalves (Rua) **X** 6
Augusta (Rua)....................... **V** 7
Aveiro (Rua de) .... **V** 9
Combatentes
  da Grande Guerra (Rua) .... **X** 12
Dom Afonso Henriques
  (Avenida)......................... **V** 13

Dr Augusto Rocha
  (Rua) .... **V** 15
Dr B. de Albuquerque
  (Rua) .... **V** 16
Dr Júlio Henriques
  (Alameda) .... **X** 21
Dr L. de Almeida Azevedo
  (Rua) .... **V** 22
Dr Marnoco e Sousa
  (Avenida)............................ **X** 24

Figueira da Foz (Rua).............. **V** 28
Guerra Junqueiro (Rua)........... **V** 30
Jardim (Arcos do).................... **X** 33
João das Regras
  (Avenida) .... **X** 34
República (Praça da)............... **V** 39
Santa Teresa (Rua de) .... **X** 40

R   Portugal dos Pequeninos

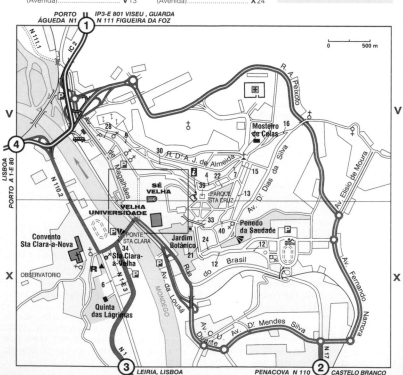

Biblioteca, Universidade Velha

Paços da Universidade – This Manueline building was endowed with a colonnaded gallery called the Via Latina in the late 18C. The central body of the building is surmounted by a triangular pediment. *(Ticket office in this section of the palace.)* A staircase leads to the first floor and the loggia, formerly for women only, which gives on to the **Sala dos Capelos** (Ceremonial Hall) where formal events such as the inauguration of rectors, the defence of theses and the conferring of degrees take place. The name derives from the cap *(capelo)* given to students on graduating. The vast hall, once the palace assembly-room, has a fine 17C painted ceiling and is adorned with a series of portraits of the kings of Portugal. Beside it is the private examination room which was remodelled in 1701. It has a painted ceiling and is hung with portraits of the former rectors.

An exterior balcony provides a beautiful **view★** of the city, the old cathedral and the more recent districts near the Mondego.

★ **Capela** – This Manueline chapel, with an elegant door, is by Marcos Pires. It is decorated with 17C *azulejos* and a painted ceiling and also possesses a fine 18C **organ loft★★**. A small **Museum of Sacred Art** adjoins the chapel.

★★ **Biblioteca** – The library was built during the reign of João V in 1724 and consists of three large rooms, where precious wood furnishings are highlighted by sumptuous baroque decorations of gilded wood. Gilt Chinese style patterns have been painted on green, red or gold lacquer work depending on the room. The ceilings painted in false perspective are by Lisbon artists influenced by Italian art. Ladders have been fitted into the shelving itself for easy access. The 30 000 books and 5 000 manuscripts are classified according to subject matter.

On leaving the university, take Rua Guilherme Moreira to the Almedina gate.

ADDITIONAL SIGHTS

★ **Mosteiro de Santa Cruz** ⊙ **(Y L)** – This monastery, which was built in the 16C on the ruins of a former monastery founded by Afonso Henriques in the 12C, is preceded by a Renaissance porch by Nicolas Chanterene and Diogo de Castilha (1520). This work has unfortunately weathered badly and, in addition, was disfigured in the 18C.

★ **Igreja** – The church's Manueline ceiling is supported by twisted columns and brackets (note the keystones around which the vaulting radiates). The walls are adorned with *azulejos* depicting the life of St Augustine.

The Renaissance **pulpit★** by Nicolas Chanterene is a sculptural masterpiece. Two bays on either side of the high altar contain the tombs of the first two kings of Portugal, Afonso Henriques and Sancho I. They are surrounded by a Late Gothic-Early Renaissance decoration, rich with flowers, figurines and medallions.

A door at the back of the chancel leads to the **Sacristia** (Sacristy) in which hang four early 16C Portuguese paintings. The visit continues with the **Sala do Capitulo** (Chapter House) which has a fine Manueline ceiling and 17C *azulejos*.

★**Claustro do Silêncio** – These Cloisters of Silence were designed by Marcos Pires in 1524 and constitute a most pure and uncluttered model of the Manueline style of architecture. The galleries are decorated with *azulejos* of parables from the Gospel. There low reliefs illustrate scenes of the Passion after Dürer engravings.

Coro Alto – *Access through the sacristy.* In the gallery at the entrance to the church are beautiful 16C wooden **stalls**★ carved and gilded by Flemish artists and the Frenchman, François Lorete. Their crowning head-pieces include armillary spheres, Crosses of the Knights of Christ and, in greatest number, castles and galleons recalling the voyages of Vasco da Gama.

Igreja de São Tiago (Y N) – This small Romanesque church gives onto the vast **Praça do Comércio**, the centre of the lower town's commercial quarter. Interesting capitals adorn its doorways.

Jardim Botânico ⊘ **(X)** – These terraced botanical gardens, which were laid out in the 18C in accordance with reforms introduced by Pombal, have a wide variety of rare trees including many tropical species.

Penedo da Saudade (X) – This wooded park and garden, a short distance from the Jardim Botânico, makes a pleasant promenade with good views of the Mondego valley.

Mosteiro de Celas ⊘ **(V)** – This is an old 12C Cistercian monastery that was rebuilt in the 16C.

The church has star vaulting. The sacristy to the right of the chancel contains a 16C **altarpiece**★ by Jean de Rouen showing St John the Evangelist and St Martin. The 13C cloisters, which are Romanesque in style with Gothic elements, have historiated capitals.

SIGHTS ON THE SOUTH BANK OF THE MONDEGO

Convento de Santa Clara-a-Velha ⊘ **(X)** – The Mondego sands have gradually reduced to ruins the beautiful Gothic church in which the body of Inês de Castro lay until it was transferred to Alcobaça *(see Alcobaça)*.

Convento de Santa Clara-a-Nova ⊘ **(X)** – The baroque church of the vast convent contains, in the chancel, the 17C silver tomb of Queen St Isabel, whose statue in wood by Teixeira Lopes is also in the church.

At the end of the lower chancel *(Coro Baixo)*, behind the wrought-iron screen, is the queen's original **tomb**★ (14C) of painted Ança stone made during her lifetime. The reclining figure dressed in the habit of the Poor Clares has its eyes wide open. The frieze encircling the tomb shows on one side the Poor Clares and their bishop, the other, Christ and the Apostles; at the foot are St Clare and two effigies of crowned saints; at the head is the Crucifixion.

Portugal dos Pequeninos ⊘ **(X R)** – This is an attraction for children where scale models of Portuguese monuments and traditional architecture including those of former overseas colonies (Brazil, Angola, Mozambique, Goa, Macao, etc.) may be seen. One of the houses contains a children's museum, the **Museu da Criança**.

Portugal dos Pequeninos

B. Brillion/MICHELIN

Quinta das Lágrimas ⊘ **(X)** – The name of this small romantic wooded park, the Villa of Tears, recalls the legend described in verse by Camoens of Inês, of Castro's murder here on 7 January 1355 by King Afonso's Chief Justice and two of his henchmen.

Miradouro do Vale do Inferno – *4km/2mi. Leave by* ③ *and take a narrow road on the right towards the Vale do Inferno (steep climb); at a fork bear right.* The belvedere provides a good **view**★ of Coimbra.

EXCURSIONS

Round tour of 87km/54mi – *About 1/2 day. Leave Coimbra by* ②, *the N 17 and after 27km/17mi bear left towards Penacova. The road affords beautiful views directly down into the Mondego Valley and of Penacova on its perched site. Cross the Mondego opposite Penacova and take the N 235.*

Luso – The radioactive properties of the waters of this spa town are used in the treatment of kidney complaints.

★★**Mata do Buçaco** – *See MATA DO BUÇACO.*

Mealhada – Mealhada, which is off the main road N 1, is famous for its roast suckling pig *(leitão assado).*

Return to Coimbra on the N 1.

★**Conímbriga** – *Round tour of 60km/37mi (twisting roads) – about 2hr 30min. Leave Coimbra by* ③, *the N 1. After 15km/9mi bear left towards Condeixa.*

★**Conímbriga** – *See CONÍMBRIGA.*

Penela – The village is overlooked by an 11 and 12C castle. From the keep, cut out of the living rock, the **panorama**★ includes the castle, the village and the Serra da Lousã to the east. The Church of Santa Eufémia, south of the castle, contains a Renaissance altarpiece of the Assumption surmounted by the Trinity, carved by the Coimbra School of Sculpture.

Return to Coimbra by N 110.

The road winds its way through green countryside.

CONÍMBRIGA★

Coimbra
Michelin map 940 or 441 L4

The Roman ruins of Conímbriga (Ruínas de Conímbriga) situated on a triangular spur bordered by two deep and narrow valleys are among the finest to be seen in the Iberian Peninsula. A Celtic city stood on this spot as long ago as the Iron Age. The present ruins, however, are those of a Roman town situated on either side of an important road which connected Lisbon and Braga; it was founded in the first century and remained prosperous over a long period. In the 3C, threatened by Barbarian invasion, the inhabitants were compelled to build ramparts, leaving some of the houses outside the wall. Material from these houses was used in the construction of the fortifications. In spite of these measures, Conímbriga fell to the Suebi in 468 and the town declined. This was to the advantage of the present town of Coimbra which takes its name from Conímbriga.

TOUR ⊙ *about 1hr*

Leave the car in front of the museum and take the path towards the ruins, following the route marked on the plan.

Cross the **Casa da Cruz Suástica** (House of the Swastika) and the **Casa dos Esqueletos** (House of the Skeletons), paved with fine mosaics, before reaching the baths and the interesting *laconicum* (a type of sauna) (**1**).

★**Casa de Cantaber** – *Parts of the house are temporarily closed.* This house, which is one of the largest in the western Roman world, is said to have belonged to Cantaber, whose wife and children were captured by the Suebi during an attack on the town in 465.

The tour begins with the private baths: the *frigidarium* (**2**) with its cold baths, the *tepidarium* (warm baths) and the *caldarium* (hot baths) (**3**) over the *hypocaust* (heated space connected with the furnace). The hypocaust's layout gives an idea of the plan for the fireplaces and the underground system of warm air circulation; a few lead pipes remain.

You then arrive at the northern entrance to the house: a colonnade (**4**) preceded the *atrium* (entrance vestibule) (**5**). As you pass from the *atrium* to the central peristyle (**6**), note an unusual stone (**7**) in the pavement, cut away to a rose tracery through which the drain can be seen. The *impluvium* (a basin for collecting rain water) (**8**) is to the left of the peristyle. Leading off from the *impluvium* were the bedrooms. From the *triclinium* (sitting and dining room) (**9**) you can see three pools. The most interesting of these pools (**10**) is encircled by columns of which one has retained its original stucco painted in red. A suite of three rooms (**11**) adjoining the wall has a lovely pool and flower beds in the shape of a cross.

Cidade Antiga – Excavations northwest of the Casa de Cantaber have uncovered the centre of the ancient town, in particular the **forum**, a hostelry and baths. To the southwest the craftsmen's quarter and the monumental baths have also been discovered.

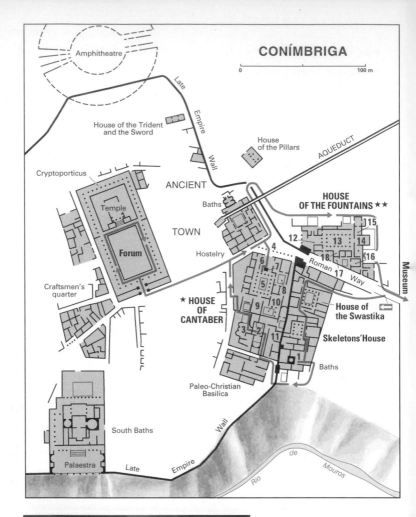

CONÍMBRIGA

Amphitheatre

House of the Trident and the Sword

House of the Pillars

AQUEDUCT

Cryptoporticus

Temple

ANCIENT

Baths

HOUSE OF THE FOUNTAINS ★★

Forum

TOWN

Hostelry

15

12

13

14

16

4

Roman

18

Way

17

6

7

Craftsmen's quarter

5

8

★ **HOUSE OF CANTABER**

9

10

House of the Swastika

Skeletons' House

3

2

11

Museum

1

Baths

Paleo-Christian Basilica

Wall

Rio

de

Mouros

South Baths

Palaestra

Late

Empire

0   100 m

ANCIENT TOWN Wall — Late Empire Wall

B. Brake/RAPHO

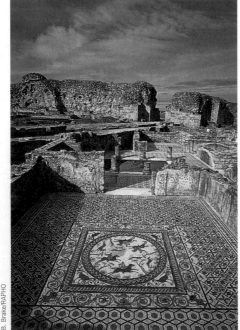

Mosaics, Casa dos Repuxos

Aqueduto – The aqueduct, which was some 3.5km/ 2mi long, brought water from Alcabideque and ended at the supply tower by the arch (reconstructed) abutting on the wall.

★★ **Casa dos Repuxos (House of the Fountains)** – *Access by footbridge to the north.* The villa, which belonged to a man named Rufus, dates from the early 2C although it was built on the site of a 1C building. The layout of the rooms is easy to follow on account of the column bases and the paving which consists largely of wonderful mosaics. Inside are the *atrium* (**12**), the peristyle (**13**) and the *triclinium* (**14**) which was bordered by a pool. Around these rooms were the living quarters and communal rooms. The **mosaics**★★ covering the floors show extraordinary variety.

In a room to the left of the *triclinium*, a fine polychrome composition (**15**) shows hunting scenes, the Four Seasons and a quadriga.

Another room (**16**) giving onto the *impluvium* presents some elegant figures at a deer hunt.

A *cubiculum* (bedroom) (**17**) has ornamental tiling with geometrical designs and plant motifs surrounding Silenus astride an ass being pulled forward by its halter.

Next door, a sitting room (**18**), opening on to the peristyle, is decorated with an outstanding mosaic: in the centre of an ornament representing wading birds, dolphins and sting rays, a marine centaur surrounded by dolphins brandishes a standard and a fish. Lastly, in the southwest corner of the peristyle, Perseus stands, holding in his right hand Medusa's head which he appears to be offering to a monster from the deep. *For the meaning of the Roman terms see Casa de Cantaber above.*

The house stands beside part of the Roman way which leads to the museum.

Museu Monográfico ⊘ – Ceramics, sculpture, epigraphs, mosaics and various small objects recount the life of the Roman town from the beginning of the Roman Empire to the end of the 6C.

COSTA DA CAPARICA
Setúbal
Michelin map 940 Q2

Costa da Caparica is the nearest seaside resort to Lisbon on the southern shore of the Tagus. With its vast beaches, which are less polluted than those on the northern shore, it is one of the most popular weekend spots with Lisbonites *(Lisboetas)*. The resort is constantly being developed; growing parallel to the ocean it is protected by a ridge of sand dunes. In season, a **small train** runs along the coast for 11km/7mi, giving access to the immensely long beach. Fishing boats, their prows adorned with a painted star or eye, may still be seen bringing in their nets helped by holiday-makers.

Miradouro dos Capuchos – *3km/2mi to the east by motorway, then bear right on a road turning off from the N 377 (follow the road signs). In front of the Convento dos Capuchos (Capuchins), turn right on to the paved lane leading to the belvedere on the cliff.*

Interesting view of the resort, the cliffs on the left of the belvedere, the Tagus estuary and the north coast as far as Cascais.

CRATO
Portalegre
Michelin map 940 O7

As early as 1350, Crato became the seat of a priory for the Order of the Knights Hospitallers of St John of Jerusalem which later became the Order of the Knights of Malta. The title of Grand Prior of Crato was bestowed up until the late 16C. The most famous incumbent was Dom António, grandson of King Dom Manuel and illegitimate son of Dom Luís, who was a pretender to the Spanish throne after the death of King Dom Henrique I in 1580. He was removed by his cousin, Philip II of Spain.

In 1356 the command of the knights' residence was transferred to the monastery-fortress in the neighbouring village of Flor da Rosa; Crato, however, retained its role as a priory. While Crato's castle was burnt in 1662 by Don Juan of Austria, several old houses may still be seen.

3km/2mi north of Crato is the village of Flor da Rosa, which has long been a manufacturing centre for pottery; the speciality is the *caçoila*, a round cooking bowl.

★**Mosteiro de Flor da Rosa** ⊘ – The monastery-fortress of the Order of the Knights of Malta was built in 1356 by Prior Álvaro Gonçalves Pereira, father of Nuno Álvares Pereira who defeated the Castilians at the Battle of Aljubarrota. It forms a compact group of fortified buildings within a crenellated perimeter wall.

The **church**★ on the right has been extremely well restored; the simplicity of its lines and the height of its nave are outstanding. The small flower-decked cloisters in the centre are robust in design but are given an overall elegance by their graceful Late Gothic network vaulting.

The refectory has beautiful vaulting supported by three twisted columns.

Vale do DOURO★★

Michelin map 940 or 441 I 5,6

Only the lower course of the Douro, which is one of the largest rivers of the Iberian Peninsula, flows through Portugal. Tradition links the river's name with that of port wine, the grapes being harvested on the valley slopes near the Spanish border.

Physical characteristics – The source of the Douro lies in Spain at an altitude of 2 060m/6 759ft in the Sierra de Urbión, one of the mountain ranges of the Iberian Peninsula. For nearly 525km/325mi the river winds its way through the Meseta before becoming, for 112km/70mi, the border between Spain and Portugal in a hilly region where its course drops rapidly as it cuts between high granite walls. Once past Barca de Alva, as it enters the last 215km/134mi of its course, the Douro becomes entirely Portuguese. The valley grows less wild, although always remaining confined by granite and shale rocks, until it opens out into the estuary commanded by Oporto. The river's annual flow is subject to heavy rain in the lower part of its course during autumn and winter and is very irregular: almost drought-like conditions above Peso da Régua contrast sharply with violent autumn and winter flood waters in the Oporto area.

The river's resources – The Douro has played an important part in the region's economic development since the 18C. The river carried the *barcos rabelos*, typical flat – bottomed craft with a tall square rig capable of shooting the rapids and used to transport fruit and, more importantly, port wine. However this trade virtually ended (except occasionally in periods of winter flooding), when roads and a railway were constructed along the valley from the Spanish border to Cinfães.

Nowadays, the aim is to harness the energy represented by the Douro Basin for the country as a whole. The project is favoured by the impermeability of the rocks, the river's own course and the narrowness of the valleys through which it flows. The dams on the Douro and its tributaries supply a high percentage of the country's requirement in hydro-electric power.

★THE VINHO VERDE REGION

1 From the Carrapatelo dam to Lamego

62km/38.5mi – about 2hr 30min – local map below

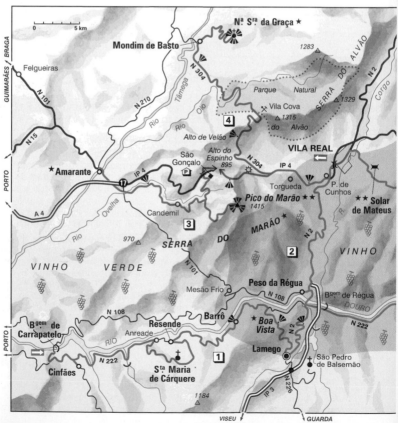

Grape picking

The lower valley of the river, near Oporto, is not the domain of the great wine of that name but that of the well known *vinho verde*, called "green" because the local climate is such that the grapes cannot fully ripen here. The real port is made much further east, from Régua to the Spanish border.

The Douro, widened by successive dams, runs hemmed in by steep hills and winds round in great twists and turns. The shale and granite slopes, more wooded on the north bank and more cultivated on the south bank, where little white villages seem to hang between the vines, terraced olive groves or corn fields, with the river below, make a very lovely landscape, despite the reminders of industrial civilisation evidenced by the railway line, the Carrapatelo dam *(barragem)*, a few factories, and the installations for transporting coal from the Pejão mines (south bank).

Two winding roads, often picturesque, sometimes built into the cliff, sometimes level with the water, hug the banks of the Douro between Porto and Peso da Régua: N 108 to the north, N 222 to the south.

Barragem do Carrapatelo – This undertaking is a dead-weight dam, 170m/558ft long with, on the south bank, a hydro-electric station and a fish ladder. In addition, on the north bank, it has a navigation lock nearly 90m/295ft long which drops 43m/141ft making it the lock with the greatest displacement in Europe.

Cinfães – Cinfães is the commercial centre for *vinho verde*.

Continue along N 222 to Anreade; turn right on the road towards Ovadas, south; 5.5km/3mi on, bear left.

Priorado de Santa Maria de Cárquere – Only the church and the funeral chapel of the lords of Resende remain, linked by a monumental arch. The church restored in the 13, 14, 16 and 17C (square crenellated tower and a Gothic chancel, the façade and nave are Manueline) still has a Romanesque doorway decorated with small columns and capitals with interlacing; the chancel under diagonal ribbed vaulting, has a door on the left with a high pediment and a double string course of billets. The chapel, which has a remarkable Romanesque window with capitals of sculpted pelicans, contains four stone sarcophagi carved with animals and inscriptions.

Return to N 222 and turn right.

Resende – Important wine production centre.

Barrô – There is a good view from the village of the valley's wooded slopes; the 12C Romanesque church *(take the path on the left on leaving the village from the east)* has a richly carved tympanum and a beautiful rose window.

After 6km/3.5mi turn right on N 226.

★**Miradouro da Boa Vista** – There is a magnificent view from this belvedere of the Douro valley. The northern bank especially, is striped with vines on stakes and terraced olive groves, there are scattered villages and the occasional *quinta* (estate) and then, crowded with the houses of Peso da Régua down by the river. High up, cut out against the sky are the dry, whitish summits of the Serra do Marão.

★★THE PORT REGION

② Round tour from Lamego
112km/70mi – about 3hr – local map below

As the local saying goes: "God created the Earth and man the Douro". One has to see the way the steep banks of the Douro have been shaped meticulously into terraces, each one comprising several rows of vines, to understand the enormous amount of work man has put into these hillsides for more than 20 centuries. The sight is particularly fascinating between mid-September and mid-October when the terraces are invaded by thousands of grape pickers. The vineyards cover an area of 42 500ha/105 000 acres and it is their grapes, which ripen in the shelter of the valley where the temperature in summer can easily reach 40°C – 106°F, that produce port.

Lamego – *See LAMEGO.*

The picturesque N 2 runs above the Corgo valley to Vila Real.

Vila Real – *See VILA REAL.*

Leave Vila Real on N 322 and continue east towards Sabrosa.

★★**Solar de Mateus** – *See Vila Real: Excursions.*

Sabrosa – The town is Magellan's birthplace.

★★**Road from Sabrosa to Pinhão** – After Sabrosa, the N 323 descends towards the Douro and overlooks the deep valley of the Pinhão. The hillsides are striped with terraces of vines and farmhouses dotted amid the greenery. 7km/4mi before Pinhão there is a fine **view**★ of a bend in the Douro and its confluence with the Pinhão river.

Pinhão – Pinhão, which stands at the junction of the Douro and Pinhão rivers, is an important port wine production centre. Wine has traditionally been sent from here by boat or by train. The **railway station** is decorated with *azulejos* illustrating the sites and the traditional costumes of the valley. Nowadays, all the wine is transported by lorry. Note the rows of white vats on the river banks.
By making an excursion eastwards to **São João da Pesqueira** *(18km/11mi of hairpin bends on N 222)* you will see the terraced hillsides of vineyards in the Torto valley. São João da Pesqueira is a large village on the plateau with an arcaded main square around which stand a chapel and white balconied houses.
After Pinhão, N 222 follows the valley westwards between shale slopes which have been terraced and contained by small drystone walls. The land is exclusively given over to vines.

Peso da Régua – This small town, at the confluence of the Corgo and the Douro, is responsible for the administration of the port wine trade. It also organises the rail transport of the wines of the Upper Douro to Oporto.
To return to Lamego, take N 2 south from Peso da Régua. The road rises through pleasantly cool countryside; from one of the bends there is a good **view** of the stepped site of Peso da Régua.

★SERRA DO MARÃO

③ From Vila Real to Amarante
④ From Vila Real to Mondim de Basto

Elvas, only a few miles from the Spanish citadel of Badajoz, is an impressive fortification still surrounded by ramparts. The town was not freed by the Christians from the Moorish occupation until 1226, while Lisbon had been liberated almost a hundred years before. Elvas subsequently resisted many assaults by the Spanish until 1580 when it was attacked by Philip II's troops.

Today Elvas is a great agricultural marketing centre, famous for its sugar plums, and is a textile manufacturing centre (cotton). Elvas also attracts tourists from Spain.

The War of the Oranges – In 1801, Spain, under pressure from Napoleon, sent an ultimatum to Portugal, demanding that Portugal end its alliance with Britain and close her ports to British ships. Portugal refused and Spain declared war, sending her troops under Godoy into the Alentejo. Olivença offered no resistance and capitulated. On hearing the news, Godoy, who had just begun the siege of Elvas, sent two orange branches cut down by his soldiers from trees at the foot of the town's ramparts, as a trophy to Queen Maria Luisa of Spain. The trophy amused the citizens of Madrid who then named the war after it.

In spite of the resistance of Elvas and Campo Major the Spanish won the war. In September peace was signed at Badajoz, Portugal lost Olivença and its lands and was obliged to close her ports to the English.

SIGHTS

★★**Muralhas** – The Elvas fortifications are the most accomplished example of 17C military architecture in Portugal. The sombre, well armoured merlons contrast with the white façades of the houses within. Fortified gates, moats, curtain walls, bastions and glacis form a remarkable defensive group completed to the south and north by the 17C Santa Luzia and the 18C Graça forts, each perched on a hill.

To fully appreciate the strength of the fortifications enjoy a tour of the city *(5km/3mi)*.

★**Aqueduto da Amoreira** – The aqueduct was constructed between 1498 and 1622 to the plans of Francisco de Arruda. It begins 7.5km/5mi southwest of the town to which it still brings water.

Enter the ramparts on the south side and go as far as Rua da Cidadela; turn left beneath the 16C Arco do Relógio which opens on to Praça da República.

Praça da República – The square, bordered to the south by the former town hall and to the north by the old cathedral, has a mosaic paving of basalt, marble and sandstone, laid in geometrical patterns.

Sé – The cathedral, which was originally Gothic, was rebuilt in the 16C by Francisco de Arruda in the Manueline style, which is particularly evident in the design of the belfry and the two lateral doorways.

The interior, whose pillars were decorated in the Manueline period, contains an 18C chancel entirely faced with marble.

Take the street on the right of the cathedral which leads to Largo de Santa Clara.

★**Largo de Santa Clara** – The *largo* is a small "square", triangular in shape, lined by houses with wrought iron grilles and façades bearing coats of arms; beneath a loggia, an Arabic door flanked by two towers remains from the original 10C town wall.

The centre of the square is occupied by an interesting 16C marble **pillory**★ which still has four iron hooks attached to the capital.

Pillory, Elvas

★**Igreja Nossa Senhora da Consolação** – The Church of Our Lady of Consolation on the south side of Largo de Santa Clara was built in the 16C in the Renaissance style. It is an octagonal building the interior of which, covered by a cupola resting on eight painted columns, is entirely decorated with fine 17C multicoloured **azulejos**★. The pulpit, supported by a marble column, has a 16C wrought iron balustrade.

Pass beneath the Arabic arch and go up the street to Largo da Alcáçova, bear left and then right into a narrow, flowered alley which ends at the castle.

Castelo ⊘ – The castle was constructed originally by the Moors and reinforced in the 14 and 16C. The 15C keep stands in the northwest corner. From the top of the ramparts there is a panorama of the town and its fortifications and the surrounding countryside scattered with olive trees and isolated farmsteads.

ERICEIRA★

Lisboa – Population 4 460
Michelin map 940 P1

The village, a lively seaside resort perched on a cliff facing the Atlantic, has preserved its old quarter around the church, its maze of alleyways and its picturesque fishing harbour. Ericeira was the scene of an historic event on 5 October 1910: King Manuel II sailed from its harbour into exile, while the Republic was being proclaimed in Lisbon.

SIGHTS

Harbour – At the foot of the cliff, strengthened with stonework shoring whose top forms a parapet for the *corniche* roads, there is a sheltered fishing beach, also protected on the north by a jetty.
From the square overlooking it, **Largo das Ribas**, there is a continual flow of spectators watching the fishing boats (small boats and trawlers being hauled up on to the sandy shore by tractors, even as far as the top of the steep road which links the beach to the *corniche*) and the unloading of the catch of fish and octopus.

Church precinct – Old cobbled alleys with lovely low white houses, their cornerstones painted blue, surround the **Igreja Matriz**. The interior of the church has a beautiful coffered ceiling and *azulejos*.

Cabo ESPICHEL★

Setúbal
Michelin map 940 Q2

Cape Espichel, at the southern tip of the Serra da Arrábida is a true World's End, beaten continuously by violent winds.
It was off this cape that **Dom Fuas Roupinho**, who had already distinguished himself before King Afonso I in the wars against the Moors, vanquished the enemy again in 1180 in a brilliant victory at sea, when Portuguese sailors, although inexperienced in this type of warfare, succeeded in capturing enemy ships.
In this desolate **setting**★ may be seen the ruins of Nossa Senhora do Cabo. This spot has been a popular pilgrimage centre ever since the 13C.
The arcaded buildings, which form a vast square, were erected during the 18C by pilgrims.

Santuário de Nossa Senhora do Cabo ⊘ – The church built in the classical style at the end of the 17C has a baroque interior.
Go round the sanctuary by the left and walk to the cliff edge.
The cliff drops a sheer 100m/350ft to the sea. To the west and below a chapel decorated with *azulejos* lies a small creek.

ESTORIL★

Lisboa – Population 25 230
Michelin map 940 P1

Estoril has developed into a sea and winter resort, favoured by a mild climate and a temperature which averages 12°C – 54°F in winter. It lies on the *corniche* road linking Lisbon and Cascais, a point on the Costa de Estoril which is famous for its luminous skies. Formerly a small village known to a few for the healing properties of its waters, Estoril now attracts an elegant international circle who come for the resort's entertainments (golf, casino and sea fishing), its sporting events (motor and horseracing, regattas), its pleasant location facing Cascais Bay, its park of tropical and exotic plants and trees, palm lined avenues, beaches of fine sand and its highly successful festivals (Festival of the Sea in July etc).

A selection of hotels in Estoril is listed under Travellers' addresses for Lisbon.

Serra da ESTRELA★

Guarda and Castelo Branco
Michelin map 940 or 441 K 6,7 L 6,7

The Serra da Estrela, a great mountain barrier 60km/40mi long by 30km/20mi wide is the highest massif in Portugal. Above the cultivated and wooded slopes appear the arid and boulder strewn summits, the tallest of which is Torro with an altitude of 1 993m/6 539ft.

Tourism is developing in this formerly isolated area: Penhas da Saúde has become a winter sports resort; Covilhã, Seia, Gouveia and Manteigas, small towns within reach of the plain, have become starting points for mountain excursions.

Geographical notes – The Serra da Estrela is a granite block extending further to the southwest from the central mountain range of Spain. It is limited to the north and south by two rock fault escarpments which, for several hundred yards, overlook the Mondego and the Zêzere valleys. The range ends abruptly in the west dominating the shale ridges of the Serra da Lousã. With the exception of the deep cleft formed in the Ice Age in the Upper Valley of the Zêzere, the relief is fairly uniform, the majority of the peaks reaching an altitude of some 1 500m/4 800ft.

Trees – pines and oaks – cease at about 1 300m/4 250ft giving way to a close carpet of grass, a few flowers and rocks. Only the valley floors are cultivated with maize and rye; the summits receive 2m/7ft of rain and snow every year, remaining frozen for nine months out of twelve. Summer is usually hot and very dry.

Formerly only a few shepherds frequented the region, seeking new pastures for their flocks; nowadays the transhumance of great flocks of sheep and herds of goats from the Mondego valley to the mountains every summer provides material for the developing wool industry at Covilhã and Fundão and the manufacture of a delicious winter cheese, the *Queijo da Serra* (mountain cheese).

★★THE MONTE DA TORRE ROAD

☐ From Covilhã to Seia

49km/30mi – about 2hr/local map facing page

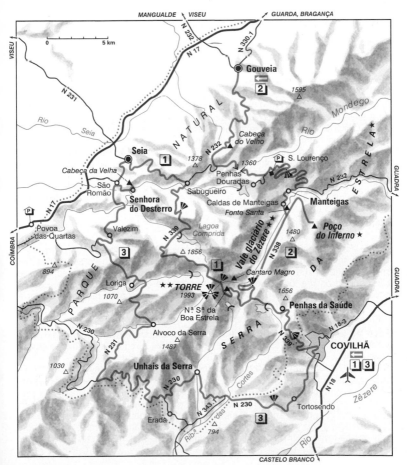

This itinerary includes the highest road in Portugal *(often closed to traffic until the end of April because of snow)*.

Covilhã – *See COVILHÃ.*

On leaving Covilhã, the road rises rapidly through pine and oak woods which soon thin out, revealing wide views.

Penhas da Saúde – Winter sports and summer holiday resort.
The landscape becomes hillier with the occasional reservoir or glacier lake.
Leave the Manteigas road on the right (see below).

After a bend bringing the road parallel with the Upper Valley of the Zêzere, the **landscape★** takes on a desolate appearance with the large quantity of worn granite boulders strewn around. A niche hollowed out of the rock on the right hand side of the road (car park) shelters a statue of Our Lady of the Holy Star (Nossa Senhora da Boa Estrela) and provides the setting for a religious festival held each year on the second Sunday in August *(see Calendar of Events)*.

There is an interesting **view★** from a belvedere arranged in a bend on the left, a short distance from the summit, of the glacial Upper Valley of the Zêzere.
The river's actual source is hidden by a 300m/900ft high granite cone, known locally as the "slender pitcher" (Cântaro Magro), which has been cut into even blocks by freezing ice.

Bear left to Torre.

★★Torre – From the summit the **panorama** includes the Mondego valley, the Serra da Lousã and the Zêzere valley.
The road continues over the crest, winding its way between rocks and moss covered boulders and around lakes.
The "long lake", Lagoa Comprida, its deep blue waters controlled by a dam parallel to the road, is the largest single expanse of water in the *serra*. The descent into the Mondego valley, where both crops and villages are to be found, is swift and the **views★★** are magnificent.

After **Sabugueiro**, a village of granite walled houses, the road drops steeply.

Seia – A small town pleasantly situated at the foot of the *serra*.

★★UPPER VALLEY OF THE ZÊZERE

② From Gouveia to Covilhã via Manteigas
77km/48mi – about 2hr 30min – local map facing page.

The route crosses the massif by way of the Upper Valley of the Zêzere.

Gouveia – A small attractive town built halfway up the side of the Mondego valley. The upper plateaux scattered with tors are soon reached; some of the granite boulders have been worn by erosion into astonishing forms, such as the Old Man's Head, **Cabeça do Velho**, which rises from a mass of rocks on the left of the road. The source of the Mondego (Nascente do Mondego – *signposted*), the longest river flowing solely in Portugal, rises to an altitude of 1 360m/4 462ft just before Penhas Douradas. The road runs past the Pousada de São Lourenço which affords a fine view of Manteigas and the Zêzere valley opposite.
The descent becomes brutal as hairpin bends twist down to the Zêzere valley; a belvedere, not far from the *pousada*, affords an upstream **view★** of the valley which is commanded by Manteigas.

Manteigas – 17C houses with wooden balconies.
At Manteigas leave the N 232 and turn right.

A little after the small spa of **Caldas de Manteigas**, note the **fish farm** ⊙ *(posto aquícola)* on the side of the road at Fonte Santa. Further on there are still a few sheepfolds, then the mountain solitude takes over. However, cultivated terraces can be seen on the lower slopes. After the bridge over the Zêzere, the road (in poor condition) continues upstream until it reaches the rock face of the glacial valley *(see below)*, it then climbs to the top.
Turn left into a narrow unsurfaced road to Poço do Inferno (6km/4mi).

★Poço do Inferno – The road occasionally affords good views of Manteigas in its setting. The Well of Hell is a wild but wooded defile given considerable beauty by a **cascade★**.
The road runs level with the edge of the ancient glacial valley where the Zêzere flows.

★★Vale Glaciário do Zêzere – This valley is a perfect example of glacial relief: U-shaped contour with consequent steep slopes, hanging tributary valleys and connecting gorges, cirque at the highest point; cascades, enormous erratic boulders strewn on the bottom, and on the slopes, scraggy vegetation.
Half-way along this rectilinear section, jagged outlines appear, which, in the front and on the right, encircle the glacial cirque, the peak of the Cântaro Magro and the Torre pyramid.

Alto Vale do Zêzere

The road bears westwards and passes near the source of the Zêzere – signposted "Cântaros" (not visible from the road but it can be reached on foot through huge boulders).

A little further on, at a fountain, there is a lovely extensive **view**★ across the glacial valley which one has just skirted.

At the final pass, take the N 339 on the left towards Covilhã.

Covilhã – Covilhã, spread over the first wooded foothills of the southern flank of the Serra da Estrela, close to the rich Zêzere valley, which at this point is known as the Cova da Beira, is both a health resort and an excursion centre, as well as being the dormitory town for the Penhas da Saúde winter sports resort.

The town is equally well-known for its *Queijo da Serra*, a strong cheese made from ewes' milk.

Sheep also supply wool which is woven in this small industrial town into yarn sufficient for two-thirds of the country's woollen industry.

★THE WESTERN SIDE OF THE SERRA

③ From Covilhã to Seia via Unhais da Serra
81km/50mi – about 2hr/local map facing page.

This route goes round the *serra* by the west along a road which runs almost constantly at an altitude of between 600 and 700m/2 000 and 2 300ft. Throughout there are interesting views to the left, first over the Zêzere valley and the Serra da Gardunha, later over the shale hillocks of the Serra da Lousã and finally towards the Mondego valley.

Covilhã – *See COVILHÃ.*

Leave Covilhã by the N 230 going south.

The Serra da Estrela's high peaks come into sight beyond Tortosendo.

Unhais da Serra – A small spa and health resort in a lovely **setting**★ at the mouth of a torrent-filled valley.

Villages such as **Alvoco da Serra** cling halfway up the hillsides or, as does **Loriga**, stand perched upon a spur in the valley.

The terraced valley floors are put to full use growing crops (maize) in even sweeps.

At São Romão turn right in the direction of Senhora do Desterro.

Senhora do Desterro – The road climbs the Alva valley to Senhora do Desterro where you leave the car.

Take the path on the left cut out of the rock which will bring you *(15min round trip on foot)* to the Cabeça da Velha (Old Woman's Head), a granite rock worn by erosion.

Return to the road which leads to Seia and to the itinerary described.

Seia – *See above.*

ESTREMOZ★

Évora — Population 7 869
Michelin map 940 P7

Approached from the south, the old town appears perched on a hill overlooking the bright whitewashed houses of the modern town below.

Estremoz, standing in a region of marble quarries, is a pleasant city, still possessing its 17C ramparts and dominated by its medieval castle. It is, and has been since the 16C, a well-known centre for Alentejo pottery which can be seen picturesquely displayed on the Rossio (main square) on market days *(Saturdays)*.

The Estremoz potteries – In addition to wide-mouthed jars *(bilhas)* and narrow mouthed jars *(barris)*, the potteries of Estremoz manufacture decorative ware in which water is kept cool and served at table. The goblets *(moringues)* with one handle and two spouts, and the kings' jugs *(púcaros dos reis)* – their name testifying to former royal favour – although unglazed are decorated with geometrical or stylised foliage motifs which are sometimes engraved and inlaid with white marble chips. A more recent and less elegant ornament is application of oak twigs. *Fidalgos* are large, big-bellied, glazed pots adorned with small bunches of flowers.

Estremoz is equally famous for its pottery figurines which are naïve in style and brightly coloured. These include figures both religious (characters from the Christmas cribs and saints) and secular (peasants at their everyday tasks, caricatures) as well as animals. They are reproduced from old designs full of realism and picturesque qualities which have lost none of their savour.

★UPPER TOWN (VILA VELHA) *1hr*

To reach the upper town, walk to the pillory on the Rossio and take a narrow uphill alley on the right. A 14C doorway marks the entrance to the old town with its Gothic and Manueline houses.

Torre de Menagem – The keep has now been converted into one of the most famous *pousadas* in Portugal. It was built in the 13C and is crowned with small pyramid shaped merlons and flanked in its upper part by galleries supported on consoles.

Enter the pousada.

On your way to the top platform, look at the lovely octagonal room with trefoil windows on the second floor. From the platform there is a circular view of the town and the Alentejo where the Serra de Ossa heights can be seen to the south.

Capela da Rainha Santa Isabel ⊘ – *Walk round the keep leaving it and King Dinis's palace on your left and go through a fine old grille gateway.*

The chapel walls are covered with beautiful *azulejos* depicting scenes from the life of **Queen Saint Isabel of Aragon**, wife of King Dinis. The Miracle of the Roses scene is the most delightful: in it, the queen, surprised by the king as she is carrying gold to distribute to the poor, opens the pleats of her skirt to banish her husband's suspicions, revealing only roses within the folds.

Igreja de Santa Maria – This square 16C church contains paintings by the Portuguese Primitives. The majority are in the sacristy which is further embellished with a marble lavabo.

Sala de Audiência de Dom Dinis – A beautiful **Gothic colonnade★** is the outstanding feature of King Dinis's Audience Chamber whose stellar vaulting dates from the Manueline period.

Queen Saint Isabel and King Pedro I both died in this room, in 1336 and 1367 respectively.

Museu Municipal ⊘ – The museum is housed in a fine building opposite the keep. Among its collections are Estremoz pottery and crib figures, religious works of art etc.

LOWER TOWN (A BAIXA) *1hr 30min*

A gateway in the 17C ramparts opens on to the modern town.

Museu Rural ⊘ – *Number 62 b on the Rossio.*

This small but interesting rural museum uses models of local crafts and costumes to portray the life of the people in the Alentejo.

Igreja de Nossa Senhora dos Mártires – *2km/1mi south on the road to Bencatel.* The church dates from 1744 and has a monumental Gothic east end. The nave, which is preceded by a triumphal Manueline arch, contains beautiful *azulejos (Flight into Egypt, The Last Supper* and *The Annunciation)* as does the chancel *(Nativity* and *Presentation in the Temple)*.

ÉVORA ★★★

Évora — Population 35 117
Michelin map 940 Q6

Évora, a walled town since Roman times, is now most attractively Moorish in character with alleys cut by arches, brilliant white houses, flower-decked terraces, openwork balconies and tiled patios.

From its rich past Évora retains several medieval and Renaissance palaces and mansions which in themselves provide a panoply of Portuguese architecture.

They are at their most impressive at night (floodlit during the season from 21.00 to midnight) standing out against a starry sky.

The Alentejo capital is today an important agricultural market and the base for several dependent crafts and industries (cork, woollen carpets, leather and painted furniture).

HISTORICAL NOTES

Évora flourished when the Romans inhabited the town, declined under the Visigoths and in 715 was occupied by the Moors. Their long rule benefited the town which became an important agricultural and trading centre at the heart of which stood the castle and mosque.

Geraldo Sempavor (Gerald the Fearless) – In the 12C internal quarrels among the Muslims encouraged the Christians under Afonso Henriques to rebel. One, Geraldo Sempavor, gained the confidence of the Muslim king of Évora and brought off a bold plot: one September night in 1165 he managed single-handedly to take the watchtower in northwest of the town, then alert the Muslim town guard who promptly hurried to the tower, leaving Gerald and his companions-in-arms to advance and take Évora without difficulty. The town then came under the rule of King Afonso Henriques.

A centre of humanism – From the late 12C, Évora was the preferred capital of the kings of Portugal and in the 15 and 16C enjoyed brilliant renown. Artists and learned men gathered at the court: humanists such as Garcia and André de Resende, the chronicler Duarte Galvão, the creator of Portuguese drama, Gil Vicente *(see GUIMARÃES)*, the sculptor Nicolas Chanterene and the painters Cristóvão de Figueiredo and Gregório Lopes. Mansions, monasteries and convents were built everywhere in the Manueline and Renaissance styles; the Moorish style of decoration was brought back into favour by several architects and formed part of a new hybrid style, the Luso-Moorish. Finally a Jesuit University was founded in 1559 at the instigation of the patron, Cardinal Dom Henrique. But in 1580, following the disaster of El-Ksar El-Kebir, Portugal was annexed by Spain and Évora declined rapidly. Although Portugal recovered its independence in the revolt of 1637 and the Portuguese Crown was restored, the town never recovered its former sparkle. In 1759, when the Marquis of Pombal expelled the Jesuits and did away with the university, the town's last brilliance was extinguished and Évora plunged into deep lethargy for centuries.

OLD TOWN (CIDADE VELHA) *3hr*

Leave the car outside the town or, in the off-season, in Largo Conde de Vila-Flor near the pousada. Set off from the Tourist Information Centre on Praça do Giraldo.

Praça do Giraldo (BZ) – The bustling town centre is a vast square partly bordered by arcades. An 18C marble fountain by Afonso Álvares stands on the site of a former triumphal Roman arch.

Rua 5 de Outubro (BYZ) – This narrow street, which climbs to the cathedral, is lined with houses bearing wrought iron balconies, as well as arts and crafts shops; number 28 has a niche decorated with *azulejos*.

★★**Sé** ⊘ **(BY)** – The cathedral was built in the late 12 and 13C in the Transitional Gothic style. While it has Romanesque characteristics, its completion was carried out under Gothic influence.

Exterior – The plain granite façade is flanked by two massive towers crowned by conical spires added in the 16C. The tower on the right consists of several turrets similar to those on the Romanesque lantern-tower over the transept. The nave and aisle walls are crenellated.

The main doorway is decorated with figures of the Apostles supported relatively high up by consoles. The sculptures were probably carved in the late 13C by French artists.

★**Interior** – The large nave, with broken barrel vaulting, has an elegant triforium. To the left, on a baroque altar, is a 15C multicoloured stone statue of the Virgin Great With Child; opposite is a 16C statue, in gilded wood, of the Angel Gabriel attributed to Olivier of Ghent.

A very fine octagonal **dome★** on squinches, from which hangs a chandelier, stands above the transept crossing. The arms of the transept are lit by two Gothic rose windows: the north one shows the Morning Star and the south the Mystic Rose. In the north transept the Renaissance archway to a chapel is decorated with a marble sculpture by Nicolas Chanterene. The south transept contains the tomb of the 16C humanist André de Resende.

ÉVORA

Giraldo (Praça do)	**BZ**	
João de Deus (Rua)	**AY**	16
República (Rua da)	**BZ**	
5 de Outubro (Rua)	**BYZ**	
Álvaro Velho (Largo)	**BZ**	3
Aviz (Rua de)	**BY**	4
Bombeiros Voluntários		
de Évora (Av.)	**CZ**	6
Caraça (Trav. da)	**BZ**	7
Cenáculo (Rua do)	**BY**	9
Combatentes		
da Grande Guerra (Av. dos)	**BZ**	10
Conde de Vila-Flor (Largo)	**BY**	12
Diogo Cão (Rua)	**BZ**	13
Freiria de Baixo (Rua da)	**BY**	15
José Elias Garcia (Rua)	**AY**	18
Lagar dos Dízimos (Rua do)	**BZ**	19
Luís de Camões (Largo)	**AY**	21
Marquês de Marialva (Largo)	**BZ**	22
Menino Jesus (R. do)	**BY**	24
Misericórdia (Largo)	**BZ**	25
Penedos (Largo dos)	**AY**	28
Santa Clara (R. de)	**AZ**	30
São Manços (Rua de)	**BZ**	31
Senhor da Pobreza (Largo)	**CZ**	33
Torta (Trav.)	**AZ**	34
Vasco da Gama (Rua)	**BY**	36
1º de Maio (Praça)	**BZ**	37

*The numbers ①, ② etc
indicate the main routes into
and out of town
They are numbered in this
way on town plans and on
Michelin maps*

A Paço dos Duques de Cadaval
B Paço dos Condes de Basto
C Casa dos Condes de Portalegre
E Casa de Garcia de Resende
F Porta de Moura
K Casa Cordovil
L Casa Soure
M¹ Museu Regional
P Pálacio de D. Manuel

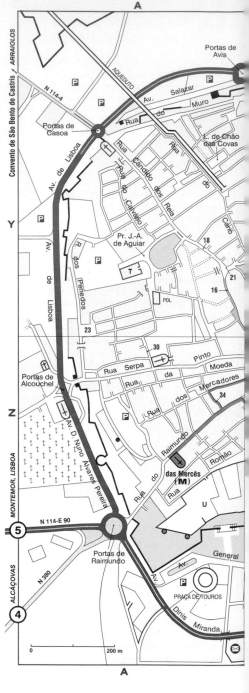

The chancel was remodelled in the 18C by Friederich Ludwig, architect of the monastery at Mafra.

★**Cadeiras do coro (Choir stalls)** – The oak stalls, which are in the gallery *(coro alto)*, were carved in the Renaissance period by Flemish artists. They are decorated with sacred and secular motifs; note in particular the scenes on the lower panels showing peasants at their everyday tasks (grape picking, pigsticking and sheep shearing).

The large Renaissance organ is thought to be the oldest in Europe.

★**Museu de Arte Sacra** – This sacred art museum contains vestments, a large collection of ecclesiastical plate, including an ivory 13C French figure-triptych of the **Virgin**★, and a 17C reliquary cross of St Lenho in silver gilt and multicoloured enamel decorated with 1426 precious stones.

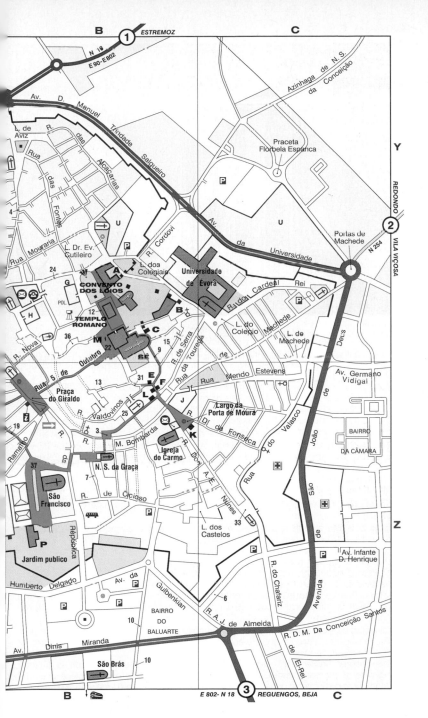

★**Claustro** – These Gothic cloisters, which were built between 1322 and 1340, have a massive appearance which is further accentuated by their granite composition, despite the elegance of rounded bays with radiating tracery.

Statues of the Evangelists stand in each of the four corners. The southwest corner provides a good view of the Romanesque belfry.

An adjoining chapel contains the 14C tomb of the founder-bishop and 14C statues of the Angel Gabriel and a polychrome Virgin whose posture shows French influence. Steps in the corners lead to the terrace where there are fine **views** of Évora.

★**Museu Regional** ⊙ (**BY M'**) – The museum is in the former 16 and 17C episcopal palace. The ground floor is devoted to Roman, medieval, Manueline and Luso-Moorish sculpture: outstanding are, a fragment of a marble **bas-relief★** of a vestal virgin (the face has disappeared), a 14C **Annunciation★** also in marble, and a 16C

Roman temple and Cathedral tower

Holy Trinity in Ança stone. Architectural features include the mullioned windows of the former town hall. There are also sculptures by Nicolas Chanterene (including the cenotaph of Bishop Afonso of Portugal).

Among the Primitive paintings on the first floor are an early 16C polyptych of the Flemish School representing the Life of the Virgin in thirteen large panels, the six panels of an altarpiece's predella, also by the Flemish School, showing the Life of Christ, a 16C triptych of the Passion in Limoges enamel, several 16C paintings by the Portuguese artists Frei Carlos and Gregório Lopes and Portuguese furnishings.

★**Templo Romano (BY)** – This Corinthian-style Roman temple erected in the 2C was probably dedicated to Diana. The capitals and bases of the columns are of Estremoz marble, the column shafts of granite.

The temple owes its relative preservation to its conversion into a fortress in the Middle Ages and its excavation only a century ago.

★**Convento dos Lóios (BY)** – The Dos Lóios or St Eligius monastery, dedicated to St John the Evangelist, was founded in the 15C.

★**Igreja** ⊙ – The church façade was remodelled after the earthquake of 1755 with the exception of the porch which protects a Flamboyant Gothic doorway. The coat of arms beneath a canopy belongs to the Melos, Counts of Olivença, for whom the church served as a mausoleum.

The nave, with lierne and tierceron vaulting, is lined with beautiful *azulejos* (1711) by António de Oliveira Bernardes, depicting the life of St Laurence Justinian, patriarch of Venice, whose writings influenced the Lóios religious. Two grilles in the pavement enable the medieval castle's cistern, on the left, and an ossuary, on the right, to be seen.

Conventual buildings – The conventual buildings have been converted into a *pousada*. The Late Gothic style cloisters were given extra height in the 16C by the addition of a Renaissance gallery.

The chapter house **door★** has outstanding architectural elegance and is a good example of the composite Luso-Moorish style *(qv)* ; the crowning piece over the doorway and the piers topped by pinnacles which serve as a framework to the door, are Gothic inspired; the columns are twisted and Manueline in style and the twin bays with horseshoe arches are, like the capitals, reminiscent of Moorish design.

Paço dos Duques de Cadaval ⊙ **(BY A)** – The Palace of the Dukes of Cadaval (presently occupied by the Direcção de Estradas de Évora – Évora Road Network Dept) is protected by two crenellated towers and has a façade that was remodelled in the 17C. It was given by King João I to his councillor, Martim Afonso de Melo, *alcalde* of Évora, in 1390. Kings João III and João V also lived within its walls at different periods.

The north tower formed part of the medieval city walls.

The Dukes of Cadaval's art gallery contains a collection of historic documents on the Cadaval family and two fine Flemish commemorative plaques in bronze, dating from the late 15C.

Retrace your steps to take the street between the Convento dos Lóios and the Museu Regional. Turn left into the street which runs perpendicular to the east end of the cathedral.

Paço dos Condes de Basto (BY B) The Palace of the Counts of Basto was built over the remains of the Roman wall including the Sertório Tower. The Gothic palace's main front has several paired Mudejar windows.

Return to the east end of the cathedral and continue round.

Casa dos Condes de Portalegre (BY C) – This is a delightful Gothic and 16C Manueline style mansion with a patio surrounded by a hanging garden and an openwork balcony.

Casa de Garcia de Resende (BZ E) – This is a 16C house in which the humanist Garcia de Resende (1470-1536) is said to have lived.
Manueline decoration adorns the three sets of paired windows on the first floor.

Porta de Moura (BZ F) – The gateway with its two towers formed part of the medieval town fortifications. A niche at the foot of the left tower contains a crucifix.

Largo da Porta de Moura (BZ) – This picturesque square is divided into two parts. On the larger of the two, in the centre, stands a beautiful Renaissance **fountain**★ which consists of a column surmounted by a white marble sphere.
Several lovely houses border the square: the 16C **Casa Cordovil (K)** on the south side has an elegant loggia with twin arcades, festooned horseshoe arches and Moorish capitals. A crenellated roof surmounted by a conical spire crowns all. On the west side, steps descend to the church of the former Carmelite Convent which has a baroque **doorway**. On the east side are the Law Courts, housed in a modern building.

Casa Soure (BZ L) – This 15C house was formerly a part of the Palace of the Infante Dom Luis. The Manueline façade has a gallery of rounded arches crowned by a conical spire.

Make for Largo da Graça by way of Travessa da Caraça.

Igreja de Nossa Senhora da Graça (BZ) This church, which was built in the 16C in the Italian Renaissance style, has a façade of granite, a portico with Tuscan columns, classical pilasters and a decoration of bosses and atlantes.

Igreja de São Francisco (BZ) – This early 16C church, which is preceded by a portico pierced by rounded, pointed and horseshoe arches, is crowned with battlements and conical pinnacles, some of which are twisted. The Manueline doorway is surmounted by a pelican and an armillary sphere, the respective emblems of João II and King Manuel.
The **interior**★, with ribbed vaulting, is surprisingly wide. The chancel contains two galleries, the one on the right, Renaissance, the one on the left, baroque. The former chapter house (access through the south transept) is furnished with a balustrade of fluted marble and turned ebony columns and, as a covering to the walls, *azulejos* depicting scenes from the Passion.

Take the door to the left of the balustrade in the former chapter house.

★**Capela dos Ossos** ⊘ – This macabre ossuary chapel was built in the 16C by a Franciscan to induce meditation in his fellow men. The bones and skulls of 5,000 people have been used to face the walls and pillars. At the entrance, the braids of young women who are about to marry are hung as ex-votos.

Capela dos Ossos

R. Leslie/HOA QUI

Jardim Público (BZ) – The public gardens are just south of the Igreja de São Francisco. Part of the **Palácio de Dom Manuel** (King Manuel's 16C palace) **(P)** – which has unfortunately been thoroughly remodelled – and the ruins of another 16C palace still stand in the gardens. Note the paired windows with horseshoe arches in the Luso-Moorish style.

The itinerary continues past the market (pottery stalls) which is held in the mornings.

Igreja das Mercês ⊙ **(AZ)** – **Museu de Artes Decorativas (M)** – The interior of the church (1670), lined with polychrome *azulejos*, houses the **Sacred Art collection** from the Museu Regional. Among the displays are a *Pietà*, statues including a small Virgin and Child (chapel on the left), two gilded altarpieces, an Indo-Portuguese oratory, and some vestments.

Return to Praça do Giraldo via Rua dos Mercadores.

TRAVELLERS' ADDRESSES

Where to stay

Estalagem Monte das Flores – *Monte das Flores, 7000 – Évora –* ☎ *(066) 254 90 – fax 275 64 – 17 rooms – 14 000$ (CC) – restaurant – parking – air conditioning.*
This charming inn, situated 6km/4mi southwest of Évora in the beautiful Alentejo countryside, is amid a group of traditional buildings offering peace and relaxation.

Hotel da Cartuxa – *Tv. da Palmeira 4, 7000 Évora –* ☎ *(066) 74 30 30 – fax (066) 74 42 84 – 85 rooms, 6 suites – 15 500$ (CC) – restaurant – parking – air conditioning.*
Modern hotel close to the city walls.

Pousada dos Lóios – *Largo Conde de Vila Flor, 7000 Évora –* ☎ *(066) 240 51 – fax (066) 272 48 – 30 rooms, 2 suites – 25 000/28 000$ (CC) – restaurant – parking – air conditioning.*
This elegant, luxurious pousada is situated in the buildings of the Lóios convent (see description below).

Eating out

O Antão – *R. João de Deus 5 –* ☎ *(066) 264 59 – 3 600$ (CC) – closed Mondays and from 23 June to 7 July.*
Good cooking at reasonable prices.

Fialho – *Tv. das Mascarenhas 14 –* ☎ *(066) 230 79 – 5 000$ (CC) – closed Mondays and from 2 to 23 September.*
Good local cuisine in a regional setting.

ADDITIONAL SIGHTS

★**Fortifications** – Considerable sections remain of the three outer walls which were required to protect the town at different periods. Traces of the 1C Roman wall, reinforced by the Visigoths in the 7C, can be seen between the Pacos dos Duques de Cadaval and dos Condes de Basto (Largo dos Colegiais). The 14C medieval wall marks the town limits to the north and west and can be seen from Estrada da Circunvalação between S and V on the town plan. The 17C fortifications now form the boundary of the public gardens to the south.

Universidade de Évora ⊙ **(Antiga Universidade dos Jesuitas) (BCY)** – The university occupies the former Jesuit University building; visit the inner courtyard.
Buildings in the 16C Italian Renaissance style surround what is known as the main **Students' Cloisters**★ (Claustro Geral dos Estudos) with its arched gallery – the whole forming a graceful inner court. Facing the entrance, the pediment over the portico to the Sala das Actas (Hall of Acts) is decorated with statues personalising the royal and the ecclesiastical universities.
The classrooms opening on the gallery are adorned with 18C *azulejos* representing the subjects taught in the different rooms – physics, history, philosophy, mathematics.

Ermida de São Brás (BZ) – This fortified 15C church has rounded buttresses covered with pepper pot roofs; the chancel is covered with a dome on squinches.

Convento de São Bento de Castris ⊙ – *3km/2mi to the northwest by* ⑤ *on N 114-1.* After passing the aqueduct built by Francisco de Arruda in the 16C, turn left to the former Monastery of São Bento de Castris.

The Manueline style **church** has network vaulting, walls covered with 18C *azulejos* illustrating the life of St Bernard, and a Gothic chapter house with traces of Renaissance influence in its decoration.

The **cloisters★** in the Luso-Moorish style are as cool and elegant as when they were first built in the 16C. Above a gallery of paired horseshoe arches is an upper gallery with basket-handle arches.

EXCURSION

Tour of Megalithic sites – *75km/47mi* – *about 3hr 30min*. The Évora region is rich in Megalithic monuments – dolmens, caves and cromlechs – that date from between 4000 and 2000 BC. To see them, you will take narrow country roads through a beautiful part of the Alentejo dotted with cork oaks.

Leave Évora by ⑤ on the plan and take the N 114 westwards towards Montemor-o-Nova. After 10km/6mi bear left for Guadalupe and follow the signs to "Cromeleque e menir dos Almendres". From Guadalupe take an unsurfaced road for 3km/2mi.

Cromeleque dos Almendres – Standing in a clearing among cork oaks are 95 granite monoliths arranged in an oval, measuring 60 x 30m/200 x 100ft.

Return to Guadalupe. On the way, near the Água de Lupe Cooperative, there is a 2.5m/8ft high menhir. From Guadalupe take an unsurfaced road to Valverde then follow the signs to "Anta de Zambujeiro" on the Alcáçovas road.

Anta do Zambujeiro – A tumulus or access gallery precedes the dolmen itself which forms a vast funerary chamber 6m/20ft high. The many artefacts discovered here are now in the Museu Regional.

Return to Valverde and head for São Brissos. Do not turn into São Brissos but continue along the road for another 2km/1.2mi.

Capela-anta de São Brissos – The chapel narthex is formed by the dolmen.

Continue westwards and turn right before Santiago do Escoural.

Gruta do Escoural ⊙ – The cave's paintings and engravings of oxen, horses and hybrid figures have been dated between 18000 and 13000 BC.

ÉVORAMONTE★

Évora – Population 935
Michelin map 940 P 6

The small fortified town of Évoramonte has a remarkable **setting★**, having been built at the top of a high hill in the Alentejo.

It was at Évoramonte on 26 May 1834 that the Convention was signed which ended the civil war and under which the liberal son of João VI, Pedro IV, Emperor of Brazil, compelled his brother Miguel I, an extremist whom he had vanquished at the Battle of Asseiceira, to abdicate in favour of his niece Maria and to go into exile.

Access – *1.5km/1mi from the modern village. Follow the signs to "Castelo de Évoramonte". After skirting the base of the 14-17C ramparts, go through the entrance gate.* The peaceful, attractive village surrounding the unusual keep consists of well-kept, low-built houses, brilliantly white with flowered balconies.

★Castelo ⊙ – The castle which was first Roman, then Moorish, then radically remodelled in the 14C, emerges as a Gothic style military monument in spite of further reconstruction in the 16C. The medieval keep is girdled by rope motifs which knot in the middle of each façade. The House of Bragança, with its motto *Despois vós, nós* (After you, us), had chosen knots as its symbol on account of the double meaning of the word *nós* (us and knots).

Inside, each of the castle's three superimposed storeys consists of a hall with nine Gothic arches resting on sturdy central pillars, those on the ground floor being massive and twisted.

Castelo de Évoramonte

From the top, there is a **panorama★** of the surrounding countryside speckled with olive trees and small white villages, and to the northeast, Estremoz.

Casa da Convenção – The house where the Convention was signed bears a commemorative plaque.

Igreja Matriz – The parish church, with its original transverse bell gable, has a distinctive outline as it stands at the end of the main street.

Use the Index to find more information about a subject mentioned in the guide – towns, places, isolated sights, historical events or figures.

FARO★

Faro – Population 28 622
Michelin map 940 U6 – Local map see ALGARVE

The capital of Algarve is sited on Portugal's most southerly headland. Faro lives on salt collected from the salt marshes in its *ria*, fishing (tunny and sardine), its cork factories and marble works, food processing (beans) and canning, its plastics and building industries.
The building of the airport nearby has turned Faro into the main arrival point for year-round visitors attracted to the seaside resorts all along the Algarve coast. The vast sand beach of Faro, situated on an island, also attracts a great many tourists.

Historical notes – Faro was already an important city when, in 1249, Afonso III recaptured it from the Moors and so marked the end of Arab power in Portugal. The king presented the city with a municipal charter and its development was such that by the 15C a printing works belonging to the Jewish community was publishing Hebraic incunabula, the first books to be printed in Portugal.
Unfortunately in July 1596, when the country was under Spanish domination, Charles Howard and Robert, second Earl of Essex, who had been sent by Elizabeth in an expedition against Cádiz, sacked and then burnt the town to the ground. As Faro sought to rise from the ruins two earthquakes in 1722 and 1755, particularly the latter, reduced all to rubble once more. It needed the vigour of Bishop Dom Francisco Gomes, the town's most famous citizen, to undertake its reconstruction. The prelate passed his entire episcopacy encouraging, advising, building and planting throughout his diocese so that the people would learn the best agricultural methods and the best trees and plants to grow for the re-establishment of the town and its environs.

The Algarve almond trees – The Algarve is famous for its beaches, but its hinterland is equally beautiful with groves of fig, orange and almond trees. Legend has it that a Moorish emir married to a Scandinavian princess who yearned for her Nordic snows, ordered a vast sweep of almond trees to be planted in his domain. One January morning, the princess was amazed to see the countryside covered in myriad almond flowers, the dazzling, snow-like whiteness of which gave her great pleasure.

★OLD TOWN

The old town lies south of the Jardim Manuel Bivar, a peaceful quarter resting in the shadow of the circle of houses which stand like ramparts around it.

Arco da Vila – The Arco da Vila is the finest of the gateways in the old Alfonso wall. It has Italian-style pilasters and, in a niche, a white marble statue of St Thomas Aquinas.

Sé – The cathedral, which was rebuilt in the 18C, stands behind a heavy porch, supporting an exterior belfry at one side. It is decorated throughout, most noticeably in the Rosary Chapel (Capela do Rosário), with 17C *azulejos*. It preserves a **bell tower** ⊙ from the earlier Gothic cathedral which affords beautiful views of the town and the coast.

Near the cathedral, the **Galeria do Trem** ⊙ (rua do Trem) and the **Galeria do Arco** ⊙ (Beco do Arco) are art galleries exhibiting works by contemporary Portuguese and international artists.

Museu Municipal ⊙ (**M²**) – The municipal museum is in the former Convent of Nossa Senhora de Assunçao which dates from the 16C and has been restored.

The archaeological collection (**Museu Arqueológico Lapilar do Infante Dom Henrique**) is housed in the cloister galleries built by Afonso Pires and contains various remains found at Milreu *(see ALGARVE)* – capitals, mosaics, a Roman tomb from the 1C AD, a 15C sarcophagus, a 16C bishop's throne and ancient weapons and coins. Moorish earthenware jars and Mudejar *azulejos* evoke the Muslim and post-Muslim periods of local art.

The **Ferreira de Almeida collection** on the first floor includes sculptures, 18C paintings and Spanish and Chinese furniture.

During the summer months, concerts (classical, jazz, *fado* etc) are held in the chapel. A programme of events is available at the Tourist Office.

ADDITIONAL SIGHTS

Sea front – The life of the resort revolves around the harbour (**doca**) which has character and a certain elegance due to the 15m/45ft **obelisk** (**A**) standing in the middle of Praça Dom Francisco Gomes, the wide avenues as well as the palms bordering Avenida da República, particularly those standing in the Jardim Manuel Bivar.

Museu Marítimo ⊙ (**M¹**) – The Maritime Museum is in the harbour-master's office. The most noteworthy exhibits are the many model ships and the displays of different types of fishing, for tunny, sardines, octopus etc.

FARO

Conselheiro Bivar (Rua) .... **A** 9
D. F. Gomes (Pr. e Rua) .... **A** 12
Ivens (Rua) .... **A** 20
Santo António (Rua de) .... **A** 27
1º de Maio (Rua) .... **A** 31

Alex. Herculano (Praça) .... **A** 3
Ataíde de Oliveira (Rua) .... **B** 4

Bocage (Rua do) .... **A** 6
Carmo (Largo do) .... **A** 7
Cruz das Mestras (Rua) .... **A** 10
Dr Teixeira Guedes
  (Rua) .... **B** 13
Eça de Queirós .... **B** 15
Ferreira de Almeida (Praça) .... **A** 16
Filipe Alistão (Rua) .... **A** 18
Francisco Barreto (R.) .... **A** 19
Lethes (Rua) .... **A** 21

Moagem (R. da) .... **A** 22
Mouras Velhas (Largo das) ...... **A** 23
Pé da Cruz (Largo do) .... **B** 24
S. Pedro (Largo de) .... **A** 25
São Sebastião (Largo de) .... **A** 28

A   Obelisco
M² Museu Municipal
M³ Museu de Etnografia Regional

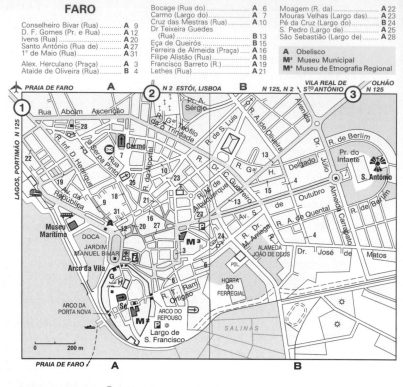

Igreja do Carmo ⊙ – This baroque church hides, abutting on its north transept near the tombs of a former graveyard, the **Capela dos Ossos**, an ossuary chapel entirely faced with bones and skulls.

Museu de Etnografia Regional ⊙ (**M³**) – This Ethnography Museum evokes traditional life in the Algarve, with photographs, paintings, everyday objects, models (one of which is a *madrague:* the huge net formerly used to catch tunny fish), reconstructions (a grocer's shop, interior of a peasant's house with the kitchen, stables and bread oven) and models displaying costumes etc.

Miradouro de Santo António ⊙ – In the courtyard is a small museum devoted to St Antony. From the belfry belvedere, at the top of some steep stairs, the **panorama★** spreads out over the town and the lagoon.

Faro beach (Praia) – *9km/6mi by ①, on N 125 and then on a signposted road on the left, or by boat – from the Arco da Porta Nova landing stage.*
This belt of sand connected with the mainland by a bridge has been turned into a beach resort. From the eastern end there is a good **view★** of Faro and its white houses reflected in the lagoon.

FÁTIMA

Santarém – Population 7 298
Michelin map 940 N4

The sanctuary at Fátima, one of the most famous in the world, stands at a place called **Cova da Iria** (alt 346m/1 135ft) in a landscape of green hills. Great pilgrimages numbering thousands of believers visit the shrine on the 13th of every month, especially on 13 May and 13 October, the dates of the first and final apparitions. However, 13 May is by far the most frequented. Many travel to the shrine on foot and, along every road that crosses the plateau, an impressive number of pilgrims may be seen.

The apparitions – On 13 May 1917, three young shepherds, **Francisco, Jacinta** and **Lúcia**, were minding their sheep at Cova da Iria when suddenly the sky lit up: the Virgin appeared before them standing in an oak tree, and spoke. Her message, which was repeated insistently and gravely at each apparition on the 13th of every subsequent month, was a call for peace. It was particularly apt since Europe had then been at war for three years, Portugal fighting with the Allies. On 13 October 1917, 70 000 people waiting for what turned out to be the last apparition, saw the rain suddenly stop and the sun shine and begin to revolve in the sky like a ball of fire. It was only in 1930 that the Bishop of Leiria authorised the celebration of belief in Our Lady of Fátima.

THE PILGRIMAGE

Basílica – Closing the end of the huge esplanade (540 x 160m/1772 x 525ft) is the neo-classical basilica (capacity: more than 300 000 pilgrims) which is extended on either side by a semicircular peristyle and dominated by a 65m/200ft tower. Inside are the tombs of Francisco and Jacinta who died in 1919 and 1920. The oldest of the three, Lúcia, is now a nun in a convent near Coimbra.

Capela das Aparições – An evergreen oak grows on the esplanade, replacing the one in which the Virgin appeared. Nearby, on the spot where the Virgin appeared, the Chapel of the Apparitions contains a statue to Our Lady of Fátima.

The great pilgrimages – The great pilgrimages include processions with burning torches, nocturnal vigils, the celebration of solemn masses on the esplanade, the benediction of the sick and finally "farewell" processions.
The fervour of the thousands of pilgrims at prayer, many of whom cover the approaches to the basilica on their knees, is deeply moving.

Nossa Senhora de Fátima pilgrimage

SIGHT

Museu de Cera ⊘ – This museum contains a beautifully rendered pageant of 28 tableaux recounting the story of the apparitions.

★THE PARQUE NACIONAL DAS SERRAS DE AIRE AND DE CANDEEIROS

The nature reserve covers an area of 35 000ha/86 450 acres in the Serra de Aire and the Serra dos Candeeiros between Batalha, Rio Maior and Fátima. The chalky heights of the *serras* pitted with caves make an impressive, arid landscape which has a certain charm. Roads bordered with a few eucalyptus wind through the park, keeping to the side of white ridges dotted with olive trees and streaked with low drystone walls. The main towns are **Porto de Mós**, the restored castle of which can be seen from afar, perched on a hillock with its strange green roof, and **Mira de Aire**, known for its handicraft work.

★**Grutas de Mira de Aire** ⊘ – *In the village, to the right of the N 243 going towards Porto de Mós.*
These caves, the biggest in Portugal, which are also called the Old Windmill Caves **(Grutas dos Moinhos Velhos)**, discovered in 1947 and then linked together by artificial tunnels, total a length of more than 4km/2.5mi *(a short section is open to visitors)* and reach a depth of 110m/360ft. The path spiralling down has 683 steps. From chamber to gallery the sight is impressive, especially in the two biggest caves, the "Grand Salon" and the "Red Chamber". The reddish tinted walls, due to iron oxide, the opalescence of the rock deposits with evocative shapes ("jewels" from the Pearl Chapel; the Medusa, the Martian, the Organ, etc), the sound of subterranean water, all exert their fascination. In the vast end gallery you can marvel at the "Great Lake" which collects all the water from the streams and the "Black River" which rises several days a year and floods the lower part of the caves.

Return by lift.

Grutas de São Mamede ⊙ – *From Cova da Iria (Fátima), 7.5km/4.5mi on the N 356 towards Batalha, take the road to Mira de Aire on the left, then the access lane to the caves on the left upon leaving the village of São Mamede.*

These are the most recently prospected caves (1971). A legend whereby bandits were said to have hurled down the body of a traveller along with his purse in their excessive haste, has led them to be called the Money Caves, **Grutas da Moeda**. One can count up to nine "chambers", and the variety of colours and folds therein, a waterfall, strange multicoloured calcarious deposits in the Shepherd's Chamber, are worth seeing.

Grutas de Alvados ⊙ – *Access by the N 361 between Alvados and Serra de San António.*

These were discovered in 1964 on the northwest flank of the Pedra de Altar hill. They extend for 450m/1/3mi across about ten chambers – linked artificially by long tunnels – each has its small limpid lake and colourful rock deposits. They have an additional attraction due to the golden colour of the walls, the number of stalactites and stalagmites joined together forming pillars, and the zigzag cracks in the ground. In the biggest chamber, 42m/138ft high, where stray animals used to fall in, remains can still be seen.

Grutas de Santo António ⊙ – *Access by the N 361 to the north of Serra de Santo António.*

These caves were discovered in 1955, near the top of the Pedra do Altar hill. An access tunnel had to be constructed for visitors. The three chambers (the main one with an area of 4 000m²/4 784sq yards is 43m/141ft high) and a short gallery all have delicate rose-coloured concretions. In one of the secondary chambers there is a small lake.

The main interest of the caves lies in the veritable forest of stalagmites found there, some of which appear as statuesque figures enacting a frozen melodrama.

FIGUEIRA DA FOZ★

Coimbra – Population 13 397
Michelin map 940 or 441 L3

Figueira da Foz, which commands the mouth of the Mondego river, is overlooked from behind by the Serra da Boa Viagem. The most unusual view of the town is from the Galã road to the south as it runs through the local salt marshes.

Figueira, which was built in the last century, lives primarily from its fishing industry (sardines and cod) and its shipyards.

Tourists congregate in the new quarter on the west side of the town, attracted by the vast beach of fine sand which lines the wide curve of Figueira Bay. This bay, previously known as Mondego Bay and overlooked by a fort of golden stone, captured from the French by students of Coimbra University but a short time before, was where Wellington landed the first British troops in August 1808. From Figueira began the advance south which was to bring the first battles of the Peninsular Campaign not far from Óbidos at Roliça and Vimeiro.

A century and a half later Figueiro presents itself as a pleasant resort where the amusements are social, sporting, and traditional – casino, concerts, theatre, swimming, tennis, regattas, and the midsummer festivals of St John on 23 and 24 June and the pardon of Our Lady of Incarnation from 7 to 9 September.

Museu Municipal Dr. Santos Rocha ⊙ – *Rua Calouste Gulbenkian.* The museum, installed along with the public library in a modern building, has an interesting archaeological section (note the stele bearing an Iberian inscription), as well as painting, sculpture and decorative art (earthenware and furniture) sections.

EXCURSION

Serra da Boa Viagem – *Round tour of 20km/12mi – about 45min. Leave Figueira da Foz heading northwest along the coastal road.*

The small fishing village and resort of **Buarcos** can be seen from the road. After going past a large cement works on the left, the road runs beside the sea to reach, again on the left, the Cabo Mondego lighthouse. The road continues through the forest of pines, acacias and eucalyptus which cloak the *serra*. Turn right towards the village of Boa Viagem.

A little before Boa Viagem, the view widens out to beautiful vistas on the right of the bay of Figueira da Foz and the mouth of the Mondego river.

Book well in advance
as vacant hotel rooms are often scarce in high season.

FREIXO DE ESPADA-à-CINTA

Bragança – Population 2 338
Michelin map 940 or 441 I 9

The shale and granite town of Freixo lies in a fertile basin before range upon range of mountains. It was the birthplace of the satirical poet **Guerra Junqueiro** (1850-1923).

★ **Igreja Matriz** – This hall church built at the end of the Gothic period has a lovely Gothic doorway adorned by a few Renaissance motifs. The interior, in which stands a fine wrought iron pulpit, is covered by network vaulting; the **chancel★**, whose vaulting is adorned with emblazoned hanging keystones, contains a gilded wood altar with turned columns and a canopy; the walls are lined with 16C painted panelling.

Pelourinho – The Manueline style pillory is crowned with a carving of a human head.

GUARDA

Guarda – Population 14 803
Michelin map 940 or 441 K8

Guarda, a pleasant health resort and the highest town in Portugal, stands at an altitude of 1 000m/3 281ft in the eastern foothills of the Serra da Estrela. Its name "protector" recalls that at one time it was the main stronghold of the province of Beira Alta near Spain. Medieval castles and fortresses are dotted throughout the region guarding the border.

Over the last few years the town has sprouted modern quarters around its medieval centre which is enclosed within the remains of ancient fortifications.

A strategic site – Taken over since prehistoric times, the site of Guarda served as a military base for Julius Caesar (so it is believed) before giving support to the Roman town of Lancia Oppidana, and then a Visigothic fortress which was soon overwhelmed by the Arab conquest. The town, recaptured from the Moors by Afonso Henriques was enlarged and fortified at the end of the 12C, under Dom Sancho I. Dom Dinis I stayed here.

After having driven back the Spanish, Guarda, nevertheless, failed to retain its role of "protector" at the time of the French invasion in 1808.

SIGHTS

Antigas fortificações – The best preserved remains of the fortifications are the Torre dos Ferreiros (Blacksmiths' Tower), the 12 and 13C keep or Torre de Menagem and the Porta d'El Rei and Porta da Estrela (King's and Star Gates).

Remains of the fortifications, Guarda

P. Mattes/EXPLORER

★**Sé** ◷ – The cathedral was begun in 1390 in the Gothic style, but as it was only completed in 1540, Renaissance and Manueline elements are clearly visible in its decoration. The granite edifice is crowned with pinnacles and trefoils which give it a certain resemblance to the monastery at Batalha.

Exterior – The northern façade is embellished with an ornate Gothic doorway surmounted by a Manueline window. In the main façade, a Manueline doorway is framed by two octagonal towers emblazoned at their bases with the coat of arms of Bishop Dom Pedro Vaz Gavião, who played an important part in getting the cathedral completed in the 16C.

★**Interior** – The lierne and tierceron vaulting over the transept crossing has a keystone in the form of a cross of the Order of Christ. In the chancel is a Renaissance altarpiece made of Ançã stone in the 16C, gilded in the 18C. Attributed to Jean de Rouen, the high relief which includes more than one hundred figures depicts, on four levels from the base to the top, scenes in the Lives of the Virgin and Jesus Christ. A 16C altarpiece in the south apsidal chapel, also attributed to Jean de Rouen, represents the Last Supper.

The Pinas Chapel which opens through a beautiful Renaissance doorway off the north aisle contains a fine Gothic tomb complete with a reclining figure.

A staircase erected at the corner of the south transept leads to the cathedral's roof, from where one can look out over the town and the Serra da Estrela.

Casa Antigas (Old Houses) – Many 16 and 18C houses bearing coats of arms are to be seen surrounding the cathedral square, Praça Luis de Camões or Largo da Sé, and lining Rua Francisco de Passos and Rua Dom Miguel de Alarcão (no 25). Overlooking the square behind the cathedral is the fine granite manor of **Solar de Alarcão**.

Museu Regional ◷ – The regional museum is housed at the foot of the ramparts in the former bishop's palace which dates from the early 17C and has preserved its Renaissance cloisters. The collections include displays of regional archaeology and ethnology as well as painting and sculpture.

THE EASTERN FORTIFIED TOWNS

Distances indicated are from Guarda – local map below

Medieval strongholds or fortified towns built in the 17-18C to protect the border, and numerous fortified small towns or villages, still seem to mount guard at the top of a hillock or a steep headland, in the heart of the Beira Alta.

★**Almeida** – *49km/30mi to the northeast.*
Less than 10km/6mi from the border, the peaceful little town of Almeida crowns a hill 729m/2 491ft high with its ramparts. Taken by the Spanish in 1762, then by the French under Massena in 1810, it has, nevertheless, kept intact its double **fortifications★**, in the form of a six pointed star in pure Vauban style, completed in the 18C. Three arched gateways *(sound horn when driving in)* with monumental porches preceded by bridges, give access to the interior, where one can see the old barrack buildings (near the north gate) which were used as a prison from 1828 to 1833, and a few lovely mansions, some covered with *azulejos.*

Castelo Bom – *39km/24mi to the east.*
Medieval fortress dating from King Dinis, this village clustered round a hill has only one ruined tower remaining, next to a Gothic gate, and a lovely 16C house.

★**Castelo Melhor** – *77km/ 47.5mi to the northeast.*
Visible from the N 222, the village clings to the flanks of a rocky peak dotted with

olive trees. A medieval **wall★** reinforced with round towers encircles the grassy and bare summit.

A Reception Centre for visits to the rock art discoveries in the Parque Arqueológico do Vale de Côa is located here *(see VALE DE CÔA)*.

Castelo Mendo – *35km/ 21.5mi to the east.*
Cobbled alleys crisscross on a rocky hillock among the remains of a Gothic wall, where the main gate is wedged between two towers. The village still has the marks of a flourishing past; a few Renaissance buildings and others dating from the Spanish domination, a 17C church; in front of it stands the highest pillory in the province (7m/23ft) dating from the 16C. It has an octagonal shaft topped by a cage with small columns. The peasant houses of granite have a flight of steps each side forming a veranda. From the summit, which has the remains of a keep and a chapel with a belfry tower, there is a view of the deep valley of the Cô river.

Celorico da Beira – *28km/17.5mi to the northwest.*
This busy small town is on the extreme north of a wooded ridge at the end of the Serra da Estrela. The square keep of the ancient castle rises up at the top, surrounded by a small wall. Extensive view.

Linhares – *49km/30mi to the west (the last 6km/3.5mi after Carrapichana are on a winding road).*
The very beautiful outer wall of the castle built at the time of Dinis I, with its two square crenellated towers, runs round the top of a granite spur dominating the Upper Valley of the Mondego. The village has a 16C pillory with an armillary sphere.

Marialva – *69km/43mi to the north.*
The remains of a castle built in 1200 cover a rocky ridge which has extensive views over the Bevesa plain. Between the ruins of the outer wall, a crenellated keep and another tower still set in its wall, there are scattered ruins of the old village, a 15C pillory, and a church with a Manueline doorway.

★Sortelha – *45km/28mi to the south.*
This 12C **stronghold★**, hemming in the old village with its picturesque granite houses, stands on a spur dominating the Upper Zêzere valley. You enter it by one of the majestic Gothic gates of the fortified wall, where the two existing square towers have their own surrounding wall, with machicolated gateways.
From the watchpath (mind the wind), there are impressive **views★** over the valley.

Other fortresses in the Guarda region are described in this guide. **Belmonte** *(22km/13.5mi to the south – see BELMONTE),* **Castelo Rodrigo** *(54km/33mi to the northeast – see PINHEL: Excursions),* **Penedono** *(74km/46mi to the north – see PENEDONO),* **Sabugal** *(33km/21mi to the southeast – see SABUGAL),* **Trancoso** *(47km/30mi to the north – see TRANCOSO).*

GUIMARÃES★★

Braga – Population 22 092
Michelin map 940 or 441 H5

In the 10C, soon after it was founded by the Countess Mumadona, Guimarães consisted of a monastery with a defensive tower and a few neighbouring houses. In the Middle Ages and later, new quarters were added to the south.

Nowadays Guimarães is a prosperous commercial city with cotton and linen spinning and weaving mills, cutlery, tanning and kitchenware industries and equally successful craft industries such as gold and silversmithing, pottery, embroidery, the weaving of linen damask and the carving of wooden yokes.

The cradle of Portugal – In 1095 Alfonso VI, King of León and Castile, bestowed the County of Portucale on his son-in-law, Henry of Burgundy. Henry had the tower at Guimarães converted into a castle and installed his wife the Princess Teresa (Tareja) there. In about 1110 Teresa bore Henry a son, **Afonso Henriques**, who succeeded his father in 1112. The young prince revolted against the notorious misconduct of his mother, who had acted as regent, and on 24 June 1128 seized power following the Battle of São Mamede. Then he campaigned against the Moors and succeeded in vanquishing them at Ourique on 25 July 1139. In the course of the campaign Afonso was proclaimed King of Portugal by his troops, a choice confirmed by the Cortes at Lamego and his cousin Alfonso VII, King of Léon and Castile in the Treaty of Zamora of 1143.

Gil Vicente (1470-1536) – The poet and goldsmith, Gil Vicente, born in Guimarães in 1470, lived at the courts of King João II and King Manuel I. He wrote plays – farces and tragicomedies – to entertain the king and the court, and mysteries *(autos)* to be performed in the churches. His forty-four plays provide a precise if satirical panorama of Portuguese society at the beginning of the 16C, while the variety of his inspiration allied to the lightness of his touch and finesse of his style make him the virtual creator of the Portuguese theatre.

CASTLE HILL

★Castelo ⊘ – In the 10C Countess Mumadona had the 28m/92ft keep built to protect the monastery and small town in its midst. The castle was later built under Henry of Burgundy and reinforced in the 15C. Seven square towers surround the keep. From the ramparts there is a wide **view** over Guimarães dominated to the south by Mount Penha.

Igreja de São Miguel do Castelo ⊘ (**A**) – This small 12C Romanesque church contains a font in which it is said Afonso Henriques was christened, in addition to a great many funerary slabs.

GUIMARÃES

Paio Galvão (Rua)................... 15
Santo António (Rua de) 19
Toural (Largo do) 22

Alberto Sampaio
  (Avenida)............................ 3
Dom A. Henriques
  (Avenida)............................ 4
Duques de Bragança (Rua) ... 6
Humberto Delgado (Avenida) 7
João Franco (Largo de) 9
Mumadona (Praça de) 10
Nuno Álvares (Rua)............... 12
Oliveira (Largo da)................ 13
Rainha (Rua da).................... 16
San Tiago (Praça de) 18
Serpa Pinto (Rua).................. 21

A   Igreja de S. Miguel do Castelo
E   Paços do Concelho
M²   Museu Martins Sarmento

★Paço dos Duques de Bragança ⊘ – The palace was built in the early 15C by the first Duke of Bragança, Afonso I, natural son of King Dom João I. The architecture shows a strong Burgundian influence particularly in the roof and the unusual 39 brick chimneys. The palace was one of the most sumptuous dwellings in the Iberian Peninsula until the 16C when the court moved to Vila Viçosa after which it was seldom visited.

The palace was thoroughly restored to its original appearance in 1933. In the front stands a bronze statue of Afonso Henriques by Soares dos Reis (late 19C).

The palace consists of four buildings with massive corner towers, surrounding a courtyard, and crowned with machicolated battlements.

Interior – The vast rooms were heated by huge fireplaces. On the first floor the eye is caught by the **ceilings★** of oak and chestnut in the Dining and Banqueting Halls and the 16 and 18C **tapestries★** (Aubusson, Flanders and Gobelins). The Tournai tapestries depicting the capture of Arzila and Tangier are in fact copies of the series woven after cartoons by Nuno Gonçalves (the originals are in the sacristy of the collegiate church in the Spanish town of Pastrana).

Other decoration includes Persian carpets, 17C Portuguese furniture, Chinese porcelain, weapons and armour as well as Dutch and Italian paintings.

THE HISTORICAL CENTRE

Wide avenues mark the limits of the historic quarter which makes a pleasant stroll with its maze of streets and squares bordered by old houses.

Convento de Nossa Senhora da Oliveira – The monastery dedicated to Our Lady of the Olive Tree was founded by Countess Mumadona in the 10C. Several buildings have since been erected in succession on this same site. Only the Gothic collegiate church with its Romanesque cloisters and chapter house (now the museum) remains.

Colegiada de Nossa Senhora da Oliveira – The main doorway of this collegiate church is surmounted by a 14C Gothic pediment. Inside, note the silver altar in the Chapel of the Holy Sacrament (Capela do Santíssimo Sacramento).

A Gothic **shrine** in front of the church commemorates the victory over the Moors at the Battle of the Salado in 1340. Legend has it that during the completion of the porch in 1342 the trunk of the olive tree, which stood in front of the church, suddenly sprouted leaves: thus, the church's name.

*Museu Alberto Sampaio ⊘ – The museum is housed in the conventual buildings. The 13C Romanesque cloisters have interesting historiated capitals. In the east corner of the cloisters is a door from the former 10C Monastery of Mumadona.

In a Gothic chapel to the right on entering is the fine **recumbent figure** in granite of Dona Constança de Noronha, wife of Dom Afonso, first Duke of Bragança. Rooms off the cloisters contain paintings of the Portuguese School, especially some by António Vaz, who was born at Guimarães, and baroque altarpieces. The chapter-house has a fine 16C coffered ceiling, and there is an interesting collection of ceramics, porcelain and *azulejos*.

On the first floor, note several statues including the 15C alabaster statue of Our Lady of Pity and a large wooden altarpiece from the 17C. The galleries that follow contain **church plate★**. Much of the collegiate church treasure was donated by Dom João I. In addition to the tunic worn by João I at the Battle of Aljubarrota, is the silver-gilt **triptych★** said to have been taken by the king from the Castilians at the battle. It shows in the centre, the Nativity, on the left, the Annunciation, the Purification and the Presentation at the Temple and on the right the shepherds and the Magi. Among other pieces of the treasure, note a silver-gilt Gothic chalice with enamel embossing, a Manueline monstrance attributed to Gil Vicente and a finely engraved 16C Manueline **cross★** depicting scenes from the Passion.

Paços do Concelho (**E**) – Facing the collegiate church is the former town hall, a 16C Manueline building with an arcaded gallery on the ground floor which has pointed arches and dates from the 14C. Beside it is the **Pousada de Oliveira**.

*Praça de São Tiago (**18**) – The small square has kept its medieval charm with its old corbelled houses with wide overhanging roofs.

Rua de Santa Maria – This follows the course of the lane that linked the monastery founded by Countess Mumadona to the castle. Best seen on foot, it is lined by 14 and 15C houses with wrought-iron grilles and carved granite cornices.

ADDITIONAL SIGHTS

Largo do Toural (**22**) – This picturesque square with a wave-like mosaic pavement is a good example of classical urban architecture. Old houses with mansard roofs surround it, their vast windows are adorned with fine wrought-iron grilles.

Museu Martins Sarmento ⊘ (**M²**) – The museum, which is housed partly in the Gothic cloisters of the Church of São Domingos, includes a large collection of archaeological exhibits from the pre-Roman cities of Sabroso and Briteiros *(see BRAGA)*.

Igreja de São Francisco – The church was built early in the 15C but was remodelled in the 17C so that only the main door and the east end have retained their original Gothic character. The capitals in the main doorway represent the legend

Altarpiece, Igreja de São Francisco

of St Francis. The interior suffered some unfortunate remodellings in the 17 and 18C. The chancel, which contains a baroque altar carved in wood and gilded, is decorated with 18C **azulejos**★ depicting the life of St Anthony.

In the **sacristy**★ ⊘ *(access through the south transept)* one can see a fine coffered ceiling ornamented with grotesques and an Arrábida marble table standing against an elegant Carrara marble column.

The chapter house, which gives onto 16C Renaissance cloisters, is closed by a fine Gothic grille.

Note, to the right of the church, a beautiful façade adorned with *azulejos*.

EXCURSIONS

Penha – *Round tour of 17km/11mi. Leave Guimarães on N 101 going towards Felgueiras. After Mesão Frio, turn right towards Penha; the road immediately begins to rise as it winds between pines and eucalyptus trees.*

Penha stands on the highest part of the Serra de Santa Catarina.

Cross the esplanade before the Basílica de Nossa Senhora da Penhal and continue along the road to the statue of St Catherine where you park your car.

There is a vast **panorama**★ of the Serra do Marão to the south and Guimarães and the Serra do Gerês to the north.

To return to Guimarães, bear left at the end of the esplanade into a narrow road, N 101-2, which winds downwards, working its way between rocks and trees.

★**Trofa** – *13km/8mi. Leave Guimarães on N 101 heading towards Amarante*. Trofa is a small village where the women make net and lace; they may be seen working and displaying their crafts (cloths and napkins) at the roadside.

Roriz – *17km/10mi. Leave Guimarães on N 105 heading south. Bear left on a sign-posted road 3km/2mi before Lordelo, N 209-2.*

An interesting Romanesque church stands beside an ancient monastery.

The exterior of this granite 11C church, **Igreja** ⊘, recalls that of Paço de Sousa. The plain but harmonious façade is pierced by a doorway adorned with capitals of carved foliage and animals, and columns embellished with shells in relief.

LAGOS ★

Faro – Population 10 504
Michelin map 940 U3 – Local map see ALGARVE

Lagos was the capital of the Algarve from 1576 to 1756. Today, in spite of great popularity with tourists, it has managed to preserve both character and charm with its fort, walls and old quarter.

The most attractive approaches to Lagos are from Aljezur in the north along the N 120 or from Vila do Bispo in the west along N 125. There are **views**★ from these two roads of the town and the development which now lines the bay. To the north of the bay rise the heights of the Serra de Monchique.

Apart from being a seaside resort and a fishing port well sheltered by the Ponta da Piedade promontory, Lagos is also an important yachting centre organising international regattas.

The harbour in the past – Lagos was an important harbour at the time of the Great Discoveries and it was from here that most of the African expeditions put to sea. It served as Prince Henry the Navigator's principal maritime base and as port of registry to Gil Eanes who, in 1434, rounded for the first time in history Cape Bojador, a point on the west coast of the Sahara which until then had been the last outpost of the habitable world. On Prince Henry's orders, one expedition followed another down the coast of Africa, each time adding to the knowledge of ocean currents and improving navigational techniques *(see Ponta de SAGRES and Cabo de SÃO VICENTE)*.

It was in the open sea off the bay that, in 1693, the French Admiral Tourville succeeded in sinking eighty ships of an Anglo-Dutch convoy commanded by Admiral Rooke who had defeated him the year before off the Normandy coast in the Battle of La Hougue.

SIGHTS

Park the car beside the harbour.

Muralhas – The ramparts were built on top of older walls between the 14 and 16C.

Praça Infante Dom Henrique (**29**) – A **statue of Prince Henry the Navigator**, inaugurated in 1960 for the 500th anniversary of his death, stands in the middle of the square. The house with arcades on the right side of the square is the former slave market, **Mercado de Escravos** (**A**). In the 15C, Europe's first slave markets were held here, following the African expeditions. The present building was reconstructed after the earthquake in 1755. It now houses temporary exhibitions.

LAGOS

Afonso do Almoida (Rua) ... 4
Cândido dos Reis (Rua)...... 7
Garrett (Rua)........................ 22
Gil Eanes (Praça)................. 25
Marquês de Pombal (Rua).. 37
Porta de Portugal (Rua da). 42

Adro (Rua do)..................... 3
Armas (Praça d')................. 5
Atalaia (Rua da).................. 6
Capelinha (Rua da)............. 9
Cardeal Netto (Rua) 10
Castelo dos Governadores . 12
Cemitério (Rua do) 13
Conselheiro J. Machado
(Rua) 15
Dr Joaquim Tello (Rua)....... 18
Dr Mendonça (Rua) 19
Forno (Travessa do)............ 21
Gen. Alberto Silveira (Rua) . 24
Henrique C. da Silva (Rua).. 27
Infante de Sagres (Rua)...... 28
João Bonança (Rua)............ 30
Lançarote de Freitas (Rua) . 33
Luís de Camões (Praça)...... 36
Marreiros Netto (Rua)........ 39
Ponta da Piedade
(Estr. da) 40
Prof. Luís de Azevedo (R.).. 43
República (Praça da).......... 44
Silva Lopes (Rua) 45
5 de Outubro (Rua)............. 46
25 de Abril (Rua)................ 48

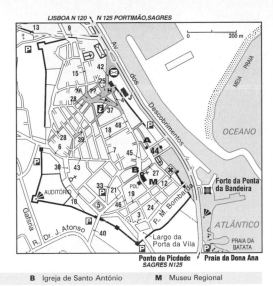

A Mercado de Escravos   **B** Igreja de Santo António   **M** Museu Regional

Take Rua Henrique Correia da Silva leading straight off the square.

★**Igreja de Santo António** ⏱ (**B**) – The plain façade gives no inkling of the exuberance and virtuosity of the **baroque decoration**★ which reigns inside. Outstanding are the ceiling painted in false relief, the Eucharistic symbols and statues of gilded wood in the chancel, the walls and the gallery ceiling.

Museu Regional ⏱ (**M**) – The regional museum adjoining the Igreja de Santo António contains an interesting archaeological collection (coins and fragments of mosaics) and an ethnographical section devoted to the Algarve (note the cork work).

Forte da Ponta da Bandeira ⏱ – The 17C fort juts out into the sea guarding a small harbour. There are boat trips from the harbour to Ponta da Piedade *(see photograph below)*. Cross the drawbridge to enter the inner courtyard. The halls contain displays on the Great Discoveries. The chapel is decorated with 17C *azulejos*. There is a **view** from the terrace of the town and the coast.

EXCURSIONS

★★**Ponta da Piedade** – *3km/2mi. From the harbour take the road leading to Sagres and at the place called Trinidad take the first road on the left as far as the lighthouse (car park).*

Forte da Ponta da Bandeira

133

The **setting**★★ of this seaside resort is what makes it especially attractive: reddish rocks worn by the ocean into swirling shaped boulders and **sea caves** contrast vividly with the clear green of the sea. *(There are boat trips to the caves ⊙).*
From behind the lighthouse, the **view**★ stretches from Cabo de São Vicente on the west to Cabo Carvoeiro on the east. By a small road on the left of the lighthouse, a belvedere affords a bird's eye view of the rocks and of the seaside resort of **Praia de Dona Ana**★.

★**Baragem da Bravura** – *14km/8.5mi. Leave Lagos by the N 125 going northeast towards Portimão.*
The road leading from Odiáxere to the Bravura Dam winds along an irrigated valley where melons, tomatoes, maize and figs all grow, before climbing the foothills of the Serra de Monchique with extensive **views** over the coastal ranges. The Odiáxere Dam closes the valley of the same name. To its west, a powered conduit directs water to the power station downstream from where it goes on to irrigate the 1 800ha/4 500 acres of agricultural land which lies between Lagos and Portimão.

LAMEGO
Viseu – Population 9 942
Michelin map 940 or 441 I6 – Local map see Vale do DOURO

Lamego is an attractive small episcopal and commercial town known for its sparkling wine and its smoked ham. It lies near the Douro Valley in a landscape of green hills covered with vines and maize.
The town, which is rich in 16 and 18C bourgeois houses, is overlooked by two hills on which stand respectively the ruins of a 12C fortified castle and the baroque Santuário de Nossa Senhora dos Remédios, famous for the annual pilgrimages held in late August-early September.

The Lamego Cortes – The first national assembly of representatives of the nobles, the clergy, and towns, was held in Lamego in 1143; it recognised Afonso Henriques as first King of Portugal and proclaimed the law of succession by which no foreigner should accede to the throne.

SIGHTS

★**Museu de Lamego** ⊙ – The museum is housed in the former episcopal palace, a majestic 18C building.
The right-hand section of the ground floor contains mainly religious sculpture from the Middle Ages to the baroque period and a fine collection of coats of arms which adorned the façades of mansions belonging to the nobility.
On the first floor two series of works – paintings and tapestries – are particularly noteworthy. The **five paintings on wood**★ (early 16C) by Vasco Fernandes were part of the altarpiece in Lamego's cathedral. From left to right they show the Creation, Annunciation, Visitation (the most outstanding in the series), the Presentation at the Temple and Circumcision. The six **16C Brussels tapestries**★ are of mythological scenes (note the myth of Œdipus and the rich composition of the Temple of Latone). On the first floor are two baroque chapels of carved and gilded wood, one of which, São João Evangelista from the Convento das Chagas, has statues and niches. There is also a Chinese room, gold and silver plate and ceramics.
The second ground-floor section contains another baroque chapel and some fine 16 and 18C *azulejos*, in particular polychromed ones from Palacio Valmor in Lisbon.

Sé – Of the original 12C Romanesque church there remains only the square belfry whose crown is 16C. The interior was redone in the 18C.

Capela do Desterro ⊙ – This chapel, built in 1640, is decorated inside with 18C carved and gilded woodwork and 17C *azulejos*; the coffered **ceiling**★ is outstanding with painted scenes from the Life of Our Lord.

Santuário de Nossa Senhora dos Remédios – A good overall view of this baroque building is gained from the bottom of the steps which lead up to it.
The 18C façade on which stucco serves to highlight the elegant granite curves, overlooks the crossed ramps of the **staircase** ornamented with *azulejos* and bristling with a multitude of pinnacles which recalls that of Bom Jesus near Braga.
The view from the church parvis *(access by car possible: 4km/2.5mi)* extends over Lamego to the heights on the horizon which border the Douro.

EXCURSIONS

Capela de São Pedro de Balsemão ⊙ – *3km/2mi east of Lamego. Follow the signs on the street opposite the Capela do Desterro.*
The 17C façade hides the sanctuary which is said to be the oldest in Portugal (7C: Visigothic period). In the small, squat interior with fishbone friezes on the walls, Roman stone has been reused. There are three naves divided by two rows of arches

supported on low columns crowned by stylised Corinthian capitals (one of which, at the chancel entrance, on the left, rests on a scrolled cushion typical of pre-Romanesque art). Note also the sarcophagus of Alfonso Pires, the Bishop of Oporto who died in 1362, carved with low reliefs of the Last Supper, the Crucifixion and a royal couple. The recumbent statue is accompanied by two angels. The painted ceiling and the baroque altarpieces date from the 17C.

The road to São João de Tarouca – *16km/10mi – about 45min. Leave Lamego south along the N 226 towards Trancoso.*

The road passes near **Ferreirim** *(2km/1.5mi on the left)* where, from 1532 to 1536, Cristóvão de Figueiredo worked with the help of Gregório Lopes and Garcia Fernandes on the altarpiece which was to adorn the monastery church.

Bear right 2km/1mi beyond the Tarouca road which branches off to the right.

São João de Tarouca – *See SÃO JOÃO DE TAROUCA.*

LEÇA DO BAILIO

Porto – Population 13 659
Michelin map 940 or 441 I4 – 8km/5mi north of Oporto

It is said that after the First Crusade, the domain of Leça do Bailio was given to brothers of the Order of the Hospital of St John of Jerusalem who had come from Palestine probably in the company of Count Henry of Burgundy, father of the first King of Portugal. Leça was the mother house of this Order (now the Order of Malta) until 1312 when this was transferred to Flor da Rosa.

★ **Igreja do Mosteiro** – This fortress church, built in granite in the Gothic period, is characterised outside by pyramid-shaped merlons emphasising the entablature by the tall battlemented tower surrounded with balconies and machicolated watch-towers, and by the very plain main façade adorned only with a door with carved capitals below and a rose window above.

The bare interior is well proportioned. The historiated capitals portray scenes from Genesis and the Gospels – of particular note are Adam and Eve with the serpent and the angel.

Several of the Hospitallers are buried here. The chancel, which has stellar vaulting, contains the 16C tomb of the Bailiff Frei Cristóvão de Cernache, which is surmounted by a painted statue (16C) and in the north apsidal chapel is the prior, Frei João Coelho's tomb, with a reclining figure by Diogo Pires the Younger (1515). The Manueline style **font**★, carved in Ançã stone by the same artist, is octagonal and rests on a pedestal adorned with acanthus leaves and fantastic animals.

LEIRIA

Leiria – Population 12 428
Michelin map 940 M3

Leiria is pleasantly situated at the confluence of two rivers, the Liz and the Lena, and at the foot of a hill crowned by a medieval castle.

Its role as a crossroads near well-known beaches – notably Nazaré – the sanctuary of Fátima and the magnificent architecture of Batalha and Alcobaça, makes it a favoured stop off place for the holidaymaker, the pilgrim and the art-loving tourist.

Craftsmanship and folklore – The Leiria region has kept alive its old tradition of popular art and folklore. The glazed and multicoloured pottery of Cruz da Légua and Milagres, the decorated glassware of Marinha Grande, the willow baskets and ornaments and the woven coverlets of Mira de Aire are among the best known crafts of the district.

The traditional festivals and customs have lost none of their spontaneity. The folklore of the Leiria Region is closely associated with that of its neighbour, the Ribatejo. The women's costume, which is not in the least showy, consists of a small black felt hat with feathers, a coloured blouse edged with lace, a short skirt and shoes with wide low heels. It differs from that of the Ribatejo only by the addition of a gold necklace and earrings. Folk dancing displays are held every year at the time of the Leiria exhibition-fair (first to last Sunday in May) and in particular on 22 May, the town's local holiday.

★CASTELO ⊙

In an exceptional **site**★, inhabited even before the arrival of the Romans, Afonso Henriques, first King of Portugal, had a fortified castle built in 1135. This castle formed part of the defence of the southern border of the kingdom of Portugal at the time, Santarém and Lisbon still being under Moorish domination. After the fall of these two cities in 1147, the castle lost its significance and fell into ruin. In the 14C, King Dinis, who undertook first the preservation and then the extension of the pine forest at Leiria, rebuilt the castle in order that he might live in it with his queen, Saint Isabel.

Tour – *About 30min*. The present buildings, modified in the 16C, were restored. After entering the first perimeter of castle walls through a door flanked by two square crenellated towers, you reach a pleasantly shaded garden courtyard. A stairway to the left leads to the centre of the castle. The royal palace is then on the left, the keep is straight ahead, and on the right the remains of the 15C chapel of Nossa Senhora da Pena with a graceful lanceolate Gothic chancel and an arcade decorated with Manueline motifs.

Paço Real (Royal Palace) – A staircase leads to a vast rectangular hall with a gallery adorned with depressed, three-centred arches resting on slender twin columns. The gallery, once the royal balcony, affords a good **view** of Leiria lying below.

LINDOSO★

Viana do Castelo – Population 837
Michelin map 940 or 441 G5 – Local map see Parque Nacional da PENEDA-GERÊS

Built like an amphitheatre against the southern flanks of one of the last mountains in the Serra do Soajo, Lindoso sets out its austere granite houses in tiered rows up to a height of 462m/1 516ft, perfectly integrated into the rocky landscape – despite the presence of a few recent constructions – and surrounded by cultivated terraces (maize, vines).

The castle stands on a hillock where there is also an unusual group of *espigueiros (see below)*.

From Ponte da Barca to Lindoso – *31km/20mi*. The road, bordered with pine trees, tangerine trees and oleanders, winds about on the wooded slope of the Serra do Soajo, with a view of the arid and rocky Serra da Peneda which rises on the other side of the Lima valley. At the crossroads with the road leading to Entre-Ambos-os-Rios, continue on the N 203 which starts a steep climb into the Parque Nacional da Peneda-Gerês and has views overlooking the meandering river, which is enlarged by a dam upstream. It ends up as a corniche road, and stops when it reaches the castle of Lindoso.

★**Espigueiros (Granaries)** – Covering a rocky platform at the foot of the castle, the sixty or more *espigueiros*, are strangely grouped together, resembling a cemetery. They are small granite buildings, perched on piles, and most of them have one or two crosses on the roof. Their very careful construction dates back to the 18 and 19C. They are still used today for drying maize.

Castelo ⊙ – Facing the border, the castle was inevitably attacked several times by the army of Philip IV of Spain during the War of Independence in the 17C. Restored, it appears again as a crenellated feudal keep in the middle of a small 17C square surrounding wall with bastions and watch turrets. From the watch-path there are views over the Lima valley and the surrounding Portuguese and Galician mountains.

Fernando António Nogueira Pessoa
1888-1935

Born in Lisbon, where he also ended his days, Pessoa was a
Modernist poet and novelist who brought Portuguese literature
into the realm of European significance.

Pessoa learned English in South Africa, where his father served
in the Portuguese diplomatic corps, and wrote his first poems in that
language. A bilingual edition of his *English Poems* was published
in Lisbon (Edições Ática) in 1994.

He returned to Lisbon at the age of 17 and put his language skills
to work as a translator. At the same time, he began contributing to
the Modernist review *Orpheu* and other avant-garde publications.
While most Portuguese literature at the time was strongly influenced
by French trends, Pessoa expressed the unique influence of his own
experiences in the English-speaking world of Durban.

In 1918, he began publishing works in English;
his first book in Portuguese, *Mensagem*,
appeared the year before his death.

Indeed, recognition in his home country came only posthumously.
His works are rich in imagery and imagination, full of reverie and
fantasy. He invented pseudonyms and published works under these
names; each of the poets he invented had a distinct voice and style.
Taken together, these works express the complex personality of one
man, whose days in Lisbon were marked out by a seemingly ordinary
existence and regular employment, and who carried within himself
surprising and extraordinary worlds of poetry.

To commemorate the centenary of Pessoa's birth, a group of scholars
began to delve into the legendary trunk packed with unpublished
work which the poet had left behind. Eventually, more than twenty-
seven thousand documents were found, which are now in the
National Library of Lisbon. Among them, a complete typescript in
English came to light, a guide to Lisbon, the city he loved so dearly.
A new bilingual edition of *Lisboa: What the Tourist Should See* has
been published with the support of local authorities. The book is not
written in the lyrical style of his poems, but with an innocent
and respectful hand. Even the famous Portuguese *saudade* seems
absent from these clear, descriptive texts, inviting the reader on
a companionable journey around the monuments, museums,
gardens and streets.

Pessoa is forever a part of the spirit of Lisbon. The opening words
to his guidebook capture the beauty of this unique city:

*...Lisbon, even from afar, rises like a vision in a dream, clear-cut
against a bright blue sky which the sun gladdens with its gold.
And the domes, the monuments, the old castles jut up above
the mass of houses, like far-off heralds of this delightful seat,
of this blessed region.*

General view of the Alfama

B. Wojtek/HOA QUI

LISBOA★★★

Lisbon – Lisboa
Conurbation 681,000
Michelin map 940 P2 or 39

140 **Travellers' addresses**
140 Where to stay
143 Eating out
145 Insider's Lisbon
145 Neighbourhoods
146 Getting around
148 Tourist information
149 Entertainment
151 Shopping
154 The Lisbon scene
158 Gardens
159 Beaches
159 Lisbon for kids
160 Perspectives

162 **Visiting Lisbon**
162 Historical notes
166 The Baixa
167 Chiado and Bairro Alto
169 Alfama
174 The Port and the Tagus
175 Expo' 98
179 Belém
182 Around Avenida
    da Liberdade
183 Gulbenkian Foundation
186 Amoreiras
187 Additional sights
189 Excursions

The Michelin maps to use with this guide:
940 and 441

Traveller's Addresses

WHERE TO STAY IN LISBON

The Michelin España Portugal Red Guide, and the extracted Portugal Hotéis e Restaurantes offer a wide selection of hotels listed by district. Those specified below have been chosen for their surroundings, character, excellent location or value for money. For further details on the different hotel classifications in Portugal *(pensão, residencial, turismo de habitação, etc.)*, please refer to the *Accommodation* chapter in the Practical Information section at the end of this guide.

The letters given immediately after the name of the hotel allow the reader to locate the hotel on the Lisbon maps in this guide.

It should be noted that prices are likely to rise during Expo'98 (May-September 1998): contact the hotel for further details. In most of the hotels prices vary according to season (high season being between spring and autumn). Special mention is made of those hotels with parking, a restaurant which serves lunch and/or dinner, and air conditioning in the rooms (highly recommended in summer for those who do not like the heat). In general, we recommend that you book your room in advance, especially in the smaller hotels.

In order to offer a choice of hotels to suit all budgets, we have classified hotels into three categories:

The **"Budget"** category offers rooms at less than 10 000$. These are usually small, simple hotels with a basic level of comfort.

"Mid-range" refers to hotels with rooms at between 13 000 to 25 000$, which have a certain amount of character.

In the **"Treat Yourself!"** category we have included hotels with particular charm, offering a high degree of comfort and ensuring a memorable stay. Naturally the cost of these hotels is in keeping with the high level of facilities provided.

Prices given generally include taxes and breakfast. The letters *CC* indicate that the hotel accepts credit cards (Visa, Eurocard/Mastercard, American Express and Diners Club).

BUDGET HOTELS

Pensão Londres (JX ❺) – *Rua Dom Pedro V. 53, 1200 Lisboa – ☎ (01) 346 22 03 – fax (01) 346 56 82 – 39 rooms – 7 000/9 800$ (CC – except American Express).*
This *pensão* occupies three floors of a handsome building on the edge of Bairro Alto, Lisbon's pulsating nightlife district. Certain rooms have original ceilings and good views of the Castelo São Jorge. A clean and well-maintained establishment offering reasonable rates in a good location.

Hotel Borges (KY ❸) – *Rua Garrett 108, 1200 Lisboa – ☎ (01) 346 19 51 – fax (01) 342 66 17 – 100 rooms – 8 500/10 500$ (CC).*
Superbly located on the Chiado's elegant shopping street only a few minutes away from the bars and restaurants of the Bairro Alto, the Borges was a favourite with many famous early 20C writers. A series of unfortunate renovations over the last decades have contributed to this rambling hotel's eclectic appearance, and a general face lift is overdue. Yet the spacious rooms, unbeatable location and reasonable rates make it worth considering. The grand breakfast room is surprisingly old-world.

Residencial Florescente (KX ❶) – *Rua Portas de Sto. Antão 99, 1150 Lisboa – ☎ (01) 346 35 17 – fax (01) 342 77 33 – 72 rooms – 5 000/7 000$ (CC) – air conditioning (certain rooms only).*
Located near the Praça dos Restauradores on a picturesque street lined with numerous restaurants and cafés, this simple *residencial* will suit visitors on a tight budget. Rooms are clean but as they can vary considerably in size and character, it is wise to look at a few before making your choice.

Residencial Sória (CP ❶) – *Rua Castilho 57, 2°, 1200 Lisboa – ☎ (01) 386 24 63 – fax (01) 387 84 45 10 rooms – 5 500/7 500$ (CC).*
Situated on the second floor of a large building close to Praça Marquês de Pombal, this *residencial* offers simple but clean rooms in a homelike atmosphere. Note that some of the rooms do not have private facilities.

Pensão São João da Praça (LZ ❷) – *Rua São João da Praça 97, 2°, 1100 Lisboa – ☎ (01) 886 25 91 – fax (01) 888 13 78 – 16 rooms (4 of which do not have private facilities) – 4 000/6 000$.*
One of the few places to stay in the picturesque Alfama district, this family-run *pensão* offers pleasant, clean and simply furnished rooms with wooden floors.

The pensão occupies the second and third floors of a handsome stone building located near the cathedral (Sé), making it within easy walking distance of the Baixa. Guests in some of the third-floor rooms will enjoy enchanting views of boats passing on the River Tagus.

Sé Guest House (LZ ❷) – *Rua São João da Praça 97, 1°, 1100 Lisboa* – ☎ *(01) 886 44 00 – 6 rooms (without private facilities) – 6 000/8 000$.*
Located one floor below the Pensão S. João da Praça (see above), this small family-run guest house offers simple, spacious, clean rooms. Guests must share bathroom facilities.
and for those on a tight budget...

Youth Hostel (Pousada de Juventude) **(CP ❸)** – *Rua Andrade Corvo 46 – Saldanha – Metro Picas* – ☎ *(01) 353 26 96.*

MID-RANGE

Hotel Britânia (JV ❹) – *Rua Rodrigues Sampaio 17, 1100 Lisboa* – ☎ *(01) 315 50 16 – fax (01) 315 50 21 – 30 rooms – 16 500/23 500$ (CC) – parking – air conditioning.*
Successfully restored to its elegant 1940s appearance, this landmark hotel designed by Cassiano Branco (architect of the Éden Teatro on the nearby Praça dos Restauradores) is both charming and comfortable. Spacious, well-appointed and quiet rooms, a good location and an understated "retro" ambience make the Britânia a good find.

Hotel Príncipe Real (JX ❺) – *Rua da Alegria, 53, 1250 Lisboa* – ☎ *(01) 346 01 16. – fax (01) 342 21 04 – 24 rooms – 15500/19500$ (CC) – panoramic restaurant – air conditioning.*
Behind this unattractive modern facade lies a charming hotel with a cosy atmosphere and attentive service. The restaurant on the top floor affords a picture postcard view of central Lisbon. Situated in a steep street near the Jardim Botânico, the hotel is close to both Avenida da Liberdade and Bairro Alto.

Albergaria Senhora do Monte (LV ❻) – *Calçada do Monte 39, 1100 Lisboa* – ☎ *(01) 886 60 02 – fax (01) 887 77 83 – 28 rooms – 16 500/25 000$ (CC) – air conditioning.*
The principal attraction of this modern hotel located off the beaten tourist trail in the residential Graça district is the outstanding views of Lisbon from all but five of the rooms. For those who want to splurge, request one of the three rooms with terrace (higher rate). Even if you choose not to stay here, you can enjoy the view from the top floor bar. Access is not very practical on foot, so plan on using taxis or the number 28 tram.

Hotel Metrópole (KY ❶) – *Praça do Rossio 30, 1100 Lisboa* – ☎ *(01) 346 91 64 – fax (01) 346 91 66 – 36 rooms – 17 000/19 000$ (CC) – air conditioning.*
Superbly situated on the bustling Praça do Rossio, the Metropole offers comfortable old-world charm in a handsome turn-of-the-century building. The restored interior is pleasant and spacious. Striking views of the Castelo São Jorge from the salon and the front rooms overlooking the often noisy Rossio.

Hotel Lisboa Tejo (KX ❸) – *Poço do Borratém 4, 1100 Lisboa* – ☎ *(01) 886 61 82/84 – fax (01) 886 51 63 – 51 rooms – 15 000$ (CC) – parking 400 metres away – air conditioning.*
This completely renovated hotel, just steps away from the Praça da Figueira in the Baixa district, offers clean and comfortable rooms at reasonable rates. Despite the double glazing, rooms on the street side tend to be noisy, while those on the courtyard side are a bit dark.

Hotel Da Torre (AQ ❼) – *Rua dos Jerónimos 8, 1400 Lisboa (Belém)* ☎ *(01) 363 62 62 – fax (01) 364 59 95 – 50 rooms – 13 500/14 700$ (CC) – restaurant – air conditioning.*
For visitors who prefer to stay in the calm and elegant Belém quarter outside the busy centre of Lisbon, this hotel facing the celebrated Mosteiro dos Jerónimos is a good option. The hotel occupies a traditional stone building with a red-tiled roof that contrasts with the 1950s and 1960s style of the interior. Rooms are spacious and quiet. Street parking is available.

TREAT YOURSELF!

York House (CQ ❺) – *Rua das Janelas Verdes 32, 1200 Lisboa* – ☎ *(01) 396 25 44 – fax (01) 397 27 93 – 36 rooms – 20 000/30 000$ (CC) – restaurant – air conditioning.*
Lisbon's best-known historic inn offers modern comfort and understated elegance in the serenity of a 17C convent. Rooms are individually appointed with taste. The handsome dining room looks onto a refreshingly verdant cobblestoned courtyard. Some visitors may find the location in the Lapa district near the Museu de Arte Antiga a bit inconvenient for visiting the city on foot.

York House

As Janelas Verdes (CQ ❶) – *Rua das Janelas Verdes 47, 1200 Lisboa –* ☎ *(01) 396 81 43 – fax (01) 396 81 44 –17 rooms – 26 000/29 800$ (CC) air conditioning.*
Just down the street from York House (see above), this handsome 18C house has been reconverted into a cosy and friendly inn appointed with personal touches. Rooms tend to be small and those facing the busy Rua das Janelas Verdes are best avoided by guests sensitive to traffic noise. A small refreshing patio garden is located in the rear.

Hotel Lisboa Plaza (JV ❶) – *Travessa do Salitre 7, 1250 Lisboa –* ☎ *(01) 346 39 22 – fax (01) 347 16 30 – 94 rooms, 12 suites – 21 000/28 000$ (CC) – restaurant – air conditioning.*
Don't be misled by the grim 1950s facade; inside, this large hotel exudes a certain intimacy and charm. Appointed in a contemporary-classic style replete with marble floors, comfortable reproduction furniture, framed prints and fresh flowers, this impeccably maintained hotel is conveniently located just off the Avenida da Liberdade. Rooms are comfortable but tend to be on the small side.

Quinta Nova da Conceição (BN ❸) – *Rua da Cidade de Rabat 5, 1500 Lisboa – Metro: Alto dos Moinhos –* ☎ *(01) 778 00 91 – fax (01) 778 00 91 – 2 rooms (a third available on special request) 17500$ (CC) – parking – closed in August.*
An oasis in the midst of unsightly modern high-rise apartment blocks, this 18C manor is Lisbon's only *turismo de habitação* accommodation. The sometimes sombre 19C interior is appointed with family furniture and mementoes. Particularly delightful are the breakfast room with its original azulejos and the manicured grounds including a swimming pool and tennis court. Given the limited capacity, advance reservation is a must. Accessible by either bus or metro.

WHERE TO STAY ON THE OUTSKIRTS OF LISBON

A pleasant alternative to staying in Lisbon itself are the resort towns along the coast (easy access by train, cool in the summer, near the sea....). For visitors who prefer staying outside the city, we have included some addresses in Estoril, Cascais and Sintra, all of which are close to Lisbon).

MID-RANGE

Casa da Pérgola – *Av. Valbom 13, 2750 Cascais –* ☎ *(01) 484 00 40 – fax (01) 483 47 91 – 10 rooms – 14 000/18 000$ – parking – air conditioning – closed from 1 December to 15 March.*
This attractive house is part of the *Turismo de Habitação* network. It has a small garden, a cosy interior and an excellent location.

Estalagem Senhora da Guia – *Estrada do Guincho, 2750 Cascais (3.5km/2mi from Cascais along the Av. 25 de Abril) –* ☎ *(01) 486 92 39 – fax (01) 486 92 27 – 41 rooms – 18 000/26 000$ (CC) – restaurant – parking – air conditioning – swimming pool.*
This beautiful villa, with its attractive location facing the sea, is surrounded by a garden with a sea-water swimming pool. Friendly service, beautiful interior decoration and some rooms with a sea view.

Hotel Inglaterra – *Rua do Porto 1, 2765 Estoril* – ☎ *(01) 468 44 61* – *fax (01) 468 21 08* – *50 rooms* – *14 300/23 100$ (CC)* – *restaurant* – *air conditioning* – *swimming pool.*
Although it has been thoroughly modernised inside, this fine hotel has managed to retain its early-20th century ambience.

Hotel Amazonia Lennox (formerly Estal. Lennox Country Club) – *Rua Eng. Álvaro Pedro de Sousa 5, 2765 Estoril* – ☎ *(01) 468 04 24* – *fax (01) 467 08 59* – *30 rooms* – *13 500/15 800$ (CC)* – *restaurant* – *air conditioning* – *parking* – *swimming pool.*
"Golf" is the decorative theme throughout this comfortable hotel, which consists of a pleasant main building and a modern annexe. The hotel also offers a beautiful garden and a swimming pool.

Quinta da Capela – *2710 Sintra (on the Colares road 4.5km/7mi from Sintra)* – ☎ *(01) 929 01 70* – *fax (01) 929 34 25* – *5 rooms, 3 suites* – *21 000/24 000$ (CC)* – *parking* – *closed from December to February.*
This old *quinta*, with its superb location in the heart of the Sintra mountains, offers a level of comfort and charm equal to its surroundings. Beautiful gardens (with a small swimming pool) and tremendous views over the surrounding countryside.

TREAT YOURSELF!

Palácio de Seteais – *Rua Barbosa do Bocage 8, 2710 Sintra* – ☎ *(01) 923 32 00* – *fax (01) 923 42 77* – *29 rooms, 1 suite* – *40 000/43 000$ (CC)* – *restaurant* – *parking* – *,air conditioning.*
The Sintra Agreement *(see SINTRA)* was signed in this elegant 18C palace. Surrounded by its own park, it is now one of the most beautiful and luxurious hotels in Portugal.

EATING OUT

The restaurants listed below have been chosen for their surroundings, ambience, typical dishes or unusual character. For a wider selection of restaurants and more detailed gastronomic information, consult the Michelin Red Guide to Portugal. The restaurants are classified by district and according to the price for a full meal: "Budget" (a meal for less than 2 500$), "Mid-range" (between 2 500$ and 6 000$), and "Treat yourself!" (more than 6 000$). It should be emphasised, however, that these prices may vary according to the number of courses ordered and the drinks which accompany the meal. A good bottle of wine can considerably increase the price of a meal.
Lunch is generally served from 12 noon until 3pm and dinner from 7pm to 10pm, although a number of restaurants serve dinner after 10pm.
For further information on Portuguese cuisine, consult the *Food and Wine* chapter in the introduction to the guide.

Baixa

BUDGET RESTAURANTS

Pizzeria Gordos – *Rua 1° Dezembro* – ☎ *(01) 346 94 95* – *(CC except American Express)* – *closed Sundays.*
This simple restaurant next to Rossio station is decorated with old *azulejos and* serves substantial pizzas and Italian dishes. An ideal spot for a quick lunch when visiting the Baixa.

MID-RANGE

Casa do Alentejo – *Rua Portas de. Sto. Antão 58* – ☎ *(01) 346 92 31* – *(CC)* – *closed from 1 to 19 August.*
An old building with Arabian-style architecture and huge rooms. Serves good regional cuisine. An association of "Alentejanos" (inhabitants of the Alentejo region) runs this amazing restaurant, where traditions are kept alive through its food and weekend shows. Saturdays: folk dances and choir singing; Sundays: morning dances. Not to be missed!

Martinho da Arcada – *Pç. Comércio 3* – ☎ *(01) 87 92 59* – *(CC – except American Express)* – *closed Sundays.*
It is said that the famous poet Fernando Pessoa wrote most of his works in this building. The restaurant has a very popular terrace under the arcades in the Praça do Comércio.

Bairro alto

BUDGET RESTAURANTS

Bota Alta – *Tv. da Queimada 35* – ☎ *(01) 342 79 59* – *(CC)* – *closed Saturday lunchtimes and Sundays.* Pleasant local restaurant. Typical cuisine.

Cervejaria Trindade – *Rua Nova Trindade 20 – ☎ (01) 342 35 06 -(CC) – closed on bank holidays.*
A Lisbon classic. The 18C azulejos in this old convent depict masonic images, creating a beautiful overall impression. The interior patio is very busy on hot summer days.

A Primavera – *Travessa da Espera 34 – ☎ (01) 342 04 77 – closed Sundays.*
One of the oldest restaurants in the district. Good traditional cuisine at reasonable prices in a tiny room full of atmosphere.

MID-RANGE

Pap'Açorda – *Rua Atalaia 57 – ☎ (01) 346 48 11 – (CC) – closed Sundays and Monday lunchtimes.*
One of the highlights of the Bairro Alto. Excellent cuisine in a theatrical décor, with performances by some of Lisbon's celebrities.

Antigo Farta Brutos – *Tv. da Espera 20 – ☎ (01) 342 67 56 – (CC) – closed Sundays.*
Good traditional cuisine full of originality served in a quiet atmosphere. Friendly service.

Sinal Vermelho – Rua das Gáveas 89 – *☎ (01) 343 12 81 – (CC) – closed Sundays.*
Very good traditional but imaginative cuisine served in light, inviting surroundings. Popular with artists and journalists.

TREAT YOURSELF!

Tavares – *Rua da Misericórdia 37 – ☎ (01) 342 11 12 – (CC) – closed Saturday lunchtime and Sundays.*
This renowned restaurant offers traditional international cuisine served with style in sumptuously decorated fin-de-siècle ambience.

Alfama/Graça

F. Vasseur/VISA

Fish marinated in white wine

MID-RANGE

Mestre André – *Cç. Sto. Estêvão 6 – ☎ (01) 87 14 87 – (American Express) – closed Sundays.*
A pleasant Alfama restaurant. A friendly atmosphere and imaginative cuisine at reasonable prices.

Lautasco – *Beco Azinhal 7-7A ☎ (01) 886 01 73 – (CC) – closed Sundays.*
This traditional restaurant in the Alfama district has but a few tables set out under a large tree in the courtyard. Good typical dishes in a village-like ambience.

Via Graça – *Rua Damesceno Monteiro 9B – ☎ (01) 887 08 30 – (CC) – closed Saturday lunchtimes and Sundays.*
Situated below the Miradouro de Nossa Senhora do Monte, this sophisticated restaurant decorated in contemporary style offers superb views of Castelo São Jorge and the centre of the city. An ideal location for a romantic dinner for two.

Casa do Leão – *Castelo de São Jorge – ☎ (01) 887 59 62 – (CC).*
This restaurant situated within the castle walls is much appreciated by tourists for its panoramic view of the city.

Alcântara/Belém

MID-RANGE

Alcântara Café – *Rua Maria Luisa Holstein 15 – ☎ (01) 363 71 76 – (CC).*
This brasserie-style café-restaurant is situated in an old factory, and adjoins the Alcântara-Mar nightclub. A young, elegant and fashionable ambience in amazing industrial-baroque décor. The entrance is slightly hidden down a dark side-street in the port area.

Caseiro – *Rua Belém 35 – ☎ (01) 363 88 03 – (CC) – closed Sundays and bank holidays.*
An eclectic décor in which onions, garlic and banknotes from around the world hang from the walls. Typical Portuguese cuisine.

Clube Naval de Lisboa – *Doca de Belém* – ☎ *(01) 363 00 61* – *(CC)* – *closed Monday lunchtimes.*
Maritime atmosphere and a very pleasant terrace with a view over the Tagus. Very busy at lunchtimes.

Other districts

MID-RANGE

Cervejaria Portugália – *Av. Almirante Reis 117* – ☎ *(01) 314 00 02* – *(CC)* – *closed bank holidays.*
One of the best brasseries in Lisbon. Spacious, airy rooms decorated with *azulejos*. Friendly, family atmosphere.

Adega da Tia Matilde – *Rua Beneficiência 77* – ☎ *(01) 797 21 72* – *(CC)* – *closed Saturday evenings and Sundays.*
Superb restaurant decorated with recent azulejos. Portuguese specialities.

O Madeirense – *Amoreiras Shopping Center* – ☎ *(01) 38 08 27* – *(CC).*
This restaurant, located in bustling modern surroundings on the first floor of the largest shopping centre in Lisbon, serves authentic Madeiran cuisine. Popular with Lisbonites.

O Funil – *Av. Elias Garcia 82A* – ☎ *(01) 796 60 07* – *(American Express)* – *closed Mondays and Sunday evenings.*
Cod à la "Funil" is one of the main specialities of this restaurant. Excellent wine list.

TREAT YOURSELF!

Casa da Comida – *Tv. das Amoreiras 1* – ☎ *(01) 388 53 76* – *(CC)* – *closed Saturday lunchtimes and Sundays.*
This immaculate, elegant restaurant in a verdant courtyard with an *azulejo*-covered fountain serves sophisticated, imaginative cuisine.

Food for thought

A particularly pleasant way of breaking the day is to have a bite to eat in one of the museum cafeterias or restaurants. These are often set in attractive surroundings (patios, gardens, modern décor) and serve traditional, family cuisine at reasonable prices. For their exact location, please refer to the museum section under *Visiting Lisbon*.

Museu Nacional do Chiado – Terrace with a view of the elegant garden decorated with bronze statues.

Museu de Artes Decorativas – Patio decorated with azulejos. Interior eating area.

Museu Nacional do Azulejo – Pleasant café-restaurant decorated with azulejos adjoining a large covered patio.

Museu Nacional de Arte Antiga – Tables set out on a garden terrace.

Centro Cultural de Belém – Cafeteria on a terrace overlooking the Tagus.

Fundação Gulbenkian – Functional cafeteria with a view of the garden.

Fundação Arpad Szenes – Vieira da Silva – A light, pleasant cafeteria inside the museum.

INSIDER'S LISBON

Neighbourhoods

Lisbon, set in a delightful valley, is a city with numerous focal points which can all be admired from the Tagus. 18C Lisbon is visible in the foreground: the Praça do Comércio with the criss-crossing network of streets in the **Baixa** district (the lower town) extending towards Rossio, the Praça dos Restauradores and the **Avenida Liberdade**, the city's main avenue, lined with shady trees. On the hill to the right stands Castelo São Jorge, surrounded by the medieval districts of **Alfama** and **Mouraria**, while the hill to the left has been taken over by the city's commercial area – the **Chiado** – and the working-class areas of **Bairro Alto** and **Madragoa** with the elegant residential districts of **Lapa**, **Alcântara** and **Belém** beyond. The areas along the Tagus and the Avenida 24 de Julho have become home to a growing number of bars and nightclubs, while the modern districts around Parc Eduardo VII and below are criss-crossed by a network of large avenues: Fontes Pereira de Melo, da República (**CP**), de Roma, de Berna etc. The suburbs continue to expand, swallowing districts such as **Restelo** (**AQ**) or **Benfica** (**AN**).

The dormitory-suburbs occupy the surrounding hills which are interspersed with fields of market gardening produce.

Compared with other capitals, Lisbon is quite a safe city; however, vistitors should always take certain precautions (do not leave bags in cars, do not tempt pickpockets etc).

Baixa (KY) – This is Lisbon's traditional shopping district and the hub of the city. Although extremely busy by day with tourists, employees from the many banks in the area, shoppers, sailors, lottery ticket vendors, shoe cleaners and passers-by, it is almost deserted by night when cars do no more than pass through the district. Its central location makes it a good departure point for visits and, as such, a practical area to make your base.

Chiado and Bairro Alto (JKY) – The Chiado, in particular Rua do Carmo and Rua do Garrett, was the city's department store district before the 1988 fire. Since its restoration, it has been occupied with shops selling international brand names, yet it has retained its book-shops and some old boutiques. The Bairro Alto, once a working-class neighbourhood, has been taken over by bars, night-clubs, restaurants and designer boutiques since the 1980s, transforming it into a fashionable district and the best-known part of the city for nightlife.

Príncipe Real (JVX) – This small, elegant district around the pleasant garden of the same name and the Rua da Escola Politécnica is home to a number of art galleries and antique shops. It is also the centre of gay nightlife in the city.

Alfama/Graça (LXY) – With its maze of narrow streets and flights of steps, courtyards and cul-de-sacs, the colourful Alfama district reveals its charms only to those who take time to explore it on foot. Its markets give it a lively atmosphere by day (in Rua São Pedro and Rua dos Remédios, and the flea-market in Campo de Santa Clara); in the evening, when its inhabitants gather in its many courtyards, it brings to mind a North African medina, and the more inquisitive visitor will find walking through the twisting semi-lit streets an enjoyable experience. Graça, situated on a hill above the Alfama, is a mainly residential district, which offers a number of excellent views of Lisbon.

Cais do Sodré (JZ) – The port area, between Praça Duque de Terceira and Praça Dom Luís I, is an eclectic mixture of sailors' bars, typical tavernas and grocery shops with cod hanging above the doorway.

Belém (AQ) – The city's main cultural events are held in the Centro Cultural de Belém, a district of Manueline monuments facing the river. This quiet, spacious district consists of villas and gardens, and is built on a hill overhanging the Tagus.

Docks – Alcântara and Santo Amaro (BQ) – Lisbon's residents have rediscovered their river, transforming the old warehouses in this area into a new centre for nightlife and leisure activities. A string of restaurants, bars and nightclubs stretch out along the docks. You'll need to take a taxi unless you have your own transportation.

Avenida 24 de Julho (BCQ) – Another hub of activity for night-owls, with the occasional bar and nightclub hidden behind an anonymous doorway (crowds around the entrance give the game away). You'll need some form of transportation to get to this part of the city, as well.

Other districts – Other areas can be found to the north of the city: **Amoreiras (BP)**, with its well-known shopping centre, **Avenida da Liberdade (CPQ)**, lined with cinemas, the Eduardo VII park and its greenhouses, **Avenida de Roma (CN)**, with its elegant boutiques and numerous cafés, **Campo Pequeno (CP)** with its bullring...

Getting around

Due to the problems caused by heavy traffic and parking problems in the narrow streets of this compact city, visitors will often find that it is much easier to get around on foot or by using the public transportation system as much as possible.

The **airport** is situated about 4km/2.5mi from the centre (Rossio). Shuttle buses (Aéro-bus) connect the airport with the Praça do Comércio and Cais do Sodré (AR) and operate from 7am to 9pm, with departures every 20min daily. A taxi from the airport to the city centre costs approximately 1 200$ with an additional charge for luggage (300$).

Lisbon on foot – The best way of exploring the old part of Lisbon – Baixa, Av. da Liberdade, Chiado/Bairro Alto and Alfama – is on foot. The climb up from Baixa to the hill of Bairro Alto can be avoided by taking the Glória or Santa Justa funiculars. The old districts of Bairro Alto and Alfama, with their narrow streets and flights of steps, can only be fully explored on foot.

Lisbon by car – The visitor will soon realise that a car in Lisbon is often more of a hindrance than a help. Traffic can be chaotic during the day and the small streets of the central districts are often choked with traffic. In addition, finding somewhere to park can be a real headache. Although parking meters have yet to make an appearance on Lisbon's streets, you will often have difficulty finding a place where you want to park. There are some new underground car-parks in Baixa (Praça dos Restauradores, Rossio, Praça do Comércio) as well as in some of the northern districts, but public parking is practically non-existent in the dense narrow streets of the Alfama and Bairro Alto. Given the excellent public transport system and the compact character of the city centre, we would advise visitors to leave their cars at home or in the hotel parking (as a general rule, however, only the larger modern hotels have their own parking).

Taxis – Numerous and cheap when compared with other European cities, taxis are a good way of getting around Lisbon. They are usually black with a green roof, or, more recently, beige. For journeys within the city, the tariff is marked on the meter. Outside the city centre, rates are calculated on a per kilometre scale.

Public transportation – In a city with as many hills as Lisbon, public transportation is a very practical, and often fun, way to get around (trams, funiculars).
The metro is run by one company and the bus, tram and funicular network by another. As a result, tickets bought in the metro are only valid on the metro system.

Timetables and tickets – The bus and tram network generally operates from 7am to 1am with a service every 11 to 15min until 9.30pm. The last number 45 bus (Cais do Sodré, Baixa, av. da Liberdade...) is at 1.55am. The funiculars stop running at 11pm. Tickets can be bought individually on both buses and trams If you are in Lisbon for a few days you can buy a "Passe turístico", valid for 4 days (1 550$) or 7 days (2 190$), offering unlimited journeys on the city's buses, trains and funiculars. Bus tickets can also be purchased for a cost of 150$ for two journeys. These tickets are on sale at the Santa Justa funicular, in metro stations and in kiosks with the sign "Venda de Passe". Bus and tram route maps can also be bought at these kiosks (1 000$). Information and free brochures are available at the Tourist Office in the Praça dos Restauradores.
There is also a guide to the capital ("Guia Urbano"), which includes maps of the transport routes and detailed maps of the districts (on sale in the main book-shops and tourist shops). Information on the buses, trams and funiculars can be obtained by phoning (01) 363 20 21.
There is no special access for handicapped passengers but a door-to-door service is carried out by mini-bus at the same price as the public transport network. This service, which operates daily from 7am to midnight, must be booked at least 2 days in advance by phoning (01) 758 56 76.

Funiculars (Elevadores) – Elevador da Bica (**JYZ**): Rua de S. Paulo / Largo do Calhariz; Elevador da Glória (**JX**): Restauradores / São Pedro de Alcântara; Elevador do Lavra (**KVX**): Largo da Anunciação / Rua da Câmara Pestana; Elevador de Santa Justa (**KY**): Rua do Ouro / Largo do Carmo.

Buses (Autocarro) – Main lines: Aero-bus: Airport/Cais do Sodré; number 45: Prior Velho/Cais do Sodré; number 83: Portela/Cais do Sodré; number 46: Est. Sta. Apolónia/Damaia; number 15: Cais do Sodré/Sete Rios; number 43: Praça Figueira/Buraca.

Metro – *The metro stations are shown on the maps in this guide.* From 1998 the system will consist of four lines: Gaivota (Pontinha / Terreiro do Paço); Girassol (Campo Grande / Rato); Caravela (Cais do Sodré / Campo Grande); and Oriente (Oriente / Alameda). These lines will be extended in the future. The metro runs from 6.30am to 1am.

M. Chaput/MICHELIN

147

Several metro stations have been decorated with azulejos by well-known Portuguese artists: Cidade Universitária (Vieira da Silva), Alto dos Moinhos (Júlio Pomar), Campo Grande (Eduardo Nery) and Rotunda (Menez).

Trams (Eléctricos) – The old trams are part of the charm of Lisbon and are a pleasant way of exploring the city. They are gradually being phased out, however, and being replaced with new, modern versions. Certain routes, such as number 28, which rattles its way through Graça, Alfama, Chiado, Estrela, to Belém, are well worth the ride.

Two lines cover the main sites:

Number 15 (Pç. da Figueira/Algés): Praça do Comércio – Museu Nacional dos Coches – Mosteiro dos Jéronimos – Museu Nacional de Arqueologia – Museu da Marinha – Padrão dos Descobrimentos – Torre de Belém.

Number 28 (Martim Moniz/Prazeres): Igreja São Vicente de Fora – Museu de Artes Decorativas – Castelo São Jorge – Sé – Baixa – Museu do Chiado – Largo do Chiado – Basílica da Estrela.

Lisbon's railway stations – Estação de Santa Apolónia (**MX**) – International routes and trains to the north of the country.

Estação do Cais do Sodré (**JZ**) – Estoril, Cascais. Departures approximately every 20min. Last train at 2.30am. Journey time: about half an hour.

Estação do Rossio (**KX**) – NW suburbs including Sintra and Leiria. Trains for Sintra depart every 20min on average. Last train at 2.30am. Journey time: approximately 30min.

Estação Sul e Sueste (**LZ**) – Alentejo and Algarve, via the ferry which crosses the river to Barreiro railway station.

Estação do Oriente (**DN**) – Intermodal transport terminal (bus, metro and train) serving the north; the station is linked to the Santa Apolónia and Sintra railway stations.

River stations – Boats and Ferries – The "cacilheiros" which serve the industrial towns on the opposite bank of the Tagus are a pleasant way of discovering the river and city. Boats leave every 15min or so during the day. Tickets can be bought at the ticket booths at the following stations.

In front of Praça do Comércio (LZ):
Estação do Sul e Sueste – Connections with Barreiro and trains running to the Alentejo and the Algarve.

Estação Fluvial do Terreiro do Paço – Serves Seixal and Montijo. Departure point for boat rides on the Tagus.

Cais da Alfândega – Serves Cacilhas.

Estação do Cais do Sodré (CQ) – Serves Cacilhas and Almada.

Estação de Belém (AQ) – Serves Porto Brandão and Trafaria.

Tourist information

Tourist Office (JKX) – Palácio Foz, Praça dos Restauradores.
☎ (01) 346 36 43 / 346 33 14
There is also an office at Lisbon airport – ☎ (01) 849 43 23 / 849 36 89.

Publications – The **Agenda Cultural** is a monthly publication providing information on cultural events in the city. It is available free of charge at the main tourist offices, hotels and kiosks. Information is also available on its web site at: portugal.hpv.pt/lisboa/agenda.

Another bilingual monthly publication (Portuguese/English), **Lisboa em**, provides a whole host of practical information as well as details of cultural events; it is available free of charge at tourist sites and some bars. English readers can pick up the monthly **What's On in Lisbon** for lists of concerts and other events (or connect from home: publituris @mail.telepac.pt)

Other publications, such as **Sete** (cultural weekly), **Público** (daily paper) and **Expresso** (weekly paper) provide details of cultural events both in Lisbon and elsewhere in Portugal.

Lisboa Card – Visitors who purchase this card can take advantage of the specific benefits it offers. These include:
– free unlimited travel on public transport (buses, metro, trams), with the exception of trams 15 and 28 (which cover a number of sites/monuments).
– free or reduced admission to most museums and cultural sites.
Price: 1 500$ (24 h); 2 500$ (48 h); 3 250$ (72 h); reductions available for children. The card can be bought at Rua Jardim Regedor 51 – Baixa – ☎ (01) 343 36 72 – open daily from 10am to 6pm, or at the Mosteiro des Jerónimos and Museu Nacional dos Coches in Belém.

Opening times of museums and monuments – In general, museums and monuments are closed on Mondays and bank holidays. For more detailed information, see the Admission times and Charges section at the back of this guide.

Boat rides on the Tagus – *Estação Fluvial du Terreiro do Paço (Estação do Sul e Sueste – opposite the Praça do Comércio)* – ☎ *(01) 887 50 58*. Two hour boat rides on the Tagus. 11am to 1pm and 3 to 5pm daily from 1 April to 31 October. 3 000$; children 6 to 12 years: 1 500$.

Changing money – Money can be exchanged in banks (open Monday to Friday from 8.30am to 3pm/commission approximately 1 000$), in some hotels (where the rate is usually not as good) and in exchange offices. Automatic change machines can also be found outside some banks. Automatic cash dispensers are now widely available throughout the city for withdrawing money using all major bank cards.

Useful numbers

To call the Lisbon area from abroad, dial 00,351 1 followed by the number. To call Lisbon from the provinces, dial 01 followed by the number.

Emergency services – 115

Duty chemist – 118

Police – 346 61 41 / 347 47 30

Telephone information – 118

Train information – 888 40 25 – Intercity trains: 790 10 04

Taxis – Rádio Táxis de Lisboa 815 50 61 – Teletáxi 815 20 76

Automatic wake-up call – 161

International telegrams – 182

Airport post-office – Open 24 hours – 849 02 45

Restauradores post-office – *Pç. Restauradores* – Open from 8am to 10pm/ 347 11 22

Lisbon Airport – 841 37 00

Tap-Air Portugal – *Pç. Marquês Pombal 3 A* – Reservations 841 50 00

Portugália – *Lisbon Airport* – Reservations 847 20 92 – 842 55 59/60/61

Tourist information on the Internet – www.distrimarketing.pt/

Entertainment

TICKETS

Tickets for shows can be bought at the following kiosks:

ABEP – *Praça dos Restauradores* – ☎ *(01) 342 53 60* – *Tickets on sale for a number of different shows: theatre, sport, concerts etc.*

Quiosque Cultural de S. Mamede – *Rua S. Mamede* – *Príncipe Real*. This and others like it have been set up by Lisbon City Hall to provide general information on the city's cultural activities.

CONCERT VENUES

Centro Cultural de Belém (**AQ**) – *Praça do Império* – ☎ *(01) 361 24 00. Internet address – www.fdescCC.pt/cCC.*
The cultural centre organises a large number of events, including concerts and temporary exhibitions. The monthly programme is available throughout the city.

Culturgest – Caixa Geral de Depósitos (**CP P**) – *Rua Arco do Cego* – ☎ *(01) 790 51 55 Internet address – www.cgd.telepac.pt/cultgest/index.htm.* This enormous building in neo-Classical style is the headquarters of the Caixa Geral de Depósitos savings bank. It houses a cultural centre with two auditoriums and two exhibition galleries. The programme of musical events is of extremely high quality, while art exhibitions on show here often include works by contemporary international artists. Information in the Agenda Cultural.

Coliseu dos Recreios (**KX**) – *Rua Portas Sto. Antão 92-104 – Baixa* – ☎ *(01) 346 16 77/8/9*. Opera, concerts and a wide range of other events are staged in this huge theatre, which was restored in 1994.

Parque Mayer (**JV**) – *Av. Liberdade* – A number of small typical theatres and restaurants with outdoor terraces can be found in this rather neglected, village-like setting in the centre of the city.

Escola Portuguesa de Arte Equestre – *Palais Nacional de QUELUZ – see under QUELUZ* – ☎ *(01) 435 89 15* – *shows every Wednesday at 11am from the end of April to the end of October (except August)*. The school, which keeps alive the tradition of Portuguese equestrian art, particularly with Lusitanian thoroughbreds, was founded by King João V at the end of the 18C.

Praça de Touros do Campo Pequeno (CP) – Av. da Republica, *Campo Pequeno* – ☎ *(01) 793 24 42* – *793 20 93* – Bullfights *(touradas)* every Thursday at 10pm from May to September in this remarkable neo-Moorish red-brick building. *See chapter on bullfighting in the Introduction* – *Traditional and Festive Portugal.*

Espaço Oikos – *Rua Augusto Rosa 40* – *Alfama* – ☎ *(01) 888 00 12.* This centre organises concerts, exhibitions, conferences and debates. Arts and crafts from 30 countries in Africa, Latin America and Asia are also on sale.

Campo Pequeno bullring

T. Perrin/HOA QUI

CINEMAS

Cine Alcântara – *Pingo Doce de Alcântara* – *Alcântara* – ☎ *(01) 363 01 55.*

ABC – Ciné Clube de Lisboa – *Rua Conde Redondo 2* – *Marquês Pombal* – ☎ *(01) 384 27 90.*

Cinema Condes – *Av. Liberdade 2* – ☎ *(01) 342 25 23.*

Cinema Tivoli – *Av. Liberdade 188* – ☎ *(01) 354 31 53.*

Cinema Xenon – *Av. Liberdade 9* – ☎ *(01) 346 84 46.*

Cinema S. Jorge – *Av. Liberdade 175* ☎ *(01) 357 91 44.* Three screens, traditional programme of current films.

Cinema Londres – *Av. Roma 7 A* – ☎ *(01) 840 13.13.*

Cinema Amoreiras – *Amoreiras Shopping Center. 2052* – ☎ *(01) 383 12 75.* Cinema complex with 10 screens and a varied programme.

Cinemateca Portuguesa – *Rua Barata Salgueiro 39* – *Av. da Liberdade* – ☎ *(01) 354 65 29.* Convivial cinema showing old films in various languages. Avant-garde Portuguese films for real cinema buffs. Snacks (quiches and cakes) are on sale in the foyer. Shows at 6.30pm and 9.30pm daily except Sundays. The Cinemateca also houses a Cinema Museum displaying documents and equipment.

THEATRES

Teatro Nacional D. Maria II (KX T[3]) – *Praça D. Pedro IV* – *Baixa* – ☎ *(01) 342 84 49.* Varied, traditional programme.

Teatro Municipal São Luís (KZ T[2]) – *Rua António Maria Cardoso 38* – *Bairro Alto* – ☎ *(01) 342 61 85.* Traditional programme.

Teatro Maria Vitória – *Parque Mayer* **(JV)** – *Av. da Liberdade* – ☎ *(01) 346 17 40* – *closed Mondays.* Plays by both foreign and Portuguese playwrights.

Teatro da Trindade (JKY T[5]) – *Rua Nova Trindade 9* – *Chiado* – ☎ *(01) 342 32 00.* Popular plays.

Comuna – *Praça de Espanha* ☎ *(01) 727 18 18.* A traditional programme of theatre, plus a bistro-style café-theatre for contemporary music concerts (rock, jazz, music from around the world) every Sunday at 10pm.

Teatro Municipal Maria Matos – *Rua Frei Miguel Contreiras 52 – Campo de Ourique* – ☎ *(01) 849 70 07.* Comedy and plays for children.

The Lisbon Players – *R da Estrela 10 – Estrela* – ☎ *(01) 887 37 89.* A group of amateur playwrights organising plays, operas etc. in English with audience participation.

MUSIC

See also Concert Venues above.

Teatro Nacional de S. Carlos (**KZ T¹**) – *Rua Serpa Pinto 9 – Bairro Alto* – ☎ *(01) 346 84 08* .Operas, ballets and classical music concerts.

Grande Auditório Gulbenkian – *Av. de Berna 45* – ☎ *(01) 793 51 31.*

Shopping

Shops are normally open from 9am to 1pm and from 3 to 7pm Mondays to Fridays. They close at 1pm on Saturdays. Shopping centres are usually open from 10am to midnight.

ARTS AND CRAFTS

A. Rocha, Lda – *Rua de São Bento 234 – São Bento.* A wide choice of crystal and glass in this factory outlet in Marinha Grande.

Albuquerque e Sousa Lda – *Rua D. Pedro V 70 – Bairro Alto.* Beautiful collections of old azulejos.

Artesanato – *Rua Castilho 61 B – Liberdade.* Souvenirs, lace, pewter, porcelain, pottery.

Atlantis – *Rua Ivens 48 – Chiado.*
Crystal from one of the country's largest manufacturers.

Constância – *Rua S. Domingos 8 – Lapa.*
Extremely attractive contemporary azulejos.

Fábrica Viúva Lamego – *Largo do Intendente Pina Manique 25. Metro Intendente. Azulejos factory.*

Madeira House – *Rua Augusta 133 – Baixa.* A selection of beautiful hand-embroidered articles.

Príncipe Real Enxovais – *Rua Escola Politécnica 12-14 – Príncipe Real.* Outstanding embroidery. This embroiderer produces table napkins with the "Vista Alegre" crockery design.

Ratton – *Rua Academia das Ciências 2C/Príncipe Real. Azulejos* designed by contemporary artists.

Sant'Anna – *Rua do Alecrim 91-95 – Chiado.* A wide choice of azulejos and porcelain from this company founded in 1741.

Trevo – *Av. Óscar Monteiro Torres 33A, Pç. de Touros.* A specialist in Arraiolos carpets.

J. N. de Soye/RAPHO

Vista Alegre – *Largo do Chiado 18 – Chiado.* This boutique sells beautiful "Vista Alegre" porcelain.

REGIONAL PRODUCTS

Cantinho Regional – *Amoreiras Shopping Center – Av. Eng. Duarte Pacheco.* Typical Portuguese specialities.

Casa Macário – *Rua Augusta 272-274 – Baixa.* Port, with vintages dating from the beginning of the century.

Manteigaria Londrina – *Rua Portas Sto. Antão 53-55 – Baixa.* Portuguese specialities such as wine, ham, dried fruit, cod etc.

Manuel Tavares, Lda – *Rua da Betesga 1A-1B.* Portuguese regional products.

MARKETS

Markets are ideal places for bargain-hunters with a multitude of inexpensive items on sale, including clothes, cotton piqué quilts, earthenware crockery, basketwork, arts and crafts, and antiques. Lively local markets are also extremely entertaining, although arrive early if you want to avoid the crowds, and watch out for pickpockets.

Feira da Ladra – *Campo Sta Clara – Alfama – Tuesdays from 7am to 1pm and Saturdays from 7am to 6pm.* Lisbon's "Feira da Ladra" flea market literally means "The Thieves' Fair". However, most vendors sell their own goods. The market is a good place to hunt for second-hand clothes, silverware, furniture, old books etc.

Mercado da Ribeira Nova – *Av. 24 de Julho – from Mondays to Saturdays from 6am to 2pm.* Wonderful food market, where colours, smells and the sales pitch of its vendors all blend together.

Feira de Carcavelos – *In the centre of Carcavelos 21km/13mi west of Lisbon on the Estoril road. Every Thursday morning* – Inexpensive clothes market selling seconds with minor – and often barely discernable – defects. A number of well-known French and British brand names are often on sale here, particularly cotton goods.

Feira de Sintra – *Largo de São Pedro à Sintra – The second and fourth Sunday of the month, all day* – This large market in one of Sintra's delighful squares sells the same goods as most other markets, plus plants and animals. Around the square you will also find small craft and antique stalls.

Feira de Cascais – *Near the Cascais bullring. The first and third Sundays of the month, all day* – Brand-name cotton clothes in addition to the usual shoes, leather bags, crockery etc.

ART GALLERIES

Art galleries usually close on Sundays.

Associação José Afonso – *Rua Voz Operário 62 – Graça.* This traditional shop also contains an art gallery which makes a point of exhibiting the work of young artists.

Feira da Ladra

Galeria 111 – *Campo Grande 113 – Campo Grande.*

Galeria 1991 – *Rua Marcos Portugal 28/30 – Príncipe Real.*

Galeria Arte Periférica – *Centro Cultural de Bélem (Shops 5 and 6).*

Galeria Graça Fonseca – *Rua da Emenda 26C/V – Chiado.* A gallery which often hosts photographic exhibitions.

Galeria Luís Serpa – *Rua Ten. Raul Cascais 1B – Príncipe Real.* Exhibitions of paintings and sculpture by contemporary artists.

Galeria Módulo – *Cç. Mestres 34 A/B – Campolide.* Contemporary artists.

Galeria Palmira Suso – *Rua das Flores 109 – Bairro Alto.* Contemporary Portuguese artists.

Galeria de S. Francisco – *Rua Ivens 40 – Chiado.* Modern painting.

Novo Século – *Rua Século 23 A/B – Bairro Alto.* Contemporary art.

Quadrum – *Rua Alberto Oliveira 52 – Roma/Alvalade.* One of Lisbon's most avant-garde galleries, located in an annexe of the Palácio de Coruchéus – accessible through the garden.

BOOKSHOPS

Livraria Antiquário – *Rua do Alecrim 40-42 – Chiado/Cais do Sodré.* Old books and a wide choice of lithographs, engravings and drawings.

Livraria Assírio & Alvim – *Av. Frei Miguel Contreiras 52.* A wide selection of books on cinema. The bookshop also organises temporary exhibitions by contemporary artists.

Livraria Barata – *Av. de Roma 11 A et D – Roma.* General bookshop with a good foreign book section.

Livraria Barateira – *Rua Nova da Trindade 16A – Baixa.* Old bookshop specialising in books on art. *Azulejo*-decorated façade.

Livraria Bertrand – *Rua Garrett 73 – Chiado.* This large, comprehensive bookshop has a maze of rooms organised by subject. Foreign books and international newspapers.

Livraria Olisipo – *Largo Trindade Coelho 7 – Bairro Alto.* Old books, prints and lithographs.

Livraria Portugal – *Rua do Carmo 70-74 – Chiado.* Good choice of coffee-table and specialist books.

ANTIQUES

Lisbon's antique shops are mainly concentrated in the following streets: **Escola Politécnica, Dom Pedro V, São Bento** and **Augusto Rosa** (Alfama).

Antiguidades Cabral Moncada – *Rua D. Pedro V 34 – Bairro Alto.* One of the best-known antique shops in Lisbon. Also organises auctions.

Abside – *Travessa dos Fiéis de Deus 14-16 – Baixa.* Very popular antique shop.

FASHION

Ana Salazar – *Rua do Carmo 87 / Av. de Roma 16^E – Roma.* One of the best boutiques for creations by the most famous designer in the Portuguese fashion industry. Women's clothes.

José António Tenente – *Travessa do Carmo 8 – Bairro Alto.* Clothes for men and women by the talented Portuguese designer who created the uniforms for Expo'98.

José Carlos – *Travessa do Monte Carmo 2 – Príncipe Real.* One of the big names in Portuguese *haute couture.*

Bazar Paraíso – *Rua do Nort 42 – Bairro Alto.* Boutique with clothes by young Portuguese designers.

Fashion Clinic – *Av. Liberdade 249.* International brand names and young designer wear.

Rosa e Teixeira – *Av. Liberdade 204.* A traditional boutique selling well-known brand names in a sophisticated setting. High quality made-to-measure clothes for men.

Loja das Meias – *Pç. D. Pedro IV – Rossio.* The first multi-brand boutique in Portugal. Off-the-peg, *haute-couture* and accessories.

Ourivesaria Aliança – *Rua Garrett 50 – Rossio.* Superb, lavishly-decorated jewellery.

Chapelaria Azevedo – *Pç. D. Pedro IV 69-72-76 – Rossio.* Hatters founded in 1886 with an old-world charm and a huge selection of hats.

Luvaria Ulisses – *Rua do Carmo 87 – Chiado.* Tiny glove shop with a huge choice of excellent quality articles.

SHOPPING CENTRE

There are several shopping centres situated outside the city centre. Of these, Amoreiras is the largest and the most interesting to visit.

Amoreiras Shopping Center (**BP**) – *Av. Eng. Duarte Pacheco.* 300 shops, a supermarket, 55 restaurants and 10 cinema screens.

The Lisbon scene

A selection of the best cafés, tea-rooms, bars and nightclubs in the capital.

One of the favourite pastimes both in Lisbon and elsewhere is to head for a bar or café after lunch and dinner for a coffee *(bica)*. Excellent cafés and pastry shops can be found all over the city as they are an important part of Portuguese life, and many an enjoyable evening begins with this time-honoured ritual.

Lisbonites like to take their time when they go out and places generally remain busy until late at night. As a general rule, the custom is to go to several places – and even several districts – in the same evening. A word of advice for night owls: clubs will not start to get busy until after midnight.

In the Bairro Alto, the evening starts in its many bars, from where you try to gauge the atmosphere of several possible venues. Next stop would perhaps be a bar/discotheque, with the evening ending in the area around the docks or on the Avenida 24 de Julho.

BAIXA

Pastelaria Suiça – *Pç. D. Pedro IV/Rossio.* One of the busiest places in the Baixa and a good meeting place. Outdoor terraces in the Rossio and Praça da Figueira, with views of the Castelo de São Jorge. Snacks, excellent cakes and fruit juices.

Café Nicola – *Rua 1º Dezembro 20.* A Lisbon landmark steeped in history. It was here that the first Portuguese woman dared to put an end to the exclusively-male character of the city's cafés.

Confeitaria Nacional – *Pç. Figueira 18B.* This old pastry shop is one of the best in Lisbon. A huge choice of pastries and traditional sweets.

Ginginha do Rossio – *Lg. S. Domingos 8.* After wandering through the Baixa, try a glass of the famous "ginginha" (cherry brandy). A unique café with a unique atmosphere!

BAIRRO ALTO/PRÍNCIPE REAL

A Brasileira – *Rua Garrett 120 – open daily from 8am to 2pm.* A well-known café with a literary tradition. Artists, fashion designers, tourists and residents all meet in this legendary establishment.

Pastelaria Benard – *Rua Garrett 104 – from 8am to midnight – closed Sundays.* Restaurant and pastry shop. Tea, lunch and dinner available at this renowned Lisbon address. Delicious pastries served in a quiet, dignified atmosphere.

A Caravela – *Rua Paiva Andradeé 8 – open from 9am to midnight.* Former Lisbon tea factory serving lunch and afternoon tea. A Chiado classic.

B. Brillion/MICHELIN

Café Nicola, Rossio

Café Rosso – *Rua Ivens 53 – open daily from 8am to 1pm.* Very pleasant terrace-café in an inner courtyard at the entrance to the renovated Chiado district.

Café No Chiado – *Largo do Picadeiro 11/12 – open from 10am to 2am Monday to Saturday and 6pm to 2am Sundays; events organised from 10pm until late at night, daily except Sundays.* This is Lisbon's first Cybernet café and is owned by the National Cultural Centre. The computers are next to the library upstairs in an old-fashioned, studious setting. The style of the restaurant-bar is modern and warm.

Solar do Vinho do Porto – *Rua S. Pedro de Alcântara 45 – open from 10am to 11pm, closed Sundays.* More than 300 different kinds of port and "vintages" can be tasted here in rooms with velvet armchairs and low tables. Glasses of port from 120$ to 2 100$.

Frágil – *Rua Atalaia 126-8 – open from 11pm to 4am – closed Sundays.* One of the classics of Lisbon nightlife. The décor in this bar-discotheque is always original and changes every three months or so. A trendy clientele of night-time regulars, celebrities, gays, yuppies etc.

Três Pastorinhos – *Rua da Barroca 111/11 – open from 11am to 2am.* Another favourite bar-discotheque where trendy Lisbonites gather when the night is still young.

Pavilhão Chinês – *Rua D. Pedro V 89 – open until 2am.* Originally a grocer's which was transformed into a bar in 1986. The walls are covered with glass cases containing a varied collection of objects, including lead soldiers, contemporary engravings, humorous ceramics and models of war planes. Billiard table at the back of the bar.

Trump's *Rua da Imprensa Nacional 104 B – Príncipe Real.* The most famous gay nightclub in Lisbon is always lively with a fun time guaranteed.

Bric a Bar – *Rua Cecílio de Sousa 82 – Príncipe Real.* More exclusive than Trump's with modern décor on two floors. Also popular with the gay community.

Targus – *Rua Diário Notícias 40 B – open from 11am to 2am.* Soul and Motown set the mood in this modern bar. The owner is one of the best-known characters of Bairro Alto nightlife.

Artis – *Rua Diário Notícias 95 – 97 – open from 8pm to 2am.* One of the long-established bars in the Bairro Alto. Famous for its jazz, Favaios moscatel and clientele of film producers, musicians and other intellectuals. It also has a beautiful collection of old wind instruments hanging from its walls.

Café Diário – *Rua Diário Notícias 3 – open from 4pm to 2am.* A bar-cum-restaurant hosting regular exhibitions, dance shows and concerts.

Tertúlia – *Rua Diário Notícias 60 – open from 7pm to 2am/closed Sundays.* This bar resembles an old Portuguese café. A pleasant place to start the evening, with live jazz bands and newspapers available for customers.

Captain Kirk – *Rua do Norte 121 – open from 6pm to 4am.* One of the current 'in' places in the Bairro Alto. Bar-discotheque with metallic décor. Youngish ambience and clientele.

Keops – *Rua da Rosa 157-159 – open from 11pm to 3.30am.* Another fashionable Lisbon bar.

Ma Jong – *Rua da Atalaia 3 – open from 7.30pm to 2am.* The Babylon of artists and cinema enthusiasts.

Ópera – *Tv. das Mónicas 65 – open Tuesdays to Fridays from 8pm to 2am and Saturdays and Sundays from 8pm to 3.30am (closed Mondays).* Young, modern atmosphere. Art exhibitions.

Snob Bar – *Rua Século 178 – open until 3am.* An elegant bar frequented by journalists and advertising executives. Snacks served until 3am.

Mássima – *Rua D. Pedro V 8 – open from 4pm to 7pm – closed Sundays and bank holidays.* An ideal spot for a well-earned rest. Try the best hot chocolate in town with milk rolls, toast or pastries.

ALFAMA/GRAÇA

Cerca Moura – *Lg. Portas do Sol – open from 10pm to 2am.* Just a few steps from the Museu de Artes Decorativas. This terrace-bar offers a splendid view of the river and the Alfama. Very lively during the summer.

Chapitô – *Rua Costa Castelo 1/7 – open from 9am to 10pm – closed Sundays.* A circus school on one of Lisbon's most pleasant terraces where after 8pm you can have a drink, listen to concerts, watch plays or enjoy other cultural events during the summer.

Bruxa Bar – *Rua S. Mamede Caldas 35 A/B – open from 10pm to 2am.* Brazilian music. Mainly popular with the over-40s.

Pé Sujo – *Lg. S. Martinho 6 – 7 – open from 10pm to 2am – closed Mondays.* Very lively Brazilian bar, where you can dance to "berimbaus", "cuícas" and "folias brasucas". Live music daily.

O Salvador – *Rua Salvador 53 – open from 9pm to 2am.* Quiet, varied music in blue and white décor. Impressive cocktail list.

Bar Anos 60 – *Lg. Terreirinho 21 – open from 9.30pm to 4am – closed Sundays.* Portuguese music from the '60s and '70s (Wednesdays). Concerts of Brazilian music the rest of the week.

Bar da Graça – *Tv. Parreira 43 – open from 9pm to 4am – closed Sundays.* One of the Lisbon bars selling Belgian beer. Live music, theatre and exhibitions by Portuguese painters.

Graça Esplananda – *Lg. Graça (Escadinhas Caracol Graça) – open from 2pm to 3am.* Enjoy a drink while contemplating a beautiful view of Lisbon from the terrace. Very pleasant in fine weather.

LIBERDADE

Hot Clube – *Pç. Alegria 39 – open Tuesdays to Saturdays from 10pm to 4am.* The oldest jazz club in Lisbon. Frequent concerts by internationally-renowned groups on Fridays and Saturdays.

CAIS DO SODRÉ

Bar do Rio – *Cais Sodré, Armazém 7 – open from 10pm to 3am.* A converted warehouse with a young atmosphere and clientele. Always popular.

British Bar – *Rua Bernardino Costa 52 – open Mondays to Fridays from 7.30am to 11pm and Saturdays from 8pm to 2am/closed Sundays.* Hardly changed since 1918. A few specialities, such as the ginger beer on tap. Good choice of beers and excellent selection of whiskies.

Ó Gillins Irish Pub – *Rua dos Remolares 8/10 – open daily from 11am to 2pm.* Very Irish atmosphere. Frequented by sailors, bankers, the young and old alike. Concerts on Friday and Saturday evenings. Jazz on Sunday afternoons.

Hennessy Irish Pub – *R do Cais do Sodré 32/38 – open daily from 11.30am to 2am (Saturdays until 4am).* Spacious pub with a plush Irish interior providing a contrast with neighbouring bars. For Irish coffee and Guinness fans.

AV. 24 DE JULHO

Plateau – *Escadinhas da Praia – open from 10.30pm to 6am – closed Sundays and Mondays.* Surprising décor of gold columns, giant fans and Pompeian wall murals. Very lively until late, young atmosphere, techno music.

Kremlin – *Escadinhas da Praia – open until 9am/closed Mondays, Wednesdays and Sundays.* Large disco and Lisbon's Mecca for techno music. Usually the last stop on the party trail.

Kapital – *Av. 24 de Julho 68 -open from 10.30pm to 4am – closed Mondays and Wednesdays.* This nightclub is very popular with Lisbonites. Elegant, airy décor on three floors, each with a bar. Terrace on the top floor.

Cinearte - Café – *Lg. Santos 2 – open Tuesdays and Wednesdays from 1pm to 1am and Thursdays to Saturdays from 1pm until the early hours.* The Catita brothers stage unique, totally surreal shows. Although incomprehensible to foreigners, it is nevertheless well worth a visit to see the theatre, music and cinema personalities who frequent the bar. On Saturdays, this constantly-teeming bar has live music. The concerts and shows never start before 2 or 3 in the morning.

B.leza – *Lg. Conde Barão 50 – 2° – open from Tuesdays to Saturdays from 10.30pm to 7am.* Situated in a 16C palace with superb ceilings. African and Latin-American music. One of the most popular places for Afro-Caribbean music.

Xafarix – *Av. D. Carlos I 69 – open from 11pm to 3am.* Various concerts daily from 1am in this very popular bar. Pleasant outdoor terrace which is very lively on summer nights.

A Paulinha – *Av. 24 de Julho 82 – open from 10pm to 4am.* Popular with people of all ages and an ideal bar in which to start or finish the evening. Good music, food and drink.

DOCAS/ALCÂNTARA/SANTO AMARO

Alcântara Mar – *Rua-Cozinha Económica 11 – open Wednesdays to Sundays from 11pm to 6am.* Red velvet, gilded wood and ancestral portraits decorate the walls of this club which was the first to be established in this trendy Lisbon district.

Salsa Latina – *Cais de Alcântara – open daily from 12.30pm to 3pm and 7pm to 11pm.* This huge bar-restaurant, with its warm designer décor, is located in the former Alcântara harbour station. Latin-American concerts daily and jazz on Wednesdays. Outdoor dining possible.

Ultramar – *Cais das Oficinas, Armazém 115, Doca Rocha Conde d'Óbidos*. Spacious bar-discotheque with superb futuristic décor akin to a voyage in Space. Very pleasant terrace directly overlooking the waterfront.

Speakeasy – *Cais das Oficinas, Armazém 115, Doca Rocha Conde d'Óbidos – open daily from 12 noon to 3pm and from 7pm to 4am, closed on Sundays*. Pleasant atmosphere in the former premises of the dock administration board. One of the best places to hear jazz (internationally-renowned groups) and popular music (Brazilian, Portuguese etc). Food also available before the concert which begins at 11pm every day (11.30pm on Saturdays).

BiStyle – *Rua Prior Crato 6*. Two floors at the back of a tiny courtyard. From 6pm the first floor moves to retro sounds, with cheese and wines by the glass on offer. From 10pm to 4am youngsters take over, dancing to 80s rock.

Rock City – *Rua Cintura Porto Lisboa, Armazém 225 – open daily from 12.30pm to 4am*. A new fashionable Lisbon club with a Rock'n Roll atmosphere.

Docks` Club – *Rua Cintura do Porto de Lisboa 226, store H, Doca Rocha Conde de Óbidos – open from 8.30am to 6am, closed Sundays*. Restaurant-bar-discotheque in a harbour warehouse. Very popular, particularly at weekends.

Blues Café – *Rua Cintura Porto Lisboa, store H, nave 3-4, Rocha Conde de Óbidos – open daily from 12.30pm to 4am (closed Sundays)*. Bar-restaurant until midnight. Rock and Blues the rest of the night.

5 ao Rio – *Doca Sto. Amaro, Armazém 5 – open from 5pm to 3am (closed Mondays)*. One of the many bars around the St. Amaro docks. Maritime décor and lively music.

7 Mares – *Doca Sto. Amaro, Armazém 3 – open daily from 12 noon to 4am*. Attractive interior and terrace to enjoy a drink or try one of its many snacks.

Cais S – *Doca Sto. Amaro, Armazém 1 – open daily from 11am to 4am (Sundays until 8pm)*. A bar decorated with large metal insects. Video wall showing sporting highlights.

Doca de Santo – *Doca Sto. Amaro – open from 12 noon to 4am*. The first bar to open at the Santo Amaro dock. Salads, fresh fruit juices and snacks day and night. Good music and pleasant terrace in summer.

Santo Amaro Café – *Doca Sto. Amaro, Pavilhão 9 e 10 – open from 2pm to 2am*. This exotic bar-café has become well-known through its original architecture. Tropical music.

BELÉM

Bar do Terraço – *Centro Cultural de Belém – Praça do Império*. Concerts are held at 7pm almost every day on the terrace of the Belém Cultural Centre. A wonderful view of the Tagus and the opposite bank.

Antiga Confeitaria de Belém – **Fábrica dos Pastéis de Belém** – *Rua Belém 84/8 – open daily from 8am to 11.30pm*. The small Belém cakes, known as *pastéis de nata*, attract great numbers of Lisbonites and tourists alike to this pastry shop. The famous mini-tarts (their recipe is a closely-guarded secret) are still made here in the old ovens which give them their highly-popular taste. They can be bought in boxes of six to take away or eaten hot in one of the pastry shop's azulejo-decorated rooms. A Lisbon institution.

M. Chaput/MICHELIN

Santo Amaro dock

Fado

Fado is the profound expression of the Lisbon soul which plunges its listeners into a gentle sadness charged with emotion. This nostalgic lament is the very expression of *saudade*, the bitter-sweet melancholy of the soul which is so difficult to translate. The best-known fado singer is undoubtedly Amália Rodrigues, who has contributed to the spread of fado around the world. A few places where you can listen to fado are listed below.

BAIRRO ALTO

Adega do Machado – *Rua do Norte 91 – ☎ (01) 342 87 13 – open Tuesdays to Sundays from 8pm to 3am.* An excellent folklore show early in the evening, followed by fado from Lisbon or Coimbra.

Adega do Ribatejo – *Rua Diário Notícias 23 – ☎ (01) 346 83 43 – open from 12 noon to 3pm and 7pm to midnight.* One of the venues with the most authentic fado. Lively atmosphere.

Arcadas do Faia – *Rua Barroca 54/56 – ☎ (01) 342 67 42 – open from 8pm to 2am (closed Sundays).* Authentic Lisbon fado in a district where fado is the traditional form of expression.

Café Luso – *Tv. Queimada 10 – open from 8pm to 2am (closed Sundays).* Very popular with tourists. Evening entertainment begins with a folklore show, followed by fado.

Mascote da Atalaia – *Rua da Atalaia 13 – ☎ (01) 347 04 08 – open from 8pm to 11pm (closed Sundays).* An anonymous address often missed by visitors. Popular with locals.

ALFAMA

O Cabacinha – *Lg. Limoeiro 9/10 – ☎ (01) 888 46 70 – Fado on Fridays and Saturdays from 9pm to 2am/Sundays from 8pm to midnight.* A venue for true fado lovers.

Parreirinha de Alfama – *Beco Espírito Santo 1 – open from 8pm to 2am – closed Sundays.* Traditional fado house popular with tourists.

Taverna del Rei – *Largo do Chafariz de Dentro 15 (corner of Rua São Pedro) – ☎ (01) 352 70 60 – open from 12 noon to 3am – closed Sundays.* Portuguese cuisine on offer while listening to some authentic fado.

OTHER DISTRICTS

Timpanas – *Rua Gilberto Rola 24 Alcântara – ☎ (01) 387 24 31 – open from 8.30pm to 2am – closed Wednesdays.* A good place to hear some excellent fado.

Senhor Vinho – *Rua Meio Lapa 18 – Lapa – ☎ (01) 397 26 81 – open daily from 8.30pm to 2am – closed Sundays – Fado at 9.45pm.* Elegant, traditional fado venue with performances by some famous artists. Traditional Portuguese cuisine and a remarkable wine list.

Gardens

One of the surprising aspects of Lisbon is the multitude of small gardens planted with exotic species. In spring, jacarandas bathe the city in a mauve tinge, while summer is the time for the purplish-blue explosion of bougainvillaea. This bold splash of colour is accompanied by the delightful scent of Lisbon's lemon trees. Most gardens are hidden behind high walls, although visitors can occasionally enjoy the sight of a few colourful overhanging branches here and there.

Jardim Botânico (JV) – See description under Visiting Lisbon- Around avenida da Liberdade.

Jardim da Estrela (BQ) – This large garden, laid out in 1852, is full of exotic species (palm trees, dragon trees etc), and has a bandstand, lakes and drinks stalls.

Jardim da Fundação Gulbenkian (CP) – Contains an open-air amphitheatre for summer concerts.

Jardim do Príncipe Real (JX 213) – Pleasant garden with an outdoor restaurant. Don't miss the very small Buçaco cedar with its impressive wide foliage.

Jardim das Amoreiras (BP) – Small, quiet garden in the middle of the attractive Praça das Amoreiras, under the Águas Livres aqueduct and close to the Fundação Vieira da Silva.

Parque Eduardo VII and greenhouse (CP) – *See description under Visiting Lisbon- Around avenida da Liberdade.*

Jardim Botânico da Ajuda and Jardim das Damas (**AQ**) – *See description under Visiting Lisbon – Belém.* This botanical garden, with its numerous trees and plants, was built by the Marquis of Pombal in 1768 just a few steps from the Palácio da Ajuda. The romantic Jardim das Damas nearby is dotted with lakes and waterfalls.

Jardim do Palácio dos Marqueses de Fronteira (**BP**) – A splendid garden decorated with a unique style of azulejos. *See description under Visiting Lisbon – Additional Sights.*

Parque Florestal de Monsanto (**APQ**) – *See description under Visiting Lisbon – Additional Sights.*

Beaches

Lisbonites have a wide choice of beaches close at hand for holidays, weekends or an hour or two after work. *See map on page 7.*

BEACHES TO THE NORTH OF LISBON

Although closer to the centre of the city, the beaches along the fast highway between Lisbon and Cascais are not as pleasant as those specified below.

Praia do Guincho – *See description under Cascais.*

Praia das Maçãs – An attractive beach with fine sand near the Azenhas do Mar.

Azenhas do Mar – A small beach (covered at high tide) with a natural swimming pool at the foot of this white-washed village perched on the cliff.

Ericeira – Family beach next to the small town of the same name.

ON THE OTHER SIDE OF THE TAGUS

To get to these beaches you will either need to cross the bridges (heavily-congested at weekends) or perhaps catch a boat.

Costa da Caparica – *Access by car via the Ponte 25 de Abril, by bus (departures from Praça de Espanha) or boat (to Cacilhas from the Terreiro do Paço river station). From Cacilhas, catch a bus to Costa da Caparica. See description under COSTA DA CAPARICA.*

Sesimbra – An attractive beach near the road, lined with restaurants specialising in grilled fish and seafood.

Portinho da Arrábida – Delightful, small sandy beach nestled in a bay.

Lisbon for kids

Jardim Zoológico – *Estr. de Benfica 158, Sete Rios – ☎ (01) 726 80 41 – See description under Life in Lisbon – Additional Sights.* A zoo, children's play area, dolphin and parrot shows.

Planetário Calouste Gulbenkian *(See map of Belém)* – *Praça Império, Belém – ☎ (01) 362 00 02 – Matinee shows for children on Saturdays at 4pm, Sundays at 11am and 4pm, Wednesdays and Thursdays at 11am, 3pm and 4.15pm.* A view of Portugal's starry skies, an imaginary voyage through the planetary system, a trip to the moon, a journey across the polar region, various films, plus eclipses of the sun and the moon are just some of the audiovisual possibilities on offer at the Planetarium.

Dolphinarium, Jardim Zoológico

Alvito – Parque de Monsanto – *Parque Monsanto, Monsanto* – ☎ *(01) 362 29 94 – open in April and May from 9am to 7pm, from October to March from 9am to 5pm, and in summer from 9am to 8pm.* Children's play areas and two swimming pools, one of which is open to the general public from July to September, for children between 3 and 14.

Parque dos Índios – *Alto Serafina, Monsanto* – ☎ *(01) 362 29 94 – open Mondays to Fridays 9am to 8pm and Saturdays and Sundays 10am to 8pm.* One of the best parks for children in the city.

Aquário Vasco da Gama – *In Dáfundo to the north of Lisbon. See description under Visiting Lisbon- Additional Sights.* An aquarium with a variety of Atlantic, tropical and freshwater species.

Museu das Crianças – *Pç. Império – Belém* – ☎ *(01) 386 21 63 – open Wednesdays from 1.30pm to 5pm and Saturdays and Sundays from 10am to 5pm.* There is also a museum with interactive teaching games for 4 to 13 year olds on the first floor of the Museu da Marinha.

Museu das Marionetas – *Lg. Rodrigues Freitas, 19 – Alfama* – ☎ *(01) 886 33 04 – open Tuesdays to Fridays from 10am to 7pm; opens at 11am on Saturdays and Sundays.* An exhibition of traditional puppets made by the São Lourenço company and a few older models.

Marionetas de Lisboa – *Av. República 101 A* – ☎ *(01) 796 57 80 – Closed in August.* A show and workshops for children between 3 and 12 years of age. Manufacture and handling of puppets.

Associação Cultural da Lanterna Mágica – *Br. Alvito, 155* – ☎ *(01) 362 27 11.* A puppet theatre for children aged 3 and above.

Cinema Tivoli – *Av. da Liberdade 188* – ☎ *(01) 354 31 53 – open from the end of February to mid-December (except July and August)*: children's matinee performances on Sundays at 3.30pm.

Teatro de Animação "Os Papa Léguas" – *Rua Prof. Santos Lucas 36 A – Benfica* – ☎ *(01) 714 23 66 – Performances from Tuesdays to Fridays at 11am and 2pm, Saturdays at 4pm and on Sundays at 11am.* Programme of events available in the local press and by telephone.

Teatro do Calvário – Teatro Infantil de Lisboa – *Rua Leão Oliveira 1 – Alcântara* – ☎ *(01) 363 99 74.* A programme of theatre for children

Teatro Infantil – Teatro Maria Matos – *Av. Frei Miguel Contreiras 52, Av. de Roma* – ☎ *(01) 849 70 07. Performances open to the public on Saturdays at 4pm and 9.30pm and on Sundays at 4pm.*

A programme of theatre for children.

Feira Popular – *Av. da República (Metro: Entre Campos) – open from April to October.* Lisbon's funfair. Rides and typical restaurants.

Catch a train to Cascais from Cais do Sodré and enjoy a pleasant trip along the Tagus and the Atlantic.

Enchanting Lisbon

A selection of our favourite things to do and see in and around Lisbon.
– Boat trips on the Tagus – the approach to the Praça do Comércio. Tram number 28 – a scenic trip in an old tram from Graça to Estrela via the Alfama, Baixa and Chiado.
– The gardens of the Palácio dos Marqueses de Fronteira. Enjoy a *"pastel de nata"* pastry and a coffee at the Fábrica dos Pastéis in Belém *(see under The Lisbon Scene – Belém above).*
– Browse around the Feira da Ladra *(see Shopping – Markets above).*
– The view of the Alfama from the Largo das Portas do Sol.
– Lunch followed by a dance matinee at the Casa do Alentejo *(see Eating Out in Lisbon – Baixa above).*
– Laze around the terrace of the Brasileira café one afternoon.
– Wander through the Bairro Alto at night.
– The collection of Lalique jewellery at the Gulbenkian Museum *(see under Visiting Lisbon – Museu Calouste Gulbenkian)*
– The Rua de S. Pedro fish market in the Alfama.

Perspectives

Spread out over seven hills overlooking the Tagus, Lisbon is a hugely picturesque city as is revealed from its many breathtaking viewpoints *(miradouros)* which have been created (often with an open-air bar or stall) to provide visitors with a pleasant spot from which to admire the city. Below is a list of the most well-known viewpoints... you will undoubtedly discover even more as you wander around the city...

Castelo de São Jorge (LY) – A view over the Baixa district and the Tagus from the extensive and attractive terraces around the castle. Panoramic restaurant (Casa do Leão) and café.

Miradouro da Senhora do Monte (LV) – Panoramic views over the entire city centre. Café.

Largo das Portas do Sol (LY) – This pleasant square lined with palm trees provides plunging views over the Alfama. Café.

Miradouro de Santa Luzia (LY) – A long terrace decked in bougainvillaea close to the Largo das Portas do Sol – views over the Alfama and the Tagus in particular. Café.

Miradouro de São Pedro de Alcântara (JX) – Attractive shaded garden with a classic view of the Baixa and the Castelo de São Jorge. The gardens below, with their splash of bougainvillaea, is a landmark which is visible from several parts of the city.

Miradouro do Alto de Santa Catarina (JZ) – Views overlooking the Tagus. Café.

Miradouro da Graça (LX) – Views of the north side of the castle. Café.

Elevador de Santa Justa (KY) – View of the Rossio and Baixa from the upper platform.

Parque Eduardo VII (CP) – A fine view looking down the Avenida da Liberdade from the terraces at the top of the park.

Miradouro de Monsanto (AP) – *In the Parque Florestal de Monsanto. Access by car.* Although slightly out of the centre, this belvedere provides sweeping views of Lisbon. The Torres das Amoreiras and Ponte 25 de Abril are particularly visible. Panoramic restaurant.

and by the river...

The *cacilheiros* which cross the Tagus offer unforgettable views of the city. The approach to the Praça do Comércio is particularly memorable.

Cristo Rei – A superb view from the statue's pedestal *(access by lift then 74 steps).*

Ponte 25 de Abril (BQ) – A magnificent panorama of Lisbon and Belém's river fronts.

Brasiliera and statue of Pessoa

Visiting Lisbon

The capital of Portugal stands midway between north and south. At the time of the Great Discoveries, Lisbon, according to the Portuguese poet Camões, was the "princess of the world... before whom even the ocean bows."

The old town was built on the northern shore of the "Straw Sea", as the bulge in the Tagus – which then runs through a wide channel into the Atlantic – was called on account of the golden reflections of the sun at this spot. Lisbon has a jumbled skyline, its buildings dotted over seven hills offering wonderfully varied views. The attraction of the city lies in its light, its pastel ochres, pinks, blues and greens, and the mosaic paving of its streets and squares – the small black and white paving-stones made of limestone and basalt known as *empedrados*. Lisbon has managed to keep the charm of its past without allowing itself to become invaded by modern buildings, except for the Amoreiras towers and the occasional bank. With its maze of narrow streets in the old quarters, its magnificent vistas along wide avenues, its lively harbour and exotic gardens, Lisbon is a delightful patchwork to explore on foot or see from ancient trams. Lisbon (or LISHBOWA, as pronounced in Portuguese) is the principal heroine of *fado*, the lyrical chants full of nostalgia *(saudade)*.

The capital is at its most light-hearted when celebrating the feasts of the popular saints in June. St Antony's is a particularly joyful occasion when young men and women *(marchas populares)* parade down Avenida da Liberdade in traditional costume.

While Lisbon bears the stamp of its past, it has set its sights firmly on the future ever since Portugal became a member of the European Community in 1986. New business districts are being developed, particularly around **Campo Pequeno** (**CP**) and **Campo Grande** (**CN**), while the Centro Cultural de Belém, which was completed in 1992, was built to further the historical and cultural importance of this part of the city. The famous post-modern towers of **Amoreiras** (**BP**), adventurous pink, blue and grey constructions by the architect Tomás Taveira, caused a sensation when they first went up, while other towers, such as the headquarters of the BNU (also by Tomás Taveira) and the Caixa Geral de Depósitos savings bank, have sprung up around Campo Grande to become landmarks within the city.

The choice of Lisbon as the site for Expo'98 *(see page 175)* has resulted in a large-scale rebuilding programme along the Tagus, particularly at the Olivais docks, near to which the exhibition will be based, and the Santo Amaro, Santos and Alcântara docks, with their new leisure facilities, which include bars, restaurants and discos.

HISTORICAL NOTES

According to legend, the town was founded by Ulysses. Historians, however, attribute the city's foundation in 1200BC to the Phoenicians who named it "serene harbour". The town soon became a port of call for Mediterranean ships sailing to northern Europe; it was conquered first by the Greeks, then the Carthaginians and, in 138 AD became Roman. Then the Barbarians invaded it and for four centuries it was under Arab rule. In AD 714 the city took the name Lissabona but it was not until 25 October 1147 when King Dom Afonso Henriques captured it, with the aid of part of the fleet from the Second Crusade, that the Arab occupation finally ended. In 1255 Dom Afonso III chose Lisbon in place of Coimbra as the capital of Portugal.

Azulejos panel showing Lisbon before the 1755 earthquake

The Age of the Great Discoveries – Lisbon benefited from the riches that accumulated after the voyage of Vasco da Gama to the Indies in 1497-9 and the discovery of Brazil by Pedro Alvares Cabral in 1500. New trade routes developed, causing a decline in the prosperity of Venice and Genoa; merchants flocked to Lisbon which was packed with small traders buying and selling gold, silver, spices, ivory, silks, precious stones and rare woods. Monuments, including the Mosteiro dos Jerónimos and Torre de Belém, were built all over the town. The decoration of these buildings, which was always inspired by the sea, became known as the Manueline style after King Manuel.

The earthquake – On 1 November 1755 during High Mass the town was shaken by an exceptionally violent earth tremor: churches, palaces and houses collapsed; fire spread from the wax candles in the churches to furnishings and woodwork; survivors rushed to take refuge in the Tagus, but a huge wave came upstream, breaking over and destroying the lower town. Lisbon's riches were engulfed.

The King, Dom José I escaped as did his minister, Sebastião de Carvalho e Melo, the future Marquis of Pombal. The minister immediately began to re-establish life in the city. In collaboration with the civil engineer Manuel de Maia and the architect Eugenio dos Santos, Pombal undertook the rebuilding of Lisbon to plans and in a style utterly revolutionary for the period. The straight wide avenues, the plain and stylised houses to be seen in the Baixa today are... Pombal's legacy.

The Lines of Tôrres Vedras – The Lines of Tôrres Vedras was the name given to a system of defence lines conceived by Wellington in 1810 to protect Lisbon from attack by the French under the command of Masséna. It was also estimated that, if necessary, British troops could be either landed or evacuated through the lines.

The lines were an assemblage of defensive positions, fortifications, embrasures and roads, rather than a continuous line. The positions, nevertheless, stretched from Tôrres Vedras, 70km/43mi north of Lisbon to Alhandra, near Vila Franca de Xira, at the furthest point inland reached by the Sea of Straw. Masséna, after a minor skirmish, during which he could personally observe the system's strength, decided not to attack in the immediate instance and later (December 1810) began what ended as the final retreat northwards out of Portugal altogether.

The Carnation Revolution – At 4.30am on April 25, 1974, Portuguese radio broadcast a message from the command of the Movement of the Armed Forces (Movimento das Forças Armadas) calling upon the population to keep calm and remain indoors. This was the beginning of the *coup d'état* led by General Antonio de Spanila against the regime instituted by Salazar and maintained by his successor Caetano. Spinola's take-over was virtually bloodless and his soldiers, with a red carnation stuck in the barrel of their rifles, were acclaimed by the citizens of Lisbon, who, ignoring the orders, surged out of their homes onto Praça do Comércio.

The Lisbonites (Lisboetas) – One of Lisbon's most endearing qualities is the friendly, approachable, easygoing character of its residents. Street vendors selling lottery tickets or hot chestnuts call out to passers-by, shoeblacks are still in evidence, housewives in some quarters still hang washing from their windows, and during football matches the entire town holds its breath for news of a goal (two of the country's three main clubs are in Lisbon: Benfica and the Sporting Club de Portugal).

In summer there is a general exodus to the popular beaches of Costa da Caparica or the more elegant resorts in Serra de Arrábida and Cascais.

Museu Nacional do Azulejo – Carlos Monteiro/ANF-IPM

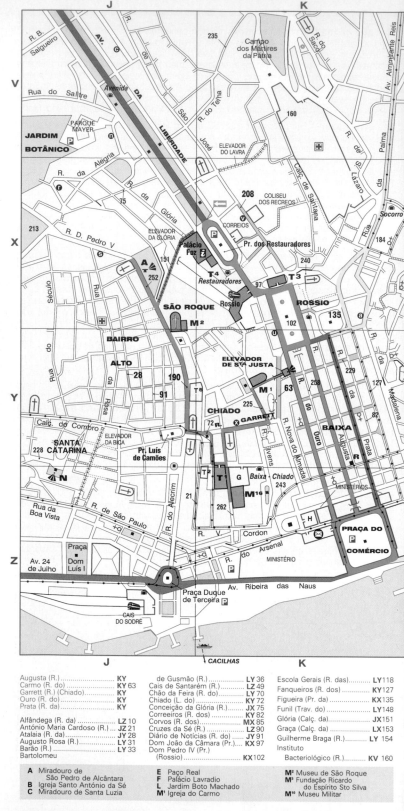

Augusta (R.) .... **KY**
Carmo (R. do) .... **KY** 63
Garrett (R.) (Chiado) ... **KY**
Ouro (R. do) .... **KY**
Prata (R. da) .... **KY**

Alfândega (R. da) .... **LZ** 10
António Maria Cardoso (R.) ... **JZ** 21
Atalaia (R. da) .... **JY** 28
Augusto Rosa (R.) .... **LY** 31
Barão (R.) .... **LY** 33
Bartolomeu

de Gusmão (R.) .... **LY** 36
Cais de Santarém (R.) .... **LZ** 49
Chão da Feira (R. do) .... **LY** 70
Chiado (L. do) .... **KY** 72
Conceição da Glória (R.) .... **JX** 75
Correeiros (R. dos) .... **KY** 82
Corvos (R. dos) .... **MX** 85
Cruzes da Sé (R.) .... **LZ** 90
Diário de Notícias (R. do) ... **JY** 91
Dom João da Câmara (Pr.) ... **KX** 97
Dom Pedro IV (Pr.)
(Rossio) .... **KX** 102

Escola Gerais (R. das) .... **LY** 118
Fanqueiros (R. dos) .... **KY** 127
Figueira (Pr. da) .... **KX** 135
Funil (Trav. do) .... **LY** 148
Glória (Calç. da) .... **JX** 151
Graça (Calç. da) .... **LX** 153
Guilherme Braga (R.) .... **LY** 154
Instituto
Bacteriológico (R.) .... **KV** 160

A Miradouro de
São Pedro de Alcântara
B Igreja Santo António da Sé
C Miradouro de Santa Luzia

E Paço Real
F Palácio Lavradio
L Jardim Boto Machado
M¹ Igreja do Carmo

M² Museu de São Roque
M³ Fundação Ricardo
do Espírito Sto Silva
M¹⁰ Museu Militar

When travelling in the Portuguese capital, use the new Michelin map 39 of Lisbon (1:10 000 scale). Use the index to locate streets, public buildings and many tourist attractions. One-way streets are indicated for motorists.

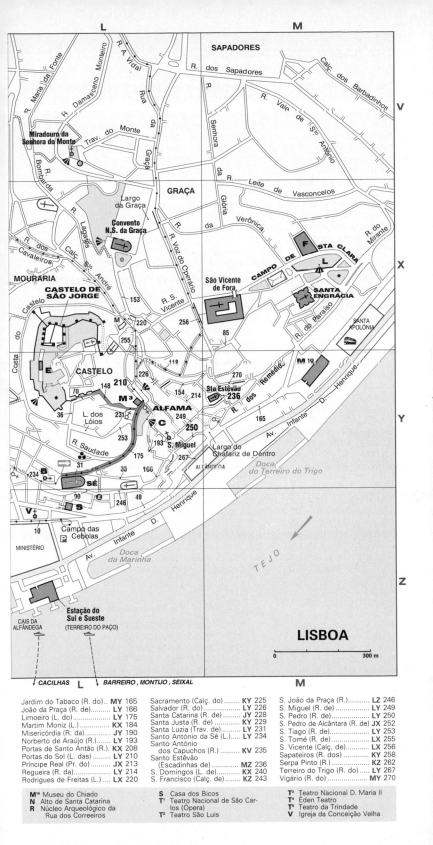

LISBOA

Jardim do Tabaco (R. do).. **MY** 165
João da Praça (R. de).......... **LY** 166
Limoeiro (L. do)................... **LY** 175
Martim Moniz (L.) .... **KX** 184
Misericórdia (R. da)............ **JY** 190
Norberto de Araújo (R.)....... **LY** 193
Portas de Santo Antão (R.). **KX** 208
Portas do Sol (L. das)........ **LY** 210
Príncipe Real (Pr. do)......... **JX** 213
Regueira (R. da)................. **LY** 214
Rodrigues de Freitas (L.) .... **LX** 220

Sacramento (Calç. do) .... **KY** 225
Salvador (R. do)................. **LY** 226
Santa Catarina (R. de) .... **JY** 228
Santa Justa (R. de) .... **KY** 229
Santa Luzia (Trav. de).......... **LY** 231
Santo António da Sé (L.)...... **LY** 234
Santo António
  dos Capuchos (R.) .... **KV** 235
Santo Estêvão
  (Escadinhas de).............. **MZ** 236
S. Domingos (L. de)............ **KX** 240
S. Francisco (Calç. de) .... **KZ** 243

S. João da Praça (R.).......... **LZ** 246
S. Miguel (R. de) .... **LY** 249
S. Pedro (R. de).................. **LY** 250
S. Pedro de Alcântara (R. de) **JX** 252
S. Tiago (R. de) .... **LX** 253
S. Tomé (R. de) .... **LX** 255
S. Vicente (Calç. de)........... **LX** 256
Sapateiros (R. dos) .... **KY** 258
Serpa Pinto (R.) .... **KZ** 262
Terreiro do Trigo (R. do) ..... **LY** 267
Vigário (R. do) .... **MY** 270

M¹⁸ Museu do Chiado
N Alto de Santa Catarina
R Núcleo Arqueológico da
  Rua dos Correeiros

S Casa dos Bicos
T¹ Teatro Nacional de São Car-
  los (Ópera)
T² Teatro São Luis

T³ Teatro Nacional D. Maria II
T⁴ Éden Teatro
T⁵ Teatro da Trindade
V Igreja da Conceição Velha

*The key on p 4 explains the abbreviations and symbols
used in the text or on the maps.*

★★THE BAIXA – 2hr

Follow the itinerary suggested on the plan.

This part of the city, which was completely devastated by the earthquake and tidal wave in 1755, was rebuilt to plans laid down by the Marquis of Pombal.

Praça dos Restauradores (**KX**) – The square owes its name to the men who in 1640 led the revolt against the Spanish and proclaimed the independence of Portugal. The event is commemorated by the obelisk in the centre. The fine red roughcast façade on the west of the square belongs to the **Palácio Foz** built by an Italian architect in the early 19C. Today it houses Lisbon's Tourist Information Centre *(Posto de Turismo)*.

Next door is the **Éden Teatro** (**KX T⁴**), designed by Cassiano Branco and opened in 1937. A part of its Art-Deco façade and its monumental stairs remain from the original building which is now occupied by the Virgin Megastore.

Avenida da Liberdade runs northeast off the square to the Parque Eduardo VII. Parallel to the avenue is **Rua Portas de Santo Antão** (**KX 208**), a picturesque pedestrian street with cinemas (Coliseu dos Recreos at no 100), cafés and traditional shops. The **Casa do Alentejo** at no 58 *(see Travellers' addresses – Eating Out)* has an unusual Moorish courtyard and a restaurant with abundant *azulejo* decoration.

Estação do Rossio (**KX**) – The station, which serves the town of Sintra, has a 19C neo-Manueline **façade**★ with wide horseshoe shaped openings.

★**Rossio** (**KX**) – Praça Dom Pedro IV, the lively main square of the Baixa, dates from the 13C and was the setting for many *autodafés*. Its present appearance is due to Pombal: 18 and 19C buildings line it on three sides, the ground floors being given over to cafés such as the famous Nicola with its art deco façade, and small shops that have kept their decoration from the beginning of the century. Among these are the tobacconist's near Nicola with *azulejos* by Rafael Bordalo Pinheiro, and the corner shop which serves *ginginha*, the well-known cherry liqueur, off Largo de São Domingos, next to a milliner's dating from the last century *(see Travellers' addresses – Shopping)*.

The north side of the square is bordered by the **Teatro Nacional Dona Maria II** (T) which was built in about 1840 on the site of the former Palace of the Inquisition. The façade, with peristyle and pediment, is adorned with a statue of Gil Vicente, the father of Portuguese theatre.

A column in the middle of the square, between the baroque fountains, bears the bronze statue (1870) of Dom Pedro IV, after whom the square is named and who was also crowned Pedro I, Emperor of Brazil. Flower stalls add a colourful surround to the fountains.

Parallel to the Rossio to the east is the **Praça da Figueira** (**KX 135**), a square of classical buildings with an equestrian statue of Dom João I in the centre. Here, the rear terrace of the famous Pastelaria Suiça *(see Travellers' addresses – the Lisbon scene)*, a café with its main façade on the Rossio, is an excellent spot for enjoying a view of the castle and the hustle and bustle of the Baixa district.

South of the square is the grid of Baixa streets, some pedestrian, which forms Lisbon's main shopping district. The streets running south between the Rossio and Praça do Comércio are named after guilds. Among them are Rua dos Correeiros (Saddlers' Street) and Rua dos Sapateiros (Cobblers's Street). The three main ones are Rua do Ouro (Goldsmiths' Street), **Rua Augusta** and Rua da Prata (Silversmith's Street).

Rua do Ouro (or Rua Áurea) (**KY**) – In the 15 and 16C, this street was the gold trading area of Lisbon; today it is lined with banks, jewellers and goldsmiths.

> ### Pedro IV or Maximilian of Mexico?
>
> The statue atop the column in the centre of the Rossio is in fact believed to have originally been cast as Maximilian of Austria, Emperor of Mexico. The boat transporting the statue to Mexico called at Lisbon when news of the emperor's assassination was heard. The captain, faced with the dilemma of what to do with the statue, left it in Lisbon and a decision was finally made to use it to replace the existing one of Pedro IV which was rather rudimentary.

Núcleo Arqueológico da Rua dos Correeiros ⊘ (**KY R**) – This important and well-presented archaeological site, located in the basement of the Banco Comercial Português, contains Roman remains which were discovered here in 1991 when the bank moved into the building. The site provides a comprehensive history of the Baixa district from its first period of occupation in the 7C BC onwards. An exhibition room by the entrance displays a number of objects from various periods which were discovered during excavations. The glass floor enables the superpositioning of construction from the Pombaline period down to the phreatic layer to be seen. The site was

Rua Augusta

used as a pottery workshop (5 – 3C BC), a necropolis (2C BC), and from the 1 – 5C AD it was an important manufacturing complex linked to the district's port and fishing activities, as shown by the presence of 25 fish-salting tanks. A mosaic dating from the 3C and an oven used for the production of ceramics dating from the Moorish period are worthy of note. Also visible is a part of the interesting Pombaline anti-seismic structure, consisting of green pine stakes knocked into the floor and submerged in water, on which the building's foundations were then laid.

★★ **Praça do Comércio (or Terreiro do Paço) (KZ)** – The finest square in Lisbon is where the Royal Palace once stood, facing the Straw Sea *(Mar da Palha)*. The palace was destroyed by the earthquake and in its memory the citizens have named the square Terreiro do Paço or the Palace Terrace.

The square was designed as a whole and is an excellent example of the Pombal style. It is 192m long by 177m wide/630ft x 581ft and lined on three sides by classical and uniform buildings with tall arcades supporting two upper storeys with red façades. Today the buildings house government departments.

A 19C baroque triumphal arch forms a backdrop to the equestrian statue of King José I. This statue by the late 18C sculptor Machado de Castro is cast in bronze and is the reason for the square also being known, particularly to the English, as Black Horse Square.

On February I, 1908, King Carlos I and his heir, Prince Luis Felipe, were assassinated on the square.

Southeast of the square is Lisbon's South Station, the **Estação do Sul e Sueste (LZ)**, which is decorated with *azulejo* panels of towns in the Alentejo and the Algarve. Passengers embark from here by ferry to the railway station on the opposite shore of the Tagus for destinations south and southeast.

★ **Elevador de Santa Justa** ⊙ **(KY)** – The lift was built in 1902 by Raul Mesnier de Ponsard, a Portuguese engineer of French origin who was influenced by Gustave Eiffel. From the upper platform there is a good **view★** of the Rossio and the Baixa.

The lift gives direct access to the Chiado quarter, which can also be reached on foot by taking Rua do Carmo and Rua Garrett.

★CHIADO AND BAIRRO ALTO – *2hr*

The name Chiado applies not only to Largo do Chiado but also to a whole district of which the main streets, Rua Garrett and Rua do Carmo, link the Rossio to Praça Luis de Camões.

The lift ascends to the area struck by fire on August 25, 1988. The four blocks of buildings damaged were mainly shops including the *Grandella* department store (since replaced by the French department store Printemps) and the *Ferrari* tearoom. More than 2 000 people lost their jobs as a result of the fire. Immediately after the event, the mayor of Lisbon entrusted the rehabilitation of the area to the well-known Portuguese architect Álvaro Siza who put forward a resolutely classical plan to reconstitute and safeguard the façades of the buildings, and to transform their interiors into pleasant patios, elegant shops and café terraces.

*Igreja do Carmo and Museu Arqueológico ⊙ (**KY M¹**) – Once through the doorway of the Carmelite Church, the visitor is struck by the atmospheric aura of the ruins; pillars soar skywards, silence reigns. The church was devastated by the earthquake on November 1, 1755.

Today, the ruins of the Gothic church, built in the late 14C by Constable Nuno Álvares Pereira, house an archaeological museum. Among the collections are Bronze Age pottery, marble low reliefs, Romanesque and Gothic tombs (including the recumbent statue of Fernão Sanchez, illegitimate son of Dom Dinis) and Spanish Arabic *azulejos.*

Ruins of the Igreja do Carmo

*Rua do Carmo and Rua Garrett (**KY**) – These elegant streets with their old-fashioned shop fronts are renowned for their bookshops, patisseries and cafés. The most famous of the latter is the **Brasileira** *(See Travellers' addresses – the Lisbon scene),* once frequented by the poet Fernando Pessoa. The centenary of his birth was celebrated in 1988. A bronze statue of the poet, portrayed in a pensive mood, has been placed at one of the tables on the terrace.

*Museu Nacional do Chiado ⊙ (**KZ M¹⁶**) – The building, originally a 13C abbey, was transformed into a contemporary arts museum in 1911. Following the 1988 fire, it was elegantly refurbished by the French architect, Jean-Michel Wilmotte. He remodelled the museum into one of open spaces, linked by connecting passageways which enable the building's original structure to be seen. The museum displays an exhibition of predominantly Portuguese paintings, drawings and sculpture from the hundred year period between 1850 and 1950. The first floor is devoted to French sculpture, including Rodin's *Bronze Age;* Canto da Maia's *Adam and Eve* is also worthy of note. Soares dos Reis' sculpture *O Desterrado (The Exile)* stands out among the works on the second floor. Various periods are represented: the **Romantic, Naturalist** *(A Charneca de Belas* by Silva Porto, *Concerto de Amadores* by Columbano, and *A Beira-Mar* by José Malhoa) and **Modernist** *(Tristezas* by Amadeo de Souza-Cardoso, *O Bailarico no Bairro* by Mário Eloy, *Nú* by Eduardo Viana, and the drawing *A Sesta* by Almada Negreiros), and a small collection of **Symbolist** and **Neo-realist** works.

The museum also has a gallery for temporary exhibitions and a good cafeteria which looks onto a pleasant garden and terrace with a view over the rooftops of Lisbon.

Teatro Nacional de São Carlos (**KZ T¹**) – This lavish theatre, situated in a calm, delightful setting, was built in 1793 in neo-Classical style with a façade inspired by La Scala in Milan. Its programme includes performances of classical music and dance.

Praça Luis de Camões – The square, with a statue of the great poet at its centre, was one of the stages for the revolution on 25 April 1974. After taking the Largo do Carmo barracks, where Marcelo Caetano was at the time, the population of the city formed a cortege for the soldiers in their assault vehicles on their way up to the Chiado, where they celebrated their regained freedom. The square is the transition zone between the Chiado and the Bairro Alto. To the south, at the bottom of the steep Rua do Alecrim, the Tagus comes into view.

Rua da Misericórdia (**JY 190**) – The street is part of the Praça Camões and borders the Bairro Alto quarter to the west of Chiado.

★**Bairro Alto (JY)** – This picturesque working-class quarter dating from the 16C has kept its character in spite of it becoming the centre for trendy fashion houses, designers, restaurants and folkloric *fado* houses over the past few years. The main shopping streets are **Rua do Diário de Not'c'as (91)** and **Rua de Atalaia (28)**. Sunsets over the Tagus are wonderful when viewed from the **Alto de Santa Catarina★ (JZ N)** belvedere with its statue of Adamastor, the giant who was transformed into the Cape of Storms (Cape of Good Hope).

★**Igreja de São Roque (JX)** – The Church of St Rock was built in the late 16C by the Italian architect Filippo Terzi, also responsible for the Church of São Vicente de Fora *(see below)*. The original façade collapsed in the great earthquake of 1755. The **interior★** decoration is strikingly elegant. The wooden ceiling painted with scenes of the Apocalypse above the nave is by artists of the Italian School. The third chapel on the right is interesting for its 16C **azulejos** and a painting on wood of the Vision of St Rock by the 16C artist Gaspar Vaz.

The chapel, **Capela de São João Baptista★★** *(4th on the left)*, a masterpiece of Italian baroque, was originally built in Rome to plans by Salvi and Vanvitelli when 130 artists contributed to its completion. After being blessed by the Pope, it was transported to Lisbon in three ships on the orders of King João V and re-erected in about 1750 in this church. All the materials used are extremely rich: the columns are of lapis lazuli, the altar front of amethyst, the steps of porphyry, the angels of white Carrara marble and ivory, the pilasters of alabaster; the flooring and the wall pictures are coloured mosaics, and the friezes, capitals and ceiling are highlighted with gold, silver and bronze. The first chapel on the left contains two paintings attributed to the school of Zurbarán *(Nativity* and *Adoration of the Magi)*, and the **sacristy** *(access through the north transept)* has a 17C coffered ceiling and paintings of St Francis by Vieira Lusitano and André Gonçalves.

★**Museu de Arte Sacra de São Roque** ⊘ **(JX M²)** – The museum abuts on the church *(access by the last door on the left as you leave the church)*. This modern-style museum contains 16C Portuguese paintings and part of the treasure from the Capela do São João Baptista of which a wooden model is on display. The furnishings and ecclesiastical plate by 18C Italian artists are outstanding for their rich baroque decoration. There is also a collection of **vestments★** in silk or lamé embroidered in gold. In the first gallery, a fine canopied altar in chased silver is framed by two silver candelabra.

★**Miradouro de São Pedro de Alcântara (JX A)** – The belvedere takes the form of a pleasant garden suspended like a balcony over the lower town with a wide **view★★** of the Baixa, the Tagus and Castelo de São Jorge on the hill opposite *(viewing table)*.

The Calçada da Gloria funicular descends to Praça dos Restauradores.

★★ALFAMA – *3hr*

Follow the itinerary suggested on the plan.

The Alfama, a district demarcated by the castle to the north, the districts of Graça and Mouraria to the northeast, and the Tagus to the south is a cobbled maze of narrow twisting streets and alleys *(becos)* cut by a multitude of steps and archways. Despite the earthquake of 1755, it has still managed to preserve its original layout and feel. The "white city" immortalised in the 1983 film by the French director Tanner, is a quarter with a North-African flavour and an Arab name: the Arabic *alhama*, meaning fountain, here recalls the hot springs in Largo das Alcaçarias. The Alfama was already in existence when the Visigoths arrived. The Roman presence is visible in the ruins of the 1C BC **Teatro Romano** in Rua da Saudade, as well as in the excavations in the cathedral. The Arabs built noblemen's mansions and the Christians churches of which most were demolished during the earthquake. The Alfama then became a quarter of seamen. Today, the houses, which are often dilapidated, are adorned with wrought-iron balconies and panels of *azulejos*, usually showing the Virgin between St Antony and St Martial.

Although the Alfama has undergone considerable restoration, including recent projects to modernise the district's infrastructure, it has, on the whole, managed to retain its authentic character.

The most pleasant way to see the Alfama quarter, which may be approached from above, Largo das Portas do Sol, or from below, alongside the Tagus, is simply to spend time wandering through the district, preferably in the morning when the market is open. The following, however, is a suggested itinerary.

★★**Sé** (Cathedral) – Lisbon's cathedral, like those of Oporto, Coimbra and Évora, was once a fortress, as can be seen from the two towers flanking the façade and its battlements. It was built in the Romanesque style in the late 12C, shortly after Afonso Henriques had captured the town with the aid of the Crusaders. The architects, it is believed, were the Frenchmen Robert and Bernard who designed

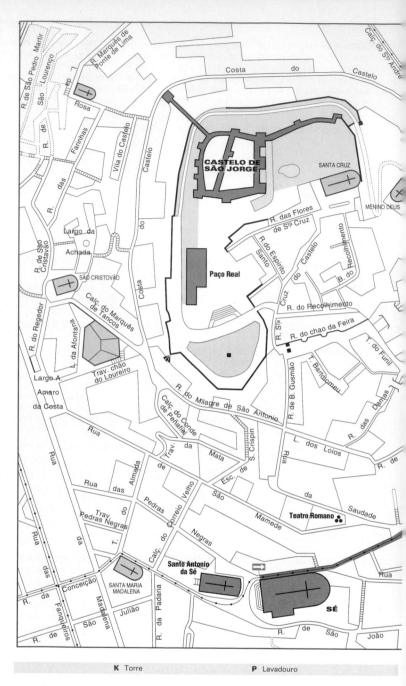

K Torre   P Lavadouro

Coimbra Cathedral. Remodelling followed each earthquake, particularly that of 1755 when the chancel collapsed, also bringing down the lantern tower over the transept. Clever restoration has given the building much of its former Romanesque appeal on the façade and in the nave, although Gothic features and the remodelling of the 17 and 18C are also apparent.

In the **interior**, the nave, supported by wide arches and graceful groined vaulting, is in plain Romanesque style. An elegant triforium runs above the aisles and the transept. The Bartolomeu Joanes Chapel, off the north aisle, containing a lovely terracotta crib by Machado de Castro, is Gothic in style.

The chancel, with its groined vaulting, was rebuilt in the 18C, but the ambulatory, pierced with lancet windows, kept the earlier Gothic style of the 14C when it was remodelled. The third radiating chapel starting from the south side contains the 14C **Gothic tombs★** of Lopo Fernandes Pacheco, companion in arms to King Afonso IV, and his wife. Note an elegant Romanesque wrought iron **grille★** enclosing a chapel near the entrance to the cloisters.

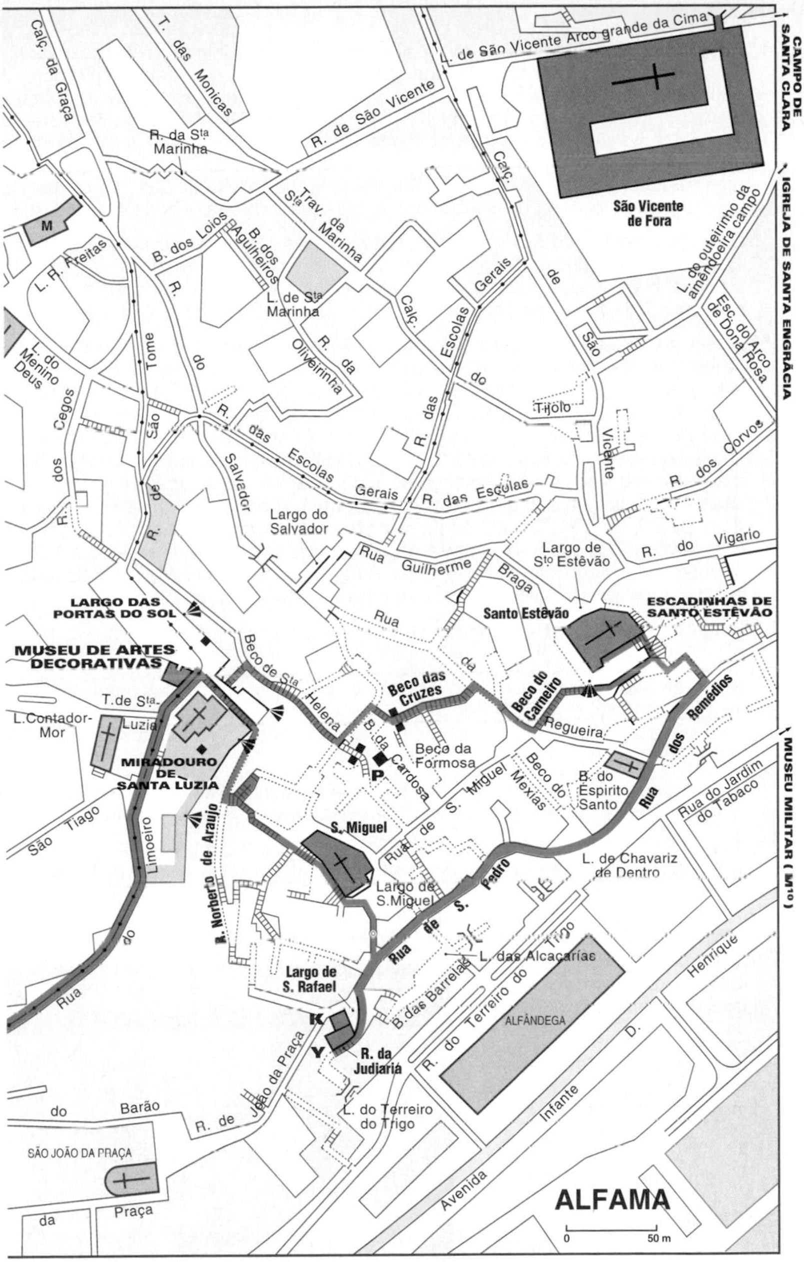

The map shows street names in the Alfama district of Lisbon, including:

CAMPO DE SANTA CLARA
IGREJA DE SANTA ENGRÁCIA
MUSEU MILITAR (M¹⁰)

São Vicente de Fora

T. das Mónicas
Calç. da Graça
L. de São Vicente Arco grande da Cima
R. da Stª Marinha
R. de São Vicente
L. R. Freitas
M
B. dos Loios
B. dos Aguilheiros
Trav. da Marinha
R.
Calç. Gerais
de
R. do
L. de Stª Marinha
L. do Menino Deus
Cebos
sop
R. do
do
R. da Oliveirinha
R. das Escolas Gerais
R. das
Escolas Gerais
de
São
Vicente
R. dos Corvos
Salvador
R. das Escolas
Largo do Salvador
Largo de Stº Estêvão
R. do Vigário
Rua Guilherme Braga
Escº. do Arco de Dona Rosa
L. do outeirinho da amêndoeira campo
LARGO DAS PORTAS DO SOL
Rua
ESCADINHAS DE SANTO ESTÊVÃO
MUSEU DE ARTES DECORATIVAS
Santo Estêvão
T. de Stª.
Beco de Stª Helena
Beco das Cruzes
Beco do Carneiro
da
R. dos Remédios
L.Contador-Mor
Luzia
Regueira
B. da Cardosa
Beco da Formosa
P
Rua do Jardim do Tabaco
MIRADOURO DE SANTA LUZIA
Rua de S. Miguel
Beco do Mexias
B. do Espírito Santo
Rua dos
São Tiago
S. Miguel
Largo de S.Miguel
Rua de S. Pedro
L. de Chavariz de Dentro
R. Norberto de Araújo
Limoeiro
Largo de S. Rafael
L. das Alcaçarias
B. das Barreiras
R. do Terreiro do Trigo
ALFÂNDEGA
Henrique
Rua
K
Y
R. da Judiaria
D.
João da Praça
Infante
L. do Terreiro do Trigo
do
Barão
R. de
SÃO JOÃO DA PRAÇA
da
Praça
AVENIDA
ALFAMA

0   50 m

Y   Casa de janelas geminadas

The rather damaged **cloisters** ⊘ *(access through the third chapel off the ambulatory)* are in the late 13C style of Cistercian Gothic: the lower gallery is supported alternately by massive buttresses and Gothic arches, above which are star-shaped oculi. The chapter house contains the tomb of Lisbon's first bishop. Excavations in the garden of the cloisters have led to the discovery of vestiges from the Phoenician (8C BC) and Roman periods, as well as the ruins of a former mosque (9 and 10C).

★ **Tesouro** ⊘ – *Access to the treasury on the right, near the entrance to the cathedral.* A staircase leads to a series of rooms displaying magnificent vestments as well as reliquaries and gold and silver plate. The impressive 18C chapter room contains the **King Dom José I monstrance**, richly decorated with 4120 precious stones.
Not far from the cathedral stands the **Igreja de Santo António da Sé** which was built on the site of the house in which St Anthony of Padua (1194-1231) was born. He is Lisbon's patron saint and a small museum, the **Museu Antoniano** ⊘, testifies to his popularity.

171

★**Miradouro de Santa Luzia** – A small terrace near the Church of Santa Luzia has been laid out as a lookout point on the remains of the old Arab fortifications. It affords an excellent **view**★★ of the Tagus, the harbour and, just below, the Alfama quarter, a maze of alleys from which rise the belfries of São Miguel and São Estêvão. The outer walls of the Church of Santa Luzia are covered with small panels of *azulejos*, one of which shows Praça do Comércio and another Lisbon's capture by the Crusaders and the death of Martim Moniz in the Castelo de São Jorge. *Azulejos* covering a wall marking the south edge of the square show a general view of Lisbon.

★**Largo das Portas do Sol** – The Sun Gateway was one of the seven gates into the Arab city. The square, situated on the other side of the Church of Santa Luzia, has a pleasant small esplanade which offers yet another wonderful **view**★★ over the rooftops, São Vicente de Fora and the river *(see photograph p 138-139)*.

★★**Museu de Artes Decorativas – Fundação Ricardo Espirito Santo Silva** ⊘ – The former palace of the Counts of Azurara (17C) and the wonderful collections it contains were bequeathed to the city of Lisbon by Ricardo Espírito Santo Silva. The museum brings to life the Lisbon of the 17 and 18C through a series of small, intimate rooms decorated with *azulejos* and frescoes on three floors. Level 4 (second floor) is quite elegant, while Level 3 displays interiors with a plainer, yet no less handsome, decorative touch. The Portuguese and Indo-Portuguese furniture is particularly interesting; there are also collections of silver, Chinese porcelain and several tapestries from the 16 and 18C. Level 3 contains a temporary exhibition room and a cafeteria with a welcoming patio. A separate decorative arts school was created in 1953.

Starting from Largo das Portas do Sol, take the steps down from **Rua Norberto de Araújo**, which are supported on one side by the Moorish town wall.

Igreja de São Miguel – Although the church is medieval in origin, it was rebuilt after the earthquake. It contains some fine baroque woodwork.

Largo de São Rafael – On the west side of this small square surrounded by 17C houses, there still stands the remains of a **tower** (**K**) which formed part of the Arab wall and later the defences of Christian Lisbon until the 14C when King Fernando had a new wall built.

Rua da Judiaria (Jewish Quarter) – In this street stands a 16C **house** (**Y**) with paired windows, above the fortifification of the old Arab wall.

Rua de São Pedro and Rua dos Remédios – These are the busiest trading streets in the Alfama, lined with small shops and local taverns. Rua de São Pedro is at its liveliest in the morning when its fish market is held. At the head of Rua dos Remédios, note on the left-hand side the Manueline door on the Igreja do Santo Espírito. Further along, at number 2 Calçadinha de Santo Estêvão, another doorway from the same period can be seen.

★**Escadinhas de Santo Estêvão** – The harmonious interplay of stairs, terrace and architecture make this one of the Alfama's most picturesque spots. As you head behind the Church of Santo Estêvão, note a balcony and a panel of *azulejos*. Climb the stairs which skirt alongside the church. At the top you are rewarded with a fine **view**★ over the rooftops, bristling with television aerials, to the harbour and the Tagus. Descend the same stairs and turn right onto Beco do Carneiro.

Beco de Carneiro – An extremely narrow street with very steep steps. At the bottom of the street to the right you will see a **public washing-place** (**P**). Look behind you for a fine view of the façade of the church of Santo Estêvão.

J. P. Lescourret/EXPLORER

Fish market, Rua de S. Pedro

Beco das Cruzes – At the corner of this street and Rua de Regueira stands an 18C house where the overhanging upper floors are supported by carved corbels. Above one of the doors a panel of *azulejos* shows the Virgin of Conception; from the same spot there is a view up the alley to where it is crossed by an arch surmounted by a cross.

Take Beco de Santa Helena back up to Largo das Portas do Sol.

Take Travessa de Santa Luzia, which leads to the castle.

★★**Castelo de São Jorge** – The castle, the heart of the city, stands in a remarkable position. Built by the Visigoths in the 5C, enlarged by the Moors in the 9C and then modified during the reign of Afonso Henriques, it has since been turned into a shaded flower garden.

After passing through the outer wall, which provides a perimeter to the old medieval quarter of Santa Cruz, you reach the former parade ground from where there is a magnificent **view**★★★ of the Straw Sea – the Mar de Palha as the Portuguese call the Tagus at this point, for the sun often gives it a gold reflection – the industrial buildings on the south bank of the river, the suspension bridge, the lower town and the Parque de Monsanto. The glacis makes a pleasant walk.

The castle's ten towers are linked by massive battlemented walls. Once through the barbican at the castle entrance, steps lead to the parapet walk and the tops of the towers which provide **viewpoints** over the town. Note in passing the door in the north wall where the Portuguese knight **Martim Moniz** stood his famous ground: at the cost of his own life, he prevented the Moors from shutting the gate while Afonso Henriques was making his attack.

The Royal Palace, **Paço Real**, built on the site of a former Arab palace, was used as the royal residence by the kings of Portugal from the 14 to 16C.

Around the Alfama

The following sights can all be reached on tram number 28.

Igreja de São Vicente de Fora – Filippo Terzi built the church between 1582 and 1627. Its name Fora, meaning beyond the wall, derives from the fact that at the time of its construction it was indeed outside the city walls.

The interior, which is covered with a fine coffered vault, is outstanding for the simplicity of its lines. On the south side of the church, the **cloisters** have walls covered in 18C **azulejos**★ illustrating the *Fables* of La Fontaine. Galleries lead to the former monks' refectory which, after the reign of Dom João IV was transformed into a pantheon for the House of Bragança.

In the convent caretaker's lodge *(portaria)* the ceiling was painted by Vincenzo Baccerelli (18C) and the large *azulejo* panel depicts the taking of Lisbon from the Moors: the Castelo de São Jorge and the cathedral are distinguishable.

★**Campo de Santa Clara (MX)** – The attractive square between the churches of São Vicente and Santa Engrácia is the setting on Tuesdays and Saturdays for the **Feira da Ladra** *(see Travellers' addresses – Shopping)*, a colourful flea-market where fine pieces of old pottery may be found among the clothes and second-hand goods. On the northern side of the square stands the graceful 18C **Palácio Lavradio (F)** which houses the military tribunal. The small **Jardim Boto Machado (L)**, offers a welcome haven of peace and tranquillity amid its exotic plants and affords a lovely view over the Straw Sea below.

★**Igreja de Santa Engrácia** ☉ **(MX)** – Begun in the 17C the church was never completed. In the form of a Greek cross, it is now surmounted by a cupola inaugurated in 1966 which completes the baroque façade. The church has since become the national pantheon with the cenotaphs of six great Portuguese men: Luis de Camões, Prince Henry the Navigator, Pedro Álvares Cabral, Vasco da Gama, Afonso de Albuquerque and Nuno Álvares Pereira.

"Like work on Santa Engrácia" has become a common expression for projects that are never completed.

Graça – This popular residential district, where several villas and working class areas from the last century can still be seen, is situated on the hill to the north of the city, overlooking the Alfama.

Igreja and Convento de Nossa Senhora da Graça (LX) – This imposing religious complex on the Graça hill dominates the city. Although the church and convent were founded in the 13C, they have been rebuilt on a number of occasions, particularly after the earthquake in 1755. Note the bell-tower constructed in 1738 next to the convent doorway. The interior is baroque in style and contains fine 17 and 18C *azulejos*. Opposite the church there is a belvedere offering an extensive **view**★ over the city, with the castle to the east and the bridge and river to the west.

Miradouro da Senhora do Monte (LV) – This affords an extensive **view**★★★ over Lisbon and in particular over the Castelo de São Jorge and the Mouraria quarter. The chapel next to the belvedere dates from 1796, although its origins can be traced back to 1147, the year of Lisbon's reconquest.

Igreja da Conceição Velha (LZ V) – The **south side★** of the transept, the only remains of the original church which collapsed in the earthquake of 1755, is a fine example of the Manueline style. The carving on the tympanum shows Our Lady of Compassion sheltering with her cloak Pope Leo X, Dom Manuel, Dona Leonor, bishops and others.

Casa dos Bicos (LZ S) – This House of Facets, faced with diamond-shaped bosses, once formed part of a 16C palace which was damaged in the 1755 earthquake. It belonged to the son of Afonso de Albuquerque, the viceroy of India. It lost its top floor in the earthquake, but was rebuilt in 1982.

THE PORT AND THE TAGUS

Porto de Lisboa – The port is one of the main places of call in Europe with docks, quays, warehouses and quayside stations extending over some 20km/12mi along the bank of the Tagus from Algés to Sacavém. Annual traffic amounts to about 15million tons, mostly in imports and capital goods. Agricultural products, essentially wine and cork, are shipped abroad through the port. Industrial complexes have developed towards Vila Franca de Xira, including grain silos, cement works, oil storage tanks, steel mills, cork factories and refrigeration plants for storing cod etc. As the four dry docks at the Rocha shipyard on the north bank of the Tagus were not large enough to take the latest tankers, a larger yard has been built by the Lisnave organisation facing Lisbon in Margueira Bay on the Tagus's south bank. This new yard, which was opened in 1967, has three dry docks, the longest (520m/1 706ft) is capable of taking the largest oil tankers. The yard, in a latitude through which 75% of the world's tankers pass, also provides repair, degassing and cleaning facilities for ships..

★**Boat trips on the Tagus** – The trips give a good view of Lisbon and its surroundings and the harbour where, in addition to the commercial traffic, Venetian style barges with large triangular sails may sometimes be seen. In the summer, some boats offer excursions along the coast between Lisbon and Cascais *(see Travellers' addresses for Lisbon – Tourist Information)*.

The crossing of the estuary in one of the regular ferries makes a pleasant trip as well as affording fine **views★★** of the city and its hills. Approaching Lisbon by boat at Terreiro do Paço is a wonderful experience, providing the visitor with the feeling of having entered the very heart of the city.

★★ **Museu Nacional do Azulejo (Convento da Madre de Deus)** ⊙ **(DP M⁹)** – *(See also under Introduction: Azulejos)*. Despite its somewhat out-of-the-way location in a relatively unattractive area alongside the port and beyond the Santa Apolónia railway station, this delightful museum is well worth a visit. The magnificent history of *azulejos*, from 15C Hispano-Moorish tiles to those manufactured today, is elegantly presented in the monastic buildings of the Convento da Madre de Deus, which was founded in the 16C and largely rebuilt after the earthquake (admire the fine Manueline doorway on the street-side façade of the church). The galleries on the ground floor are arranged around the great cloister and display fine examples of *azulejos* imported from Seville during the 15 and 16C; these are predominantly of Italian majolica style, which was adopted by the first Portuguese workshops. Particularly worthy of note is the altarpiece of Nossa Senhora da Vida (1580) depicting a nativity scene.

Leave the cloister and enter the church through a low choir, whose walls have preserved their 16C Seville *azulejos*. The 18C **church★★**, and the baroque altar in particular, is resplendent with gilded woodwork. The nave has a coffered vault with panels painted to illustrate scenes from the Life of the Virgin; high on the walls paintings represent on the left and right respectively the lives of St Clare and St Francis; the lower parts of the walls are covered with 18C Dutch tiles.

Before heading upstairs, pass through the delightful small **Manueline cloisters** adorned with their original 16 and 17C coloured *azulejos*. The first floor has attractive 17 and 18C *azulejo* panels representing animals, battles and scenes of everyday life. The splendour and opulence of the chapel dedicated to Santo António, and the **chapter house★** in particular, is impressive. Of particular note amid this rich decoration are the panels in the ceiling with gilt frames set with 16 and 17C paintings including portraits of King João III and his queen, Catherine of Austria, which are attributed to Cristóvão Lopes. The walls are adorned with paintings of the Life of Christ.

In the great cloister admire the famous **panoramic view of Lisbon** prior to the earthquake – a fine blue and white composition of 1300 *azulejos*, 23m/75ft in length *(see photograph on p 162-163)*.

The other rooms, which are used for temporary expositions, illustrate the continuity of *azulejo* art through modern works such as those adorning some of Lisbon's metro stations by well-known artists such as Júlio Pomar and Vieira da Silva.

The museum's restaurant-café *(located near the entrance)*, with its interior patio decorated with appetite-whetting *azulejos* of hams, rabbits and other tempting titbits, is a refreshing and restful spot in which to have a drink or a meal.

EXPO'98 –
THE WORLD EXPOSITION IN LISBON (DN)

The theme of the last world exposition of the 20C, to be held in Lisbon from the 22 May – 30 September 1998, is: "The Oceans, a Heritage for the Future".

Portugal's aim is to present and re-affirm its own history and culture, which is so closely connected to the sea. The event coincides with the commemoration of the 500th anniversary of Vasco da Gama's voyage to India. However, the other aim of EXPO'98 is to provide an international forum for issues such as the importance of the oceans as a vital resource and the urgent need to ensure their preservation. With this in mind, the UN has declared 1998 the "International Year of the Oceans".

More than 135 countries will be taking part in EXPO'98, the site of which will be spread over a 60ha/148 acre area, 1km/0.6mi wide and 2km/1.2mi long, alongside the River Tagus next to the Doca dos Olivais in the eastern part of the city. After the event, most of the pavilions will be re-used, transforming the district and its residential areas into EXPO URBE, one of Lisbon's sites of the future, which will be served by the large Oriente intermodal transport station, designed by the architect Santiago Calatravza, and the **Vasco da Gama bridge**, to the north.

Main pavilions – The permanent buildings are located around the dock. To the south is the marina, which will receive a flotilla of craft from around the world throughout the exposition. The **Portuguese National Pavilion**, designed by Siza Vieira, has two distinct parts: the pavilion itself, which will present exhibits on the importance and impact of Portuguese maritime voyages, and the Ceremonial Square, which will be the venue for all official ceremonies. The latter is covered by an enormous wave-shaped roof which appears to be suspended in mid-air. After Expo'98, the pavilion will become the headquarters of a major institution. The **Oceans Pavilion**, which has been designed by the American architect Peter Chermayeff, has a transparent, undulating cover which is secured by steel cables, similar to a real sailing ship. Four tanks containing animals and vegetation will re-create the eco-systems of coastal areas in the Arctic, Indian, Pacific and Atlantic Oceans around an enormous central tank, the largest aquarium in Europe. This pavilion will remain open to the public after EXPO'98, as the Lisbon Oceanarium. The **Knowledge of the Seas Pavilion**, built by the Portuguese architect Carrilho da Graça, will show visitors the various techniques developed by people throughout history to develop a better understanding and knowledge of the oceans. At the end of the exposition, the building, which calls to mind the bridge of a ship, will be used as a scientific and cultural centre for maritime affairs. The **Water Gardens** opposite are reserved for entertainment and leisure. The **Utopia Pavilion**, meanwhile, an impressive building shaped like an upturned ship, with an exposed wooden framework, will house an amphitheatre during the exposition, which will be used to present multimedia shows devoted to the myths and literature of the sea. After EXPO'98, this will become Lisbon's **Multipurpose Pavilion**, a 16 000-capacity arena for sporting events, concerts and conventions. Next door is the **Norte International Area**, which will replace the FIL (Feira Internacionale de Lisboa/Lisbon International Fair), which has become too small for the demand, once the world exposition has finished and then house the **Lisbon Exhibition Centre**. The **Vasco da Gama Tower**, to the north, will provide superb views over the whole site and the Tagus. Its panoramic restaurant will stay open after 1998 and will have a cable car next to it. The **Garcia da Orta Gardens**, which have been planted with Mediterranean, Oriental and tropical flora, provide a pleasant area in which to walk along the river.

Organising your visit

Information – At the Information Centre by the South Gate. Information ☎ 0800 22.1998 (toll-free, from Portugal only) and (01) 831 94 16.

Access – There are three main entrances, in addition to the river port. Whether you are travelling by metro, bus or train, you will arrive at the Estação do Oriente intermodal transport station and gain access to the site through the West Gate. Access for cars is via the North Gate. Coaches will stop at the South Gate.

Tickets and opening hours – The Exposition site is open daily from 22 May to 30 September 1998 between 9am and 3am the following morning. A day at Expo'98 is divided into two periods: EXPO-Day and EXPO-Night. Approximate entrance costs (in escudos): 1 day: 5 000$; 3 days: 12 500$; 3 months: 50 000$. Night-time tickets (8pm/3am) are also on sale. Prices as follows: 1 night: 2 000$; 3 months: 25 000$. There is a a 50% discount for children and senior citizens; group reductions are also available.

A night-time visit can be a pleasant alternative, particularly on very hot days. As the pavilions close at 8pm, it is the area by the river which then becomes the main centre of events. The aim of EXPO-Night is to offer visitors entertainment and large cultural events which will mainly be staged in the Jules Verne auditorium, the open-air amphitheatre and in the videotech *(videoádio)*. The bars and restaurants on the site will of course stay open.

Accommodation – This should be booked as far in advance as possible, given the millions of visitors who will be visiting Lisbon during the course of the event. Hotels are available near the Estação do Oriente in addition to accommodation in the city and its suburbs.

Eating Out – Expo'98 has numeruous restaurants serving a huge variety of cuisine at prices to suit everyone: *haute cuisine*, international, home cooking, self-service, fast-food restaurants and stalls, spread across the exposition site.

Shopping – In addition to the shops on the EXPO site itself, special franchise stores are also open. Goods are also on sale at shops inside the pavilions of participating countries.

INTERNET: Full details are available on the EXPO'98 Web Site: http://www.expo98.pt

Museu da Água da EPAL ⊘ (**DQ M⁸**) – The museum traces the history of water supply to Lisbon and more particularly of the Águas Livres (Free Water) project drawn up by the engineer Manuel de Maia. Attempts to bring water to Lisbon from springs at the foot of the Serra de Sintra had begun in 1571, but it wasn't until King Dom João V gave his permission in 1731 that the aqueduct was built (1732 to 1748). The water it brought ran into the Mão d'Água des Amoreiras reservoir (1752-1834) and was then channelled to the fountains and water pipes of the town. In 1880 the third link in the chain, the Barbadinhos pumping station, was built. The combined system managed to supply the town with water for almost two and a half centuries until 1967. Today the pumping station is a museum.

Tour – The exposition hall displays instruments and documents which trace the history of water supply to Lisbon from the time of the Romans.

The **Barbadinhos Steam Pumping Station** (Estação Elevatória a Vapor dos Barbadinhos) was built within the grounds of a former monastery from which it took its name. It is a magnificent example of industrial architecture from the late 19C which successfully combines brick, wood, cast-iron and copper. One of the four powerful steam engines on show is put through its paces for the benefit of visitors.

The museum also runs the **Aqueduto das Águas Livres** and the **Mãe d'Água das Amoreiras** *(see below under AMOREIRAS)*.

Museu Militar ⊘ (**MY M¹⁰**) – The former 18C arsenal on the banks of the Tagus has preserved its outstanding woodwork as well as *azulejos* and interesting **ceilings**★ mainly illustrating battle scenes. Models, paintings and in particular numerous local and foreign weapons from the 16 to the late 19C, some manufactured on the spot, recall Portugal's military past.

★★★ **Museu Nacional de Arte Antiga** ⊘ (**BQ M⁷**) – *Rua das Janelas Verdes.*

The Museum of Ancient Art, which is housed in the 17C palace of the Counts of Alvor and in a modern annexe built in 1940, has an outstanding collection of works of art of which some were confiscated from monasteries when religious orders were suppressed in 1833. The displays of paintings, sculptures and decorative arts from the 12 to the early 19C all reflect the history of Portugal, in so far as they are by Portuguese or European artists who lived in or travelled to Portugal, or are items from former Portuguese colonies.

The main wealth of the museum lies in the Portuguese Primitives of which the major work is the famous **polyptych of the Adoration of St Vincent**★★★ painted between 1460 and 1470 by Nuno Gonçalves. The panels of this previously unknown polyptych were discovered

---

The Wellington Plate

The Portuguese government offered a sumptuous 1 000-piece service of banquet silver to the Duke of Wellington in gratitude both for his delivery of the nation from French invaders. The service was made in the Lisbon Arsenal to designs by the court painter Domingos Antonio Sequeira. It took 142 craftsmen the better part of five years to complete. Pieces from the service, including the 26ft-long centrepiece, are on display in Apsley House in London and were regularly used by the duke for the Waterloo banquets. The Museu Nacional de Arte Antiga has some of the drawings.

① St Vincent	⑨ Knights	⑮ His eldest son, Fernando
② King Afonso V	⑩ The Archbishop of Lisbon	⑯ His youngest son, João
③ Prince João, future João II	accompagnied by two canons	⑰ A moorish knight
④ Prince Henry the Navigator	⑪ The Chronicler, Gomes Eanes	⑱ A cleric proffering
⑤ Queen Isabel	de Azurara	St Vincent's skull
⑥ Isabella of Aragon, her mother	⑫ Cistercians from Alcobaça	⑲ A jew
⑦ Nuno Gonçalves	⑬ Fishermen and pilots	⑳ A beggar before the saint's coffin
⑧ Prince Fernando	⑭ Fernando, Second Duke of Bragança	

The Adoration of St Vincent in the Museu Nacional de Arte Antiga

in an attic in the monastery of São Vicente da Fora in 1882 and provide a precious document on contemporary Portuguese society. The figures standing around St Vincent, the patron saint of Portugal, include Prince Henry the Navigator and all kinds of people from different social ranks: princes, prelates, knights, monks and fishermen. The work, which shows some debt to the tapestries of the period, is outstanding for its flaming colours and realistic expressions.

The masterly **Annunciation★** by Frei Carlos (1523), is a remarkable example of Luso-Flemish painting, a style which developed as a result of intense exchange between Lisbon and the Low Countries. The depiction of the figures is Flemish while the composition is original. Among other Portuguese works are the *Cook Triptych* by Grão Vasco and the *Martyrdom of the Eleven Thousand Virgins* which comes from the Igreja da Madre de Deus. It is an unsigned work showing the arrival in Portugal of the relics of Santa Auta which were given by the Holy Roman Emperor Maximilian I to his cousin Dona Leonor in 1509.

Notable among the paintings from other European schools is the extraordinary **Temptation of St Anthony★★★** by Hieronymus Bosch. It is one of his mature works in which hybrid creatures mix in a weird underworld with human figures, plants and animals. Mention should also be made of the *Virgin and Child* by Memling, *St Jerome* by Dürer, *Virgin, Child and Saints* by Hans Holbein the Elder and the **Twelve Apostles★** by Zurbarán.

Museu Nacional de Arte Antiga – J. Pessoa/ANF-IPM

Japanese Namban screen (detail)

177

One of the rooms contains precious **Nambans** or **Japanese screens**★★ showing the arrival of the Portuguese on the island of Tane-ga-Shima in 1543. The Japanese called the Portuguese *Namban-jin* meaning barbarians from the south and the art that ensued came to be known as Namban. Each of the six-fold screens is a wonderful document on how the Portuguese were viewed by the Japanese. These latter were particularly fascinated by the long noses, bushy moustaches, baggy breeches, round hats and the black skin of some of the sailors. The two screens attributed to Kano Domi show goods being unloaded and a procession of Portuguese carrying gifts through the streets of Nagasaki. Two other screens attributed to Kano Naizen show a departure from Goa and an arrival in Japan. As the Japanese artist was not familiar with the Indian continent, he gave its architecture a Chinese flavour.

There is also a rich collection of gold and silver plate of which the finest piece is the **monstrance from the Mosteiro de Belém** (1506) attributed to Gil Vicente who, it is believed, made it out of gold brought back from the Indies by Vasco da Gama. Of note also are the 16C Indo-European caskets and the rich collection of furniture, tapestries and Arraiolos carpets.

The more recent section of the museum houses the **chapel**★ from the former Carmelite Convent of Santa Alberto, which is outstanding for its gilded woodwork and its 16-18C *azulejos*.

The museum also has a shop, as well as a restaurant with a pleasant, quiet patio.

Docas de Santo Amaro and Alcântara (**BQ**) – The dock area along the river was formerly occupied by warehouses and river facilities. It has recently been transformed into a fashionable district with a multitude of esplanades, bars, restaurants and discos for every taste *(see Travellers' addresses – The Lisbon Scene)*. It is a pleasant place for a stroll in the late-afternoon, or at night when the atmosphere is at its liveliest.

★**Ponte 25 de Abril** (**Suspension Bridge**) (**BQ**) – Until 1966 there were no bridges over the Tagus below Vila Franca de Xira, and Lisbon, therefore, was only connected with the country's southern province and the industrial area on the river's south bank (Barreiro, Almada, Cacilhas) by ferry. In 1962 construction of a suspension bridge began; it was opened in August 1966 as the Salazar Bridge and renamed after the Carnation Revolution. The bridge was constructed from steel purchased from the United Kingdom and the USA. This suspension bridge, with an overall length of 2 278m/approx 1.5mi, has the longest central span in Europe – 1 013m/3 323ft. The bridge is 70m/230ft above the waters of the Tagus and is suspended from two pylons 190m/623ft high while the world record foundations go 80m/262ft below the river bed to stand on basalt rock. The bridge was constructed to carry not only the present road traffic but also a double railway line below.

The **view**★★ from the bridge is especially interesting looking from south to north: the light façades of the town buildings can be seen rising in tiers – to the east lie the medieval quarters of the Alfama, dominated by the Castelo de São Jorge, in the centre is the Baixa with neo-classical houses standing majestically along the banks of the Tagus and in the west the Torre de Belém recalls the sumptuous days of the 16C.

T. Adina/EXPLORER

Ponte 25 de Abril

Cristo Rei ⊘ – *Leave Lisbon by ② on the map. 3.5km/2mi from the south toll gate of the suspension bridge, turn right at the second motorway exit to take the Almada road. Then follow the signs and leave the car in the car park near the monument.*

The enormous statue of Christ in Majesty (28m/92ft high) was erected in 1959 in thanks to God for having spared Portugal during the Second World War. It is a slightly smaller replica of the statue of Christ the Redeemer in Rio de Janeiro. From the pedestal *(access by lift; plus 74 steps)* which is 85m/279ft above ground level and 113m/371ft over the Tagus, there is a **panoramic view★★** over the Tagus Estuary, the old quarters of Lisbon and the plain to the south as far as Setúbal.

★★BELÉM – *allow 1 day*

It was from Belém (Portuguese for Bethlehem) that sailing ships set forth to brave the Ocean Sea and discover hitherto unknown lands and continents.

Starting from Praça do Comércio, either drive alongside the Tagus or take tram number 15 to Belém.

Cloisters, Mosteiro dos Jerónimos

★★★Mosteiro dos Jeronimos – In 1502, on the site of a former hermitage founded by Prince Henry the Navigator, the King, Dom Manuel, undertook to build this magnificent Hieronymite monastery which is considered to be the jewel of Manueline art. This style of art served to glorify the great discoveries of the age; in this case that of Vasco da Gama who, on his return from the Indies, had moored his caravels in Restelo harbour near Belém. The architects of the monastery, benefiting from the riches then pouring into Lisbon, were able to throw themselves into an ambitious, large-scale work. The Gothic style adopted by the Frenchman Boytac until his death in 1517 was modified by his successors who added ornamentation typical of the Manueline style with its diverse influences: João de Castilho, of Spanish origin, added a Plateresque form to the decoration, Nicolas Chanterene emphasised the Renaissance element, while Diogo de Torralva and Jérôme de Rouen, at the end of the 16C, brought in a classical note. Only the buildings added in the 19C, west of the belfry, detract from the monastery's overall architectural harmony.

★★★Igreja de Santa Maria ⊘ – The **south door**, the work of Boytac and João de Castilho, combines a mass of gables, pinnacles and niches filled with statues. Crowning all is a canopy surmounted by the Cross of the Order of the Knights of Christ. A statue of Prince Henry the Navigator adorns the pier, and two low reliefs showing scenes from the life of St Jerome, the tympanum. The windows on either side of the doorway have richly decorated mouldings.

The **west door**, sheltered beneath the 19C porch which leads to the cloisters, is by Nicolas Chanterene. It is adorned with very fine statues, particularly those of King Manuel and Queen Maria being presented by their patrons. Represented above the doorway are the Annunciation, the Nativity and the Adoration of the Magi.

The **interior** is outstanding for the beauty of the stonework, carved throughout in great detail but never in such a way as to obscure the architectural lines, as for instance in the network **vaulting★★** of equal height over the nave and aisles.

This vaulting withstood the earthquake of 1755, standing on paired columns uniform in sculptural decoration but ever more slender as their distance from the transept increases. The decoration on the pillars and the magnificent vaulting over the transept crossing are by João de Castilho. The transepts are baroque, designed by Jérôme de Rouen, son of Jean de Rouen, and contain the tombs of several royal princes. In the chancel, which was reconstructed in the classical period, are the tombs of Dom Manuel I and Dom João III and their queens.

Beneath the gallery of the *coro alto* at the entrance to the church are the neo-Manueline tombs of Vasco da Gama and also Camões, whose recumbent figure wears a crown of laurel leaves.

★★★ **Cloisters** ⊘ – This masterpiece of Manueline art is fantastically rich in sculpture. The stone is at its most beautiful when it takes on the warm golden tint of the late afternoon sun. The cloisters, forming a hollow square of which each side measures 55m/170ft, are two storeys high. The ground level galleries with groined vaulting by Boytac have wide arches with tracery resting upon slender columns, and Late Gothic and Renaissance decoration carved into the massive thickness of the walls. The recessed upper storey by João do Castilho is less exuberant but more delicate in style. The chapter house contains the tomb of the writer Alexandre Herculano. The sacristy leading off the east gallery and the monks' refectory off the west gallery both have lierne and tierceron vaulting.

A staircase leads to the church's **coro alto** which affords another view of the vaulting. The graceful Renaissance stalls carved out of maple are by Diogo de Carça.

Museu Nacional de Arqueologia ⊘ – The museum is in the 19C wing of the Mosteiro dos Jeronimos. A large gallery contains displays of pottery, weapons, jewellery, stelae, and so on, illustrating the different stages of the country's history from Antiquity to the Roman period. Megalithic exhibits include stelae and menhir-statues; the Iron Age is represented by weapons and examples of the strange granite sculptures of boars called *Berrões* which are common in northeast Portugal; the Roman period is particularly well covered with, among others, a small 1C bronze statue labelled Fortune and a 3C marble sarcophagus of a little girl.

★ **Tesouro** – The treasury includes a rich collection of archaic goldwork from excavation sites throughout Portugal and features some magnificently worked gold pieces: bracelets, torques and ear rings.

★★ **Museu da Marinha** ⊘ – This museum, containing a remarkable collection of **models★★★** of seafaring craft over the centuries is located on both sides of the esplanade of the **Calouste Gulbenkian Planetarium** in two separate buildings: the west wing of the Mosteiro dos Jeronimos and the modern Galliot Pavilion *(Pavilhão das Galeotas)*.

Once through the entrance, take the stairs in front of the door on the right. On the mezzanine, the room devoted to the Far East displays porcelain and Asiatic ships, as well as a set of 15C Japanese armour.

The Sala da Marinha de Recreio, a room dedicated to pleasure craft on the upper floor, includes a small collection of models of 18 and 19C yachts. The Sala da Marinha Mercante (Merchant Navy Room) opposite recalls the history of merchant shipping in Portugal, with interesting exhibits such as the *Santa Maria* and the *Infante Dom Henrique*, which transported soldiers to the ex-colonies, and the *Neiva* oil tanker. The Sala da Construção Naval at the far end provides an informative look at naval construction techniques.

Return to the main floor.

Main building – Giant sandstone statues of historical figures (including Henry the Navigator) and ancient cannon can be seen in the entrance hall.

On the ground floor there is an immense room devoted to the Discoveries and the Navy, from the 15 to the 18C, with old maps and very accurate and often magnificent models of sailing ships, caravels and frigates, including the 18C vessel, the *Principe de Beira*, which would have been used mainly in navigation schools. There are displays of figureheads and navigational instruments such as 15C astrolabes. Warships of the 19 and 20C can also be seen (small scale models of gunboats, frigates and corvettes, and modern submarines) as well as a fishing fleet (the Henrique Seixas Collection) with models of various kinds of boats which used to fish in the estuaries or along the Portuguese coast: a *muleta* from Seixal with its many sails, a *calão* from the Algarve, a *galeão* from Nazaré etc. Models of boats used for river navigation include frigates of the Tagus and *rabelos* of the Douro. In the last room there is a reconstruction of the royal stateroom of the yacht *Amelia* (late 19C).

The exit leads to the Pavilhão das Galeotas.

Pavilhão das Galeotas – This pavilion contains seven magnificent ceremonial galliots. The most impressive is that decorated by the French ornamentalist Pillement and built in 1778 for the wedding of the future King João VI. There is also a whole arsenal of naval cannon, shells and torpedoes, as well as three sea-planes, including the *Santa Cruz*, in which Sacadura Cabral and Gago Coutinho made the first crossing of the south Atlantic in June 1922.

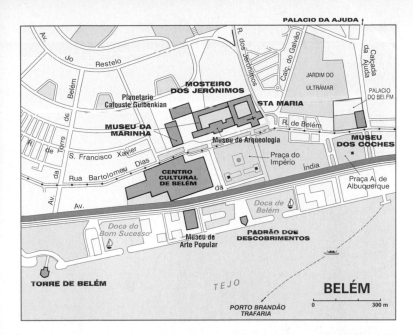

★Centro Cultural de Belém – This immense building standing opposite the Mosteiro dos Jerónimos and made of the same attractive limestone was designed by the architects Vittorio Gregotti and Manuel Salgado. Construction began in 1987 and was completed in 1990. The complex plays a prominent role in the cultural life of Lisbon and, to a certain extent, Portugal as well, and comprises a conference centre, two theatres (one of which is for opera), a museum and a huge exposition centre, all dependent upon the Discoveries Foundation. The centre presents a varied programme of music, theatre and dance by Portuguese and foreign artists, and also hosts contemporary exhibits covering painting, sculpture, architecture and photography. The complex also has several bars, a restaurant, and a cafeteria with a terrace offering a view over the Tagus.

Museu de Arte Popular ⊙ – The museum, which is situated opposite the Centro Cultural de Belém, is all that remains of the 1940 Portuguese Exposition. Although generally short on explanation, the museum does contain an interesting display of traditional objects, utensils, crockery, furniture, costumes, accessories, rugs and a collection of carts from the provinces of Portugal.

Padrão dos Descobrimentos ⊙ – The 52m/170ft Monument to the Discoveries by the sculptor Leopoldo de Almeida erected in 1960 beside the Tagus on the 500th anniversary of the death of Prince Henry the Navigator, represents the prow of a ship with the prince pointing the way to a crowd of important figures. Among them, on the right side, are King Dom Manuel carrying an armillary sphere, Camões holding verses from *The Lusiads* and the painter, Nuno Gonçalves.

From the top of the monument *(access by lift)* there is a view of the Tagus, the Belém monuments and western Lisbon, and at a closer range, just below, of the marble mosaic at the foot of the monument representing a compass; in the centre is a map of the world.

★★★Torre de Belém ⊙ – This elegant Manueline tower was built between 1515 and 1519 in the middle of the Tagus to defend the river mouth and the Mosteiro dos Jer-nimos. Today it stands at the water's edge on the north bank, the river having altered course during the earthquake in 1755. It is an architectural gem; the Romanesque-Gothic structure is adorned with loggias like those in Venice and small domes like those in Morocco where the tower's architect, Francisco de Arruda had travelled. Jutting out to command the mainstream is an artillery platform, protected by battlements, each of which is decorated with a shield of the Cross of the Order of Christ.

On the keep terrace, facing the sea, is a statue of Our Lady of Safe Homecoming. The tower is five storeys high ending in a terrace. On the ground floor one can see openings through which prisoners were thrown into the often waterlogged dungeons below. On the third floor, paired windows with elegant balconies, a magnificent Renaissance loggia surmounted by the royal arms of Manuel I and two armillary spheres mellow the granite tower's original architectural severity.

★★Museu Nacional dos Coches ⊙ – The museum founded in 1904 by Queen Amelia is housed in the former royal riding school of the Palácio do Belém, now the official residence of the President of the Republic. It has a splendid collection of carriages (coaches, four-wheelers, litters etc.) the oldest of which is the magnificently painted four-wheeler that Philip II of Spain brought to Portugal in the late 16C.

Torre de Belém at night

The most notable examples are the three huge ambassadorial coaches at the back of the hall that were built in Rome in 1716 for the Marquis de Fontes, Portugal's ambassador extraordinary to the Vatican at the time of Pope Clement XI. The decoration on these masterpieces of Italian baroque illustrates Portuguese discoveries and conquests in allegorical form. João V's coach bears beautiful paintwork by Antoine Quillard and is adorned with sculptures. A room on the first floor devoted to Queen Amelia contains her portrait and a fine ceremonial cloak.

★**Palácio da Ajuda** ⊘ (**AQ**) – This former royal palace (18-19C) to the north of Belém was built after the earthquake, yet was never completed. It was the residence of the Portuguese monarchs, Dom Luís and Dona Maria Pia, from 1862 onwards. Its two floors offer a succession of rooms with painted ceilings and an interior richly filled with furniture, tapestries, statues (by Machado de Castro, among others) and decorative objects from the last century, which combine to create one of Europe's most perfect romantic buildings. The ceiling in the Winter Garden (Jardim do Inverno), with its covering of chalcedonic agate is worth seeing, as is the surprising Sala de Saxe, a salon decorated with figures and items in Saxony porcelain. Several of the rooms, such as the queen's bedroom and dining room, have a more intimate appearance with a lived-in feel due to the abundance of personal objects contained within them. The top-floor rooms (the Throne Room, the Ballroom, with its three crystal chandeliers, and the Ambassadors' Room) are generally more spacious and ostentatious. Dom Luís' art studio, with its carved wooden furniture and neo-Gothic decoration, comes as a rather unexpected surprise within this ensemble. The palace now houses part of the Ministry for Cultural Affairs.

At the top of the Calçada da Ajuda is the **Jardim Botânico da Ajuda**, which is connected to the romantic **Jardim das Damas** (18C) with its waterfalls and ponds. It was here that the ladies of the Court would enjoy pleasant strolls.

AROUND AVENIDA DA LIBERDADE – *allow half a day*

★**Avenida da Liberdade** (**JV**) – The Avenida da Liberdade, 1 300m long and 90m wide – 1mile x 295ft, is the most majestic of Lisbon's avenues. On either side late 19C buildings and more recent constructions house hotels and company offices for travel, insurance, air transport etc. The pavements are covered in black and white mosaics made from limestone and basalt. To the north, the Avenida leads to the **Praça do Marquês de Pombal** (**CP**), Lisbon's nerve centre, where several wide avenues converge. In the centre of this circular "square", ringed by large hotels, stands a

Y. Travert/DIAF

monument to the Marquis of Pombal. Inscriptions round the base of the monument recall the great man's most important ministerial achievements.

Take Avenida Fontes Pereira de Melo then Avenida António Augusto de Aguiar on the left.

★ **Parque Eduardo VII** (**CP**) – This formal, elegant landscaped park, crowning Avenida da Liberdade, was named after King Edward VII of England on the occasion of his visit to Lisbon in 1902 to reaffirm the Anglo-Portuguese Alliance. There is a magnificent **vista**★ from the upper end of the park over the Baixa district and the Tagus, dominated on either side by the castle and the Bairro Alto hills.

★ **Estufa fria** ⊘ – Wooden shutters in the cold greenhouse provide protection from the extremes of summer heat and winter cold. The many exotic plants displayed grow beside fishponds or cooling waterfalls near small grottoes.

★ **Jardim Botânico** ⊘ (**JV**) – *(Entrance through the Faculdade de Ciências in Rua da Escola Politécnica or Rua da Alegria).* The botanical gardens stretching across the hillside not far from Avenida da Liberdade were laid out for scientific purposes in 1873 and are now run by the Science Academy. They rate among the finest in Europe for subtropical plants.

With their magnificent avenue of palm trees the gardens are a haven of peace in the midst of a busy quarter of Lisbon.

GULBENKIAN FOUNDATION

Calouste Gulbenkian, an Armenian oil magnate and patron of the arts born in Istanbul in 1869, was nicknamed "Mister 5%" on account of his five per cent share in the profits of the Iraq Petroleum Company. His keenness for collecting started at a very early age with the acquisition of a few old coins, and was to lead to the creation of an outstanding collection of works of art over a period of forty years. On his death in 1955 he bequeathed his immense fortune to Portugal and a year later the Calouste Gulbenkian Foundation was set up. This is a private institution which runs its museums in Lisbon as well as an orchestra, a ballet company and a choir. It also provides student grants, finances research, organises exhibits and manages two branches, one in London, the other in Paris.

The foundation's headquarters, set in beautiful gardens, consist of a complex of modern buildings which house the Gulbenkian Museum, the Modern Art Centre, four multi-purpose lecture halls, of which one is open-air, a conference centre, two large galleries for art exhibitions and a library with 152 000 books.

★★★ **Museu Calouste Gulbenkian** ⊘ (**CP**) – The museum, set in spacious, airy, tastefully laid out rooms giving onto the gardens, was especially designed for the Gulbenkian collections which consist of selected exhibits of great value and beauty. They are particularly rich in Oriental and European art and are beautifully presented. The lower floor displays contemporary art exhibitions.

Ancient art – Antiquity is represented by works from Egypt (an alabaster bowl about 2700 years old, a stone statuette of "Judge Bes", a bronze sun-boat, and a silver-gilt mask for a mummy dating from the 30th Dynasty), the Graeco-Roman world (a superb 5BC Attic crater, jewellery, the head of a woman attributed to Phidias, iridescent Roman vases, and a magnificent collection of gold and silver coins) and Mesopotamia (9BC Assyrian stele and a Parthian urn).

> **Unexpected treasures**
>
> Lisbon is full of unusual sights hidden away in unexpected places. In Campo dos Mártires da Pátria (**KV**) for instance, a statue of **Doctor Sousa Martins** (1843-1897) stands surrounded by candles and marble ex-votos. The doctor, who never abandoned hopeless cases, has become a cult figure.

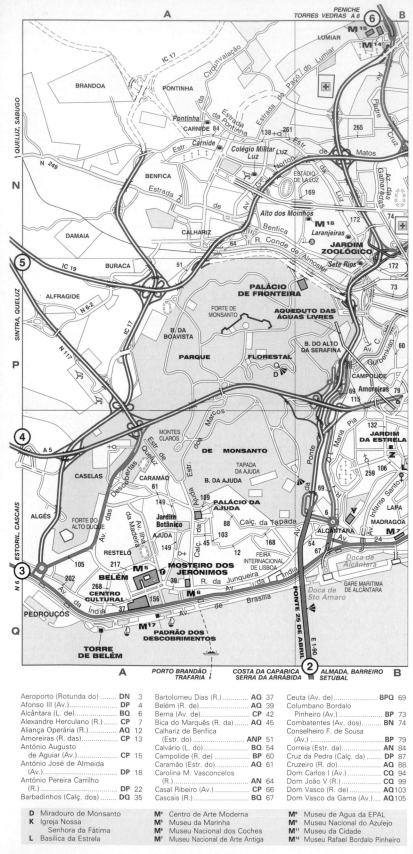

Aeroporto (Rotunda do)	**DN**	3	
Afonso III (Av.)....................	**DP**	4	
Alcântara (L. de)..................	**BQ**	6	
Alexandre Herculano (R.)......	**CP**	7	
Aliança Operária (R.)............	**AQ**	12	
Amoreiras (R. das)...............	**CP**	13	
António Augusto			
de Aguiar (Av.)...................	**CP**	15	
António José de Almeida			
(Av.).................................	**DP**	18	
António Pereira Carrilho			
(R.)..................................	**DP**	22	
Barbadinhos (Calç. dos)	**DQ**	35	

Bartolomeu Dias (R.)	**AQ**	37	
Belém (R. de)......................	**AQ**	39	
Berna (Av. de).....................	**CP**	42	
Bica do Marquês (R. da).......	**AQ**	45	
Calhariz de Benfica			
(Estr. do).........................	**ANP**	51	
Calvário (L. do)...................	**BQ**	54	
Campolide (R. de)	**BP**	60	
Caramão (Estr. do)..............	**AQ**	61	
Carolina M. Vasconcelos			
(R.)..................................	**AN**	64	
Casal Ribeiro (Av.)...............	**CP**	66	
Cascais (R.)........................	**BQ**	67	

Ceuta (Av. de).....................	**BPQ**	69	
Columbano Bordalo			
Pinheiro (Av.)	**BP**	73	
Combatentes (Av. dos).........	**BN**	74	
Conselheiro F. de Sousa			
(Av.)			
Correia (Estr. da).................	**AN**	84	
Cruz da Pedra (Calç. da)	**DP**	87	
Cruzeiro (R. do)...................	**AQ**	88	
Dom Carlos I (Av.)...............	**CQ**	94	
Dom João V (R.)	**CQ**	99	
Dom Vasco (R. de)...............	**AQ**	103	
Dom Vasco da Gama (Av.)....	**AQ**	105	

D	Miradouro de Monsanto	
K	Igreja Nossa	
	Senhora de Fátima	
L	Basílica da Estrela	

M⁴	Centro de Arte Moderna	
M⁵	Museu da Marinha	
M⁶	Museu Nacional dos Coches	
M⁷	Museu Nacional de Arte Antiga	

M⁸	Museu de Agua da EPAL	
M⁹	Museu Nacional do Azulejo	
M¹¹	Museu da Cidade	
M¹²	Museu Rafael Bordalo Pinheiro	

Domingos Sequeira (R.)	**BQ**	106
Duque de Saldanha (Pr.)	**CP**	112
Engenheiro		
Duarte Pacheco (Av.)	**BP**	115
Escola Politécnica (R. da)	**CQ**	120
Espanha (Pr. de)	**CP**	124
Ferreira Borges (R.)	**BQ**	132
Fonte (R. da)	**AN**	138
Fontes Pereira de Melo		
(Av.)	**CP**	139
Forças Armadas		
(Av. das)	**CN**	142
Galvão (Calç. do)	**AQ**	149
Império (Pr. do)	**AQ**	156
João de Barros (R.)	**AQ**	168
João de Freitas Branco (R.)	**BN**	169
Joaquim António		
de Aguiar (R.)	**CP**	171
Laranjeiras (Estr. das)	**BNP**	172
Londres (Pr. de)	**DP**	177
Marquês da Fronteira (R.)	**CP**	181
Miguel Bombarda (Av.)	**CP**	186
Mirante (Calç. do)	**AQ**	189
Mouzinho de Albuquerque		
(Pr.)	**CN**	192
Pascoal de Melo (R.)	**DP**	196
Pedro Alvares Cabral (Av.)	**CQ**	199
Pedrouços (R. de)	**AQ**	202
República (Av. da)	**CP**	216
Restelo (Av. do)	**AQ**	217
Rovisco Pais (Av.)	**DP**	222
S. Bento (R. de)	**CQ**	237
S. Filipe de Nery (R.)	**CP**	241
Saraiva de Carvalho (R.)	**BQ**	259
Seminário (R. do)	**AN**	261
Telheiras (Estr. de)	**BN**	265
Torre de Belém (Av.)	**AQ**	268
Xabregas (R. de)	**DP**	271
5 de Outubro (Av.)	**CNP**	273

M¹⁴ Museu Nacional do Trajo	**M¹⁹** Fundação Arpad Szenes-Vieira da Silva	**X** Biblioteca Municipal
M¹⁵ Museu Nacional do Teatro	**P** Caixa Gairal de Depósitos	**Y** Palácio das Necessidades
M¹⁷ Museu de Arte Popular	**W** Mãe d'Agua des Amoreiras	**Z** Casa Fernando Pessoa
M¹⁸ Museu da Música		

Near Eastern– The finest pieces in this vast collection are the pottery and carpets. The sumptuous woollen and silk carpets, which are mainly Persian, date from the 16 and 17C as do the shimmering Prusa velvets from Turkey. The pottery (12-18C), silk costumes and lamps from the mosque of Alep are as finely worked as Persian miniatures. There are also collections of poetry (displayed in rotation), Korans and Armenian manuscripts.

Far Eastern art – Chinese art is mainly represented by magnificent porcelain (a 14C Taoist bowl; a 17C vase of the hundred birds) and "rough stones" (an 18C green nephrite bowl); Japanese exhibits include prints and a selection of lacquerware from the 18 and 19C.

European Art – This section begins with **medieval religious art**, represented by some beautiful carved **ivories**, illuminated manuscripts and books of hours.

15, 16 and 17C painting and sculpture – The *Presentation at the Temple* by the German artist **Stephan Lochner** was one of Gulbenkian's first acquisitions. The Flemish and Dutch schools are well represented with a *St Joseph* by **Van der Weyden**, an admirable *Annunciation* by **Dirk Bouts**, a magnificent *Old Man* by **Rembrandt** and a masterly *Portrait of Helen Fourment* by **Rubens**.

From the Italian school there is a delightful *Portrait of a Young Woman* attributed to **Ghirlandaio**.

The rooms that follow are mainly devoted to the decorative arts: furniture and furnishings (luxurious creations by Cressent, Jacob, Oeben, Riesener, Garnier and Carlin), tapestries, including the beautiful *Children's Games* series made in Ferrara after cartoons attributed to Guilio Romano, and gold and silver plate, particularly the masterpieces of table silverware by A. Durand and F.T. Germain. The 18C French school of painting, famous for its portraits and festive scenes, is represented here by **Lancret** *(Fête Galante)*, **Hubert Robert** *(Gardens of Versailles)*, **Quentin de la Tour** *(Portrait of Mademoiselle Sallé* and *Portrait of Duval de l'Epinoy)*, and **Nicolas de Largillière** *(Portrait of M. et Mme. Thomas-Germain)*. Among the sculptures note the proud *Diana* in white marble by Houdon.

18C English painting includes works by **Gainsborough** (a lovely *Portrait of Mrs. Lowndes-Stone)*, **Romney** *(Portrait of Miss Constable)*, **Turner** *(Quillebœuf)*, and **Thomas Lawrence**.

A gallery on **Francesco Guardi** is hung with scenes of the life and festivals of Venice. The 19C French school is represented by **Henri Fantin-Latour** *(La Lecture)* the Impressionists, including **Manet** *(Boy with Cherries* and *Blowing Bubbles)*, **Degas** *(Self-portrait)*, and **Renoir** *(Portrait of Mme. Claude Monet)*, a number of canvases by Corot *(Bridge at Mantes,Willows)*, as well as a fine collection of bronzes *(Spring)* and marble sculptures *(Benedictions)* by **Rodin**.

Pendant by René Lalique

Museu Calouste Gulbenkian, Lisboa

In the last room there is an extraordinary collection of works from the Art Nouveau period by the French decorative artist **René Lalique** (1860-1945), a personal friend of Calouste Gulbenkian. The detail in them, particularly in the beautiful jewels, is quite remarkable.

★**Centro de Arte Moderna** ⊙ (**CP M⁴**) – The centre, which was built by the British architect Sir Leslie Martin in 1983, has an interesting, roomy design in which plants have been incorporated, giving the impression of a screen of greenery. It houses modern works by Portuguese artists from 1910 to the present day.

Among the artists are Vieira da Silva, Amadeo Souza-Cardoso, Almada Negreiros and Julio Pomar. Several sculptures, including the *Reclining Woman* by **Henry Moore**, are exhibited in the gardens surrounding the centre.

Around the Gulbenkian

Igreja de Nossa Senhora de Fátima (**CP K**) – This modern church is adorned with beautiful **stained-glass windows★** by Almada Negreiros.

Biblioteca municipal (**CP X**) – The library is housed in the 16C Galveias Palace opposite the neo-Moorish **bullring** at Campo Pequeno.

AMOREIRAS (BP)

This district is dominated by the Torres das Amoreiras and the Aqueduto das Águas Livres. The name recalls the mulberry trees which existed here to produce silkworms used in the manufacture of silk.

Torres das Amoreiras

Torres das Amoreiras – The famous pink, grey and black post-modern towers designed by the architect Tomás Taveira were completed in 1983. They are situated close to one of the entrances to the city and can be seen from afar. They comprise three floors, and contain offices, luxury apartments, restaurants and a large shopping centre *(see Travllers' addresses for Lisbon – Shopping).*

★**Fundação Arpad Szenes – Vieira da Silva** ⊘ (**CP M¹⁹**) – This foundation is located on one side of the leafy Praça das Amoreiras, next to the Águas Livres aqueduct. It is a fine 18C workshop which has been remodelled in a sober, elegant manner by the architect Sommer Ribeiro. Maria Helena Vieira da Silva (1908-1992), who lived a great part of her life in Paris with the artist Arpad Szenes, is one of Portugal's most famous artists of the 20C.
The museum displays a small collection of exhibits bequeathed by the artists, in addition to works donated by collectors and institutions.

★**Aqueduto das Águas Livres** ⊘ (**BP**) – The aqueduct built between 1732 and 1748 *(see Museu da Água)* measures a total of 58km/36mi, including all its ramifications. 34 of its arches stride across the Alcântara valley. The tallest is 65m/213ft high with a span of 29m/95ft. The best view of the aqueduct is from Avenida de Ceuta, north of the N7 motorway bridge.

Mãe d'Água das Amoreiras ⊘ (**CQ W**)   Water from the Águas Livres aqueduct flows into the reservoir which is housed in a building completed in 1834 *(see Museu da Água).* Inside, one can see the water flow and the Arca d'Água or "water arch" basin which has a depth of 7m/23ft and a capacity of about 5 500m³ cubic metres/194 433cubic feet. Beside the building is the former recording station where the levels were recorded for the water to be channelled to the city's fountains. Today, it is a centre for exhibitions, concerts and plays.

ADDITIONAL SIGHTS

★★**Palácio dos Marqueses de Fronteira** ⊘ (**ABP**) – *Take the metro to Sete Rios, followed by a 20min walk along Rua das Furnas and Rua São Domingo de Benfica.* The palace, which stands to the north of the Parque de Monsanto near Benfica, was built as a hunting lodge by João Mascarenhas, the first Marquis of Fronteira, in 1670. While a strong Italian Renaissance influence is apparent, particularly in the layout of the gardens, the palace is one of the most beautiful Portuguese creations with its **azulejos**★★ of outstanding quality and variety. Inside the palace, the *azulejos* in the Victory Room depict with a touch of naivety the main events in the War of Restoration in which the first Marquis of Fronteira distinguished himself. The dining room is adorned with 17C Delft tiles, the first to be imported into Portugal. Outside, on the terraces and in the gardens, not a bench, a pool or a stretch of wall has been left untouched; every conceivable flat surface has been decorated with small ceramic tiles. Some depict country scenes of the seasons and work in the fields, others more stately, solemn subjects like the twelve horsemen in the Kings' Gallery which are reflected in a pool, while others still strike a humorous note as in the bestiary with its cats and monkeys.

★★**Jardim Zoologico** ⊘ (**BN**) – *Metro: Sete Rios.* The park, which is both a lovely garden and a zoo, is laid out in the 26ha/64 acres of the Parque das Laranjeiras, which includes the rose-coloured palace of the Counts of Farrobo, visible to the right of the entrance. The lower part includes the rose garden, a variety of other

Gardens, Palácio Fronteira

flowers and enclosures for the 2 500 zoo animals, many of which are exotic species. For an overview of the zoo and its animals, take the cable car (20min) above the garden. A small train (15min) goes around the main sites.

The rarest exhibits are a pair of pandas and a pair of white rhinoceros from South Africa. The zoo organises shows featuring parrots, reptiles and dolphins several times daily, the colourful and attractive **dolphinarium**, however, can only be visited during shows. Temporary exhibitions are organised for children. The zoo also has a picnic area and a popular restaurant.

★**Parque Florestal de Monsanto** (**APQ**) – This hilly, wooded park is dissected by roads affording panoramic **views**★ of Lisbon, particularly of the Monsanto belvedere (D).

★**Museu da Música** ⊘ (**BN M**[18]) – The small museum, which is located inside the Alto dos Moinhos metro station, contains a wide variety of musical instruments and publications from the 16 – 20C, including a set of baroque harpsichords and a large collection of string and wind instruments. Concerts are organised in the exhibition area, which also contains several interactive multimedia stations.

★**Basilica da Estrela** (**BQ L**) – *Tram number 28.* The white baroque edifice was built at the end of the 18C. Inside, the transept crossing is covered by a fine **cupola** topped by a lantern tower. Note also a Christmas crib with life size figures carved by Machado de Castro.

The **Jardim da Estrela´** opposite the basilica is one of the most beautiful gardens in Lisbon with its varied display of exotic plants and trees.

Casa Fernando Pessoa ⊘ (**BQ Z**) – *Rua Coelho da Rocha, 16-18.* The house where the poet Pessoa spent the last 15 years of his life has been refurbished and the modern setting now serves as a cultural centre specialising in Portuguese poetry as well as an exhibition centre for painting and sculpture. The works of Pessoa and his archives are also assembled here.

Palácio das Necessidades (**BQ Y**) – *Calçada das Necessidades.* The former royal palace, now the Ministry for Foreign Affairs, was built for Dom João V's brothers in the 18C.

Museu da Cidade ⊘ (**CN M**[11]) – *Campo Grande, 345. Metro: Campo Grande.* The municipal museum stands above Campo Grande – unfortunately near the motorway interchange – in the graceful 18C Palácio Pimenta built during Dom João V's luxurious reign. The different stages in the history of Lisbon may be traced through Roman, Visigothic, Arab and medieval remains. The emblem of the city, a caravel transporting the body of St Vincent guided by ravens, may be seen on the many coats of arms displayed. A model of Lisbon in the early 18C gives an idea of the city before the earthquake as do the *azulejos* of Torreiro do Paço square showing the Royal Palace still in place. The palace kitchens are adorned with *azulejos* of country scenes. The first floor is devoted to ceramics and engravings of Lisbon. Note the famous *Fado* canvas by Malhoa.

Museu Rafael Bordalo Pinheiro ⊙ (**CN M¹²**) – *Campo Grande, 382. Metro: Campo Grande.* The museum, which stands across the Campo Grande from the Museu da Cidade, contains collections of drawings, caricatures and particularly **ceramics★** by Rafael Bordalo Pinheiro (1846-1905). He was a prolific artist and together with his brother and sister had some influence on social life in Lisbon at the end of the 19C. Among other things, he was responsible for the great success of the ceramics factory at Caldas da Rainha.

★**Museu Nacional do Traje and Museu Nacional do Teatro** – *Estrada do Lumiar, 12* (**BN**).
The Estrada do Lumiar runs through a district of fine estates past the **Quinta de Monteiro-Mor**, a vast property with two palaces. One has been converted into a Costume Museum, the other into a Theatre Museum. There is a pleasant restaurant in a pavilion near the Costume Museum.

★**Museu Nacional do Traje** ⊙ (**M¹⁴**) – The graceful palace of the Marquis of Angeja now holds outstanding costume exhibitions. The beautifully presented collections bring a whole era, or a town or profession, to life, through the art of dress.
Below the palace, the attractive botanical gardens, **Jardim Botânico do Monteiro-Mor** ⊙ with their pools and a rich variety of plants, lie in a wild, hilly setting.
The palace of Monteiro-Mor, which was rebuilt after a fire, now houses the **Museu Nacional do Teatro** ⊙ (**M¹⁵**). This holds temporary exhibitions on drama-related themes.

Aquário Vasco da Gama ⊙ – *In Dafundo, on the N 6, by* ③ *on the map.* There are numerous tanks with marine plants, fish and shellfish from both hemispheres, as well as ponds with turtles and seals. Upstairs, there is a room with displays of stuffed sea creatures.

EXCURSIONS – *See map of principal sights on page 7.*

★★**Sintra** – *See SINTRA.*

★★**Queluz** – *See Palácio Nacional de QUELUZ.*

★**Estoril** – *See ESTORIL.*

★**Cascais** – *See CASCAIS.*

Costa da Caparica – *See COSTA DA CAPARICA.*

Sesimbra – *See SESIMBRA.*

Serra da LOUSÃ★

Coimbra and Leiria
Michelin map 940 M4-5 and L5

Wooded hills and crests, where the bare rock takes on a violet hue, make up the mountain landscape of the Serra da Lousã where the highest point, at Alto do Trevim, reaches an altitude of 1 202m/3 934ft. The range, consisting of shale ridges and a few harder quartz rock crests, ends in the north in a sheer drop to the Lousã basin. To the south, the Zêzere valley divides it from the Serra da Gardunha, which on the east is overlooked by the granite mass of the Serra da Estrela.
In the past, the local inhabitants, living in scattered hamlets of low-lying houses built of shale, subsisted on mediocre crops of rye and maize grown on terraces and the raising of sheep and goats. The hillsides have been planted with maritime pines in an effort to combat soil erosion.

FROM POMBAL TO COIMBRA VIA THE SERRA

124km/77mi – about 3hr (not including tour of Coimbra)

Pombal – *See Pombal.*
From Pombal take the IC 8 towards Ansião.
The road from Pombal to Pantão winds over chalky hills dotted with olive trees, oaks, pines and eucalyptus.
The countryside becomes greener and hillier as the chalk gives way to marl, which is used in some of the local brickworks. The **drive★** has great variety as *corniche* roads follow the mountain contours, and views of cultivated valleys below and bare peaks alternate with wooded stretches of countryside.

Figueiró dos Vinhos – Figueiró dos Vinhos is a small town known for its earthenware pots and bowls. The **church**, with a chancel decorated in 18C *azulejos* illustrating the life of John the Baptist, has a fine Trinity in the south chapel.
Between Figueiró dos Vinhos and Lousã, the N 236-1crosses the Serra da Lousã, the southern slope of which, at first wooded, gets barer as it rises.

Castanheira de Pêra – On the main street of the town. opposite a school. there is a strange public garden with yew trees. box trees and thuyas clipped into amusing shapes.

After Castanheira a belvedere at a right hand turn affords a wide **view**★. beyond onto a curtain of pine, below onto a tributary valley of the Zêzere, higher up on to a crest-line. with the Zêzere valley behind it. then a second crestline and the Tagus basin. The **descent**★ into Lousã is swift. the *corniche* road affording attractive glimpses of the Arouce valley.

Candal – The old village of Candal stands in an unusual setting where fine grey schist houses may be seen stepped up the slope.

★**Miradouro de Nossa Senhora da Piedade** – The **view** from the belvedere plunges down into the Arouce valley where a medieval castle and minute white chapels can be seen on the valley floor. Opposite. surrounded by crop-covered terraces, stands the perched village of **Casal Novo**.

A little further on Lousã and the Mondego valley can be seen.

Lousã – Lousã. like **Foz de Arouce** to the north. possesses a considerable number of 18C patrician houses.

After crossing the Lousã basin and passing through Foz de Arouce. the road *(the N 236 and later the N 17 on the left)* follows the course of the Ceira and Mondego Valleys before reaching Coimbra.

★★**Coimbra** – *See COIMBRA: 3hr.*

Palácio and Convento de MAFRA★★

Lisboa

Michelin map 940 P2

Mafra monastery stands some twenty-five miles northwest of Lisbon. Its impressive size and baroque style. in which marble proliferates, testify to the rich reign of King João V, the Magnanimous. The monument has often been compared to the Escorial Monastery in Spain on account of its size, its proximity to the capital as well as the fact that it was built in fulfilment of a vow and played the role of royal palace and religious centre. Its austerity is softened by baroque decoration.

The fulfilment of a vow – In 1711 King João V, having no children after three years of marriage. vowed to build a monastery if God would grant him an heir.

A daughter. Barbara. was born. later to become Queen of Spain.

In 1717. work was entrusted to the German architect Friedrich Ludwig although the plans and decoration were more those of Roman artists under the Marquis de Fontes. Portuguese ambassador to the Holy See. Gold from Brazil financed the construction on a grandiose scale. The monastery was originally intended for thirteen monks but ended up accommodating 300 as well as the entire royal family. In order to do this the king called in two additional architects. which explains why some of the architectural detail is Germanic. some Italian and some Portuguese.

50 000 workers spent thirteen years on the vast buildings which cover 4ha/10 acres of ground and include a basilica. a palace and a monastery with 4 500 doors and windows. The complex extends eastwards into a park with a perimeter wall 20km/12mi long. The materials came from Portugal (Leiria pinewood. Pero Pinheiro marble and Santarém lime). from the Netherlands and Belgium (the bells). France (liturgical items). Brazil (precious woods) and Italy (walnut wood. statues from Rome and Florence and Carrara marble).

The Mafra School – João V took advantage of the presence of so many foreign artists at Mafra to found a school of sculpture. The first principal was the Italian. Alessandro Giusti. and among the teachers were such men as José Almeida. Giovanni António of Padua. who carved the main statues in the cathedral at Evora and. particularly. Joaquim Machado de Castro (1731-1822). The school's studios. patronised by the Canons Regular of St Augustine. who formerly occupied the monastery. produced many marble statues and several jasper and marble altarpieces. often embellished with low-reliefs. which may now be seen in the basilica.

TOUR *1hr 30min*

The 220m/722ft long façade is flanked at either end by Germanic-style wings surmounted by bulbous domes. The basilica stands in the centre of the façade.

★★**Basílica** – The basilica. like the flanking wings. is built of marble. its façade breaking the monotony of the main face by its whiteness and its Baroque decoration. The towers (68m/223ft tall) are joined by a double row of columns; niches high up contain Carrara marble statues of St Dominic and St Francis and below of St Clare and St Elizabeth of Hungary.

The peristyle is adorned with six statues of which the most remarkable is that of St Bruno.

The church **interior** is strikingly elegant in its proportions and in the marble ornamentation. The rounded vaulting rests upon fluted pilasters which also divide the
lateral chapels, each of which contains statues and an altarpiece in white marble
with a low relief carved by sculptors from the Mafra School.

The jasper and marble altarpieces in the transept chapels and the chancel pediment are also by the Mafra School. Note especially the fine marble altarpiece of
the Virgin and Child in the chapel off the north aisle and the sacristy and lavabo
where marble of every description may be seen. Four delicately worked arches at
the transept crossing support a magnificent rose and white marble **cupola★** which
rises to a height of 70m/230ft.

The bronze candelabra and six fine organs dating from 1807 are also remarkable.

Palace and Monastery ⊘ – *Third door to the left of the basilica.* The tour pro-
ceeds through a museum of comparative sculpture, the monks' infirmary, the
pharmacy, the kitchens and a museum of sacred art.

On the second floor, the royal apartments form a long succession of galleries, with
the Queen's Pavilion at one end and the King's at the other.

The ceilings are painted and the rooms have been refurnished. The palace reached
the height of its splendour at the beginning of the 19C under Dom João VI but
when this king left for Brazil in 1807, he took with him some of the decorative
items and furniture that had adorned Mafra.

Convento de Mafra

Y. Travert/DIAF

The grandiose and harmoniously proportioned **Audience Room** (Sala da Bênção) gives onto the basilica. It was from this gallery with its columns and mouldings faced with coloured marble, that the royal family attended mass. The bust of Dom João V is by the Italian master, Alessandro Giusti.

The Trophy Room, the monks' cells and the beautiful **library** (biblioteca)★, a hall 83.60m/274ft long, with magnificent rose, grey and white marble flooring are also of interest. The wooden bookshelves are rococo in style and contain 40 000 works from the 14 to the 19C.

ADDITIONAL SIGHT

Igreja de Santo André ⊘ – *In the old town (vila velha).*
Built in the late 13C, this small church presents three naves and a pentagonal apse with quadripartite vaulting.
At the entrance stand two fine Gothic sepulchres of Diego de Sousa and his wife. According to a local legend, Pedro Hispano, the future Pope John XXI (13C), was a priest here.

MANGUALDE

Viseu – Population 8 055
Michelin map 940 K6

The medieval town of Mangualde is today a busy agricultural and commercial centre.

Palácio dos Condes de Anadia – This 17C seigneurial estate has a rococo-style façade.

Igreja da Misericórdia – *Enter by the courtyard of the adjoining school.* The church, which dates from the 18C and is built at right angles, is a charming one with its small baroque façade adorned with statues, and on the courtyard side its first floor gallery with granite colonnades and balusters.
Inside, in the nave, *azulejos* depict the Last Supper, the Miraculous Draught of Fishes, St Martin etc. In the chancel, which has a gilded coffered ceiling and altars decorated with *azulejos*, note the carved wooden brackets on which to hang lamps.

Bairro Antigo (Old Quarter) – In front of the palace and fountain is the old part of Mangualde: winding alleys, small granite houses huddled together around the belfry.

EXCURSION

Penalva do Castelo – *12km/7.5mi on N 329-1, to the northeast.*
On the western side of this small town, the **Casa da Ínsua** ⊘, also known as Solar dos Albuquerques, is a manor house dating from 1775. It rises majestically with its battlemented façade in a pleasant landscape of woods and orchards. One can visit the chapel dating from 1690, as well as the park which is planted with huge trees (sequoias, eucalyptus) and the very carefully kept garden where camelias, magnolias and exotic plants grow.

Serra do MARÃO★

Porto and Vila Real
Michelin map 940 and 441 I6 – Local map see VALE DO DOURO

The Serra do Marão is a block of granite and shale bounded to the east by the Corgo, to the west by the Tâmega and to the south by the Douro. The dislocations caused by the mountain range's upheaval in the Tertiary Era are the reason for its variation of altitude; the wildness and desolation of the landscape are due to intense erosion.

FROM VILA REAL TO AMARANTE

70km/44mi – about 1hr 30min – Itinerary ③ on the Vale do DOURO local map

Vila Real – *See VILA REAL.*
Leave Vila Real by the Oporto road (IP 4), heading west.
As soon as the road reaches the slopes maize, pine and chestnut trees replace vineyards, apple orchards and olive groves; starting at Parada de Cunhos, there are **views** to the right of the serra's foothills and of Vila Real in its hollow.
After Torgueda leave the N 304, the Mondim de Basto road (see below) on your right. The road (IP 4) continues to climb, soon overlooking to the right the valley and to the left beautiful **views**★ of the summit of the Marão, which is the highest of the serra's peaks.
At the Alto do Espinho pass leave IP 4 and take the road south towards the Pico do Marão. You pass the Pousada de São Gonçalo located above pine-covered slopes. Continue for several miles then bear left.

The road rises up through a mineral landscape of laminated crystalline rocks and shale and ends on a ledge near the summit where the chapel of Nossa Senhora da Serra and a television relay station may be seen.

★★**Pico do Marão** – Alt 1 415m/4 642ft. The summit, topped by an obelisk, commands a magnificent **panorama** of the serra's bare peaks.

Return to the road and continue westwards to Amarante via Candemil.

The steep and winding descent to Amarante continues along a corniche road above the Ovelha river, a tributary of the Tâmega, which is well stocked with trout. Shortly before Candemil the road enters an enclosed rocky valley.

The last part of the drive through a green landscape of growing crops, pines and chestnut trees affords attractive views to the right of the tributary valleys of the Tâmega.

The N 15 drops down to the Tâmega valley before reaching Amarante.

★**Amarante** – *See AMARANTE.*

FROM VILA REAL TO MONDIM DE BASTO

61km/38mi – about 1hr 30min – Itinerary 4 on the Vale do Douro local map.

Leave Vila Real westwards on IP 4 described above, then bear right on N 304.

The road climbs to the Alto de Velão pass from where there is a **view** to the left of the upper basin of the Olo river. You cross the western end of the beautiful **Parque Natural do Alvão** dotted with jumbled granite rock formations, then begin the **descent★** to Mondim de Basto in the Tâmega valley.

Leave Mondim de Basto on N 312 to the north and then bear right on a forest road which climbs between rocks and pine trees.

★**Capela do Nossa Senhora da Graça** *Leave the car at the bottom of the majestic staircase (68 steps) which leads to the chapel. From the steeple (reached by 54 steps and rungs) there is a vast* **panorama** *of the Tâmega valley, Mondim de Basto and the Serra do Marão.*

MARVÃO★★

Portalegre – Population 309

Michelin map 940 N 7 – Local map see Serra de SÃO MAMEDE

Marvão is a fortified medieval village perched like an eagle's nest atop a granite wall on one of the peaks (865m/2 838ft) of the Serra de São Mamede near the Spanish border. The access road which circles the rocky crag by the north gives one a good idea of the military value of this outstanding **site★★**.

When in 1833 the Alentejo became the scene of the civil war, the liberals and the extremists fought for possession of the Marvão stronghold because of its impregnability. The liberals captured it by surprise in December 1833, repulsing a counter attack by Dom Miguel I's troops the following month.

Marvão

★THE VILLAGE *2hr*

After circling the ramparts, take a look at the Gothic doorway of the Igreja de Nossa Senhora da Estrela, before entering the village through the double doors flanked by curtain walls, watch towers and battlements.

A narrow alley leads to a square with a pillory where you may leave the car.

The village stronghold is cut by small streets, covered alleys and white houses with balconies bright with flowers, wrought-iron grilles and Manueline windows; several chapels have Renaissance doorways.

In the Rua do Espírito Santo which leads to the castle, there are two magnificent 17C wrought-iron **balustrades**★.

Igreja de Santa Maria – The 13C church at the foot of the castle now houses the Tourist Office and a local museum, the **Museu Municipal de Marvão** ⊘ (megaliths, Roman stelae and copies of old maps of Marvão).

★**Castelo** – The late-13C castle standing on the western edge of the crag was remodelled in the 17C. It consists of a series of perimeter walls dominated by a square keep. Go through the first fortified gate and immediately to the right take the stairs which lead down to a **cistern**★. Ten wide arches are reflected in the water. A second fortified gate leads into the first courtyard where the parapet walk affords fine **views**★ of the white village stretching out below the castle. In the second courtyard, which contains the keep, take the stairs to the right up to the parapet walk and follow it round to the keep. Impressive downward **views**★★ give a good idea of the various walls and particularly of the crenellated towers and watch towers built on the overhanging rocks. The vast **panorama**★★ extends to the jagged mountain ranges of Spain in the east, the Castelo Branco region and Serra da Estrela in the north and the Serra de São Mamede in the southwest.

MÉRTOLA

Beja – Population 3 347
Michelin map 940 T7

The small white town of Mértola suddenly emerges from the middle of the lonely Alentejo countryside, rising in a tiered amphitheatre up a hillside overlooking the confluence of the Guadiana and Oeiras rivers. Dominating the town are the restored keep and ruined walls of its 13C fortified castle. The former mosque, now converted into a church, testifies to Mértola's Arab past.

Igreja-Mesquita ⊘ – The square plan and forest of pillars reveal the church's origin; look at the ancient *mihrab* behind the altar, the niche from which the Imam conducted prayers, and outside at the doorway leading to the sacristy.

On leaving the church take the first street on the right.

At Rua da República, a small **museum** ⊘ displays Moorish pottery (9-12C).

MIRANDA DO DOURO★

Bragança – Population 1 841
Michelin map 940 or 441 H 11

Miranda stands perched on a spur above the Douro valley. It is an old town with its own special dialect, somewhat similar to Low Latin, and known as *mirandês*.

Guarding the entrance to the village from a hillock, are the ruins of a medieval castle which was destroyed by an explosion in the 19C.

The town's income comes from its numerous shops (clothes, shoe and gold) serving its Spanish neighbours who cross the border to shop.

The Pauliteiros Dance – The local men gather on holidays and especially on the feast-day of St Barbara on the third Sunday in August, to perform the Pauliteiros Dance. Dressed in white flannel kilts, black shirts with multicoloured embroideries and black hats trimmed with scarlet ribbons and covered in flowers, the men step out a rhythmic stick dance. The striking of the sticks or *paulitos* recalls the sword-fighting of long ago which perhaps formed the original basis of the dance.

Sé ⊘ – The former cathedral built according to a plan by Gonçalo de Torralva and instructions from Miguel de Arruda *(see Art – The Manueline Period)*, has an austere granite façade with two quadrangular bell-towers. The three- nave interior, with its ribbed vaulting, a 16C edifice of granite, contains a series of gilded and carved wood **altarpieces**★: the one in the chancel by the Spaniards Grégório Hernandez and Francisco Velázquez Juan Muniátegui, depicts the Assumption, round which are scenes from the Life of the Virgin, the Evangelists and several bishops. The whole is crowned with a calvary. On either side of the chancel, the 18C gilded wood stalls are embellished with painted landscapes.

An amusing statuette of the Child Jesus in a top hat stands in a glass display case in the south transept. He is much loved and venerated by the people of Miranda. On the Day of the Kings (dia dos Reis), a festival takes place, in which four boys carry the statue in a wooden frame during the procession.
There is a good view down from the cathedral terrace to the Douro flowing below. Opposite the cathedral, the ruins of the episcopal palace cloisters can be seen.

★**Museu Regional da Terra de Miranda** ⊘ – This former 17C Town Hall located in the historical centre of the town now houses an interesting and varied ethnographic museum displaying looms, archaeological finds (Stone, Bronze and Iron Age tools, Roman steles), old toys, regional costumes, a traditional bedroom and kitchen, weapons, coins, agricultural tools, ceramics and ritual costumes worn during the winter solstice, when those wearing masks with startled expressions have the right to do anything they are unable to do the rest of the year. This tradition is believed to have its origins in ancient initiation and fertility rituals.

EXCURSIONS

★**Baragem de Mirando do Douro** – *3km/2mi by a narrow road to the east.*
Miranda is the first of the five dams constructed on the international section of the Douro *(see VALE DO DOURO)* where it forms the border between Portugal and Spain. It is a buttressed dam, erected in a rocky defile and measures 80m/262ft high by 263m/863ft along its crest.

★**Baragem de Picote** – *27km/17mi by the Mogadouro road, N 221, and then N 221-6 on the left after Fonte da Aldeia.*
After going through Picote, a village created to house those involved in the construction of the dam, you pass, on your right, a road leading to a viewpoint over the enclosed Douro valley. The Picote Dam, which is a vaulted dam, uses the granite slopes of the Douro as support; it is nearly as high at its crest as it is long – 100m x 139m/328ft x 456ft.

MIRANDELA

Bragança – Population 8 192
Michelin map 940 or 441 H8

Although Mirandela is Roman in origin, the town visible today was founded by Dom Afonso II. It looks down upon the Tua, which is spanned by a long Romanesque bridge, rebuilt in the 16C, which is 230m long and has 20 different arches.
It is an elegant, flower-decked town with many gardens and lawns and various options for visitors, such as a boat trip on the Tua river, a journey by train along the old railway line connecting Mirandela with Carvalhais, or a visit around the city by minitrain.

Palácio dos Távoras ⊘ – This beautiful 18C palace, now occupied by the town hall, stands at the top of a hill. Its three-part granite façade (with the middle part the highest) is topped with curved pediments and crowned by spiral pinnacles.
A statue of Pope John Paul II sits in the middle of the square, with a more recent church to one side.

★**Museu Municipal Armindo Teixeira Lopes** ⊘ – This interesting museum, housed in the town's cultural centre, is devoted to sculpture and painting. It has been created from donations from the children of Armindo Teixeira Lopes, and contains more than 400 works by 200 predominantly Portuguese artists from the beginning of the century to the present day. These include Vieira da Silva, Tapiès, Cargaleiro, Nadir Afonso, Graça Morais, José Guimarães, Júlio Pomar and Teixeira Lopes. The museum also organises temporary exhibitions by contemporary artists.

EXCURSION

Romeu – Pop 478. *12km/7mi to the northeast.*
In the heart of the Trás-os-Montes, Romeu, together with **Vila Verdinho** and **Vale do Couço**, form a group of colourful villages gay with flowers, in a landscape of valleys wooded with cork oaks and chestnuts.
Recent restoration work has given them a new lease of life.

Museu das Curiosidades ⊘ – The museum contains the personal collection of Manuel Meneres, the benefactor of all three villages. In one room are early machines such as typewriters, sewing machines, stereoscopes and a phenakistoscope – predecessor of the cinema; in another room are objects of all kinds, each containing a music box – a chair, dolls, clocks.
On the ground floor note the old velocipede and several vintage cars (1909 Ford).

Serra de MONCHIQUE★

Faro

Michelin map 940 U4 – Local map see ALGARVE

The cool heights of the Serra de Monchique in the Algarve hinterland with their eucalyptus, cork-oak, chestnut and pine trees make a pleasant retreat for summer visitors and afford fine views of the region.

The Serra de Monchique is a volcanic block which rises more than 900m/2 953ft above the surrounding shale ridges, forming a barrier against the sea mists which condense upon it; the resulting water flows down owing to the impermeable nature of the rock. This humidity and the heat combine to produce a lush and varied vegetation, including orange trees and maize on the cultivated terraces, and arbutus trees, carobs and rhododendrons in the wild.

The volcanic nature of the area has given rise to medicinal springs which at **Caldas de Monchique** are used for the treatment of rheumatism and skin ailments.

FROM PORTIMÃO TO PICO DA FÓIA

30km/19mi – about 2hr

Portimão – *See PORTIMÃO.*

Leave Portimão on N 124 to the north.

After Porto de Lagos bear left on to the N 266; the road climbs up into the wooded Serra de Monchique. Beyond the junction to Caldas de Monchique, in a wide bend to the left, a belvedere *(viewing table)* affords a bird's eye **view** of the spa and the terraces of maize surrounding it. Southwards the hills cluster around Portimão.

The road crosses the slopes of the Fóia and Picota peaks, which are covered with pines, cork oaks and eucalyptus. Large syenite quarries are worked for the building industry.

Monchique – Attractively nestled on the verdant east side of Pico da Fóia, this small town possesses a **church** known for its Manueline doorway. The twisted columns are in the form of regularly knotted cables which end in unusual pinnacles.

From the belvedere situated on the fair ground *(access by the street which is an extension of the Fóia road)*, there is an interesting view of the terraced quarters facing Alto da Picota (alt 773m/2 536ft).

In Monchique bear left on to the N 266-3 towards Pico da Fóia.

The **road★** goes up the slopes of the Fóia, the highest point in the range. After a few miles' drive beneath the pines and eucalyptus, the **view★** opens out to the south in a right bend (cross and fountain): from left to right can be seen the Gulf of Portimão, Lagos Bay, Odiáxere Lake and, in the far distance, the Sagres Peninsula.

★**Pico da Fóia** – Alt 902m/2 959ft. A radio-television relay and a restaurant share this rocky site. From the summit (obelisk) there are extensive **views★** of bare ridges to the north and wooded heights to the west.

MONSANTO★★

Castelo Branco – Population 1 902

Michelin map 940 M7

Monsanto clings to the foot of a granite hill in the middle of a plain. It is visible from afar in a chaotic mass of rocks which blends in with the rocks of its castle. The origins of the village date from pre-history, when it was linked with pagan rituals; it was subsequently occupied by the Romans, and in 1165 was handed over by Dom Afonso Henriques to Gualdim Pais, master of the Knights Templar, who built the impregnable citadel.

Every year in May *(see Calendar of Events)*, young girls throw pitchers of flowers from the ramparts to commemorate the defiant throwing out of a calf when the castle was once bitterly besieged and those inside wished to convince the assailants that they would never be starved into capitulation.

★**Village** – Steep and rough alleys cut across the village of old granite houses. The façades, some of which are emblazoned, are pierced by paired windows and, in some cases, Manueline style doorways.

Capela de Santo António – This Manueline chapel in the village has a doorway with four ogival archivolts.

Capela de São Miguel – This Romanesque chapel next to the castle is now in ruins, yet it has preserved its four archivolts and historiated capitals.

★**Castelo** – An alley and later a steep path lead through an impressive rock chaos to the castle, where it is not unusual to find hens or rabbits in openings formed in the rocks, and the odd pig or sheep sheltering within a Roman ruin. Although

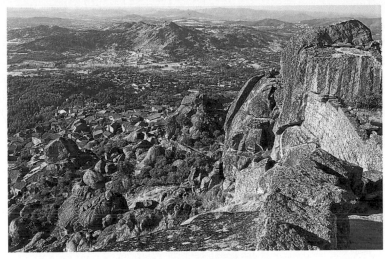

J. P. Garcin/DIAF

Monsanto – an impregnable site

it was rebuilt by Dom Dinis, countless sieges have since reduced to a ruin. From the top of the keep, an immense **panorama**★★ spreads northwest over the wooded hills of the Serra da Estrela and southwest over the lake formed by the Idanha dam, the Ponsul valley and, in the distance, Castelo Branco. As you return to the village note several tombs carved into the living rock.

MONSARAZ★★

Évora – Population 1 290
Michelin map 940 Q7

The old fortified village of Monsaraz occupies a strategic position in an outstanding **site**★★ on a height near the Guadiana valley on the border between Portugal and Spain. When it lost its military role it also lost its importance in favour of Reguengos de Monsaraz. Because of this the town has retained much of its historic character.

SIGHTS

Leave the car in front of the main gate.

★**Rua Direita** – The street retains all its original charm as it is still lined with 16 and 17C whitewashed houses, many flanked by outside staircases and balconies with wrought iron grilles. All the village monuments may be seen in this street which leads to the castle.

Antigo Tribunal ⊘ – The former court building, which is on the left side of Rua Direita, can be distinguished by the pointed arches above its doors and windows. Inside an interesting fresco depicts true and false Justice (bearing a crooked stick) with, above, a Christ in Majesty with upraised arms.

Igreja Matriz – The parish church contains the 14C marble tomb of Tomás Martins on which are carved figures in a funeral procession (monks and knights led by a priest), and, at the foot, falcons at the hunt.

S. Cordier/EXPLORER

Pelourinho – The pillory dates from the 18C.

Hospital da Misericórdia ⊘ – The Misericord Hospital (16C), which stands opposite the parish church, possesses a beautiful meeting hall on the first floor.

Castelo – The castle was rebuilt by King Dom Dinis in the 13C and given a second perimeter wall with massive bastions in the 17C. The parapet walk commands a magnificent **panorama**★★ of the Alentejo with its olive groves and cork-oak plantations.

MONTEMOR-O-NOVO

Évora – Population 6 458
Michelin map 940 QS

Montemor-o-Novo, a small peaceful town and agricultural market in the Alentejo, stretches out at the foot of a hill which is crowned by the ruins of a medieval fortified city. The **ramparts**, the construction of which goes back to Roman times, offer a good viewpoint over the countryside dotted with olive trees.

Montemor-o-Novo was the birthplace of **St John of God** (1495-1550) a Franciscan of exemplary charity who founded the Order of Brothers Hospitallers. The statue in the square before the parish church shows the saint carrying a beggar, whom he had found on a stormy night. The town's present hospital, named after the saint, was founded in the 17C.

MONTEMOR-O-VELHO

Coimbra – Population 2 572
Michelin map 940 or 441 L3

The town of Montemor-o-Velho in the fertile Mondego valley is dominated by the ruins of a citadel built in the 11C to defend Coimbra against the Moors, who were occupying the province of Estremadura in Spain.

If coming from Coimbra, take the road to the right on entering the village, cross the first perimeter wall and enter the castle courtyard.

★**Castelo** ⊘ – Of the original castle there remains a double perimeter wall, oval in shape, battlemented and flanked by many towers; the north corner is occupied by the church and the keep. From the top of the ramparts there is a **panorama**★ of the Mondego valley spread with vast rice fields, a few fields of maize and groves of poplar trees. On the southeast horizon lies the Serra da Lousã.

MOURA

Beja – Population 8 427
Michelin map 940 R7

Moura, the Town of the Moorish Maiden, stands grouped round the ruins of a 13C castle. It is also a small spa, the bicarbonated calcium waters of which are used in the treatment of rheumatism. The Pisões-Moura spring, a few miles from the town, provides a table water (Água de Castelo) which is widely sold in Portugal.

The legend of Salúquia – If the legend is to be believed, the town acquired its name – Vila da Moura – and the design on its coat of arms – a young girl dead at the foot of a tower – from the fate of Salúquia, the daughter of a local Moorish lord. Salúquia waited in vain on her wedding morning for her fiancé, a lord from a neighbouring castle. He had been ambushed and slain with all his escort by Christian knights who then stripped the dead of their clothes and dressed themselves in them. They thus entered and seized the castle – Salúquia, in despair, hurled herself to death from the top of the tower.

SIGHTS

★**Igreja de São João Baptista** – The Gothic Church of St John the Baptist is entered through an interesting Manueline **doorway** decorated with armillary spheres. Inside an elegant twisted white marble column supports the pulpit; the chancel, with network vaulting, contains a beautiful baroque Crucifixion group and the south chapel is adorned with 17C *azulejos* representing the Cardinal Virtues.

Opposite the church are the **thermal baths** (Estabelecimento Termal) and a public garden.

Mouraria – This quarter recalls by its name the former Moorish occupation, which only ended in 1233 with the liberation of the town. The low houses lining the narrow streets are sometimes ornamented with panels of *azulejos* or picturesque chimneys.

NAZARÉ★

Leiria – Population 10 265
Michelin map 940 N2

Nazaré lies in an exceptional **site**★★ with its long beach dominated to the north by a steep cliff. The town has three distinct quarters: **Praia**, the largest, which runs alongside the seafront, **Sítio** built on the clifftop and **Pederneira** on a hill. The name of Nazaré comes from a statue of the Virgin brought back from the town of Nazareth in Palestine by a monk in the 4C.

Nazaré's fishing folk – Nazaré was famous in the past for the costumes and traditions of its fishing community. The men wearing check shirts and trousers and long woollen bonnets would haul their boats up the beach with the aid of logs

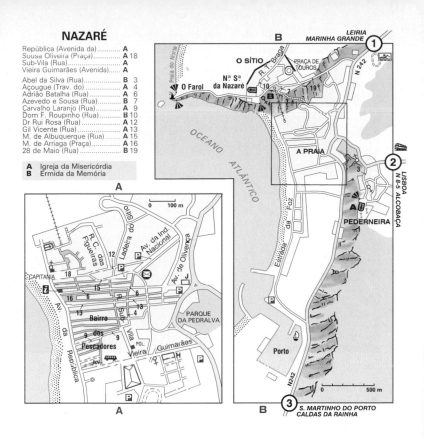

NAZARÉ

República (Avenida da)	**A**	
Sousa Oliveira (Praça)	**A** 18
Sub-Vila (Rua)	**A**
Vieira Guimarães (Avenida)	**A**
Abel da Silva (Rua)	**B** 3
Açougue (Trav. do)	**A** 4
Adrião Batalha (Rua)	**A** 6
Azevedo e Sousa (Rua)	**B** 7
Carvalho Laranjo (Rua)	**A** 9
Dom F. Roupinho (Rua)	**B** 10
Dr Rui Rosa (Rua)	**A** 12
Gil Vicente (Rua)	**A** 13
M. de Albuquerque (Rua)	**A** 15
M. de Arriaga (Praça)	**A** 16
28 de Maio (Rua)	**B** 19

A Igreja da Misericórdia
B Ermida da Memória

(see CANTANHEDE: Excursions, Praia da Mira) under the watchful eye of their womenfolk who would all be dressed in black but with skirts which showed the hems of seven petticoats of different colours, worn one over the other.

Today these costumes are barely in evidence and the fishing boats have been moved to the new harbour.

PRAIA (B)

Praia is the name of the lower town with its geometrically laid out streets giving onto the beach of fine sand. There are many hotels, restaurants and souvenir shops.

Bairro dos Pescadores (**A**) – The fishermen's quarter stretches between Praça Manuel de Arriaga and Avenida Vieira Guimarães.
Small whitewashed cottages line either side of the alleys leading down to the quayside.

Harbour – South of the beach a harbour now shelters the fishing boats. Part of the catch is sold in the market (sole, whiting, perch, coalfish, hake, skate, mackerel and especially sardines). Another part goes to the local canneries, while the fish the men's families eat are left to dry on the beach.

SÍTIO (B)

The Sítio quarter may be reached by car or on foot (up a flight of steps) although the funicular ⊘ is more enjoyable (see plan).

Miradouro – The belvedere built on the edge of the cliff overlooking the sea from a height of 110m/361ft, affords a fine **view**★ of the lower town and the beach.

Ermida da Memória ⊘ (**B**) – This minute chapel, near the belvedere, commemorates the miracle which saved the life of the local lord, Fuas Roupinho *(see ESPICHEL)*. One misty morning in 1182 Roupinho on horseback was giving chase to a roe deer which suddenly somersaulted into the air off the top of the cliff. Just as the horse, galloping at top speed, was about to do the same thing, Dom Fuas implored Our Lady of Nazaré for help and the horse stopped, saving the life of its rider.
The façade, the roof and the two floors inside the chapel are covered with *azulejos*: those of the façade on the side facing the sea evoke the knight's jump; those of the crypt, the miracle of the Marian intercession. In the staircase leading to the crypt a recess still has the footprint which the horse is said to have left on the rock face.

General view of Nazaré

Igréja de Nossa Senhora da Nazaré – This imposing church built at the end of the 17C is on the main square where the annual festival dedicated to its patron saint takes place. It has a façade with a forepart forming a gallery, and a baroque doorway opening at the top of a semicircular flight of steps.

The interior has a profusion of *azulejos*: those of the transept depict Biblical scenes.

Farol (Lighthouse) – *800m/0.5mi west of the church.*

The lighthouse is built on a small fort at the furthermost promontory of a cliff. Behind, and lower down, a path with steps and a parapet wall and then an iron staircase (at an angle of 34° – watch out for vertigo) leads to a point *(15min Rtn)* overlooking a magnificent **seascape★★**: a chaotic mass of jagged rocks through which the sea swirls furiously; on the right one can see the northern beach (Praia do Norte) where the waves surge in great rollers. Go round the headland a little, towards the left; you get a beautiful view over the gashed rockface of the Sítio cliffs and the Bay of Nazaré.

PEDERNEIRA (B)

Pederneira, on a cliff to the east of Praia, is the original centre of Nazaré.

Igreja da Misericórdia (A) – The 16C church at the end of the main street, Rua Abel da Silva, has a wooden roof and also an unusual colonnade abutting on its south wall.

There is a fine **view★** of the town and the Sitío quarter from the church terrace.

Portuguese Water Dog

The Portuguese water dog is classified by breeders as a Working dog. Robust, an adept swimmer and diver, it is a medium-sized dog with a wavy or curly coat, stands 50-56cm (20-22 in) and weighs 19-25kg (42-55lb). It has a fluffy mop of hair around its head, a long, curled tail, and resembles a cross between a standard poodle and an Irish water spaniel, both of which probably contributed to the breed. The dogs, now few in number, are black, brown, white, black and white, or brown and white. Developed along the Algarve coast by fishermen who trained them to retrieve fishing nets and tackle as well as to guard their boats, the breed is recognized by international Kennel Clubs.

EXCURSION

São Martinho do Porto – *13km/8mi south. Leave Nazaré by ③, N 242.*

The seaside resort of São Martinho do Porto lies to the north of a salt-water lake connected to the sea by a narrow channel pierced between tall cliffs.

Take the O Facho road.

A viewpoint offers an interesting **view★** of the surf and the cove. The hamlet of **Alfeizerão**, 5km/3mi east of São Martinho do Porto, is well known for its *pão de ló*, a delicious egg pastry.

Óbidos, which commands a vast sweep of countryside consisting of green valleys and heights topped by the occasional windmill, has managed to keep its proud medieval character through the ages. The fortified city, protected by its perimeter wall, flanked by small round towers and massive square bastions, once commanded this part of the coastline.

The silting up of its bay created a lagoon (Lagoa da Óbidos) which deprived the town of its coastal position and today Óbidos stands 10km/6mi inland.

The Queen's perquisite — Óbidos, freed from Moorish domination in 1148 by Afonso Henriques, immediately began rebuilding feverishly: the walls were consolidated, towers rebuilt, the delightful white houses refurbished so that the city already had a most attractive appearance when in 1282 it was visited by the king, Dom Dinis, accompanied by his young wife, Queen Isabel. The king made a gift of Óbidos to Isabel, and future monarchs repeated this gesture to their consorts until 1833.

The Óbidos net — In 1491 the *infante* drowned in the Tagus at Santarém. His body was recovered in a fisherman's net. It was to her town of Óbidos that Queen Leonor, the child's mother and wife of Dom João II, came to hide her sorrow and seek peace. The net upon the town's pillory is a reminder of this sad event.

Josefa de Óbidos — Josefa de Ayala, born in Sevilla in 1634 and better known under the name of Josefa de Óbidos, came to live in the town when very young and stayed here until her death in 1684.

Some paintings use indecisive colours and blurred line effects; her still lifes in rich colours are more popular.

The first confrontation: Wellington and Junot — Wellington, in advance of his troops in the march south at the beginning of the Peninsular Campaign, reached Óbidos and saw ahead the French army drawn up, under Laborde, some eight miles away at the village of Roliça. On 17 August 1808 the two armies met and the British gained their first, but inconclusive action.

Within four days both sides had been reinforced and battle was rejoined: this time thirty miles south of Óbidos at the village of Vimeiro. Wellington took full advantage of the terrain, including the famous ridge and Vimeiro Hill, to win a conclusive victory. A change of command in the British forces failed to follow up the victory and instead the Sintra Convention was signed.

TRAVELLERS' ADDRESSES

Where to stay

Mansão da Torre — *On the Caldas da Rainha road 2.5km/1.5mi to the northeast of Óbidos* — ☎ *(062) 95 92 47 — fax (062) 95 90 51 — 41 rooms — 10 500/13 500$ (CC) — restaurant — parking — air conditioning.*
Comfortable hotel in a rustic setting, with a beautiful garden, tennis court and swimming pool.

Estalagem do Convento — *R. D. João d'Ornelas, 2510 Óbidos* — ☎ *(062) 95 92 16 — fax (062) 95 91 59 — 31 rooms — 13 000/15 200$ (CC) — restaurant.*
An attractive inn set in an old convent. A rustic atmosphere, with pleasant and spacious rooms.

Pousada do Castelo — *Paço Real, 2510 Óbidos* — ☎ *(062) 95 91 05 — fax (062) 95 91 48 — 9 rooms — 25 000/28 000$ (CC) — restaurant — air conditioning.*
The former palace of Óbidos today houses a comfortable *pousada* elegantly decorated in an old-world style.

Eating out

Alcaide — *R. Direita* — ☎ *(062) 95 92 20 — 3 000/3 650$ (CC) — closed Mondays.*
Its central location, beautiful views of the town and simple traditional cooking make this a very popular restaurant.

A Ilustre Casa de Ramiro — *R. Porta do Vale* — ☎ *(062) 95 91 94 — 4 200/5 300$ (CC) — closed Thursdays and in January.*
Fine traditional cuisine served in an old country house.

Pousada do Castelo — *see above.*

Óbidos and its walls

★★THE MEDIEVAL CITY *1hr 30min*
Park the car outside the ramparts.

Porta da Vila – The inside walls of this double zigzag gateway are covered with 18C *azulejos*.

★**Rua Direita** – A paved channel runs through the centre of this narrow main street which is bordered with white houses bright with geraniums and bougainvillaeas. There are craft shops, restaurants and art galleries.

★**Praça de Santa Maria** – The church square stands below the main street and forms an attractive scene.

Pelourinho – The 15C pillory surmounting a fountain bears the coat of arms of Queen Leonor. Note the net, a reference to the tragic drowning of the *Infante (see above)*.

Igreja de Santa Maria ⊙ – It was here that the young King Afonso V married his eight-year-old cousin, Isabella, in 1444.
The **interior★** is noteworthy for its walls entirely covered with blue 17C *azulejos* depicting large plant motifs. In the chancel, in a bay on the left, a Renaissance **tomb★** is surmounted by a *Pietà* accompanied by the Holy Women and Nicodemus returning from burying the body of Our Lord. This outstanding work is attributed to the studio of Nicolas Chanterene *(qv)*. The retable at the high altar is adorned with paintings by João da Costa.

Museu Municipal ⊙ – The small municipal museum houses a statue of St Sebastian dating from the 15 or 16C and also a 17C polychrome *Pietà*. The "Josefa de Óbidos" room, in the first basement, contains various works by this artist, while exhibits in another room include mementoes of the war against Napoleon (a relief map of the region, weapons and unusual coffers made of transparent hide). The second basement displays medieval and Luso-Roman archaeological remains.

Continue to the very end of the main street to the ramparts. Follow the signs to the Pousada.

An English Governor

General **William Carr** (1768-1854) served in the distant British colonies at the end of the 18C. In 1807, as France and Spain signed a treaty of alliance, Portugal strengthened ties with Great Britain and prepared for war. Carr was assigned to take command of the Portuguese forces. The royal family remained in Brazil during this time, despite pleas for the king's return, and Carr took full advantage of his power.
Named Viscount of Beresford after a string of victories resulting in the Sintra Accord (which allowed defeated French soldiers to return home), the general was appointed Regent of Portugal by João VI, who remained in Rio de Janeiro until 1821. By then, Beresford's tyranny had provoked a conspiracy against him; a year before the monarch's return, liberal forces compelled the general to flee the country. These same liberals obliged João to accept (1822) a liberal constitution, the first step in the Portuguese experiment with the institutions of constitutional government.

★★ Muralhas – *The best access points are near the Porta da Vila or the Castelo.* The walls date from the Moorish occupation but were restored in parts in the 12, 13 and 16C. Along the north side, the highest, are the keep and the castle towers. The sentry path commands pleasant **views★** over the fortified city of whitewashed houses with their blue or yellow borders and gardens, and the surrounding countryside.

Castelo – *This is now a Pousada.*
The castle was converted into a royal palace in the 16C. Its façade has paired Manueline windows with twisted columns and a Manueline doorway surmounted by two armillary spheres.

ADDITIONAL SIGHTS

Aqueduto – The aqueduct outside the town dates from the 16C.

Santuário do Senhor da Pedra ⊘ – The sanctuary stands north of the town, beside the N 8. It is a baroque edifice and was built to a hexagonal plan between 1740-7. In a glass case above the altar is a primitive stone cross dating from the 2 or 3C; on it is a strange little figure whose arms are in the form of a cross. Niches round the nave contain baroque statues of the Apostles.
A coach, which is kept in the sanctuary, was used to transport the statue of the Virgin from the church of Santa Maria in Óbidos to the church of Nossa Senhora in Nazaré *(qv)* during the festival on 8 September.

EXCURSION

Lagoa de Óbidos – *17km/10.5mi about 1hr. Head for Peniche and at Amoreira turn right going north.*
The road, after crossing Vau, reaches the southern tip of the lagoon and then continues round it through pine trees. A little before the loop at the end of the road there is a vista over the sea to the left and the lagoon to the right. You then emerge facing the village of Praia (on the opposite bank); the **view** is of the pass, the stretch of water and the beaches.

OLHÃO

Faro – Population 13 151
Michelin map 940 U6 – Local map see ALGARVE

Olhão is a sardine and tuna fishing port and canning centre. It is built on the Algarve coast at a point where long coastal sandbanks lying offshore have been developed into beaches, of which some (Ilha da Armona) may be reached by boat. In spite of its picturesque Moorish village appearance with bustling narrow alleys, cube-shaped white or pale blue houses stepped with terraces and corner chimneys, Olhão's history does not go back to the Arabic occupation. It was founded in the 18C by fishermen who came to the spot by sea from the Ria de Aveiro and its architectural style came about through its commercial contacts with North Africa.

Viewpoints – The bridge over the railway at the entrance to the town affords a good view of the white houses piled up so close together.
An unusual **panorama★** of the whole town may be had from the belfry of the parish church, **Igreja Matriz** ⊘, standing in the main street *(access through the first door on the right as you enter the church).*
Many of the houses are covered by stepped exterior terraces *(açoteias and mirantes)* connected by small stairways.
Finally you can take a pleasant walk in the **Parque Joaquim Lopes** beside the river; from the park you can see the fishing port and the vast flat expanse of the islands and the offshore bars, as far as the lighthouse at Cabo de Santa Maria. There is a covered market near the park which on Saturdays is crowded with stalls and country folk.

OLIVEIRA DO HOSPITAL

Coimbra – Population 3 074
Michelin map 940 or 441 K6

Hills clad with vines, olive, and pine trees, form the setting of Oliveira do Hospital, the name of which recalls the 12C Order of the Hospitallers of St John of Jerusalem, now the Knights Templar of Malta *(see LEÇA DO BAILIO).*

★ Igreja Matriz ⊘ – The parish church, originally Romanesque, was reconstructed in the baroque period.
The interior, covered by a fine ceiling painted in false relief, includes the 13C funerary chapel of the Ferreiros containing the late 13C tombs of Domingos Joanes and his wife. The reclining figures of Ança stone reflect in the delicacy of their carving the evolution from the Romanesque to the Gothic style.

An equestrian **statue★** of a 14C medieval knight reminiscent of the one in the Museu Nacional Machado de Castro in Coimbra has been fixed to the wall above the tombs. Also noteworthy is a beautiful 14C stone **altarpiece★** of the Virgin Mother between St Joachim and St Anne.

EXCURSION

Igreja de Lourosa ⊙ – *10km/6mi to the southwest on N 230, N 17 and a road on the left. Excavations in progress.*
This pre-Romanesque church which probably dates as far back as 950 was built in the form of a basilica, low and squat, with a porch in front. It was restored in 1921 (façade and chancel).
The interior is typically Mozarabic with its horseshoe arches dividing it into three naves, and supported by short round pillars (ancient Roman columns), and by the small, elegant windows with two bays at each gable end of the central nave. A primitive Romanesque lintel can be seen in the false transept on the right.
Excavations have revealed the remains of a baptistry, and both underneath the nave and outside the sanctuary, numerous sepultures.
Near the church there is a 15C bell tower and a Manueline pillory.

OPORTO

see PORTO

OURÉM

Santarém – Population 4 498
Michelin map 940 N 4

The fortified city of Ourém, south of Vila Nova de Ourém, was built around the top of a hillock, the actual summit of which is occupied by the remains of a castle.
The town lived through a period of sumptuous richness in the 15C when the fourth count of Ourém, Dom Afonso, the bastard son of João I and nephew of Constable Nuno Álvares Pereira, converted the castle into a palace and built several other monuments. At the time more than 2 000 people lived within the city walls.

SIGHTS

Leave the car at the entrance to the town and take a road on the left which leads up to the castle.

The arms adorning the fountain at the entrance to the village are those of Count Dom Afonso.

Castelo – Two advanced towers appear on either side of the road; note the unusual brick machicolations crowning the walls all round the castle. *Go through the porch of the right tower.*
A path leads to a point where one may view a former tunnel. Steps go up to a square tower commanding the entrance to an older triangular castle; in the castle courtyard is a Moorish underground cistern dating from the 9C. Walk round the parapet path to view the belfry of the basilica at Fátima over to the west, the town of Pinhel to the northwest, Vila Nova de Ourém to the northeast and Serra da Lousã in the far distance.
A path leads to the village and the collegiate church.

Colegiada – Enter through the south transept. A door immediately to the right opens onto a stairway down to the crypt with its six monolithic columns. The Gothic and highly ornate white limestone **tomb** of Count Dom Afonso in the crypt has a recumbent figure attributed to the sculptor Diogo Pires the Elder. Two lifting mechanisms are engraved on the tomb.

PAÇO DE SOUSA

Porto – Population 3 536
Michelin map 940 or 441 I4

Paço de Sousa has retained from a former Benedictine monastery, founded early in the 11C, a vast Romanesque church (restored) in which lies the tomb of Egas Moniz, the companion in arms of Prince Afonso Henriques, whose loyalty to his royal leader has remained a legend.

A model of honesty – Alfonso VII, King of Léon, to put an end to the claims of independence of the County of Portugal, lay siege to Lanhoso where the Queen Regent Dona Teresa *(see GUIMARÃES)* was established and later, in 1127, to Guimarães, where her son, the Infante Afonso Henriques, was installed. The prince had only a small handful of men with which to oppose his enemy, and so he dispatched his former tutor **Egas Moniz** to plead before the king. In exchange for the king's abandoning the siege of Guimarães, Moniz swore, in the name of the prince, to recognise the sovereignty of the King of Léon. But in 1130, the danger over, Afonso Henriques forgot his promise and led another uprising against the king. Egas Moniz, accompanied by his wife and children, departed immediately for Toledo where he appeared before Alfonso VII dressed as a penitent with bare feet and a cord about his neck, prepared to pay with his life the ransom for his prince's treason. Moniz's honesty won him a pardon.

Igreja do Mosteiro de São Salvador – The church façade has a tiers-point doorway with recessed orders ornamented with motifs which are repeated on the surround of the rose window. The capitals are decorated with foliage. The tympanum is supported on the left by a bull's head and on the right by an unusual head of a man. On the tympanum on the left, is a man carrying the moon, on the right is a man carrying the sun. Two friezes of Lombard arcading run along the sides of the church.

Inside, the three aisles with pointed arches shelter, on the left, a naïve statue of St Peter and, on the right near the entrance, the 12C tomb of Egas Moniz. Low reliefs carved somewhat crudely on the tomb depict the scene at Toledo and the funeral of this loyal preceptor.

A battlemented tower stands to the left of the church.

PALMELA★

Setúbal – Population 14 444
Michelin map 940 Q3 – Local map see SERRA DA ARRÁBIDA

This picturesque white town is built up in tiers on the northern slope of the Serra da Arrábida at the foot of a mound crowned by a large castle which became the seat of the Order of St James in 1423.

Means to an end – In 1484, one year after the execution of the Duke of Bragança *(see VILA VIÇOSA)*, King João II learned of a new plot intended to overthrow him in favour of the Duke of Viseu, his brother-in-law. In August, when the king was at Alcácer do Sal and about to return to Setúbal down the Sado river, he avoided an ambush by changing plans and returning by road. However, upon his arrival at Setúbal he sent to Palmela for the Duke of Viseu, received him in his bedchamber and stabbed him to death. The Bishop of Évora, the instigator of the plot, was imprisoned in Palmela Castle and died a few days later, probably by poisoning.

SIGHTS

★**Castelo** ⊘ – *Follow the signs to the Pousada. Leave the car in the outer yard.* The castle, now partly converted into a *pousada*, stands on a sort of promontory commanding the surrounding countryside. The castle was constructed in three different periods: enter first the perimeter erected at the end of the 17C and based on the French military engineer Vauban's system: next go up a zigzag path to the second, somewhat clumsy line of fortifications probably constructed by the Moors. Bearing left you pass near the ruins of a one time mosque, transformed into a church (Santa Maria) and then destroyed in the earthquake of 1755. Finally you reach the keep and the parade ground which date from the late 14C. Below ground is the dungeon in which the Bishop of Évora was imprisoned.

★**Panorama** – From the top of the keep (64 steps) there is a beautiful view westwards of the Serra da Arrábida; southwards of a line of windmills, Setúbal, the Tróia Peninsula and the Atlantic; eastwards of the Alentejo Plain; and northwards of the village of Palmela and, on a clear day, Lisbon and the Serra de Sintra.

Antigo convento de Sant'Iago – The western extremity of the castle is occupied by the Church and Monastery of St James which were erected in the 15C by the Knights of St James, who had installed themselves in the castle in 1186. The conventual buildings are now a *pousada*.

The **church** constructed in transitional Romanesque style, is a well-proportioned building of great simplicity. The Romanesque barrel vaulting of the nave extends over the Gothic chancel; the walls are covered with *azulejos*, 16C in the chancel and 18C in the nave. Carved into the flooring is the blazon of the Order of the Knights of St James. The tomb of Jorge de Lencastre, the son of João II and last Master of the Order, may be seen in a Manueline bay off the north aisle.

Igreja de São Pedro ⊘ – The church, which is in the upper part of the town at the foot of the castle walls, dates from the 18C.

The interior is entirely lined with **azulejos★** depicting scenes from the life of St Peter; outstanding are those in the south aisle illustrating the miraculous catch of fish, Christ walking on the waves and the crucifixion of St Peter.

Braga, Viana do Castelo and Vila Real

Michelin map 940 F5, G5 and G6

Peneda-Gerês, Portugal's only **National Park**, was established in 1971 and covers 72 000ha/178 000 acres in the northern districts of Braga, Viana do Castelo and Vila Real. It is in the shape of a horseshoe, the two halves encircling the southwest point of the Spanish province of Orense with which it shares over 100km/60mi of border.

It is a very hilly region where the relief has been eroded into an awesome landscape of jumbled granite rocks and scree. The valleys of the Lima, Homem and Cávado rivers divide the region into *serras* – da Peneda, do Soajo, da Amarela and do Gerês. The Serra da Peneda has the highest average rainfall in the whole of Portugal.

The park consists of three regions. The first, in the north, is of the very wild part of the **Serra da Peneda** which is crossed by a road currently under repair. The second and most popular region is that of the Serra do **Gerês** in the south where tourists are also attracted by the spa. The third section, in the east, the **Barroso** region is around the Paradela dam.

For drivers wishing to cross from the Peneda section to Gerês, the quickest route is through Spain.

The park is designed to protect the natural sites, archaeological remains, flora (oaks, Scots pines and firs, lilies, ferns etc) and fauna (stags, wild horses and golden eagles) of outstanding interest. In spite of its ruggedness, the park has a considerable population living in its numerous hamlets.

★★FROM RIO CÁVADO TO PORTELA DO HOMEM

① Northwards from the N 103

20km/12mi – about 3hr

N 304 branches north from N 103 between Braga and Chaves and begins winding downhill through an attractive landscape of rocks and heather. After 2km/1mi you pass the beautifully situated São Bento *pousada* with its panoramic view of the Caniçada reservoir.

★**Confluente de Caniçada** – Two bridges cross successively the Cávado and its tributary, the Caldo, turned into reservoir-lakes by the Caniçada Dam (which is 10km/6mi to the west). The first bridge crosses over a submerged village which appears when the water level drops.

Coming from the first bridge onto the peninsula between the two lakes, take N 308 on the right at the intersection, and then immediately cross the second bridge. Head for Gerês.

Parque Nacional da Peneda-Gerês – View of the Caniçada

B. Brillion/MICHELIN

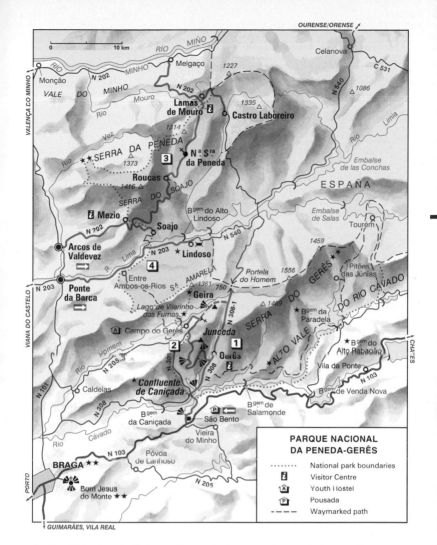

Gerês – This pleasant little spa lies at the bottom of a wooded gorge. Its waters, rich in fluorine, are used in the treatment of liver and digestive disorders.

Gerês is the main centre for excursions into the national park. The Visitor's Centre, the **Centro de Informação do Parque** is just beyond the thermal cure centre.

After Gerês, the road is lined first with hydrangeas, then winds up through woods of pines and oaks. 8km/5mi from Gerês you reach the nature reserve preceded by a picnic area beside a stream.

The road climbs gently through woods and crosses the Homem river which races through a rocky course. It continues to the Homem Pass defile and the Spanish border.

Turn back and take the track on the right towards Campo do Gerês. The track crosses the remains of a Roman road at two points: after 1.3km/0.8mi and 2km/1.2mi.

★**Remains of the Roman Way (Geira)** – The milestones on the side of the road are the remains of the Roman Way (Via Romana) which stretched some 320km/200mi between Braga and Astorga in Spain via the Homem Pass. The stones bore commemorative or honorific inscriptions to the emperor (of the Flavian dynasty in the 1C) or sometimes the provincial governor. *Bracara Augusta*, the ancient name for Braga, may be seen on some.

The track continues, affording lovely views of, and then skirting the **Represa de Vilarinho das Fumas**, a blue-water reservoir set in a wild, rocky landscape.

Return to the car.

The road rises gradually through woods to cross the Homem river, which at this point is a rushing mass of water over the rocks. The road continues to the Portela do Homempass and the border with Spain.

★★SERRA DO GERÊS

② From Gerês to the Vilarinho das Furnas reservoir
15km/9mi – allow 2 hours

From Gerês take N 308 to the south then turn right.

★★**Uphill road to Campo do Gerês** – This road with tight hairpin bends offers good views of the Caniçada reservoir and of the superb rock falls and some precariously perched boulders.
When the road stops climbing turn right to follow the signpost "Miradouro de Junceda" and Gerês. 4km/2.4mi further on a track (3km/1.8mi) in very poor condition leads left to the viewpoint.

★**Miradouro de Junceda** – A bird's eye view of Gerês and its valley.
Return to the main road and continue on to Campo do Gerês. At a crossroads in the middle of which stands an ancient Roman milestone bearing a sculpture of Christ.
Continue along the road to the right to reach the Vilarinho das Furnas reservoir. On the left the vaulted dam is built in a rocky and wild setting. The track which runs along side the reservoir (footpath) leads to the Roman way described above.

★★SERRA DA PENEDA

③ From Arcos de Valdevez to Melgaço
70km/44mi – a good half day

This itinerary takes you through the wildest part of the park.

Arcos de Valdevez – The towers of two churches dominate this pleasant little town on the banks of the Vez river.
The road from Arcos to Soajo rises first among chestnuts, pines and plane trees, through a terraced landscape scattered with houses surrounded by vineyards, then it crosses a wilder region of moorland.

Mezio – This stands at the entrance to the national park. An information centre gives details on the park, its geological features, flora and fauna.
The road for Peneda begins 2.5km/1.5mi further on, but keep going towards Soajo.

Soajo – This is an isolated village with a wonderful group of granaries or **espigueiros**★ for drying grain. The granite constructions built on piles date from the 18 and 19C.
Return to the junction with the Peneda road, which you take.

The landscape becomes grandiose – mountains strewn with granite blocks; extraordinarily shaped boulders. Several hamlets line the road.

Roucas – The village stands in the midst of terraces scattered with *espigueiros*. Women in black may be seen working in the fields.

Espigueiros or granaries

Mosteiro de Nossa Senhora da Peneda – The sanctuary, which stands in a magnificent **setting**★ at the foot of a granite cliff, is preceded by 300 steps climbed by devotees during the famous pilgrimage which attracts crowds from the whole region in early September. Pilgrims walked or rode to the site before the road was built.

Lamas de Mouro – This is another entrance to the park with an information centre and a camp site.

Castro Laboreiro – The village has preserved several traditional houses built of granite as well as the ruins of a castle which afford an extensive view of the rock-strewn landscape.

Return to Lamas de Mouro and take the Melgaço road.

④ From Ponte da Barca to Lindoso

31km/19mi – See Lindoso.

PENEDONO

Viseu – Population 912
Michelin map 940 or 441 J7

The town of Penedono, perched on a rocky crest 947m/3 106ft high in the Beira Alta. is overlooked on its northern side by a fortified castle, graceful and triangular.

Castelo ⊘ – A 16C **pillory** stands before the steps leading up to the castle. Pass through the ramparts and turn left towards the simple entrance gate which is flanked by two battlemented turrets. The view from the parapet walk extends south over the village to the Serra da Estrela in the distance and northwards to the mountainous plain which precedes Trás-os-Montes.

PENICHE

Leiria – Population 15 267
Michelin map 940 N 1

Peniche, which was built to command access to the mile long promontory, is today Portugal's second most important fishing port (crayfish, sardines, tunny etc). Catches are preserved in the town's canneries. Peniche's other source of prosperity is its dockyard. The remains of ramparts and the powerful looking citadel recall the former military role played by the city. A pleasant public garden planted with palm trees surrounds the Tourist Information Centre (Posto de Turismo) on Rua Alexandre Herculano.

The revival of handmade lace – Peniche has been trying to revive its former speciality of bobbin lace since the end of the 19C. To encourage this revival, an apprentice school has been set up at the town's Industrial and Business School *(avenida 25 de abril)*. On the first floor there is an exhibition of samples from past and present production. Lacemakers can also be seen working at the Casa de Trabalho das Filhas de Pescadores *(rua do Calvário)*, and handmade lace can still be bought in the town *(avenida do Mar)*.

SIGHTS

Cidadela – An ancient 16C fortress, converted in the 17C into a Vauban-style citadel. It stands proudly with its invulnerable high walls and sharp edged bastions topped with watch towers. Until 1974 it was a state prison, then it became an emergency city for refugees from Angola. It dominates both the harbour to the east and the sea to the south.

Harbour – To the southeast of the town, it lies in a cove which is almost enclosed by two jetties. The esplanade *(Largo da Ribeira)* which surrounds it, at the foot of the citadel, is always the scene of a highly colourful spectacle with the **return of the fishing fleet**★, under the unceasing overhead ballet of the squawking seagulls when the catch of sardines, tunny fish or crayfish is unloaded.

Igreja de São Pedro – The 17C chancel was embellished in the 18C with gilded woodwork into which were incorporated four huge canvases dating from the 16C and attributed to the father of Josefa de Óbidos.

EXCURSIONS

★**Cabo Carvoeiro** – This is a 2km/1.2mi long peninsula with shores consisting of piles of flat laminated rock formations.
Leave Peniche heading north and bear left on N 114.

Papoa – *Beyond a school and a water tower, take the lane to the right and park the car after 500m/1/3mi. 30min on foot.* Papoa, a small peninsula grafted like a spur onto Cabo Carvoeiro, still has, on the widest part, a windmill and the ruins of a fort which was the northern counterpart of the citadel in Peniche. To get there, take the footbridges to a promontory where you overlook the high cliffs and

Ph. Roy/EXPLORER

Cabo Carvoeiro

the rocks which rise out of the sea, one of which is called the Crows' Stone (Pedra dos Corvos). Go as far as the monument at the highest point to have the full **panorama**★ which extends to the east and the Baleal headland, its island and the coast further on, scalloped out by the Obidos Lagoon; to the northwest over Berlenga; to the west over the cliffs as far as Remédios; to the south over Peniche. *Return to N 114.*

The road twists and turns following the precipitous coastline, where the numerous crevices are much appreciated by anglers.

Several look-out points offer bird's eye views over the cliffs; the one situated in the axis of the Capela dos Remédios has an admirable view over a strange concentrated mass of piles of flat laminated rocks.

Capela de Nossa Senhora dos Remédios – The chapel, in the small whitewashed village of Remédios, stands in a little courtyard of monkey-puzzle trees. It has a tiny hexagonal belfry and is faced inside with beautiful 18C **azulejos**★ attributed to the studio of António Oliveira Bernardes. On the right are the Nativity and the Visitation, on the left the Presentation in the Temple. The ceiling is painted with an Assumption.

Beyond Remédios the vegetation dies away to be replaced by a kind of moorland which continues to the foot of a **lighthouse** (farol). From the lighthouse there is an impressive **view**★ of the ocean, an isolated rock known as the Crows' Ship (Nau dos Corvos), and, in the distance, the squat shape of the island of Berlenga.

★★**Ilha da Berlenga** – *Access by boat. See ILHA DA BERLENGA.*

PINHEL

Guarda – Population 3 237
Michelin map 940 or 441 J8

Pinhel, an old village and former fortified outpost on a mountainous shelf near to Spain, has many houses decorated with coats of arms and beautiful wrought iron balconies. In the main square, planted with acacia trees, stands a pillory consisting of a monolithic column topped by a pretty lantern turret.

The road approaching Pinhel from the southwest (N 221) crosses a countryside covered with olive trees and vines; towards the end, near the town, there is a large group of wine vats, with very prominent white pointed domes.

Museu Municipal ⊙ – This small municipal museum contains prehistoric and Roman remains, religious works of art (Ança stone altarpiece attributed to Jean de Rouen), weapons and Portuguese pewterware and earthenware. Upstairs, there is a collection of naive folk art and other paintings.

EXCURSIONS

Serra da Marofa – *20km/12mi – about 1hr 30min. Leave Pinhel on N 221 going north.*

The road linking Pinhel and Figueira de Castelo Rodrigo was known locally as the **Accursed Road** because of the danger presented by its countless bends when crossing the Serra da Marofa.

The road, after passing through a rich agricultural region, gradually becomes more and more hemmed in between rock strewn slopes before entering the green Côa Valley. On emerging it traverses the wild and stony **Serra da Marofa**, to reach the Figueira de Castelo Rodrigo Plateau which is planted with fruit trees.

To the left, the *serra's* highest peak, with an altitude of 976m/3 202ft commands an interesting view of the ruins of the fortified village of Castelo Rodrigo on a height nearby.

Castelo Rodrigo – An important city since the Middle Ages, it was superseded in the 19C by Figueira de Castelo Rodrigo. Good views of the surrounding area.

Figueira de Castelo Rodrigo – In the town an 18C baroque church contains many gilded wood altars.

Antigo Convento de Santa Maria de Aguiar – *2km/1mi to the southeast of Figueira*. This is now private property. The church, which lacks all furnishings and has a very tall central aisle, is a Gothic edifice built to a Cistercian plan.

Barca de Alva – *20km/12mi to the north of Figueira*. The blossoming of the almond trees between late February and mid-May, provides a delightful spectacle – a sea of pink flowers.

★ **Estrada de Almeida** – *25km/15.5mi to the southeast*. This route provides a picturesque link between Pinhel and Almeida. *Take N 324 southeast of Pinhel*. The road then comes to a desolate plateau strewn with enormous blocks of granite forming a lunar **landscape**★. After Vale Verde you cross a tributary of the Côa river by a narrow old humpback bridge.

2.5km/1.5mi further on, at a crossroads turn left on N 340: the road then crosses a bridge over the Côa river and rejoins N 332, which one takes to the left to reach Almeida.

POMBAL
Leiria – Population 12 469
Michelin map 940 M4

The town of Pombal at the foot of its medieval castle evokes the memory of the Marquis of Pombal who acquired a property locally and died here in 1782.

The despotism of the Grand Marquis – Born in Lisbon in 1699 into a family of the petty nobility, Sebastião de Carvalho e Melo began life in the diplomatic service. Thanks to the support of his uncle, a canon of the Chapel Royal, he was sent first to London, where he became interested in the flourishing national economy, and then on to Vienna. On the death of Dom João V in 1750, his successor King José I called Carvalho to power. The minister undertook the task of improving the nation's finances and achieved considerable success, promulgating numerous decrees by which, among other things, the Royal Bank was founded and traffic in slavery of the natives of Brazil was abolished. In 1755 the earthquake gave him the opportunity to demonstrate his capacity for organisation and planning *(see LISBON: Historical notes)*.
Simultaneously he sought to consolidate the absolute power of the monarchy by expelling the over powerful Jesuits (1759) and reducing the power of the nobles. On 2 September 1758 the king was wounded in an attack as he was returning from a private meeting with Maria-Teresa of Távora. Only in December did Carvalho decide to act, arresting the Marquis of Távora and his family. They were broken on the wheel and burned while their accomplices were hanged.
In 1759 the minister became Count of Oeiras and ten years later the king bestowed on him the title of Marquis of Pombal. But the death of Dom José I in 1777 showed the frailty of such created power; Pombal had to face a number of enemies. In 1781 he was banished from the Court and retired to his lands where he died the following year.

Castelo ⊘ – *15min. Take the Ansião road on the right at the corner of the Palácio de Justiça and, on reaching a Cross, bear sharp right into a narrow surfaced road which rises steeply. Leave the car at the foot of the castle.*
The castle, which was built originally in 1161 by Gualdim Pais, Grand Master of the Order of the Knights Templar, was modified in the 16C and restored in 1940. From the top of the ramparts, overlooked by the battlemented keep, there is a view of Pombal to the west and the foothills of the Serra da Lousã to the east.

PONTE DE LIMA
Viana do Castelo – Population 2 655
Michelin map 940 or 441 G4

The small town between Viana do Castelo and the Parque Nacional da Peneda-Gerês has a long historical past. The Romans built a strategic bridge at this point, which was part of the Roman Way between Braga and Astorga in Spain. Later, in the early 12C, Queen Tareja (Teresa) came to live in Ponte de Lima and granted it local privileges.
Ponte de Lima's wealth of ancient buildings has earned it the status as a pilot town for the restoration of Portuguese architectural heritage. Its streets are lined with Romanesque, Gothic, Manueline, baroque and neoclassical constructions while its environs are particularly rich in manor houses *(solares)* and seigneurial country estates *(quintas)*. The latter are built of granite, adorned with coats-of-arms on gateways, and covered galleries, and date from the 16, 17 and 18C.

The **Associacão do Turismo de Habitação**, an association which arranges accommodation for tourists in beautiful country homes or "casas rusticas", was set up in Ponte de Lima in the 1980s.
Today the organisation arranges accommodation in homes throughout northern Portugal *(see Practical Information)*.

SIGHTS

★**Ponte** – The bridge, after which the town was named, has 16 rounded arches alternating with openwork piers with cutwaters. It was built by the Romans – five of the original arches remain – and then rebuilt in the 14C by Dom Pedro I who was also responsible for the ramparts and fortified gateways.

Largo Principal – The main square has an 18C fountain with an armillary sphere.

Palácio dos Marqueses de Ponte de Lima – The façade with its Manueline windows dates from 1464. Today the building houses the Town Hall.

Igreja Matriz – The church, which was altered in the 18C, has a Romanesque doorway with recessed orders decorated with a double string course of billets. The interior has numerous statues dating from different periods, and in the side chapels there are two baroque altarpieces.

Igreja-Museu dos Terceiros ⊘ – The complex comprises two churches and some conventual buildings. Note the 16C Hispano-Moorish *azulejos* and the **Igreja dos Terceiros** decorated with a rare collection of **woodwork★**. The sacred art section around the cloisters contains religious ornaments and ancient statues.

PORTALEGRE

Portalegre – Population 15 876
Michelin map 940 07 – Local map see SERRA DE SÃO MAMEDE

A strategic position near the border in olden times, the town was endowed with a fortified castle by King Dinis I in 1290, but only a few ruins remain.
Portalegre, opulent and famous in the 16C through its tapestries, found a new prosperity at the end of the 17C when silk mills were established in the town. The bourgeois of the time filled the neighbourhood with baroque houses and mansions which may be seen to this day.
Portalegre is the starting point for the excursion in the Serra de São Mamede.

PORTALEGRE

Luís de Camoes (Rua)...............13
5 de Outubro (Rua)...................21

Alex. Herculano (Rua) 3
Bairro Ferreira e Rainho...........4
Comércio (Rua do)....................6
Elvas (Rua de) 7
Figueira (Rua da)......................9
G.G. Fernandes (Rua)...............10
Luís Barahona (Rua)................12
Mouzinho de Albuquerque
  (Rua)......................................15
República (Praça da) 16
Sé (Largo da)............................18
Sé (Rua da)...............................19

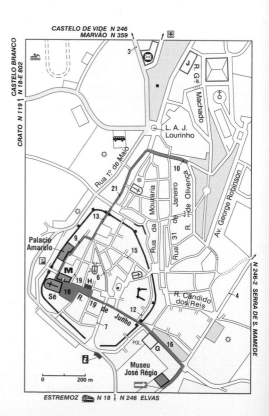

M Museu Municipal

SIGHTS

Follow the route marked on the town plan.

Museu José Régio ⊘ – The collection of regional, religious and folk art assembled by the poet José Régio (1901-69) is the most interesting part of the museum, which is in the house where he lived: there are numerous 16 to 19C crucifixes and naive statuettes of St Antony, as well as antiques.

Rua 19 de Junho – This street is lined with 17 and 18C houses.

Sé – The cathedral's 18C façade is characterised by the marble columns of the main doorway, wrought iron balconies and granite pilasters. The 16C interior contains in the second chapel on the right, a fine compartmented altarpiece on the Life of the Virgin and, in the sacristy, where the walls are clad with *azulejos*, an 18C cope chest.

Museu Municipal ⊘ **(M)** – Installed in the former diocesan seminary, this municipal museum contains a rich collection of sacred art: a Spanish *Pietà* in gilded wood dating from the end of the 15C, a 16C altarpiece in polychrome terracotta, a magnificent 17C tabernacle in ebony, four ivory high reliefs (18C Italian School), an 18C ivory crucifix, 16C gold and silver plate.
Also on display are 17-18C Arraiolos carpets, pieces of furniture including a beautiful Dutch wardrobe, earthenware (Hispano-Moorish, 16-17C Portuguese) as well as 17 and 19C porcelain from China.

Palácio Amarelo – The "yellow" palace façade, unfortunately in a poor state of repair, has some beautiful, ornate 17C ironwork.

EXCURSION

✶**Serra de São Mamede** – *See Serra de SÃO MAMEDE.*

PORTIMÃO

Faro – Population 26 172
Michelin map 940 U4 – Local map see ALGARVE

Portimão is a fishing port nestled at the back of a bay. The best **view★** is at high tide from the bridge across the Arade at the end of the bay. The town is also an industrial centre specialising in boat building and the canning of tunny and sardines. The seaside resort of **Praia da Rocha★★** contains the town's famous beach.

Largo 1° de Dezembro – The benches of this small square are covered with 19C *azulejos* portraying various episodes from Portuguese history.

EXCURSIONS

★★**Praia da Rocha** – *See PRAIA DA ROCHA.*

Serra de Monchique – *See Serra de MONCHIQUE.*

Portugal and the Jesuits

During the period of the Great Discoveries the Jesuits played an important role in the mission field. Dom João III showed an interest in the followers of St Ignatius and the founding of the Society of Jesus in 1540. In 1542 St Francis Xavier, the Apostle of the Indies, started preaching in India, the Spice Islands and Japan. The Jesuits engaged in trade. These first encounters (1540s) between the Portuguese and the Japanese are amusingly depicted on the Namban screens. The lanky figures of the Jesuits in their black cloaks are easily identifiable from the colourful, gold braided attires of the merchants. Persecution began at the beginning of the 17C and the Jesuits took refuge in Macau, the trading base on the Chinese coast. The Marquis of Pombal fought a constant battle to reduce the power and wealth of the Jesuits. He expelled them from the missions in Brazil, prohibited the Jesuits from engaging in trade, forbade them to preach or to teach and on 3 September 1759 all the members of the Society of Jesus were outlawed and expelled from Portugal.

PORTO★★

Oporto – Porto – Population 302 535
Michelin map 940 14

Oporto, Portugal's second largest city and capital of the north, has a population of over a million including that of its suburbs. It has a reputation for being hard-working, sombre and austere and yet when the sun shines it comes alive with vitality and colour. Undaunted by the steep terrain, Oporto occupies a magnificent **site★★**, its houses clinging to the banks of the Douro, the legendary river that ends here after its long course through Spain and Portugal.

Not least among the city's claims to fame, are its internationally celebrated port wines which are matured in the **Vila Nova de Gaia** wine lodges.

The best **general view★** of Oporto is from the terrace of the former Convento de Nossa Senhora da Serra do Pilar (**EZ** – *see below*).

The historical centre of the city was declared a World Heritage site by UNESCO in 1996.

The city – The traditional city **centre** spreads across a network of shopping streets around Praça da Liberdade and São Bento station. This is very lively during the day with its crowds of people, its old-fashioned shop fronts in Rua Santa Catarina, Formosa, Sá da Bandeira and Fernandes Tomás, and its numerous cake shops and tea rooms full of students in their black capes.

The working districts of **Ribeira** and **Miragaia** near the Douro have been restored and renovated over the last few years. Oporto's nightlife is now centred in Ribeira with its many fashionable restaurants.

The quarter also provides a good selection of moderately priced restaurants and bars and is the best place to look for two of the local dishes, tripe or *tripas à modo do Porto* and cod or *bacalhau à Gomes de Sá*.

Oporto's business centre has been moving gradually westwards around **Avenida da Boavista** between Oporto and Foz. Major banks, businesses and shopping centres are springing up in modern tower blocks.

Economy – A large percentage of Portuguese industry is carried out in Oporto and the surrounding area. Major industries include textiles (cotton), metallurgy (foundries), chemical (tyres), food (canning), leather and ceramics. Horticultural produce (nurseries and gardens) is also important as, of course, is the wine trade with export worldwide.

The bridges – The river banks are linked by three technically outstanding bridges. "Oporto has laid its Eiffel Towers out horizontally to serve as bridges", wrote the Frenchman Paul Morand before the building of the Arrábida bridge. The quotation is a wonderfully apt description of the 19C constructions.

Porto and the Luís I bridge

The **Ponte Ferroviária Maria★** (**FZ**), a railway bridge which is the furthest upstream and the most graceful, was designed by the French engineer Eiffel and completed in 1877. It is entirely made of metal and its single arch has a span of 350m/1 148ft.

The **Ponte Rodoviária Luís I Road★★** (**EZ**), a road bridge, is the most spectacular of Oporto's bridges with two superimposed road tracks, allowing it to serve both upper and lower levels of the town on both banks. It is the symbol of Oporto, as is the Eiffel Tower for Paris. It has a span of 172m/564ft and was built in 1886 by the Belgian firm of Willebroeck on the same lines as Eiffel's railway bridge.

The **Ponte Rodoviária Arrábida Road** (**BV**), which is the furthest downstream and is used by the motorway which goes through Oporto, is a particularly bold structure; it was built between 1960-3. It crosses the Douro in a single reinforced concrete span of nearly 270m/886ft.

Both the road bridges provide interesting viewpoints over the town.

HISTORICAL NOTES

Portucale – At the time of the Romans, the Douro was a considerable obstacle to communication, between north and south Lusitania. Two cities faced each other across the river, controlling the estuary: Portus (the harbour) on the north bank, Cale on the south.

ed Lusitania but Christian resistance prevented them
gion between the Minho and the Douro. It was this
e, that the Princess Dona Tareja (Teresa), daughter
a dowry in the form of a county to her husband
this same county was to be one of the mainsprings
s name to the whole country *(see INTRODUCTION).*

unty of Portucale, Oporto (O Porto in Portuguese,
eloped trading relations with northern Europe and
15C its shipyards helped to create the Portuguese
of Prince Henry the Navigator, who came from this
which in 1415 took part in capturing Ceuta from
To feed the fleet, all the cattle in the region were
being left with only the offal – from which they
tripe eaters.

igland and Portugal signed the **Methuen Treaty** which
tured goods – wool especially – to the Portuguese;
per Douro found a ready market in Britain.
ading centre in Oporto in 1717 and little by little
roduction of port wine from the harvesting of the

the wine trade the Marquis of Pombal founded
which he gave a monopoly control of the wines
ontrol annoyed many small Portuguese producers
set fire to the company's local offices. Pombal
ere condemned to death.

os borrachos – the drunkards' rebellion – was by
the inhabitants of Oporto for their love of liberty.
btaining a royal edict which barred all noblemen
s. Later, on 29 March 1809, fleeing before the
General Soult, they rushed the pontoon bridge
undreds were drowned. A plaque near the Luís I

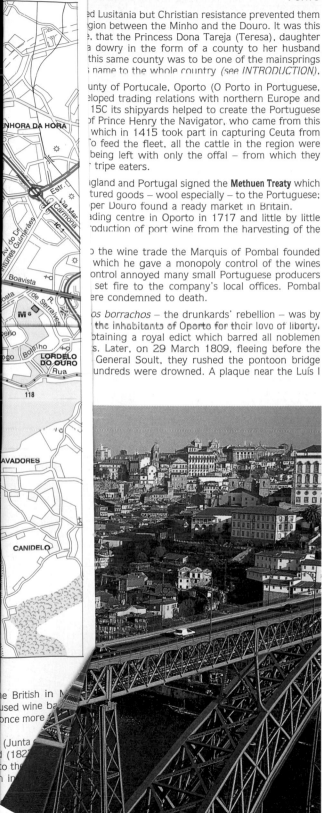

Y. Travert/DIAF

e British in
used wine ba
once more

(Junta
(182
to the
in

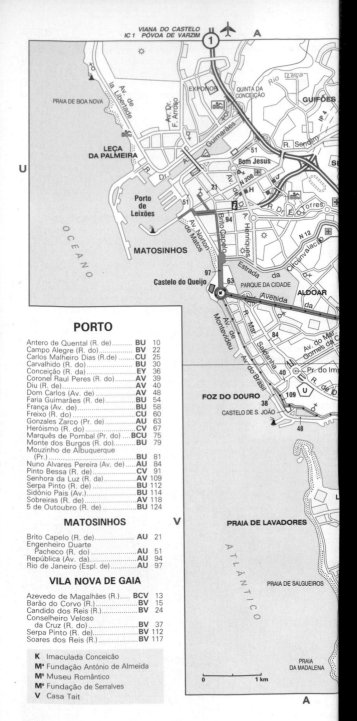

PORTO

Antero de Quental (R. de)	**BU**	10
Campo Alegre (R. do)	**BV**	22
Carlos Malheiro Dias (R.de)	**CU**	25
Carvalhido (R. do)	**BU**	30
Conceição (R. da)	**EY**	36
Coronel Raul Peres (R. do)	**AV**	39
Diu (R. de)	**AV**	40
Dom Carlos (Av. de)	**AV**	48
Faria Guimarães (R. de)	**BU**	54
França (Av. de)	**BU**	58
Freixo (R. do)	**CU**	60
Gonzales Zarco (Pr. de)	**AU**	63
Heróismo (R. do)	**CV**	67
Marquês de Pombal (Pr. do)	**BCU**	75
Monte dos Burgos (R. do)	**BU**	79
Mouzinho de Albuquerque (Pr.)	**BU**	81
Nuno Alvares Pereira (Av. de)	**AU**	84
Pinto Bessa (R. de)	**CV**	91
Senhora da Luz (R. da)	**AV**	109
Serpa Pinto (R. de)	**BU**	112
Sidónio Pais (Av.)	**BU**	114
Sobreiras (R. de)	**AV**	118
5 de Outoubro (R. de)	**BU**	124

MATOSINHOS

Brito Capelo (R. de)	**AU**	21
Engenheiro Duarte Pacheco (R. do)	**AU**	51
República (Av. da)	**AU**	94
Rio de Janeiro (Espl. de)	**AU**	97

VILA NOVA DE GAIA

Azevedo de Magalhães (R.)	**BCV**	13
Barão do Corvo (R.)	**BV**	15
Candido dos Reis (R.)	**BV**	24
Conselheiro Veloso da Cruz (R. do)	**BV**	37
Serpa Pinto (R. de)	**BV**	112
Soares dos Reis (R.)	**BV**	117

K	Imaculada Conceição
M⁴	Fundação António de Almeida
M⁵	Museu Romântico
M⁶	Fundação de Serralves
V	Casa Tait

The pontoon bridge was blown up by Soult at the approach of t[...]
1809, but Wellington managed to get a force across the river in dis[...]
and so surprised and captured the town. The pursuit which followed [...]
the French out of Portugal.

In 1820 Oporto rebelled against the English occupation, the assembly [...]
subsequently convened and succeded in drafting and having adopte[...]
constitution for the whole country. But in 1828 Dom Miguel I came [...]
ruled as an absolute monarch which brought about a new rebellio[...]
1833 a liberal monarchy was restored.

On 31 January 1891, Oporto once more rebelled, under the influer[...]
licans who had initiated disturbances throughout the country – but [...]
not to be declared until 1910 in Lisbon.

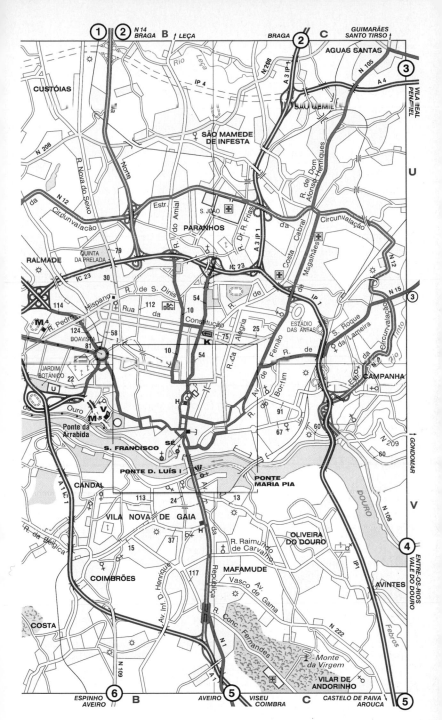

★★OLD OPORTO

Terreiro da Sé (**EZ 108**) – In the middle of the vast esplanade overlooking the old town stands a neo-Pombaline pillory. The square is bordered by the massive cathedral, the former episcopal palace dating from the 18C and a 14C granite tower.

★Sé ⊘ (**EZ**) – The cathedral began as a fortress church in the 12C and was considerably modified in the 17 and 18C. The main façade, flanked by two square, domed towers, has a 13C Romanesque rose window and a baroque doorway.

A baroque loggia, attributed to the architect Nasoni, was added in 1736 to the north face.

Inside, the narrow Romanesque nave is flanked by aisles on a lower level. Note three 17C marble stoups, each supported by a statue and, in the baptistry, a bronze relief of the Baptism of Christ, by the sculptor Teixeira Lopes.

TRAVELLERS' ADDRESSES

Where to stay

BUDGET HOTELS

Rex – *Praça da República 117, 4000 Porto* – ☎ *(02) 200 45 48 – fax (02) 208 38 82 – 21 rooms – 8 000$ – parking.*
Small hotel in an old town house. Intimate atmosphere with a few original ceilings remaining. The number of French guests is explained by the Alliance Française nearby.

Hotel da Bolsa – *R. Ferreira Borges 101, 4050 Porto* – ☎ *(02) 202 67 68 – fax (02) 31 88 88 – 36 rooms – 10 000/12 000$ (CC) – air conditioning.*
An interesting address due to the proximity of the lively Ribeira district. Beautiful 19C façade; the interior has been completely refurbished in a rather dull modern style. The top-floor rooms offer wonderful views of the port.

Castelo Santa Catarina – *R. de Santa Catarina 1347, 4000 Porto* – ☎ *(02) 59 55 99 – fax (02) 55 06 613 – 25 rooms – 7 500$ – parking.*
This astonishing fairy-tale style villa complete with a crenellated tower, extensive terraced gardens and massive reproduction furniture provides reasonably priced, comfortable (if somewhat "kitch") accommodation close to Oporto's centre.

MID-RANGE

Grande Hotel do Porto – *R. de Santa Catarina 197, 4000 Porto* – ☎ *(02) 200 81 76 – fax (02) 31 10 61 – 100 rooms – 14 000$ (CC) – restaurant – air conditioning.*
Although this landmark hotel has lost much of its former splendour, its public areas still retain an old fashioned charm. The rooms are appointed in a basic modern style. Its location on a bustling pedestrian shopping street in the centre is a plus for those visiting the city on foot.

Casa do Marechal – *Av. da Boavista 2652, 4100 Porto* – ☎ *(02) 610 47 02 – fax 610 32 41 – 5 rooms – 23 000$ (CC) – restaurant – parking – air conditioning.*
This small guest house outside Oporto's historic centre combines the comfort and service of a fine hotel in an intimate and elegant setting.

TREAT YOURSELF!

Infante de Sagres – *Praça D. Filipa de Lencastre 62, 4050 Porto* – ☎ *(02) 200 81 01 – fax (02) 31 49 37 – 68 rooms – 25 000/27 000$ (CC) – restaurant – air conditioning.*
The centrally-located Infante de Sagres, close to the Praça da Liberdade, is the most prestigious hotel in Oporto with a charm all of its own. Its interior contains wood-panelling, period furniture and stained glass.

Eating out

Mercearia – *R. Cais da Ribeira, 32* – ☎ *(02) 200 43 89 – 3 500$ (CC)*
One of the numerous cafés, bars and restaurants in Ribeira overlooking the port, the Mercearia restaurant is situated in pleasant surroundings and serves fine cuisine at reasonable prices. The first floor enjoys lovely views of the port.

Churrascão do Mar – *R. João Grave 134 (north of the historic centre on the corner of Rua da Constitução)* – ☎ *(02) 609 63 82 – 4 000/6 000$ (CC) – Closed Sundays in August.*
Seafood specialities served in an old mansion.

Mesa Antiga – *R. de Santo Ildefonso 208* – ☎ *(02) 200 64 32 – 2 500/4 900$ (CC) – Closed on Sundays.*
Traditional cuisine beautifully served in a family atmosphere.

Escondidinho – *R. de Passos Manuel 144* – ☎ *(02) 483 90 14 – 2 000$.*
Traditional cuisine in a regional setting.

At Leça da Palmeira *(8km north-west of the centre of Oporto near Leixões port)*
Two restaurants reputed for their seafood specialities.

Garrafão – *R. António Nobre 53* – ☎ *(02) 995 16 60 – 8 900$ (CC) – Closed on Sundays and from 15 to 30 August.*

O Chanquinhas – *R. de Santana 243* – ☎ *(02) 995 18 84 – 4 600$ (CC) – parking – Closed on Sundays.*

Oporto nightlife

In Portugal, the saying goes that Oporto works while Lisbon has fun. Nevertheless, there is a rich and varied nightlife in Oporto, with something for everyone.

In order to fully appreciate Oporto's unique location, visit the **Vila Nova de Gaia**, on a terrace opposite the town, and watch the setting sun; or have a drink at **Rock's** bar *(R. Rei Ramiro 288)*, situated in a beautiful old residence.

An old Oporto favourite, either during the day or at the end of the afternoon, is the **Majestic Café** *(R. de Santa Catarina 112)*, with its *fin de siècle* décor.

The restaurant-bar **Café na Praça**, close to the Torre dos Clérigos, is open late and is a good place to start your evening.

You can then choose between staying in Oporto or moving on to Foz or Matosinhos.

The port – The Ribeira district, along the river, is a must for all night-owls. The elegant **Aniki-Bóbó** bar *(R. Fonte Taurina 36/38 – closed Sundays and Mondays)* is frequented by architects, painters, photographers etc. If you are looking for a more typical atmosphere, try the **Duque** *(R. da Lada 98)*, in the same district.

Original music can be enjoyed at the **Marechal** *(R. Augusto Nobre 451)* which has a beautiful outdoor terrace.

In the Boavista district, the **Labirinto** *(R. Nossa Senhora de Fátima 334)* is a pleasant art-gallery/bar, while the **Swing** nightclub *(R. Júlio Dinis 766 – Parque Itália)* plays 70s/80s and techno music.

Foz – **The Praia da Luz** bar *(Av. do Brasil)* has a lovely outdoor terrace.

The **Foz Clube** (restaurant, bar and nightclub), near Castelo do Queijo, is frequented by the wealthy youth and jet-set of the city, while **Industria** *(Centro Comercial da Foz – Av. do Brasil 843 – open Sundays to Wednesdays)*, a large nightclub with a number of rooms, is one of Oporto's most popular night spots. The pleasant **Trinta-e-Um** bar *(R. do Passeio Alegre 564)* and the more recent floating bar, **Barquimedes**, are both located in Foz Velha.

Matosinhos – This is currently the city's liveliest area at night. Jazz groups can be heard at B Flat *(Tv. Glória 57)* or the **Heritage** *(R. D. João I 292)*. The **Via Rápida**, on Manuel Pinto de Azevedo *(open Thursdays to Sundays)*, is a large nightclub with several bars.

Better still, take time to stroll through the district, as there are always surprises and new places waiting to be discovered.

The transept and chancel were modified in the baroque period. The Chapel of the Holy Sacrament which opens off the north transept contains a very fine **altar**★ with a chased silver altarpiece worked by Portuguese silversmiths in the 17C.

Claustro – *Access through the south transept*. The 14C cloisters are decorated with **azulejos**★ panels, illustrating the Life of the Virgin and Ovid's *Metamorphoses*, made by Valentim de Almeida between 1729 and 1731. From these cloisters one may see the original Romanesque cloisters which contain several sarcophagi. A fine granite staircase leads to the terrace decorated with *azulejos* by António Vital and to the chapter-house which has a coffered ceiling painted by Pachini in 1737 depicting allegories of moral values.

Behind the cathedral is the delightful **Museu Guerra Junqueiro** *(see below)*.

Terreiro da Sé is a good departure point for a wander through the old town with its flights of steps and narrow alleyways. Many of the houses are being restored. The **Igreja de São Lourenço dos Grilos** (**EZ A**), a church built by the Jesuits in the 17C, is now the headquarters of the Grand Seminary.

On reaching Rua Mouzinho da Silveira, cross over to Largo de São Domingos. Leading off from it is the picturesque Rua das Flores.

Rua das Flores (**EYZ**) – The narrow street leading up to São Bento Station is bordered by traditional shops and 18C houses with coats-of-arms adorning the façades. It was once the main street for jewellers as well as gold and silversmiths. The **Santa Casa da Misericórdia** ⊙ (**B**) beside the baroque Igreja da Misericórdia, contains an outstanding painting from the Flemish School called **Fons Vitae**★ or the Fountain of Mercy, donated by King Manuel I in about 1520. The donor, his queen and their eight children are shown in the foreground. The origin of the painting remains a mystery. It has been attributed to different people including Holbein, Van der Weyden and Van Orley, although it was probably the work of a Portuguese artist who drew his inspiration from Flemish painters.

Return to Largo de São Domingos and then take Rua Belomonte.

Museu Etnográfico ⊘ **(DZ M³)** – The ethnography museum is housed in an 18C mansion built by Nasoni. Its baroque façade fills an entire side of the delightful Largo de São João Novo. The life and customs of the region are evoked through collections of religious works of art, costumes, ceramics, furniture, toys, decorated yokes, etc.

Palácio da Bolsa ⊘ **(EZ)** – The Stock Exchange was built in 1834 by the Associação Comercial do Porto which is still there to this day.
A fine carved granite and marble staircase leads to the old Trade Hall, the Gold Room and the **Arabian Hall★**. The latter, which is a pastiche of the Alhambra in Granada, is ovoid in shape and decorated with stained-glass windows, arabesques and carved woodwork in imitation of Moorish stucco.
The metal construction opposite the Stock Exchange is the **Mercado Ferreira Borges** (**C**) which houses temporary exhibitions.

★★Igreja de São Francisco ⊘ **(EZ)** – The Gothic church has kept its fine rose window and 17C doorway. The original restraint of the edifice was in keeping with the Fran-

ciscan order's ideal of poverty. However, in the 17C the order became extremely powerful with the result that privileges and material possessions were bestowed upon it. This is borne out by the triumph of **baroque decoration★★** inside: altars, walls and vaulting disappear beneath a forest of 17 and 18C carved and gilded woodwork, representing vines, cherubim and birds. The **Tree of Jesse★** in the second chapel on the left is particularly noteworthy, as is the high altar. Beneath the gallery, to the right on entering the church, is a polychrome granite statue of St Francis dating from the 13C.
The wealth of decoration so shocked the clergy that worship was discontinued in the church.
Casa dos Terceiros de São Francisco (House of the Third Order of St Francis) – The building houses a permanent collection of sacred art with objects from the

Igreja de São Francisco

J. P. Garcin/DIAF

16-20C. The crypt contains the sarcophagi of Franciscan friars and nobles. An ossuary is also visible in the basement through an iron railing.

Casa do Infante (EZ D) – *Rua da Alfândega.* This is where Prince Henry the Navigator is traditionally believed to have been born. It was the town Customs House from the 14 to 19C. It has a fine façade and vaulted rooms in which exhibitions are held.

★Cais da Ribeira (EZ) – The quayside dominated by the tall outline of the Luís I bridge is the most picturesque spot in Oporto. Ancient houses festooned with colourful laundry look down from a great height on the waterfront with its fish and vegetable market. Several old boats lie moored at the water's edge. The district is also lively in the evening.
Cross the Douro by the Luís I bridge to reach the wine lodges *(5min on foot – see WINE LODGES below).*

THE CENTRE

Praça da Liberdade and Praça do General Humberto Delgado (EY) – These two squares in the city centre form a vast open space dominated by the Town Hall. Among the streets surrounding them is the pedestrian **Rua de Santa Catarina (FY)**, which has the city's smartest shops and the famous Café Majestic. The **Mercado Muncipal de Bolhão (FY F)**, the municipal market, located between Rua de Fernandes and Rua Formosa, is colourful and two-tiered.

Igreja and Torre dos Clérigos ⊙ (**EY**) – The baroque church built by the architect Nasoni between 1735-1748 forms a backdrop to the steep Rua dos Clérigos. The oval plan of the nave bears out the Italian influence. Dominating the church is the 75.60m/248ft high **Torre dos Clérigos★**, Oporto's most characteristic monument, which in the past served as a seamark to ships. The extensive **panorama★** from the top takes in the city, the cathedral, the Douro valley and the wine lodges.

Rua das Carmelitas (**EY 27**) – Note, at no 144, the neo-Gothic façade of the **Lello & Irmão Bookshop** (1881) with its extraordinary double, two-way staircase. A small bar on the first floor is an ideal place to relax among the bookshop's many works.

Igreja do Carmo and Igreja das Carmelitas (**EY R**) – The two baroque churches stand side by side. Carmo Church is decorated on the outside with a large panel of *azulejos* dating from 1912 showing Carmelites taking the veil.

Museu Nacional Soares dos Reis ⊙ (**DY**) – The museum, which is housed in the 18C Palácio dos Carrancos, has been recently remodelled by the Oporto architect Fernando Távora. It exhibits permanent collections of Portuguese paintings and sculpture from the 19 and 20C, as well as works from the 17C and 18C. A gallery is also available for temporary exhibitions. Most interesting among the sculptures are those by **Soares dos Reis** (1847-1889), particularly that of the **Exile★** (O Desterrado) and the statue of the Count of Ferreira. Portuguese painting between 1850 and 1950 is represented by canvases by Silva Porto, Henrique Pousão, who was influenced by the Impressionists and Symbolists, José Malhoa, João Vaz and Columbano.
Older paintings on display include Portuguese works by Frei Carlos, Gaspar Vaz, Vasco Fernandes and Cristóvão de Figueiredo, and foreign works by Francis Clouet *(portraits of Marguerite de Valois and Henri II of France)*, Quillard, Pillement, Teniers, Troni and Simpson. The museum also contains a collection of old ceramics, gold articles and sacred art. Particularly worthy of note are two 17C Namban screens illustrating the arrival of the Portuguese in Japan.

ROMANTIC OPORTO

West of the Palácio de Cristal gardens, where the greenhouse, after which the palace was named, once stood, is Rua Entre-Quintas which leads to some fine 19C town houses.

Museu Romântico ⊙ (**BX M⁵**) – The Romantic Museum is housed in Quinta da Macieirinha. The romantic aspect of the place derives from its architecture, sash windows, park and, in particular, its history. It was here that the abdicated King of Sardinia, Charles Albert, retired in 1849 and died two months later. The decoration of paintings, Empire and English style furniture and stucco work lends the house a note of individual charm. There are beautiful views of the Douro valley from the windows.

Solar do Vinho do Porto ⊙ – *Below the Museu Romântico.* This is the headquarters of the Port Wine Institute. Hundreds of different types of port may be tasted in very pleasant surroundings.

Casa Tait ⊙ (**BV V**) – Situated across the street from the above, Casa Tait holds exhibitions and contains an interesting **coin and medal collection** illustrating the history of Portugal.

Port wine lodge

Y. Travert/DIAF

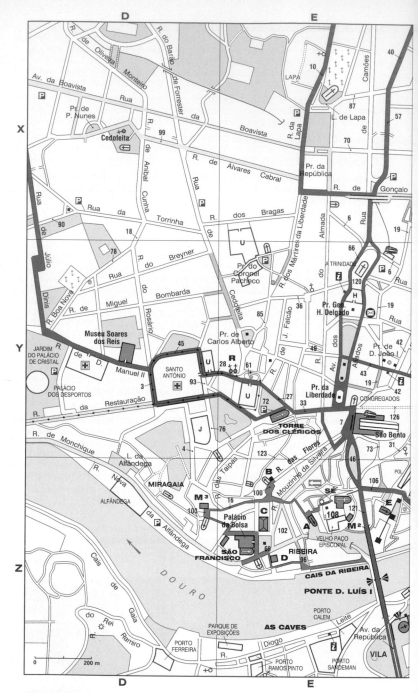

★WINE LODGES ⊘ (DEZ)

The city's wine lodges cover several acres on the south bank of the Douro in the lower quarter of **Vila Nova da Gaia**. More than 58 port companies are established in the area. In the olden days, boats known as *barcos rebelos* would transport the wines of the Upper Douro some 150km/90mi along the river to the lodges where they would be transformed into port. Today tanker-lorries unload their precious cargo into steel vats although some of the larger manufacturers still keep *barcos rebelos* loaded with barrels on view opposite their lodges.

Approximately twenty wine lodges may be toured including those of Cálem, Sandeman, Ramos Pinto and Ferreira. The slow process of transforming wines into port is explained. The wine is stocked in immense vats (containing about 100 000 litres/26 400 imperial gallons) for several years before being decanted

F

82

R. de Latino Coelhos

Pr. da Rainha D. Amélia

Almada (R. do) .... **EXY**
Carmelitas (R. das) .... **EY** 27
Clérigos (R. dos) .... **EY** 33
Dr. António Emilio
  de Magalhães (R. do) .... **EY** 42
Dr. Magalhães Lemos
  (R. do) .... **EY** 43
Fernandes Tomás (R. de) ... **EFY**
Flores (R. das) .... **EXY**
Formosa (R.) .... **EY**
Passos Manuel (R. de) .... **FY** 88
Sá da Bandeira (R. de) .... **FXY**
Santa Catarina (R. de) .... **FY**
31 de Janeiro (R. de) .... **EY** 126

Alberto Aires Gouveia
  (R. de) .... **DY** 3
Albuquerque (R. Af. de) ..... **DYZ** 4
Alferes Malheiro (R. do)... **EXY** 6
Almeida Garrett (Pr. de) .... **EY** 7
Antero de Quental (R. de) ... **EX** 10
Augusto Rosa (R. de).......... **FZ** 12
Belomonte (R. de) .... **EZ** 16
Boa Hora (R. da) .... **DXY** 18
Bonjardim (R. do) .... **EXY** 19
Carmo (R. do) .... **DEY** 28
Cimo da Vila (R. de)............ **EY** 31
Coolho Neto (R. de) .... **FY** 34
Dr. Tiogo de Almeida
  (R. do) .... **DY** 45
Dom Afonso Henriques
  (Av.) .... **EYZ** 46
Dona Filipa de Lencastre
  (Pr. de) .... **EY** 49
Entreparedes (R. de)........... **FY** 52
Faria Guimarães (R. de)....... **EX** 54
Fonseca Cardoso (R. de)...... **EX** 57
Gomes Teixeira (Pr. de) .... **EY** 61
Guedes de Azevedo
  (R. de) .... **FXY** 64
Heróis e Mártires
  de Angola (R. dos)............. **EY** 66
Infante Dom Henrique
  (Pr. e R. do) .... **EZ** 69
João das Regras (R. de)....... **EX** 70
Lisboa (Pr. de)................... **EY** 72
Loureiro (R. do)................. **EY** 73
Mártires da Patria
  (Campo dos) .... **DEY** 76
Maternidade (R. da)............. **DY** 78
Nova de São Crispim (R.) .... **FX** 82
Oliveiras (R. das)................ **EY** 85
Paraíso (R. do) .... **EFX** 87
Piedade (R. da)................... **DX** 90
Prov. Vicente José
  de Carvalho (R. do).......... **DY** 93
Ribeira (Pr. da) .... **EZ** 96
Sacadura Cabral (R.)........... **DX** 99
São Domingos (L. de)......... **EZ** 100
Cão João (R. de) **F7** 102
São João Novo (Pr. de)....... **DZ** 103
São Lázaro (Passeio de) ...... **FY** 105
Saraiva de Carvalho (R. de) .. **EZ** 106
Sé (Terreiro da) .... **EZ** 108
Soares dos Reis (L. de) .... **FY** 115
Trinidade (R. da)................ **EY** 120
Vimara Peres (Av.)............. **EZ** 121
Vitoria (R. da).................... **EYZ** 123

X

Cristóvão

64

Campo
24 de Agosto

R. do Bonfim

Y

115

Pr. da
Bathala

105

52

Av. de Rodrigues de Freitas

R. de Alexandre Herculano

Alameda das
Fontainhas

Passeio das Fontainhas

Gustavo

Eiffel

PONTE
MARIA PIA

Z

Simão

Cabo

N.ª S.ª da Serra
do Pilar

OBSERVATÓRIO

NOVA   DE   GAIA

F

A São Lourenço dos Grilos
B Casa da Misericórdia
C Mercado Ferreira Borges
D Casa do Infante
E Santa Clara
F Mercado de Bolhão
M² Museu Guerra Junqueiro
M³ Museu Etnográfico
R Carmo e Carmelitas

into 535 litres/118 gallon barrels in which the porous nature of the wood assists in the ageing process. On view are enormous chestnut casks as well as metal vats and modern bottling methods. Only quality wines passed by the Wine Institute *(Instituto do Vinho)* are allowed into the lodges.

ADDITIONAL SIGHTS

Estação de São Bento (EY) – The railway station, which serves trains bound for the Minho and Douro areas, has been in operation since 1896. The walls of the waiting room are covered with *azulejos* painted by Jorge Colaço in 1930.
They show traditions from the north of Portugal (country scenes and *romerias*) as well as important historic events such as João I's entry into Oporto *(top right)* and the capture of Ceuta by the Infante Dom Henrique (Prince Henry), who had left Oporto in 1415 *(bottom right)*.

★**Igreja de Santa Clara** ◷ (**EZ E**) – The church, which dates from the Renaissance, has kept its original granite doorway with figures in medallions. The rather austere exterior contrasts with the profuse decoration of 17C **carved and gilded woodwork**★ inside. The ceiling is Mudejar in style.

Museu Guerra Junqueiro ◷ (**EZ M²**) – The 18C mansion with its lovely garden is a haven of peace just a short distance from the busiest part of town. It belonged to the poet Guerra Junquerio who collected beautiful furniture, gold and silver plate, religious statues and tapestries throughout his life.

Particularly noteworthy are the Hispano-Moorish pieces of pottery from the 15 and 16C, Portuguese furniture, 16C Flemish tapestries and a fine collection of polychrome wooden figures of the Virgin, most of which are Flemish.

Fundação António de Almeida ◷ (**BU M⁴**) – Throughout his lifetime the rich industrialist António de Almeida put together a fine **collection of gold coins**★ (Greek, Roman, Byzantine, French and Portuguese) which is exhibited in the house where he lived. The interior decoration includes antique furniture and porcelain.

★**Fundação de Serralves** ◷ (**Museu de Arte Contemporânea**) (**AU M⁶**) – *Take Avenida da Boavista from the city centre and turn left on Avenida do Marechal Gomes da Costa which is distinguishable by a black pyramid-shaped monument. Access also by tram.* The Casa de Serralves complex which stands in a magnificent 18ha/44 acre **park**★, is an outstanding example of 1930s architecture with Art Nouveau decoration inside by the Frenchman Lalique. The buildings designed by the architect Alvaro Siza will house the future National Museum of Contemporary Art. At present, Casa de Serralves is an important cultural centre for temporary exhibitions, symposiums and concerts.

Inside, note the architecture, decoration, graceful **forged iron grilles**★ designed by Lalique and the luxurious inlaid parquet floors on the first floor.

Igreja da Cedofeita ◷ (**DX**) – This is the city's oldest church and dates from the 12C. It is a fine example of early Romanesque architecture although it has been transformed over the centuries, particularly in the 17C. The original Romanesque portal adorned with a Lamb of God, and the barrel vaulting in the nave, are intact.

Igreja da Imaculada Conceição ◷ (**BU K**) – The Stations of the Cross and the frescoes in this interesting modern church (1939-47) are by the Portuguese painter Guilherme Camarinha.

Antigo Convento de Nossa Senhora da Serra do Pilar (**EFZ**) – *Across Luís I bridge in Vila Nova de Gaia.* The old convent above the city affords one of the finest views of Oporto including the remains of the 14C walls to the right of Luís I bridge. It is a curious building erected in the 16 and 17C in the form of a rotunda which is said to have been designed by Filippo Terzi. The Renaissance **cloisters**★ are also circular.

Typical Porto houses

B. Barbier

FROM OPORTO TO MATOSINHOS

8.5km/5mi via Avenida da Boavista.

Foz do Douro (AUV) – The name means the mouth of the Douro river. This residential area is also a seaside resort with a well-known beach which ends at **Castelo do Queijo** (Cheese Castle) **(AU)**, a fort which once guarded the Douro estuary.

Port of Leixões (AU) – The approach is along the inner harbour and docks. The port, which was begun in the late 19C, transformed in the 1930s and completed in 1985, serves as a backup to the harbour on the Douro which has suffered periodic silting by the river. It provides an excellent outlet for local industrial production. The building of a tankers' wharf and an oil refinery has opened up possibilities for industrial expansion. Leixões is Portugal's second largest port as well as an important harbour for sardine fishing.

Matosinhos (AU) – The town is mainly known for its modern architectural creations from the Oporto School. Its leader, Álvaro Siza, designed Matosinhos Town Hall in 1981.

Igreja Bom Jesus de Matosinhos – The 18C baroque façade bristling with pinnacles and four torches is further enriched with several coats of arms. Inside, the outstanding woodwork in the chancel is immediately noticeable; the carvings portray scenes from Christ's Passion. The very old statue of Christ carved in wood, standing at the high altar, attracts a large yearly pilgrimage *(see THE CALENDAR OF EVENTS)*. A beautiful coffered ceiling covers the nave and chancel.

PÓVOA DE VARZIM

Porto – Population 23 846
Michelin map 940 or 441 H3

Póvoa de Varzim is partly an old fishing port and partly an elegant and modern seaside resort. It is also the birthplace of the great novelist Eça de Queirós (1845-1900).

★**Fishermen's quarter (Bairro dos pescadores)** – South of the beach, the low houses of the fishermen's quarter line the fishing harbour where boats may be seen sheltered in the bay.

EXCURSION

Romanesque churches of Rio Mau and Rates – *15km/9mi – about 1hr.*
Leave Póvoa de Varzim by the Oporto road (N 13) going south, and after 2km/1mi turn left onto the N 206 towards Guimarães.

Rio Mau – *Turn right opposite the post office onto an unsurfaced road.* The small Romanesque Igreja de São Cristóvão is built very plainly of granite; the rough decoration of the capitals in the doorway contrast with the more detailed ornamentation on the **capitals**★ in the triumphal arch and in the chancel which is later in date.

2km/1mi beyond Rio Mau, take a road on the left to Rates (1km/0.5mi).

Rates – The granite Igreja de São Pedro was built in the 12 and 13C by Benedictine monks from Cluny on the orders of Count Henry of Burgundy.
The façade is pierced by a rose window and a door with five arches, of which two are historiated, and capitals decorated with animals and other figures; on the tympanum a low relief presents a Transfiguration. The south door is adorned with a honeycombed archway sheltering a low relief of the Holy Lamb.
The interior is well proportioned and contains beautiful Romanesque capitals.

Join us in our constant task of keeping up-to-date.
Please send us your comments and suggestions.

Michelin Tyre PLC
Tourism Department
The Edward Hyde Building
38 Clarenson Road
WATFORD Herts WD1 1SX - U.K.
Tel: 01923 415000
Fax: 01923 415250
Internet: www.michelin-travel.com

PRAIA DA ROCHA★★

Faro

Michelin map 940 U4 – Local map see ALGARVE

Praia da Rocha was made famous by a group of English writers and intellectuals who settled there between 1930 and 1950. Since then, the village has grown into one of the largest seaside resorts in the Algarve and one of the most popular, even in winter. It owes its fame to its climate, its exceptionally high number of sunny days and its vast beach which extends into a series of emerald green **creeks★**. These curve dramatically between red and ochre-coloured cliffs pitted with caves.

Praia da Rocha on the Algarve coast

★**Miradouro** – From a viewpoint on the promontory to the west of the resort near the Dos Castelos creek, there is an overall vista on one side of the long, gently sloping beach dominated by the resort's white buildings, and on the other of the series of creeks sheltered by cliffs.

Forte de Santa Catarina – The fort commands the mouth of the Arade from the west and, along with the fort of **Ferragudo** on the far bank, guards the entrance to Portimão bay. It was built in 1621 to protect Silves and Portimão from Spanish and Moorish attacks.

Palácio Nacional de QUELUZ★★

Lisboa

Michelin map 940 P2

The **Royal Palace of Queluz**, just a few miles west of Lisbon, takes the visitor right back into the heart of the 18C. In the formal gardens adorned with pools and statues, overlooked by the roughcast, pastel-coloured rococo façades with their many windows, one almost expects to come upon a romantic scene from a painting by Watteau. Although inspired by Versailles, the smaller proportions of Queluz Palace make it more intimate.

From hunting lodge to royal palace – At the end of the 16C, the land belonged to the Marquis of Castelo Rodrigo who had a hunting lodge here. After the restoration of the Portuguese monarchy and Dom João IV's accession to the throne, the property was confiscated and, several years later in 1654, became the residence of the *Infantes*. Dom Pedro (1717-1786) son of Dom João V and the future Dom Pedro III, was the first *infante* to show a real interest in the estate and decided to build a palace. From 1747 to 1758, the Portuguese architect Mateus Vicente de Oliveira, who had studied at the Mafra school, built the main façade as well as the wing which would later contain the **Throne Room★** *(see following page)*. In 1758, while he was busy rebuilding Lisbon after the earth-quake, work continued with the French architect, Jean-Baptiste Robillon, who had studied under Gabriel. He altered and appointed both the Sala do Trono and the Sala da Música, and then built the West Wing which was named after him. A final and third stage of building saw the construction of the Dona Maria Wing between 1786 and 1792. While the overall style of the palace is rococo, architectural differences between the three periods are apparent.

Although the palace was intended for festivals, music and merriment, it was often the scene of drama such as the madness of Queen Maria I (1734-1816) towards the end of her life.

★**Palácio Nacional** ⊘ – Queluz palace is also a museum of decorative art as can be seen in the series of rooms adorned with beautiful objects and furniture.
The sumptuous **Sala do Trono**★ (Throne Room), recalls the Hall of Mirrors in Versailles. Magnificent Venetian crystal chandeliers hang from the shallow-domed ceiling decorated with allegorical illustrations and supported on caryatids. Note also the ceilings in the Music Room (Sala da Música) and the rooms of the three princesses.
The Sala dos Azulejos is so called on account of the wonderful multi-coloured 18C *azulejos* depicting landscapes of China and Brazil. The Sala da Guarda Real (Royal Guard Room) contains a fine 18C Arraiolos carpet. The **Sala dos Embaixadores** (Ambassadores Hall), decorated with marble and mirrors, has a painted ceiling of a concert at the court of King Dom José and diverse mythological motifs.
Beyond the Queen's Boudoir, French rococo in style, lies the **Sala Don Quixote** where eight columns support a circular ceiling, and paintings of Cervantes's hero decorate the walls. In the Sala das Merendas (Tea Room), embellished with gilded woodwork, are several 18C paintings of royal picnics.

★**Gardens (Jardins)** – The gardens were designed by the French architect J.B. Robillon in the style of the 17C French landscape gardener, Le Nôtre. Clipped box trees, cypresses, statues and pools surrounded by banks of flowers make up the gardens as a whole. Individual attractions include the Amphitrite Basin from where there is a pleasant view of the Neptune Basin and the main façade rebuilt by Robillon in the Gabriel style and, lower down, an Italian style park with pools, cascades, green arbours and bougainvillaeas. The walls of the **Grand Canal** are covered in 18C *azulejos* of river and sea ports between which flows the Jamor river (often reduced to a mere trickle). In the past the royal family went boating along the canal. Opposite, note the façade of the Robillon Wing, fronted by a magnificent **Lion Staircase**★ (Escadaria dos Leões) which is extended by a beautiful colonnade.

Palácio Nacional de Queluz

Y. Travert/DIAF

SABUGAL

Guarda – Population 2 164
Michelin map 940 441 K8

The small city of Sabugal, grouped on a hillock round its fortified castle, dominates the peaceful Côa valley, a tributary of the Douro.
The town, which was founded by Alfonso X of León in the beginning of the 13C, became Portuguese in 1282 on the marriage of Isabel of Aragon and King Dom Dinis of Portugal.

Castelo ⊘ – The castle's present appearance dates from the late 13C; a double crenellated perimeter wall, flanked by square towers with pyramid-shaped merlons, encloses an impressive pentagonal keep with battlemented overhangs.

Ponta de SAGRES
and Cabo de SÃO VICENTE★★

Faro

Michelin map 940 U3 – Local map see ALGARVE

The windswept headland falling steeply to the sea, a kind of world's end at the south-west extremity of mainland Europe, has a stirring historical past. It was here, facing the Atlantic Ocean, the great unknown, that Prince Henry the Navigator retired in the 15C to found the Sagres School of Navigation which would prepare the way for the Great Discoveries.

The Sagres School – After the capture of Ceuta in 1415, Prince Henry retired to Sagres where he gathered around him the most famous Arab astronomers, cartographers from Majorca and mariners of the day, and founded a School of Navigation. Theories were tested and put to practical use in expeditions which set out on longer and longer voyages *(See LAGOS)*.

Improvements in the astrolabe and the sextant and increased knowledge in their use, enabling calculations to be made far out to sea, led to the prince's introduction of navigation by the stars: mariners who had been used to a chart and compass as guides and had gauged their position from an estimate of the distance travelled, learned to calculate their latitude from the height of the stars above the horizon and chart their positions with greater accuracy.

Cartography also improved. To the Mediterranean portolano were added maps of the Atlantic which, although they ignored points of latitude, nevertheless demonstrated Portuguese supremacy in the cartographic field.

Finally the demands of the voyages compelled the Portuguese to design a new type of ship which revolutionised navigation – the **caravel**. This long boat with a shallow draught and a small area of canvas could carry a good-sized crew and had all the advantages of traditional ships without their disadvantages. Its wider hull and high sheathing increased security; the large number of masts enabled it to carry square as well as triangular lateen sails. The use of a stern rudder made them easier to handle.

SIGHTS

★★**Ponta de Sagres** – The headland is partially occupied by the remains of a **fortress** (fortaleza) built in the 16C and considerably damaged during the earthquake in 1755 and rebuilt by the New State in the 40s. The entrance tunnel leads into a vast court-yard with an immense wind compass with a diameter of 43m/141ft on the ground. While the buildings are said to be the former School of Navigation and Prince Henry's house, these, in fact, no longer stand since they were sacked by Drake in 1587.

Ponta de Sagres may be explored by car or on foot (about 1hr).

Cabo de São Vicente

Views* from the promontory open out westwards onto St Vincent's bay and Cabo de São Vincente and eastwards onto the Lagos coast. Two marine caves in which the deep rumbling of the sea can be heard add to the atmosphere and the wild beauty of the setting.

**Cabo de São Vicente   Cape St Vincent, the most southwesterly point of continental Europe, towers above the ocean at a height of 75m/246ft. It has always been considered a sacred spot – the Romans called it *Promontorium Sacrum*. Its present name derives from a legend recounting how the vessel containing the body of St Vincent after he had suffered martyrdom in Valencia in the 4C ran aground at the cape. The ship, guarded by two ravens, remained here for centuries before continuing its way to Lisbon which it reached in 1173.

The cape has also served as a backcloth to several British naval victories, notably in 1759 against the French, in 1780 by Admiral Rodney against the Spanish and in 1797 when Nelson's tactical genius was first revealed in a battle with the Spanish. The old fortress on the point has been converted to a lighthouse. The **views**** of cliffs stretching ever northwards and of Ponta de Sagres to the east are impressive, particularly at sunset.

Forte de Beliche – This small fortress on the Cabo de São Vicente road now houses a hotel and restaurant. There is also a beautiful chapel and a fine **view** of the headland, Ponta de Sagres.

Ship Ahoy

One of Portugal's most significant contributions to maritime history is the **caravel**. This type of light sailing ship, developed by Portuguese fishermen, was widely used in the 15-17C in Europe, particularly for exploring uncharted seas. Caravels were rigged with lanteen (triangular) sails, which enabled them to sail to windward (taking advantage of a wind from the side of the ship). These elegant craft, which superseded the oared galley, generally measured about 23m/75ft in length, with two or three masts (later versions added a fourth with square rigging for running before the wind). The caravel was capable of remarkable speed, and was well-adapted to long voyages. Two of the three ships under the command of Christopher Columbus in 1492, the *Niña* and the *Pinta*, were caravels.

SANTA MARIA DA FEIRA

Aveiro – Population 4 877
Michelin map 940 or 441 J4

The castle of Santa Maria da Feira stands on a wooded height facing the town which lies scattered over the opposite hillside.

*Castelo ⊙ – The 11C castle was reconstructed in the 15C by the local baron, Fernão Pereira, whose coat of arms can still be seen above the entrance. It is an interesting example of Portuguese Gothic military architecture. A keep flanked by four tall towers with pepperpot roofs overlooks a fortified perimeter wall whose entrance is defended on its eastern side by a barbican. A postern gate leads to the parade ground. Follow the wall walk; latrines can still be seen. Stairs lead to the 1st floor of the keep where there is a vast Gothic hall; the upper platform (60 steps) affords a panorama of the castle's fortifications, the town, the surrounding wooded hills and the coastline, where one can make out the Ria de Aveiro in the distance.

Igreja da Misericórdia – The church's chancel, under a coffered ceiling, has a lovely gilded altarpiece. In a south chapel there are some unusual statues, one of which is a Saint Christopher, 3m/10ft high.

SANTARÉM

Santarém – Population 20 034
Michelin map 940 O3

Santarém, on a hill on the north bank of the Tagus, overlooks the vast Ribatejo plain, of which it is the chief town. Its strategic position has made it the scene of several battles since Mohammedan times. It was recaptured from the Moors in 1147 by Alfonso I and later became a royal residence, appreciated by several kings for its setting and its proximity to Lisbon. From this rich past, Santarém retains several monuments, mostly Gothic, dotted about the town's attractive old quarter.

Santarém is well known for Portuguese bullfighting. Performances as well as folk dancing and a procession of *campinos* take place at the annual Ribatejo Fair.

St Irene – Irene, a young nun in a convent near Tomar, was assassinated in 653 by a monk called Remigo whose advances she had refused. Her body, thrown in the Tagus, was washed up at the foot of the former Roman city of Scalabis. The king of the Visigoths, who had recently been converted to Christianity, gave the town the new name of Saint Irene or Santarém to commemorate the event.

OLD TOWN

Igreja do Seminário (A A) – 17C. The baroque façade of this former Jesuit college has as its main feature the superimposition of several storeys outlined by cornices and pierced by windows and niches, which gives the church more the appearance of a palace than a place of worship. The niches contain statues of Jesuits whose symbol (Christ's monogram) is above the main doorway. The curvilinear pediment crowning the façade is flanked by heavy scrolls and pyramids.

The **interior** remains austere in spite of the marble incrustations decorating the altar and the pilasters. The single nave is covered with a ceiling painted to represent the Immaculate Conception and Jesuit evangelical activities overseas.

The frieze of 18C *azulejos*, which lines the corridor walls throughout the building, begins in the vestibule of the former monastery *(entrance to the right of the church)*.

Igreja de Marvila (B) – This 16C church has a graceful Manueline doorway. The interior is lined with *azulejos*, the most interesting being those known as carpet or *tapete azulejos*, painted in many colours with plant motifs, which date from 1620 and 1635.

★**Igreja de São João de Alporão – Museu Arqueológico** ⊘ **(B)** – This Romanesque Gothic church contains archaeological collections. In addition to Arab and Roman pottery, *azulejos* and chinaware, the church's narrow nave has an interesting collection of sculpture, including funerary steles and capitals (two Arabic). The fine Flamboyant Gothic style **tomb** of Duarte de Meneses, Count of Viana, was erected by his wife to contain a tooth, the only relic of her husband who had been killed by Moors in North Africa.

The beautiful stone balcony to the left of the entrance was carved by Mateus Fernandes.

Torre das Cabaças ⊘ **(B)** – There is a good overall **view** of Santarém from the top of Calabash Tower which faces the church of São João de Alporão.

Chimes from the tower bell formerly regulated the life of the city.

Portas do Sol ⊘ **(B)** – From the wall near the Sun Gate, from which the garden has taken its name, one can look straight down on to the Tagus.

★**Igreja da Graça** ⊘ **(B)** – This Gothic church of 1380 has a fine Flamboyant façade with a lovely rose window that has been carved out of a single block of stone.

The beautiful **nave** has been restored to its original pure lines. The church contains several tombs including, in the south transept, that of Dom Pedro de Meneses, first Governor of Ceuta *(see Introduction – The Great Discoveries)*. The 15C tomb, which rests on eight lions and bears the recumbent figures of the count and his wife, is carved with leaf motifs and coats of arms. On the pavement of the south apsidal chapel can be seen the funerary stone of the navigator Pedro Álvares Cabral who discovered Brazil in 1500. In the chapel off the south aisle, a panel of 18C *azulejos* shows St John the Baptist between St Rita and St Francis.

ADDITIONAL SIGHTS

Igreja de Santa Clara ⊘ **(B)** – This vast Gothic church was once part of a 13C convent. The lack of a doorway on the façade intensifies the bare appearance of the church's exterior.

Inside, the narrow 72m/236ft long nave ends with a beautiful rose window above the 17C tomb of Dona Leonor, founder of the convent. The church also contains the original 14C tomb of Dona Leonor. On either side of it are Franciscan monks and Poor Clares, at the foot St Francis receiving the stigmata, and at the head the Annunciation.

★**Miradouro de São Bento (B)** – The belvedere affords a vast **panorama**★ of the Tagus plain and Santarém where the main buildings can easily be distinguished.

Fonte das Figueiras (B) – This 13C fountain, against a wall, is covered by a porch roof crowned with pyramid shaped merlons.

Mercado (A) – The walls of the market are covered with *azulejos* dating from the turn of the century.

Capela de Nossa Senhora do Monte (A) – The 16C chapel stands in the middle of a horseshoe shaped square. The façade is bordered on both sides by an arcaded gallery with capitals adorned with leaf motifs and heads of cherubim. At the east end is a 16C statue of Our Lady.

SANTARÉM

Capelo Ivens (Rua) .... **AB** 9
Serpa Pinto (Rua) .... **AB**

Alex. Herculano (Rua) .... **A** 3
Alf. de Santarém (Rua) .... **B** 4
Braamcamp Freire (Rua) .... **B** 6

Cândido dos Reis (Largo) .... **A** 7
G. de Azevedo (Rua) .... **A** 10
João Afonso (Rua) .... **A** 12
Miguel Bombarda (Rua) .... **B** 13
Piedade (Largo da) .... **A** 15
São Martinho (Rua de) .... **B** 16
Teixeira Guedes (Rua) .... **A** 18
Tenente Valadim (Rua) .... **B** 19

Vasco de Gama (Rua) .... **A** 21
Zeferino Brandão (Rua) .... **A** 22
1º de Dezembro (Rua) .... **B** 24
5 de Outubro (Avenida) .... **B** 25
31 de Janeiro .... **A** 27

A Igreja do Seminário

EXCURSION

Alpiarça– *10km/6mi east. Leave Santarém by* ② *on N 114.* This small farming centre across the Tagus below Santarém is home to a manor, now a museum.

★**Casa dos Patudos** ⊘ – The manor built in 1905 belonged to José Relvas (1858-1929), a statesman and art lover who collected some outstanding works of art. On his death, the manor became a museum.

The vast house contains a remarkable series of **tapestries and carpets**★ dating from the 17 to the 19C. There are more than 40 Arraiolos carpets, of which one, a unique example, embroidered in silk, dates from 1762. Some of the carpets are made of Indo-Portuguese silk. Castelo Branco bedspreads and Aubusson tapestries are also shown. A rich collection of **china and porcelain**★ includes pieces from Portugal, France, Germany and the Far East – some of the ware is displayed in the dining-room.

Paintings adorn the museum's walls. In the Primitives gallery there are some intersting 16C Luso-Flemish pictures and a beautiful Italian *Mother and Child*. Also on display are Portuguese paintings (by Josefa de Óbidos and Silva Porto) including portraits of José Relvas's family (by José Malhoa), and sculptures (by Soares dos Reis, Teixeira Lopes and Machado de Castro).

One of the rooms in the house is faced with 18C *azulejos* illustrating the life of St Francis of Assisi.

SANTIAGO DO CACÉM

Setúbal – Population 6 777
Michelin map 940 R3

Santiago do Cacém clings to the hill crowned by a castle built long ago by the Knights Templar. There is a good **view**★ of the site from N 120 at the town's southern exit.

Castelo – Two restored perimeter walls encircle the ruins of the castle whose interior is now planted with cypress trees and occupied by a graveyard. Walk round the ramparts to see the panorama which extends as far as Cabo de Sines.

Museu Municipal ⊘ – In the former prison, several rooms have been set up depicting the costumes and traditions of Alentejo.

Roman Ruins of Miróbriga ⓒ – *1km/0.5mi. Leave the town on the Lisbon road, the N 120 going north; at the top of a hill, bear right (signpost) on a narrow road, then left on a dirt road. Leave the car at the last layby.*

Miróbriga was probably a fairly large centre from the 1 to the 4C as the scattered ruins testify. They appear in a pleasant country setting dotted with cypresses. A Roman road leads to the **baths** below. The different water channels, baths and resting rooms are easily distinguishable. Returning uphill, you go past the inn and reach the **forum**, around which stood administrative and religious buildings. Excavations have shown that this was occupied during the Iron Age (4C BC) by a temple. 1km/0.5mi further on are the remains of the hippodrome where the famous horses from Lusitania once raced.

SÃO JOÃO DE TAROUCA
Viseu – Population 1 054
Michelin map 940 or 441 I6

The former Monastery of Tarouca, overlooked by the heights of the Serra de Leomil, lies squat in a hollow in the fertile Barossa valley.

Igreja ⓒ – The church, erected in the 12C by Cistercian monks, was considerably remodelled in the 17C when the interior was given baroque decoration. The side chapels contain several pictures attributed to the painter, Gaspar Vaz; a picture of **St Peter★** *(3rd south chapel)* is outstanding.

In the north transept the walls are lined with 18C *azulejos* depicting scenes from the life of John the Baptist and the Baptism of Christ. The monumental 14C granite tomb decorated with low reliefs of a boar hunt contains the remains of Dom Pedro, Count of Barcelos, bastard son of Dom Dinis. Dom Pedro was the author of the *General Chronicle of 1344* and is considered to be the greatest Portuguese writer of the Middle Ages. The *azulejos* in the chancel illustrate the life of St Bernard. The sacristy also contains fine *azulejos*.

Serra de SÃO MAMEDE★
Portalegre
Michelin map 940 N7,8 O7,8

The Serra de São-Mamede is a small island of greenery in an arid and stony region; its relatively high altitude (highest point: 1 025m/3 363ft) and the impermeable nature of the soil combine to provide sufficient humidity for a dense and varied vegetation.
The triangular shaped massif is composed of hard rock which has resisted erosion; the variations in level on the west face were accentuated by a fault.

ROUND TOUR FROM PORTALEGRE
73km/45mi – about 2hr 30min – local map right

Portalegre – *See PORTALEGRE.*
Leave Portalegre to the east then turn northwards
The road rises through the woods, affording attractive views of Portalegre and the surrounding countryside.

Follow the signs to São Mamede.

★**São Mamede** – From the top, where there is a radio and television relay station, there is a vast **panorama★**, which extends south over the Alentejo, west and north over the Serra de São Mamede and east over range after range of the Spanish *sierras*.

Return to the main road. It runs through a landscape of bare moors bristling in places with pines. The descent is swift to the green and wooded plain.

★★**Marvão**– *See MARVÃO.*

★**Castelo de Vide; Monte da Penha**– *See CASTELO DE VIDE.*

Return to Portalegre on the Carreiras *corniche* **road★**.

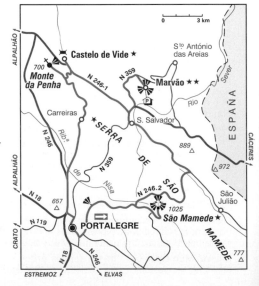

SERNANCELHE

Viseu – Population 1 060
Michelin map 437 or 441 J7

The old town of Sernancelhe occupies a rocky height in the Beira Alta. It was once a commandery of the Order of Malta which built the castle now standing in ruins.

Igreja – The façade of this Romanesque church, flanked by a squat square belfry, is pierced by a beautiful rounded doorway in which one of the arches is adorned with an unusual frieze of archangels. The tympanum is carved with plant motifs. Two niches on either side of the door shelter six granite statues of the Evangelists St Peter and St Paul.

Pelourinho – *Opposite the church.* The pillory (16C) is topped by a cage.

Solar dos Carvalhos – This elegant baroque manor-house (18C) with a façade flanked by pilasters, belongs to the Marquis of Pombal's family.

Christ – *Take a road which begins to the left of the church and goes towards the castle. It ends in a flight of steps.*
Shortly afterwards, on the right protected by a porch, is a fine stone Calvary (14C). Continuing, one soon gets a view of the church and then of the village.

SERPA

Beja – Population 9 200
Michelin map 440 S7

Serpa, a market town in the Lower Alentejo east of the Guadiana river, crowns a hilltop overlooking vast plains of wheat fields interspersed with rows of olive trees. The town has kept its ramparts which partially surmount an **aqueduct**.
The approach from Beja is impressive.

TOUR *1hr 30min*

The fortified gate, the **Porta de Beja**, leads through the ramparts into the white-washed town, which makes for a pleasant stroll. The main square, the **Largo dos Santos Próculo e Hilarião**, with its olive and cypress trees, is dominated by the façade of the Igreja de Santa Maria. A street on the right leads to the **castle**. The entrance looks like a romantic 19C engraving with its crumbling tower which now forms a porch. There is a good view of the town from the sentry path.

Museu Etnográfico ⊘ – *Largo do Corro.* The displays in this small, well-presented museum illustrate the traditions and crafts of the region.

Capela de Guadalupe – *1.5km/1mi. Follow signs to the Pousada.* The bare, white Moorish building with domes overlooks the valley affording wonderful views of the surrounding countryside.

SESIMBRA

Setúbal – Population 8 138
Michelin map 440 Q2 – Local map see Serra da ARRÁBIDA

Sesimbra occupies a pleasant site in an inlet at the foot of the southern slope of the Serra da Arrábida. Its beach is popular with Lisbonites.
Sesimbra is a centre for harpooning as well as deep-sea fishing for swordfish. These sports provide a counterpoint to the more traditional fishing methods, the town's main activity.

SIGHTS

The town – The small fishing harbour has grown into an important seaside resort with modern buildings surrounding the centre, which has nonetheless preserved its steep, sometimes stepped streets which lead down to the sea.
Along these picturesque alleyways you may see washing hanging out to dry alongside the day's catch. The many restaurants along the shore serve grilled fish and seafood.

Igreja Matriz – *Halfway up the hill.* Inside is a 17C pulpit in local pink marble and a triumphal arch with Manueline style motifs. A gilded wood altarpiece stands in the 18C chancel.

The beach – This is alive with holiday-makers during weekends and in the summer. The rest of the time it reverts to fishermen who may be seen disentangling and mending their lines and nets on either side of **Santiago Fort**.

Fishing boats

★The harbour – This leans picturesquely against the foot of the cliff, away from the town.
The large fleet of trawlers, decorated with an eye or a star on the prow, bring in sardines, sea-bream, conger eels, swordfish and shellfish every morning and evening; some of these are sold by auction.

Castelo– *6km/4mi northwest on a steep uphill road.*
The castle, on the crest of a bare ridge at an altitude of more than 200m/700ft, occupies a first-class defensive position which the first King of Portugal, Afonso Henriques, captured from the Moors in 1165, almost eighteen years after freeing Lisbon.
From its crenellated walls surrounding the cemetery there are fine **views★** of Sesimbra and its harbour.

SETÚBAL★

Setúbal – Population 97 762
Michelin map 940 Q3 – Local map see Serra da ARRÁBIDA

Setúbal, situated in the foothills of the Serra da Arrábida *(qv)* and on the north bank of the wide Sado estuary, is an industrial town, a port and a tourist centre. It has an old quarter with narrow alleys which contrast sharply with the wide avenues of the modern town. The town's moscatel wine and orange marmalade are popular.
Two Portuguese celebrities were born in Setúbal – the opera-singer **Luísa Todi** (1754-1833) and the poet **Manuel Barbosa do Bocage** (1765-1805), whose original works earned him censorship and exile.

A busy port – The town's commercial activities are various: cement, standing as the town does close to the slopes of the *serra*, development of the salt marshes on either bank of the Sado, the assembling of lorries and cars, chemicals, fish canning and the marketing of agricultural produce grown in the region. The shipbuilding industry here is highly developed: at present shipyards are being built at Setenave which when finished will have a greater capacity than those at Lisbon.
Setúbal is Portugal's third port after Lisbon and Oporto (Leixões). It consists of a fishing port (sardines) with a fleet of about 2 000 boats, a pleasure boat marina and a commercial port. The latter is in contact with the great maritime cities of Germany, the Netherlands, Spain and Great Britain.
Trade consists primarily of importing coal and phosphates and exporting cement and paper pulp.

Portuguese oysters – The region of Setúbal, like that of Faro, is a production area for molluscs which when eaten are known as Portuguese oysters *(ostras)*. The Portuguese prefer their oysters cooked rather than live. In fact, few are eaten in the country so oyster farmers direct their activites primarily towards the production of seed oysters; Setúbal virtually holds the monopoly in this Portuguese export trade.

★CASTELO DE SÃO FILIPE

Take Avenida Luísa Todi to the west then follow the signs to the Pousada.

The fortress overlooking the town has been partially converted into one of Portugal's most beautiful *pousadas*. It was built in 1590 on the orders of King Philip II of Spain in an attempt to control the animosity of the inhabitants of Setúbal and to prevent the English from establishing themselves in Tróia. The castle is equipped with ramps and stepped bastions.

Cross a covered passage to a chapel with 18C *azulejos* attributed to Policarpo de Oliveira Bernardes which illustrate the life of St Philip.

There is a wide **panorama★** from the top of the ramparts: to the east lie Setúbal harbour and shipyards, Sado Bay and the Tróia Peninsula; northwest, the Castelode Palmela and, west and south, the Serra da Arrábida.

OLD QUARTER (BAIRRO ANTIGO)

Between Avenida Luísa Todi, Praça Almirante de Reis and Santa Maria church, lies the picturesque old quarter with its narrow streets (many of which are pedestrian) and its interesting monuments.

★**Igreja de Jesus** – This church, constructed of Arrábida marble in 1491, was designed by the architect Boytac and is the first example of a building with Manueline decoration.

It is a Late Gothic building, judging by its Flamboyant doorway – twin doors with bracketed arches framed in ringed columns – and its three lines of vaulting of equal height which make it into a hall church.

Manueline art is seen to particular advantage in the amazingly twisted pillars supporting the vaulting and in the spiral ribs of the vault above the chancel.

The walls of the nave and chancel are partly covered with 17C *azulejos*.

Museu de Jesus ⊘ (**M¹**) – The museum is in the Gothic cloisters of the Igreja de Jesus.

The upper galleries house a large collection of 15 and 16C Portuguese Primitives. All these **paintings★** are said to be by the anonymous artist known as the Master of the Setúbal Altarpiece; some, however, attribute them to two other 16C artists, both members of the Lisbon School, namely Gregório Lopes and Cristóvão de Figueiredo.

Igreja de Jesus, Setúbal

In spite of the influence of the Flemish School (stiff attitudes, realistic details) a certain increase in warm tones should be noted, also the imprint on the faces of verisimilitude and mysticism, and especially the expression of the Virgin and the Saints before the Crucifixion and St Francis when receiving the stigmata.

The lower galleries contain 15-18C *azulejos*.

Igreja de São Julião – The trefoil door in the north face of the church is Manueline. Two columns, twisted like cables, frame the door and rise above it in a moulding before ending in pinnacles. Inside, beautiful 18C *azulejos* depict the life of St Julian.

Museu Regional de Arqueologia e Etnografia ⊘ (**M²**) – The museum contains prehistoric objects (an idol cut out of bone, Bronze Age pottery vase) and Luso-Roman coins, collections of folk art and crafts, costumes, small scale models of boats; the textile industry, agriculture, wood and iron handicrafts are depicted by animated models. There are also numerous panels and decorative motifs made of cork.

Álvaro Castelões (Rua).................... 7
António Girão (Rua)........................ 9
Augusto Cardoso (Rua de)............. 13
Bocage (Rua do)........................... 18
Dr Paula Borba (Rua).................... 25
Santo António (Largo de)............. 44

Alexandre Herculano
  (Av. de) 3
Almirante Reis (Praça do) 4
Almocreves (Rua dos)...................... 6
Arronches Junqueiro (Rua) 12
Bocage (Praça do) 16
Clube Naval (Rua)........................ 20
Combatentes da Grande Guerra
  (Av.)... 21
Defensores da República
  (Largo dos) 22

Dr António J. Granjo (Rua)............ 24
Exército (Praça do)........................ 27
Major Alfonso Pala (Rua do)....... 33
Mariano de Carvalho (Av.).......... 34
Marquês de Pombal (Praça) 37
Mirante (Rua do) 38
Occidental do Mercado (R.)........ 39
Tenente Valadim (Rua)................. 43
Trabalhadores do Mar
  (Rua dos) 45
22 de Dezembro (Av.) 46

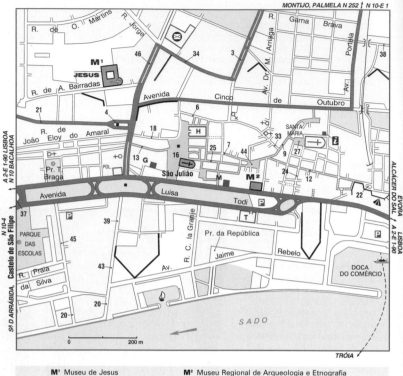

M¹ Museu de Jesus   M² Museu Regional de Arqueologia e Etnografia

PENÍNSULA DE TRÓIA

The Tróia Peninsula, an immense strip of fine sand barring the Sado estuary, lined with dunes and pine trees, has been heavily developed for tourism all along the north and west coasts: hotels, residential villas and high-rise blocks already make it a kind of city, facing the Serra da Arrábida.

Access

By road: *98km/61mi. Go round the estuary of the Sado river on N 10, N 5, N 253 and N 253-1.*

By ferry ⊙: *crossing, 15min.*

Roman ruins at Cetóbriga ⊙ – *4km/2.5mi from the pier, 2.5km/1.5mi along a sandy though practicable road off N 253-1.*
Some of the remains of an important Roman town destroyed by the sea in the early 5C have been excavated in a pleasant site beside the Sado lagoon. They include an installation for salting fish, a sepulchral vault, the remains of a temple decorated with frescoes, and some baths.

SILVES★

Faro – Population 9 845
Michelin map 940 U4

Of the ancient city of Xelb with its many mosques, the Moorish capital of the Algarve, the magnificence of which was said to eclipse even that of Lisbon, there remain the red sandstone walls of a castle standing above the white-walled town which rises in tiers up the hillside. Thanks to its protected position inland, in the foothills of the Serra de Monchique, Silves has managed to preserve its character with its steep, cobbled streets.

★**Castelo** ⊙ – *Leave the car in the cathedral square and go through a gate in the perimeter wall to the castle.*

The sentry path around the magnificently restored crenellated ramparts affords good **views** of the town and surrounding countryside: northwest of the irrigated Arade valley, cork factories, and behind, the Serra de Monchique; south, of peach and almond orchards and, in the far distance, the coast. Inside the fortress with its gardens of oleanders are two large underground water cisterns.

Sé – The cathedral was built on the site of a former mosque. The 13C Gothic nave and aisles have a beautiful and striking simplicity; the chancel and transept are of the later Flamboyant Gothic style. The numerous tombs are said to be of the Crusaders who helped to capture the town in 1242.
Note the **Manueline door** opposite the cathedral's entrance.

Museu Arqueológico ⊙ – The archaeological museum is housed in a modern building beside the town walls, built around a large 12-13C cistern. The collections retrace the history of the region beginning with the Palaeolithic Age. Note the menhirs and the funerary stelae from the Iron Age. The Moorish period with its ceramics and architectural displays is particularly well presented.

Cruz de Portugal (The Portuguese Cross) – *At the eastern exit of the town on the N 124, the São Bartolomeu de Messines road.*
The 16C Calvary shows, on one side, Christ crucified, and on the other, a *Pietá*.

Muslim domination

In 711 Muslim subjects of the Umayyed Caliphate in Damascus invade the Iberian Peninsula.
In 722 the victory of the Visigothic King Pelayo at Covadonga in Asturias in Spain marks the beginning of the Christian War of Reconquest which is to last 700 years.
The following dates mark important steps in the *Reconquista* of present-day Portugal:

867   Oporto falls to the Christians.
1064   Coimbra is reconquered by Fernando I of Castile.
1147   Lisbon is freed by the first King of Portugal, Dom Afonso Henriques.
1189   Silves succombs temporarily after a seige by Sancho I.
1249   The capture of Faro marks the end of the Reconquest in Portugal.
The Algarve had been under Moorish occupation for over 600 years.
Unlike Spain, Portugal has few architectural remains that show an Islamic influence apart from the mosque at Mértola in the Alentejo and several city walls such as those in Silves.

SINTRA★★

Lisboa – Population 20 574
Michelin map 940 PI – Local map see Serra de SINTRA

Only half an hour from Lisbon, Sintra, built right up against the north slope of the *serra*, is a haven of peace and greenery. For six centuries the town was the favourite summer residence of the kings of Portugal and today remains a holiday resort for wealthy Lisbon families who have built delightful mansions or *quintas*. In the 19C several English Romantic poets, including Lord Byron, stayed here.
Three different areas make up the town of Sintra: the old town (Vila Velha), grouped round the royal palace, the modern town (Estefânia), and the former village of São Pedro. The latter is famous for its market of secondhand goods held on the second and fourth Sundays of each month.
Sintra's popularity, particularly during weekends, is reflected in the old town's many antique and craft shops, smart boutiques, restaurants and tea-rooms where one may sample the local gastronomic speciality: delicious small tarts known as *queijadas*.
Sintra's "cultural landscape" was declared a World Heritage site by UNESCO in 1995.

The Convention of Sintra – Wellington's victory at Vimeiro in August 1808 was followed by an armistice and subsequently an agreement, known as the Convention of Sintra (30 August 1808). Under this the British made some material gains and the French were granted a passage home on board British ships with their arms and baggage. The terms distressed the Portuguese, who renamed the Dutch Ambassador's residence, where the Convention was signed, the **Seteais** or House of the Seven Sighs. This is now a luxury hotel, the Palácio de Seteais.

★Palácio Real ⊙ – The royal palace's irregular structure is due to the additions made during different periods; the central edifice was erected by Dom João I at the end of the 14C and the wings by Dom Manuel I early in the 16C. Apart from the two tall conical chimneys, the paired Moorish style *(ajimeces)* and Manueline windows are the most striking features of the exterior.

Palácio Real, Sintra

The interior is interesting for its remarkable decoration of 16 and 17C **azulejos**★★. The finest embellish the dining room or Arabic Hall (Sala dos Árabes), the chapel and the Sirens' Hall (Sala das Sereias). The **Sala dos Brasoes** (Armoury), which is square, is covered with a **ceiling**★★ in the form of a dome on squinches, the dome itself consisting of coffers painted with the coats of arms of Portuguese nobles of the early 16C/the missing blazon is that of the Coelho family who conspired against Dom João II. The **Sala das Pegas** (Magpie or Reading Room) has a ceiling painted in the 17C with magpies holding in their beaks a rose inscribed with the words: *por bem* – for good – words pronounced by Dom João I when his queen caught him about to kiss one of her ladies-in-waiting. To put an end to the gossip the king had as many magpies painted on the ceiling as there were ladies at court.

A fine Venetian chandelier adorns the queen's audience chamber.

★**Museu de Arte Moderna** ⊘ **(Colecção Berardo)** – This museum, which is housed in the town's former casino, was opened in 1997 to exhibit the valuable private collection of the benefactor, J. Berardo. It contains works from the second half of the 20C, and represents the avant-garde artistic trends which developed after 1945. The exhibits, which are shown on a rotating basis, include works by Dubuffet (the oldest on display), Gilbert & George, David Hockney, Jeff Koons, Joan Mitchele, Richter, Rosenquist, Stella, Tom Wesselmann, Andy Warhol etc. The museum also contains a cafeteria, a bookshop and a gift shop.

A selection of hotels in Sintra is listed under Travellers' addresses for Lisbon.

Serra de SINTRA★★
Lisboa
Michelin map 940 Pl

The Sintra Range is a granite block forming a mountain barrier with the Cruz Alta with an altitude of 529m/1 736ft as its highest point. Rain from the Atlantic falls upon the impermeable rock giving rise to the dense vegetation which covers the whole massif and largely masks the granite spikes left exposed by the erosion of other rocks. The flora is varied: oaks, cedars, tropical and subtropical trees, bracken, camellias etc. The beauty of the landscape has been sung by poets, including Gil Vicente, Camões *(The Lusiads)*, Southey and **Byron** *(Childe Harold)*:

> ... Cintra's mountain greets them on their way
> ....
> The horrid crags, by toppling convent crowned,
> The cork trees hoar that clothe the shaggy steep,
> The mountain moss by scorching skies imbrowned,
> The sunken glen, whose sunless shrubs must weep,
> The tender azure of the unruffled deep,
> The orange tints that gild the greenest bough,
> The torrents that from cliff to valley leap,
> The vine on high, the willow branch below,
> Mixed in one mighty scene, with varied beauty glow.

★★PARQUE DA PENA ⊙

From Sintra to Cruz Alta
5km/3mi – about 2hr/local map below

South of Sintra the very beautiful **Parque da Pena**★★ covers 200ha/500 acres on the granite slopes of the Serra de Sintra; the park is planted with rare species of trees, both nordic and tropical, and there are a great number of lakes and fountains. It should be visited on foot to fully appreciate its great charm, but the motorist in a hurry can simply drive along the small roads which cross it, or at least go to the top of the two culminating points; the Palácio da Pena stands on one, and the Cruz Alta (High Cross) on the other.

★★**Sintra** – *See SINTRA.*

Leave Sintra on the road to Pena, southwards.

After skirting on the right the Estalagem dos Cavaleiros, where Lord Byron planned *Childe Harold*, the road rises in a series of hairpin bends.

At the crossroads with the N 247-3, turn left to Pena.

★**Castelo dos Mouros** ⊙ – *30min round trip on foot from the car park.*
The Moors' Castle, built in the 8 or 9C, still has a battlemented perimeter wall guarded by four towers and a ruined Romanesque chapel.
From the royal tower, which is climbed by a series of staircases, there is a commanding **view**★ of Sintra and its palace, the Atlantic coast and the Castelo da Pena perched on its height.

Go through the wrought iron gate at the entrance to the Parque da Pena and leave the car in the car park.

★★**Palácio Nacional da Pena** ⊙ *see illustration p. 54-55* – The palace, which is perched on one of the highest peaks of the range, was built in the middle of the 19C by the King-Consort Prince Ferdinand of Saxe-Coburg, around a former Hieronymite monastery dating from the 16C. Its eccentric architecture evokes some of Ludwig II of Bavaria's castles although it predates them by 30 years. It is a pastiche in which several styles merge with varying degrees of success: Moorish, Gothic, Manueline, Renaissance and baroque. The palace's eclecticism is further accentuated by the fact that it has been repainted in bright colours.

A drawbridge leads through a Moorish doorway to the palace courtyard onto which opens a passageway surmounted by an impressive Triton arch. Inside, the remains of the monastery, the Manueline cloisters and the chapel – with an alabaster altar by Nicolas Chanterene – are decorated with *azulejos*. They contrast strangely with the rest of the palace: the audience chambers, reception rooms and bedrooms furnished in the 19C style with a profusion of hangings, tapestries, heavy furniture, sofas, pouffes, mirrors and stucco decoration.

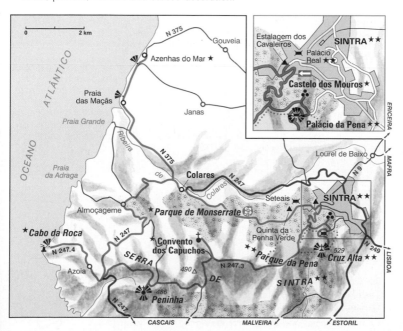

From the terraces there are fine **views★★** of the whole region from the Atlantic coast to the Tagus, straddled by the suspension bridge. The Cruz Alta and the statue of the palace architect, Count Eschwege, standing as a medieval knight on a rock, can be distinguished in the nearby *serra*.

★★**Cruz Alta (viewpoint)** – *It is possible to drive right to the foot of the cross*. From this summit, topped by a cross, there is a **panoramic view** over the whole massif (except Sintra) and the surrounding plain, as far as Lisbon to the south (behind the palace).

★ROUND TOUR OF THE SERRA

From Sintra *30km/19mi – about 3hr – see local map*

★★**Sintra** – *See SINTRA.*

Leave Sintra on the road towards Pena then turn onto the N 247-3 towards Cabo da Roca.

★**Convento dos Capuchos** ⊘ – The Capuchin Monastery, set in a striking landscape of jumbled rocks, was built in the 16C. The many tiny, precarious monks' cells were cut out of the living rock and the walls lined with cork, the best insulator at the time.

Return to the N 247-3 and take the narrow road opposite which leads to Peninha.

The road passes through countryside dotted with enormous rocks.

Peninha – A small **chapel** ⊘ with an interior lined with 18C *azulejos*, showing scenes from the life of the Virgin, stands on this hilltop (486m/1 594ft).

The panoramic **view★★** from the chapel terrace includes the vast Praia do Guincho in the foreground.

One can go directly to Cabo da Roca by heading towards Azóia.

★**Cabo da Roca** – The Serra da Sintra ends in a sheer cliff, the Cabo da Roca or Cape Rock, nearly 140m/459ft above the sea. This cliff is continental Europe's most westerly point. The sea pounds furiously below at the rocks and cliffs, wearing the coastline to the north away into inlets and small harbours.

Return to the N 247 and continue to Colares.

Colares – Colares is a small town known for its red and white table wines – wines grown from vines on sandy soil, velvety and light with a bouquet.

From here one may continue northwards to **Azenhas do Mar★** *(6km/4mi)* via the seaside resort of **Praia das Maçãs**. The approach to Azenhas do Mar gives a good general view of the town's **setting★** with its houses rising in tiers up a jagged cliff at the foot of which the Atlantic heaves and breaks. A small creek in a hollow in the cliff face has been made into a seawater swimming pool.

From Colares return to Sintra on the narrow and hilly N 375.

★**Parque de Monserrate** ⊘ – The landscape **park★** surrounding the neo-Oriental palace built by Sir Francis Cook in the 19C contains many different species of trees and plants including cedars, arbutus, bamboos, bracken etc, which stand beside pools and waterfalls.

The great English eccentric, traveller, writer and man of great wealth, **William Beckford**, sublet the previous house on the site and added an English garden with several romantic follies. Later English owners maintained the tradition of stocking the garden with the finest new species.

On the way to Sintra one passes, on the left, the 16C Quinta de Penha Verde, the former mansion of a Viceroy of India. An arch of the mansion straddles the road. Further on, again on the left, can be seen the early 19C monumental entrance to the Palácio-Hotel de Seteais *(see SINTRA)*.

The Practical Information section at the end of the guide lists :
– local or national organisations providing additional information
– events of interest to the tourist
– admission times and charges for the sights.

TAVIRA★

Faro — Population 7 282
Michelin map 940 U7 — Local map see ALGARVE

Tavira has a pleasant setting on an estuary of the Séqua river at the foot of a hill girded by the remains of ramparts built by King Dinis. The Roman bridge and Moorish walls testify to the town's long history.
The earthquake in 1755 demolished most of Tavira's buildings and silted up the harbour thus cutting the town off from the coast. In the past Tavira was an important centre for tuna and today continues some of its fishing activities. The local beach is on an offshore bar.

SIGHTS

Park in the town centre near Praça da República.

The centre of Tavira is extremely attractive with its narrow streets, river banks lined with gardens, and a lively covered market.
From Praça da República one can see the **Roman bridge** and, on the other side of the river, some beautiful houses. To visit the old quarter, go through Misericórdia Arch where you will see the Renaissance doorway of the **Igreja da Misericórdia**. By turning left in front of the church you come to the moorish castle, **Castelo dos Mouros**, which has some fine gardens within its crenellated walls. Higher up the hill is the **Igreja de Santa Maria do Castelo** which has preserved its Gothic doorway and stands facing the Largo de Graça, an attractive sloping square with flowers and shade. From here take Avenida da Liberdade which leads back to the centre.

EXCURSIONS

Praia da Ilha de Tavira — *2km/1.2mi, followed by a boat trip.* The road crosses salt marshes to the pier where boats leave regularly for the beaches on Tavira island in summer.

TOMAR★★

Santarém — Population 14 821
Michelin map 940 N4

Tomar stretches along the banks of the Nabão at the foot of a wooded hill crowned by a fortified castle built in 1160 by Gualdim Pais, Grand Master of the Order of the Knights Templars. Within the castle grounds stands the Convento de Cristo.

Convento de Cristo

From Knights Templars to Knights of Christ – In the early 12C, at the height of the Reconquest, the border between Christian and Moorish territories passed through the Tomar area. The military Order of the Knights Templars, founded in Jerusalem in 1119, built a convent-fortress in Tomar in 1160 which became the headquarters for the Order in Portugal. In 1314, at the request of Philip the Fair, Pope Clement V ordered the suppression of the Templars. A new Order, the Knights of Christ, was then founded by King Dinis in Portugal in 1320. It took over the possessions of the Knights Templars and most of its soldiering monks were from the former Order. The headquarters for the new Order were first set up in Castro Marim in the Algarve and then moved to Tomar in 1356. The golden period of the Knights of Christ was at the beginning of the 15C when Prince Henry the Navigator was Grand Master (1418-1460). The Order's vast fortune enabled him to finance expeditions for the Great Discoveries; armed caravels bore the Order's emblem, a large red cross, on their sails. The Portuguese explored the coast of Africa, rounded the Cape of Good Hope and reached the Indies. In Tomar, the wealth of this period is expressed in the rich Manueline decoration.

The Tabuleiros Festival – Every two years Tomar celebrates the Festa dos Tabuleiros which keeps alive the ceremonies organised by the Brotherhood of the Holy Spirit – an Order founded by Queen Saint Isabel in the 14C to distribute bread, wine and meat to the poor of the town. At the festival, young girls, dressed in white, walk in procession through the streets bearing on their heads a *tabuleiro* or platter. The *tabuleiro* is piled up until it is as tall as the girl bearing it; thirty loaves are threaded on reeds and fixed into a willow basket which is adorned with foliage, paper flowers and blades of wheat. The festival lasts four days, the procession being followed by secular festivities, folk dancing and fireworks.

★★CONVENTO DE CRISTO ◎ *1hr*

The 12C walls crowning the summit of the hillock dominating the town enclose the Convent of Christ which was begun in the 12C and only completed in the 17C. The result is a museum of different Portuguese architectural styles.

Leave the car in the car park outside the walls.

Once inside, cross the garden of clipped box trees which precedes the convent.

★**Igreja** – The church doorway, which is reminiscent of the Plateresque style in Salamanca, Spain, is by the Spanish architect Juan de Castilla, successor of Diogo de Arruda. To the former church of the Templars, which now forms the east end of the church, King Manuel added a nave, linking it to the rotunda by means of an arch which he commissioned Diogo de Arruda to design.

★★**Charola dos Templários** – The Templar's Rotunda was built in the 12C on the model of the Holy Sepulchre in Jerusalem. The two-storey octagonal construction is supported by eight pillars. An ambulatory with a ring vault divides the central octagon from the exterior polygon which has sixteen sides. The paintings decorating the octagon are by 16C Portuguese artists and the polychrome wooden statues date from the same period.

Nave – The 16C nave by Diogo de Arruda is outstanding for the exuberance of its Manueline decoration.

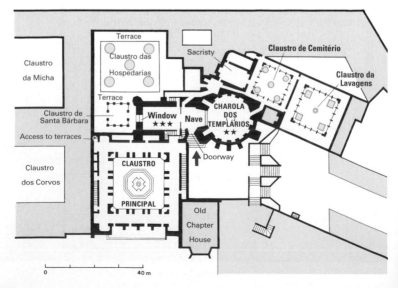

★Conventual buildings (Edifícios conventuais) – The conventual buildings are spread around several cloisters.

Claustro Principal – The great cloisters were mainly built between 1557 and 1566 by the architect Diogo de Torralva, a fervent admirer of Palladio, one of the architects of the Italian Renaissance. The cloisters are also known as Claustro dos Felipes in memory of Philip II of Spain who assumed the crown of Portugal here in 1581. The cloisters are Renaissance in style with two storeys, the ground level gallery having Tuscan columns, the upper, Ionic. The bare simplicity of the cloisters makes a surprising contrast with the Manueline style decoration of the nave which, unfortunately, is partly hidden by the cloisters. The most outstanding features of the decoration are on three windows of which only two are visible. The first may be seen to the right on entering the cloisters but the second, the most famous, is below, in the Santa Barbara Cloisters (Claustro de Santa Bárbara).

A spiral staircase in the east corner of the cloisters leads to terraces from which there is a good overall view of the convent.

The Manueline window at Tomar

★★★Window (Janela) – This window is the most amazing example of Manueline style ornament to be seen in Portugal. It was designed by the architect Diogo de Arruda and sculpted between 1510 and 1513. The decoration which rises from the roots ① of a cork oak, supported on the bust of a sea captain ②, climbs two convoluted masts. Among the profusion of plant and marine motifs can be seen coral ③, ropes ④, cork for use in the construction of ships ⑤, seaweed ⑥, cables ⑦ and anchor chains ⑧. The whole is crowned with the royal emblems of Manuel I – a blazon and armillary spheres – and the cross of the Order of Christ, which recurs as a motif on the balustrades surrounding the nave. The window is "moored" by cables to two turrets which bear the same decorative stamp. These are encircled, one by a chain, representing the Order of the Golden Fleece, and the other by a ribbon, the Order of the Garter.

Gothic cloisters (Claustros góticos) – The **Claustro do Cemitério**, with plant motif capitals, and the **Claustro da Lavagens**, both east of the rotunda, were built in the 15C at the behest of Prince Henry the Navigator.

ADDITIONAL SIGHTS

Capela de Nossa Senhora da Conceição ⊘ – The chapel stands halfway down the hill on the left as you descend from the convent into the town. It is a lovely Renaissance building with delicately carved capitals.

Igreja de São João Baptista – *Praça da República*. This late 15C Gothic church flanked by a Manueline belfry has a beautiful Flamboyant **door★**, which is said to be the work of a French artist, as is the fine Flamboyant pulpit standing on the north side of the nave. In the north aisle hangs a *Last Supper* by Gregório Lopes (16C).

Sinagoga ⊘ – *Rua Joaquim Jacinto 73*. The synagogue was built between 1430 and 1460 but it was only used as a place of worship until 1497 when the Jews were expelled from Portugal. A Lusitanian Hebrew museum now occupies the premises. Note the earthenware pitchers in the main hall where pillars support a vaulted ceiling. They were used to improve the acoustics of the room.

TORRE DE MONCORVO

Bragança – Population 3 154
Michelin map 940 or 441 I8

Arriving from the east along the N 220 you will get a general **view★** of the town as it lies grouped together in a vast landscape of arid mountain scenery above a fertile valley planted with olive groves and vineyards near the confluence of the Douro and Sabor rivers.

The Serra do Reboredo to the southeast contains rich iron ore deposits.

The town is embellished with various 17C and 18C mansions (Solar dos Pimentéis, Casa dos Távoras); it is also known for its *amêndoas cobertas*, a sort of nut sweetmeat.

Igreja Matriz – This imposing 16C and 17C church, with its buttress reinforcements and austere façade, has a prominent tower in its centre with a Renaissance doorway with round curves. Its entablature is completed with sculptures in shell-shaped baroque niches. The interior, with its three naves and ribbed vaulting, contains a fine 17C retable, with, in its north transept, an interesting wooden triptych painted to illustrate the life of St Anne, mother of the Virgin, and her husband, Joachim. On the right, is their first meeting; on the left, their marriage; and in the centre, the presentation of the Infant Jesus to his grandparents.

TRANCOSO

Guarda – Population 884
Michelin map 940 or 441 J7

The ramparts of the citadel, which are still intact, can be seen from far away on the high plateau which extends the Serra da Estrela to the north. The best overall view is obtained from a rocky hillock (north of the town) near a calvary on the side of the road to Meda.

The city, which knew glory in the 13 and 14C, reached its peak when the marriage of Dom Dinis and Queen Saint Isabel of Aragon took place on 24 June 1282 within its walls.

★Fortifications – *To fully appreciate these powerful fortifications go round the city by car.*
The 9C wall, which has been rebuilt several times, is topped by pyramid shaped merlons and flanked by massive square bastions. Two of its gates are decorated.

Castelo ⊙ – Dominated by a square keep, it occupies the northeast corner of the wall; from the top of the ramparts, the view extends to the hilly landscape of the Beira Alta.

Pelourinho – The pillory, an octagonal column supporting a small lantern crowned by an armillary sphere and the cross of the Order of Christ, stands in the centre of the town.

Old houses (Casas Antigas) – The façades of some of the houses in the town's narrow alleys are adorned with coats of arms and balconies.

Parque Arqueológico do VALE DO CÔA★★

Guarda
Michelin map 940 or 441 I8

The **Parque Arqueológico do Vale do Côa** is situated in the northeast of the country on the border between Trás-os-Montes and Beira Alta in an isolated and majestic natural setting. The archaeological park was created to preserve one of the world's most important open-air sites for Paleolithic rock art alongside the Côa river, close to its confluence with the Douro.

The discovery – The landscape has hardly changed since the age when Cro-Magnon people made rock engravings of animals living in nature. As a result of the area's isolation, the rock art in the Côa valley has been preserved to the present day; one could even say that it has been perpetuated over the course of history with every age leaving its mark engraved in the stone as travellers passed through the region. The railway bridge at the mouth of the Côa marks the modern age.

In 1992, during the construction of a dam at Canada do Inferno, rocks with engravings from the Paleolithic period (between 30 000 and 10 000 years ago) were discovered. Following protracted debates concerning the possibility of continuing work on the dam, which would have raised the water level by 130 metres, at the beginning of 1996 the new government made the decision to suspend the project, preferring to preserve this exceptional paleolithic art site.

To date, about 150 rocks with engravings have been discovered, of which 18 can be visited. Other sites containing ornamented rocks have also been discovered (some of which are under water); as a result, the park is in a state of continual flux due to the innumerable discoveries being made by current excavations.

The park, which was opened in August 1996, extends over 17km/10mi along the river, and is centred on three main areas of engravings: Penascosa, Ribeira de Piscos and Canada do Inferno.

Paleolithic rock art – The Paleolithic Age was the oldest, and longest (2.5 million years), era in the history of humanity and corresponds to the Stone Age. The oldest engravings in the Vale do Côa, identifiable by the species of animals represented, come from the Upper Paleolithic, or Solutrean Age and are 20.000 years old. Paintings discovered in the Lascaux caves in France and Altimira in Spain certainly date from the

View of Ribeira de Piscos site

same period (cave art is known as parietal art). Rock engravings can also be seen at Siega Verde in the Duero (Douro) valley in Spain, just 60km/37mi from the Vale do Côa site, although discoveries on this site date from a later era.

Engraving techniques used in the Côa valley, (where paintings may have been made as well), are of three main types: **abrasion**, which consisted of creating a deep groove through the repeated use of an instrument (a fragment of stone) along a marking, **pecking**, a succession of points hammered into the rock using a stone, and occasionally finished off using the abrasion technique, and **fine line incision**, which resulted in finer markings which are more difficult to distinguish. The animals most frequently represented were the horse, aurochs and mountain goat. In general, the same rock was used to depict various animals, with one drawing added on top of another. What is particularly special about art in the Côa valley is the exceptional beauty of the engravings, the representation of the shape and movement of the animals through the simple, firm lines.

VISIT ⊘

Penascosa – *Visit: 1hr 40min, including 40min round trip by jeep.* – The Reception Centre at **Castelo Melhor** *(see GUARDA)* is located in an old schist house which is typical of the region. The building is a successful marriage between the preservation of a traditional architectural structure and a modern interior, with multimedia sites connected to the Internet and a conference and slide-show room. The attractive outdoor terrace is a pleasant place to have a drink while you are waiting for your visit to start.

The jeep ride provides beautiful views of the surrounding hills planted with vines used for Port wine, particularly the famous Quinta da Ervamoira. Penascosa is the most accessible of the three sites and contains engraving which are the most legible in the park. It is located alongside the river, which has created a beach in this part of its course, and jeeps can park just a few metres from the rocks. The site is best visited in the afternoon, when the light is at its best for viewing the engravings which for the most part were created by pecking or abrasion. The movement of animals has been reproduced to an extraordinary degree here, particularly in a mating scene, in which a mare is mounted by a horse with three heads to interpret the downward movement of its neck. Seven rocks can be visited here at present.

Ribeira de Piscos – *Visit: 2hr 30min, including 1hr round trip by jeep and 40min return on foot*. The Reception Centre is in the village of **Muxagata**, where a 16C pillory can also be seen. It occupies a fine 16C house which has been restored.

The visit in itself is an extremely pleasant stroll along the river bank. The engravings, particularly fine line incisions, are dispersed over the hills and are not as easily discernible. However, one quite visible drawing shows two horses crossing their heads, with their dorsal lines bringing to mind two wings. The grace and purity of the engraving are moving in their beauty. A human figure on a panel to the side dates from the same period and is also worthy of note. Five engraved panels are currently on display.

Canada do Inferno – *Visit: 1hr 40min, including 20min round trip journey by jeep and 20min return on foot.* Jeeps depart from the **park headquarters** *(sede do parque)* in **Vila Nova de Foz Côa** *(see VILA NOVA DO FOZ CÔA).*

This site is situated in the steepest part of the river valley, where a canyon has formed, 130m/426ft deep, making access a little more difficult. From here the suspended work on the dam 400m/1/4mi downstream can be seen. The best

Paleolithic rock art, Penascosa

time of day to see the engravings, the majority of which are fine line incisions, is in the morning. Although Canado do Inferno is the most interesting of the three sites, many rocks are under water, and only six are currently visible. Another interesting fact proving the continuity of rock art over the centuries has been the discovery of several 17C engravings with religious themes.

USEFUL INFORMATION

Access – The easiest way of getting to the Vale do Côa is by car.

From Lisbon: *387km/242mi via Albergaria-a-Velha, allow 5hr.* From Oporto: *214km/134mi via Mirandela, allow 3hr 30min.* From Madrid: *398km/249mi, allow 5hr.*

Organising your visit – *see Admission times and charges section at the end of the guide for opening times, entrance fees and reservations.* Visits must be reserved at least two months in advance. Visitors should head directly to the Reception Centre *(Centro de Recepção)* of the site they are planning to visit at least 15minutes before their scheduled departure (Castelo Melhor for Penascosa, Muxagata for Ribeira de Piscos, and the park headquarters at Vila Nova de Foz Côa for Canada do Inferno). Transport to the sites is by 8-seater jeep (children are counted as an adult in the vehicles). Visits are led by specially-trained young guides from the region. The Park reserves the right to temporarily cancel visits during bad weather (rain). Exact timings for visits shall be sent when reservations are made.

Two days should be allowed for those wishing to see all three sites. We recommend Penascosa for those visitors only able to visit one site.

Don't forget... Suitable footwear, boots in winter, a hat in summer, a bottle of water; keep your hands free if at all possible (use a rucksack) to make walking easier, particularly in Canada do Inferno and Ribeira de Piscos, where the uneven terrain and slopes force visitors to occasionally hold onto vegetation and stones. Visitors who are sensitive to heat should avoid the summer months, when temperatures here can reach 40°C (104°F).

Plan ahead!

To plan your route, the sights to see, to select a hotel or a restaurant, Internet users can log in at www.michelin-travel.com

In France, consult the French videotex service Minitel 36 15 MICHELIN.

VALENÇA DO MINHO*

Viana do Castelo – Population 2 474
Michelin map 940 or 441 G3

Valença, on a hillock overlooking the south bank of the Minho and facing the Galician town of Tui, has stood guard for centuries over Portugal's northern border and the river. The main road from Santiago de Compostela to Oporto crosses the river by a metal **bridge** built by Gustave Eiffel in 1884. The old town is an unusual double city, consisting of two fortresses in the style of Vauban and a single bridge spanning a wide ditch and continuing through a long vaulted passage.

Valença is very popular with the Spanish who come to buy cotton goods and table linen.

  ★ Fortified Town (Vila Fortificada) – *Access by car from the south on a shaded road off N 13.* Each fortress, unchanged since the 17C, is in the shape of an irregular polygon with six bastions with double redans and watch towers, in front of which are the defensive outworks and two monumental doorways, north and south, emblazoned with the arms of the kingdom and the governor. Old cannon are still in position on the battlements.

From the north side of the ramparts there is a fine **view★** over the Minho valley, Tui and the Galician mountains.

Each stronghold is an independent quarter with its own churches and picturesque narrow cobbled streets, fountains, shops, and houses sometimes decorated with statues at the corners.

EXCURSIONS

★★ Monte do Faro – *7km/4mi. Leave Valença on N 101 going towards Monção; bear right towards Cerdal and shortly afterwards left to Monte do Faro.* The road rises rapidly through the pines; views open out ever wider as one climbs. Leave the car at the last roundabout and walk up the path to the summit 565m/1 854ft which lies to the left of the road. From the summit, the **panorama★★** is very extensive indeed: to the north and west lies the Minho valley scattered with white houses grouped in villages and dominated in the distance by the Galician mountains; to the east is the Serra do Soajo and southwest the wooded hills of the coastal area and the Atlantic.

Vale do Minho – *From Valença to São Gregório 52km/32mi, leave Valença on N 101, to the east.*

The Portuguese bank of the Minho on the east side of Valença is the most interesting. The river, which at the beginning is majestically spread out, becomes hemmed in until it is practically invisible between the steep green slopes. The road is cobbled and winding, thickly bordered with trees (pines, eucalyptus and even palm trees) and climbing vines which make the well known *vinho verde (qv)*. It passes through large wine-making villages.

Monção – This attractive little town overlooking the Minho is also a spa whose waters are used in the treatment of rheumatism. Several old houses, the **Igreja Matriz** (parish church) which has preserved some of its Romanesque features, the **belvedere★** over the Minho and surrounding countryside, and the well-known local Alvarinho wine all make Monção a pleasant place to stop.

3km/1.8mi south on the road towards Arcos de Valdevez, one may see, on the right, the early 19C **Palácio da Brejoeira** which was modelled on the Palácio da Ajuda in Lisbon.

Below the road the vines, fields of maize and pumpkins grow on terraces facing the smiling slopes of the Spanish side, dotted with perched villages. The abundance of cultivation and the isolated houses (roughcast in vivid colours) are particularly striking.

After Melgaço, N 301 rises offering wonderful **views** of the Minho, still very hemmed in, before reaching São Gregório (border post).

VIANA DO ALENTEJO

Évora – Population 3 674
Michelin map 940 R5

This agricultural town in the vast Alentejo Plain, away from the main roads, hides an interesting church behind its castle walls.

  Castelo ⊙ – The **castle's ramparts** present fortified walls flanked at each corner by a tower with a pepperpot roof surrounding the pentagonal shaped edifice. The entrance porch is adorned with worn capitals decorated with animals, including tortoises, lions etc. The castle courtyard extends along the north side of the church.

Igreja – The church façade surmounted by conical bell turrets and merlons has a fine Manueline **doorway*** : a slender twisted column serves as the supporting pier for twin arches framed by two candlestick shaped pilasters; it also supports the tympanum which is decorated with stylised flowers and the cross of the Order of Christ in a medallion surmounted by the Portuguese coat of arms: a gable formed by a twisted cable ends in a type of pinnacle flanked by two armillary spheres.

The interior, which is Romanesque remodelled in the Manueline style, is outstanding for its size. The walls are decorated at their base with 17C *azulejos*, the chancel has a fine Crucifix.

VIANA DO CASTELO★★

Viana do Castelo – Population 15 356
Michelin map 940 or 441 G3

Viana do Castelo, lying on the north bank of the Lima estuary at the foot of the sunny hillside slope of Santa Luzia, is a pleasant holiday resort.

A humble fishermen's village in the Middle Ages, that suddenly attained fantastic prosperity in the 16C when, following the Great Discoveries, its fishermen set sail to fish for cod off Newfoundland and trade with the Hanseatic Cities. It was during this period that the Manueline and Renaissance houses were built which today make the old town so attractive. After a period of decline following the independence of Brazil in the beginning of the 19C and the civil war, Viana has once again become an active centre for deep sea fishing; industries (wood, ceramics, pyrotechnics, and boat building) and crafts (costumes and embroidery) also contribute to the town's prosperity.

Romaria of Our Lady in Sorrow (Nossa Senhora da Agonia) – The festival which is held in August *(see Calendar of Events)*, is one of the most famous in the Minho region. It includes a procession, bull running in the barricaded streets, fireworks on the Lima, a parade of carnival giants and dwarfs, illuminations and traditional folklore events. A festival of regional dancing and singing is also held, and on the last day a procession in regional costumes winds its way through the streets of the town.

★★**Miradouro de Santa Luzia** – *4km/2.5mi on the road from Santa Luzia, or 7minutes by the funicular*. Viana belvedere is on the hill of Santa Luzia, which rises to the north of the town and is topped with a modern basilica, a place of pilgrimage. By car one approaches it by a cobbled road with a series of hairpin bends which climbs pleasantly among pines, eucalyptus and mimosas.

Basílica de Santa Luzia ⊙ – Built in neo-Byzantine style, it has a large parvis in front of it and a monumental staircase. The interior is lit by three rose windows; the chancel and the apse under the domes are decorated with frescoes. 57m/187ft above the ground the central dome's lantern turret (142 steps starting in the sacristy – very narrow passageway at the end of the climb) has a magnificent **panoramic view**★★ over Viana do Castelo and the Lima estuary, and to the southeast on the horizon, the towering wooded heights of the Barcelos region, scattered with white villages; beyond the harbour, guarded by the 16C São Tiago de Barra Fortress, the ocean foams along the immense beaches of fine sand.

Festival of Nossa Senhora da Agonia

VIANA DO CASTELO

Bandeira (Rua da) .... **B**
Combatentes da Grande
  Guerra (Av. dos)................ **AB** 7
República (Praça da)............... **B** 18

Cândido dos Reis
  (Rua) .... **B** 3
Capitão Gaspar de Castro
  (Rua) .... **B** 4
Carmo (Rua do)....................... **B** 6
Conde da Carreira (Av. da) ..... **A** 9
Dom Afonso III (Av.) .... **B** 10

Gago Coutinho (R. de)............ **B** 12
Humberto Delgado (Av.).......... **A** 13
João Tomás da Costa (Largo) . **B** 15
Luís de Camões (Av.)............. **B** 16
Sacadura Cabral (Rua) .... **B** 19
Santa Luzia (Estrada) .... **A** 21
São Pedro (Rua de)................ **B** 22

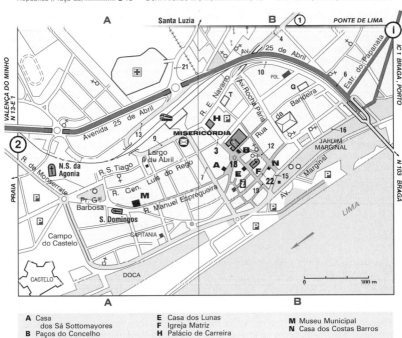

A Casa
  dos Sá Sottomayores
B Paços do Concelho

E Casa dos Lunas
F Igreja Matriz
H Palácio de Carreira

M Museu Municipal
N Casa dos Costas Barros

★THE OLD QUARTER (BAIRRO ANTIGO)

By wandering at random through the old quarter with its pedestrian streets, one comes across many houses with armorial bearings on the façades and some interesting examples of Renaissance and Manueline architecture.

★**Praça da República** (**18**) – The 16C buildings, including **Casa dos Sá Sottomayores** (**A**), surrounding the vast square make up a graceful, picturesque ensemble.

Chafariz – João Lopes the Elder built the fountain in 1553, crowning its several basins with sculptured decoration supporting an armillary sphere and a cross of the Order of Christ.

Paços do Concelho (**B**) – Only the façade of the former town hall has retained its original 16C appearance. It bristles with merlons above, has pointed arches at ground level, and on the first storey has windows crowned with the coat of arms of Dom João III, the armillary sphere or emblem of Dom Manuel I and the town's coat of arms which features a caravel, as many sailors from Viana do Castelo took part in the Great Discoveries.

★**Hospital da Misericórdia** – This 1589 Renaissance hospice, with Venetian and Flemish influence in its style was designed by João Lopes the Younger. Its noble façade, to the left of the monumental doorway, rises from a massive colonnade with Ionic capitals as two tiers of loggias supported on atlantes and caryatids.
The adjoining **Igreja da Misericórdia** ⊘ was rebuilt in 1714. It is decorated with *azulejos* and gilded woodwork dating from the same period.

Rua Cândido dos Reis (**3**) – Some of the houses fronting the street have Manueline façades. Particularly noteworthy is **Palácio de Carreira** (**H**) which houses the present Town Hall. Its beautiful Manueline front is strikingly symmetrical. **Casa das Lunas** (**E**), is Italian Renaissance in style, but also has some Manueline features.

Igreja Matriz (**F**) – The church dates from the 14 and 15C, but the two crenellated towers flanking the façade are Romanesque, their crowning Lombard blind arcades supported by carved modillions. The Gothic doorway has a series of three historiated archivolts which rest on statue columns of St Andrew, St Peter and the Evangelists; the outer archivolt shows Christ surrounded by cherubim holding the emblems of the Passion.
Inside, in the baptistry, a carved, polychrome wooden panel (17C) represents the Baptism of the Infant Jesus. In the third chapel on the left there is a fine 16C painting on wood.

The 15C house, north of the church, is said to have belonged to **João the Elder**.

Rua de São Pedro (**22**) – The street is lined with old mansions. Of particular interest is the Manueline window of **Casa dos Costas Barros** (**N**).

★**Museu Municipal** ⊙ (**M**) – The museum is housed in the former 18C palace of the Barbosa Macieis. The interior walls are covered with lovely **azulejos**★★ depicting distant continents, hunting and fishing scenes and receptions painted by Policarpo de Oliveira Bernardes in 1721. These *azulejos* together with some fine wooden ceilings decorate the rooms on the first floor which contain an outstanding collection of **Portuguese glazed earthenware**★ (from Lisbon, Coimbra, etc) said to be the largest in Portugal.
The rooms on the ground floor, with coffered ceilings of varnished wood, contain some sumptuous cabinets, including one from Italy made of ivory and tortoiseshell, some fine 17C Indo-Portuguese furniture, carved or inlaid, local ceramics, a small Virgin and Child in ivory as well as some prehistoric remains. The adjoining courtyard has a collection of stone work: statues, votive offerings and tombstones.

Igreja de São Domingos – The church built in 1570 has a Renaissance façade. Inside is the tomb of the founder of the church, Bartolomeu dos Mártires, Archbishop of Braga.

Igreja de Nossa Senhora da Agonia – This delightful baroque chapel is known for the pilgrimage which takes place on 15 August each year.

VILA DO CONDE

Porto — Population 20 245
Michelin map 940 or 441 H3

Vila do Conde at the mouth of the Ave, birthplace of the poet José Régio, is a seaside resort, active fishing harbour and industrial centre (shipbuilding, textiles and chocolate making).
The town is well-known for its pillow-lace and its festivals. The Feast of St John *(see Calendar of Events)* is the occasion for picturesque processions by the *Mordomas* adorned with magnificent gold jewellery and by the *Rendilheras*, the town's lacemakers in regional costumes.

SIGHTS

★**Convento de Santa Clara** ⊙ – The monumental edifice rises impressively above the Ave River. Behind the 18C façade are 14C buildings. Today the convent is a reformatory and only the church and cloisters are open to the public.

Igreja – The church, which was founded in 1318 and designed as a fortress, has retained its original Gothic style. In the west face is a beautiful rose window.
The interior, with a single aisle, has a coffered ceiling carved in the 18C. The Capelada Conceição *(first chapel on the left)*, built in the 16C, contains the Renaissance **tombs**★ of the founders and their children. Wonderfully detailed reliefs have been carved into the Ança stone. The low reliefs on the sides of the tomb of **Dom Afonso Sanches** represent scenes from the Life of Christ; that at the head shows St Clare preventing the Saracens from entering the Convent of St Clare at Assisi. The reclining figure on the tomb of **Dona Teresa Martins** is dressed in the habit of a nun of the Franciscan Tertiaries. Scenes of the Passion are depicted on the sides and St Francis receiving the stigmata is shown at the head. The children's tombs have the Doctors of the Church *(left tomb)* and the Evangelists *(right tomb)* carved upon them.
A fine grille divides the nave from the nun's chancel.
The arches of the 18C cloisters can still be seen to the south of the church; the fountain in the centre of the close is the terminal for the 18C aqueduct from Póvoa de Varzim.
From the church terrace there is a good view of the small town bounded on its south side by the Ave and on its west by the sea.

Igreja Matriz – This fortified church was erected in the 16C in the Manueline style by Biscayan artists, which explains the existence of the fine Plateresque doorway. The tympanum is decorated with a small statue of St John the Baptist protected by a canopy and surrounded by the symbols of the Evangelists.
The tower to the left of the façade dates from the end of the 17C. Inside are altars and a gilded wooden pulpit dating from the 17 and 18C.

Pelourinho – *Opposite the parish church.* The pillory, originally Renaissance but restyled in the 18C, supports the arm of justice brandishing a sword.

EXCURSION

Azurara – *1km/0.5mi south.* The village has a fortified, 16C Manueline **church** crowned with crenellations. Facing the church is a beautiful cross, also Manueline.

VILA FRANCA DE XIRA

Lisboa – Pop 19 823
Michelin map 940 P3

On the west bank of the Tagus, Vila Franca de Xira, this industrial town of the Ribatejo Plain, is known for its festivals and bullfights.

The city comes alive, particularly in July (see Calendar of Events), at the time of the Festival of the **Colete Encarnado**, the *campinos'* "red waistcoat" festival. The visitor can see picturesque processions of *campinos* and bulls running loose through the streets. Folk dancing, bullfights, open air feasts (grilled sardines) and sometimes boating regattas on the Tagus complete the festivities.

The arenas are on the southern side of the town, on the road to Lisbon (N 10), opposite an unusual raised cemetery with flowered pergolas.

Muse Etnográfico ⊙ – This small museum has a few paintings and sculptures relating to the region or the art of bullfighting, and particularly 19C traditional costumes (fishermen, peasants, cattle breeders) and 18 and 19C *campinos*.

Miradouro de Monte Gordo – *3km/2mi to the north on the Rua António Lucio Baptista, passing under the motorway, then on a surfaced road which climbs steeply.*

From the belvedere, between two windmills at the top of the hill, there is a **panoramic view** to the west and north over the other hills covered with woods and vineyards (among which you can see the farmhouses – *quintas*); to the east over the Ribatejo Plain which stretches to the Ponte de Vila Franca crossing the Tagus; to the south over the first two islands in the river's estuary.

EXCURSION

Alverca do Ribatejo – *8km/5mi southwest on N 1, then follow signs to the Museu do Ar.*

A hangar at the military aerodrome has been converted into an Aviation Museum, **Museu do Ar** ⊙. The history of Portuguese aviation is retraced through a collection of photographs, archives and, in particular, genuine old planes and replicas such as the Blériot XI, the 1908 Demoiselle XX, which was piloted by the Brazilian Santos-Dumont, and the 1920 Santa Cruz flying boat which was the first to cross the South Atlantic.

VILAMOURA

Faro
Michelin map 940 U5 – Local map see ALGARVE

The resort of Vilamoura and its southeast neighbour **Quarteira** have huge tourist complexes all along their seafronts. Quarteira's high-rise blocks line a wide avenue beside Vilamoura's holiday villages, hotels, three golf courses and a vast marina which can accommodate several hundred yachts. The ruins of a Roman city come as a surprise among all these modern constructions.

Roman ruins of Cerro da Vila ⊙ – *On the northeast corner of the marina.* The excavations undertaken here since 1964 have revealed a Roman city underneath Moorish and Visigothic remains. Apart from a patrician villa dating from the 1C with private baths and a cellar, there are also wells, a crematorium, silos, stables, a wine press and, below, the ruins of 3C public baths. These baths once stood near the harbour (quayside wall) before the sea retreated and were used by sailors. Beautiful panels and fragments of mosaics, some polychrome, others black and white, still adorn the floors and pools (the latter subsequently converted into salting vats and fishtanks).

The small museum, installed in the warden's house, contains displays from the site.

VILA NOVA DE FOZ CÔA

Guarda – Population 3 869
Michelin map 940 or 441 I8

In a landscape of bare hills, this small isolated but cheerful village, made lively by students, stretches across a long ridge with vine-covered slopes. Since 1992 the town has become famous through the discovery of Paleolithic rock art in the bed of the Côa valley, just a few kilometres away.

Igreja Matriz – The parish church has a remarkable Manueline granite **façade★**, a belfry porch, and a doorway surrounded with clustered pilasters and topped by an archivolt decorated with floral and shell motifs under a lintel where the armillary spheres frame a 16C *Pietà* in limestone.

The interior has three naves where the painted wooden ceiling is supported by leaning columns giving the impression of being open to the sky; the carved capitals represent human heads. Baroque altarpieces of gilded wood decorate the apse and a south chapel.

Pelourinho – This is a beautiful Manueline pillory in granite, the stock encircled with cable moulding and the top sculpted with small columns and statues under an armillary sphere and a lily.

EXCURSIONS

Parque Arqueológico do VALE DO CÔA – *See Parque Arqueológico do VALE DO CÔA.*

VILA REAL

Vila Real – Population 13 876
Michelin map 940 or 441 I6 – Local map see Vale do DOURO

Vila Real, or Royal Town, is a lively small town, enhanced by numerous patrician houses dating from the 16 and 18C. It stands grouped on a plateau among vineyards and orchards at the foot of the Serra do Marão.
Fine black pottery is made in the surrounding countryside and can be bought in the town, particularly on 28-29 June when quantities are brought in for the St Peter's Fair *(Feira de Sâo Pedro)*.
Vila Real is also known for its car racing circuit.

SIGHTS

The main sights are to be found in the vicinity of Avenida Carvalho Araújo.
From the central crossroads by the cathedral go down the avenue on the right.

Sé – This former conventual church built at the end of the Gothic period has preserved certain Romanesque details. These are particularly noticeable in the treatment of the capitals in the nave.

Y. Travert/DIAF

Solar de Mateus

Casa de Diogo Cão – *At number 19 (door-plate).* So-called because, according to tradition, the well-known navigator, Diogo Cão, was born here. The façade was remodelled in the 16C in Italian Renaissance style.

Câmara Municipal – Built at the beginning of the 19C, the town hall has a lantern pillory in front, and a remarkable monumental stone staircase with balusters in the Italian Renaissance style.

Continue along towards the cemetery which you skirt round on the right.

Cemetery Esplanade (Esplanada do Cemitério) – This shaded walk, on the site of the old castle, overlooks the junction of the Corgo and Cabril rivers. In direct line with the cemetery and behind it there is a **view** looking steeply down into the Gorges of the Corgo and its tributary. Further to the left, there is an extensive view over the Corgo Ravine and the houses which overhang it.

Return to Avenida Carvalho Araújo, turn right and climb upwards.

Tourist Information Centre (Poste de Turismo) – *At number 94.* It occupies a 16C house which has a lovely Manueline façade.

From here take the first road on the right (by the law courts) to the Igreja de São Pedro.

Igreja de São Pedro – St Peter's Church is decorated in the chancel with 17C multicoloured *azulejos* and a fine coffered **ceiling★** of carved and gilded wood.

EXCURSION

Mateus – *3.5km/2mi to the east on N 322 towards Sabrosa.* Chestnut trees, vines and orchards herald the approach to the village of Mateus, famous for the manor belonging to the Counts of Vila Real and the rosé wine made on the estate.

★★ **Solar de Mateus** ⊘ – Dating from the first half of the 18C, this creation by Nicolau Nasoni is a perfect example of Portuguese baroque architecture.

Behind lawns planted with cedars, followed by a garden laid out with clumps of boxwood and a tree-covered walk, appears the **façade★★** of the manor, preceded by a mirror of water. The central section of the manor is set back, and has a beautiful balustraded stairway and a high emblazoned pediment, surrounded by allegorical statues. The main courtyard is protected by an ornamental stone balustrade. The windows upstairs are topped with moulded gables. Beautiful pinnacles top the roof cornices.

To the left of the façade there is a tall elegant baroque chapel built in 1750, also by Nasoni.

Inside the palace there are magnificent carved wooden ceilings in the main hall and the main salon, a rich library (numerous old French editions), some furniture (Portuguese, Spanish, Chinese and 18C French painted wood), and in two rooms which have been made into a museum **copperplate engravings** by Fragonard and Baron Gerard, precious fans, liturgical objects and vestments, a 17C altar and religious sculptures, one of which is a 16C ivory crucifix.

VILA REAL DE SANTO ANTÓNIO

Faro – Population 13 379
Michelin map 940 U7 – Local map see ALGARVE

The border town was founded by the Marquis of Pombal in 1774 as a counterpoint to the Andalusian city of Ayamonte on the opposite bank of the Guadiana. The new town, which was built in five months, is a fine example of the town planning of the day with its grid plan streets and whitewashed houses with distinctive roofs.

Vila Real has become one of the largest fishing and commercial ports on the Algarve and is also a considerable fish canning centre. Yachts for export are also built here. Links with Spain are provided by a ferry service and, since 1992, a bridge *(north of the town)*. Vila Real de Santo António is very popular with the Spanish who cross over to buy cotton goods (table linen, sheets, towels etc).

SIGHTS

Praça do Marquês de Pombal – This is the main square in the centre of the Pombaline quarter. It is surrounded with orange trees and paved with a black and white mosaic radiating from a central obelisk. Pedestrian streets around the square are lined with shops selling cotton goods.

The banks of the Guadiana – The white houses of Ayamonte can be clearly seen from the beautiful gardens on the river bank.

EXCURSIONS

Monte Gordo – *3km/2mi west.* On the far side of the pinewoods is the modern resort of Monte Gordo with miles of sandy beach.

Castro Marim – *See CASTRO MARIM.*

VILA VIÇOSA★

Évora — Population 4 282
Michelin map 940 P7

Vila Viçosa, grouped on a hillside slope where oranges and lemons grow, is a town of shade *(viçosa)* and bright flowers. Vale Viçosa, as this village was first called, was granted a charter in 1270 by Alfonso III under its new name, Vila Vicosa (the charter was renewed in 1512). It was at one time the seat of the dukes of Bragança and also the residence of several kings of Portugal.

Since the fall of the monarchy in 1910 Vila Viçosa has become a quiet little town making a living from various crafts such as pottery and wrought iron as well as the marble quarries in the environs. While the centre around Praça da República is fairly lively, the atmosphere in the town near the ducal palace and the old quarter is more like that of a museum-city, evoking the sumptuous past of the Bragança family.

North of the town is a huge park of 2 000ha/4 950 acres which was formerly the Bragança hunt.

Only a few miles away, on 17 June 1665, the Battle of Montes Claros was fought, which confirmed Portugal's independence from Spain.

The ducal court – It was as early as the 15C that the second Duke of Bragança, Dom Fernando, chose Vila Viçosa as the residence of his court. The execution of the third duke, Dom Fernando *(see below)*, however, annihilated the ducal power and it was only in the following century that court life became really sumptuous.

In the palace, built by Duke Jaime, great seignorial festivals and princely marriages followed one after the other as did gargantuan banquets, theatrical performances and bullfights.

This golden age ended in 1640 when the eighth Duke of Bragança acceded to the throne of Portugal as Dom João IV.

The execution of the Duke of Bragança – On his succession to the throne in 1481, King João II instituted stern measures to abolish the privileges granted by his father, King Alfonso V, to the nobles who had taken part in the Reconquest.

The first to be brought low was the Duke of Brangança, brother-in-law of the king, the richest and most powerful nobleman in the land, and already guilty of plotting against the monarchy. After a summary trial, the duke was executed in Évora in 1483.

★TERREIRO DO PAÇO

Paço Ducal ⊙ – The Ducal Palace overlooks the Terreiro do Paço, in the centre of which stands a bronze statue of Dom João IV by Francisco Franco.

Tired of the discomfort of the old castle which dated from the time of King Dom Dinis, the fourth duke, Dom Jaime I, began the construction of the present palace in 1501. The plan consists of two wings at right angles, the main wing in white marble being 110m/311ft long.

The interior is now a museum. The well of the staircase to the first floor is adorned with wall paintings depicting the 15C Battle of Ceuta and the 16C Siege of Azamor by Duke Dom Jaime I.

Main wing – This wing is decorated with 17C *azulejos*, Brussels and Aubusson tapestries and Arraiolos carpets.

The rooms are embellished with finely painted ceilings representing a variety of subjects including David and Goliath, the adventures of Perseus, the Seven Virtues, etc. There are also portraits of the Braganças by the late 19C Portuguese painters Columbano, Malhoa and Sousa Pinto and (Sala dos Tudescos) in the Teutonic Hall, paintings by the 18C French artist Quillard.

The west face looks over a boxwood tree topiary.

Transverse wing – The wing comprises the apartments of King Carlos I (1863-1908), who was a talented painter and draughtsman, and Queen Amelia. There is an interesting 16C triptych attributed to Cristovão de Figueiredo illustrating scenes from the Calvary in the chapel.

The 16C Manueline style cloisters are beautifully cool.

★ **Museu dos Coches** – The collection complements that of the Museu Nacional dos Coches in Lisbon.

More than 70 coaches, four-wheelers and carriages dating from the 18 to the 20C are displayed in four buildings including the **Royal Stables★** built at the request of King José I in 1752. The stables, with room for hundreds of horses, are 70m/230ft long with a vaulted roof resting on marble pillars.

Among the carriages, note number 29, the landau in which Dom Carlos I and his son were assassinated on 1 February, 1908. The condition and the variety of exhibits are outstanding; there are mail coaches, charabancs, phaetons, landaus, four-wheelers and state carriages.

On leaving the museum the "Knot Gate" *(see facing page)* stands beside the Lisbon road.

★Porta dos Nós – The so-called Knot Gate is one of the last remains of the 16C perimeter wall. The House of Bragança, whose motto was *Despois vós, nós* (After you, us), chose knots as emblems on account of the two meanings of the word *nós* (us or we and knots).

Return to the Terreiro do Paço.

Convento dos Agostinhos – The church, which was rebuilt in the 17C by the future Dom João IV, stands at the east end of the Terreiro do Paço and is now the mausoleum of the dukes of Bragança. Bays in the chancel and the transept contain the veined white marble ducal tombs.

Antigo Convento das Chagas – The building on the south side of the Terreiro do Paço was founded by Joana de Mendonça, the second wife of Duke Dom Jaime I. The walls of the church, which serves as the mausoleum for the duchesses of Bragança, are covered in *azulejos* dating from 1626.

Porta dos Nós

OLD TOWN (VILA VELHA)

Leave the car outside the ramparts.

The castle and ramparts built at the end of the 13C on the order of King Dinis were reinforced with bastions in the 17C. The crenellated walls flanked with towers still gird the old town.

Enter through a gateway cut into the ramparts. The alleys are lined with whitewashed houses, their lower sections painted with bright colours. A narrow street leads to the western glacis on which stand the **Igreja da Conceição** and a 16C **pillory** *(pelourinho)*.

Castelo – The castle, which has been modified since the earliest parts were built in the 13C, is surrounded by a deep moat. The tour includes the original building's dungeons.

An archaeological museum, **Museu Arqueológico** ⊘, on the first floor, displays a collection of Greek vases.

The sentry path affords views of the old town.

VISEU★

Viseu – Population 21 454
Michelin map 940 or 441 K6

The town of Viseu has developed in the region of the famous Dão vineyards in a wooded and somewhat hilly area on the south bank of the Pavia, a tributary of the Mondego.

It is an important centre of agriculture (rye, maize, cattle and fruit) and crafts (lace, carpets, basketmaking and black clay pottery).

Its egg sweetmeats *(bolos de amor, papos de anjo, travesseiros de ovos moles, castanhas de ovos)* are a speciality.

Viseu School of Painting – Viseu, like Lisbon, had a flourishing school of painting in the 16C. It was led by two masters, Vasco Fernandes and Gaspar Vaz, in their turn greatly influenced by Flemish artists such as Van Eyck and Quentin Metsys.

Gaspar Vaz, who died about 1568, developed his style at the Lisbon School. He was gifted with a brilliant imagination and knew how to give great intensity of expression to forms and draped figures. The landscapes he painted keep their regional flavour, nevertheless.

His principal works, still showing considerable Gothic influence, hang in the Igreja de São João de Tarouca.

The early works of **Vasco Fernandes** (1480-*c*1543), to whom legend has given the name of Grão Vasco – Great Vasco – reveal Flemish influence (altarpieces at Lamego – in the regional museum – and Freixo de Espada-à-Cinta). His later work showed more originality, a distinct sense of the dramatic and of composition, a richness of colour and a violent realism inspired by popular and local subjects particularly in his portraits and landscapes. His principal works are in the Viseu museum.

The two masters probably collaborated in the creation of the polyptych in Viseu cathedral, which would explain its hybrid character.

★OLD TOWN (CIDADE VELHA) *2hr*

Follow the route marked on the plan starting at Praça da República.

Old Viseu has all the attraction of an ancient town with narrow alleys paved with granite sets and Renaissance and classical corbelled houses emblazoned with coats of arms.

Praça da República (or Rossio) (33) – Facing the town hall, this pleasant tree planted square is the town's lively centre.

Porta do Soar – Go through this gate built in the town wall by King Dom Afonso in the 15C to enter the old town.

★**Adro da Sé (36)** – The peaceful cathedral square in the heart of the old town is lined with noble granite buildings: the Museu de Grão Vasco, the cathedral and the Igreja da Misericórdia.

★★ **Museu Grão Vasco** ⊘ (**M¹**) – The museum is the former Palácio dos Três Escalões, which was built in the 16C and remodelled in the 18C.

The ground floor is devoted to 13-18C sculpture. Outstanding are the 14C **Throne of Grace**★ of which only a representation of God the Father remains, and the 13C *Pietà*; some 16C Spanish-Arabic *azulejos* and Portuguese porcelain (17 and 18C) are also interesting.

On the first floor are works by Portuguese painters of the 19 and early 20C.

With the exception of one room which contains paintings by **Columbano** (1857-1929) including a self-portrait, the second floor is devoted to the **Primitives**★★ of the Viseu School. Particularly noteworthy is the painting of **St Peter on his Throne**, one of Vasco Fernandes's masterpieces. While it is a copy of the one in São João de Tarouca attributed to Gaspar Vaz, it shows great originality in the portraiture of St Peter who, set against a Renaissance background, has a coarse, serious face wih a rather sad expression. Another major work by Grão Vasco is the **Calvary** in which the figures in the windswept landscape are depicted with forceful violence. The fourteen paintings, which comprise the altarpiece which stood formerly in the cathedral, are by a group of artists from the Viseu School: the *Descent from the Cross* and the *Kiss of Judas* are among the best. In the *Adoration of the Magi*, the Black King has been replaced by an Indian from Brazil, as the country had just been discovered by Pedro Álvares Cabral in 1500.

Museu Nacional Grão Vasco – J. Pessoa/ANF-IPM

St Peter by Grão Vasco

VISEU

Andrades (Rua dos) 4
Comércio (Rua do)............. 10
Direita (Rua)...................... 13
Formosa (Rua) 21
Fran. Alex. Lobo (Rua.)...... 22

Alexandre Herculano (Rua) 3
Arvore (Rua da) 6
Augusto Hilário (Rua)......... 7
Chão do Mestre (Rua)........ 9
Conselheiro Macedo (Rua) 12
Dom Duarte (Rua)............... 15
Dr M. de Aragão (Rua) 16
Emídio Navarro (Avenida)... 18
Escura (Rua)...................... 19
G. Barreiros (Rua) 24
Gen. Humberto Delgado
   (Largo) 25
Hospital (Rua do).............. 27
Infante D. Henrique
   (Avenida) 28
Maj. Leop. da Silva (Rua)... 30
Nunes de Carvalho (Rua)... 31
República (Praça da).......... 33
São Lázaro (Rua)................ 34
Sé (Adro da)...................... 36
Senhora da Piedade (Rua da) 37
Vigia (Calçada da) 39
Vitória (Rua da) 40

A Torre de Menagem
M¹ Museu de Grão Vasco

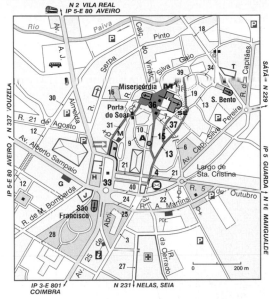

Also from the Viseu School are *The Last Supper* and *Christ in the House of Martha*.

★**Sé** – This Romanesque church was considerably remodelled between the 16 and 18C.

The façade was rebuilt in the 17C, the central statue among the six which ornament the façade is of São Teotónio, patron saint of Viseu.

Inside, the reconstruction of the Manueline vaulting in the 16C transformed the edifice into a hall church.

The roof, which rests on Gothic pillars, is supported by twisted **liernes**★ which form knots at regular intervals; the keystones are decorated with the arms of the founder bishop and the royal mottos of Afonso V and João II (the latter's symbol is a pelican). The chancel is 17C; the barrel vaulting shelters a monumental baroque **altarpiece**★ of gilded wood; above the high altar is a 14C Virgin carved in Ança stone. The north chapel is decorated with *azulejos* dating from the 18C.

Stairs lead from the north transept to the gallery *(coro alto)* where there is a wooden lectern brought from Brazil in the 16C and an amusing statue of an angel musician. Go to the first floor of the cloisters where the chapter house contains a **treasury of sacred art** ⊙ (Tesouro de Arte Sacra) including two 13C Limoges enamel reliquary caskets, a 12C Gospel in a 14C binding and a crib by Machado de Castro. The **cloisters** are Renaissance. The ground level gallery, where the arches rest on Ionic columns, is decorated with 18C *azulejos*. In the Chapel of Our Lady of Mercy there is a fine 16C low relief of the Descent from the Cross which is said to be by the Coimbra School.

A beautiful doorway in the transitional Gothic style leads from the cloisters back into the cathedral.

Igreja da Misericórdia – This baroque building has an attractive rhythmic façade in contrast to its white walls and grey granite pilasters.

The central section, focused beneath an elegant pediment, is pierced by a pretty baroque doorway surmounted by a balcony.

Old Houses (Casas Antigas) – The following are worthly of note: in the **Rua Dom Duarte** (**15**) a keep (Torre de Menagem) (**A**), embellished with a lovely Manueline window; in the picturesque narrow, bustling **Rua Direita** (**13**), 18C houses with balconies supported on wrought iron brackets; in the **Rua dos Andrades** (**4**) (south of the Rua Direita), corbelled houses; and in the **Rua da Senhora da Piedade** (**37**), houses built in the 16C.

Take the Rua Direita before returning to Praça da Sé via Rua Escura.

ADDITIONAL SIGHTS

Igreja de São Francisco – St Francis's is a baroque church ornamented with *azulejos* and gilded wood.

Igreja de São Bento – The church has beautiful 17C **azulejos**★.

Consult the key on p 4
to interpret all the information provided on town plans.

Madeira landscape: Paúl do Mar

Madeira
and the Azores

The Madeira Archipelago

The Madeira Archipelago consists of the main island which has the greatest area (740km²/286sq mi) and the largest population (254 880), the island of Porto Santo (42km²/16sq mi), lying 40km/25mi to the northeast, and two groups of uninhabited islands, the Ilhas Desertas or Empty Isles, 20km/12mi from Funchal and the Ihlas Selvagens or Wild Isles, situated near the Canaries, 240km/150mi away.

A HOLIDAY IN MADEIRA

Access by air – There are direct flights twice a week from the UK and daily flights from Lisbon *(see Practical Information for connections between London and Lisbon, and the USA and Lisbon)* to Funchal Airport, Madeira and from Funchal to Porto Santo.

When to go? – The temperature is mild throughout the year with an average of 16°C/61°F in January and 22°C/72°F in July. Rain falls in March, April and October.

To choose a hotel or restaurant in Madeira, consult the current *Michelin Red Guide España Portugal*. Funchal has most of Madeira's hotels although Machico near the airport is an alternative for places to stay as is the island of Porto Santo. Other hotel or boarding house accommodation is dotted about Madeira island in Santana, Porto Moniz, São Vicente and Ribeira Brava. There are also two *pousadas* – Pico Arieiro and Vinháticos – in the heart of the countryside.

Madeira by car – Madeira has spectacular landscapes which may be explored from the places to stay mentioned above by following the routes described hereafter. Taxis may be used for short distances and cars hired for longer ones. There are also many regular bus services.

Madeira on foot – Madeira is becoming increasingly popular with ramblers who have a wide choice of walks. Some paths follow the *levada* network, while others take mountain routes around Pico Ruivo. The paths are rated according to difficulty. The Direcção Regional de Turismo runs several mountain huts but they are not open all year and have to be booked in advance. Some of the walks including Pico Ruivo, Balcões, Levada do Norte to Estreito do Lobos, and Rabaçal are described in this guide.

For ramblers, we recommend the tourist map of Madeira available on the island and the book, *Landscapes of Madeira*, by John and Pat Underwood.

Flowers – Madeira attracts flower enthusiasts, one of the reasons for its popularity with the English. There are a great many botanical gardens and parks, particularly around Funchal, including Quinta das Cruces in Funchal and Quinta do Palheiro Ferreiro in the environs.

Beaches – Madeira island itself has practically no beaches so swimmers have to make do with swimming pools which are sometimes salt water. The island of Porto Santo, however, has Portugal's most beautiful beach – 8km/5mi of white sand with an ideal temperature for most of the year. The water is a little cool in winter.

Other sports – These include golf at the Campo da Serra and Campo de Peleiro clubs, angling and deep-sea fishing.

MADEIRA★★★

Madeira stands out in the Atlantic Ocean, a volcanic island mass rising high above the ocean swell.
The "pearl of the Atlantic", 900km/559mi from Lisbon, offers tourists a climate which is mild as well as vegetation which is subtropical and transforms the island into a blossoming garden all year round, and a landscape, beautiful and varied, which opens out into vast panoramas.

HISTORICAL AND GEOGRAPHICAL NOTES

Discovery and colonisation – The discovery of Madeira marks the beginning of the first period in the era of the Great Portuguese Discoveries. In 1419, **João Gonçalves Zarco** and Tristão Vaz Teixeira, leaders of an expedition dispatched by Prince Henry the Navigator, landed first on the island of Porto Santo, after having been diverted by a storm and later on Madeira itself in what was later known as Machico Bay. The island appeared to be uninhabited and entirely covered in woodland and they, therefore, named it the wooded island, *a ilha da madeira*.
The navigators reported their discovery to Prince Henry, who commanded them to return the following year to proceed with its colonisation and settlement.
The prince divided the territory into three *captaincies*: Zarco received the land centred on Funchal and extending south of an imaginary line drawn from Ponta do Oliveira to Ponta do Tristão; Tristão Vaz Teixeira received Machico and all the rest of the island and **Bartolomeu Perestrelo** the neighbouring island of Porto Santo. Shortly after the lieutenants had become established Prince Henry made their titles hereditary but in 1497, to avoid further abuses which the explorers' heirs were making of their authority, the islands were restored to the Crown.

Terrace farming

MADEIRA

In the early 19C during the period of the Napoleonic Wars the island of Madeira was twice occupied by British troops, first in 1801 and later from 1807 to 1814. A few years after Portugal became a Republic in 1902, the archipelago achieved internal self government under the Statute of Neighbouring Islands.

Volcanic character – Madeira, together with Porto Santo and the Desertas, rose from the bed of the Atlantic during a period of volcanic eruption in the Tertiary Era. It is divided from the Selvagens and Canary Islands and the continent of Africa by an ocean bed some 2 000m/6 000ft deep and a marine trough which reaches a depth in places of 4 512m/14 804ft. Later underwater upcasts and convulsions accentuated the geological development of the island. The island's volcanic origin is also visibly confirmed in the Curral das Freiras crater where the principal heights in Madeira's central relief are to be found; the several lakes and volcanic craters and the prismatic basalt piles bordering the valleys and coastline also confirm this theory.

Erosion has modified the relief: streams have created steep-sided valleys, waves have bitten into the cliffs, wearing them away to shingle.

A turbulent landscape – Madeira is an island of escarpments, outcrops and a mountain chain of over 1 200m/3 950ft culminating in high peaks such as Pico Ruivo (1 862m/6 109ft). The chain crosses the island from Ponta de S. Lourenço to Ponta do Tristão, dropping to 1 007m/3 304ft at its centre at the Encumeada Pass from which several minor formations radiate. The island is thus divided into two distinct sectors. One presents a wild and turbulent landscape where high peaks abut deep precipices at whose feet torrents *(ribeiras)* follow courses through to the sea. The only flat area is the Paúl de Serra, a desert-like and inhospitable plateau extending for some 20km²/8sq mi at a height of 1 400m/4 593ft in the centre of the island, which is only inhabited by grazing sheep.

The rock and cliff-lined shore is broken at frequent intervals by estuaries where small fishing villages have become established. The rare beaches which exist are of pebbles. The only sandy beach is at Praínha, to the east of Machico.

A privileged climate – Madeira, which is almost at the same latitude as Casablanca, on the whole enjoys a temperate climate. Mild and with no extremes, the mean temperature only varies from 16° to 21°C/61° to 70° F from winter to summer. The weather is best on the south coast, which is well protected from the northerly and northeasterly winds by the mountains: rain is scarce and when it falls, does so in downpours in March, April and October; the summer is very dry. The temperature of the water varies between 18° and 20°C/64° and 68°F and so makes bathing pleasant almost every season of the year. Apart from occasional sea mists the light is excellent.

Inland, where the land rises, has lower and less stable temperatures. Clouds formed by seawater evaporation collect round the peaks, keeping the air cool and producing considerable humidity in the mountainous regions which are transformed by the abundant spring and autumn rains into the island's watershed.

A luxuriant vegetation – The climate and relief of Madeira combine to produce three distinct vegetation zones. The subtropical area which extends from sea level to about 300m/1 000ft includes the north and south coasts where sugar cane, bananas and some vegetables are grown – Barbary figs have invaded all the non-irrigated areas along the south coast. The area from 300 to 750m/1 000 to 2 500ft is the warm, temperate or Mediterranean zone where vines and cereals such as maize, wheat and oats all flourish.

European and tropical fruits grow well: oranges, pears, apples, mangoes.

The area from 750 to 1 300m/2 500 to 4 300ft is an ancient forest zone, which dates back to the Tertiary Era and is known as **Laurissilva**. The forest once covered part of Europe but was destroyed by glaciation; these islands are the only places where it has been preserved. It consists of many endemic species such as the til *(Oreodaphne jetens)*, sesame, vinhático, heaths and tree laurels. The forest cover plays an essential part in protecting the ground against erosion, as well as ensuring the harnessing and permeation of rainwater. Among the crests, over 1 300m/4 300ft, there are pastures and bracken. In order to preserve this vast natural heritage, more than two-thirds of the surface area of the island has been converted into a nature reserve.

Flowers – The whole island of Madeira is a mass of flowers; every hillside, every garden and roadside verge is covered with hydrangeas, geraniums, hibiscus, agapanthus, bougainvilleas, fuchsias and euphorbias. Certain species such as orchids, anthuriums and strelitzias (or Birds of Paradise) are grown in large quantities for export. There are also several species of flowering trees – mimosas, magnolias, sumaumás and jacarandas.

Population of Madeira – Other settlers followed the Portuguese colonists to the island; these included Jews, Moors, and African slaves to work in the sugar cane plantations. In the 18C the English also came to settle. In spite of the island's fertility and the intensive cultivation Madeira does not have sufficient land to provide for all her inhabitants. The density of population (presently 350 inhabitants per square kilometre) forces many of its younger generation to make their homes abroad, mainly in Brazil, Venezuela and Canada.

Rouxaime/JACANA

Agapanthus

M. Viard/JACANA

Mimosa

F. Lieutier/JACANA

Orchid

R. Konig/JACANA

Strelitzia

S. Fiore/JACANA

Hibiscus

G. Laurent/JACANA

Magnolia

Rouxaime/JACANA

Anthurium

Terraces and levadas – To clear the soil the early colonists set fire to the forests; this fire, it is said, burned for seven years, sparing a few areas of original forest. Once cleared, the land had to be brought under cultivation. The peasants hauled earth in hods on their backs (for no draught animals have ever been able to acclimatise to the island) to build the **poios** or terraces into the hillsides which now give the island its characteristic appearance. The minute parcels of earth are not ploughed but hoed. Madeira's agricultural prosperity, however, is due to irrigation. The island is an enormous natural reservoir; rainwater seeps through the volcanic ash to the impermeable layer of laterite and basalt where it collects, forming subterranean reserves of water from which springs rise. From a very early stage, the peasants began channelling water from these springs, creating a network of irrigation furrows known as **levadas**. In 1900 the network was 1 000km/621mi long; it has since more than doubled. In 1939 the Portuguese government developed a scheme for irrigation and hydroelectricity. Water is harnessed at an altitude of 1 000m/3 300ft, channelled to hydroelectric power stations and thence to the fields where it is redistributed by supervisors known as *levadeiros*. The allocation system, whereby lifegiving water from the peaks is brought to the fields in the less favoured areas near the coast, is governed by strict laws. The construction of the *levadas*, when one considers the relative lack of technical knowledge and equipment, represents a prodigious undertaking, for these aqueducts and tunnels have been made to follow the contour lines as naturally as possible. Where they cling to the rock face over breathtaking drops, the men who built them did so from wickerwork baskets suspended in mid-air. Among the main *levadas* are the Levada do Norte, Levada dos Tornos and Levada do Furado.

Maintenance paths run alongside the *levadas* giving ramblers a wonderful opportunity to see the island's magnificent landscape.

Crops and cultivation – Sugar cane was imported from Sicily in 1492. An export market for sugar developed to Castile, England and Flanders but in the 16C was exposed to competition from Brazil and so Madeira turned to wine-making (*see below*).

Today, one of the island's main crops is the banana. Most of the banana plantations are on the south coast around Ribeira Brava.

Madeira wine – The cultivation of vineyards was introduced to Madeira in the 15C. The stock, which was imported from Crete and planted in the rich and sunny volcanic soil along the south coast, produced a good quality wine, later famous in England as Malmsey. Madeira wine acquired a certain prestige in Europe: the Duke of Clarence drowned in a butt of Malmsey, François I (King of France, 1515-47) offered it to his guests and later Admiral Lord Nelson was known to be partial to it.

In 1660 the commercial treaty between England and Portugal encouraged the export of the wine and increased production. Overseas buyers, for the most part English (Blandy, Leacock and Cossart Gordon), were drawn to Madeira by the prosperous trade which reached its height in the 18 and 19C.

In 1852 the vines were decimated by phylloxera. A few Englishmen, including Charles Blandy, were determined to re-establish the vineyards. In 1872 Thomas Leacock succeeded in overcoming the blight which had attacked the renewed vineyards.

There are three principal wines. **Sercial**, made from grapes whose vines originally came from the Rhine valley, is a dry wine with a good bouquet; it is amber in colour and is served chilled and drunk as an aperitif. **Boal** originates from Burgundy; the rich, full-bodied flavour of this red-brown wine makes it primarily a dessert wine. **Malmsey**, the most famous, is rare today; again a dessert wine, honeyed in flavour with a deep red, almost purple colour.

A medium sweet all-purpose wine, **Verdelho**, a Muscatel and *Tinto* or red wine are also produced.

The grape harvest begins at the end of August. The bunches of grapes are brought to the press and from there the juice is transported to Funchal. This was traditionally done by men known as *borracheiros*, carrying skin bottles on their backs, each with a capacity of at least 40 litres/9 gallons. As the wine ferments in the cask various processes are performed: it is fortified with small amounts of alcohol, clarified with the aid of egg whites or isinglass and submitted to heat. This last operation known as *estufagem* or heating, the most notable characteristic of the Madeira method, consists in stocking the wine in barrels and casks for at least three months in cellars heated to a temperature of 45°C/113°F. The maturing period then follows. The properties of heat with regard to wine were discovered during sea voyages to the tropics in the 18C.

At one time, barrels of Madeira were used as ballast in ships making the long journey to India or America; the trip there and back gave the wine ample time to heat.

Vintage Madeira made from the best wines in exceptionally good years may be consumed up to and over 150 years later. There is a story which tells how Napoleon put in to Madeira on his way to St Helena in 1815 and was given a cask of wine by the British Consul. On the emperor's death, the consul reclaimed the cask, which had not been broached, and bottled the contents. More than a century later, in 1936, an Englishman was able to boast that he had enjoyed the emperor's wine, by then some hundred and twenty years old.

Madeira embroidery – Embroidery is one of the mainstays of the island's economy. Madeira embroidery owes its origin to an Englishwoman. In 1856 **Miss Phelps**, the daughter of a wine importer, started a workroom where she set women to embroider designs after the manner of *broderie anglaise*. The work was sold for charity. Samples of the embroidery reached London and were received with such enthusiasm that Miss Phelps decided in future to sell the work abroad. In less than a century embroidery became one of Madeira's major resources; today 30 000 women are employed, sewing, usually in the open air – although there are a few workshops in Funchal. The embroidery on linen, lawn or organdie is very fine and very varied in design.

ART

Art in Madeira is almost entirely religious. The churches with their treasures constitute the major part of the island's artistic heritage.

With the arrival of the first colonists, the island began to be scattered with churches and chapels built in the Portuguese eccleslastical style. Prosperity brought artistic riches, commercial exchanges increased and, through contact with Flanders, Flemish art reached Madeira. Thanks to the gifts and bequests of rich merchants, of Knights of the Order of Christ, of King Manuel I, and of the captains and their descendants between whom the island had been divided, the churches became even more important artistically. The interiors, in contrast to the façades which often continued to be built with a certain austerity of style, were adorned with altarpieces and triptychs brought from Antwerp, Lisbon or Venice in exchange for cargoes of sugar. The benefactors are frequently represented within the churches.

Architectural styles reached Madeira only after some delay and their evolution was also slower than on the Portuguese mainland. The earliest churches are Romanesque, Gothic or Manueline. In the 17 and 18C their interiors were over-embellished with baroque ornament while the majority of new churches erected were almost entirely in the baroque style.

Their white façades, although often influenced by the Italian Renaissance, remain somewhat restrained except where the details are outlined in black basalt scrollwork. Usually a doorway surmounted by a semicircular arch and a window pierces the face, which is always flanked by one or two square belfries topped by a pyramid shaped roof, covered, in the traditional manner, with faience tiles. The main door is lined by an inner door, a *paravent*, made of precious woods and marquetry.

Inside, the single naves are roofed with barrel vaulting, baroque frescoes being painted directly on to the wood. The altarpieces have a striking exuberance; a profusion of pictures, of which many are of interest, still hang upon the walls and lovely filigree silver lamps can usually be seen adorning the chancels; finally the sacristy is often a fine chamber containing a vestment cupboard and a beautiful baroque fountain.

The palace of the counts of Carvalhal, now the Funchal town hall, and the town hall in Santa Cruz are elegant examples of the island's domestic architecture.

FOOD

Fare in restaurants includes meat grilled on skewers *(espetadas)*, cinnamon spiced roasts, tunny steaks *(bifes)*, fried corn and, for dessert, honey cakes and delicious fruits.

★★FUNCHAL Population 48 239

The island's capital rises in tiers of white houses up the open slopes of a vast amphitheatre around a beautiful bay. The summits of the encircling green hills overlooking the town are often wrapped in mist and cloud. When the early settlers arrived they found the heights covered in wild fennel, hence the name Funchal meaning fennel garden.

The remarkable setting, the luxuriant vegetation, the *quintas*, hotels, nightlife and sports facilities (swimming, tennis, water-skiing and fishing), combine to form a popular city resort, attracting visitors from many countries year round.

Funchal is also a busy outlet for the island's main products. The commercial harbour is recognisable at a distance by its long breakwater, the **pontinha** (**BZ**), which was built in the late 18C to link an islet to the main island and has since been lengthened twice. It plays an important role since most of the goods arriving in Madeira come by sea. It also serves as a mooring quay for cruise ships. The pleasure boat harbour faces central Funchal where shops, government services and most of the town's historical monuments may be found. East of this quarter stretch the alleyways of the old town. The area to the west towards Câmara do Lobos with its large modern hotels, caters to tourists, while Funchal's residents tend to live in the higher part of town. There is a brilliant firework display each year at midnight on 31 December.

Zarco and the founding of Funchal – João Gonçalves Zarco, born in Tomar of humble origin, abducted the daughter of a noble family whom he wished to marry. He sought the protection of the Infante, who took him into his service and invested him as a knight.

FUNCHAL

Alfândega (R. da) .... **BZ** 3
Aljube (R. do) .... **BZ** 4
Bettencourt (R. do) .... **CY** 9
Chafariz (Largo do) .... **CZ** 19
Dr Fernão de Ornelas (R.) .... **CZ** 28

João Tavira (R.) .... **BZ** 39
Phelps (Largo do) .... **CY** 58
Pretas (R.das) .... **BY** 61
Aranhas (R. dos) .... **ABZ** 6
Autonomia (Pr. da) .... **CZ** 7
Brigadeiro Oudinot
  (R.) .... **CY** 10

Carne Azeda (R. da) .... **BY** 12
Carvalho Araújo (R.) .... **AZ** 15
Conceição (R. da) .... **CY** 22
Conselheiro
  Aires Ornelas (R.) .... **CY** 24
Conselheiro
  José Silvestre Ribeiro (R.).. **BZ** 25
Encarnação (Calç. da) .... **BY** 30

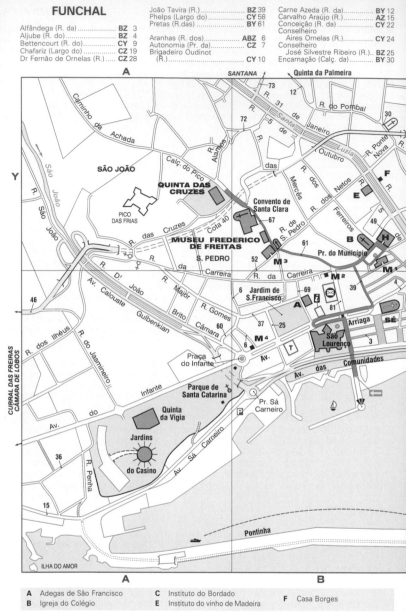

A Adegas de São Francisco
B Igreja do Colégio
C Instituto do Bordado
E Instituto do vinho de Madeira
F Casa Borges

Zarco distinguished himself by his courage at the Battle of Tangier and in the capture of Ceuta when he was struck in the eye by an arrow. He joined Tristão Vaz Teixeira in the discovery of Madeira and the following year returned to the island to settle with his family in Funchal, remaining there as ruler for more than forty years until his death (1467). On this site, at the meeting of three river mouths, he drew the plan for the town and gave out land to the colonists to farm. In 1508 King Manuel granted a charter to the town which had by then grown prosperous from its sugar trade (the town's crest includes four sugar loaves).

The centre

Follow the itinerary indicated on the town plan.

Avenida das Comunidades Madeirenses or Avenida do Mar (BCZ) – This wide promenade bordered with flowers runs parallel to the shore and the marina. Stretching along the quayside below the avenue is a row of restaurants and cafés, one of which is established on a boat that belonged to the Beatles.
There is a fine **view★** of the town from the end of the jetty.

Avenida Arriaga (BZ) – This is Funchal's main street. The jacaranda trees along it are covered in purple flowers throughout the spring. The **Jardim Público de São Francisco** is an interesting botanical garden with a wide variety of plants. Between the

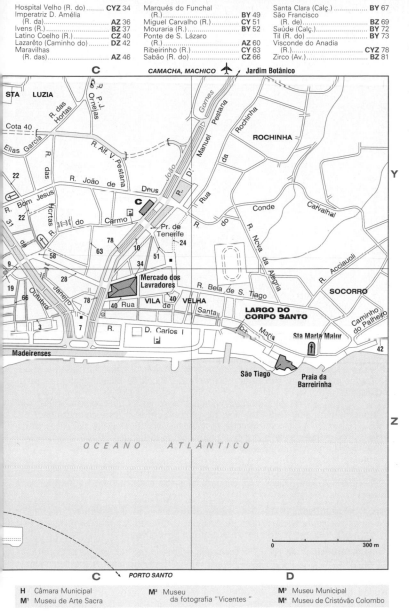

Hospital Velho (R. do) .... **CYZ** 34	Marqués do Funchal	Santa Clara (Calç.) .... **BY** 67
Imperatriz D. Amélia	(R.) .... **BY** 49	São Francisco
(R. da) .... **AZ** 36	Miguel Carvalho (R.) .... **CY** 51	(R. de) .... **BZ** 69
Ivens (R.) .... **BZ** 37	Mouraria (R.) .... **BY** 52	Saúde (Calç.) .... **BY** 72
Latino Coelho (R.) .... **CZ** 40	Ponte de S. Lázaro	Til (R. do) .... **BY** 73
Lazarêto (Caminho do) .... **DZ** 42	(R.) .... **AZ** 60	Visconde do Anadia
Maravilhas	Ribeirinho (R.) .... **CY** 63	(R.) .... **CYZ** 78
(R. das) .... **AZ** 46	Sabão (R. do) .... **CZ** 66	Zirco (Av.) .... **BZ** 81

The Madeira Archipelago

H Câmara Municipal	**M²** Museu
M¹ Museu de Arte Sacra	da fotografia "Vicentes"
	M³ Museu Municipal
	M⁴ Museu de Cristóvão Colombo

garden and the tourist information centre (Turismo) are the cellars, **Adegas de São Francisco**★ ⊘ (**BZ A**), the oldest in Funchal. They are housed in a former Franciscan monastery dating from the 16C. The tour, which includes the cooper workshop, the cellars in which the precious wine is aged and a small museum, finishes with a free wine-tasting.

Opposite the cellars is **Forte de São Lourenço**, which is still occupied by the army and serves as residence to the Commandant of Madeira.

★**Sé** (**BZ**) – This cathedral, which was built by Knights of the Order of Christ at the end of the 15C, was the first Portuguese cathedral to be constructed overseas.

The style is Manueline; the façade is plain, the white rough stucco being relieved by black basalt and red tufa rock. The apse, decorated with openwork balustrades and twisted pinnacles, is flanked by a crenellated square belfry the roof of which, pyramid in shape, is tiled with *azulejos*.

In the nave, slender columns support arcades of painted lava rock while above, and also over the transept, extends a remarkable *artesonado* **ceiling**★ in which ivory inlays in the cedar wood have been used to emphasise the stylistic motifs.

The stalls which adorn the chancel date from the 17C but are, nevertheless, Manueline in style. On the upper part, set against a blue background, are gilded statues of Apostles, Doctors of the Church and saints which bear a primitive stamp. The

Y. Travert/DIAF

View of Funchal port

cheekpieces are ornamented with interesting caricatures carved in sesame wood: grotesque animals and people add a humorous touch to Biblical, satiric or fabulous scenes.

An attractive 16C retable adorned with paintings from the Flemish school surmounts the high altar. Note the delicate vaulting crowning the composition.

To the right of the chancel, the chapel dedicated to the Holy Sacrament is worth a visit. The chapel's style is decidedly baroque as evidenced by the abundance of gilded wood and marble throughout.

The pulpit and font are crafted from Arrábida marble.

The visit of the cathedral can be concluded with a look at the small market to the rear of the cathedral where local vendors display a colourful and fragrant array of flowers.

Praça do Município (BY) – The square is bordered to the south by the former episcopal palace, now the Museu de Arte Sacra (Sacred Art Museum), to the east by the town hall and to the north by the former college.

Câmara Municipal (BY H) – The town hall, formerly the 18C palace of Count Carvalhal, is surmounted by a tower which still proudly dominates the surrounding houses. The inner courtyard is decorated with *azulejos*.

Museu de Arte Sacra ⊘ **(BY M¹)** – The Museum of Sacred Art is housed in the former episcopal palace which has a beautiful arcaded gallery overlooking the square. It contains fine religious items and liturgical ornaments but its main interest lies in a collection of **paintings★** on wood from the 15 and 16C Portuguese and Flemish Schools. From the Portuguese School, note the triptych depicting *St James and St Philip* between the donors of the painting (an *Annunciation* can be seen on the back). Among paintings from the Flemish School are a *Descent from the Cross* attributed to Gérard David, in which the figures show great nobility in bearing; a full-length portrait of *St James the Less*, patron of Funchal, in a red toga, attributed to Thierry Bouts; a surprisingly realistic portrayal of *Mary Magdalene*, standing sumptuously robed before a magnificent landscape; a triptych attributed to Quentin Metys of *St Peter* in a sumptuous red mantle; an *Annunciation*, a portrait of *Bishop St Nicholas*, a *Meeting between St Anne and St Joachim*, a *Crucifixion* which is full of movement, and an *Adoration of the Magi*, a beautiful composition by the Antwerp School from the church at Machico.

Igreja do Colégio (BY B) – The Church of St John the Evangelist, which abuts on a monastery now converted into a university, was built early in the 17C in the Jesuit style.

The austere white façade, which is pierced by numerous windows with black surrounds, has also been hollowed out to form four statuary niches. These contain marble figures on the upper level of St Ignatius and St Francis Xavier, and on the lower of St Francis Borgia and St Stanislas.

The nave, paved with *azulejos*, is superabundantly decorated with exuberant baroque altars ornamented with bunches of grapes.

The sacristy to the left of the chancel is an elegant room with a fine ceiling with painted squinches, a frieze of *azulejos* and a magnificent vestment cupboard with gilt locks.

Museu da Fotografia "Vicentes" ⊘ (**BZ M²**) – Rising up at the far end of a patio which serves as a café-restaurant is a house façade reminiscent of those in New Orleans. This is the former mid-19C studio of Vincente Gomes da Silva, the first in a long line of photographers. Cameras and glass plates have been reverently preserved and the studio itself has been reconstituted with its original decor. The photos in the many albums displayed provide a wonderful testimony to life in Madeira during the 19C.

Museu Municipal ⊘ (**BY M³**) – The former mansion of Count Carvalhal now houses an aquarium and a natural history museum. The aquarium contains various sea creatures from the waters around Madeira, including red scorpion fish, mantis shrimps and morays. Among the natural history museum's many stuffed and mounted animals are some impressive sharks, horned rays and white-bellied seals.

★**Museu Frederico de Freitas** ⊘ (**BY**) – This large town house, the former mansion of Dr Frederico de Freitas, is divided into two museum sections. The first, the part that gives onto Calçada Santa Clara contains engravings, drawings and water-colours illustrating Madeira through the centuries.

The more intimate second part on the first floor shows the interior of a middle-class home in the 19C. Its English furniture has been preserved as have its 'sugar chest' cupboards *(see Quinta das Cruzes below)*, musical instruments and cabinets adorned with ivory and whalebone. The small patio with its plants and paving stones is a delightful haven of peace.

Convento de Santa Clara ⊘ (**BY**) – The convent was built in the 17C on the site of the church founded in the 15C by Zarco to provide a burial place for his family. His two granddaughters who founded the original convent of the Order of St Clare are buried here.

Inside the church, which was tiled between the 16 and 18C with *azulejos*, lying at the far end, is Zarco's Gothic tomb supported by lions.

★★**Quinta das Cruzes** ⊘ (**AY**) – Zarco's former mansion has been converted into a museum of decorative arts (Museu de Artes Decorativas).

On the ground floor, low-ceilinged rooms, which served formerly as wine stores, now contain 16C Portuguese furniture collected from private houses in Funchal. There are a great many cabinets – the most widely used type of furniture in the 17C – as well as cupboards and chests known as *caixa de açucar* or sugar chests made with wood taken from boxes in which Brazilian sugar was once transported. At the back of the last room stands a Flemish altarpiece of the Nativity dating from

Mercado dos Lavradores

the second half of the 15C. A glass case contains some of the treasure found in the wreck of a Dutch galleon from the East India Company that ran aground at Porto Santo in 1724.

The rooms on the first floor contain a rich collection of 18 and 19C English furniture in the Hepplewhite and Chippendale style.

The house stands in a botanical garden with kapok, dragon and monkey-puzzle trees. Orchids and a multitude of other types of flowers can be seen in a hot house. Part of the garden has been converted into an archaeological section with a small lapidary museum containing a piece of the Funchal pillory erected in the late 15C and demolished in 1835, as well as two beautiful Manueline windows.

Eastern Funchal

Mercado dos Lavradores (CZ) – This worker's market, which is now housed in a modern building, is particularly lively in the morning. At the entrance, flower sellers in traditional Madeiran costume (striped skirts, corselets and leather boots) sell bunches of flowers in myriad colours.

Baskets and stalls overflowing with fruit and vegetables ring the central patio. The liveliest section, however, is the fishmarket adorned with panels of *azulejos*.

Vila Velha (Old Town) (CDZ) – This is where the original town was founded in the 15C. Today, the narrow streets are lined with the homes of fishermen and craftsmen. There are a lot of taverns, bars and restaurants.

Igreja da Santa Maria Maior (DZ) – The church's elegant 18C baroque façade, with scrollwork of black lava rock standing out against the white roughcast, has a plain door. The Apostle St James the Less is honoured before this doorway each year on May Day in remembrance of the miracles of 1523 and 1538, when epidemics of the plague were dissipated.

Inside, note the painted barrel vaulting.

Barreirinha beach stretches out below the church.

Forte de São Tiago (DZ) – The fort was built in 1614. Its yellow walls rise above the shore where fishing boats lie moored beside small blue and white striped huts.

★**Largo do Corpo Santo (DZ)** – This delightful little square in front of Corpo Santo chapel is the heart of old Funchal. It comes alive at mealtimes when its fish restaurants begin to fill.

Instituto do Bordado ⊘ **(CY C)** – Several rooms in the embroidery institute have been converted into a museum where magnificent old examples of Madeiran workmanship are displayed.

Instituto do Vinho de Madeira ⊘ **(BY E)** – The institute, which was founded to promote Madeira wine, offers free wine-tastings. Opposite are the cellars of the Borges wine company, Casa Borges **(F)**.

Western Funchal

Jardins do Casino (AZ) – Funchal casino was built in 1979 by the Brazilian architect Óscar Niemeyer. Interestingly, it bears some resemblance to the cathedral in Brazil's capital, Brasilia. The casino stands in a park of beautiful exotic trees.

Quinta da Vigia (AZ) – The vast pink mansion between Casino Gardens and Santa Catarina Park is the headquarters of the Regional Government of Madeira.

Parque de Santa Catarina (AZ) – The park, which forms the setting for Santa Catarina chapel built by Zarco in 1425, overlooks Avenida das Comunidades Madeirenses and the harbour. It contains a statue to Christopher Columbus. A second statue, of Prince Henry the Navigator, beneath a large arch made of volcanic stone, can be seen on the way from the park towards Avenida Arriaga.

Museu Cristóvão Colombo ⊘ **(BZ M⁴)** – *Diogo, number 48 Avenida Arriaga.* Throughout his life Mário Barbeito de Vasconcellos (1905-85) pursued his passion for putting together a collection on Christopher Columbus. It consists of books, cartoons, engravings, maps etc. and one of the three copies of the **Psalterium★**, the first account of the discovery of the New World which appeared in 1516 and was written in Chaldean, Arabic, Hebrew and Greek.

Northern Funchal

★**Jardim Botânico** ⊘ – *Take Rua Dr Manuel Pestana* **(DY)** *towards the airport, then follow the signposts "Jardim Botânico".* The botanical gardens, where outstanding examples of Madeiran flora grow, have been laid out in terraces overlooking the *ribeira* valley in the grounds of the old Quinta de Bom Sucesso. The elegant white house with green shutters contains a small old style museum with wooden display cases showing botanical, geological and zoological collections; note the vulcanised wood.

From the topmost belvedere, there is a **view★** of Funchal harbour and immediately below of the terraced valley of Ribeira de João Gomes.

The Madeira Archipelago

Quinta da Palmeira – *Take Rua da Carne Azeda heading north (**BY**) then bear left on Rua da Levada de Santa Luzia. The entrance to the Quinta is just before a left bend; its name is in white shingle inlaid in the roadway. Although it is a private property one may walk in the gardens. Leave the car near the entrance gate.*
The terraces of the well kept park overlook Funchal. There are fine *azulejo* benches and a Gothic stone window. This window was formerly in the house in which, it is said, Christopher Columbus stayed when he lived in Funchal.

Excursions

★★**Quinta do Palheiro Ferreiro** ⊘ – *10km/6mi. Leave Funchal on Rua Dr Manuel Pestana (**DY**) towards the airport. Take the first road towards Camacha and after several bends turn right on a narrow cobbled road signposted Quinta do Palheiro Ferreiro. Go through the entrance gate to the quinta and follow the avenue of plane trees to a car park near the villa. Private property.*
The vast mansion is set in a well kept **park** approached by paths lined with camellias. There are over 3 000 plant species. The park is a pleasure to wander through, with its remarkable specimens of exotic trees and beds of rare flowers.

★★**Eira do Serrado and Curral das Freiras** – *Round trip of 34km/21mi. 2hr. Leave Funchal on Avenida do Infante.*
São Martinho – In São Martinho the parish church stands at the top of a "peak" 259m/850ft high.
As you come to the cemetery, turn right.

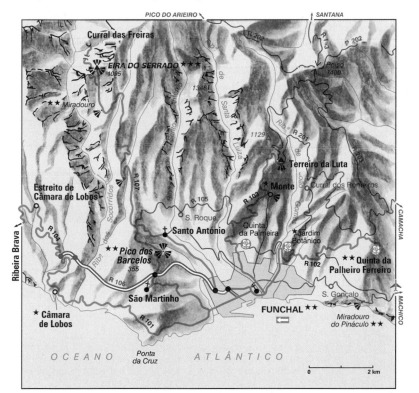

★★**Pico dos Barcelos** – The viewpoint (alt 355m/194ft), surrounded by aloes and masses of flowers, affords a panorama of Funchal set at the foot of the mountain ranges, the ragged outlines of which can be distinguished massed to the north. One can also see Santo António lying snugly in its valley and clustered round its village church, as well as São Martinho, the church of which stands out silhouetted against the sea.
Continue along the road towards Eira do Serrado.
Several kilometres further on, beyond a wood of eucalyptus trees, the road nears the Ribeira dos Socorridos – River of Survivors – named after the survivors who took refuge in its course when the island was set on fire. There is an impressive **sight**★ of the deep defile caused by a volcanic fracture through which the stream flows, and to the south, its opening to the sea and the few houses of Câmara de Lobos.

The road runs through pine and eucalyptus woods soon affording wide views of the valley. There is a magnificent **view**★★ from a point on the left, of the defile where the face has been cut into terraces for cultivation and where the occasional white house has been built.

A right fork takes you to Eira do Serrado where you leave the car.

★★★ **Eira do Serrado** – A path *(10min round trip on foot)* goes round the Pico do Serrado (1 095m/359ft) on the right to a viewpoint. The panorama is outstanding: the white houses of the village of Curral das Freiras lie scattered around mountain ravines.

Take the road which runs down to Curral das Freiras.

This road, which has taken the place of the old path which zigzagged down the steep hillsides, has been cut out of the completely vertical rock face and passes through two tunnels to reach the village.

Curral das Freiras – Curral das Freiras lies in an enclosed **setting**★ at the foot of a grandiose cirque of extinct volcanoes. It belonged to the sisters of the Convent of St Clare who took shelter here when French pirates pillaged Funchal in 1566. The event was commemorated in the name of the village, which in Portuguese means the "nuns' shelter". The church stands in a small square surrounded with cafés.

As you return uphill pause on leaving the village at a paved terrace on your left, to get an interesting **view**★ of the circle of mountain peaks.

Leave the Pico dos Barcelos road on your right as you enter Funchal.

Santo António – This is Funchal's smart residential quarter. It has an 18C baroque church.

Return to Funchal by Caminho de Santo António which drops rapidly into the town centre.

★ **Monte** – *7km/4mi. About 1hr.* Monte, at an altitude of nearly 600m/1 970ft, is a country resort much appreciated for its cool climate and rich vegetation. Enhancing the surroundings further are several *quintas*, in their lovely gardens. The Quinta do Monte, which lies below the former Belmonte Hotel, became the house of the last Emperor of Austria and his family when they went into exile and came to live on the island in 1921. Karl I died in the house the following year. His wife Empress Zita was the grand-niece of Dom Pedro IV.

Igreja de Nossa Senhora do Monte – The church rises from a hillock in the centre of a park. It was built on the site of a chapel erected in 1470 by Adam Gonçalves Ferreira, who with his twin sister, Eva, were the first children to be born on the island of Madeira. The façade with a baroque pediment, great windows and arcaded porch is highly decorative.

The church contains, in a chapel to the left of the nave, the iron tomb of Emperor Karl I of Austria. A tabernacle worked in silver above the high altar shelters a small cloaked statue of Our Lady of the Mountain, the patron saint of Madeira. The figure which was discovered in the 15C at Terreiro da Luta at the spot where the Virgin appeared to a young shepherdess, is the goal of a popular pilgrimage held on 14 and 15 August each year.

At the foot of the church stairway is the departure point for the traditional cane sledges or *carros de cesto*. Two men in white drive these toboggans at great speed down Caminho do Monte.

Walk down Largo dos Barbosas to the left of the staircase.

Largo dos Barbosas leads to a small square shaded by plane trees. It is overlooked by the chapel, **Capela de Nossa Senhora da Conceição**, which was built in the baroque style in 1906. From the square there is a view across the wooded valley of the Ribeira de João Gomes to the locality of Curral dos Romeiros.

Terreiro da Luta – *15km/9mi from Funchal and 2km/1mi from Monte.*
When the bombardment of Funchal by German submarines in 1917 ceased, the Bishop of Funchal made a vow to erect a monument to the Virgin, provided peace followed quickly.

The monument to Our Lady of Peace, completed in 1927, stands where Our Lady of the Mountain is said to have appeared. Encircling the monument are anchor chains from the torpedoed ships. There is a view of Funchal.

★ **From Funchal to Ribeira Brava via Cabo Girão** – *30km/19mi west. About 1hr. Leave Funchal on Avenida do Infante.*

★ **Câmara de Lobos** – Câmara de Lobos or Seals' House was so named on account of the great number of seals (*lobos marinhos* in Portuguese) on the shores when Zarco first arrived.

The picturesque town is built round a harbour well protected by two cliffs of volcanic rock. By walking westwards alongside the harbour one has an overall view of the town **setting★**. The white houses with their red tiled roofs stand scattered on terraces among banana-trees. Below, on the shingle beach, brilliantly coloured boats lie drawn up in the shade of palm and plane trees with their bizarre black nets suspended on willow frames to dry.

In the upper part of the town, a pergola ornamented viewpoint directly overlooks the shingle beach and, on the right, the Ribeiro do Vigário.

At the crossroads with the main road, overlooking the harbour, is the small terrace where Winston Churchill used to come to paint, when he visited the island in 1950.

Continue along the road.

Banana plantations give way to vineyards for the vine is virtually the only crop in the region of Estreito de Câmara do Lobos. Beneath the low vines vegetables are grown so as not to waste an inch of valuable land. Malmsey and Verdelho are made from the white grape; Tinto from the black. Above 500m/1 500ft in the Jardim da Serra region vines are grown on espaliers, their grapes producing the well-known Sercial.

Câmara de Lobos

Estreito de Câmara do Lobos – This small bustling village off R 101 is dominated by its white parish church which stands on a vast terrace.

A narrow road beside the church leads to the upper village and the Levada do Norte.

★**Walk along the Levada do Norte** – *2hr round trip.* The *levada* leads to the valley of the Ribeira de Caixa. This enchanting spot is set between cultivated terraces. As you walk among the flowers, only the sound of the water breaks the silence.

Return to R 101 and continue westwards.

The approaches to Cabo Girão are clad with pinewoods and eucalyptus groves.

Bear left towards Cabo Girão.

★**Cabo Girão** – From the belvedere built at the tip of the vertical cliff there is an extensive view of the coastal plain as far as Funchal Bay. The sea crashes 580m/1 900ft below. Even the slenderest ledges on the cliff face are striped by the regular curves of vines planted in terraces.

The road continues through terraced land and banana plantations before descending abruptly to Ribeira Brava.

Ribeira Brava – *See RIBEIRA BRAVA.*

★EAST COAST OF MADEIRA

Itinerary 1 on the map p. 275

This itinerary is along one of the sunniest of Madeira's coasts, and the one with the mildest climate. Rivers flowing from the mountains have formed ravines and inlets along which villages have grown. The often desolate countryside bears traces of terraces that were once cultivated. The shape of the coastline has been slightly altered by the airport which juts into the sea.

1 Round tour starting from Funchal – *90km/56mi – about 4hr – Leave Funchal on Rua de Conde Carvalhal. Head for the airport.*

★★**Miradouro do Pináculo** – *2km/1mi beyond São Gonçalo.* A belvedere on a rocky promontory *(pináculo)* affords, through the flowers on its pergola, a wonderful view of Funchal, lying spread out at the end of its beautiful bay. Cabo Girão stands out on the horizon. The Desertas can be seen far out to sea.

Caniço – Caniço is a small town whose inhabitants live by fishing and the cultivation of bananas and sugar cane. Ponta do Garajou and Ponta do Oliveira now form a residential zone with hotels and apartment blocks. On Ponta do Garajou stands a tall statue of **Christ in Majesty** raised by a Madeiran family.

Santa Cruz – Santa Cruz, a fishing village edged with a shingle foreshore, possesses several Manueline monuments, mementoes of the early period of colonisation.
The **Igreja São Salvador**★ borders the main square, the centre of which is a public garden. It was erected in 1533 and is said to be the oldest now standing on the island. The exterior is white, flanked by a belfry with a pyramidal roof. At the end the apse is girdled by a balustrade of crosses. The interior, divided into three aisles, is covered with a painted ceiling. The chancel, where the vaulting is supported on twisted columns, contains a metal memorial plaque to João de Freitas. The tomb of the Spinolas is in the north aisle off which lies a beautiful Manueline chapel.
The former **Domus Municipalis**, with beautiful Manueline windows, stands on the other side of the church square. The small street on the east side of the square leads to the present **town hall** *(Câmara Municipal)*, a fine 16C building.
The road skirts the airport which was built in 1966.

★**Miradouro Francisco Álvares Nóbrega** – A road to the left leads to this belvedere named after a Portuguese poet, known also as the Lesser Camões (1772-1806), who sang Madeira's praises. From the belvedere there is a view of Machico and the Ponta de São Lourenço.

Machico – The town of Machico, situated at the mouth of the fertile Ribeira de Machico valley, is divided by a river: the fishermen's quarter, the Banda d'Além, lies on the east side, the old town on the west. It was at Machico that Zarco and his companions landed. The following year, Tristão Vaz Teixeira was invested by Prince Henry as Governor of the Captaincy of Machico.

The lovers of Machico – There is a legend that in 1346 an English ship sank in a tempest at the mouth of the river. Robert Machim and Ana d'Arfet, who had fled from Bristol to get married in spite of their parents' opposition, survived the shipwreck but died a few days later. Their companions took to sea again on a raft, were captured by Arab pirates and taken to Morocco. The story of their adventure was told by a Castilian to the King of Portugal who thereon decided to equip an expedition to find the island. When Zarco landed at Machico he found the lovers' tomb at the base of a cedar tree and named the village after the young Englishman, Machim.

Igreja Matriz – The Manueline parish church built at the end of the 15C stands in a square shaded by plane trees. The façade is pierced by a lovely rose window and a doorway adorned with capitals carved with the heads of animals. The side doorway, a gift from King Manuel I, consists of paired arches supported on white marble columns. The nave has an interesting painted ceiling.
A Manueline arch in the north wall leads to the Capela de São João Baptista, which serves as pantheon to those who donated the church.

Capela dos Milagres – As ruler, Tristão Vaz Teixeira had a chapel constructed in 1420 on the east bank of the river on the site of the English lovers' tomb. This Chapel of Miracles was destroyed by river floods in 1803. The original Manueline doorway was reinstalled when it was rebuilt. In 1829 Robert Page, an English merchant, maintained that he had found the cedar cross which had originally stood upon the grave of Robert Machim and Ana d'Arfet.

Take the Caniçal road.

There are views, as the road rises, of the Upper Valley of Machico dominated by mountain summits. The road leaves the valley through a tunnel bored through the base of Monte Facho.

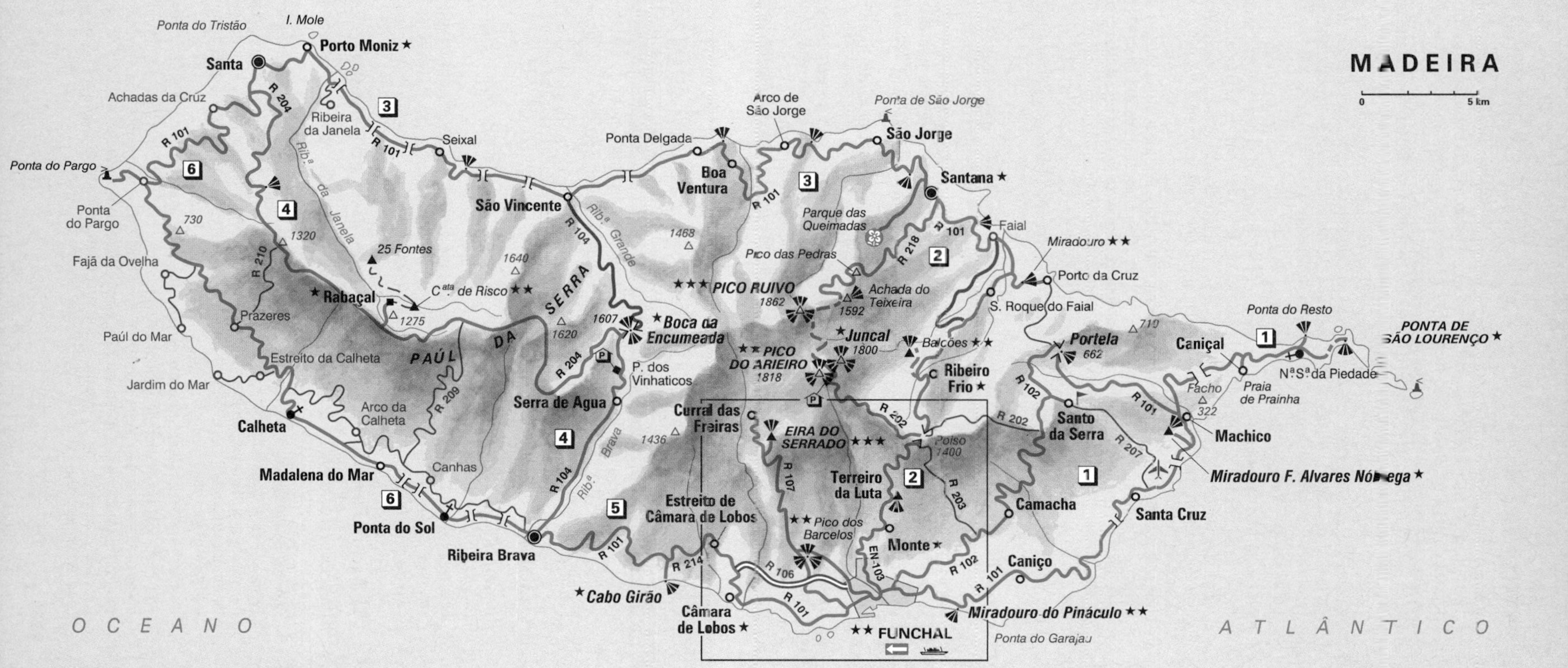
MADEIRA
0
5 km
Ponta do Tristão
I. Mole
Porto Moniz ★
Santa
Achadas da Cruz
Ribeira da Janela
Seixal
Ponta do Pargo
Ponta do Pargo
Fajã da Ovelha
Paúl do Mar
Jardim do Mar
Calheta
Madalena do Mar
Ponta do Sol
Ribeira Brava
Estreito da Calheta
Prazeres
Arco da Calheta
Canhas
★ Rabaçal
25 Fontes
Cªᵗᵃ de Risco ★★
1275
1320
730
1640
1620
1607
PAÚL DA SERRA
Ribª da Janela
R 101
R 204
R 210
R 209
R 104
R 204
São Vincente
Ribª Grande
Ponta Delgada
Boa Ventura
Arco de São Jorge
Ponta de São Jorge
São Jorge
Santana ★
Faial
Parque das Queimadas
Pico das Pedras
Achada do Teixeira
1592
1468
★★★ PICO RUIVO
1862
★ Boca da Encumeada
P. dos Vinhaticos
Serra de Agua
Ribª Brava
★★ PICO DO ARIEIRO
1818
★ Juncal
1800
Balcões ★★
Ribeiro Frio ★
Miradouro ★★
Porto da Cruz
S. Roque do Faial
Portela
662
710
Curral das Freiras
1436
EIRA DO SERRADO ★★★
Poiso
1400
Terreiro da Luta
★★ Pico dos Barcelos
Monte ★
Estreito de Câmara de Lobos
★ Cabo Girão
Câmara de Lobos ★
★★ FUNCHAL
EN-103
R 106
R 107
R 202
R 203
R 102
R 101
R 214
R 218
R 207
Camacha
Caniço
Santo da Serra
Santa Cruz
Machico
Facho
322
Praia de Prainha
Caniçal
Ponta do Resto
Nª Sª da Piedade
PONTA DE SÃO LOURENÇO ★
Miradouro F. Alvares Nóbrega ★
Miradouro do Pináculo ★★
Ponta do Garajau
OCEANO ATLÂNTICO

Caniçal – After losing its role as a station for whaling when this was banned in 1981, Caniçal stagnated for a few years before regaining its status as a major Portuguese port, this time for tunny fishing which has become an important activity as the port facilities and canning factory testify.

A small Whaling Museum, **Museu da Baleia** ⊙, near the old harbour below the village illustrates the importance of the whaling industry from 1940 to 1981. A film *(25min)* shot in Caniçal in 1978, shows the whalers struggling with their huge catch. The whaling boat on display seems but a frail barque beside the life-size model of a sperm whale. Other exhibits include harpoons, model boats and scrimshaw (engraved sperm whale teeth and bones).

Continue to Ponta de São Lourenço.

★Ponta de São Lourenço – The headland of red, black and ochre-coloured volcanic rocks stretches far out into the sea. Although it is battered by waves and winds (there are windmills), it is the only place on the island with a sand beach, **Praínha**. This lies sheltered at the foot of a hillock upon which stands the hermitage of **Nossa Senhora da Piedade**.

The road continues to a parking area near Abra Bay. A footpath leads to a viewpoint overlooking some extraordinary rocks. There are impressive **views★★** from here, as from the **Miradouro Ponta do Resto** *(narrow road to the left before the chapel)*, of the sheer cliffs on the island's northern coast.

Return to Machico and take the road to Portela.

As you climb, the banana and cane sugar plantations of the valley floor give way to pine and eucalyptus trees.

Boca da Portela – At the Portela Pass (alt 662m/2 172ft) crossroads, go up to look at the view from the belvedere overlooking the green Machico valley.

Santo da Serra – Santo da Serra, which was built on a forest covered plateau (pines and eucalyptus) at an altitude of 800m/2 500ft, has become popular with the residents of Funchal as a country resort with a cool climate in a restful setting. The two golf courses are well-known to enthusiasts.

Go from the main square where the church stands, into the Quinta da Junta park, formerly the property of the Blandy family. At the end of the main drive lined with azaleas, magnolias and camellias, a belvedere provides a bird's eye view of the Machico valley; in the distance can be seen the Ponta de São Lourenço and, in clear weather, a white speck which is the island of Porto Santo.

The Camacha road goes through a wooded area where occasional fields of early vegetables draw one's attention to the odd hamlet.

A signpost on the left marks a viewpoint over the Levada dos Tornos which flows across the valley on the far hillside.

Camacha – Camacha is a village set in the woods at an altitude of 700m/2 300ft. It is famous for its basketwork and equally for its group of folk dancers and musicians. The lively but graceful dances are accompanied by chords from a *braguinha*, a four string guitar, while the rhythm is accentuated by an amusing looking stick caparisoned with a pyramid of dolls and castanets, known as a *brinquinho*.

Follow the signs back to Funchal.

★★TOUR OF THE ISLAND

Itineraries **1**, **2**, and **4** on the map p. 275. Starting from Funchal – *220km/137mi – allow two days.*

The following tour of the island covers Madeira's main sights. It can be done in a day but if you wish to go on some of the walks we advise you to allow at least two days with a stopover in Santana, for instance.

2 From Funchal to Santana via Pico do Arieiro

This section of the itinerary describes the journey north from Funchal up to the island's highest peaks and then the descent to the north coast.

Leave Funchal by ①.

Beyond Terreiro da Luta the road, which is lined with flowering hedges, rises in hairpin bends through pine and acacia woods. With the increase in altitude the landscape becomes more barren and the only trees are a few scattered junipers and evergreen oaks.

At the Poiso Pass (Boca do Poiso), take the road on the left to the Pico Aceiro.

The road follows the crest line of the mountains in the centre of the island and there are, therefore, good views from it of both the south coast and Funchal, and the north coast. Flocks of sheep graze on desolate moorlands. At Chão do Arieiro the road passes below a weather station at an altitude of 1 700m/5 578ft. The road ends near the Pousada do Pico do Arieiro.

★★ Miradouro do Pico do Arieiro – There is a magnificent panorama of the mountain ranges in the central part of the island from the Arieiro belvedere built on the very summit of the mountain at an altitude of 1 818m/5 965ft. The landmarks include the Curral das Freiras crater, the distinctive outline of the crest of the Pico das Torrinhas (turrets) and, standing one before the other, the Pico das Torres and Pico Ruivo. To the northeast are the Ribeira da Metade, the Penha d'Águia (Eagle's Rock) rock spike and the Ponta de São Lourenço.

A path has been constructed from Pico do Arieiro to Pico Ruivo.

Around the Pico do Arieiro

H. Veiller/EXPLORER

★ Miradouro do Juncal – A well designed path goes round the summit of Pico do Juncal – 1 800m/5 906ft – to the belvedere *(15min round trip on foot)* from which there is an attractive view along the full length of the Ribeira da Metade valley, which runs into the sea below Faial near a curious rock spike, the Penha d'Águia. The Ponta de São Lourenço can also be seen.

Return to Poiso and take the road on the left going to Faial.

The road descends in a series of hairpin bends through pines and tree laurels whose dense growth gives an indication of the humidity to be found on the north coast.

★ Ribeiro Frio – Near a little bridge over the Ribeiro Frio (meaning cold river) stands a restaurant, settled in a pleasant site amid the greenery at an altitude of 860m/2 822ft.

The slopes overlooking the site are rich in plant species and now form a forestry park, the Parque Florestal da "Flora da Madeira". Given the suitably cool climate and environment, a trout farm has been set up.

The **Levada do Furado**, which irrigates these slopes as far as Porto da Cruz and Machico, passes through Ribeiro Frio. One may walk along it eastwards to the Portela Pass *(3hr 30min)* or westwards as far as Balcões.

★★ Balcões – *40min round trip on foot. Take the path to the left of the bend below Ribeiro Frio.* The path runs alongside the Levada do Furado through passages hewn out of the basalt rock to the Balcões belvedere. This stands in the Metade valley on a hillside surrounded by the last of the high mountains. The view extends from the upper valley, which begins among jagged peaks (Pico do Arieiro, Pico das Torres and Pico Ruivo) to the more open valley with its richly cultivated slopes which runs down to the coast. The town of Faial can be seen to the left of Penha da Águia.

Return to the road and head for Faial.

Continuing along the course of the valley you will come to **São Roque do Faial**, a village perched on a long crest between two valleys. The houses with tiled roofs covered in vines are surrounded by small, terraced market gardens, willow plantations and orchards scattered with straw thatched byres *(palheiros)*.

Turn right towards Portela.

From the bridge over the Ribeira de São Roque there is an attractive view of the Faial valley and the village perched on the clifftop. Bananas, sugar cane and vines are grown on the sunniest slopes.

Head for Porto da Cruz.

A belvedere built on the left side of the road affords one of the island's most interesting **views★★**, that of Porto da Cruz, a village nestled at the foot of a cliff bordered by a shingle beach.

At Porto da Cruz turn round and make for Faial.

4km/3mi from Faial, two belvederes on the right provide an overall **view★** of Faial, the Penha d'Águia, the village of São Roque at the confluence of the Metade and São Roque valleys and, on the horizon, the Ponta de São Lourenço.

★**Santana** – Santana, at an altitude of 436m/2 433ft, a coastal plateau, is one of the prettiest villages on the island. The villagers once lived in attractive cottages made of wood with pointed thatched roofs. Gardens enclosed by box hedges and bright with flowers surrounded the cottages, some of which may still be seen today in among modern buildings, particularly around Queimadas.

Parque das Queimadas – *Bear left off the main road onto Caminho das Queimadas, of which a 3km/1.8mi stretch is in poor condition.*
The road leads to some thatched cottages belonging to the government, at

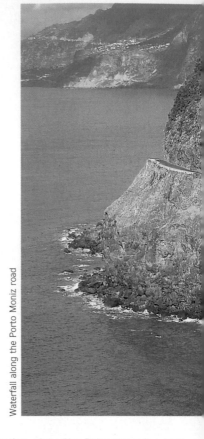

Waterfall along the Porto Moniz road

883m/2 897ft. In a peaceful **setting★** at the foot of the Pico Ruivo slopes is a beautiful park where the trees stand reflected in a small pool. Some rather difficult paths, which are not advisable in the wet, lead off from here to Pico Ruivo and the Caldeirão Verde crater (*1hr 30min walk*).

Pico das Pedras and Achada do Teixeira – *10km/6mi.* The road from Santana runs to Pico das Pedras with its botanical research station and continues to a parking area at Achada do Teixeira. A path leads from here to Pico Ruivo. A short distance along this path there is a fine **view★★** of the Pico Ruivo massif. From the viewpoint behind the building near the car park one can see Faial and, in the foreground, a basalt formation known as **Homem em Pé** (the Man Standing).

② From Santana to Santa *70km/44mi*

As you leave Santana there is a splendid panorama to your left of the chain of mountains. The road, pleasantly lined with hydrangeas, arum and cana lilies, crosses coastal valleys where the sunny hillsides bear a variety of crops.

São Jorge – São Jorge's 17C **church** is astonishingly rich in its baroque ornament. This totally unexpected abundance in a country parish church recalls the sumptuous period of King João V. The decoration includes a ceiling painted in false relief, *azulejos*, a gilded wooden altarpiece, paintings, twisted columns and, in the sacristy, an elegant vestment cupboard and a pretty baroque fountain.
Before beginning the descent to **Arco de São Jorge**, a belvedere to the right of the road affords a wide **vista★** of the coast as it curves to form the São Vicente bay. Below lies the small valley, worn into a series of steps by erosion, in which Arco de São Jorge was built.
Many vines grow on trellises on the more sheltered slopes, for this is a region which produces Sercial wine.

Boa Ventura – This small village lies scattered among vineyards in a pretty setting on a hill dividing two valleys *(lombos)*.

3km/2mi on there is a beautiful **view★** to the right over the harsh coastline which, beyond the nearby Moinhos river, sweeps away in a series of headlands and inlets. To the left is **Ponta Delgada** with its white church and seawater swimming pool.

G. Durand/DIAF

Beyond Ponta Delgada, the coast becomes even more rugged. The road passes beneath an immensely high cliff. The trellised vines are, by now, protected from the wind by broom hedges giving the landscape a chequered appearance.

São Vicente – São Vicente stands in a protected site at the mouth of the river of the same name, grouped in a cliff hollow a little way from the sea. It makes a pleasant stop with its recently renovated houses huddled around the church. At the point where the river flows into the sea, a rock has been hollowed out to form the Capela de São Vicente.

★★ The road from São Vicente to Porto Moniz – The cost of the road built in 1950 earned it the nickname the "gold road". It was boldly cut into the side of a cliff which plunges vertically to the sea below. Its narrowness – (lay-bys have been planned) – and successive tunnels make it a really impressive drive.

The falls which drain the Paúl da Serra can be seen cascading down the slopes and in some places the road dips close enough to the sea to be sprayed by waves. Vines have managed to brave the inhospitable terrain.

3km/2mi from Seixal the road passes through a long tunnel over which a waterfall pours. A belvedere, at the far end, provides a good **viewpoint★** of the well-known site.

Seixal – This village occupies a pleasant **setting★** surrounded by vineyards on a promontory which ends in a series of reefs.

Three small islands *(ilhéus)* rise out of the sea at the mouth of the Ribeira da Janela. The largest is pierced by a sort of window *(janela)* which has given its name to the river and the village. At a distance from the bridge the unusual formation of this rock islet can be clearly seen.

★ Porto Moniz – Porto Moniz provides the only sheltered harbour along the north coast. Protection is afforded by a low-lying flat tongue of land which stretches out towards a rounded islet, the Ilhéu Mole, on which stand a few fishermen's cottages. Whaling was carried out until 1980. Today, Porto Moniz is equipped with hotels and restaurants making it a convenient place to stay.

North of the village the coast is strewn with a mass of pointed **reefs★** among which a seawater swimming pool has been constructed. Before you approach the pool go and take a look down from the balconies which overhang the chasms and natural arches hollowed out by the sea in the black lava rocks.

The road, on leaving Porto Moniz, climbs in hairpin bends up the cliff which dominates the village. Two successive belvederes afford plunging **views**★ of Porto Moniz, its houses and other buildings huddled halfway up the slope round the church and surrounded by fields divided squarely by broom hedges.

Santa – At Santa, short for Santa Maria Madalena, a curious belfry resembling a minaret flanks the white church.

Beyond Santa bear left onto the 204 towards Paúl da Serra and Encumeada, or take itinerary 6 *to follow the coast in the opposite direction.*

4 From Santa to Ribeira Brava via Paúl da Serra
55km/34mi

The 204 road, which is very pleasant and a good deal faster than the coast road, links the west of the island, near Santa, to the Boca da Encumeada. It crosses the high plateau pastures, the only flat surface on the island, where cattle can be seen grazing. In winter when the clouds descend, however, the area is best avoided.
Between Santa and Rabaçal the road follows the mountain crests affording fine views of both sides of the island and particularly of the **Ribeira da Janela**. This very green, steep-sided valley with its laurels and heather is the longest on the island.

★**Rabaçal** – A narrow road *(4km/2.4mi)* twists and turns through the shrubs to the Rabaçal mountain huts (Casas de Rabaçal) set in a wild and remote spot. This is a favourite Sunday picnic site with Madeirans.

★★**Cascata de Risco** – *50min walk round trip from the hut.* A cool path alongside the Levada de Risco leads to a magnificent waterfall which drops about 330ft into a pool in the Ribeira da Janela valley.
Another path, which branches off the Risco, leads to the **25 springs** along the Levada das 25 Fontes *(allow at least 2hr round trip on foot)*.

Paúl da Serra – This vast plain, atypical of Madeira in its unending flatness and aridity, is grazed in summer by flocks of sheep. In winter it becomes a marshland *(paúl)*. The plain is cut by many paths and tracks for excursions which penetrate deep into the centre of the island.
Some sections of the road between Paúl da Serra and Encumeada overlook the south side of the island affording fine views of the mountain tops dominating the coast and its banana plantations.

★**Boca da Encumeada** – A belvedere in the Encumeada Pass at an altitude of 1 007m/3 304ft, in a depression in the mountain chain, looks down over both sides of the island. There is a general view of Madeira's two central valleys which occupy a volcanic fault area between the Paúl da Serra plateau and the mountain ranges near Pico Ruivo.
The **Levada do Norte**, which passes beneath the road and descends to Serra de Água before irrigating the region between Ribeira Brava and Câmara do Lobos, is 60km/38mi long. It was built in 1952 and is one of the newest irrigation channels in Madeira.
From the Pousada dos Vinháticos, there are views over the valleys which have been carved into terraces at the bottom.

Serra de Água – The village of Serra de Água has been built in a pretty **setting**★ halfway up a slope in the Riveira Brava valley surrounded by abundant crops.
The river flows through a narrow valley of gentle contours. The plant life is rich and varied with mostly willows and black poplars along the water's edge.

From Ribeira Brava to Funchal – *35km/22mi. Drive described going in opposite direction (see FUNCHAL: Excursions).*

★SOUTHWEST COAST OF MADEIRA From Funchal

Tour of 145km/90mi – allow one day – Itineraries 5 and 6 on the map p. 275.

South-western Madeira has a much sunnier climate than the northern coast and its slopes are thick with banana trees and all sorts of flowers. It is a densely populated region. The road between the villages twists and bends persistently, hugging the curves of the contour lines. To facilitate access to this part of the coast, a new road, which follows the shoreline and is punctuated by tunnels, now runs between Ribeira Brava and Calheta.

5 From Funchal to Ribeira Brava – *See Funchal: Excursions.*

6 From Ribeira Brava to Santa – *70km/44mi*

Ribeira Brava – The small town of Ribeira Brava or Wild River was built at the mouth of the river which bears the same name, between two hillsides covered in plantations of bananas and other agricultural products. A bustling, shaded avenue runs the length of the beach and leads to a small quay. A tower, the remains of a small 17C fort, testifies to battles of old with raiding pirates.

In the centre of the town on a square where the cobbles have been laid to form a mosaic, stands a proud little 16C **church** flanked by a belfry with a decorative blue and white tiled roof. The church has been remodelled but still retains the original pulpit and an interesting Manueline font.

Leave Ribeira Brava on the road that runs west alongside the shoreline. The lie of the land has necessitated numerous tunnels.

Ponta do Sol – Set at the foot of slopes covered in banana trees is a 15C **church** with a belfry ornamented with faience tiles. Inside, over the chancel, is a painted cedarwood ceiling in the Moorish style reminiscent of the one at Calheta.

Madalena do Mar – The village stands grouped between two large rocks beside a black shingle beach.

Calheta – The **church**, which stands on the right at a bend in the road, dates from 1639 and is interesting for its Moorish ceiling over the chancel. Motifs, similar to those on Funchal Cathedral's ceiling, are seen here grouped in squares.

Beyond Calheta you return to the old, extremely winding road that runs to the west of the island.

The west coast of Madeira has fewer inhabitants and is more isolated than other parts of the island. The road, banked on either side by a profusion of flowers, crosses a green countryside where occasional cultivated terraces can be seen scattered amid the laurel woods, briar trees, eucalyptus and pines.

The road passes near the headland, **Ponta do Pargo**, the westernmost tip of Madeira and so called because sailors from Zarco's ship when out exploring caught a huge type of gilt-head *(pargo)* offshore at this spot. The lighthouse is half hidden by a hill.

Continue along the west coast to the junction with the 204.

Return to Funchal via Paúl da Serra – the itinerary ④ *is described above.*

★★★PICO RUIVO

Pico Ruivo, Madeira's highest point, stands at an altitude of 1 862m/6 109ft. Its slopes are covered in giant heathers and from the summit there is an incomparable panorama. The peak can only be reached on foot. Several paths lead to the mountain refuge hut *(casa-abrigo)*.

Access from Pico do Arieiro – *8km/5mi on foot, about 4hr round trip. This is the best-known approach and a most rewarding hill walk. However, the absence of a safety rail in some places and the unevenness of the terrain make the walk hazardous, particularly for people subject to vertigo.*

Pico Ruivo

T. Perrin/HOA QUI

The path begins by following a rock crest line which, on the left, overlooks the Curral das Freiras valley and, on the right, that of the Ribeira da Metade.
After the tunnel through the Cabo de Gato peak, a second tunnel avoids the climb up to the Pico das Torres. On leaving the tunnel one sees a vast circle of mountains, the source of the upper tributaries of the Ribeira Seca. The remains of a remarkable volcanic chimney lie not far from the path.

Access from Achada do Teixeira *(Itinerary* 2 *described above) – This is a much easier, quicker route. 1 hour's walk on a paved pathway to the refuge at Pico Ruivo. From here there is a 15-minute walk to the Ruivo summit. Allow the same time for the return.*
A good plan, if one can arrange local means of transport, is to set out from Pico do Arieiro, continue to Achada do Teixeira and beyond to Queimadas and Santana. From Pico do Arieiro to Achada do Teixeira allow 3hr 30min; 6hr for the whole trip.

Panorama from the Pico Ruivo summit *from left to right one can see:*
– towards the east, the wild valleys of the Ribeira Seca, the Ribeira da Metade and the Ribeiro Frio as they disappear behind the mountains on their way to the sea. In the far distance is the Ponta de São Lourenço;
– near, to the southeast, is the Pico das Torres and behind it the Arieiro; to the right of this the Cidrão (1 802m/5 912ft);
– to the south and west are the Curral das Freiras cirque and the Ribeira dos Socorridos defile; above stands the Pico Grande: 1 657m/5 437ft overlooking all, including the distinctive Torrinhas (meaning turrets), and the Casado (resembling a blackcurrant); in the distance lies the Paúl da Serra;
– to the northwest, the Caldeiro do Inferno (Hell's Cauldron) crater;
– to the north, the valleys of the north coast separated by long lines of hills;
– and to the northeast, São Jorge and Santana on their coastal plateau.

PORTO SANTO★

Funchal – Population 5 000
Michelin map 940 fold 40

The island of Porto Santo, though only 40km/27mi to the northeast of Madeira, could not be more different. With a total population of 5 000 and an area of 42km²/16sq mi it is less densely inhabited – 241 inhabitants to the square mile – and geographically consists of a large plain edged to the northeast and southeast by a few so called "peaks", of which the highest, the Facho, has an altitude of only 517m/1 696ft.
Except in winter when the damp turns the fields green, nothing grows on the chalky soil and the landscape has an ochre tinge, resembling a desert.
A vast **beach of golden sand★** stretching 7km/4mi along the southern shore and a climate milder (mean annual temperature: 19°C/67°F) and drier than that of Madeira, attract tourists to this island.

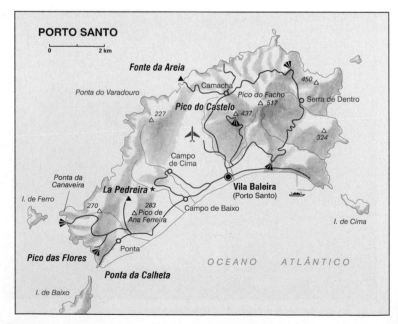

The inhabitants of Porto Santo live by fishing and cultivating cereals, tomatoes, melons, watermelons and figs. The island's vines produce an excellent very sweet white wine which is less well known, however, than the local mineral water. The therapeutic value of this water has made it popular not only on the island but also in Madeira and in Portugal, to which it is exported.

HISTORICAL NOTES

One year after the island had been discovered the first captain, **Bartolomeu Perestrelo**, arrived. The year was 1420. Perestrelo had the unfortunate idea of bringing rabbits to Porto Santo and the island suffered thereafter from the destruction they caused and their proliferation. He, nevertheless, succeeded in bringing a certain prosperity to the devastated island. For a long time the authorities on the mainland of Portugal ignored Porto Santo's existence so that the inhabitants were left to defend themselves against the Barbary Coast pirates and French corsairs and privateers, who continued at intervals to pillage and murder until the 18C. In addition the island suffered several periods of drought and famine.

Christopher Columbus – Christopher Columbus first came to the island when he was charged by a Portuguese merchant to buy a cargo of sugar in Madeira. He sailed on to Porto Santo where he married Isabela Moniz, the daughter of the administrator, Bartolomeu Perestrelo. He left for Funchal, where he lived for some time with his friend, João Esmeraldo, studying the theories then current in navigation and which were later to inspire his voyages of exploration.

Access – By plane or boat ⊘.

Tour of the island – As a complete tour takes 3 or 4 hours it is therefore possible to make a day trip to Porto Santo from Madeira. One can tour the island by taxi, hired car, or by bicycle. If you plan on spending several days, why not visit the island on foot? The island's main interest is its beautiful sandy beach which attracts tourists and Madeirans alike. During summer it can be crowded so it is best to book a hotel ahead of time.

The beach on Porto Santo

J. Ducange/TOP

SIGHTS

Vila Baleira – Vila Baleira is a fitting capital for the island.
At the centre of the town is the **Largo do Pelourinho★**, an attractive square shaded by palm trees. Around it stand some fine white buildings including the church and an emblazoned edifice which houses the town hall.
An alleyway to the right of the church leads to the house of Christopher Columbus, **Casa de Cristóvão Colombo** ⊘. One can see two rooms where he lived with his wife and, in an annexe, engravings and maps recalling events from his life including his various voyages.
Rua Infante Dom Henrique, a wide street bordered by palm trees, leads off Largo do Pelourinho to a garden in which stands a statue to Christopher Columbus. Beyond, the jetty affords an overall view of the town.

The Madeira Archipelago

Tour of Pico do Facho – *30min*. A road from Vila Baleira runs all the way round Pico do Facho affording fine views of different parts of the island including the capital, the harbour, Pico de Ana Ferreira in the west and the island's long beach. The road crosses undulating countryside, deserted but for cattle and sheep guarded by a few shepherds whose thatched-roof cabins may be seen here and there.

Pico do Castelo – A road climbs up the side of the wooded peak to a lookout point where there is a general view of the island chequered with crops in patch-work fields.

Fonte da Areia – This fountain in the sands flows near cliffs which overlook a wild and rocky coast, worn into strange shapes by erosion.

★**A Pedreira** – *Take the road parallel to the beach towards the headland, Ponta da Calheta. Beyond the Porto Santo Hotel, bear right onto a track which after 2km/1.2mi leads to a quarry.*
A Pedreira, which stands on the slope to Pico de Ana Ferreira, is a spectacular basalt rock formation of organ pipes soaring skywards.

Pico das Flores and Ponta da Canaveira – *Take the Ponta da Calheta road and then turn onto the track that runs alongside the riding school.*
You first reach Pico das Flores where there is a fine **view** of cliffs and Baixo islet. The track continues to Morenos, a pleasant picnic site, then to the headland, Ponta da Canaveira. There is a wonderful **view**★ of Ilhéu de Ferro (Iron Islet) with its beautiful red-toned rocks and its lighthouse as well as of the surrounding creeks which are wild and inhospitable.

Ponta da Calheta – This point, which lies separated from Baixo Islet by a channel dangerously strewn with reefs on which the sea breaks incessantly, has a beach spiked with black basalt rocks. It is an unusual and memorable spot.

The Azores Archipelago

For many people the Azores are still a *terra incognita*. They are often confused with the Canaries or Madeira, and are thought of as a group of wild islands somewhere in the Atlantic Ocean, with dense, tropical vegetation, beaches lined with coconut palms and an eternally blue sky. This last characteristic stems from the anticyclone (synonymous with fine weather) which made the name Azores famous. In fact, the nine islands, which share the same latitude as Lisbon and are two hours by plane from Portugal, are more like Ireland, albeit a volcanic Ireland. As for the beaches, the few there are have black sand. The Azores are dotted over an area of 600km/373mi. The air is pure and the quality of the light is such that it intensifies the colours, particularly the green of the shrubs, the blue of the hydrangeas in summer and the dark mauve shades of the volcanic rocks.

In spite of their remoteness, the islands form part of the European continent and in so far as they belong to Portugal are members of the European Union.

Goshawks – The first Portuguese to discover the islands were struck by the presence of birds which reminded them of a type of sparrow-hawk, the goshawk (*açor* in Portuguese). The birds were in fact buzzards, but the name remained.

GEOGRAPHY

Layout of the archipelago – There are three distinct groups of islands between latitudes 36°55N and 39°43 N. The eastern group consists of São Miguel and Santa Maria, the central one of Terceira, Graciosa, São Jorge, Faial and Pico, and the western group of Flores and Corvo. The total surface area is 2 335sq km/902sq mi, less than a third of that of Corsica. Santa Maria, the easternmost island, is 1 300km/808mi from Portugal, and Flores, the westernmost, is 3 750km/2 330mi from North America.

Formation – The geological origins of the Azores are not as yet thoroughly known and have been difficult to date. Like other islands belonging to archipelagos in the Atlantic, they are volcanic. Their formation dates from the Quaternary Era with the exception of Santa Maria where Tertiary soil from the Miocene period has been found. The islands, which emerged from ocean depths of over 6 000m/19 700ft, are among the youngest in the world. The archipelago originated from a weak zone where the Atlantic rift meets the fault line which separates the African and Eurasian continental blocks. Apart from Corvo and Flores, which belong to the American plate and have a North-South relief line, the Azores form part of the Eurasian plate with an East-West relief line.

Ever since the islands were settled in the 15C they have been subject to intense seismic and volcanic activity including the upheaval of the Sete Cidades caldera in 1440, eruptions in the Lagoa do Fogo crater in 1563, lava flows known as *misterios* on Pico (in 1562, 1718 and 1720) and Faial (in 1672), as well as eruptions on São Jorge (1808). Volcanic activity continues (fumaroles, geysers, hot springs) and, from time to time, volcano erupts (Capelinhos on Faial in 1957) or an earthquake (Terceira in 1980).

A great many eruptions have also been noted beneath the sea. Their presence is marked by a bubbling of the water, emissions of gas and clouds of steam. The most spectacular of these occurred in 1811 when an islet 90m/295ft high, with a perimeter of 2 000m/6 562ft, appeared off the coast of São Miguel. The captain of an English frigate, who had been watching the eruption, hoisted the Union Jack on the islet and named it *Sabrina* after his ship. But the islet disappeared shortly afterwards taking with it the flag and the dream of a new colony!

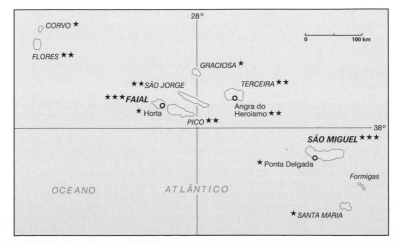

J. P. Garcin/DIAF

Slopes of the Pico volcano

Physical appearance – Vulcanian or explosive volcanic activity on the islands has given rise to large amounts of ash and the formation of **calderas** or vast craters formed either by explosion or, in larger cases, collapse. Further explosions inside and around these calderas have formed small cones. Unusual examples of lava flows resulting from effusive types of eruptions, can be seen on the islands of Pico and Faial where they are known as **misterios**.

As for the island's coastlines, most consist of black cliffs dropping sheer to the sea. One of the most characteristic features of intense erosion by the sea is the **fajã**, a collapsed cliff face which forms a type of platform, the most striking of which can be seen at São Jorge. There are also basalt organ pipe formations resulting from the crystallisation of volcanic rocks.

HISTORY

In the 14C, the islands were mentioned in several accounts of voyages and appeared in portolanos (navigation manuals), including the Catalan Atlas of 1375, charted with imaginary boundaries and relief. At a very early stage, some historians identified them with Atlantis which according to Plato was an island west of the Pillars of Hercules. By the time Prince Henry the Navigator had founded the School of Navigation at Sagres in the early 15C, he had heard reports about these "sea islands" and decided to send out an expedition to investigate. Santa Maria was discovered in 1427. Prince Henry then assigned Brother Gonçalo Velho, a Knight of the Order of Christ, to take possession of the island. Velho was awarded the captaincy of Santa Maria and São Miguel in 1444. As in Madeira, each island was put under the command of a donee-captain who was responsible for its settlement and economic development, and often invested his entire fortune in the venture. In 1494 Dom Manuel I did away with these hereditary titles which had led to the abuse of power. Some of the central islands were captained by Flemings including Jacomo de Bruges in Terceira, Wilhem van der Haegen in São Jorge and Josse van Huerter in Faial, who encouraged their country-men to join them. The Flemish were known locally as Os Flamengos.

By 1452 all the islands had been discovered but not all were settled immediately: Terceira in 1450, Pico and Faial in 1466, Graciosa and São Jorge in 1480 and Flores and Corvo only a century later.

In the 16C the Azores were involved in the succession to the throne after King Sebastiao's death. One of the pretenders to the crown, Dom António, Prior of Crato, had taken refuge in Terceira where he obtained such support from the islanders that he was proclaimed king in 1582 in spite of the fact that Philip II of Spain had been reigning over Portugal for the last two years. In 1583 the Spanish troops got the upper hand and the Prior of Crato fled to France.

In the 19C the Azores were the scene of political struggles between constitutionalists under Dom Pedro IV and absolutists under Dom Miguel. On the death of João VI in 1826, his son Pedro IV, who had been appointed Emperor Pedro I of Brazil, left the throne of Portugal to his daughter Maria II under the regency of his brother Miguel. The latter, however, took over the crown with the help of his absolutist supporters. In 1831, followers of Dom Pedro IV and his daughter sailed from São Miguel with several thousand soldiers, landed at Mindelo near Oporto, overcame Dom Miguel's troops and set up a constitutional regime in 1834.

From an economic point of view, some of the islands prospered rapidly thanks to the cultivation of plants such as woad and orchil which were used in the dye industry. But the great wealth of the Azores sprang from its role as a port of call between Europe and the colonies in South America. In the late 19C Faial became famous as a relay point for intercontinental cables.

THE AZORES TODAY

Population – The Azores have a mixed population. Early settlers were heterogeneous: landless Portuguese, Moorish captives, and Flemings sent by the Duchess of Burgundy, the daughter of King Dom João I. In the 19C, American families came to settle in Faial and São Miguel.

Today the estimated population is 237 795; in 1960 it was 327 000. A large proportion of each new generation has tended to emigrate. In the 17C people mostly went to Brazil, and later to the United States (Massachusetts and California). More than 130 000 islanders emigrated to North America between 1955 and 1974. Those who have emigrated remain faithful to their roots and return to the islands regularly. In summer, the Luso-Americanos, or emigrants to the United States and Canada, make up the majority of tourists. Today, however, emigration seems to be stabilising.

Economy – The main source of livelihood in the Azores is **farming**, particularly dairy farming which accounts for a quarter of Portugal's total production. Dutch cattle are a common sight throughout the islands. São Miguel has also specialised in the large scale cultivation of tea, tobacco, beet, and especially pineapples which are grown under glass. Crops are grown according to the altitude: potatoes, bananas and vines up to 150m/500ft; maize and fodder crops between 150-400m/500-1 300ft, and pastures above 400m/1 300ft.

The Azores export their foodstuffs to Portugal and Azorean colonies in North America. Although **fishing** has diminished since sperm whaling was banned, it is still an important activity. Almost 90% of Portuguese tunny is fished in these waters.

São Miguel and Terceira, the archipelago's two most densely populated islands (between them they make up three quarters of the entire population), are the centres for most of the administrative and economic bodies. In order to allow the islands to develop on an equal footing, each one has its own airport, served by the regional airline, SATA.

Administration – Since 1976 the Azores have been an Autonomous Region with an Assembly and a Regional Government. The Regional Parliament of 50 members sits in Horta, the main town of Faial. Each island is represented by a minimum of two members of Parliament plus a number of representatives in proportion to the island's population. The offices of the President of the Autonomous Region are in São Miguel and the ministries are spread between Faial, São Miguel and Terceira. The residence of the Minister of the Republic is in Angra do Heroismo in Terceira. The University is based in Ponta Delgada in São Miguel with a branch at Angra do Heroismo.

On the archipelago's **flag** are nine stars representing the nine islands, with a goshawk or açor in the middle of the escutcheon. Until 1976 the bird was shown in a huddled position protected by one of its wings, now it is in full flight.

THE AZORES ANTICYCLONE, CLIMATE AND VEGETATION

The French geographer Elisée Reclus wrote the following in the middle of the 19C: "The aerial currents start in this central area of the maritime basin on their way to the Iberian Peninsula, France and the British Isles. The cable which will link the Azores with European observatories will be of immense importance to meteorologists; it is at the crossroads of the great aerial currents that the master station will thus be established, telegraphing probable weather conditions for Western Europe several days in advance." In 1893 Reclus's prediction was realised: an underwater cable was laid between Faial and the European continent to transmit information from the weather stations in Faial, Flores, São Miguel, Terceira and Santa Maria to the Paris observatory. The Azores anticyclone arises because the Azores archipelago lies in the contact zone between cold currents from the North Atlantic and warm ones from the tropical Atlantic. It is at this point that the two high atmospheric pressures merge – the warm, subtropical ones on the one hand and the Arctic intensified ones on the other.

Climate – The weather changes extremely quickly in the Azores; it is commonly said that each of the four seasons can be experienced in a single day. Clouds tend to settle thickly over highland regions, leaving the coast in full sunshine.
The climate is mild and very humid throughout the year, with a humidity rate that can reach 80% and average temperatures of 14°C/57°F in winter and 23°C/73°F in summer.

Vegetation – The vegetation on the Azores is very dense and varied on account of the humidity, latitude and volcanic soil. Tropical species thrive beside European plants giving a surprising combination of sequoias, dragon trees, tulip trees, jacarandas, pines, beeches, monkey-puzzle trees, palms and cedars. The most characteristic tree is the Japanese cryptomeria.
The variety of flora is even more striking in the case of flowers. The most emblematic of the Azores is the **hydrangea** which is either be white or blue depending on the season. It grows wild alongside tropical species like the canna.

WHALING

In *Moby Dick*, Herman Melville mentions the Azores as a good recruiting ground for seamen: "No small number of these whaling seamen belong to the Azores, where the outward bound Nantucket whalers frequently stop to augment their crews from the hardy peasants of these rocky shores." As from the 17C, whaling was carried out in the ocean around the Azores, organised first by the English and then by the Americans. The latter equipped large sailing ships and put to sea for expeditions that sometimes lasted for years. Many Azoreans joined them and so found a means of emigrating to the United States. In 1870 when oil was discovered and replaced whale blubber as fuel, American whalers became scarce and the Azoreans decided to hunt from their own shores. They built swift, streamlined craft called *baleeiras* in which they hunted sperm whale or *baleias*, the most common type of cetacean in these waters. Watchmen scoured the horizon permanently for schools of whales and as soon as they saw the signal spout of water blown out by a whale as it surfaced, they raised the alarm. Preparations for action immediately ensued with men rushing to the harbour, putting to sea and giving chase. As soon as they approached the whale the harpooner would aim for a spot behind the eye. The beast would plunge, dragging the harpoon rope with it. This unwound so quickly that the place where it rubbed against the side of the boat had to be watered repeatedly so as not to catch fire. Twenty minutes later the whale resurfaced to breathe, at which point a second harpoon was thrust. And so the struggle continued, often for hours, raging like a bullfight at sea.
Once dead, the sperm whale was towed to a whaling factory like the one at Cais do Pico where it was cut up and the blubber, bones, liver and precious spermaceti used in the cosmetics industry were collected. Whaling continued until 1981 and many Azoreans still look back nostalgically to the dangerous days of hunting. It was an important source of income for the islanders and while it has been partly replaced by tunny fishing, the gap it has left in the economy has caused many of the young to emigrate.

Scrimshaws

Th. Vogel/EXPLORER

J. P. Garcin/DIAF

Empire of the Holy Ghost

ARCHITECTURE

While some Gothic and Manueline monuments have survived the earthquakes and volcanic eruptions in the Azores, most of the churches, convents and palaces date from the baroque period. The baroque style developed in the 18C, a period of great wealth on account of the gold which came across from Brazil to the Azores, especially to the towns of Ponta Delgada and Angra do Heroisma. The decorative splendour inside the churches contrasts completely with the austere, monumental façades framed in volcanic rock and takes the form of gilded altarpieces, *azulejos*, jacaranda wooden lecterns adorned with ivory, ceilings carved in cedarwood or painted in false relief, and silver altars. Some of the public buildings such as the town hall at Ponta Delgada in São Miguel and that at Velas in São Jorge, as well as some of the palaces such as Bettencourt at Angra do Heroismo and others in Ponta Delgada and Ribeira Grande also date from the same period.

In the 19C, some of the great American families that had grown rich from trade or prospered from orange plantations, built sumptuous mansions in Ponta Delgada, Furnas and Horta. An example is Thomas Hickling's palace in Ponta Delgada, now the São Pedro Hotel. The style of building was derisively known as "orange architecture" since it was the orange plantations that produced such wealth.

Rural architecture has been preserved in most of the islands particularly in Santa Maria and Terceira where the influence of the Alentejo and Algarve can be seen in the whitewashed houses, the immense chimneys and the brightly coloured borders painted to outline the façades.

TRADITIONS

As is often the case in remote islands, traditions have been kept very much alive in the Azores although they are now beginning to die out. Traditional dress is only worn during festivals. An example is the **capote**, a cape with an enormous hood stiffened with whalebone which masks the face completely.

Festivals, however, have managed to retain their importance. Crowds of people from all over the Azores and from the colonies across the Atlantic gather at Ponta Delgada to celebrate Cristo dos Milagres on the fifth Sunday after Easter. All the islands but most particularly Terceira celebrate the feast of the **Holy Ghost**, when a gift-bearing emperor is elected. Brightly-coloured buildings known as Empires of the Holy Ghost *(Império do Espíritu Santo)* are used to house objects for this festival.

The São Pedro cavalcade is held at Ribeira Grande in São Miguel on 29 June and a sea festival, with boats from all the islands, takes place in Faial during the feast of Nossa Senhora da Guia in August.

All the information such as entry formalities, accommodation, post and tele-communications, currency, changing money etc. which is also relevant for the rest of Portugal, is contained in the chapter on Practical Information at the end of the guide.

Time difference

The time in Portugal is 1 hour ahead of GMT or the same as BST; there is no alteration at any season of the year. There is a time difference of 2 hours between continental Portugal and the Azores: when it is 8am in Lisbon it is 6am in the Azores.

Telephone

To call the Azores from the United Kingdom, dial 00 (Ireland 16) + 351 + 96 for São Miguel and Santa Maria, 95 for Terceira, Graciosa and São Jorge, and 92 for Faial, Pico, Flores and Corvo. To make an international call from the Azores, dial 00 then the country code (44 for the United Kingdom, 353 for Ireland, 001 for the United States), the area code and the number.

Tourist Information

Regional Tourism Directorate: Casa do Relógio, Colónia Alemã, 9900 Horta, Faial. ☎ (92) 2 38 01 /2/3.

Delegação de Turismo:

São Miguel: Avenida Infante Dom Henrique, 9500 Ponta Delgada. ☎ (96) 2 57 43 or 2 51 52.

Terceira: Rua dos Artistas, 35, 9700 Angra do Heroismo. ☎ (95) 2 61 09.

Faial: Rua Vasco da Gama, 9900 Horta. ☎ (92) 2 22 37.

Information centres:

Santa Maria: Aeroporto de Santa Maria, 9580 Vila do Porto. ☎ (96) 8 63 55.

Graciosa: Praça Fontes Pereira de Melo, 9880 Santa Cruz. ☎ (95) 7 21 25.

Pico: Rua Conselheiro Terra Pinheiro, 9950 Madalena. ☎ (92) 62 35 24.

São Jorge: Rua Conselheiro Dr. José Pereira – 9800 – Velas ☎ (95) 4 24 40.

Flores: 9970 – Santa Cruz das Flores – ☎ (92) 5 28 42.

Corvo: please enquire at Faial as the island does not have a tourist information centre.

When to go

The most pleasant season to visit the Azores is between May and September when there is less rain. The temperatures are mild and the hydrangeas are in full bloom. In October there can be thick fog and the rest of the year the weather is often dull although winters can sometimes be fine.

What clothes to take

Whatever the season it is best to take a raincoat, good walking shoes and a pullover. Warm clothes are required in winter. It is never cold in summer except at high altitudes; light trousers and dresses are ideal.

How to get there

It is only possible to get to the Azores from Europe by air. All flights are automatically via Lisbon since the only airline to the Azores is the Portuguese TAP which has flights to Ponta Delgada (São Miguel), Lajes (Terceira) and Horta (Faial). There are also regular air links between the Azores, Madeira (enquire at TAP) and North America.

Language

The Portuguese spoken in the Azores is slightly different from that on the continent on account of various archaisms. However, staff in all tourist information centres, hotels, restaurants and car hire firms speak English, French and German.

Banks

All the islands except Corvo.

Transport between the islands

SATA *(Av. Infante D. Henrique, 55 – Ponta Delgada – ☎ (96) 2 22 55)* the local airline, has flights to all the islands. Some are only once or twice a week so take this into account when organising your trip if you wish to visit several islands.

In London information on SATA flights may be obtained from TAP Air Portugal. In the summer there are boat connections between the islands in the central group several times a week. Crossings can be long: 4 hours between Terceira and Graciosa, 3hr 30min between Terceira and São Jorge and 1hr 15min between São Jorge and Pico.

There are boat links between Faial and Pico several times a day *(30min crossing)* and between Flores and Corvo daily in the summer *(2hr both ways)*. The Portuguese Tourist Office provides boat timetables.

Transport on the islands

Taxis: Each of the islands has a good many green and black taxis which generally run excursions for a fixed sum.

Car hire: There are car hire firms on all the islands. Cars on some of the smaller islands, such as Graciosa and Flores, are not always in good condition and it is advisable to check the brakes.

Buses: The main islands have a regular bus service.

Roads

On the whole, the roads are in fairly good condition, though minimally signposted.

Accommodation

Tourist accommodation varies greatly depending on the island. São Miguel (Ponta Delgada and Furnas), Terceira (Angra do Heroísmo and Praia da Vitória) and Faial (Horta) are well equipped while the smaller islands often only have two or three hotels. There are no hotels on Corvo.

It is best to book ahead of time in the tourist season.

Prices are comparable to those on the continent. A luxury hotel costs between 10 000 and 20 000 Escudos while residential hotels and boarding-houses cost between 5 000 and 10 000 Escudos. The cheapest accommodation is with local families whose addresses may be obtained from tourist offices.

Camp sites are beginning to develop on some of the islands.

Restaurants, food and drink

There are a good many reasonably-priced restaurants in the Azores. Grilled fish served with chilled *vinho verde* is delicious as are local specialities such as the *Furnas cozido*, a kind of hotpot stewed in underground ovens hollowed out of the hot volcanic earth.

Sports and leisure

Walking – This is one of the most popular pastimes in the Azores. The most pleasant islands to walk on are Pico for the climb up the volcano, São Jorge with its wonderful coastal rambles, Flores and Corvo for their caldera and São Miguel which has a wide choice of walks. See the suggestions below for books to read on rambling.

J. P. Garcin/DIAF

Swimming – There are not many beaches in the Azores apart from those on São Miguel (long ones on the south coast), Santa Maria (São Lourenço Bay and Praia Formosa), Faial (Porto Pim, Praia do Almoxarife and Praia do Norte) and Terceira (Praia da Vitória). Swimming is possible on the other islands in natural swimming-pools that have been hewn out of the lava. Local children swim in the harbours.

Diving – The coastal waters around the Azores are very beautiful and a number of diving clubs have been set up in São Miguel, Terceira and Faial.

Sailing – The main pleasure boat harbours are at Horta, Angra do Heroísmo and Ponta Delgada.

Golf – There are three main golf courses on the Azores – one on Terceira near Lajes and two on São Miguel, at Furnas and near Ribeira Grande.

Spas – Several spas have been developed to take advantage of the therapeutic waters from hot springs. There are baths at Furnas on São Miguel, Veradouro on Faial and Carapacho on Graciosa.

Calendar of Events

Festivals for village patron saints are held throughout the year. All the islands also celebrate the well-known feast of the Holy Ghost.
The following is a selection of the main festivals:

5th Sunday after Easter
São Miguel.......................... Santo Cristo Festival at Ponta Delgada
29 June
São Miguel.......................... São Pedro Cavalcade at Ribeira Grande
Last week in June
Terceira................................ Midsummer's Day (St John) Festival with processions and bullfights
22 July
Pico...................................... Madalena Festival
Week of 1st to 2nd Sunday in August
Faial..................................... Sea Festival at Horta harbour with boats
15 August
Santa Maria .... Island Festival. Election of Holy Ghost emperor

Essential sightseeing on each of the islands

São Miguel: Sete Cidades★★★, Furnas★★ and Lagoa do Fogo★★
Santa Maria: Baía do São Lourenço★★
Terceira: Angra do Heroísmo★ and Algar do Carvão★★
Graciosa: Santa Cruz★ and Furna de Enxofre★★
Faial: Horta★, Caldeira★★ and Capelinhos★★★
Pico: Ascension of Pico★★★
São Jorge: Short tour of the island (allow 4hr)★★
Flores: Tour of the island (allow 4hr)★★
Corvo: Caldeirão★

Books to read

Novels

Mau tempo no canal by Vitorino Nemésio. A novel describing life on the islands at the beginning of the century.

Walking in the Azores

Landscapes of the Azores by Andreas Stieglitz (Sunflower)
The Azores – Garden Islands of the Atlantic by David Sayers and Albano Cymbron.

SÃO MIGUEL★★★

Ponta Delgada – Population: 125 915
Surface area: 747sq km/288sq mi; Length: 65km/40mi; Width: 16km/10mi
Main towns: Ponta Delgada, Ribeira Grande
Highest point: 1 103m/3 619ft

Access: *There are direct flights daily to and from Lisbon, Madeira, North America and the other islands in the Azores archipelago.*

Length of stay: *If you are short of time, it is possible to see Ponta Delgada, Sete Cidades and Furnas in two days. However, you should allow a minimum of four days for a thorough visit.*

São Miguel, which is the largest of the Azorean islands and has the densest population (more than half of the total population), forms the eastern group of islands with Santa Maria. It is known as the green island or *ilha verde*. In spite of a certain amount of modernity for which neighbouring islanders nickname it Japan, one can still see traditional scenes such as milk churns being transported on horse-drawn carts.
The island draws more visitors than any other in the archipelago on account of its many attractions including its magnificent landscapes, its pretty country roads bordered by plane trees and banks of hydrangeas, its volcanic activity, beaches and tourist facilities.

Historical notes – São Miguel was discovered by Brother **Gonçalo Velho Cabral**, a Knight of the Order of Christ, in 1444. As a donee-captain, Velho was given responsibility for the development of the island which was soon settled by colonists from the Alentejo, the Algarve, Estremadura, as well as by Jews, Moors and even Bretons (one of the villages is still called Bretanha).
In 1640, after the restoration of Portuguese independence from Spain, São Miguel became an important centre between America and Europe and strong links were set up with Brazil. The island prospered greatly as the many churches and mansions from this period testify. The orange trade with England was another source of wealth but in 1860 the orange groves were devastated by disease and so the farmers turned to growing tobacco, tea, chicory and above all, pineapples.

Geography – São Miguel consists of two volcanic mountain massifs divided by a depression which is covered in lava from recent volcanic eruptions and stretches between Ponta Delgada and Ribeira Grande. The oldest massif, in the east, is dominated by Pico da Vara at an altitude of 1 103m/3 619ft. The island's most impressive landscape features are its craters which contain lakes: Sete Cidades, Lagoa do Fogo and Furnas. Volcanic activity is still abundantly apparent today in the form of geysers and bubbling mud springs *(solfatares)* at Furnas, Ribeira Grande and Mosteiros. The jagged coastline, particularly in the north and east, consists of sheer cliffs at the foot of which are sometimes narrow beaches of black sand. The gentler, southern coast has wider beaches at Pópulo, Água de Alto, Ribeira Chã, Vila Franca do Campo and Ribeira Quente.
The main activities of the island are the cultivation of pineapples, which are grown in more than 6 000 glasshouses, the rearing of dairy cattle, canning, cottage industries and tanning.

★PONTA DELGADA Population 21 000

Ponta Delgada is the archipelago's main town as well as the seat of the Regional Government and the University.
It became capital of the island in 1546 and fortifications were built in the 16 and 17C to protect the town from pirate attack. As a result of the town's prosperity in the 18 and 19C many churches and mansions were built. In 1831, the Portuguese expedition in which 3 500 Azoreans took part, left from Ponta Delgada harbour to sail for the continent and proclaim a constitutional charter which would put Maria II on the throne.

Sights

The **historical quarter** of Ponta Delgada is set back from **Avenida do Infante Dom Henrique**, a wide boulevard lined with black and white pavement that runs alongside the harbour. The quarter is a tight network of streets along which stand fine 17 and 18C mansions. Open spaces are provided by squares and public gardens shaded by monkey-puzzle trees.

Praça Gonçalo Velho Cabral – On the square stand the statue of Gonçalo Velho who discovered the island, and the 18C **Town Gates** which consist of three archways set in basalt. Extending from the square is the **Largo da Matriz** **(22)** which is dominated by the tall façade of the 16C church of São Sebastião and the interesting baroque **Town Hall** (Paços do Conselho) **(H)** dating from the 17C.

Igreja Matriz de São Sebastião (A) – The 16C parish church, which was built on the site of a former chapel, is famous for its graceful **Manueline doorway★** in white limestone. The stone was brought from Portugal.

PONTA DELGADA

Ant. J. N. Silva (Rua) 3
Contador (Rua do) 7
João Moreira (Rua)..................... 16
L. V. Bens (Rua)......................... 19
Matriz (Largo da) 22

Calhau (Rua do)......................... 4
Clerigos (Rua dos) 6

Cor. Silva Leal (Rua) 9
Dr L.M. Camara (Rua)................ 10
Eng. José Cordeiro (Rua) 12
Ernesto do Canto (Rua).............. 13
João de Melo Abreu (Rua)......... 15
Kopke (Avenida)....................... 18
Machado dos Santos (Rua)........ 21
Melo (Rua do)........................... 24
Mercadores (Rua dos)............... 25

Vasco da Gama (Praça).............. 27
2 de Março (Largo)..................... 28
5 de Outubro (Praça)................. 30

A	Igreja Matriz de São Sebastião
B	Convento de Nossa Senhora da Esperança
H	Paços do Concelho

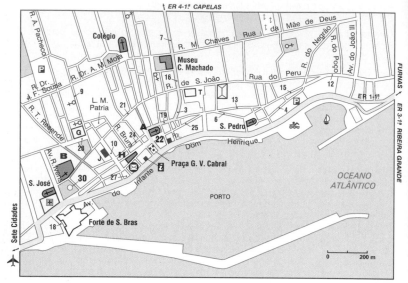

The interior is noteworthy for the vaulting in the chancel and the gilded baroque statues of the Evangelists on the high altar. The sacristy to the left of the chancel is decorated with *azulejos* and has some beautiful 17C furniture made of jacaranda. The **treasury** to the right of the chancel contains gold and silver plate as well as some extremely precious 14C vestments from Exeter Cathedral in England.

Forte de São Brás – This fort was built in the 16C and remodelled in the 19C. The vast **Praça Cinco de Outubro** (or Largo de São Francisco) (**30**) with a bandstand and a huge tree stretches out before the fort. Two large churches give onto the square: the Igreja de São José, which was part of a former Franciscan convent, and the Igreja de Nossa Senhora de Esperança.

★**Convento de Nossa Senhora da Esperança** (**B**) – The convent houses the statue of **Cristo dos Milagres** (Christ of Miracles) which attracts a large crowd – including many emigrants who return for the occasion – during the Santo Cristo Festival on the 5th Sunday after Easter. The statue is believed to have been given by Pope Paul III to nuns who petitioned in Rome for the setting up of their convent near Ponta Delgada in the 16C. Inside, the long narrow church is divided by a wrought-iron grille. Kept at some distance behind the grille are the church treasures including the statue of Santo Cristo together with rich gold and silver plate and polychrome *azulejos* by António de Oliveira Bernardes.

Outside the church, at a corner of the building beneath an anchor carved in the wall and inscribed with the word *Esperança* is the spot where the Azorean poet **Antero de Quental** (1842-1891) committed suicide.

Igreja de São José – The church belonged to a 17C Franciscan monastery which is now a hospital. Inside, the vast nave is covered in wooden vaulting painted in false relief. The late 18C chapel of Nossa Senhora das Dores has a baroque façade.

Igreja de São Pedro – 17 and 18C. The church overlooks the port and faces the **São Pedro Hotel**, the former residence of Thomas Hickling. Behind the church's graceful façade is a rich baroque interior with gilded altarpieces and ceilings painted in false relief. The chapel to the right of the chancel contains the 18C **statue of Our Lady of Sighs★**, one of the most beautiful statues in the Azores.

Museu Carlos Machado ⊙ – The museum is housed in the 17-18C Santo Andres Monastery. The church contains two magnificent wrought-iron grilles *(above and below)*. The museum displays an interesting collection of early 16C paintings including two delightful **panels★** in the style of the Master of Sardoal (early 16C), one of St Catherine and St Barbara and the other of St Margaret and St Apollonia. In the same room can also be seen an anonymous series of paintings depicting martyrs. The baroque sculpture section contains a good many angel candelabra.

Igreja do Colégio – The church of the former Jesuit College stands behind the museum. Its unusual baroque façade, which looks more like that of a palace than a church, was added in the 18C.

★★★① SETE CIDADES AND THE WEST OF THE ISLAND

80km/50mi – allow half a day.
Take the airport road from Ponta Delgada and then the fork marked Sete Cidades.

★**Pico do Carvão** – A lookout point at this spot dominates a large area of the island affording views of the centre, the northern coast and Ponta Delgada.
The road runs past a moss-covered aqueduct and then some small lakes including **Lagoa do Canário** which is surrounded by botanical gardens.

★★★**Sete Cidades** – Sete Cidades, the natural wonder of the Azores, is a caldera with a circumference of 12km/7mi. It is best seen from the **Vista do Rei★★★** belvedere south of the crater. The view takes in the twin lakes, one green, the other blue, and the village of Sete Cidades at the bottom of the crater. The area on the left, partly occupied by a small volcanic cone, is like a scene from Switzerland with cows quietly grazing the green pasture in among pine trees. The caldera is believed to have been formed in 1440 when an eruption is thought to have completely changed the lie of the land in this part of the island. Mariners sailing past the island before its colonisation described it as being dominated at each end by a peak. Several years later, by the time the first Portuguese settled on the island, the western peak had disappeared in a volcanic explosion and in its place was a caldera described at the time as a "burnt" mountain on account of the calcined volcanic rocks which covered it.
The extraordinary site has inspired many legends including one about seven bishops who fled Portugal on the arrival of the Moors and took refuge in the "undiscovered islands" where they were believed to have built the seven cities of Sete Cidades.
An unsurfaced but practicable road (marked Cumeeiras) leads from Vista do Rei along the edge of the crater (allow 2 hours if you wish to walk). There are views of both sides of the crater, inside and out. The road crosses another one leading down to Sete Cidades. Beyond the village are the lakes.
The road runs across a bridge built between the two lakes. On the other side of the bridge a path to the left leads to a picnic area beside the blue lake, Lagoa Azul. The choice of route back to Ponta Delgada from Sete Cidades depends upon the amount of time you have at your disposal:
– if you have about 1 hour, take the road that skirts the lake, **Lagoa de Santiago** and climbs back up to Vista do Rei, then the road which begins near Monte Palace.

Sete Cidades, São Miguel

J. P. Garcin/DIAF

295

This descends between banks of hydrangeas to join the road to Ponta Delgada.
– if you have at least 3 hours, head northwest to **Miradouro do Escalvado★** on the
coast which affords a fine view of Mosteiros and its rocks, then continue along a
winding road to Capelas where you head south to Ponta Delgada via Fajã de Cima.

★★ACHADA DAS FURNAS

The **Achada valley** is an idyllic site set in a crown of hills and mountains. The best
views of it are from the Pico do Ferro and Salto do Cavalo belvederes *(see below)*.
The name Furnas meaning caves derives from the hollows in the ground from which
spurt hot springs and sulphurous, bubbling mud geysers which can be identified
from a distance by their jets of steam. The vegetation surrounding the charming,
whitewashed town of Furnas is exceptionally luxuriant thanks to the area's warm,
moist soil and the humidity.

Furnas – Apart from being a wonderful place in which to relax and go for walks,
Furnas is also popular for its waters which are used in the treatment of respiratory ailments, rheumatism and depression.

★★**Caldeiras** – The extraordinary sulphurous waters in the area with their volcanic ema-
nations and vapours boil at temperatures of around 100°C/212°F. Known as
caldeiras, the geysers punctuate the landscape like so many spewing mouths
opening from a bubbling hell below. One of them, Pêro Botelho, is named after a
man who died here after a fall. The locals boil up maize cobs in the natural caul-
drons in no time and proffer them to tourists.

★★**Parque Terra Nostra** ☉ – The park was laid out by Thomas Hickling in the 18C and
is now cared for by the Praia e Monforte family. It contains a remarkably diverse
range of plant species with hibiscus, azaleas, hydrangeas and tropical plants and
flowers thriving in the shade beneath Japanese larches. The avenues are bordered
by magnificent royal palms.
In front of the house there is a large oval swimming-pool into which flows yel-
lowish, warm, ferruginous spring water. Bathing is possible but be warned that
one's costume may take on a rust colour.
The old part of the Terra Nostra Hotel, which forms part of the property, has interesting architecture dating from the thirties.

★**Lagoa das Furnas** – *3.5km/2mi along the Ponta Delgada road.* Clouds of steam
rising up from the northwest shores of the vast lake lying at the foot of steep
slopes mark the presence of geysers. The warm earth has been hollowed out and
cemented to form underground ovens with large wooden lids. The local speciality,
a kind of hotpot known as *cozido*, is cooked inside the ovens.

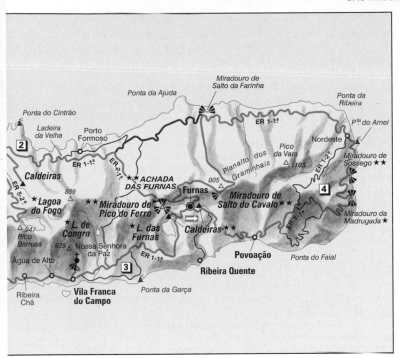

Excursion

Ribeira Quente – *8km/5mi from Furnas.* The road between Furnas and Ribeira Quente is one of the most attractive on the island and several picnic sites have been developed along it. At a point between two tunnels an impressive waterfall can be seen cascading down to the right. The village of Ribeira Quente or Hot River is mainly known for its beach warmed by the hot springs after which the place is named.

★★THE CENTRE OF THE ISLAND

② From Ponta Delgada to Furnas *71km/44mi – 4hr*

Take the Lagoa road east of Ponta Delgada. Beyond Lagoa head north towards Remédios and Pico Barrosa.

★★**Lagoa do Fogo** – An eruption in the 16C formed a crater lake which was given the name Fire Lake. Today this is a peaceful, majestically beautiful spot with the clear water of the lake covering the crater floor. A white sand beach borders the lake on one side, a sheer cliff face on the other.
The road continues downhill towards Ribeira Grande. Steam clouds hang above the geothermal power station which produces part of the island's electricity supply.

Ribeira Grande – Ribeira Grande, the second largest town on the island, has some fine 16-18C mansions including **Solar de São Vicente** which houses the arts centre.
The vast garden square in the middle of town, alongside which flows the Ribeira Grande, is surrounded by interesting buildings including the **Town Hall** dating from the 16 and 17C with its double staircase and square tower (note the Manueline window), and the **Igreja do Espírito Santo** with its elaborate baroque façade. The church is also known as the Dos Passos Church as it contains the statue of Christ (Senhor dos Passos) which is carried in traditional processions.
The large 18C **Igreja de Nossa Senhora da Estrela** stands at the top of a wide flight of steps. Inside, the walls and ceilings are painted and, as elsewhere on the island, the gilt altarpieces are richly decorated.

Head south from Ribeira Grande following signs to Caldeiras.

Caldeiras – This is an active volcanic area heralded by a group of small fumaroles. There is a thermal establishment and some springs that produce a well-known mineral water.

Return to the coast road and head east.

The coast is a series of capes and bays within which nestle small beaches like that of **Porto Formoso**.

Take the Furnas road.

★★Miradouro de Pico do Ferro – The view stretches across the whole Furnas valley, taking in the village, Terra Nostra park and the lake.

Furnas – *See above.*

③ From Furnas to Ponta Delgada *52km/32mi – 3hr*

Leave Furnas on the Ponta Delgada road. After 16km/10mi turn right and 3km/1.8mi further on turn left. After 330 yards you reach a fork; turn right and continue for another 550 yards.

★Lagoa do Congro – To reach Lagoa do Congro, an emerald green lake at the bottom of a crater, you leave the pastureland with its hydrangea hedges and follow a footpath *(40min round trip)* which leads rapidly down the crater slopes through thick vegetation and magnificent trees.

Vila Franca do Campo – The town, the island's early capital, was partly destroyed by an earthquake in 1522. Facing the town is a volcanic **islet** which appeared when a crater subsided. In the town centre is a beautiful square with a public garden dominated by the Gothic **Igreja de São Miguel.**

Standing on a rise above Vila Franca is the **Capela de Nossa Senhora da Paz** which is approached by a flight of steps rather like a small scale version of that of Bom Jesus at Braga on mainland Portugal. There is a fine **view★** of the coast, Vila Franca and the sea of white hothouses in which pineapples are ripened.

Once past the long **Água do Alto beach** one can turn south to the headland, **Ponta da Galera**, with the delightful little harbour of Caloura and attractive holiday homes.

Água de Pau – *Follow the signs to Ermita and Miradouro (20min round trip on foot).* The lookout point affords an interesting view★, to one side, Ponta da Caloura and a volcanic cone covered right to the top in a patchwork of fields, and to the other, the hermitage which stands out against a mountain background.

The road continues along the coast past a series of beaches including those of Lagoa and Pópulo to Ponta Delgada.

④ THE EAST OF THE ISLAND From Furnas
85km/53mi – about 4hr

The road climbs from Furnas eastwards onto the Graminhais plateau. There is a beautiful view of the Furnas valley from **Miradouro de Salto do Cavalo★★**. The road continues to the coast where the **Salto da Farinha** belvedere beyond Salga affords a good view of the north coast.

★★The East Coast – The eastern part of the island has a strikingly beautiful coastline which may be admired from a series of garden lookout points and picnic sites. These are popular with local families who gather for barbecues on weekends. The most spectacular views are from belvederes south of the village of Nordeste: **Miradouro do Sossego★★** and **Miradouro da Madrugada★**. Cliffs drop sheer to the sea in breathtakingly steep escarpments and sometimes end in a narrow shingle strand. Beyond Miradouro da Madrugada a narrow winding road 2km/1.2mi long leads to the beach at Lombo Gordo. This part of the coast is dominated by **Pico da Vara**, the sad scene of a plane crash in 1949 which cost the lives of the French violinist Ginette Neveu and the boxer Marcel Cerdan.

Povoação – This is the first place on the island to have been settled (povoação means population). The village stands at the mouth of a picturesque valley under intense cultivation.

Furnas – *See above.*

*Every year
the Michelin Red Guide España Portugal
and the Michelin Red Guide Portugal
revise the selection of top-ranking restaurants and
review culinary specialities and local wines.
They also include a selection of simpler restaurants
offering carefully prepared dishes which are often regional
specialities... at a reasonable price.
It is worth buying the current edition.*

SANTA MARIA★

Ponta Delgada — Population: 5 922
Surface area: 97sq km/37sq mi; Length: 17km/11mi; Width: 9.5km/6mi
Main town: Vila do Porto
Highest point: 590m/1 936ft.

Access: *There are regular flights between Santa Maria and the neighbouring island of São Miguel.*

Length of stay: *Allow a whole day for an unhurried tour of the island.*

Santa Maria is one of the least visited islands of the Azores and yet it is one of the most pleasant with its warm climate, its **beaches** and its delightful countryside dotted with white houses. These have tall cylindrical chimneys and are painted with brightly coloured borders to outline the façades. The landscape one first sees on arrival in Santa Maria is somewhat unexpected: a dry plateau of yellow grass that looks more like Texas than the Azores. A host of metal huts testifies to the role of Atlantic aircraft carrier the island played for the Americans during the Second World War. In 1947, the air-

House on Santa Maria

B. Brillon/MICHELIN

port was converted for use by civil international traffic. Today, the huts are partly used by Portuguese air traffic controllers for this part of the Atlantic, and the former officers' mess, now the Airport Hotel, still has an atmosphere of the kind encountered in American films of the forties. Several kilometres beyond the airport the landscape changes to the green countryside typical of the Azores.

Historical notes – In 1427, Santa Maria was spotted by early Portuguese caravels and several years later came under the captaincy of Gonçalo Velho Cabral. It was settled by a small group of pioneers who mainly came from the Algarve, which explains the similarity between the architecture on the island and that of southern Portugal.

Geography – Santa Maria is the nearest of the Azorean islands to Portugal and is also the southernmost and the warmest of the archipelago. It consists of a plateau which extends into hills, culminating with Pico Alto, the island's highest point at an altitude of 587m/1 936ft. Santa Maria is the only island in the Azores with sedimentary Tertiary soil in the form of limestone from the Miocene period, which has given rise to white sand beaches.
37km/23mi northeast of Santa Maria is **Formigas**, a nature reserve of eight islets.

An island of dyes – The original wealth of the island came from the cultivation of woad and the gathering of orchil. Woad was exported for use in the dyeing industries in Flanders and Spain until it was superseded by indigo blue from Brazil, while orchil, a type of lichen that gives a brown dye and grows on rocks beside the sea, was collected in perilous conditions from the coast and exported until the mid 19C.

SIGHTS

Vila do Porto – The town is set in the south of the island between Cabo Marvão and Cabo Força. It stretches along a strip of basalt plateau between two ravines which join to form a creek. Among the buildings dating from the 16 and 17C are the **Convento de Santo António**, now the public library and the Franciscan monastery, now the **Town Hall**. The **Igreja de Nossa Senhora da Assunção**, which was originally founded in the 15C and then rebuilt in the 19C, has preserved Gothic and Manueline features in its doorways and windows.

299

Almagreira – Below the village lies Praia Bay and its "beautiful beach" or **Praia Formosa**, one of the finest in the Azores.

★★**Pico Alto (view)** – *Take the road to the left and drive for 2km/1.2mi.* The view from the top of Pico Alto (590m/1 936ft) takes in the whole island. Note the scattered houses of Santa Bárbara stretching away to the east.

Santo Espírito – In the village, which stretches lengthways for some distance, is the **Igreja de Nossa Senhora da Purificação** with a white façade set off by black lava carvings. Beyond Santo Espírito the road descends to **Ponta do Castelo** through a very dry landscape dotted with aloes and cacti, in the middle of which stands a lighthouse. Lower still is **Maia**, a former whaling station now popular for its swimming-pool hollowed out of the rocks.

Return to Santo Espírito and head towards Baía do São Lourenço. Make a right turn just before you get there and go to the **Miradouro do Espigão**★★ which affords a most beautiful view of the bay.

★★**Baía do São Lourenço** – The bay, once a crater that has since been invaded by the sea, is an outstanding site with concave slopes covered in terraced vineyards. Bordering the narrow beaches around the turquoise water are houses occupied only in the summer season.

Santa Bárbara – The houses are scattered over the hills and along the steep coastline bordering Tagareite Bay. The **church** was rebuilt in 1661 and is a fine example of popular architecture.

Anjos – The small fishing harbour popular in summer for its natural rock swimming-pool is mainly known for its history.
A statue of **Christopher Columbus** recalls that the Genoese explorer is believed to have stopped here on his return from his first voyage of discovery and to have attended Mass in the **Capela da Nossa Senhora dos Anjos**. The chapel altar consisting of a triptych of the Holy Family

Baía de São Lourenço, Santa Maria

B. Brillion/EXPLORER

with St Cosmas and St Damian is believed to have come from the caravel that brought Gonçalo Velho to the island.

TERCEIRA★★

Angra do Heroísmo – Population: 55 706
Surface area: 402sq km/155sq mi; Length: 29km/18mi; Width: 17.5km/11mi
Main towns: Angra do Heroísmo and Praia da Vitória
Highest point: 1 023m/3 356ft

Access: *There are regular flights between Terceira and Lisbon, some cities in North America and the other islands in the archipelago.*
In summer, the boat connecting the central group of islands calls at Terceira several times a week.

Length of stay: *Allow two days to tour the island and spend some time in Angra do Heroísmo.*

Terceira, the Portuguese word for third, was the third island in the archipelago to be discovered. It is also the third largest island, after São Miguel and Pico. While its landscape is less striking than those of the other islands, Terceira is more interesting on a human level in terms of architecture, traditions and festivals.

Historical notes – In the early days of its discovery Terceira was known as the Island of Jesus Christ. Settlement began in 1450 under the auspices of Jacomo de Bruges who established a small colony at Porto Judeu and Praia da Vitória.

The economy of the island was soon oriented towards farming, mainly cereals and the cultivation of woad. During the succession to the Portuguese throne, the pretender Dom António, **Prior of Crato**, took up residence on the island and gained local support for his cause.

But in 1580, Philip II of Spain came to power and sent Spanish troops to conquer the island. Their attempt to land in **Baía da Salga** – among them were Cervantes and Lope de Vega – ended in failure and was all the more humiliating since they were driven back into the sea by a herd of 1 000 cows that had been desperately rounded up by an Augustinian friar.

In 1583 other troops managed to take control of the island and up until 1640 when the Portuguese dynasty was restored, Angra do Heroísmo was a port of call for richly-laden Spanish galleons returning from Peru and Mexico. The island, and in particular the town of Angra do Heroísmo, once again played an important role during the political struggles in the 19C.

Geography – Terceira is a tableland overlooked in the east by the Serra do Cume, the remains of Cinco Picos, the island's oldest volcano. The central area is demarcated by a vast crater known as Caldeira de Guilherme Moniz which is surrounded by other volcanic formations. To the west is the Serra da Santa Bárbara, the island's most recent and highest (1 021m/3 350ft) volcanic cone with a wide crater.

The islanders live essentially from farming, cultivating maize and vines, as well as stock rearing. Terceira is the granary of the Azores.

Traditional architecture – Throughout the island are the typical whitewashed houses with wide canopies, sash windows and enormous flat chimneys. These chimneys are like those in the Alentejo and the Algarve, the regions from which the early settlers originated. The stone frames around the windows extend below into different shapes, perhaps a flower, or a rosette. Beside each house stands a maize dryer or *burra do milho* which adds a rural touch.

Impérios – The Azorean tradition of the worship of the Holy Ghost is particularly strong in Terceira. Every quarter in each village has its little chapel known as an *império* or "empire" of the Holy Ghost. The chapels look like salons, their picture windows adorned with net curtains. Most of them date from the 19 or early 20C and were originally built of wood.

The Holy Ghost chapels are maintained by brotherhoods whose chief task is to organise festivals. The festivals follow a ritual that dates back to the early days of colonisation when the islanders would call upon the Holy Ghost in times of natural disaster. They were originally intended to be charitable events and one of their main functions was to provide meals for the poor.

During today's festival an emperor is still elected by the people. He is presented with a sceptre and crown on a silver platter and is crowned by a priest. He is then accompanied to the *Império do Santo Espírito* where he receives the gifts to be distributed to the poor and then invites the whole village to take part in the feast which is followed by a traditional *tourada da corda (see below)*.

The island of bulls – Terceira is famous for its **touradas à corda** which take place during village festivals. A bull with a long rope about its neck and its horns adorned with baubles is held by four men in white coats and grey trousers. The animal is allowed to rush at crowds of men who speed away leaving the bravest to taunt the bull by opening a large black umbrella beneath its muzzle.

Another bullfighting event, the **tourada**, which is conducted on horseback against locally reared bulls, is held regularly in the bullring at Angra do Heroísmo and attracts large crowds from all over the island.

★★ANGRA DO HEROÍSMO Population 12 000

The town set in the curve of a wide bay or *angra* and dominated by Monte Brasil, is without doubt the most beautiful haven in the archipelago.

Angra do Heroísmo is home to the Minister of the Republic and to a branch of the University of the Azores.

The architecture is particularly interesting in that it is a synthesis of different features: Portuguese, Brazilian – the streets are strangely like those of Ouro Preto – and even English and American.

Historical notes – In 1474 the town became the headquarters of a captaincy and in 1534 Pope Paul III raised it to the level of a bishopric. By the 16C it had become a busy port, expressing its wealth in fine buildings constructed within the grid-iron street plan which exists to this day. With the restoration of Portuguese sovereignty in 1640, Angra regained its status as the economic, political and religious centre of the Azores which it kept until the 19C.

Angra do Heroísmo

The title "do Heroísmo" was bestowed upon the town by Queen Maria II in memory of the heroism shown by the inhabitants during the onslaught by Dom Miguel's supporters in the 19C.

The 1980 earthquake – On January 1 a violent earthquake shook the town and demolished a large part of it without taking any lives. In 1983 Angra do Heroísmo was given World Heritage status by Unesco and the outstanding work carried out has since restored its former beauty.

Sights

Historical quarter – Beyond the Bahía de Angra, where caravels and galleons once moored, lies the geometric street plan that follows the original layout. The houses within the square of streets bordered by the harbour, Rua Direita, Rua da Sé and Rua Gonçalo Velho, are adorned with wrought-iron balconies and window and door frames made of stone that set off the pastel colours of the façades.

Sé – The cathedral is the Episcopal See of the Azores. Building began in 1570 on the site of a 15C church and was completed in 1618. The austere design is in keeping with the architecture prevalent during Philip II's reign. The cathedral was badly damaged both by a fire and the 1980 earthquake. Inside, there is carved wooden vaulting and a fine silver altarpiece in the chancel. The collection of 17C sculptures by Masters of the Cathedral of Angra show a Spanish and Oriental influence.

Palácio dos Bettencourts ⊘ (**A**) – The 17C mansion in the baroque style houses the public library and the city archives. *Azulejos* inside illustrate episodes from the history of Terceira.

Igreja da Misericórdia – The late-18C church overlooks the bay.

Praça da Restauração or Praça Velha (**28**) – The 19C **Town Hall** or Paços do Concelho looks onto the square.

Igreja do Colégio – The collegiate church was built by the Jesuits in the middle of the 17C. Of particular interest are the carved cedarwood ceiling, the delft earthenware in the sacristy and the many altarpieces and Indo-Portuguese ivory statues.

Palácio dos Capitães-generais (**D**) – The former Jesuit college was converted into the Palace of the Captain-Generals after the expulsion of the Society of Jesus by the Marquis of Pombal. The palace was largely rebuilt in 1980 and painted white and yellow. Today it houses the offices of the Regional Government of the Azores. It was in this palace that President Pompidou of France held a meeting with President Nixon in 1971.

Jardim Público Duque da Terceira – The gardens of exotic trees and flowers stand in the former grounds of the Monastery of São Francisco.

Convento de São Francisco: Museu de Angra ⊘ (**M**) – The museum displays collections of weapons, musical instruments, ceramics, porcelain, furniture and paintings, including some 16C panels of St Catherine.

Igreja de Nossa Senhora de Guia – This vast church with painted pillars forms part of the São Francisco Monastery and contains some of the museum collections. It was built in the 18C on the site of a chapel where Vasco da Gama buried his brother Paulo who died on his return from a voyage to the Indies.

Igreja de São Gonçalo – The 17C church adorned with *azulejos* has interesting cloisters.

Alto da Memória – The obelisk was erected on the site of the town's first castle in memory of Dom Pedro IV. There is a fine view of the town and Monte Brasil.

Castelo de São João Baptista – The fortress stands at the foot of Monte Brasil and commands the entrance to the harbour. It was built during the Spanish domination of Portugal and was first called the St Philip Fortress. It is one of the largest examples of military architecture from 16 and 17C Europe.
The Igreja de São Baptista inside the fortress was built by the Portuguese to celebrate the departure of the Spanish.

★★**Monte Brasil** – To benefit fully from the site one must climb to the Pico das Cruzinhas, passing the fortress of São João Baptista on the way. There is a view of the Monte Brasil crater and an outstanding **panorama**★★ of Angra from the commemorative monument or *padrão*.

Fortaleza de São Sebastião – This was built during the reign of King Sebastião and dominates Pipas harbour.

ANGRA DO HEROISMO

Alfândega (Pátio da) 3
Barreiro (Can. do) 4
Canoa Verdeo (Rua doc) 6
Carreira dos Cavalos (Rua)....... 7
Ciprião Figueiredo (Rua)............. 9
Conceição (Rua)........................ 10

Cons. José Silvestre Ribeiro
  (Rua)............................. 12
Covas (Alto das) 13
Dr Aníbal Bettencourt.............. 15
Faleiro (Rua do) 16
Gaspar Corte Real (Estrada)...... 18
Gonçalo Velho (Rua)............... 19
Jacomo de Bruges (Avenida)...... 21
M. Terras (Rua das)............... 22

Miragaia (Rua da) 24
Oliveira (Rua da) 25
Palácio (Rua do)...................... 27
Restauracão (Praça da) 28
Santo Espirito (Rua do) 30

A Palácio dos Bettencourts
D Palácio dos Capitães-Generais
M Museu de Angra

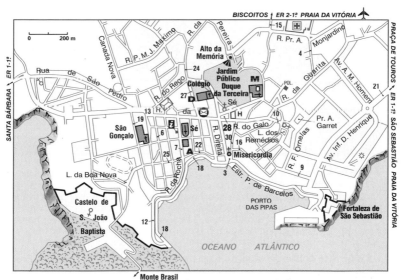

1 TOUR OF THE ISLAND from Angra do Heroísmo
85km/53mi – Allow one day

The coast road between Angra do Heroísmo and the village of São Mateus is lined by country estates with fine houses *(quintas)*. There is a beautiful view of São Mateus.

São Mateus – The picturesque fishing village is dominated by its church, the tallest on the island.

The west of the island is dotted with charming little villages such as the summer resorts of **Porto Negrito** and **Cinco Ribeiras**. There are also views of the islands of Graciosa, São Jorge and Pico.

Santa Bárbara – The 15C village **church** contains a statue of St Barbara in Ançã stone (from mainland Portugal).

Serra da Santa Bárbara road – *Head towards Esplanada then bear left onto a forest road which climbs to the summit.* The road affords wonderful panoramas of the island. From the top there is a view of the vast crater of the **Caldeira de Santa Bárbara**.

Return to the road, bear left, continue to the junction with the road between Angra do Heroísmo and Altares. Turn left.

★**Biscoitos** – The name *biscoitos* has been given to the strangely-shaped layers of lava which flowed up from the earth during volcanic eruptions and formed a lunar landscape. Natural **swimming-pools** have been hewn out of the rock and are popular in summer.

Biscoitos is famous for its vines or *curraletas*, protected by stone walls beneath which they grow. A Wine Museum, **Museu do Vinho** ⊙, displays the equipment in which generations of wine-growers have made *verdelho*, a sweet aperitif wine containing an average of nine grape varieties which once appeared on the tables of some of Europe's leading houses. Dry and sweet *verdelho*, which is produced exclusively from verdelhe stock, is produced and bottled by the museum itself. Note the old Roman type of winepress which could be transported and used by the whole community.

Take the Angra road from Biscoitos and bear left towards Lajes.

The terrain in the centre of the island has suffered from volcanic upheaval which has left craters like the vast Caldeira de Guilherme Moniz.

Follow signs to Furnas do Enxofre.

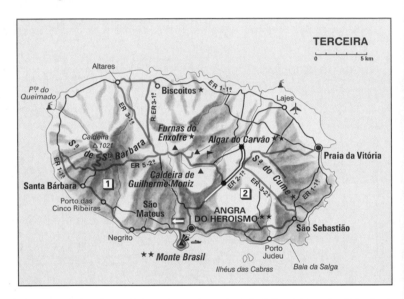

★**Furnas do Enxofre** – *Follow the path to the left (after taking the Estrada do Cabrito at the Pico da Bragacina crossroads) until you reach a small car park. 10min round trip on foot.* You soon reach a wild landscape over which vapours cloud. These are fumaroles which rise up from sulphur wells in the ground. The air is hot and there is a strong smell. The sulphur crystallises into beautiful bright yellow flowers; in some places a red colour dominates, spreading over the ground and rocks. Furnas de Enxofre is a surreal world of colour, light and steam.

Caldeira de Guilherme Moniz – As the road descends between Furnas do Enxofre and Algar do Carvão one can catch glimpses of the immense crater with its 15km/ 9mi perimeter. The flat green crater floor is covered in thick vegetation.

★★**Algar do Carvão** ⊙ – A tunnel some fifty yards long leads to the base of a volcanic chimney, a sort of moss-covered well of light 45m/148ft high. You continue down into an enormous cave which was formed by escaping gases when the lava cooled. Above is a series of majestic overlapping arches of different colours: beige, obsidian black and ochre. Several siliceous concretions have formed milky white umbrella shapes on the cave walls. Below, the arches can be seen reflected in a pool.

The road connects with the Via Rápida which leads back to Angra do Heroísmo. One can also follow itinerary ② in the opposite direction to return to Angra.

② FROM ANGRA DO HEROÍSMO TO PRAIA DA VITÓRIA
35km/22mi – 2hr

The strange rocks, Ilhéus Cabras, a short distance beyond Angra look as though they have been sawn through the middle.

São Sebastião – The village was the first site to be settled on the island and has preserved some old monuments.

*Igreja de São Sebastião – The Gothic church built in 1455 has a graceful doorway and chapels with Manueline and Renaissance vaulting. The nave has some interesting 16C frescoes, illustrating on the left, the Last Judgement, and on the right, St Martin, St Mary Magdalene and St Sebastian set in a medieval castle.

Opposite the church is the **Império do Espírito Santo** decorated with romantic paintings. A commemorative monument or *padrão* stands in the neighbouring square.

Beyond São Sebastião take ER 3.2 left to Serra do Cume, then a road right which climbs to the top.

*Serra do Cume – The gentle slopes of this eroded volcano form a patchwork of fields divided by low stone walls where Dutch cows can be seen grazing. At certain times of the day, particularly in the evening, the countryside takes on a lush bucolic air.

The tourada in São Sebastiao

Praia da Vitória – The "Praia" in the name derives from the beautiful white sand **beach** which stretches the full length of the bay, and the "da Vitória" commemorates the battle in 1829 between Liberals and supporters of Dom Miguel.

A harbour sheltered by a breakwater some 1 400m/1 500yds long serves as a dock for ships, while the Lajes air base nearby, which was established by the British in 1943 and enlarged by the Americans in 1944, is still used by the United States air force and serves as a port of call for heavy transport aircraft.

Praia da Vitória is a lively place when the weather is fine and the beach and surrounding cafés fill with people.

The old town centre has been preserved and has a 16C **Town Hall** and an old parish church.

Igreja Matriz – This large church was founded by Jacomo de Bruges, the island's first donee-captain. Its main doorway, a gift from the King, Dom Manuel, is Gothic in style, while another portal, a side entrance, is Manueline. The rich interior decoration includes *azulejos* and gilt altarpieces.

GRACIOSA*

Angra do Heroísmo

Surface area: 61sq km/24sq mi; Length: 12.5km/8mi; Width: 8.5km/5mi
Population: 5 189
Main town: Santa Cruz da Graciosa – Highest point: 398m/1 306ft

Access: *There are regular flights between Terceira and Graciosa and boat connections between the two islands several times a week.*

Length of stay: *One can tour the island in a few hours although it is pleasant to spend time strolling through Santa Cruz or driving along narrow country roads.*

Graciosa or "gracious" island owes its name to its attractive main town, Santa Cruz, its countryside of well-tended vineyards and fields of maize, and its villages bright with flowers set at the foot of gently rolling hills dotted with windmills. Graciosa is the second smallest island after Corvo and has the lowest altitude (the highest point, Pico Timão, rises to 398m/1 306ft). The whole of the eastern part of the island is occupied by a vast crater.

Historical notes – Graciosa was probably discovered by sailors from Terceira and then settled by Portuguese families from the Beira and Minho regions as well as by Flemings. In 1810 the French writer and diplomat Chateaubriand spent some time in the Santa Cruz Monastery and mentioned his stay in *Memoirs from beyond the Tomb*.

Windmills – The Dutch style windmills with their pointed, onion shaped tops that pivot in the direction of the wind are a rather surprising feature of the island's landscape.

The Azores Archipelago

★SANTA CRUZ DA GRACIOSA Population 2 000

Santa Cruz is a delightful small town with its bright white house façades set off by volcanic stone. The centre forms a charming scene with its two pools, once watering holes for livestock, surrounded by majestic monkey-puzzle trees, and in which are reflected the outlines of the church and several town mansions. Down by the harbour with its fishermen's cottages, the locals remember the great whaling days of the past.

Igreja Matriz – This church was first built in the 16C and reconstructed two centuries later. Inside, the **panels★** at the high altar by 15C Portuguese Primitives illustrate the Holy Cross (Santa Cruz) as well as Pentecost, recalling the worship of the Holy Ghost which is still a strong tradition in the Azores. A chapel on the left contains Flemish statues of St Peter and St Anthony.

Museu Etnográfico ⊘ – The collections housed in a former mansion evoke traditional island life through various displays including tools, clothes and pottery. Note the large winepresses and the millstone used for grinding maize which was drawn by an ox.

An annexe to the museum in the harbour contains a whaling boat *(a video on whaling is also shown)*.

Ermidas do Monte da Ajuda – The three hermitages devoted to São João, São Salvador and **Nossa Senhora da Ajuda** dominate the town and can be reached on foot *(20min)* or by car. There is a beautiful **view★** of Santa Cruz.

Excursion

★**Farol da Ponta da Barca** – *4.5km/3mi west of Santa Cruz.* There is a view from the lighthouse of the headland of red rocks plunging to a bright blue sea.

INLAND

Praia – The old village stretches alongside its harbour and the beach after which it is named.

GRACIOSA

★★**Furna do Enxofre** ⊘ – *The best time to visit is between 1100 and 1400 when the sun shines into the cave.*

Furna de Enxofre is in the middle of a vast caldeira or crater. A tunnel has been dug through one of the sides of the crater giving access by car. Once inside the crater the road zigzags down to the entrance of the chasm. From here a path and then a spiral staircase (184 steps) lead down to the chasm. The cave itself is immense – 220m/722ft long by 120m/394ft wide. It contains a lake of hot sulphurous water which gurgles and boils. The steps were built in 1939; before that, one had to follow the example of Prince Albert of Monaco who visited the cave in 1879 by climbing down a rope ladder.

Furna Maria Encantada – *Leave the caldeira. Once through the tunnel take the first road left. About 100 yards further on there is a sign on the right to Furna de Maria Encantada. A path reinforced by logs leads up to a rock above the road (5min). A natural tunnel in the rock about ten yards long opens onto the crater affording a good overall view.*

The road continues around the crater. There are views over Graciosa island with Terceira in the distance.

Carapacho – Carapacho is a small spa as well as a seaside resort. The hot springs that rise from the sea bed are used for therapeutic purposes, particularly in the treatment of rheumatism.

The star ratings are allocated for various categories :
– regions of scenic beauty with dramatic natural features
– cities with a cultural heritage
– elegant resorts and charming villages
– ancient monuments and fine architecture
– museums and picture galleries.

FAIAL★★★

Horta

Surface area: 173sq km/67sq mi; Length: 21km/13mi; Width: 14km/9mi

Population: 14 920

Main town: Horta – Highest point: 1 043m/3 422ft.

Access: *There are direct flights from Lisbon to Horta and regular flights between Faial and the other islands. Boats connect Faial and the port of Madalena on Pico island (30min) several times a day, and Faial, São Jorge and Terceira several times a week in summer.*

Length of stay: *Allow at least two days to explore Horta and tour the island.*

The blue island, as Faial is also known, owes its name to the mass of hydrangeas that flower there in season. There is a magnificent view from Faial of Pico's volcano, while Faial itself has some interesting volcanic features such as the Caldeira crater and the Capelinhos volcano. The island's particular charm derives from Horta, the main town and pleasure boat harbour, its attractive villages, windmills and beaches (Porto Pim, Praia do Almoxarife and Praia da Fajã).

Historical notes – The island's first inhabitant was a hermit. He was followed by the Fleming Josse van Huerter who set out to look for silver mines. After an unsuccessful attempt by northern Portuguese to settle the island, Josse van Huerter – who thanks to the intervention of the Duchess of Burgundy, the daughter of King João I of Portugal, was appointed donee-captain in 1468 – obtained permission to bring his countrymen to settle. Farming and the cultivation of plants for the dye industry brought Faial a certain amount of prosperity but it was in the 19C that Horta became famous for its harbour, and trade began to develop.

Capelinhos, the birth of a volcano – The headland on the west of the island is covered in ashes from Capelinhos, the volcano that rose up from the depths of the ocean in 1957. On September 27, there was a huge eruption under the sea accompanied by gaseous emissions and clouds of steam that reached a height of 4 000m/13 000ft. A first islet surfaced only to disappear a short time afterwards. Then a second islet-volcano formed and was joined to Faial by an isthmus of lava and ash. For thirteen months, up until October 24, 1958, volcanic activity continued in the form of underwater explosions, lava flows, eruptions and showers of ash that covered the village of Capelo and the lighthouse. As Capelinhos volcano rose, so the water level of the lake inside Faial's crater or caldeira, fell. By the end of the eruption the volcano had increased the size of Faial by 2.4sq km/0.9sq mi, although marine erosion has since reduced this to 1sq km/0.38sq mi. Over 300 houses were destroyed and alternative lodging had to be found for 2 000 people.

★HORTA Population 6 000

Horta stretches out alongside a bay which forms one of the rare sheltered anchorages in the archipelago. This is where Josse van Huerter, after whom the town is probably named, came to settle.

Anglo-Saxon influence is apparent in Horta's architecture and in the names of some of the properties including The Cedars. This heritage comes down from the **Dabneys**, a family of wealthy American traders and consuls who held a lot of sway on the island in the 19C. When they left, American presence in Faial continued through trans-atlantic cable companies.

Since 1976 Horta has been the seat of the Parliament for the Autonomous Region of the Azores as well as the headquarters for administrative bodies including the Ministry for Tourism.

Meteorology and telegraphic cables – Towards the end of the 19C, several scientists including Elisée Reclus and Prince Albert I of Monaco realised that the Azores anticyclone had considerable influence on the weather in western Europe. They concluded that if information on the anticyclone could be transmitted rapidly to the continent, the weather there could be forecast several days ahead of time. This resulted in the laying of a telegraphic cable between Faial and Lisbon in 1893. And so the weather forecast came into being. Eight years later King Dom Carlos I came to Faial to lay the first stone of a weather station.

Between 1900 and 1928 Horta became an important anchoring point for underwater cables linking Europe and America. English, German, American, French and Italian companies employed cosmopolitan staff who lived in lodgings around Rua Cônsul Dabney, including the small Western Union buildings that now house the Faial Hotel. After the Second World War the cables were abandoned little by little giving way to radio-telephone and communications provided by increasingly regular air transport. By 1960 their use had ceased altogether.

In the 1930s, Faial was a port of call and a refuelling station for sea-planes and it was not uncommon to see one or more of these aircraft afloat in Horta harbour.

Sights

★**Marina da Horta** – The marina is where sailors on their journey across the Atlantic congregate. It has become a kind of open air art gallery since each crew leaves a visual trace of its stay, otherwise, as the superstition goes, some mishap will befall it.

Historical quarter – The quarter is dominated by the imposing façades of its churches which face the sea. It comprises the area around **Rua Conselheiro Medeiros, Rua W. Bensaúde** and **Rua Serpa Pinto** which are lined with 18 and 19C shops and houses surmounted by unusual wooden upper storeys. This main thoroughfare leads to **Praça da República**, a charming square with a bandstand sheltered by monkey-puzzle trees. The market gives onto the square. The striking façade of the **Sociedade Amor da Pátria** building dating from 1930 and decorated with a frieze of blue hydrangeas, can be seen in the northeast corner of the square on Rua Ernesto Rebelo.

Igreja Matriz de São Salvador – This vast 18C church, which formerly belonged to the Jesuit College, has some fine *azulejos* and interesting baroque furniture.

Museu da Horta ⊙ – The museum housed in the former Jesuit College, traces the history of the town, in particular the laying of the underwater cables. There is also an extraordinary collection of **items made of fig-tree pith**★ carved by Euclíades Rosa between 1940 and 1960. These miniatures, depicting monuments, sailing ships and scenes of everyday life, required countless hours of work.

Forte de Santa Cruz – The fort was begun in the 16C, enlarged at a later date and now houses an inn.

"Chez Peter" Café – The café, a popular meeting place for sailors, contains the **Museu do Scrimshaw** ⊙.

Among the items on display are sperm-whale teeth engraved by whalers. There are scenes of whale hunting on the older teeth while more recent engravings include portraits of well-known yachtsmen such as Sir Francis Chichester and the Frenchman Eric Tabarly.

★★**Monte da Guia** – *A road leads up to the summit of Monte da Guia.* Horta bay is sheltered by two volcanoes linked to the mainland by isthmuses. The first volcano, Monte Queimado dominates the harbour and is linked by an isthmus to the second, Monte da Guia.

From the top of Monte da Guia, beside the **Ermida de Nossa Senhora da Guia**, there is a view of **Caldeira do Inferno**, a former crater that has been filled in by the sea.

As you return to Horta there is a good **view**★ of the town and the beach at Porto Pim. Porto Pim inlet was originally protected by fortifications.

TOUR OF THE ISLAND *80km/50mi from Horta – allow 5hr.*

Take the airport road from Horta and drive along the southwest coast.

The road leads past **Castelo Branco** headland, so named on account of its white cliffs, and continues to **Varadouro**, a small spa. Natural swimming-pools have been hewn out of the lava.

Follow signs to Capelinhos.

You cross Capelo village with the ruins of houses that were destroyed when Capelinhos erupted in 1957.

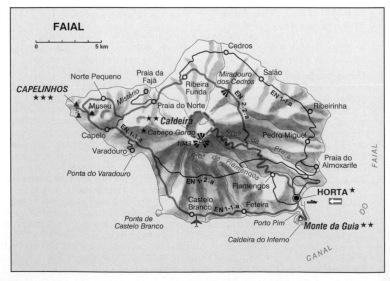

Capelinhos volcano

J. P. Garcin/DIAF

★★★ **Capelinhos** – *The best way to explore the volcano is to see it on foot. Park below the lighthouse and then allow for a walk of at least 1 hour.* The landscape of the volcano, so recent it is still devoid of vegetation, is fascinating. The volcano's very structure, with its ash, bombs (solidified lava) and scoria, is gradually being eroded by the sea, and the different mineral colours of ochre, red and black stand out against the green of the rest of the island.

Before reaching the lighthouse, you arrive at a house that has been rebuilt and now contains a **museum** ⊙ which traces the different phases of the eruption from 1957-8.

Between Capelinhos and Praia do Norte the road passes through Norte Pequeno where the houses are still buried in ash, then crosses a *mistério* or lava flow that is covered in thick vegetation consisting of hydrangeas, cedars and mango trees. Praia do Norte has a black sand beach known as Praia da Fajã. The coast beyond Praia do Norte becomes steep with a succession of lookout points.

Beyond Ribeira Funda bear right onto the road for Horta and Caldeira.

The road crosses a patchwork of fields separated by hydrangea hedges. There is a fine view from the **Miradouro dos Cedros**. After entering the **Ribeiro dos Flamingos** you join up with a road that rises in zigzags through hydrangeas, roses and cryptomerias to Caldeira and its crater.

★★ **Caldeira** – *Walk through a short tunnel into the crater.* Caldeira's vast crater is 400m/1 312ft deep with a diameter of 1 450m/4 757ft. It is a nature reserve covered in cedars, ferns, junipers, moss and various other species found on the island. The floor of the crater is very flat and the contours of the former lake which emptied during the eruption of Capelinhos can be clearly seen.

A path leading round the crater takes about 2 hours. A second path, which is for experienced walkers and can be dangerous if one does not have the right footwear or if the ground is slippery, leads down into the crater (Allow at least 5hr round trip). Beside the crater is **Cabeço Gordo★** *(45min round trip walk from Caldeira car park),* a lookout point at an altitude of 1 043m/3 422ft, with wonderful views of the islands of Pico and São Jorge and, in clear weather, of Graciosa.

Return to Horta through Ribeira dos Flamengos.

PICO★★

Horta

Surface area: 447sq km/173sq mi; Length: 42km/26mi; Width: 15km/9mi
Population: 15 302
Main towns: Madalena, Lajes and São Roque – Highest point: 2 351m/7 713ft.

Access: *There is a boat shuttle service between Horta on Faial and Madalena on Pico several times a day. In summer, boats call in at Cais do Pico from Terceira and São Jorge several times a week.*
There are also flights to Pico.

Length of stay: *One may tour Pico island in a day from Faial. However, if you wish to climb the volcano, allow at least one night on the island.*

Pico is a long island only 7km/4mi east of Faial. It is the second largest island in the archipelago after São Miguel and is dominated by the volcano after which it is named. The small population is spread between the different coastal villages.

Geography – The island is in fact a volcano upon which the cone of Pico sits. At 2 351m/7 713ft, it is the highest point in the whole of Portugal.
Recent volcanic activity is visible in the form of **misterios** or "mysteries". These are lava flows which occurred during eruptions after the island had been settled and so destroyed various cultivated areas. The humus layer has not yet had time to build itself up again on the burnt black earth and so it is not possible to farm the land. The result is a series of lunar landscapes with lichen-covered lava or, on the other hand, a contrasting tangle of luxuriant, riotous vegetation which is completely impenetrable. The most striking *misterios* are those of **Praínha** (1572), **Santa Luzia** (1718) and **São João** (1720).

Historical notes – Settlers from northern Portugal began to arrive on the island in 1460 and Pico became part of the captaincy of Faial.
Originally, the farming economy was based on the cultivation of cereals, woad for blue dye, as well as wine-growing. A new activity developed at the end of the 18C. This was whaling, which became an important source of income and was only stopped in 1981.

Pico wines – The vines grown on lava terrain produced a wine known as **verdelho** which enjoyed international acclaim for over 200 years and was particularly appreciated in England, America and Russia (where it appeared on the tables of the tsars). Then the vines were attacked by vine-mildew in the middle of the 19C. Little by little, the wine trade is being built up again on the island.

★★★PICO VOLCANO

Pico island's greatest attraction is the ascension of its volcano. This is a perfect cone with regular sides which is sometimes snow-capped in winter but which, more often than not, is hidden by cloud. They gather on the top or ring the volcano like a scarf; whatever the case, Pico is rarely completely cloud-free.

Allow at least 7 hours for the walk (3hr to climb to the crater, 30min to walk round it, 1hr to climb up to and down from Pico Pequeno and 2hr 30min to come right down again). The walk is fairly difficult and tiring on account of the difference in altitude and the volcanic rocks one has to walk over. Strong climbing shoes are an absolute must. It is a good idea to take at least 1 litre of drinking water per person or 1.5 litres if the weather is hot. Most walkers like to climb at night to be able to reach the summit as the sun rises. In this case it is best to have a guide (enquire at the Tourist Office or at your hotel). Otherwise, during the day and when the weather is fine, the path is easy to follow.

Access: *Taxis from Madalena can drive you to the beginning of the path. If you have a car, take the central road and turn right after 13km/8mi. A narrow road climbs for 5km/3mi up to the path.*

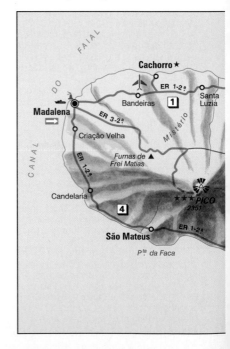

After about a 20-minute walk, you reach a cave (be careful not to slip), after which the path continues on to the right through ferns, heather and dwarf pines *(about 15min)*. You then reach the first of the cement stakes that line the path right up to the crater. The path becomes quite difficult and you sometimes have to scramble up with the help of your hands. The view stretches out over small volcanic cones at the foot of Pico. After a 3-hour climb you reach the crater which is 30m/98ft deep. It is an impressive sight – a bare, tortured landscape forming a circle with a 700m/2 297ft perimeter. **Pico Pequeno** (70m/ 230ft) rises at the far end to form the mountain summit. This may be climbed *(the ascent is very steep – allow 1hr there and back)*. The fumaroles and smell of sulphur at the top remind one that a volcano is never completely dormant. On a clear day the **panorama★★★** takes in São Jorge island stretching out like some sea monster, and Faial island with its volcano, Capelinhos. In the far distance are Graciosa and Terceira.

On the way back to Madalena, the cave at **Furnas de Frei Matias** *(a 5-minute walk from the road)* is a series of long underground galleries stretching out between mossy wells of light *(take a torch)*.

TOUR OF THE ISLAND

① From Madalena to São Roque *28km/17mi – 2hr*

Madalena – This harbour, into which boats sail from Horta 7km/4mi west, is protected by two rocks, Em Pé (meaning upright) and Deitado (meaning recumbent), which are home to colonies of sea birds. Madalena itself is a pleasant little town centred around the **Igreja de Santa Maria Madalena**. This has a graceful 19C façade and a 17C interior decorated with rich altarpieces of gilded wood.

★**Cachorro** – *After Bandeiras bear left off the main road and follow the signs.* The small village built of lava stretches out behind the airport landing strips beside black rocks and cliffs. These have been eroded into caves into which the sea rushes and roars. Most of the buildings were once storehouses for wine.

The road continues through the villages of **Santa Luzia** and **Santo António** whose plain-looking church contains a baroque altarpiece in the naive style.

★**São Roque do Pico** – The town grew prosperous when it was a whaling centre. Nowadays, if a whale is spotted on the horizon, the signal is given and boats take tourists out to have a look.

Cais do Pico – This is São Roque's harbour. It possesses the archipelago's only **whaling factory** which was closed down in 1981. Whales, and particularly sperm-whales, caught off the central group of islands, were towed here to the quayside to be cut up. The factory front bears the words "Vitaminas, Óleos, Farinhas, Adubos, Armações Baleeiras Reunidas Lda" which translates as: vitamins, oil, flour, fertiliser, and the name of the co-operative. The whale blubber was melted down to produce

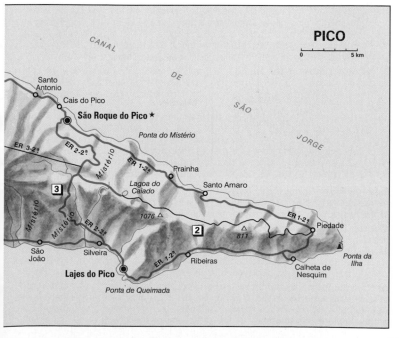

Pico Volcano

oil, the liver was mashed for vitamins, the meat was milled into flour for animal fodder and the bones were ground into fertiliser. A streamlined whaling boat is on display to illustrate the sporting skill and danger of the hunt.

Convento and Igreja de São Pedro de Alcântara – The baroque building stands out against the volcano in the background. It has an interesting façade, and inside, the chancel is adorned with *azulejos* and an abundantly decorated altarpiece.

Igreja de São Roque – *This is in a different part of town, beyond the centre, on the sea front.* The church is a large 18C building decorated inside with statues, jacaranda wood furniture inlaid with ivory, and a silver lamp donated by Dom João V.

From São Roque to Lajes do Pico There are two possible itineraries.

2 Via the coast – *50km/31mi, allow 2hr 30min. This itinerary is for those who have the time and who don't mind winding roads.*
The villages along this route include **Praínha**, which is well-known for its *misterio* and natural swimming-pools, **Santo Amaro** with its shipbuilding yard, and **Piedade** and the attractive countryside at the end of the island. The itinerary continues along the southeast coast which is steep and bordered by projecting ledges of lava upon which are the fishing villages of **Calheta de Nesquim** and **Ribeiras**.

3 Via the centre of the island – *32km/20mi including an excursion to Lagoa do Caiado – allow 1 hr. Take the Lajes road which soon rises to cross the centre of the island. After 10km/6mi take the road left marked Lagoa do Caiado and continue for 5km/3mi.*
The centre of the island, which lies at an altitude of 800-1 000m/2 625-3 280ft, is often covered in cloud. There are a good many small crater lakes and the vegetation consists of strange low plants, some of which are indigenous species. *A road crosses the island from east to west affording good views of beautiful countryside (if one is lucky enough to be travelling on a clear day). After visiting Lagoa do Caiado, return to the main road and continue towards Lajes.*

Lajes do Pico – This was the first settlement on the island. The main activity from the 19C, up until 1981, was whaling. Lajes, a small, quiet, white town in the middle of maize fields, extends into a lava plateau known as a Fajã *(see SÃO JORGE).*

★ **Museu dos Baleeiros** ⊘ – The Whaling Museum is housed in a former boat shelter in the harbour. The fine **scrimshaw collection** contains engraved sperm-whale teeth and ivory walrus tusks. The early examples of the art show barely sketched stippled patterns while the more finely-worked later items were carved in the round. A streamlined whaling boat (baleeira) is displayed with all the equipment used during a hunt.

Ermida de São Pedro – By continuing along the quayside you arrive at a white chapel. It is the oldest on the island and has an attractive altarpiece in the naive style. Beside the chapel stands the **Padrão** monument, erected in 1960 to commemorate the five hundredth anniversary of the settlement of the island.

★★④ From Lajes to Madalena – Misterios and vineyards
35km/22mi – allow 1hr 30min

The road crosses the *misterios* on either side of **São João** which date from an eruption in 1718 and partly destroyed the village. Picnic areas and paths for exploring the region have been laid out along the misteries.

São Mateus – The village is dominated by its impressive church. In the old days the inhabitants of some of the hamlets around São Mateus were wine-growers. The road crosses through vineyards closed off by low lava walls. These are so closely spaced that there are sometimes only three or four rows of vines between each wall. The countryside is striking with the black of the lava walls contrasting sharply with the soft green of the abandoned vines and the deep blue of the sea beyond. The picture is completed by several small buildings used for storing wine. The road passes through **Candelaria** and **Criação Velha**, the village in which *verdelho* wine originated, before reaching Madalena.

SÃO JORGE★★
Horta
Surface area: 246sq km/95sq mi; Length: 56km/35mi; Width: 8km/5mi
Population: 10 219
Main town: Velas – Highest point: 1 067m/3 500ft.

Access: *There are flights between São Jorge and the other islands throughout the year. In summer, the boat that plies between the islands in the central group of the archipelago calls at São Jorge several times a week.*

Length of stay: *Allow a full day to tour the island by car.*

The cigar-shaped island stretches out parallel to Pico. Its wild, grandiose landscapes make a splendid environment for walking *(see book suggestions for ramblers in the Practical Information section).*

Geography – The island of São Jorge consists of a single, large, elongated volcano. It lies in the middle of the archipelago, and all the other islands in the central group can be seen from its uplands. Pico da Esperança is the highest point with an altitude of 1 053m/3 455ft.
Small cones in the middle of the island have resulted from recent volcanic eruptions. On the coast, the steep cliffs which drop sheer to the sea extend onto unusual basalt platforms level with the water. These **fajãs**, as they are known, are the remains of eroded cliff faces that have collapsed. Their soil is fertile, hence the orchards and fields. They were once densely populated areas but those that do not have good road connections have been abandoned.

Historical notes – In 1443 the first settlers to arrive on the island were Flemings brought by Wilhelm van der Haegen whose name was changed to Guilhermo da Silveira. The island was colonised rapidly and in 1483 João Vaz Corte Real was appointed donee-captain. The island's main wealth originally came from plants such as woad and orchil which were exported to Flanders for the dye industry. In the 18C the island was pillaged by Duguay-Trouin, a French pirate who brought with him 700 men. São Jorge has experienced several earthquakes of which the latest, in 1980, caused a lot of damage and forced some of the population to emigrate.

Cheeses and bedspreads – São Jorge is well-known for its large round cheeses. These are made in increasingly modern dairies with milk from Dutch cows which can be seen grazing on pastures among hydrangeas. The cheeses are exported. Bedspreads, the island's other speciality, are woven on rudimentary wooden looms.

VELAS

Velas has grown on a fajã near the Baía de Entre-Morros. (The word *morro* means hillock.)
The small town has preserved several old buildings including the 18C **Paços do Concelho** (Town Hall), of Azorean baroque style with twisted columns on either side of its doorway, and the 18C **Portas do Mar**, a gateway remaining from the old ramparts. The 16C church of São Jorge has an interesting façade.

From Velas to Ponta dos Rosais – *14km/9mi west.* The road runs alongside Baía de Entre-Morros, crosses Rosais village and continues to **Sete Fontes**, an attractive forest with a picnic area. There are also some animals, including deer, in enclosures. You can continue to Ponta da Rosais by car although it is extremely pleasant to walk the distance *(2hr 30min round trip).* There are fine views of both sides of the island. At the sea-battered headland there is a lighthouse and an islet.

The Azores Archipelago

★★TOUR OF THE ISLAND

83km/52mi – 4hr

The North Coast –

Take the Santo António road out of Velas.

The north coast is particularly steep with wonderful views. While the villages of Toledo, Santo António and Norte Pequeno are right near the sea, they stand at an altitude of 500m/ 1 640ft. The road, which is lined by a high hedge of hydrangeas, leads from one viewpoint to another, revealing impressive vistas of the coast.

★★**Fajã do Ouvidor** – The *fajã* with its hamlet is the largest on the north coast. The lookout point above it affords a bird's eye view of a flat stretch of land covered in cultivated fields and houses, dominated by a sheer cliff.

★★**Miradouro da Fajã dos Cubres** – The landscape viewed from this lookout point, on the road beyond Norte Pequeno, is highly characteristic of São Jorge. Seen from the side, the *fajãs* look like a series of festoons curving round the base

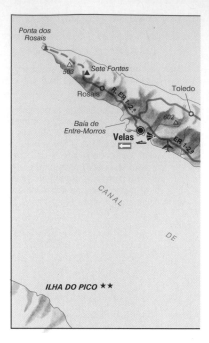

of sheer escarpments. The most impressive, **Fajã da Caldeira do Santo Cristo**, is occupied by a lagoon that has been made into a nature reserve to protect its clams, a particular type of scallop-shell only found here.

The road from the north coast to the village of Ribeira Seca on the south coast crosses beautiful woodland criss-crossed by hedges of hydrangeas. The **view**★★ is particularly fine from the **Miradouro de Urzal**.

The South Coast

The relief on the south coast is gentler than that on the north and the region is more densely populated. There is a succession of villages along the shore. The coast continues to Topo headland, although the itinerary suggested here begins at **Ribeira Seca** and includes **Serra do Topo** and **Fajã de São Jorge**. The most hospitable part of the coast is between Calheta and Velas where the villages have been developed into seaside resorts with swimming-pools and camp sites.

Calheta – This fishing village has preserved some old houses.

Manadas – The picturesque hamlet is mainly known for its **Igreja de Santa Bárbara**★ ⊙ which is on the seashore (narrow road down). It dates from the 18C and is one of the prettiest churches in the Azores. The very rich interior decoration was directed by an Italian artist. The finely worked **cedarwood ceiling**★ is adorned with naive sculptures like that of St George slaying the dragon. The *azulejos* relate the story of St Barbara. There are some fine cupboards for copes and other vestments in the sacristy.

Urzelina – The village, which was rebuilt after the volcanic eruption in 1808, was named after the island's brown lichen or orchil *(urzela)*. A tower emerges out of the lava beneath which the church lies buried. Small windmills still functioning beside the shore stand out against Pico island in the background.

A lookout point on the road approaching Velas gives an interesting **aerial view** of the town.

WALKS

The whole of São Jorge lends itself wonderfully to walking. The walk below is particularly special and includes the northern *fajãs*.

★**The Fajã de Caldeira and Fajã dos Cubres walk** – *3hr. Bring good walking shoes. The itinerary begins beyond Ribeira Seca and ends at Fajã dos Cubres. Arrange for a taxi to come and collect you at the end. Take the path which begins on the left of the road between Ribeira Seca and Topo, 5.5km/3.4mi from the junction with the road from Norte Pequeno.*
A very steep, paved path with occasional steps leads down to sea level. One then crosses several *fajãs* with their orchards and hamlets where most of the houses have been abandoned. The *fajãs* include Fajã da Caldeira, Fajã dos Tijolos, Fajã do Belo and lastly, Fajã dos Cubres. There are magnificent views all along the way.

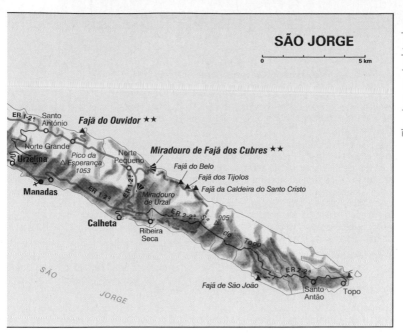

SÃO JORGE

0   5 km

ER 1-2ª   Santo
          António   **Fajã do Ouvidor ★★**
Norte Grande
Urzelina   Pico da   Norte   **Miradouro de Fajã dos Cubres ★★**
                Esperança   Pequeno
                1053   *Fajã do Belo*
Manadas   *Fajã dos Tijolos*
                            Miradouro   ▲ *Fajã da Caldeira do Santo Cristo*
                            de Urzal
          Calheta   ER 2-2ª   S.ª   905
                Ribeira   do   Topo
                Seca
                                                    ER 2-2ª
                            Fajã de São João   Santo   Topo
                                                        Antão

SÃO
    JORGE

View from the Miradouro da Fajã dos Cubres

FLORES★★
Horta
Surface area: 143sq km/55sq mi; Length: 17km/11mi; Width: 12.5km/8mi
Population: 4 329
Main town: Santa Cruz das Flores – Highest point: 914m/3 000ft.

Access: *Flores is only accessible by air from the other islands.*

Length of stay: *It is possible to tour the island in a day although it is well worth taking the time to stroll and go for walks. An extra day is required for an excursion to the island of Corvo.*

The island of flowers is the most westerly of the Azorean islands and the western-most point in Europe. Along with its sister Corvo, Flores lies at quite some distance from the other islands in the archipelago. It is 236km/147mi from Faial. Flores is thinly populated, very rugged and its wild landscapes are among the most majestic in the Azores. Its luxuriant vegetation is explained by the very high rainfall; it rains on average nearly 300 days a year.

The French scientific observatory that was set up on Flores in 1966 closed in June 1993. Over the last few years its role has changed from weather station to relay base for the space station at Kourou in French Guyana.

Historical notes – It is believed that the Fleming, Wilhelm van der Haegen, tried to settle the island but was discouraged by its remoteness and settled on São Jorge instead. It wasn't until the 16C that farmers from the continent arrived to cultivate cereals and grow woad and orchil for the dye industry.

Geography – The plateau in the middle of the island has an average altitude of 550m/1 804ft and is dominated by Morro Alto (914m/3 000ft). The magnificent land-scape is punctuated by seven crater lakes of which the most striking is Lagoa Funda. Between the plateau and the sea there are deep valleys formed by erosion; waterfalls plunge down steep cliffs into thick vegetation.

The abundant sources of water were tapped in the past to power the many small water-mills built out of black lava on streams all over the island. Farmers used them to grind the wheat and maize they grew on terraced hillsides. Today, the island's main resources derive from farming and stock rearing.

SANTA CRUZ DAS FLORES Population 2 000

Santa Cruz, the island's administrative centre, is a quiet, pleasant town with a small harbour. The whaling boats moored here are remnants of an era when sperm-whale hunting was an important activity.

Museu Etnográfico ◷ – The museum, set up in an old house, displays several reconstituted interiors of traditional homes as well as a collection of items illus-trating the inhabitants' way of life on the island. This was centred around fishing and whaling – there are some scrimshaw pieces – and work in the fields.

Convento de São Boaventura ◷ – The 17C building, once a Franciscan monastery, has been restored to house part of the museum. The baroque chancel in the church shows a Hispano-Mexican influence.

★★TOUR OF THE ISLAND
68km/42mi – about 4hr

Take the Lajes road out of Santa Cruz.
The road twists and turns with the relief, dipping into deep ravines and running alongside mountain ridges. It affords superb views above the banks of bright red and yellow cannas and blue hydrangeas that line it.

Fazenda das Lajes – The **Igreja do Senhor Santo Cristo** with its *azulejo* decoration on the façade, is one of the most representative exam-ples of Azorean religious architecture.

Lajes The island's second largest town thrives on its harbour activities and a major radio station.

Once past Lajes, take the road south. Turn right towards Lagoa Funda.

★★**Lagoa Funda** – Lagoa Funda, meaning deep lake, is a crater lake that stretches out for mi below the road at the foot of steep slopes covered in hydrangeas. After 3km/1.8mi you reach a rudimentary parking area where, to the right, and at a great depth, one can see the end of Lagoa Funda and, to the left, at road level, **Lagoa Rasa**.

Return to the road, and 600m/660yds beyond the 25km mitone, look up to see the Rocha dos Bordões rock formation.

★★**Rocha dos Bordões** – Masses of flowers can be seen bursting from basalt organ pipes. These high, vertical stria were formed when the basalt solidified. More can be seen several hundred yards further on where they flank a waterfall at a bend in the road.

Take the Mosteiro road.

The road passes near the village of **Mosteiro**, which is set in enchanting countryside with the sea in the background, runs alongside an abandoned hamlet and then links up with the main road.

A little further on take the road to Fajāzinha and Fajā Grande.

Fajāzinha – As the road approaches Fajāzinha there is a beautiful **view**★★ from above of the village setting. The **Igreja de Nossa Senhora dos Remédios** dates from the 18C. The 300m/984ft Ribeira Grande waterfall is in the vicinity.

Fajā Grande – This is the island's seaside resort. A long shingle beach stretches out at the foot of an impressive cliff over which waterfalls plunge. The most spectacular of these waterfalls may be reached from the Ponta da Fajā road.

Cascata (Waterfall) – *Turn right towards Ponta da Fajā. Continue for 400m/ 440 yards and stop at the first bridge. Take the track on the left of the bridge as you stand looking towards the cliff. 20min round trip on foot.* The track follows the stream and passes three water-mills. The waterfall plunges from the top of the cliff onto a ledge where it divides into a multitude of smaller cascades and then loses itself in a natural basin among moss and hydrangeas.

Return to the main road and head for Santa Cruz. Turn left towards the lakes.

Lagoa Seca and Lagoa Branca – The road runs alongside the Lagoa Seca crater where the lake has dried up. Lagoa Branca or White Lake can be seen a little further on, on the left.

CORVO★

Horta
Surface area: 17sq km/6.5sq mi. Length: 6.5km/4 mi; Width: 4km/2.4 mi
Population: 393
Only town: Vila Nova do Corvo – Highest point: 718m/2 356ft.

As a rule, there are boat excursions ⊙ from Flores to Corvo every day during the summer. The boat leaves Santa Cruz harbour at 1000, arrives at Corvo at 1200 and returns between 1600 and 1800. It is advisable to book in advance through your hotel. A large, black, sea-battered rock rises out of the water 15 nautical mi northeast of Flores. This is Crow Island, the visible part of Monte Gordo (718m/2 356ft), a marine volcano. As there is no protected bay, access is difficult. In 1452, Corvo was the last of the islands in the archipelago to display the Portuguese flag and settlement only began in the middle of the 16C. A remote community of farmers and herders began to develop. In winter, for weeks on end, it was impossible for boats to moor so communication with Flores was made through lighting fires on a hillock. Nevertheless, in spite of the island's isolation, its inhabitants had a reputation for bravery and American whalers arrived at the end of the 18C and into the 19C to recruit sailors.

SIGHTS

Vila Nova do Corvo – When the boat docks, it is greeted by people with their motorised cultivators and small trailers who are awaiting the arrival of basic products. The 400 or so inhabitants of the island live in the small village with its winding streets and simple architecture. The black stone façades have mostly been white-washed and many of the houses have added on a pig sty.

The **Igreja de Nossa Senhora dos Milagres** has preserved a 16C Flemish statue.

Vila Nova do Corvo may well be the smallest and least populated district in Portugal, yet it possesses an airport. By walking alongside the landing strip you reach some disused windmills near the shore, and opposite, a restaurant run by the local council.

Caldeira do Corvo

★**Caldeirão** – *6km/3.7 mi from Vila Nova. The restaurant runs* **jeep excursions** ⊘ *to the caldera (45 min round trip)*. One can also walk there along the road. (*3 hr round trip*). There is a difference in altitude of 550m/1 804ft. Bring warm clothes as the uplands are often covered in cloud and can be cool. The road to Caldeirão crosses beautiful countryside brightened by hedges of hydrangeas. The central crater has a perimeter of 3.4km/2mi and is 300m/984ft deep. Two blue lakes lie at the bottom and in them are some islets. According to tradition, these islets have the same layout as the islands in the Azores archipelago (with the exception of Flores and Corvo). The slopes of the crater were once cultivated and the side facing the lookout point is still crisscrossed by stone walls.

Practical information

Planning your trip ———————— 322

Getting there ———————————— 323

Getting around ————————————— 323

Accommodation ——————————— 325

Eating out —————————————— 326

General information ——————————— 326

Shopping ————————————————— 328

Recreation —————————————— 329

Calendar of events ———————— 331

Further reading ———————————— 333

Glossary ———————————————— 334

Admission times and charges ———— 336

Index ————————————————— 357

A window in the Alfama, Lisbon

Practical information

Planning your trip

Portugal has a relatively mild climate. However, the best time to visit the country depends on the region you wish to visit. The north is cooler than the south, particularly in Trás-os-Montes, where winter can be especially harsh. For a tour of the whole country, spring or autumn are the best seasons.

Spring – Spring is the best time to visit the south of the country if you wish to avoid the heat of summer and the masses who flock to the beaches in the Algarve. It is also the season when the flowers which adorn so many houses come into full bloom and the countryside is green.

April offers the added attractions of Holy Week festivities and numerous folklore events for visitors.

Summer – Inland, the summer months are hot and dry, but in the coastal areas the heat is tempered by sea breezes. Many *Romarias*, festivals, feast days and sporting events take place during the summer months *(see the Calendar of Events)* and of course it's the best time to head for the beaches. Average sea temperatures are as follows: 16/19°C - 61/66°F on the west coast; 21/23°C - 70/73°F on the Algarve coast. Average summer temperatures for the major towns and cities are: Oporto - 20°C; Lisbon - 26°C; Évora - 29°C; Faro - 28°C.

Autumn – In the north with the chestnut trees and the vineyards, the countryside takes on some lovely tints. The Douro Valley with its many vineyards becomes a hive of activity during the grape harvest (mid-September to mid-October). Autumn is also the ideal time to visit the Minho and Trás-os-Montes regions. Average temperatures in these two regions: 13°C/55°F and 8°C/45°F respectively (between October and December).

Winter – On the Algarve coast, where bathing is possible from March to November (sea temperature: 17°C; air temperature: 18°C), along the Costa de Estoril (sea temperature: 16°C; air temperature: 17°C), and, above all, in Madeira and the Azores (sea and air temperature: 21°C) where winters are mild and sunny. The Algarve is transformed at the end of January when the almond trees are in blossom.

In winter skiers flock to the winter sports centres in the Serra da Estrela.

Useful addresses

In Portugal

For general information on the country, contact:

– **ICEP** (Investimentos, Comércio e Turismo de Portugal). Posto de Turismo – Praça dos Restauradores, Palácio Foz, Lisboa. ☎ (01) 346 33 14/346 36 43

– **Direcção Geral de Turismo** - Avenida António Augusto de Aguiar, 86, 1050 Lisboa – ☎ (01) 357 50 86; Praça Dom João I, 25-4°, 4000 Porto. ☎ (02) 200 58 05.

Tourist Information Centres – All Portuguese towns have a Tourist Information Centre, known as Posto or Comissão de Turismo or simply Turismo, marked on Michelin town plans with an i. The addresses of individual Tourist Offices are listed in the Admission times and charges section.

Portuguese National Tourist Offices:

London: 22/25A Sackville Street, London WIX 1DE, ☎ (0171) 494 14 41.

New York: 590 Fifth Avenue 4th floor, New York NY 10036-4704, ☎ (212) 354 44 03.

Toronto: 60 Bloor Street West, Suite 1005, Toronto, Ontario N4W 3B8, ☎ 921 73 76.

Dublin: Knocksinna House, Knocksinna, Fox Rock, Dublin 18, ☎ (01) 289 35 69.

Formalities – Despite the new law which came into force on 1 January 1993 authorising the free flow of goods and people within the EU, it is nonetheless advisable that travellers should be equipped with some valid piece of identification such as a **passport**. Holders of British, Irish and US passports do not require a visa to enter Portugal, although visas may be necessary for visitors from some Commonwealth countries, and for those planning to stay longer than 3months. US citizens should obtain the booklet *Your Trip Abroad* ($1.25) which provides useful information on visa requirements, customs regulations, medical care, etc for international travellers. Apply to the Superintendent of Documents, P.O. Box 371954, Pittsburgh, PA 15250-7954. ☎ 202-783-3238.

Customs Regulations – Tax-free allowances for various commodities within the EU have increased with the birth of the Single European market. The HM Customs and Excise Notice 1 A *Guide for Travellers* explains how recent changes affect travellers within the EU. The US Customs Service (P.O. Box 7407, Washington, DC 20044. ☎ 202-927-5580) offers a publication *Know Before You Go* for US citizens.

Pets (cats and dogs) – A general health certificate and proof of rabies vaccination should be obtained from your local vet before departure.

Getting there

By air – Various international airlines operate regular services to the international airports in Portugal (Lisbon, Oporto and Faro). Contact airlines and travel agents for information and timetables.

BA and TAP operate daily flights from London to Lisbon (2hr 30min), Oporto (2hr) and Faro (3hr 15min). TAP operates flights from Manchester to the above airports and to Madeira and the Azores via Lisbon.

TAP Portugal, 19 Lower Regent Street, London SW1Y 4LR, ☎ (0171) 839 1031.

TAP and TWA operate daily flights from New York to Lisbon (6hr 30min). There are numerous connecting flights from other major American cities (Atlanta, San Francisco, Chicago, Boston, Dallas/Fort Worth).

TAP ticket office, 521 Fifth Avenue, New York 10017, ☎ 212-661-4359 or toll-free for information and reservations ☎ 800-221-7370.

There are numerous possibilities for fly-drive holidays.

By sea – There are no direct ferry services between Great Britain and Portugal however Brittany Ferries operate a car-ferry service between Plymouth and Santander in northern Spain 2 to 3 times a week. Distances from Santander are 600 miles to Lisbon, 500 miles to Oporto and 800 miles to the Algarve. Brittany Ferries' Agents: Millbay Docks, Plymouth PL1 3EW, Devon, ☎ (01752) 22,1321.

Modesto Pineiro & Coy, 27 Paseo de Pereda, Santander, Spain, ☎ (942) 21 45 00.

Across the Channel then on through France and Spain – There is now the choice between the Channel Tunnel and the numerous cross-Channel services (passenger and car ferries, hovercraft, SeaCat). The distance to Lisbon by road when you have landed from the car ferry or taken the Channel Tunnel is about 2 100km/1 300mi. The most direct route is via Bordeaux, Irun and then either San Sebastian or Valladolid or Burgos, Salamanca, Vilar Formosa and Coimbra to Lisbon.

By rail – The train journey from London (Victoria Station) to Lisbon is via Paris, where there is a change of railway stations. British Rail offers a wide range of services to the Channel ports and French Railways (SNCF) operates an extensive network of lines including many high-speed passenger trains and motorail services throughout France. Information and bookings from:

British Rail International, Ticket and Information Office, PO Box 303, Victoria Station, London SW1V 1JY, ☎ (0171) 834 23 45 (enquiries only)

French Railways, 179 Piccadilly, London W1V 0BA, ☎ (0171) 409 35 18.

By coach – Regular coach departures are operated from London to the following destinations in Portugal: Coimbra, Faro, Guarda, Lagos, Lisbon, Mangualde, Oporto and Viseu.

Eurolines, 52 Grosvenor Gardens, Victoria, London SW1W 0A 4, ☎ (0171) 730 82 35.

Getting around

BY CAR

Documents – Nationals of EU countries require a national driving licence; nationals of non-EU countries require an international driving licence (obtainable in the the US from the American Automobile Association).

For the vehicle it is necessary to have the registration papers (log-book) and a national identification plate of the approved size.

Insurance – An International Insurance Certificate (Green Card) is compulsory. Third party insurance is also compulsory in Portugal. Special breakdown and get-you-home packages are a good idea (AA, Five Star RAC, National Breakdown, Europ-Assistance). Members of the American Automobile Association should obtain the brochure "Offices to Serve You Abroad".

If the driver of the vehicle is not accompanied by the owner, he or she should have written permission from the owner to drive in Portugal.

Driving regulations and general information – The minimum driving age is 17. Traffic drives on the right. It is compulsory for the front-seat passengers to wear seat belts when not driving in urban areas. The rules of the road are the same in Portugal as in other continental countries and Portugal uses the international road sign system.

Motorways – The Portuguese road network includes over 300km/186mi of motorways. Tolls are payable on some motorways and bridges.

Speed limits – Maximum speed limits are 120km/h / 75mph on motorways *(autoestrada)*; 90km/h / 56mph on dual carriageways *(estrada com faixas de rodagem separades)*; 90km/h / 56mph on other roads; 60km/h / 37mph in built-up areas.

Breakdown service – The Portuguese Automobile Club (Automovel Club de Portugal), Rua Rosa Arújo 24, Lisboa 1200, ☎ (01) 356 39 31, offers members of equivalent foreign organisations medical, legal and breakdown assistance.

Petrol – Super (97-96 octanes), normal (92-90 octanes) and diesel are generally available but not all petrol stations sell unleaded petrol *(gasolina sem chumbo)*. Credit cards are accepted in most petrol stations but visitors are strongly advised to have other means of payment with them. Petrol stations are generally open from 7am - midnight, although some open 24 hours a day.

Car hire – The major car hire firms have offices in all large towns. Cars may be hired from branches at airports, main stations and large hotels. The minimum age to qualify for car hire is 21. The Department of State publishes a pamphlet *A Safe Trip Abroad* which is available from the Superintendent of Documents, P.O. Box 371954, Pittsburgh, PA 15250-7954. ☎ 202-783-3238. Fly-drive schemes are operated by major airlines. Major car hire companies include Avis – ☎ (01) 346 26 76, Hertz – ☎ (01) 381 24 30, and Europcar – ☎ (01) 940 77 90.

Michelin's route planning service, available on the Internet, proposes various routes to drivers (shortest, quickest etc), distances between towns and cities, as well as details of restaurants and bars. Internet address: **www.michelin-travel.com** (there is a charge for using this service).

Road maps – Michelin map 990 at a 1: 1 000 000 scale covers the whole of the Iberian Peninsula, while map 940 at a 1: 400 000 scale, covers Portugal. Map 940 has an index and an enlarged inset map of Lisbon. Map 39 covers the city of Lisbon.

36 15 MICHELIN Minitel Service – Michelin Travel Assistance (AMI) is a computerised route-finding system offering integrated information on roads, tourist sights, hotels and restaurants. 36 15 MICHELIN is a French Telecom videotex services available in France and to foreign subscribers.

Railway station, Aveiro

BY AIR

TAP operates flights from Lisbon and Oporto to Madeira (Funchal) and from Lisbon to the Azores (Ponta Delgado on São Miguel). Local airlines operate inter-island flights in the Azores. Internal flights are the most practical way of travelling from the north to south, although prices tend to be relatively high.

International airports - Lisbon, Oporto, Faro, Funchal and Porto Santo (on Madeira), Ponta Delgada, Santa Maria and Terceira (in the Azores).

Journey times: Lisbon - Oporto: 30min; Lisbon - Faro: 30min; Lisbon - Funchal: 1hr 30min; Lisbon - Ponta Delgada: 1hr 30min.

BY TRAIN

Portuguese Railways – Caminhos de Ferro Portugueses (CP) has a rather sparse rail network linking major cities and an inter-city service. The rápidos or express trains are fast and punctual and some are first class only. The directos or inter-city trains are slower, make more stops and have both first and second class compartments. The regionais are often slow, run late and are overcrowded.

There is a tourist pass which is valid on the entire rail network for a period of 7, 14 or 21 days. For further information call (01) 888 40 25. Internet address: http://www.cp.pt

BY COACH

Portugal's national coach network (Rodoviária Nacional) is extremely extensive and covers all parts of the country. For information, contact: Rodoviária Nacional - Avenida Casal Ribeiro, 18 B – 1200 Lisboa; ☎ (01) 357 77 15.

Accommodation

Hotels – The **Michelin Red Guide España Portugal** is revised annually and is an indispensable complement to this Green Guide with information on hotels and restaurants including category, price, degree of comfort and setting. Towns underlined in red on the Michelin map 940 are listed in the current Red Guide with a choice of hotels and restaurants. The Portuguese Tourist Board also publishes a list with hotel categories ranging from one-star to five-star establishments. In Portugal hotel prices are inclusive of VAT (5% or 16%) and the price of breakfast is almost always included in the cost of the room.

Pousadas – The state-owned *pousadas* are marked by a ☺ sign on the Map of Places to Stay in the Introduction and on the Michelin map 940. Special mention should be made of thirty-odd Portuguese *pousadas*, most of which are extremely comfortable, restored historic monuments (castles, palaces and monasteries) in beautiful sites or excursion centres. The *pousadas* are very popular and usually full so it is always wise to book in advance. For further information, contact ENATUR, Avenida Santa Joana Princesa 10, 1700 Lisboa, ☎ (01) 848 12 21.

Estalagems – These are similar types of establishments, often refurbished historic buildings, but they are privately owned.

Residencial – These comfortable guest houses are almost on a par with some hotels but they do not serve meals.

Pensão – More modest guest house.

Bed and breakfast – Again the type of accommodation on offer is varied, although the term **Turismo de Habitação (TH)** usually covers historic houses and manors. There are numerous establishments in northern Portugal but again it is necessary to book in advance. In the north, contact Associação do Turismo de Habitação, Praça da República, 4990 Ponte de Lima, ☎ (058) 94 27 29; in Lisbon, Direcção Geral do Turismo, Rua António Augusto de Aguiar, 86, 1050 Lisboa – ☎ (01) 388 12 28.
For accommodation in rural houses apply to **ANTER (Associação de Turismo no Espaço Rural)**, either through the Direcção Geral do Turismo at the address specified above, or to ANTER, Rua 24 de Julho, 1-1° – 7000 Évora, ☎ (066) 74 45 55.

Camping – *(see △ sign on Michelin map 940)*. The local tourist information centres provide a list of official camp sites. The official classification awards stars (★ to ★★★★) to state owned sites and lists private ones. The international camping carnet is obligatory. Independent camping outside official sites is not allowed in Portugal. Details on camping and caravanning are supplied by the Federação Portuguesa de Campismo, Av Coronel Eduardo Galhardo, 24D, 1170 Lisboa ☎ (01) 812 68 90/1 or 812 69 00. It is advisable to book in advance for popular resorts during summer.

Youth Hostels (Pousadas de Juventude) – Portugal's 22 youth hostels (including two in the Azores) are open to travellers with an International Card. For further information, contact MOVIJOVEM - Pousadas de Juventade, Av. Duque de Avila, 137, 1050 Lisboa, ☎ (01) 313 88 20. Hostelling International/American Youth Hostel Association (☎ 202-783-6161) offers a publication *International Hostel Guide for Europe* listing properties throughout Europe. Youth hostels are located in the following Portuguese towns and cities from north to south: Vila Nova de Cerveira, Vilarinho das Furnas, Foz do Cávado, Braga, Oporto, Ovar, Mira, Penhas da Saúde, Coimbra, Leiria, São Martinho do Porto, Praia da Areia Branca, Sintra, Oeiras, Lisbon, Sines, Alcoutim, Vila Real de Santo António, Portimão and Lagos. In addition, there are two youth hostel in the Azores: one in Angra do Heroísmo (Terceira) and one in Ponta Delgada (São Miguel).

Eating out

Restaurants – The Portuguese keep fairly similar hours to the British and Americans. As a general rule, restaurants serve lunch from noon to 2.30pm and dinner from 7pm onwards.

A wide selection of gourmet restaurants can be found in the **Michelin Red Guide España Portugal** and **Portugal**. All towns with a restaurant listed in the Michelin Red Guide are underlined in red on the Michelin map 940.

A further selection of restaurants is also listed in the Lisbon, Oporto, Coimbra, Óbidos, Évora and Faro under *Travellers' addresses*.

In some of the more popular restaurants, particularly in the north, two prices are written by the same item. The first is for a full portion *(dose)* and the second is for the half-portion *(meia dose)*. Hors-d'œuvres are often served prior to the meal (cheese, cured ham, spicy sausage, olives, tuna croquettes etc) and are added to the bill if eaten. It is customary to leave a tip of about 10% of the total bill. For further information on Portuguese food and wine, please consult the relevant chapters in the Introduction to this guide.

J. P. Lescouret/EXPLORER – Palácio de Fronteira

General information

Opening times – **Monuments, museums and churches:** Monuments and museums are generally open 10am to 12.30pm and 2pm to 6pm. Some churches are only open during service early in the morning or in the evening. For more detailed information, please consult the Admission times and charges chapter at the back of the guide.

Shops are generally open weekdays 9am to 1pm and 3pm to 7pm (some department stores stay open during the lunch hour). Most shops are closed on Saturday afternoons and most all day Sunday. Shopping centres are the exception as they are open every day of the week from 10am to 11pm.

Entertainment – Evening performances begin about 9.30pm and *fados* at about 10.30pm.

Currency – The Portuguese unit of currency is the Escudo (represented by the dollar sign $) comprising 100 Centavos. Approximate exchange rate £1 = 300$; 1 USD = 181$. There are no restrictions on the amount of currency (Portuguese or other) that foreigners may bring with them into Portugal.

Changing money, Credit Cards – Banks, airports and some stations have exchange offices. Commissions vary so check before cashing.

All major credit cards (American Express, Diners Club, Eurocard, Visacard, Access and MasterCard) are accepted but always check in advance. MULTIBANCO is a national network of automatic cash dispensers which accept international credit cards and enable cash withdrawal 24 hours a day.

Banks – Banks are generally open Mondays to Fridays 8.30am to 3pm, closed on Saturdays. These times are subject to change, especially in summer. Most banks have cash dispensers which accept international credit cards *(see above)*.

Tipping – The bill is usually inclusive of service charges and VAT (10%). An extra tip can be left for special service. 10% of the fare or ticket price is the usual amount given to taxi drivers and cinema and theatre usherettes.

Time differences – Mainland Portugal is one hour ahead of GMT and 2 hours ahead in summer. Madeira is 1 hour behind mainland Portugal and the Azores are 2 hours behind.

Public Holidays

1 January	15 August
Shrove Tuesday	5 October (Republic Day)
Good Friday	1 November (All Saints' Day)
25 April (Liberation Day)	1 December (Independence Day)
1 May (Labour Day)	8 December
10 June (Death of Camões national holiday)	25 December Corpus Christi

In addition to the list below each town or locality celebrates the feast day of its patron saint (St Anthony in Lisbon – 13 June; St John in Oporto – 24 June). For local holidays contact the Tourist Information Centres.

Post Offices *(Correios)* – Post Offices are open weekdays from 0900 to 1800; the smaller branches may close for lunch from 12.30pm to 2.30pm. The main post offices in large towns and those in international airports have a 24-hour service.

Stamps *(selos)* are sold in post offices and shops displaying the sign CTT Selos. Current prices for letters and postcards are as follows: Portugal – 49$; Europe (EU countries) – 80$; Europe (non-EU countries) – 100$; Rest of the world – 140$. The **Michelin Red Guide España Portugal** gives the post code for every town covered. Letter boxes and phone booths are red.

Telephone – Phonecards are now widely used and can be purchased at Telecom Portugal shops, post offices and some kiosks and *tabacarias*. There are two types of cards: Portugal Telecom, which operates in and around Lisbon and Oporto, and Credifone, which are generally used in the rest of the country. In-

---

Some useful telephone numbers

International directory enquiries: 098
ATT : 05017-1- 288
MCI : 05017-1-234
Sprint : 05017-1-877
English-speaking international operator: 098 (intercontinental service) or 099 (European service).
Police and ambulance: 115

---

ternational calls may be made from modern phone boxes or from post offices; in bars and hotels be prepared to pay more than the going rate. For **international calls** dial: 00 44 for the United Kingdom; 00 353 for Ireland; 00 1 for the United States and Canada) followed by the area code and the number. For internal calls from one area to another keep the 0 in front of the area code then dial the number. The **Michelin Red Guide España Portugal** gives the area code for each town listed.

Foreign country codes are listed inside telephone booths.

To call Portugal from the United Kingdom or Ireland dial 00 351 + area code (without the first 0) + number.

Newspapers: The main Portuguese newspapers are the following: *O Diário de Notícias*, *O Correo da Manhã*, and *O Público*. Oporto has its own daily newspaper; *O Jornal de Notícias*. Weekly publications include *O Expresso*, which has the widest readership, *O Seminário, O Independente* and *O Jornal*.

Foreign Embassies and Consulates in Portugal

British Embassy: Rua São Domingos à Lapa 37, 1200 Lisboa, ☎ (01) 396 11 91.

Consulates: Rua da Estrela 4, 1200 Lisboa, ☎ (01) 395 40 83.
Avenida da Boa Vista, 3072 Porto, ☎ (02) 618 47 89.
Largo Francisco A Maurício 7-1°, 8500 Portimão,☎ (082) 41 78 00.
Quinta do Bom Jesus, Rua das Almas 23, Pico da Pedra, 9600 Ribeira Grande, Açores. ☎ (096) 498 115.
Avenida de Zarco 2/PO Box 417, 9000 Funchal, Madeira, ☎ (091) 220 161.

American Embassy: Avenida das Forças Armadas Sete Rios, 1600 Lisboa, ☎ (01) 72 57 17.

Canadian Embassy: Avenida da Liberdade, 144-156-4°, 1200 Lisboa, ☎ (01) 347 48 92.

Consulates: Honorary Consul in Faro.

Embassy of Ireland: Rua da Imprensa, à Estrela 1-4°, 1200 Lisboa, ☎ (01) 396 75 69.

Portuguese Embassies and Consulates

Portuguese Embassy, London, ☎ (0171) 235 5331; Portuguese Consulate, London, ☎ (0171,581,8722).
Portuguese Consulate, Manchester, ☎ (0161) 834 1821.
Portuguese, Washington DC 20009.
Consulates in Boston, Chicago, Houston, Los Angeles, Miami, New Orleans, New York and San Francisco.

Medical treatment – British citizens should apply to the Department of Health and Social Security for **Form E 111**, which entitles the holder to urgent treatment in case of an accident or unexpected illness in EU countries. On arrival in Portugal, exchange the form at the Segurança Social for a booklet of health coupons.

Since medical insurance is not always valid out of the United States, travellers are advised to take out supplementary medical insurance with specific overseas coverage. Chemists *(farmácia)* or pharmacists are open weekdays 0900 to 1300 and 1500 to 1900, Saturdays 0900 to 1300.

Electric current – 220 volts AC (some of the older establishments may still have 110 V). Plugs are two-pin.

Shopping

WHAT TO BRING HOME

Traditional Portuguese crafts will catch your eye, and the prices are attractive, too. From the north to the south, variety is found in the choice of colours and natural materials. In Viana do Castelo, look for hand-embroidered linen and cotton (table-cloths and napkins, shirts, aprons etc.) and the classic filigree jewellery, silver or gold. Embroidered bedspreads are a good buy in Castelo Branco; hand-made rugs in Arrailos, and many places offer ceramics (Caldas, da Rainha, Coimbra etc.) and pottery (Barcelos, Alentejo, Algarve). Woodworkers make decorative objects, kitchen utensils, toys; tinsmiths are famous for *almutelias*, recipients for olive oil; glass makers are active in Marinha Grande; azulejos tiles are found everywhere, as are objects and kitchenware made of copper (including the typical *cataplana* from the Algarve). For more information, see the chapter on *Traditional and festive Portugal* in the Introduction to this guide.

Kid Kervella/HOA QUI

Recreation

WATER SPORTS

Sailing – There are ample opportunities for this sport in Portugal with its long coastline, the Tagus estuary and the inland stretches of water. Many northern European yachtsmen stop over at a Portuguese port as they sail round to the Mediterranean. In season it is possible to hire boats with or without crew. Apply to the Federação Portuguesa de Vela, Doca de Belém, 1300 Lisboa, ☎ (01) 364 11 52.

Coastlines where sailing is possible are marked by a yacht sign on the Map of Places to Stay in the Introduction and on Michelin map 940. Marinas marked on Michelin Map 940 have been selected because of their facilities and infrastructure. Check weather bulletins before heading out to sea.

Seaside resort, Costa Nova

Windsurfing – Although this sport can be practised all around the coast the most important areas are around Estoril (Praia do Guincho) and Lisbon, the Algarve coast and the Madeira Islands. In these areas you are sure to be able to hire boards and find a school. There are strict rules concerning windsurfing and it is best to enquire at the local surfing school or club.

Scuba diving – The more rugged coastlines (Berlenga Island, Peniche and Sesimbra coast) offer ideal conditions for this sport. The sea caves along the Algarve coast between Albufeira and Sagres are popular with scuba divers.

Aquaparks – These are mainly located around Lisbon and in the Algarve *(see under ALGARVE)*. Further information can be obtained from Tourist Offices.

Beaches – Michelin Map 940 and the Map of Places to Stay in the Introduction highlight the best beaches. The Portuguese coastline is a series of beaches from north to south.

The best known are the great sandy stretches of the **Algarve** (Costa Algarvia) where both the climate and temperature of the sea (17°C in winter, 23°C in summer) are pleasant. The **Costa Dourada** (coastline of the Planicies region) between Cabo São Vicente and Setúbal is a more rugged coastline with tiny curves of sand at the foot of imposing cliffs and a colder and rougher sea (15°C in winter and 19°C in summer).

The **Costa de Lisboa** from Setúbal to Cabo da Roca includes the pleasant, well sheltered beaches of the Serra de Arrábida, the great expanse of dunes of the Costa da Caparica south of the Tagus and the very crowded beaches of Cascais and Estoril so popular with Lisbonites.

The Costa de Prato extending from Cabo da Roca to Aveiro has flat sandy beaches. North of Nazaré the fishermen's boats can be seen high up on the beaches. The Costa Verde from the Douro northwards to the Spanish border has fine sandy beaches backed inland with a pleasantly green countryside.

Many of Portugal's beaches are supervised and it is important to heed the flags: red – it is forbidden to enter the sea even to paddle; yellow – no swimming; green – it is safe to paddle and swim; blue and white chequered – beach temporarily unsupervised.

FISHING

Freshwater angling – This is done mostly in the north for trout, salmon, barbel and shad (Rio Minho and the Douro) and in the numerous mountain torrents of the Serra de Estrela (carp, barbel and trout).

A fishing permit can be obtained from the Direcçao Geral dos Serviços Florestais e Aquícolas *(address see above)* or from the Federação Portuguesa da Pesca Desportiva, Rua Sociedade Farmacêutica 56-2°, 1100 Lisboa, ☎ (01) 356 31 47. Enquire at the local tourist information centres for the opening dates of the fishing season.

Sea angling – In the north the catch usually includes skate, cod, dogfish and sea perch while in the south Mediterranean species are more common.

B. Barbier

GOLF

Portugal's mild climate enables golfers to play all year round. The country has a wide selection of courses to choose from, several of which are of championship standard, especially in the Algarve. Details may be obtained from the Federação Portuguesa de Golf, Rua General Ferreira Martins, 10-5°C, 1495 Lisboa, ☎ (01) 410 76 83 and from Tourist Offices.

Golf courses with the number of holes and their telephone numbers are listed in the current Michelin Red Guide España Portugal under the nearest town and are indicated on the Michelin Map 940.

OTHER SPORTS

Football – The Portuguese are great football (soccer) fans and the teams with the greatest following are Oporto's FC Porto and Lisbon's Benfica and Sporting. Tickets for the matches of the big three are difficult to obtain as there are so many season-ticket holders. Games are played on Sunday afternoons.

Bullfights – The season begins at Easter and ends in October. For further information, contact local Tourist Offices.

Spas – Portugal's tradition of elegant spas with casinos, pump-rooms and exclusive hotels dates from the late 19C. Although they have lost some of their elegance the country's 40 or so spas still cater for a wide variety of ailments. The Map of Places to Stay in the Introduction and Michelin map 940 indicate some of the more important ones. For a small selection of spas in the Trás-os-Montes region, see under CHAVES.

For further information, contact the Associação das Termas de Portugal, Avenida Miguel Bombarda, 110-2° Dt°, 1050 Lisboa – ☎ (01) 794 05 74. Internet: http://www.supra.pt/termas-portugal.

Shooting – Shooting is very popular in southern Portugal and the game includes pigeon, duck, quail, partridge, hare, rabbit and fox. A temporary shooting licence may be obtained from the Direcção Geral dos Serviços Florestais e Aquícolas, Av. João Crisóstomo 26-28, Lisboa, ☎ (01) 315 61 32; for northern Portugal, Divisão de Caça e Pesca nas Águas Interiores, Praça dos Pavoeiras, 56-2°, 4000 Porto, ☎ (02) 200 48 24.

To bring a shotgun into the country a deposit must be made at the customs. If you come via Spain an authorisation is required to carry arms.

To plan a special itinerary:

*– consult the map of **Touring Programmes** which indicates the recommended routes, the tourist regions, the principal towns and main sights*

*– read the descriptions in the **Sights** section which include Excursions from the main tourist centres.*

Michelin Maps nos *940 **and** 441 indicate scenic routes, interesting sights, viewpoints, rivers, forests...*

Calendar of events

Detailed calendars of events are published by the local Tourist Information Centres. The following list is a selection of the most well-known events.

Map references in parentheses (U5) are given for places not featured in this guide, but referred to on Michelin map 940.

Week preceding Shrove Tuesday

Ovar (J4) .... Carnival: procession of floats.

Torres Vedras (O2) .... Carnival: procession of floats.

Loulé (U5) .... Carnival and Almond Gatherers' Fair.

Holy Week

Braga .... Holy Week ceremonies and processions.

Easter Sunday

Loulé (U5) .... Pilgrimage in honour of Our Lady of Pity. Repeated on the following two Sundays.

29 April to 3 May

Barcelos .... Festival of Crosses, Pottery Fair and folk dancing.

3 to 5 May

Sesimbra .... Festival in honour of Our Lord Jesus of the Wounds: fishermen's festival dating from the 16C. Procession on 4 May.

First Sunday after 3 May

Monsanto .... Castle festival.

Second weekend in May

Vila Franca do Lima ... Rose Festival: Mordomias procession in which the mistress of the house bears on her head a tray of flowers arranged to represent one of the many provincial coats of arms.

12 and 13 May

Fátima .... First great pilgrimage. Candlelight procession at 2130 on the 12th and International Mass on the 13th. These take place every evening on the 12th and 13th of every month until October.

Second half of May

Leiria .... Fair and agricultural machinery exhibition with town festival on 22 May (processions, celebrations, etc).

Third Tuesday after Whitsun

Matosinhos .... Pilgrimage in honour of Senhor of Matosinhos: folk dancing.

6, 7, 8 June

Amarante .... St Gonsalo Festival.

First fortnight in June

Santarém .... National Agricultural Show: folklore.

12 - 29 June

Lisboa .... Popular saints' festival: marchas.

13 June

Vila Real .... St Anthony's Festival: procession, fireworks. St Anthony's Festival from 6 - 17 June.

23 to 24 June (St John)

Braga .... St John's Midsummer Festival.
Porto .... Popular saints' festival.
Vila do Conde .... Lacemakers' procession.

Last week in June - first week in July

Póvoa de Varzim .... St Peter's Festival.

28 - 29 June

Sintra .... St Peter's Fair.
Vila Real .... St Peter's Fair.

First week in July (every 4 years - next festival in 1999)
Tomar .... Tabuleiros Festival.

July and August
Estoril .... Handcrafts fair: all the Portuguese regions are represented.

First weekend in July (even years)
Coimbra...................... Festival of the Queen, Saint Isabel of Portugal.

First weekend in July
Vila Franca de Xira.... Festival of the Red Waistcoats.

26 July to 17 August
Setúbal....................... St James' Fair: bullfights and folk groups.

In July and part of August
Aveiro .... The Ria Festival with a competition for the best decorated prow.

First weekend in August
Guimarães .... St Walter's Festival: fair, decorated streets, giants procession.
Peniche...................... Festival in honour of Our Lady of Safe Travel.

Third week in August
Viana do Castelo........ Pilgrimage in honour of Our Lady of Sorrow.

Third Sunday in August
Miranda do Douro ..... St Barbara's Festival: dance of the Pauliteiros.

End of August - beginning of September
Lamego .... Romaria of Our Lady of Remedies.

First week in September
Palmela .... Grape harvest Festival: benediction of the grapes, running of the bulls through the streets, fireworks, etc.

8 September
Mirando do Douro ..... Pilgrimage in honour of Our Lady of Nazo at Póva *(11km 7miles north)*: a fair precedes the pilgrimage and a festival ends the celebrations.

Beginning 8 September
Nazaré........................ Romaria of Our Lady of Nazareth.

4 - 12 October
Vila Franca de Xira.... Handicrafts Fair, running of the bulls through the streets, touradas.

Second Sunday in October
Nazaré .... National Gastronomy Fair: food, handicrafts, folklore.

12 and 13 October
Fátima .... Last annual pilgrimage.

Third Sunday in October
Castro Verde .... October Fair which goes back to the 17C: agricultural show and handcrafts.

First fortnight in November
Golegã .... National Horse Show and the Feast of St Martin: benediction of the horses, a tradition dating back to the 17C.

The days of the week

While Monday in Portuguese is the second day of the week *(segunda-feira)*, Tuesday the third *(terça-feira)*, Wednesday the fourth *(quarta-feira)*, Thursday the fifth *(quinta-feira)* and Friday the sixth *(sexta-feira)*, Sunday, the first day of the week, remains that of the Lord *(domingo)* and Saturday, the seventh, the sabbath *(sábado)*.

This denomination is believed to have originated in the 6C when São Martinho, Bishop of Braga, took the Christians to task for using the traditional calendar dating from the time of the Chaldeans and thereby dedicating each day to a pagan divinity: the Sun, the Moon, Mars, Mercury, Jupiter, Venus and Saturn.

Further reading

CONTEMPORARY PORTUGAL

Contemporary Portugal – R A H Robinson (Allen and Unwin)

In Search of Modern Portugal, the Revolution and its Consequences – L S Graham and D L Wheeler (University of Wisconsin Press)

The Portuguese: The Land and its People – Marion Kaplan (Penguin)

Living in Portugal – S Thackeray

HISTORY

The Portuguese Seaborne Empire 1415-1825 – C R Boxer (Harmondsworth)

Portugal and its Empire: The Truth – Antonio De Figueiredo (Gollancz)

Portugal: Birth of Democracy – R Harvey (Macmillan)

Portugal, A Short History – H V Livermore (Edinburgh University Press)

A New History of Portugal – H V Livermore (Cambridge University Press)

Portugal: 50 Years of Dictatorship – A de Figueiredo (Harmondsworth)

Wellington at War, 1794-1815 by A James Brett

Wellington's Peninsular Victories by M Glover

Carlota Joaquina: Queen of Portugal by M Cheke (Sidgwick & Jackson)

Dictator of Portugal: A Life of the Marques de Pombal (Sidgwick & Jackson)

Henry the Navigator by J Ure (Constable & Co)

The Moors in Spain and Portugal by J Read (Faber & Faber)

A SAMPLING OF PORTUGUESE AUTHORS

Selected poems – Pessoa (1982 edition)

Selected Prose – Pessoa (1988 edition)

Lisboa : What the Tourist should see – Pessoa – (bilingual edition Livros Horizonte)

The Lusiads – Camões – translated by Sir R Fanshawe (Centaur Press)

Esau and Jacob – Machado de Assis translated by H Caldwell (Owen)

Travels in My Homeland – Almeida Garrett

The Blacksmith of Santarém (play) – Almeida Garrett

The Wheat and the Chaff – Fernando Namora

The Jungle and *The Mission* – Ferreira de Castro

The Cement Forest – Paço de Arcos

EARLY TRAVELLERS

These works, although long out of print, can make interesting reading.

Journal of a Voyage to Lisbon (1754) by Henry Fielding

Journals of a Residence in Portugal (1801) by Robert Southey

Historical Memoirs of My Own Time (1815) by Sir N William Wraxall

A Visit to Portugal, 1866 – Hans Christian Andersen

Recollections of an Excursion to the Monasteries of Alcobaça and Batalha – William Beckford edited by B Alexander (Centaur Press)

They Went to Portugal by Rose Macaulay (Penguin)

MISCELLANEOUS

The Wines of Portugal by J Read (Faber & Faber)

The Story of Port by S Bradford (Christie's Wine Publications)

The Factory House at Oporto – *Its historic role in the Port Wine trade* by C Hel (Christie's Wine Publications)

Portuguese Cooking by Hilaire Walden (Apple Press)

Gastronomy of Spain and Portugal by Maite Manjou (Garamond)

Lisbon by Manfred Hamm and Werner Radasewsky (Verlag)

Porto by Werner Radasewsky and Gunter Schneider (Verlag)

Madeira: Pearl of the Atlantic – J and S Farrow

The Art of Portugal 1500-1800 by RC Smith (Weidenfeld & Nicholson)

Churches of Portugal by Carlso de Azevedo (Scala Books)

The Finest Castles in Portugal by Júlio Gil (Verbo)

Portuguese Gardens by H Carita and H Cardoso (The Antique Collectors' Club)

Glossary

COMMON WORDS

bank; exchange	banco; câmbio	petrol; oil	gasolina; óleo
boat	barco	please	(se) faz favor
bus; tram	autocarro; eléctrico	post office; stamp	correio; selo
car	carro	river; stream	rio; ribeira
car park	parque de estacionamento	ruins	ruínas
		sir	senhor
chemist	farmácia	square	largo; praça
customs	alfândega	station; train	estação; comboio
doctor	mêdico	street; avenue	rue; avenida
entrance; exit	entrada; saída	thank you	
expensive	caro	(said by a man)	obrigado
good afternoon	boa tarde	(said by a woman)	obrigada
good morning	bom dia	today	hoje
goodbye	adeus	toll	portagem
guide	guia	tomorrow morning	amanhã de manhã
halt	paragem	tomorrow evening	amanhã à tarde
I beg	desculpe	to the left	à esquerda
your pardon		to the right	à direita
information	informações	town; quarter,	cidade;
large; small	grande; pequeno	district	bairro
letter; postcard	carta; postal	where; when	onde? quando?
letter-box	caixa de correio	yes; no	sim; não
light	luz	where is?	onde é...?
madam	minha senhora	the road to ...?	a estrada para ...?
(married woman)		at what time ...?	a que hora ...?
madam (single	menina	how much ...?	quanto custa ...?
woman), miss		road works	obras
much; little	muito; pouco	danger	perigo
noon	meio-dia	prohibited	prohibido

TOURIST VOCABULARY

abadia	abbey	ilha	island
albufeira	reservoir	local	site
andar	storey	mata	wood
baixa	town centre	mercado, feira	market, fair
barragem	dam	miradouro	belvedere
Câmara	town hall	paço, palácio	palace, castle
Municipal		parque	park
capela	chapel	porto	harbour, port
casa	house	praia	beach
castelo	castle, citadel	quinta	country property
centro urbano	town centre	Sé	cathedral
chafariz	fountain	século	century
chave	key	solar	manor-house
citânia	prehistoric city	tapete, tapeçaria	tapestry
convento, mosteiro	convent, monastery	tesouro	treasure, treasury
		torre	tower
cruz; cruzeiro	cross; calvary	torre de managem	keep
escada	stairs, steps	túmulo	tomb
excavaçâoes	excavations	vista	view, panorama
fechado, aberto	closed, open	dirigir-se a...	apply to...
igreja	church	pode-se visitar?	may one visit?

RESTAURANT TERMINOLOGY

NB: for a more detailed restaurant terminology consult the **Michelin Red Guide España Portugal** or **Portugal**

açucar	sugar	gelo	ice cream; ice cube
água; copo	water; glass		
(pequeno)	(small)	jantar, ceia	dinner
almoço	breakfast	lista	menu (à la carte)
azeite	olive oil	óleo	peanut oil
café com leite	coffee with milk	pão	bread
carne	meat	peixe	fish
cerveja	beer	pimenta, sal	pepper, salt
conta	bill	prato do dia	dish of the day
ementa, carta	menu	sumo de fruta	fruit juice
fresco	cold, chilled	vinho tinto	red wine

A FEW TYPICAL DISHES

Açorda de Mariscos	Bread soup with clams and prawns, mixed with garlic, eggs, coriander and spices
Amêijoas à Bulhão Pato	Small clams cooked in olive oil, garlic and coriander
Arroz de Marisco	Rice with clams, shrimp, mussels and coriander
Bacalhau	Cod
Cabrito	Roast goat
Caldeirada	Spicy fish and seafood stew
Caldo verde	Potato and cabbage stew
Canja de Galinha	Chicken bouillon with rice and hard egg yolks
Carne de porco à Alentajana	Diced pork in olive oil, garlic and coriander sauce, served with potatoes and small clams
Cataplana	Steamed seafood with pieces of ham
Chouriço	Smoked sausage
Cozido	Pot roast with meat, sausage and vegetables
Feijoada	Beans prepared with pork, cabbage and sausage
Gaspacho	Cold vegetable soup
Leitão assado	Grilled suckling pig, served hot or cold
Presunto	Smoked ham
Salpição	Spicy smoked ham
Sopa à Alentajana	Garlic and bread soup, served with a poached egg and coriander
Sopa de Feijão verde	Green bean soup
Sopa de Grão	Chickpea soup
Sopa de Legumes	Vegetable soup
Sopa de Marisco	Seafood soup
Sopa de Peixe	Fish soup

A. Tovy/EXPLORER

Mordomas procession during
the Rose Festival at Vila do Lima

Admission times and charges

As admission times and charges are subject to modification due to increases in the cost of living, the information printed below is for guidance only.

The following list details the opening times and charges (if any) and other relevant information concerning all sights in the descriptive part of this Guide accompanied by the symbol ⊙. The entries given below are listed in the same order as they appear in the Guide.

The prices quoted apply to individual adults but many places offer reduced rates for children, senior citizens, or families. Prices are given in Escudos (written $).

The times are those of opening and closure but remember that some places do not admit visitors during the last hour or half hour.

Most tours are conducted by Portuguese-speaking guides but in some cases the term "guided tours" may cover groups visiting with recorded commentaries. Some of the larger and more popular sights may offer guided tours in other languages. Enquire at the ticket desk or book stall.

For most towns the address and/or telephone number of the local Tourist Information Centre, indicated by the symbol ⬛, is given below. Generally most efficient, these organisations are able to help tourists find accommodation and provide information on exhibitions, performances, guided tours, market days and other items of interest locally.

City tours are given regularly during the tourist season in Coimbra, Faro, Lisbon, Oporto and Viana do Castelo. Apply to the Tourist Information Centre.

A

ABRANTES
⬛ Largo da Feira, ☎ (041) 2 25 55

Castelo – Igreja de Santa Maria – Visits to the Church from 9am to 1pm and 2pm to 6pm (10am on Saturdays, Sundays and holidays); free admission; ☎ (041) 37 17 24.

ALCOBAÇA
⬛ Praça 25 de Abril, ☎ (062) 4 23 77

Mosteiro de Santa Maria – Open 9am to 5pm (7pm from October to March); closed 1 January, Good Friday, Easter Sunday and 25 December; 400$; free admission on Sundays until 2pm; no visits allowed between 11am and 12 noon during mass; ☎ (062) 4 34 69.

Museu da Junta Nacional do Vinho – Guided tours (45min) from 9am to 12.30pm and 2pm to 5.30pm (10am to 12.30pm and 2pm/6pm on Saturdays and Sundays from May to September); closed Mondays and holidays from May to September and Saturdays, Sundays and holidays from October to April; free admission; ☎ (062) 4 22 22.

ALGARVE

Estói: Ruínas Romanas de Milreu – Open 9am to 12 noon and 2pm to 5pm Tuesday to Sunday; closed Mondays.

Casa da Cultura António Benes – Museu Etnográfico do Trajo Algarvio – Open 10am to 1pm and 2pm to 5pm; closed mornings on Saturdays, Sundays and holidays; 100$; ☎ (089) 84 26 18.

Loulé: Museu Municipal – Open 9am to 5.30pm; Saturdays from 10am to 5.30pm; closed Sundays; free admission.

Vila do Bispo: Igreja – Open every morning except Wednesday; ☎ (082) 6 64 00.

ALMANSIL

Capela de São Lourenço – Open 9.30am to 1pm and 2.15pm to 5.30pm Monday to Saturday; closed Sundays.

Centro Cultural de São Lourenço – Open daily 10am to 7pm; ☎ (089) 39 54 75.

Castelo de ALMOUROL

Tour – The castle can be reached directly by boat from 9am to 6pm (100$ round trip). For further information, contact the Tourist Office in Vila Nova da Barquinha; ☎ (049) 71 02 75.

Castelo de Almourol

AMARANTE
B Rua Cândido dos Reis, ☎ (055) 43 22 59

Museu de Amadeu de Souza Cardoso – Open 10am to 12 noon and 2pm to 5pm; closed Mondays and holidays; 200$; ☎ (055) 43 26 63.

ARMAÇÃO DE PÊRA
B Av. Marginal, ☎ (082) 31 21 45

Boat trip – To hire a motorboat, apply to the fishermen on the beach; 2 500$ per person.

Capela de Nossa Senhora da Rocha – Open all day; in the nearby creek boats can be hired to visit the caves; ☎ (089) 44 23 25.

AROUCA

Igreja do Mosteiro Open 8am to 5pm.

Museu – Guided tours (45min) 10am to 12 noon and 2pm to 5pm; closed Mondays, 1 January, Good Friday, Easter Sunday, 1May and 25 December; 350$; ☎ (056) 94 33 21.

Serra da ARRÁBIDA

Portinho da Arrábida: Museu Oceanográfico – Open 10am to 4pm Tuesdays to Fridays; 3pm to 6pm weekends; closed Mondays; 300$; ☎ (065) 40 32.

AVEIRO
B Rua João Mendonça 8, ☎ (034) 2 36 80 or 2 07 60

Antigo Convento de Jesus: Museu – Guided tours (30min – 1 hour 30min) 10am to 1.30pm and 2pm to 5pm (unaccompanied visits in July and August); closed Mondays, 1 January, Good Friday, Easter Sunday, 1May and 25 December; 250$; free admission on Sundays and mornings of holidays; ☎ (034) 2 32 97 and 38 31 88.

Ria de AVEIRO

Boat trips – Allow a whole day for the complete tour including 3 hours of relaxation on shore. Departures daily from Aveiro's Central Canal from 15 June to 15 September at 10am (return around 5pm). For information and reservations apply to the Tourist Information Centre in Aveiro; Região de Turismo da Rota da Luz, Rua João Mendonça 8, 3800 Aveiro; 2 340$ (children 1 170$); ☎ (034) 2 36 80 and 2 07 60.

Reserva Natural das Dunas de São Jacinto – Guided tours Mondays, Tuesdays, Wednesdays, Fridays and Saturdays from 9am to 9.30am and 2pm to 2.30pm; closed Thursdays, Sundays and holidays; ☎ (034) 33 12 82.

Ílhavo: Museu – Open 9am to 12.30pm and 2pm to 5.30pm; closed Mondays and holidays and Tuesday and Sunday mornings; 100$; ☎ (034) 32 17 97.

Vista Alegre: Museu – Open 9am to 12.30pm and 2pm to 4.30pm (5pm on Saturdays, Sundays and holidays); closed Mondays, 1 January, Good Friday, Easter Sunday, 1May and 25 December; free admission; ☎ (034) 32 50 40/46.

Avoid visiting a church during a service.

B

Quinta da BACALHOA

Gardens – Guided tours (30min) 11am to 1pm; closed Sundays and holidays; 250$; ☎ (01) 218 00 11.

BARCELOS
🅱 Largo da Porta Nova (Torre de Menagem), ☎ (053) 81 18 82 or 81 21 35

Ruínas Paço dos Condes de Barcelos: Museu Arqueológico – Open 9am to 5.30pm (until 6.30pm from May to September); closed 1 January, Good Friday, Easter Sunday, 1May and 25 December; free admission; ☎ (053) 82 12 51.

Mosteiro da BATALHA

Visit – Open 9am to 5pm from October to March and 9am to 6pm from April to September; closed 1 January, Good Friday, Easter Sunday, 1May and 25 December; 400$; free admission on Sundays and holidays until 2pm; ☎ (044) 9 64 97.

BEJA
🅱 Rua Capitão Francisco de Sousa 25, ☎ (084) 32 21 01

Antigo Convento da Conceição: Museu da Rainha Dona Leonor – Open 9.45am to 12.30pm and 2pm to 5.15pm; closed Mondays and holidays; 100$, free on Sundays and holidays; ☎ (084) 32 33 51.

Castelo – Open 10am to 1pm and 2pm to 6pm; closed Mondays, 1 January, 25 December and local holidays; 100$, free on Sundays and holidays; ☎ (084) 32 21 01/05.

Igreja de Santo Amaro: Visigothic art section – Same opening times as the Museu da Rainha Dona Leonor (the same ticket is used).

Excursion

São Cucufate: Roman villa – Open 9am to 12.30pm from Wednesday to Saturday (9am to 12 noon on Sundays) and from 2pm to 5.30pm from Tuesday to Sunday; closed Mondays, 27 April and 5May.

BELMONTE

Castelo – Open daily from 10am to 12.30 and from 2pm to 5pm. Closed 1 January, Holy Friday, Easter Sunday 1May and 25 December; no admission charge.

Igreja de São Tiago – Guided tours from 10am to 12.30pm and 2pm to 5pm. Closed 1 January, Easter and 25 December; free admission. For visits, contact the Belmonte Tourist Information Centre, Praça da República, 6250 Belmonte; ☎ (075) 91 14 88.

Panteão dos Cabrais – Guided tours from 10am to 12.30pm and 2pm to 5pm. Closed 1 January, Easter and 25 December; free admission. For visits, contact the Belmonte Tourist Information Centre, Praça da República, 6250 Belmonte; ☎ (075) 91 14 88.

Capela de Santo António – Visitors are asked to collect the key from Father José Martins in the parish of Belmonte.

Igreja Matriz – Open during the day. If closed, please contact Father José Martins in the parish of Belmonte.

Ilha da BERLENGA

Access – There is a regular boat service to the island from Peniche between 15 May and 20 September; round trip fare 2 500$ per person; crossing time: 45min; apply for information to Viamar, Residencial Aviz – 2520 Peniche or contact the Tourist Information Centre. ☎ (062) 78 21 53.

Boat trip – Apply to the company Berlenga Turpesa de Tiago & Bernardo, Rua Marechal Freire de Andrade, 90 r/c – 2520 Peniche; ☎ (062) 78 99 60 AND 78 23 14.

BRAGA
🅱 Av. da Liberdade 1, ☎ (053) 2 25 50

Sé – Guided tours (approximately 1 hour) from 8.30am to 12.30pm and 1.30pm to 6.30pm (5.30pm in winter); 300$; ☎ (053) 2 33 17.

Capela dos Coimbras – Visits of the interior only during Holy Week from 9am to 7pm.

Museu dos Biscainhos – Guided tours (30min) 10am to 12.15pm and 2pm to 5.30pm; last entrance at 11.45am and 5pm; closed Mondays; 250$; free admission on Sundays and mornings of holidays; ☎ (053) 21 76 45.

Capela da Nossa Senhora da Penha de França – Open 7.30am to 12 noon. Closed during August. If closed during these times, please contact the gate of Lar D.Pedro V or call (053) 2 26 52.

Excursions

Santuário de Bom Jesus do Monte – Funicular to the top 8am to 8pm daily (departures every half an hour); 100$ one way.

Capela de São Frutuoso de Montélios – Open 10am to 12.30pm and 2pm to 5.30pm (until 6.30pm from October to March); closed Mondays and Tuesdays.

BRAGANÇA

∎ Av Cidade de Zamora, **☎** (073) 38 12 73

Castelo and Museu Militar – Open 9am to 12 noon and 2pm to 5pm (until 5.30pm in summer); closed Thursdays, national holidays and 22 August (local holiday); 200$; free admission on Sunday mornings; **☎** (073) 2 23 78.

Domus Municipalis – Closed. For visits apply to Rua da Cidadela n° 24 (inside the ramparts).

Museu do Abade de Baçal – Open Tuesdays to Fridays 10am to 5pm, Saturdays, Sundays and holidays 10am to 6pm; closed Mondays, 1 January, Good Friday, Easter Sunday, 1May and 25 December; 250$; free admission on Sundays and holidays until 2pm; **☎** (073) 33 15 95.

BRAVÃES

Igreja de São Salvador – Open 8am to 6.30pm; **☎** (058) 4 21 97.

Mata do BUÇACO

Tour – Free admission at any time.

Convento dos Carmelitas Descalços – Open from 10am to 12.30pm and 2pm to 5.30pm; closed Fridays; 100$; **☎** (031) 93 92 26.

Museu Militar – Open from 10am to 5.30pm; closed Mondays, 1 January, Good Friday, Easter Sunday and 25 December; 200$; **☎** (031) 93 93 10.

C

CALDAS DA RAINHA

∎ Rua Eng° Duarte Pacheco, **☎** (062) 83 10 03
∎ Praça da República (only open during the summer), **☎** (062) 3 45 11

Museu José Malhoa – Open 10am to 12.30pm and 2pm to 5pm; closed Mondays, 1 January, Good Friday, Easter Sunday, 1May and 25 December; 250$, free admission on Sunday mornings; **☎** (062) 83 19 84.

CAMINHA

∎ Rua Ricardo Joaquim de Sousa, **☎** (058) 92 19 52

Igreja Matriz – Open daily for Mass..

CARAMULO

∎ Estrada Principal do Caramulo, **☎** (032) 86 14 37

Museu do Caramulo – Open 10am to 1pm and 2pm to 5pm (6pm from 1 April to 19 October); closed 24 and 25 December; 700$ **☎** (032) 86 14 83.

CARVOEIRO

Algar Seco – To visit the sea caves apply to the fishermen in Algar Seco and on Carvoeiro beach.

CASCAIS

∎ Rua Visconde da Luz, **☎** (01) 486 82 04 or 486 70 44

Museu-Biblioteca dos Condes de Castro Guimarães: Museum – Guided tours (30min) 10am to 5pm; closed Mondays and holidays; 200$; free admission on Sundays; **☎** (01) 483 08 56.

Biblioteca dos Condes de Castro Guimarães – Open 10am to 5pm (1pm on Saturdays); closed Sundays, holidays and Saturdays in July, August and September; **☎** (01) 484 08 61, ext. 406.

CASTELO BRANCO

∎ Alameda da Liberdade, **☎** (072) 2 10 02

Museu Francisco Tavares Proença – Currently closed for restoration work. Usual opening times are 10am to 12 noon and 2.30pm to 5pm; closed Mondays, 1 January, Good Friday, Easter Sunday, 1May and 25 December; 200$; **☎** (072) 2 42 77.

Jardim do Antigo Paço Episcopal – Open 9am to 5pm (8pm on Saturdays, Sundays and holidays); closed 25 December; 20$; **☎** (072) 2 10 02.

Convento da Graça and Museu de Arte Sacra da Misericórdia – Guided visits from 9am to 12 noon and 2pm to 6pm; closed Saturdays, Sundays and holidays; **☎** (072) 2 44 54, ext. 57.

Excursions

Penamacor: Igreja da Misericórdia – Open 9am to 5pm Monday to Saturday; **☎** (077) 9 41 33.

Convento de Santo António – Open 9am to 5pm; closed Sundays and holidays; **☎** (077) 9 41 33.

CASTELO DE VIDE
i Rua Bartolomeu Álvares da Santa, 81-83, ☎ (045) 9 13 61/2

Castelo – The castle is always open. The keep is open from 9am to 7pm. Free admission.

CASTRO MARIM

Castelo – Open daily 9am to 6pm; free admission; ☎ (081) 53 12 32.

CASTRO VERDE

Igreja de Nossa Senhora da Conceição – Apply to the priest at Residência Paroquial, Avenida Humberto Delgado; ☎ (086) 2 21 76.

CHAVES
i Terreiro de Cavalaría, ☎ (076) 33 30 29

Museu da Região Flaviense – Open 9am to 12.30pm and 2pm to 5.30pm (only open in the afternoon at the weekend); closed Mondays and holidays; 100$; ☎ (076) 33 29 65/6/7.

Torre de Menagem: Museu Militar – Open 9am to 12.30pm and 2pm to 5.30pm (only open in the afternoon at the weekend); closed Mondays and holidays; 100$; ☎ (076) 33 29 65/6/7.

Caldas de Chaves – Guided visits (30min) from 8am to 12 noon and 5pm to 7pm (opens at 9am from October to May); closed Sunday and holiday afternoons, Easter and Christmas; free admission; ☎ (076) 33 29 66.

Termas de Vidago – Open from 8am to 12 noon and 4pm to 7pm; closed Sundays and from 1 October to 31May; ☎ (076) 9 73 56/7/8.

Termas de Pedras Salgadas – Open from 8am to 12 noon and 4pm to 7pm; closed Sundays and from 1 October to 31May; ☎ (076) 9 73 73/4.

Caldas Santas de Carvalheldos – Open from 1 July to 30 September. For information call ☎ (076) 4 21 16.

COIMBRA
i Largo D. Dinis, ☎ (039) 3 25 91
i Praça da República, ☎ (039) 3 32 02

Sé Velha – Open 10am to 7pm; closed Fridays and some holidays; 100$; ☎ (039) 2 52 73.

Museu Nacional Machado de Castro – Open 9.30am to 5.30pm; closed Mondays; 250$; free admission on Sunday mornings; ☎ (039) 2 37 27.

Universidade Velha – Open 9.30am to 12 noon and 2pm to 5pm; closed 25 December; includes visit to library, chapel and Sala dos Capelos, 500$; ☎ (039) 410 98 41.

Mosteiro de Santa Cruz – Open from 2pm to 6pm, Sundays 4pm to 6pm; Mass is from 10.30am to 12.30pm; 200$, including visit to the sacristy and cloister; ☎ (039) 2 29 41.

Jardim Botânico – Open 9am to 6pm; ☎ (039) 2 28 97.

Mosteiro de Celas – Open 10am to 12 noon and 2pm to 6pm.

Door of Universidade Velha chapel, Coimbra

Convento de Santa Clara-a-Velha – Closed for restoration work.

Convento de Santa Clara-a-Nova – Guided tours (20min) from 9am to 12 noon and 2pm to 5pm; closed Sundays and Mondays; 100$; ☎ (039) 44 16 74.

Portugal dos Pequeninos – Open summer 10am to 7pm, winter 10am to 5pm; 600$, 100$ children under 10.

Quinta das Lágrimas – Open 9am to 5pm; 150$; ☎ (039) 44 16 15.

CONÍMBRIGA

Ruins – Open 9am to 1pm and 2pm to 8pm (10am to 6pm from 15 September to 14 March); 350$ (includes Ruins and Museum); free admission on Sunday and holiday mornings; ☎ (039) 94 11 77.

Museu Monográfico – Open 10am to 1pm and 2pm to 6pm; closed Mondays; 350$ (includes Museum and Ruins); ☎ (039) 94 11 77.

CRATO

Mosteiro de Flor da Rosa – Guided visits from 10am to 12.30pm and 2pm to 6.30pm; closed Tuesdays and holidays; 100$.

D – E

ELVAS
🛈 Praça da República, ☎ (068) 62 22 36

Castelo – Open 9am to 1pm and 3pm to 6pm (9am to 12.30pm and 2pm to 5.30pm from November to February); closed 1 January, 1 May and 25 December; free admission.

Cabo ESPICHEL

Santuário de Nossa Senhora do Cabo – Open 9am to 1pm and 3pm to 6pm; ☎ (01) 2 23 57 43.

Serra da ESTRELA

Caldas de Manteigas: Fish Farm – Open 8am to 12 noon and 1pm to 5pm; ☎ (075) 98 15 05.

ESTREMOZ
🛈 Largo da República, ☎ (068) 2 25 38
🛈 Rossio do Marquês de Pombal, ☎ (068) 33 20 71

Capela da Rainha Santa Isabel Guided tours from 10am to 12.30pm and 2pm to 6pm. If the chapel is closed (between April and September), ask at the Igreja de Santa Maria or contact Father D. Júlio Esteves, Rua S. Francisco Xavier, 46-1°.

Museu Municipal: Museu Arqueológico e Etnológico – Open 10am to 12.30pm and 2pm to 5pm (3pm to 7pm from April to September); closed Mondays and holidays; 170$; ☎ (068) 33 20 71/2.

Museu Rural – Open 10am to 12.30pm and 3pm to 5pm (6.30pm in summer); closed Sundays, Mondays and holidays; 100$.

ÉVORA
🛈 Praça do Giraldo, ☎ (066) 2 26 71

Sé – Open 9am to 12 noon and 2pm to 4.30pm; closed Mondays and 25 December; 350$; ☎ (066) 2 69 10.

Museu Regional – Open 10am to 12.30pm and 2pm to 5pm; closed Mondays and holidays; 200$, free admission on Sunday mornings; ☎ (066) 2 26 04.

Convento dos Lóios: Igreja – Open from 10am to 12.30pm and 2pm to 5pm; closed Mondays and holidays; 500$; ☎ (066) 2 47 14.

Paço dos Duques do Cadaval: Art Gallery – Closed in 1997 and 1998 for restoration work; ☎ (066) 2 47 14.

Igreja de São Francisco: Capela dos Ossos – Open 8am to 1pm and 2.30pm to 5.30pm (6pm in summer); Sundays and holidays 2.30pm to 5.30pm (6pm in summer); 50$; ☎ (066) 2 45 21.

Igreja das Mercês: Museu de Artes Decorativas – Open 10am to 12.30pm and 2pm to 5pm; closed Mondays and holidays; the church is an annexe of the Museu Regional above; the same ticket is valid for both museums; ☎ (066) 2 26 04.

Universidade de Évora – Open 8am to 6.30pm Monday to Friday, 10am to 2pm and 3pm to 6pm weekends and holidays; closed on weekday holidays; 200$ on Saturdays and Sundays; free admission on other days; ☎ (066) 74 49 69.

Convento de São Bento de Castris – Open 9am to 12 noon and 2pm to 5pm; closed Saturdays, Sundays and holidays; ☎ (066) 3 35 66.

Excursion

Gruta do Escoural – Open 9am to 12 noon and 1.30pm to 5.30pm (5pm on Saturdays, Sundays and holidays); closed Mondays, Tuesday mornings, 1 January, Good Friday, Easter Sunday, 1 May and 25 December; free admission. To visit the cave apply to IPPAR – Instituto Português do Patrimônio Arquitectónico e Arqueológico, Rua Burgos, 5; ☎ (066) 2 21 38.

EVORAMONTE

Castelo – Open 10am to 12.30pm and 2pm to 5pm; closed Mondays, 1 January, Good Friday, Easter Sunday, 1 May and 25 December; 250$.

F

FARO
🖪 Rua da Misericórdia 8 – 12, ☎ (089) 80 36 04 or 80 36 67

Sé: Bell-tower – Open 10am to 12 noon and 2pm to 7pm (9.30am to 1pm on Sundays and holidays); 200$; ☎ (089) 82 24 05.

Galeria do Arco: Galeria de Art Contemporáneo – Open Monday to Friday 9am to 1pm and 2pm to 6pm; 10am to 2pm and 3pm to 7pm weekends; closed holidays; free admission; ☎ (089) 81 38 82.

Galeria do Trem – Same opening times as Galeria do Arco; ☎ (089) 80 41 97.

Museu Municipal – Open 9am to 12 noon and 2pm to 5pm; closed Saturdays, Sundays and holidays; 110$; ☎ (089) 82 20 42.

Museu Marítimo – Open 2pm to 5pm; closed Saturdays, Sundays and holidays; 100$; ☎ (089) 80 36 01.

Igreja do Carmo – Open Mondays to Saturdays 10am to 1pm and 3pm to 5pm; closed Sundays; access to Capelo dos Ossos; 120$.

Museu de Etnografia Regional – Open 9.30am to 5.30pm; closed Saturdays, Sundays and holidays; 300$; ☎ (089) 2 76 10.

Miradouro de Santo António: Museum – Open 10am to 12.30pm and 2pm to 5.30pm; closed Saturdays, Sundays and holidays; 110$; ☎ (089) 80 25 09.

FÁTIMA
🖪 Av. D. José Alves Correia da Silva, ☎ (049) 53 11 39

Museu de Cera – Open November to March 10am to 5pm, from April to October 9.30am to 6.30pm; closed 25 December; 650$; ☎ (049) 53 21 02.

Serra de Aire and Serra de Candeeiros:

Grutas de Mira de Aire – Guided tours (40min) from 9.30am to 6pm (9am to 7pm in May, June and September and 9am to 8pm in July and August); 500$; ☎ (044) 44 03 22.

Grutas de São Mamede – Guided tours (20-25min) 9am to 5pm (6pm from April to June and 7pm from June to September); 500$; ☎ (044) 9 03 02.

Grutas de Alvados – Guided tours (20-25min) 9.30am to 1pm and 2pm to 5.30pm October to March (6pm in April and May, 7pm in July and September, 8.30pm in June and August); 500$, children between 6 and 12 years of age, 350$; ☎ (044) 44 07 87 and 2 36 89.

Grutas de Santo António – Guided tours (20-25min) 9.30am to 1pm and 2pm to 5.30pm October to March (6pm in April and May, 7pm in July and September, 8.30pm in June and August); 500$, children between 6 and 12 years of age, 350$; ☎ (049) 2 36 89 and 84 18 76.

FIGUEIRA DA FOZ
🖪 Av. 25 Abril, ☎ (033) 2 21 26 or 2 26 10

Museu Municipal Dr. Santos Rocha – Open 9am to 12.30pm and 2pm to 5.30pm; closed Mondays and holidays; ☎ (033) 2 45 09.

G – I

GUARDA
🖪 Edifício da Câmara Municipal (Largo do Município), ☎ (071) 22 18 17 and 22 22 51

Sé – Open 9am to 12 noon and 2pm to 5pm; ☎ (071) 21 12 31

Museu Regional – Open 10am to 12.30pm and 2pm to 5.30pm; closed Mondays, 1 January, Good Friday, Easter Monday, 1May and 25 December; free admission on Sunday mornings; ☎ (071) 21 34 60.

GUIMARÃES
🖪 Almeda de São Dâmaso, 86, ☎ (053) 41 24 50
🖪 Praça de Santiago, ☎ (053) 51 51 23, ext. 184

Castelo – Open 9.30am to 5.30pm (6.30pm from July to September); closed Mondays, 1 January, Good Friday, Easter Monday, 1May and 25 December; free admission; ☎ (053) 41 22 73.

Igreja de São Miguel do Castelo – Open daily 9.30am to 5.30pm (6.30pm from July to September); ☎ (053) 41 22 73 .

Paço dos Duques de Bragança – Guided tours (30min) from 9.30am to 5.30pm (6.30pm from June to September); closed 1 January, Good Friday, Easter Monday, 1May and 25 December; 400$; free admission until 2pm on Sundays and holidays; ☎ (053) 41 22 73.

Museu Alberto Sampaio – Guided tours (45min) 10am to 12.30pm and 2pm to 5.30pm; closed Mondays, Good Friday, Easter Sunday, 1May and 25 December; 250$, free admission on Sunday mornings; ☎ (053) 41 24 65.

Museu Martins Sarmento – Guided tours (30min) from 9.30am to 12 noon and 2pm to 5pm (open 10am on Sundays); closed Mondays, holidays and 24 June (local holiday); 200$; ☎ (053) 41 59 69.

Igrega de São Francisco – Sacristy open 9am to 12 noon and 3pm to 5pm; closed Sundays and Mondays; ☎ (053) 51 25 07..

Excursion

Roriz: Igreja – Open 8am to 7pm.

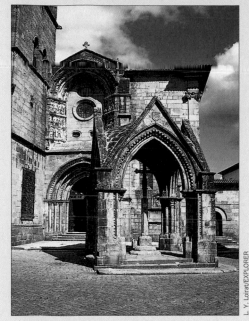

Colegiada de Nossa Senhora da Oliveira, Guimarães

L

LAGOS
🛈 Largo Marquês de Pombal, ☎ (082) 76 30 31

Igreja de Santo António and Museu Regional – Open 9.30am to 12.30pm and 2pm to 5pm; closed Mondays and holidays; 320$; free admission on Sundays; ☎ (082) 76 23 01.

Forte da Ponta de Bandeira – Open 10am to 1pm and 2pm to 6pm; closed Sunday afternoons, Mondays and holidays, 320$; free admission on Sundays; ☎ (082) 76 14 10.

Excursion

Ponta da Piedade: sea caves – Tour by boat in summer; times to be discussed with local fishermen; apply to Avenida dos Descobrimentos, Fortaleza do Pau da Bandeira, Praia de Dona Ana, Ponta da Piedade.

LAMEGO   🛈 Av. Visconde Guedes Teixeira, ☎ (054) 6 20 05

Museu de Lamego – Open 10am to 12.30pm and 2pm to 5pm; closed Mondays, 1 January, Good Friday, Easter Sunday, 1May, 8 September and 25 December; 250$, free on Sunday mornings; ☎ (054) 6 20 08.

Capela do Desterro – Apply to Sra Aurora Rodrigues, Rua Cardoso Avelino, n° 11-2° or call (054) 6 37 88.

Excursion

Capela de São Pedro de Balsemão – Open 10am to 12.30pm and 2pm to 5pm; closed Mondays and 1May; ☎ (054) 6 29 76.

LEIRIA   🛈 Jardim Luís de Camões, ☎ (044) 82 37 73 and 81 47 48

Castelo – Open 9am to 5.30pm (6.30pm in summer); closed 1 January and 25 December; ☎ (044) 81 39 82.

LINDOSO

Castelo – Guided tours 8.30 to 12.30pm and 2pm to 5.30pm; closed Mondays; 200$; ☎ (058) 6 74 05.

LISBOA   🛈 Praça dos Restauradores (Palácio Foz), ☎ (01) 346 33 14 or 346 36 43

Baixa

Núcleo Arqueológico da Rua dos Correeiros – Guided tours (45min) Thursdays at 3pm, 4pm and 5pm, Saturdays at 10am, 11am, 12 noon, 3pm, 4pm and 5pm, free admission. Visitors are asked to give two days' notice if possible to Dr. Camilo Melo, Rua dos Correeiros, 9 – 1100 Lisboa; ☎ (01) 422 44 66 and 321 17 00.

Elevador de Santa Justa – Open daily; 150$; ☎ (01) 363 20 21.

Chiado

Igreja do Carmo – Closed temporarily.

Museu do Chiado – Open 10am to 6pm (2pm to 6pm on Tuesdays); closed Mondays and Tuesday mornings; 400$; free admission on Sundays and holidays until 2pm; ☎ (01) 343 21 48/9.

Museu de Arte Sacra de São Roque – Open 10am to 5pm; closed Mondays and holidays; 150$; free admission on Sundays; ☎ (01) 346 03 61, ext. 380.

Alfama

Sé: Cloisters – Open 8am to 5pm; closed holidays; 100$; ☎ (01) 886 67 52

Treasury – Open 10am to 5pm; closed Sundays and holidays; 400$.

Museu Antoniano – Open 10am to 1pm and 2pm to 6pm; closed Mondays, 25 April and holidays; 165$; ☎ (01) 886 04 47.

Museu de Artes Decorativas – Fundação Ricardo Espírito Santo Silva – Open 10am to 5pm; closed Tuesdays, 1 January, Easter Sunday, 1 May and 25 December; 800$; ☎ (01) 888 21 83/5.

Igreja de São Vicente de Fora – Guided tours from 10am to 6pm; closed Mondays, 1 January, Good Friday and 15 December; 300$; ☎ (01) 885 36 65.

Igreja de Santa Engrácia – The national pantheon is open 10am to 5pm; closed Mondays, 1 January, Easter Sunday, 1 May and 25 December; 250$; free admission on Sundays and holidays until 2pm; ☎ (01) 888 15 29.

The Port and the Tagus

Museu Nacional do Azulejo (Convento da Madre de Deus) – Open from 10am to 6pm; closed Mondays, Tuesday mornings, Good Friday, Easter Sunday, 1 May and 25 December; 350$; free admission on Sunday mornings; ☎ (01) 814 77 47.

Museu da Água da EPAL – Open 10am to 12.30pm and 2pm to 5pm; closed Sundays, Mondays and holidays; 200$; free admission on 22 March, 18 May and 1 October; ☎ (01) 813 55 22.

Museu Militar – Open 10am to 5pm; closed Mondays and holidays; 300$, free admission on Wednesdays; ☎ (01) 888 21 31

Cristo Rei – Car park: 100$; access by lift from 9am to 7pm (6pm in winter): 250$; ☎ (01) 275 10 00.

MNAA – P. Ferreira/ANF-IPM

Panel of Polyptych of St Vincent, Museu Nacional de Arte Antiga, Lisbon

Museu Nacional de Arte Antiga – Open Wednesdays to Sundays 10am to 6pm; Tuesdays 2pm to 6pm; closed Mondays and holidays; 500$; ☎ (01) 396 41 51.

Belém

Mosteiro dos Jerónimos: Igreja de Santa Maria – Open 10am to 5pm; closed Mondays, 1 January, Easter Sunday, 1 May and 25 December.

Cloisters – Same opening times as the church above; 400$; ☎ (01) 362 00 34.

Museu Nacional de Arqueologia – Open 10am to 6pm; closed Mondays, Tuesday mornings, 1 January, Good Friday, Easter Sunday, 1 May and 25 December; 350$; free admission on Sundays and holidays until 2pm; ☎ (01) 362 00 00.

Museu da Marinha – Open 10am to 5pm; closed Mondays and holidays; 300$; ☎ (01) 362 00 01.

Museu de Arte Popular – Open 10am to 12.30pm and 2pm to 5pm; closed Mondays, 1 January, Good Friday, Easter Sunday, 1 May and 25 December; 300$; free admission on Sunday mornings; ☎ (01) 301 12 82.

Padrão dos Descobrimentos – Open 9.30am to 6.45pm; closed Mondays, 22 June and holidays; 320$; ☎ (01) 301 90 25.

Torre de Belém – Open 10am to 5pm; closed Mondays, 1 January, Easter Sunday, 1May and 25 December; 400$.

Museu Nacional dos Coches – Open 10am to 6pm; closed Mondays, 1 January, Good Friday, Easter Sunday, 1 May and 25 December; 450$; free admission on Sunday mornings; ☎ (01) 361 08 50 and 361 08 57.

Museu Nacional dos Coches, Lisbon

Palácio Nacional da Ajuda – Guided tours from 10am to 5pm; closed Wednesdays, 1 January, Good Friday, Easter Sunday, 1 May, 25 December and all through February (maintenance); 400$, free admission on Sundays until 2pm; ☎ (01) 363 70 95 and 362 02 64.

Parque Eduardo VII: Estufa Fria – Open 9am to 5.30pm (4.30pm from 1 October to 21 March); closed 1 January, 25 April, 1 May and 25 December; 95$; ☎ (01) 388 22 78.

Jardim Botânico – Open 9am to 8pm Monday to Friday (10am at weekends); closes at 6pm in winter; closed 1 January and 25 December; 200$; ☎ (01) 396 15 21/2/3.

Gulbenkian Foundation

Museu Calouste Gulbenkian – Open from 10am to 5pm Tuesdays to Sundays (from June to September open 2pm to 7.30pm Wednesdays and Saturdays, and 10am to 5pm on Tuesdays, Thursdays, Fridays and Sundays); closed Mondays and holidays; 500$; free admission on Sundays, ☎ (01) 793 51 31.

Centro de Arte Moderna – Open 10am to 5pm; closed Mondays and holidays; 500$, free admission on Sundays; ☎ (01) 795 02 41.

As Amoreiras

Fundação Arpad Szenes – Vieira da Silva – Open 12 noon to 8pm (10am on Sundays and Mondays); closed Tuesdays and holidays; 500$, free admission on Mondays; ☎ (01) 388 00 53/44.

Aqueduto das Águas Livres – Guided tours for groups with reservations on Wednesdays and Saturdays; apply at least a fortnight in advance to Museu da Água da EPAL, Rua do Alviela 12, 1100 Lisboa; ☎ (01) 813 55 22.

Mãe d'Água das Amoreiras – Open during exhibitions and for group visits only; apply at least a fortnight in advance to Museu da Água da EPAL, Rua do Alviela 12, 1100 Lisboa; 300$; ☎ (01) 813 55 22.

Additional sights

Palácio dos Marqueses de Fronteira – Guided tours (1 hour) daily Mondays to Saturdays at 11am and 12 noon from October to May and at 10.30am, 11am, 11.30am and 12 noon from June to September; closed Sundays and holidays; 1000$ (1 500$ on Saturdays); ☎ (01) 778 20 23.

Jardim Zoológico – Open 10am to 8pm (6pm from October to March); 1 650$; ☎ (01) 726 93 49.

Museu da Música – Open 1.30pm to 8pm; closed Sundays, Mondays and holidays; 300$; ☎ (01) 355 84 57.

Casa Fernando Pessoa – Open 10am to 6pm (1pm to 8pm on Thursdays); closed weekends and holidays; free admission; ☎ (01) 396 81 90/99.

Museu da Cidade – Open 10am to 1pm and 2pm to 6pm; closed Mondays; 330$; free admission on Sundays; ☎ (01) 759 16 17.

Museu Rafael Bordalo Pinheiro – Open 10am to 1pm and 2pm to 6pm; closed Mondays and holidays; 260$, free admission on Sundays; ☎ (01) 759 08 16.

Museu Nacional do Traje – Open 10am to 6pm; closed Mondays, 1 January, Good Friday, Easter Sunday, 1May and 25 December; 400$; free admission on Sundays from 10am to 2pm; ☎ (01) 759 03 18.

Jardim Botânico de Monteiro-Mar – Open 10am to 5.30pm (6.30pm from April to October); closed Mondays; 200$.

Museu Nacional do Teatro – Open 10am to 6pm; closed Mondays; Tuesday mornings, 1 January, 25 April, Good Friday, Easter Sunday, 1 May and 25 December; 400$; free admission on Sundays from 10am to 2pm; ☎ (01) 757 25 47/94.

Aquário Vasco da Gama – Open 10am to 6pm (6.30pm from 15 June to 30 September); 300$ adults, 150$ for under 18s (400$ and 200$ from 15 June to 30 September); free admission on Sundays from 10am to 1pm.

M

MAFRA Av. 25 de Abril, ☎ (061) 81 20 23

Palace and Monastery – Guided tours (1 hour 15min) 10am to 5.30pm (9.30am to 6pm in July, August and September); closed Tuesdays, Good Friday, Easter Sunday, 1May, Ascension Thursday (local holiday) and 25 December; 400$, free on Sundays and holidays from 9am to 12 noon; ☎ (061) 81 18 88.

Biblioteca do Convento de Mafra

Igreja de Santo André – Ask for the key at the Casa da Cultura; ☎ (061) 5 14 16.

MANGUALADE

Excursion

Penalva do Castelo: Casa da Insua – Guided tours (30min) 10am to 12 noon and 1.30pm to 6pm; 300$; ☎ (032) 64 22 22.

MARVÃO
2 Rua Dr. Matos Magalhães, ☎ (045) 9 32 26

Igreja de Santa Maria: Museu Municipal de Marvão – Open 9am to 12.30pm and 2pm to 5.30pm; 150$; ☎ (045) 9 31 04.

MÉRTOLA
2 Largo Vasco da Gama, ☎ (086) 6 25 73

Igreja-Mesquita – Open 9.30am to 12.15pm and 2.15pm to 5.15pm; closed Mondays; when closed apply to Sister Teresa; ☎ (086) 6 25 50.

Museu – Open 9am to 12.30pm and 2pm to 6pm; (on Saturdays, Sundays and holidays visits by guided tour only – 2 hr 30min) – apply to the Tourist Information in Mértola; 500$; ☎ (086) 6 25 73.

MIRANDA DO DOURO
2 Largo do Menino Jesus da Cartolinha, ☎ (073) 4 11 32

Sé – Open 10am to 12.15pm and 2pm to 4.45pm; closed Mondays, 1 January, Good Friday, Easter Sunday, 1 May, 10 July and 25 December.

Museu Regional da Terra de Miranda – Open 10am to 12.30pm and 2pm to 5.15pm (5.45pm from May to September); closed Mondays and Sunday afternoons from October to April; 150$; free of charge on Sunday mornings; ☎ (073) 4 11 64.

MIRANDELA
2 Praça do Mercado, ☎ (078) 2 57 68

Museu Municipal Armindo Teixeira Lopes – Open 9.30am to 12.30pm and 2pm to 6pm; closed Saturdays, Sundays and holidays; free admission; ☎ (078) 26 57 68.

Excursion

Romeu: Museu das Curiosidades – Open 12 noon to 4pm (6pm from April to September); closed Mondays, first Sunday in September and 25 December; 250$; ☎ (078) 9 31 34.

MONSARAZ
2 Largo D. Nuno Álvares Pereira, ☎ (066) 5 51 36

Antigo Tribunal – Open 9am to 7pm; 200$; ☎ (066) 5 13 15.

Hospital da Misericórdia – Open 10am to 5pm; ☎ (066) 5 51 41.

MONTEMOR-O-VELHO
2 Praça da República (Câmara Municipal), ☎ (039) 68 91 14

Castelo – Open 9am to 12.30pm and 2pm to 5pm; closed Mondays, Good Friday, Easter Sunday and 25 November; free admission; ☎ (039) 2 95 90.

N

NAZARÉ
2 Av. da República, ☎ (062) 56 11 94

O Sítio: funicular – The funicular operates daily from 7.30am until midnight; closed in March; 85$ per person; ☎ (062) 56 11 53.

Ermida da Memória – Open 9am to 7pm; ☎ (062) 55 17 95.

O

ÓBIDOS
2 Rua Direita, ☎ (062) 95 92 31

Igreja de Santa Maria – Open 9.30am to 12.30pm and 2.30pm to 5pm (7pm from April to September); ☎ (062) 95 96 33.

Museu Municipal – Open 10am to 12.30pm and 2pm to 6pm; closed 1 January, 11 January (local holiday) and 25 December; 250$; free admission on Sunday mornings; ☎ (062) 95 92 63.

Santuário do Senhor da Pedra – Open 9.30am to 12.30pm and 2.30pm to 7pm; closed Mondays; normally closed from October to March, although the key can be obtained by calling (062) 95 96 33.

OLHÃO
2 Largo da Lagoa, ☎ (089) 71 39 36

Igreja Matriz – Open from 9am to 12 noon and 3pm to 6pm; closed Saturday afternoon and all day Monday; 100$; ☎ (089) 70 51 17.

OLIVEIRA DO HOSPITAL
2 Casa da Cultura de Oliveira, Rua do Colégio, ☎ (038) 5 91 19

Igreja Matriz – Open 9am to 6pm.

Excursion

Igreja de Lourosa – Open daily at any time; ☎ (038) 5 71 26; when closed apply to Dona Maria do Patrocínio.

P

PALMELA
⊞ Castelo de Palmela, **☎** (01) 235 21 22

Castelo – Open daily with the exception of one part of the castle which opens from 9am to 1pm and 2pm to 8pm; closed Mondays; **☎** (01) 233 21 22.

Igreja de São Pedro – Visitors are requested to apply to the "Casa Parroquial" near the church; **☎** (01) 235 00 25.

PENEDONO

Castelo – Open from 9.30am to 12.30pm and 2.30pm to 7pm (6pm on Saturdays, Sundays and holidays); closed Good Friday and Easter Sunday; free admission; **☎** (054) 5 41 50 or 6 57 70; if closed apply to Sr. Luís Martins in the building next to the castle.

PINHEL

Museu Municipal – Open 9am to 12.30pm and 2pm to 5.30pm Mondays to Fridays and 10am to 12 noon and 2pm to 5pm on Saturdays, Sundays and holidays; 100$; **☎** (071) 4 33 05.

POMBAL
⊞ Largo do Cardal, **☎** (036) 40 23 23

Castelo – Open 8am to 5pm Monday to Friday; 8am to 12 noon and 1pm to 5pm on Saturdays, Sundays and holidays; free admission; **☎** (036) 2 61 01/2.

PONTE DE LIMA
⊞ Praça da República, **☎** (058) 74 16 52

Igreja-Museu dos Terceiros – Open 10am to 12 noon and 2pm to 5pm; closed Tuesdays.

PORTALEGRE
⊞ Estrada de Santana 25, **☎** (045) 2 18 15 or 2 84 53
⊞ Galeria Municipal – Rossio, **☎** (045) 33 13 59

Museu José Régio – Guided tours (30-45min) from 9.30am to 12.30pm and 2pm to 6pm; closed Mondays and holidays; 250$. **☎** (045) 2 36 25.

Museu Municipal – Guided tours (30-45min) from 9.30am to 12.30pm and 2pm to 6pm; closed Tuesdays and holidays; 250$. **☎** (045) 33 06 16, ext. 344.

PORTO
⊞ Rua Clube dos Fenianos 25, **☎** (02) 31 27 40
⊞ Rua Infante D. Henrique 73, **☎** (02) 200 97 70

Sé – Open 9am to 12 noon and 2.30pm to 5.30pm; cloisters 250$; **☎** (02) 31 90 28.

Santa Casa da Misericórdia – Guided tours 9am to 12.30pm and 2pm to 5.30pm; closed weekends and holidays; 300$; **☎** (02) 200 09 41/4.

Museu Etnográfico – Closed temporarily; **☎** (02) 200 20 10.

Ribeiro district in Porto

Palácio da Bolsa – Guided tours (20-30min) 9am to 1pm and 2pm to 6pm; visits every 20min from April to October (last admission 12.40pm and 5.40pm); from April to November visits every 30min (last admission 12.30pm and 5.30pm); closed weekends and holidays from November to March; 700$; ☎ (02) 200 44 97.

Igreja de São Francisco – Open 9.30am to 12.30pm and 2pm to 6pm daily (5pm on weekdays from October to April); 500$; ☎ (02) 200 04 41.

Igreja and Torre dos Clérigos – Access to the tower and bells from 10am to 12 noon and 2.30pm to 5pm; 100$; ☎ (02) 200 17 29.

Museu Nacional de Soares dos Reis – Open from 10am to 12.30pm and 2pm to 5.30pm; closed Mondays, 1 January, Easter Sunday, 25 April, 1 May and 25 December; 350$; free admission on Sunday mornings.

Museu Romântico – Guided tours (20min) from 10am to 12 noon and 2pm to 5pm (Sundays 2pm to 5.30pm); closed Mondays and holidays; 150$; free admission on Saturdays and Sundays; ☎ (02) 609 11 31.

Solar do Vinho do Porto – Open 11am to midnight; closed Sundays and holidays; ☎ (02) 69 77 93 or 69 47 49.

Casa Tait – Open 10am to 12 noon and 2pm to 5.30pm (6pm on Saturdays, Sundays and holidays); ☎ (02) 606 82 45.

Wine lodges – Guided tours (20min) from 9.30am to 12 noon and 2pm to 5.30pm; open weekends and holidays by appointment only; free admission; ☎ (02) 30 50 02.

Igreja de Santa Clara – Open 9.30am to 11.30am and 3pm to 6pm; closed weekends; ☎ (02) 31 48 37.

Museu Guerra Junqueiro – Closed for building work; ☎ (02) 31 36 44.

Fundação António de Almeida – Guided tours (30min) from 2.30pm to 5.30pm; closed Sundays, holidays and throughout August; 100$; ☎ (02) 606 74 18.

Fundação de Serralves: Museu de Arte Contemporânea – Open Monday to Friday 2pm to 6pm; Saturdays and Sundays 10am to 8pm (until 8pm from 1 March to 31 October); closed Mondays, 1 January and 25 December; 400$; free admission on Sundays from 10am to 2pm; ☎ (02) 618 00 57.

Igreja da Cedofeita – Ask for the key at the church next door; ☎ (02) 200 56 20.

Q

QUELUZ
🚇 Av. Dr. Miguel Bombarda (railway station); ☎ (01) 924 16 23

Palácio Nacional – Open 10am to 1pm and 2pm to 5pm; closed Tuesdays and holidays; 400$; ☎ (01) 924 16 23.

S

SABUGAL

Castelo – Open 9.30am to 1pm and 2pm to 6pm (6.30pm on Sundays); closed Tuesdays and Wednesdays; free admission; ☎ (071) 610 10 40.

SANTA MARIA DA FEIRA
🚇 Rua dos Descubrimentos, ☎ (056) 37 20 32

Castelo – Open in summer 9am to 12.30pm and 2.30pm to 7pm and in winter from 9.30am to 12.30pm and 2.30pm to 5pm; closed Mondays; ☎ (056) 37 22 48.

SANTARÉM
🚇 Rua Capelo e Ivens 63, ☎ (043) 39 15 12

Igreja de São João de Alporão: Museu Arqueológico – Open 9.30am to 12.30pm and 2pm to 6pm (5.30pm Saturdays and Sundays); closed Mondays and holidays; 200$, free admission on 19 and 28 March, 18 May and 11 September; ☎ (043) 39 15 10/7.

Torre das Cabaças – Undergoing restoration.

Igreja da Graça – Temporarily closed for building work; ☎ (043) 2 55 52.

Igreja de Santa Clara – Open 9.30am to 12.30pm and 2pm to 5.30pm; closed Mondays and holidays; ☎ (043) 2 55 52.

Excursion

Alpiarça: Casa dos Patudos – Guided tours (1 hour); 10am to 12.30pm and 2pm to 5pm; closed Mondays, Tuesdays, 2 and 25 April, Easter Sunday, 1May and 25 December; 350$; ☎ (043) 5 43 21.

SANTIAGO DO CACÉM
🖪 Praça do Mercado Municipal, ☎ (069) 82 66 96

Museu Municipal – Open from 10am to 12 noon and 2pm to 5pm; closed Saturday and Sunday mornings, Mondays and holidays; free admission; ☎ (069) 82 73 75.

Miróbriga: Roman ruins – Open from 9.30am to 12.30pm and 2pm to 5.30pm (open until 12 noon on Sundays), closed Mondays, 1 January, Good Friday, Easter Sunday, 1 May and 25 December; 300$; free on Sunday and holiday mornings; ☎ (069) 2 38 03.

SÃO JOÃO DE TAROUCA

Igreja – Open 10am to 12 noon and 2pm to 5pm; closed Mondays; ☎ (054) 67 98 49 (Sr. Caetano).

SERPA
🖪 Largo D. Jorge 2, ☎ (084) 5 37 27/29

Museu Etnográfico – Open 9am to 12.30pm and 2pm to 5.30pm (6.30pm during the summer); closed Mondays and holidays; free admission; ☎ (084) 5 37 27.

SETÚBAL
🖪 Tv. Frei Gaspar, 10, ☎ (065) 52 42 84
🖪 Praca do Quebedo (Posto da C.M.), ☎ (065) 53 42 22

Museu de Jesus – Open from 9am to 1pm and 2.30pm to 5pm; closed Mondays; free admission; ☎ (065) 52 47 72.

Museu Regional de Arqueologia e Etnografia – Open from 9am to 12.30pm and 2pm to 5.30pm; closed Sundays, Mondays, holidays and Saturdays in August; ☎ (065) 3 93 65.

Península de Tróia

Crossing the estuary to Península de Tróia – By ferry (20min) departures every hour from the Doca de Recreio.

Cetóbriga: Roman ruins – Currently closed to visitors; ☎ (065) 4 41 51.

SILVES
🖪 Rua 25 de Abril, ☎ (082) 44 22 55

Castelo – Open 9am to 8pm from 1 June to 15 September (until 6pm from 16 September to 31 March); until 7pm from 1 April to 31 May); 250$; free admission on 3 September; ☎ (082) 44 56 24.

Museu Arqueológico – Open 10am to 5pm; closed national and local (3 September) holidays; 300$; ☎ (082) 44 48 32.

SINTRA
🖪 Praça da República (Edifício do Turismo), ☎ (01) 923 11 57 or 923 39 19

Palácio Real – Open from 10am to 1pm and 2pm to 5pm; closed Wednesdays, days of official ceremonies, 1 January, Good Friday, Easter Sunday, 1May, 29 July and 25 December; 400$; free admission on Sunday mornings; ☎ (01) 923 00 85.

Museu de Arte Moderna de Sintra (Colecção Berardo) – Open Wednesdays to Sundays 10am to 6pm and Tuesday afternoons 2pm to 6pm; closed Mondays; 600$; ☎ (01) 924 81 70.

Serra de SINTRA

Parque da Pena – Open 10am to 5pm (6pm in summer); free admission; ☎ (01) 923 51 16/66.

Castelo dos Mouros – Same times as the Parque da Pena, ☎ (01) 923 51 16/66.

Palácio Nacional da Pena – Open 10am to 5pm (6.30pm from 1 July to 15 September); closed Mondays, 1 January, Good Friday, Easter Sunday, 1May, 29 June and 25 December; 400$; free admission on Sundays and holidays until 2pm; ☎ (01) 923 02 27 or 924 08 61.

Convento dos Capuchos – Open 10am to 7pm (5pm in winter); 200$; ☎ (01) 923 01 37.

Peninha – Closed for restoration work; ☎ (01) 923 51 16.

Parque de Monserrate – Open 9am to 5pm (7pm from June to October); opens at 10am from November to February; closed 1 January, 1May, 29 June and 25 December; 200$; ☎ (01) 923 51 16 or 923 12 10 (visits must be organised two weeks in advance).

The Michelin on-line route planning service is available on a pay-per-route basis, or you may opt for a subscription package. This option affords you multiple route plans at considerable savings.
Plan your next trip in minutes with Michelin on Internet: www.michelin-travel.com.
Bon voyage!

T

TOMAR

 Av. Doutor Cândido Madureira, ☎ (049) 32 26 01 or 32 24 27

Convento de Cristo – Open daily 9.15am to 12.30pm and 2pm to 5pm; 400$; ☎ (049) 31 34 81.

Capela de Nossa Senhora da Conceição – Open 11am to 12.15pm; ☎ (049) 31 34 81; for visits please apply to the Convento de Cristo.

Sinagoga – Open 9.30am to 12.30pm and 2pm to 5.30pm; closed Wednesdays and holidays; free admission.

TRANSCOSO

Castelo – Guided tours from 9.30am to 12.30pm and 2pm to 5.30pm; if closed please apply to the Tourist Information Centre ☎ (071) 9 11 47 or the Posta da Guarda Nacional Republicana.

Y. Travert/DIAF

Convento de Cristo, Tomar

V

Parque Arqueológico do VALE do CÔA

Headquarters: Avenida Gago Coutinho, 19A – 5150 Vila Nova de Foz Côa; tel (079) 76 43 17; fax (079) 76 52 57.

Castelo Melhor Reception Centre: ☎ (079) 7 33 44

Muxagata Reception Centre: ☎ (079) 76 42 98

Visits must be organised at least two months in advance during the high season.

Guided tours of the Penascosa (by jeep from the Castelo Melhor Reception Centre), Ribeira de Piscos (by jeep from the Muxagata Reception Centre) and Canada do Inferno (by jeep from the park headquarters in Vila Nova de Foz Côa) sites.

Variable visiting times depending on natural light conditions.

Closed Mondays, 1 January, 1May and 25 December; approximate admission fee: 500$ per visit.

VIANA DO ALENTEJO
⊞ Câmara Municipal, ☎ (066) 9 31 06

Castelo – Open 10am to 12.30pm and 2pm to 6pm; closed Mondays; ☎ (066) 9 31 04/06.

VIANA DO CASTELO
⊞ Rua do Hospital Velho, ☎ (058) 82 26 20 or 2 49 71

Basílica de Santa Luzia – Open 9am to 7pm (Sunday Eucharist between 11am and 12 noon); free admission to the basilica; 70$ for access to dome and 100$ charge for lift; ☎ (058) 82 31 73.

Igreja da Misericórdia – Guided tours from 9.30am to 12.30pm and 2pm to 5.30pm; (Sunday Eucharist between 11.30am and 1pm); ☎ (058) 82 23 50.

Museu Municipal – Open 9.30am to 12.30pm and 2pm to 5.30pm; closed Mondays and holidays; 145$; ☎ (058) 82 06 78.

VILA DO CONDE
⊞ Rua 5 de Outobro, ☎ (052) 64 27 00

Convento de Santa Clara – Guided tours (15min) from 9am to 12.15pm and 2.30pm to 5.30pm; ☎ (052) 64 27 00.

VILA FRANCA DE XIRA
⊞ Av. Almirante Cândido dos Reis 147-149 r/c, ☎ (063) 260 53

Museu Etnográfico – Guided tours from 10am to 12.30pm and 2pm to 6pm; closed Mondays and holidays; ☎ (063) 2 30 57.

VILA FRANCA DE XIRA

Excursion

Alverca do Ribatejo: Museu do Ar – Open 10am to 5pm; closed Mondays, 1 January, Easter Sunday and 24 and 25 December; free admission; ☎ (063) 958 27 82.

VILAMOURA

Cerro da Vila: Roman ruins – Open 9am to 12.30pm and 2pm to 5pm (8pm in summer); closed 1 January and 25 December; 200$; ☎ (089) 31 21 53.

VILA REAL   ❸ Av. Carvalho Araújo 94, ☎ (059) 32 28 19

Excursion

Solar de Mateus – Guided tours (45min) from 9am to 6pm; closed 25 December; 980$ for full visit, 600$ for the gardens; ☎ (059) 32 31 21.

VILA VIÇOSA

Paço Ducal – Guided tours (1 hour) in summer from 9am to 1pm and 3pm to 5.30pm (until 6pm on weekends) and in winter from 9am to 1pm and 2.30pm to 5pm (2pm to 5pm on weekends); closed Mondays and holidays; 1 000$; ☎ (068) 9 86 59.

Castelo – Museu Arqueológico – Closed for renovation.

VISEU   ❸ Av. Gulbenkian, ☎ (032) 42 20 14

Museu Grão Vasco – Open from 9.30am to 12.30pm and 2pm to 5.30pm; closed Mondays, 1 January, Good Friday, Easter Sunday, 1May and 25 December; 250$, free on Sunday mornings; ☎ (032) 42 20 49.

Sé: Tesouro de Arte Sacra – Guided tours (30min) from 9am to 12 noon and 2pm to 5pm; closed Saturday and Sunday mornings, Wednesdays and first two weeks in July; 200$; ☎ (032) 42 88 18.

The Madeira Archipelago

MADEIRA

Tour of the Island – For information on bus itineraries (many options at varying prices) ask at the Direcção Regional de Turismo, Avenida Arriaga, 18, Funchal, ☎ (091) 22 90 57.

FUNCHAL

🅱 Av. Arriaga 18, ☎ (091) 22 90 57

Adegas de São Francisco – Guided tours (approx. 1 hour 30min, including wine-tasting) from 9am to 7pm (until 2pm on Saturdays; closed Sundays, 1 January, 25 and 26 December and holidays; 500$; ☎ (091) 22 30 65 or 22 80 58.

Museu de Arte Sacra – Open 10am to 12.30pm and 2.30pm to 6pm, Sundays 10am to 1pm; closed Mondays and holidays; 400$; ☎ (091) 22 89 00.

Museu da Fotografia "Vicentes" – Open 2pm to 6pm; closed weekends and holidays; 150$; free admission on 18 May; ☎ (091) 22 50 50.

Museu Municipal – Open 10am to 6pm (12 noon to 6pm on weekends); closed Mondays, 1 January, Easter Sunday and 25 December; 250$; free admission on Sundays; ☎ (091) 22 97 61.

Museu Frederico de Freitas – Temporarily closed for restoration.

Convento de Santa Clara – Guided tours (45-60min) from 10am to 12 noon and 3pm to 5pm; ☎ (091) 74 26 12.

Quinta das Cruzes – Open 10am to 12.30pm and 2pm to 6pm; closed Mondays, 1 January, Carnival, Good Friday, Easter Sunday, 25 April, 1May, 10 June, 1 July, 15 and 21 August, 5 October, 1 November, 1, 8, 25 and 26 December; 350$, free admission on weekends; ☎ (091) 74 13 82/84/88.

Instituto do Bordado – Open from 10am to 12.30pm and 2.30pm to 5.30pm; closed weekends and holidays; free admission; ☎ (091) 22 31 41.

Instituto do Vinho de Madeira – Open 9am to 12 noon and 2pm to 5pm; closed weekends and holidays; free admission; ☎ (091) 22 25 76.

Museu Cristóvão Colombo – Open 9.30am to 1pm and 3pm to 7pm; closed Saturday afternoons, Sundays and holidays; 200$; ☎ (091) 23 33 57.

Jardim Botânico – Open 8am to 6pm; closed 25 December; 300$, children 100$; ☎ (091) 200 20 00.

Quinta do Palheiro Ferreiro – Open 9.30am to 12.30pm; closed weekends, 1 January, 28 March, Good Friday, 1May, 25 and 26 December; 850$; ☎ (091) 79 30 44 or 79 49 84.

Quinta das Cruzes, Funchal

Y. Travert/DIAF

East Coast

Caniçal: Museu da Baleia – Open 10am to 12 noon and 2pm to 6pm; closed Mondays, 1 January, 1 May, 25 and 26 December; 200$; ☎ (091) 96 14 07.

PORTO SANTO   🖪 Vila Baleira, 9400 Porto Santo, ☎ (091) 98 23 61 or 98 34 05

Access – By plane: TAP operates between 5 and 7 daily flights both ways between Madeira and Porto Santo. The first flight from Funchal to Porto Santo leaves at 8am, the last flight from Porto Santo to Funchal leaves at 9.30pm; the flight takes 15min and the return journey is approximately 15 160$; for further information call (091) 23 92 10.

By boat: Sailing time 2hr 45min. The boat leaves Funchal at 8am and sets out on the return journey from Porto Santo at 6pm (except Tuesdays); the frequency of service may be increased at busy times of year; day return price: 9 000$, return on a different day: 7 450; further information from Porto Santo Line, Rua da Praia, 4; ☎ (091) 22 65 11.

VILA BALEIRA

Casa de Cristóvão Colombo – Open Mondays to Fridays 9.30am to 12.30pm and 2pm to 5pm, Saturdays 9.30am to 12 noon; closed Saturday afternoons, Sundays and holidays; free admission; ☎ (091) 98 34 05.

The Azores Archipelago

SÃO MIGUEL
🆔 Av. Infante D. Henrique, 9500 Ponta Delgada, ☎ (096) 2 57 43 or 2 51 52

Ponta Delgada

Museu Carlos Machado – Open 9.30am to 12.30pm and 2pm to 5.30pm, weekends 2pm to 5.30pm (10am to 12.30pm and 2pm to 5pm from October to April); closed Mondays and holidays; 200$; free admission on Sundays; ☎ (096) 2 38 14.

West of the Island

Furnas: Parque Terra Nostra – Open from 10am to 5pm; 400$; children 200$; ☎ (096) 5 43 34

TERCEIRA
🆔 Rua Recreio dos Artistas, 35, 9700 Angra do Heroísmo, ☎ (095) 2 61 09

Angra do Heroísmo

Palácio dos Bettencourt: Biblioteca – Open from 9am to 7pm Monday to Friday and 9.30am to 12 noon on Saturdays (open until 5pm Monday to Friday in summer); closed Sundays and holidays; ☎ (095) 2 26 90/7.

Convento de São Francisco: Museu de Angra – The museum is closed; ☎ (095) 2 31 47.

Tour of the Island

Biscoitos: Museu do Vinho – Open 9am to 7pm (10am to 4pm in winter); closed Sundays (only in winter) and Mondays; free admission; ☎ (095) 9 84 04.

Algar do Carvão – Open 3pm to 5pm from 1 June to 30 September; 2-3 days' notice is required at other times; 300$; contact "Os Montanhelros", Rua da Rocha, 9700 Angra do Heroísmo; ☎ (095) 2 29 92.

GRACIOSA
🆔 Praça Fontes Pereira de Melo, 9880 Santa Cruz, ☎ (095) 7 21 25

Santa Cruz da Graciosa

Museu Etnográfico – Guided tours from 9am to 12.30pm and 2pm to 5.30pm; closed weekends and holidays; open 2pm to 5pm on weekends from May to September; 200$; free admission on Sundays; ☎ (095) 7 24 29.

Inland

Furna do Enxofre – Guided tours from 11am to 4pm; closed Thursdays, 1 January, 25 April and 25 December; 100$; ☎ (095) 7 21 25.

FAIAL
🆔 Casa do Relógio, Colonia Alemã, 9900 Horta, ☎ (092) 2 38 01/2 /3

Horta

Museu da Horta – Guided tours from 9.30am to 12.30pm and 2pm to 5.30pm (10am to 12 noon and 2pm to 5pm in winter); open 2pm to 5.30pm on Saturdays; closed Mondays and holidays (open from 2pm to 5.30pm on local holidays); 200$; free admission on Sundays; ☎ (092) 2 33 48.

Museu do Scrimshaw – Open 9.30am to 1pm and 2pm to 6.30pm (6pm on weekends); closed 1 January and 25 December; 200$; ☎ (092) 2 23 27.

Tour of the Island

Museu dos Capelinhos – Open 10am to 1pm and 2.30pm to 5.30pm; closed Sunday mornings and Mondays; ☎ (092) 9 51 65.

PICO
🆔 Rua Conselheiro Terra Pinheiro, 9950Madalena, ☎ (092) 62 35 24

Lajes do Pico

Museu dos Baleeiros – Open from 9.30am to 12.30pm and 2pm to 5pm (in winter from 10am to 12 noon and 2pm to 5pm); open Saturday and Sunday afternoons in summer only, closed Saturdays, Sundays and Mondays (in winter) and holidays; 200$; free admission on Sundays and 29 June (local holiday); ☎ (092) 67 22 76.

SÃO JORGE
🆔 Rua Conselheiro Dr. José Pereira, 9800 Velas, ☎ (095) 4 24 40

Manadas

Igreja de Santa Bárbara – Guided tours from 9.30am to 12 noon and 2pm to 5.30pm (Mondays to Fridays only); for visits, contact Sr. Rev. Francisco António Lousa; ☎ (095) 4 41 53.

Fajãzinha, Ilha das Flores, Azores

FLORES

🅱 Santa Cruz das Flores, ☎ (092) 5 28 42

Santa Cruz das Flores

Museu Etnográfico and Convento de São Boaventura – Guided tours (1hr) from 9am to 12.30pm and 2pm to 5.30pm, 2pm to 5.30pm Saturdays and Sundays from May to September; closed weekends October to April and holidays; 200$; ☎ (092) 5 21 59.

CORVO

Boat excursions – Bookings for the boat from Flores to Corvo need to be booked in advance on ☎ (092) 5 22 89; Round trip 4 000$; children 2 000$.

Caldeirão – Ascent by jeep 1 000$; ☎ (092) 5 61 15.

Index

Albufeira *Faro* .... Towns, sights and tourist regions followed by the name of the district.
NB The sights in the Archipelagos of Madeira and the Azores are an exception as they are followed by the name of the island and not the district.

Gama, Vasco da................. People, historical events, artistic styles and local terms explained in the text.

Torre de Belém .... Sights in important towns.

Main sights in Coimbra, Evora, Lisboa and Porto are listed under these headings.

A

Abrantes *Santarém* 56
Accommodation 325
Achada das Furnas
 São Miguel 296
Achada de Teixeira
 Madeira 278
Achada Valley *São Miguel*
 296
*Afonso Henriques,
 Afonso I* 18, 129
Afonso, João 28
Afonso, Jorge 30
Afonso Sanches, Dom
 250
Água de Alto *São Miguel*
 298
Água de Pau *São Miguel*
 298
Aguiar da Beira *Guarda*
 56
Aire, Serra de 15,125
Albufeira *Faro* 56
Albuquerque, Afonso de
 25
Alcobaça *Leiria* 27, 57
Alcoforado, Mariana 76
Alfeizerão *Leiria* 120
Algar do Carvão *Terceira*
 304
Algarve 59
Algar Seco *Faro* 89
Alicatados technique 35
Aljezur *Faro* 64
Aljubarrota, Battle of 19,
 73
*Almada Negreiros, José
 de* 32
Almagreira *Santa Maria*
 300
Almansil *Faro* 64
Almeida *Guarda* 128
Almeida, Estrada da
 Guarda 211
Almeida Garrett 38
Almendres, Cromeleque
 dos *Évora* 121
Almourol, Castelo
 de *Santarém* 65

Alpiarça *Santarém* 231
Alter do Chão
 Portalegre 65
Alto, Pico do *Santa Maria*
 300
Alto Rabagão, Barragem
 do *Vila Real* 95
Alvados, Grutas de *Leiria*
 126
Alvão, Parque natural de
 Vila Real 15, 193
Álvares, Afonso 30
Álvares, Baltazar 30
Álvares Cabral, Pedro 19,
 24, 77
Álvares Pereira, Nuno 77
Alverca do Ribatejo
 Lisboa 251
Alvoco da Serra *Guarda*
 113
Amado, Jorge 39
Amarante *Porto* 65
Ança *Coimbra* 88
Ança stone 88, 97
Andrade, Eugénio de 39
Angra do Heroísmo
 Terceira 301
Anjos *Santa Maria* 300
*António, Dom Prior of
 Crato* 287, 301
Antunes, Bartolomeu 36
Antunes, João 30
Architectural terms 33
Arco de São Jorge
 Madeira 278
Arcos de Valdevez *Viana
 do Castelo* 208
Areia, Fonte da *Porto
 Santo* 284
Aresta technique 35
Arieiro, Pico do *Madeira*
 277
Armação de Pêra *Faro* 66
Arouca *Aveiro* 66
Arrábida, Serra da
 Setúbal 15, 66
Arraiolos *Évora* 68
Arraiolos carpets 68
Arrifana *Faro* 64
Arruda, Diogo de 29
Arruda, Francisco de 29
Arruda, Miguel de 30

Aspa, Torre de *Faro* 63
Aveiro *Aveiro* 68
Aveiro, Ria de *Aveiro* 70
Avis *Portalegre* 71
Azenhas do Mar *Lisboa*
 240
Azores Anticyclone 287
Azores Archipelago 285
Azulejos 35
Azurara *Porto* 250

B

Bacalhau 49
Bacalhoa, Quinta da
 Setúbal 72
Balcões *Madeira* 277
Balhas 44
Barca de Alva *Guarda*
 211
Barca, Ponta da *Graciosa*
 306
Barcelos *Braga* 72
Barcelos cock 72
Barcelos, Pico dos
 Madeira 271
Barriga, Praia da *Faro* 64
Barril, Praia do *Faro* 59
Barrô *Viseu* 108
Batalha, Mosteiro da
 Leiria 27, 73
Beckford, William 240
Beja *Beja* 76
Beliche, Forte de *Faro*
 229
Belmonte *Castelo Branco*
 77
Berlenga, Ilha da *Leiria*
 15, 78
Bessa Luís, Agustina 38
Bico *Aveiro* 71
Biscoitos *Terceira* 304
Boa Ventura *Madeira* 278
Boa Viagem, Serra da
 Coimbra 126
Boa Vista, Miradouro da
 Viseu 108
Boca do Inferno *Lisboa*
 90

Bocage, Manuel M B do 38, 234
Bom Jesus do Monte Braga 80
Bordalo Pinheiro, Columbano: see Columbano
Bordalo Pinheiro, Rafael 36, 189
Botelho, João 39
Boticas Vila Real 95
Boytac/Boittaca 29
Braga Braga 78
Bragança Bragança 82
Bragança, Duke of 254
Bragança, House of 20, 82
Bravães Viana do Castelo 84
Bravura, Barragem da Faro 134
Brejoeira, Palácio da Viana do Castelo 247
Buarcos Coimbra 126
Buçaco, Battle of 85
Buçaco, Mata do Aveiro 84
Bullfighting 46
Burgau Faro 63
Burgundy, Henry of 18
Byron 238

C

Cabeço da Neve Viseu 89
Cabeço Gordo Faial 309
Cabeço do Velho Guarda 112
Cabo da Roca Lisboa 240
Cabral, Gonçalo Velho 293
Cacela Velha Faro 59
Cachorro Pico 311
Cais do Pico Pico 311
Caldas da Rainha Leiria 87
Caldas de Manteigas Guarda 59, 112
Caldas de Monchique Faro 196
Caldas do Gerês 207
Caldeira Faial 309
Caldeirão Corvo 318
Caldeira de Guilherme Moniz Terceira 304
Caldeira de Santa Bárbara Terceira 303
Caldeiras São Miguel 296
Caldeiras 286
Calendar of Events 331
Caldo verde 48
Calheta Madeira 281
Calheta São Jorge 314
Calheta de Nesquim Pico 312
Calheta, Ponta da Porto Santo 284
Camacha Madeira 276
Câmara de Lobos Madeira 273

Caminha Viana do Castelo 87
Camoens: see Camões
Camões, Luís de 37
Campo do Gerês Braga 208
Canario, Lagoa do São Miguel 295
Canaveira, Ponta da Porto Santo 284
Candal Viseu 190
Candeeiros, Serra dos Santarém 15, 125
Candelaria Pico 313
Caniçada, Confluente de Braga 206
Caniçal Madeira 276
Caniço Madeira 274
Cantanhede Coimbra 88
Cão, Diogo 24
Capelinhos Faial 309
Capuchos, Convento dos Lisboa 240
Caramulinho Viseu 89
Caramulo Viseu 89
Caramulo, Serra do Viseu 89
Carapacho Graciosa 227
Caravel 228
Cardoso Pires, José 38
Carnation Revolution 21, 163
Carr, William 202
Carrapateira Faro 64
Carrapatelo, Barragem do Viseu 107
Carvalho, Maria Judite de 39
Carvão, Pico do São Miguel 295
Carvoeiro Faro 89
Carvoeiro, Cabo Leiria 209
Casal Novo Coimbra 190
Cascais Lisboa 15, 90
Castanheira de Pêra Leiria 190
Castelejo, Praia do Faro 64
Castelo, Pico do Porto Santo 284
Castelo Bom Guarda 128
Castelo Branco Castelo Branco 90
Castelo Branco, Ponta de Faial 308
Castelo Branco, Camilo 38
Castelo de Vide Portalegre 92
Castelo Melhor Guarda 128
Castelo Mendo Guarda 128
Castelo Rodrigo Guarda 211
Castilho, João and Diogo de 29
Castilho, António F de 38
Castro, Inês de 57
Castro Laboreiro Viana do Castelo 209

Castro Marim Faro 15, 93
Castro Verde Beja 93
Cávado, Alto vale do Rio Braga/Vila Real 93
Cávado, Rio 206
Celorico da Beira Guarda 128
Centum Cellas Castelo Branco 78
Cerro da Vila Faro 251
Cetóbriga Setúbal 236
Ceuta, Capture of 19, 23
Chamilly, Count 76
Chanterene, Nicolas/Nicolau 30
Chaves Vila Real 95
Chulas 44
Churchill, Winston 273
Cinco Ribeiras Terceira 303
Cinema 39
Cinfães Viseu 107
Citânia de Briteiros Braga 82
Coimbra Coimbra 97
  Casa do Arco 98
  Convento de Santa Clara-a-Nova 102
  Convento de Santa Clara-a-Velha 102
  Igreja de São Tiago 102
  Jardim botânico 102
  Miradouro do Vale do Inferno 102
  Mosteiro de Celas 102
  Mosteiro de Santa Cruz 101
  Museu da Criança 102
  Museu Nacional Machado de Castro 99
  Paço de Sub-Ripas 98
  Penedo da Saudade 102
  Porta de Almeidina 98
  Portugal dos Pequeninos 102
  Quinta das Lágrimas 102
  Sé Velha 98
  Torre de Anto 98
  Travellers' addresses 98
  Velha Universidade 100
  Coimbra School of Sculpture 97
Colaço, Jorge 36
Colares Lisboa 240
Columbano 32, 256
Columbus, Christopher 24, 283
Concelhos 17
Congro, Lagoa de São Miguel 298
Conímbriga Coimbra 103
Conservation areas 15
Corda seca technique 35
Cordoama, Praia da Faro 64
Correia, Natália 38
Corridinho 44
Corte Real, Gaspar 25
Corvo 317
Costa da Caparica Setúbal 15, 105
Costa Nova Aveiro 71
Cova da Iria Santarém 124
Covilhã Castelo Branco 113
Crato Portalegre 105

Criação Velha *Pico* 313
Cruz Alta *(Pena) Lisboa* 240
Cruz Amarante, Carlos da 31
Curral das Freiras *Madeira* 271

D – E

Dabneys, The 307
Days of the week 332
Deus, João de 38
Dias, Bartolomeu 24
Districts 17
Douro, Vale do 106
Eanes, Gil 23
Eastern Fortified Towns *Guarda* 128
Eça de Queirós 38
Eira do Serrado *Madeira* 271
Elvas *Portalegre* 109
Empedrados 41
Encumeada, Boca da *Madeira* 280
Ericeira *Lisboa* 110
Ernestine Wettins, The 23
Escalvado, Miradouro *São Miguel* 296
Escoural, Gruta do *Évora* 121
Escovinho 44
Espichel, Cabo *Setúbal* 110
Espigueiros 41, 136, 208
Esposende *Braga* 15
Estoril *Lisboa* 110
Estreito de Câmara de Lobos *Madeira* 273
Estrela, Serra da *Guarda/Castelo Branco* 15, 111
Estremoz *Évora* 114
Estremoz potteries 114
Évora *Évora* 115
  Sé (Cathedral) 115
  Capela dos Ossos 119
  Casa Cordovil 119
  Casa dos Condes de Portalegre 119
  Casa de Garcia de Resende 119
  Casa Soure 119
  Convento de São Bento de Castris 120
  Convento dos Lóios 118
  Igreja das Mercês 120
  Igreja de Nossa Senhora da Graça 119
  Igreja de São Francisco 119
  Ermida de São Brás 120
  Fortificacoes 120
  Jardim público 120
  Largo da Porta da Moura 119
  Museu das Artes decorativas 120
  Museu Regional 117
  Paço dos Condes de Basto 118
  Paço dos duques de Cadaval 118
  Palácio de Dom Manuel 120
  Porta de Moura 119
  Praça do Giraldo 115
  Rua 5 de Outubro 115
  Templo romano 118
  Travellers' addresses 120
  Universidade 120
Évoramonte *Évora* 121
Évoramonte, Convention of 121
Expo'98 175

F

Facho, Pico do *Porto Santo* 284
Fado 43
Faial 307
Fajã 286, 313
Fajã da Caldeira do Santo Cristo São Jorge 314
Fajã de São Jorge São Jorge 314
Fajã do Ouvidor *São Jorge* 314
Fajã dos Cubres, Miradouro *São Jorge* 314
Fajã Grande *Flores* 317
Fajãzinha *Flores* 317
Falperra, Serra da *Braga* 82
Fandango 44
Faro *Faro* 122
Faro, Monte do *Viana do Castelo* 247
Faro, Praia de *Faro* 124
Fátima *Santarém* 124
Fazenda das Lajes *Flores* 316
Fernandes, Garcia 30
Fernandes, Mateus 29
Fernandes, Vasco 30, 183
Ferreira, António 31
Ferreira, Vergilio 38
Ferreira de Castro 38
Ferreirim *Viseu* 135
Ferro, Pico do *São Miguel* 298
Festivals 331
Figueira da Foz *Coimbra* 126
Figueira de Castelo Rodrigo *Guarda* 211
Figueiredo, Cristóvão de 30
Figueiró dos Vinhos *Leiria* 189
Flag 17
Flamengos, Ribeira dos *Faial* 309
Flor da Rosa, Monasterio de *Portalegre* 105
Flores 316
Flores, Pico das *Porto Santo* 284
Fogo, Lagoa do *São Miguel* 297
Fóia, Pico da *Faro* 196
Food 48
Formigas *Azores* 299
Foz de Arouce *Coimbra* 190
Foz do Douro *Porto* 225
Francisco Alvares Nóbrega, Miradouro *Madeira* 274
Franco, Francisco 32
Freguesias 17
Frei, Carlos 30
Freitas, Nicolau de 36
Freixo de Espada-à-Cinta *Bragança* 127
Fuas Roupinho, Dom 110
Funchal *Madeira* 265
Furna do Enxofre *Graciosa* 306
Furna Maria Encantada *Graciosa* 306
Furnas *São Miguel* 296
Furnas do Enxofre *Terceira* 304
Furnas de Frei Matias *Pico* 311
Furnas, Lagoa das *São Miguel* 296

G

Galera, Ponta da *São Miguel* 298
Gama, Vasco da 19, 24
Gand, Olivier de 29
Garrett, Almeida 38
Geira *Braga* 207
Geraldo Sempavor 115
Gerês *Braga* 207
Gerês, Serra do *Braga* 208
Girão, Cabo *Madeira* 273
Giusti 31
Glossary 334
Golegã *Santarém* 332
Gonçalves, Nuno 29
Goshawks 285
Gota 44
Gouveia *Guarda* 112
Graciosa 305
Grão Vasco: see Fernandes, Vasco
Great Discoveries 23, 163
Grilo, João Mario 39
Guarda *Guarda* 127
Guimarães *Braga* 129

H – I – J

Handicrafts 42
Henriques, Francisco 30
Henry the Navigator, Prince 23
Herculano, Alexandre 38
Horta *Faial* 307
Houdart 30
Huguet, Master 28
Ibne-Mucane 90

Ilhavo *Aveiro* 71
Impérios 301
Irene, Saint 229
Isabel of Aragon, Queen Saint 114
John of God, St 198
Jesuits 213
Joana, Saint 69
João I 19, 71, 73
João II 19
João V 20
João VI 20
Jorge, Lídia 38
José I 20
Juncal, Miradouro do *Madeira* 277
Junceda, Miradouro de *Braga* 208
Junqueiro, Guerra 38, 127

L

Lace 209
Lagoa Branca *Flores* 317
Lagoa Funda *Flores* 317
Lagoa Seca *Flores* 317
Lagoa Rasa *Flores* 317
Lagos *Faro* 132
Lajes *Flores* 317
Lajes do Pico *Pico* 312
Lamas do Mouro *Viana do Castelo* 209
Lamego *Viseu* 134
Laprade 31
Laurissilva 262
Leça do Bailio *Porto* 135
Leiria *Leiria* 135
Leixões *Porto* 225
Leonor, Queen 87
Levada 264
Levada do Norte *Madeira* 273, 280
Lindoso *Viana do Castelo* 136
Linhares *Guarda* 128
Lino, Raúl 32
Lisboa *Lisboa* 138
  Alfama 169
  Alto de Santa Catarina 169
  Amoreiras 186
  Aquário Vasco da Gama 189
  Aqueduto das Águas Livres 187
  Avenida da Liberdade 182
  Bairro Alto 167
  Baixa 166
  Basílica da Estrela 188
  Beco das Cruzes 173
  Beco de Carneiro 172
  Belém 179
  Biblioteca municipal 186
  Campo de Santa Clara 173
  Casa do Alentejo 166
  Casa dos Bicos 175
  Casa Fernando Pessoa 188
  Castelo de São Jorge 173
  Centro Cultural de Belém 181
  Centro de Arte moderna 186
  Chiado 167
  Cristo Rei 179
  Dona Maria II National Theatre 166
  Elevador de Santa Justa 167
  Escadinhas de Santo-Estêvão 172
  Estação do Rossio 166
  Estação do Sul e Sueste 167
  Expo'98 174
  Fado 158
  Feira da Ladra 173
  Fundação Arpad Szenes-Vieira da Silva 187
  Fundação Gulbenkian 183
  Fundação Ricardo do Espírito Santo Silva 172
  Graça 173
  Hotels 140
  Igreja da Conceição Velha 175
  Igreja da Madre de Deus 175
  Igreja de Nossa Senhora de Fátima 186
  Igreja, Convento de Nossa Senhora da Graça 173
  Igreja de Santa Engrácia 173
  Igreja de Santa Maria 179
  Igreja de Santo António da Sé 171
  Igreja de São Miguel 172
  Igreja de São Roque 169
  Igreja de São Vicente de Fora 173
  Igreja do Carmo 168
  Jardim Boto Machado 173
  Jardim botânico 183
  Jardim Botânico da Ajuda 182
  Jardim Botânico de Monteiro-Mor 189
  Jardim da Estrela 188
  Jardim das Damas 182
  Jardim Zoológico 187
  Largo das Portas do Sol 172
  Largo de São Rafael 172
  Mãe d'Água das Amoreiras 187
  Miradouro da Senhora do Monte 173
  Miradouro de Santa Luzia 172
  Miradouro de São Pedro de Alcântara 169
  Mosterio dos Jerónimos 179
  Museu Antoniano 171
  Museu arqueológico do Carmo 168
  Museu da Água da EPAL 176
  Museu da Cidade 188
  Museu da Marinha 180
  Museu da Música 188
  Museu de Arte popular 181
  Museu de São Roque 169
  Museu des Artes decorativas 172
  Museu do Chiado 168
  Museu dos Coches 181
  Museu do Trajo 189
  Museu Gulbenkian 183
  Museu militar 176
  Museu nacional de Arqueologia 179
  Museu Nacional de Arte Antiga 177
  Museu Nacional do Azulejo 175
  Museu Nacional do Teatro 189
  Museu Rafael Bordalo Pinheiro 189
  Núcleo Arqueológico da Rua dos Correeiros 166
  Paço Real 173
  Padrão dos Descobrimentos 181
  Palácio da Ajuda 182
  Palácio das Necessidades 188
  Palácio dos marqueses de Fronteira 187
  Palácio Foz 166
  Palácio Lavradio 173
  Parque Eduardo VII 183
  Parque Florestal de Monsanto 188
  Planetarium 180
  Ponte 25 de Abril 178
  Port 175
  Praça do Comércio 167
  Praça dos Restauradores 166
  Praça Luis de Camões 168
  Praça Marquês de Pombal 182
  Quinta de Monteiro-Mor 189
  Railway stations 148
  Restaurants 143
  Rossio 166
  Rua Augusta 166
  Rua da Judairia 172
  Rua da Misericórdia 168
  Rua de São Pedro 172
  Rua do Ouro 166
  Rua dos Remédios 172
  Rua Garrett 168
  Rua Portas de Santo Antão 166
  Sé (Cathedral) 169
  Teatro Nacional de São Carlos 168
  Terreiro do Paço 167
  Torre de Belém 181
  Travellers' addresses 140
Lisbon: see Lisboa
Lisbon School 30
Literature 37
Letters from a Portuguese Nun 76
Lobo Antunes, António 38
Lopes, Fernando 39
Lopes, Gregório 30
Lourenço, Eduardo 39
Loriga *Guarda* 113
Loulé *Faro* 61, 331
Lourosa, Igreja de *Coimbra* 204
Lousã, Serra da *Coimbra/Leiria* 189
Lousã *Coimbra* 190
Ludwig, Friedrich 31
Luís I, 20
Luso *Aveiro* 103
Luso-Moorish Style 29
Luz de Tavira *Faro* 59

M

Machado de Castro, Joaquim 31
Machico *Madeira* 274
Madalena *Pico* 311
Madalena do Mar *Madeira* 281
Madeira Archipelago 260
Madeira 261
Madeira Wine 264
Madeira embroidery 265

Madrugada, Miradouro da São Miguel 298
Mafra, Convento de Lisboa 190
Mafra School, 190
Magalhães, Fernão de (Magellan) 10, 26
Maia Santa Maria 300
Majolica technique 35
Malhão 32
Serra de Malcata, Guarda 15
Malhoa, José 32, 87
Manadas São Jorge 314
Mangualde Viseu 192
Manteigas Guarda 112
Manuel I 19
Manuel II 20
Manueline architecture 28
Marão, Pico do Vila Real 193
Marão, Serra do Porto/Vila Real 192
Mardel 31
Maria II 20
Marialva Guarda 128
Marofa, Serra da Guarda 210
Martins, Dr Sousa 183
Martins, Dona Teresa 178
Martins, Oliveira 38
Marvão Portalegre 193
Mateus Vila Real 253
Matosinhos Porto 225
Mealhada Aveiro 103
Mello Breyner, Sofia de 38
Mendes Pinto, Fernão 38
Methuen Treaty 50, 215
Mértola Beja 194
Mezio Viana do Castelo 208
Minho, Vale do Viana do Castelo 247
Mira de Aire Leiria 125
Mira de Aire, Grutas de Leiria 125
Miranda do Douro Bragança 194
Miranda do Douro, Barragem de Bragança 195
Mirandela Bragança 195
Miróbriga Setúbal 232
Moeda, Grutas da Leiria 126
Misterios 286, 310
Moinhos Velhos, Grutas das Leiria 125
Moliceiros 70
Moncão Viana do Castelo 247
Monchique Faro 196
Monchique, Serra de Faro 196
Mondim de Basto Vila Real 193
Moniz, Egas 205
Moniz, Martim 173
Monsanto Castelo Branco 196

Monsaraz Évora 197
Monserrate, Parque de Lisboa 240
Montalegre Vila Real 95
Monte Madeira 272
Monte da Ajuda, Ermidas do Graciosa 306
Monte da Guia Faial 308
Monte Gordo Faro 253
Monte Sameiro Braga 82
Monteiro, João César 39
Montemor-o-Novo Évora 198
Montemor-o-Velho Coimbra 198
Montesinho, Parque natural 15, 83
Mosteiro Flores 237
Moura Beja 198
Mouranitos, Praia dos Faro 64
Mouros, Castelo dos Lisboa 239
Muslims 237

N – O

Namora, Fernando 38
Napoleonic Wars 20
Nasoni, Nicolau 31
Nature Reserves 15
Nazaré Leiria 198
Nemésio, Vitorino 38
Nossa Senhora da Conceição, Capela de Madeira 272
Nossa Senhora da Piedade, Miardouro Coimbra 190
Nossa Senhora da Graça, Capela de 193
Nossa Senhora da Peneda, Mosteiro de Viana do Castelo 209
Nossa Senhora do Monte, Igreja de Madeira 272
Nunes Tinoco, João 30
Óbidos Leiria 201
Óbidos, Josefa de 30, 201
Óbidos, Lagoa de Leiria 203
Odeceixe Faro 64
Olhão Faro 203
Oliveira Bernardes, António and Polycarpo de 36
Oliveira, Carlos de 38
Oliveira do Hospital Coimbra 203
Oliveira, Manoel de 39
Oliveira, Marquês de 32
Oporto: see Porto
Oranges, War of the 20, 109
Ourém Santarém 204
Ovar Aveiro 331
Oysters, Portuguese 234

P

Paço de Sousa Porto 204
Padrões 42
Palheiro Ferreiro, Quinta do Madeira 271
Palmela Setúbal 205
Papoa Peniche 209
Paradela, Represa da Vila Real 94
Pargo, Ponta da Madeira 281
Paúl da Serra Madeira 280
Paúl de Arzila Coimbra 15
Paúl do Boquilobo Santarém 15
Pauliteiros Dance 44, 194
Pedras, Pico das Madeira 278
Pedras de El Rei Faro 59
Pedreira, A Porto Santo 284
Pedro II 20
Pedro IV, Maximilian of Mexico 166
Pedro V 20
Pelourinhos 41
Pena, Palácio da Lisboa 239
Pena, Parque da Lisboa 239
Penalva do Castelo Viseu 192
Peneda-Gerês, Parque nacional da Braga 15, 206
Peneda, Serra da Viana do Castelo 206
Penedono Viseu 209
Penela Coimbra 103
Penha Braga 132
Penha, Monte da Portalegre 92
Penhas da Saúde Castelo Branco 111
Peniche Leiria 209
Peninha Lisboa 240
Pereira, António 36
Perestrelo, Bartolomeu 261, 283
Perim 44
Pero, Master 28, 100
Peso da Régua Vila Real 108
Pessoa, Fernando 38, 137, 188
Philip II of Spain 20
Pico 310
Pico, Volcano 310
Pico Pequeno Pico 311
Picote, Barragem de Bragança 195
Piedade Pico 312
Pináculo, Miradouro do Madeira 274
Pinhão Vila Real 108
Pinhel Guarda 210
Pinoucas, Monte Viseu 89

Pinto, José António Jorge 36

Pires the Elder, Diogo 28

Pires the Younger, Diogo 29

Pitóes das Júnias *Vila Real* 94

Poço do Inferno *Guarda* 112

Pombal *Leiria* 211

Pombal, Marquês de 20, 211

Ponte da Barca *Viana do Castelo* 136

Ponta da Piedade *Faro* 133

Ponta Delgada *Madeira* 278

Ponta Delgada *São Miguel* 293

Ponta do Castelo *Santa Maria* 300

Ponta do Sol *Madeira* 281

Ponte de Lima *Viana do Castelo* 211

Portalegre *Portalegre* 212

Portela, Boca da *Madeira* 276

Portimão *Faro* 213

Portinho da Arrábida *Setúbal* 67

Porto *Porto* 214
  Bolhão Municipal Market
  Cais da Ribeira 220
  Casa do Infante 220
  Casa Tait 221
  Estação de São Bento 223
  Fundação António de Almeida 224
  Fundação de Serralves 224
  Igreja da Imaculada Conceição 224
  Igreja das Carmelitas
  Igreja da Cedofeita 224
  Igreja do Carmo 221
  Igreja dos Clérigos 221
  Igreja de São Lourenço dos Grilos 219
  Igreja de São Francisco 220
  Igreja de Santa Clara 224
  Lello & Irmao Bookshop 221
  Mercado Ferreira Borges 220
  Museu de Arte Contemporânea 224
  Museu etnográfico 220
  Museu Guerra Junqueiro 224
  Museu romântico 221
  Museu Soares dos Reis 221
  Nossa Senhora da Serra do Pilar, Convento 224
  Palácio da Bolsa 220
  Praça da Liberdade 220
  Praça do General H Delgado 220
  Rua das Carmelitas 221
  Rua das Flores 219
  Rua de Santa Catarina 220
  Santa Casa da Misericórdia 219
  Sé 217
  Solar do Vinho do Porto 221
  Terreiro da Sé 217
  Torre dos Clérigos 221
  Travellers' addresses 218
  Wine lodges 222

Porto de Mós *Leiria* 125

Porto Formosa *São Miguel* 297

Porto Moniz *Madeira* 279

Porto Negrito *Terceira* 303

Porto Santo *Porto Santo* 282

Porto, Silva 32

Portucale County 214

Portuguese Water Dog 200

Port Wine 50, 215

Pousadas 325

Pousão, Henrique 32

Povoação *São Miguel* 298

Póvoa de Varzim *Porto* 225

Practical Information 320

Praia *Graciosa* 306

Praia da Barre *Aveiro* 71

Praia da Mira *Coimbra* 88

Praia da Rocha *Faro* 226

Praia das Maças *Lisboa* 240

Praia da Vitória *Terceira* 305

Praia de Dona Ana *Faro* 134

Praia do Guincho *Lisboa* 90

Prainha *Pico* 312

Protected landscapes 15

Public Holidays 327

Q – R

Queimadas, Parque das *Madeira* 278

Queluz, Palácio *Lisboa* 226

Quental, Antero de 38, 294

Quinta do Lago *Faro* 62

Rabaçal *Madeira* 280

Rates *Porto* 225

Régio, José 38

Reis, António 39

Remédios, Capela de Nossa Senhora dos *Leiria* 210

Resende *Viseu* 108

Ria Formosa, Parque natural *Faro* 15, 59

Ribeira Brava *Madeira* 280

Ribeira da Janela *Madeira* 280

Ribeira Grande *São Miguel* 297

Ribeira Quente *São Miguel* 297

Ribeiras *Pico* 312

Ribeira Seca *São Jorge* 314

Ribeiro, Aquilino 38

Ribeiro, Bernardim 37

Ribeiro Frio *Madeira* 277

Rio Mau *Porto* 225

Risco, Cascata do *Madeira* 280

Rocha, Paulo 39

Rocha dos Bordões *Flores* 317

Rodrigues, Amália 44

Romaria 44

Romeu *Bragança* 195

Roriz *Porto* 132

Rosais, Ponta dos *São Jorge* 313

Roucas *Viana do Castelo* 208

Rouen, Jean de 30

Ruivo, Pico *Madeira* 281

S

Sá Carneiro, Mario de 38

Sá de Miranda, Francisco 37

Sabrosa *Vila Real* 108

Sabugal *Guarda* 227

Sabugueiro *Guarda* 112

Sado estuary *Setúbal* 15

Sagres, Ponta de *Faro* 228

Sagres School 21, 228

Saias 44

Salazar 20

Salema *Faro* 63

Salga, Baía de *Terceira* 301

Salto da Farinha *São Miguel* 298

Salto do Cavalo, Miradouro *São Miguel* 298

Sameiro, Monte *Braga* 82

Santa *Madeira* 280

Santa Bárbara *Santa Maria* 300

Santa Bárbara *Terceira* 303

Santa Bárbara, Igreja de *São Jorge* 314

Santa Bárbara, Serra da *Terceira* 303

Santa Cruz *Madeira* 274

Santa Cruz das Flores *Flores* 316

Santa Cruz da Graciosa *Graciosa* 306

Santa Luzia, Basílica de *Viana do Castelo* 248

Santa Luzia, Miradouro de *Viara do Castelo* 248

Santa Luzia *Pico* 311

Santa Maria, 299

Santa Maria da Feira *Aveiro* 229

Santa Maria de Aguiar, Convento de *Guarda* 211

Santa Maria de Cárquere, Priorado de *Viseu* 107

Santana *Funchal* 203

Santa Rita 32

Santarém *Santarém* 229

Santiago, Lago de *São Miguel* 295

Santiago do Cacém *Setúbal* 231
Santo Amaro *Pico* 312
Santo António, Grutas de *Leiria* 126
Santo António *Madeira* 272
Santo António *Pico* 311
Santo da Serra *Madeira* 276
Santo Espírito *Santa Maria* 300
Santos, Eugénio dos 31
Santos, Manuel dos 36
São Brissos, Capela-anta *Évora* 121
São Cucufate *Beja* 77
São Fructuoso de Montélios, Capela de *Braga* 82
São Jacinto *Aveiro* 71
São Jacinto (Reserva natural das dunas) *Aveiro* 15, 71
São Jõao *Pico* 313
São João da Pesqueira *Viseu* 108
São João de Tarouca *Viseu* 134, 232
São Jorge 313
São Jorge *Madeira* 278
São Lourenço, Baía do *Santa Maria* 300
São Lourenço, Ponta de *Madeira* 276
São Mamede, Grutas de *Leiria* 126
São Mamede, Serra de *Portalegre* 15, 232
São Martinho *Madeira* 271
São Martinho do Porto *Leiria* 200
São Mateus *Pico* 313
São Mateus *Terceira* 303
São Miguel 293
São Pedro de Balsemão, Capela de *Viseu* 134
São Roque do Faial *Madeira* 277
São Roque do Pico *Pico* 311
São Sebastião *Terceira* 304
São Vicente *Madeira* 279
São Vicente, Cabo de *Faro* 15, 229
Sapiães *Vila Real* 95
Saramago, José 38
Sardoal, Master of 30
Saudade 43
Scrimshaw 308, 312
Sebastião I 19
Seia *Guarda* 112
Seixal *Madeira* 279
Senhora do Desterro *Guarda* 113
Sequeira, Domingos António de 31
Sernancelhe *Viseu* 233

Serpa *Beja* 233
Serpa Pinto 20
Serra de Agua *Madeira* 280
Serra do Cume *Terceira* 305
Serra do Topo *São Jorge* 314
Sesimbra *Setúbal* 233
Sete Cidades *São Miguel* 295
Sete Fontes *São Jorge* 313
Setúbal *Setúbal* 234
Severa, Maria 44
Silva Porto 32
Silveira, General 65
Silves *Faro* 236
Sintra *Lisboa* 237
Sintra, Convention of 237
Sintra, Serra de *Lisboa* 15, 238
Siza, Álvaro 32
Soajo *Viana do Castelo* 208
Soares dos Reis 31, 221
Sortelha *Guarda* 129
Sosseqo, Miradouro de *São Miguel* 298
Sousa Pinto 32
Souza Cardoso, Amadeo de 32, 65
Sports 329

T

Tabuleiros 46, 241
Tagus estuary *Lisboa* 15
Talha dourada 31
Taveira, Tomás 32
Tavira, Ilha de 241
Tavira Faro 241
Távora, Fernando 32
Teixeira, Manuel 31
Teixeira Lopes, António 31
Templars, Knights 241
Terceira 300
Terra Nostra, Parque *São Miguel* 296
Terreiro da Luta *Madeira* 272
Terzi, Filippo 30
Three Marias, the 76
Todi, Luisa 234
Tomar *Santarém* 241
Tordesillas, Treaty of 19, 24
Torga, Miguel 38
Torralva, Diogo de 30
Torre, Monte da *Castelo Branco* 111
Torre de Moncorvo *Bragança* 243
Torreira *Aveiro* 71
Torres Vedras *Lisboa* 163
Tourada 46, 222

Trancoso *Guarda* 244
Travanca *Porto* 66
Trofa *Porto* 132
Tróia, Península de *Setúbal* 236
Turiano, João 30

U – V – W – Y – Z

UNESCO 53
Unhais da Serra *Castelo Branco* 113
Urzal, Miradouro de *São Jorge* 314
Urzelina *São Jorge* 315
Vale do Côa, Parque Archeológico do *Guarda* 244
Vale do Couço *Bragança* 195
Vale do Inferno, Miradouro do *Coimbra* 102
Vale do Lobo *Faro* 62
Valença do Minho *Viana do Castelo* 247
Varadouro *Faial* 308
Vara, Pico de *São Miguel* 298
Varziela *Coimbra* 88
Vasco de Gama: see Gama
Vaz, Gaspar 30, 255
Velas *São Jorge* 313
Venda Nova, Reservoir *Vila Real* 94
Verdelho 230
Viana do Alentejo *Évora* 247
Viana do Castelo *Viana do Castelo* 248
Vicente, Gil 37, 129
Vicente, Mateus 31
Vieira, António 38
Vieira da Silva, Maria Helena 32
Vieira, Domingos 30
Vieira, Jacinto 31
Vieira Lusitano 31
Vila Baleira *Porto Santo* 283
Vila da Ponte *Vila Real* 94
Vila do Bispo *Faro* 63
Vila do Conde *Porto* 250
Vila do Porto *Santa Maria* 299
Vila Franca de Xira *Lisboa* 251
Vila Franca do Campo *São Miguel* 298
Vila Franca do Lima *Viana do Castelo* 331
Vilamoura *Faro* 251
Vila Nogueira de Azeitão *Setúbal* 67

Vila Nova da Gaia *Porto* 214
Vila Nova de Foz Côa
 Guarda 251
Vila Nova do Corvo *Corvo*
 317
Vila Real *Vila Real* 252
Vila Real de Santo
 António *Faro* 253
Vilarinho das Furnas
 Braga 208

Vila Verdinho *Bragança*
 195
Vila Viçosa *Évora* 254
Vinho verde 51, 106
Vira 44
Viseu *Viseu* 255
Viseu School 30, 255
Vista Alegre *Aveiro* 71
Waterparks *Algarve 63*
Wellington 177, 201

Whaling 287
Windsor, Treaty of 21
Wine 50
Ypres, Jean d' 29
Zambujeiro, Anta do
 Évora 121
Zarco, João Gonçalves
 261, 265
Zêzere, Vale glaciário
 do Guarda 112